• Praise for This Book •

This is a complete guide for qualitative researchers, emerging or experienced, and provides new ways to think about the vital role of qualitative studies!
–Jacalyn M. Griffen, Fresno Pacific University

This book is a great addition to the library of qualitative books for graduate students. Each chapter has examples to use and offers the nuance and complexities that are inherent in qualitative inquiry.
–Anne M. Hornak, Central Michigan University

The chapter authors provide clear, practical, and vibrant examples of their strategies. Individually, each chapter gives care to how the authors have used the strategy in the past. Collectively, the chapters provide a wealth of unique and innovative analysis approaches for all qualitative researchers to consider.
–Peggy Shannon-Baker, Georgia Southern University

As an instructor of qualitative research courses, I know this text will be immediately useful for my students. Each chapter calls to mind a student who could benefit from its contents. The whole book is written in a way that's accessible and down-to-earth, and it will appeal to graduate students especially; I've picked up some new techniques too!
–Jane West, Mercer University

ANALYZING AND INTERPRETING QUALITATIVE RESEARCH
After the Interview

Edited by

Charles Vanover
University of South Florida

Paul Mihas
University of North Carolina at Chapel Hill

Johnny Saldaña
Arizona State University

Los Angeles | London | New Delhi
Singapore | Washington DC | Melbourne

FOR INFORMATION:

SAGE Publications, Inc.

2455 Teller Road

Thousand Oaks, California 91320

E-mail: order@sagepub.com

SAGE Publications Ltd.

1 Oliver's Yard

55 City Road

London EC1Y 1SP

United Kingdom

SAGE Publications India Pvt. Ltd.

B 1/I 1 Mohan Cooperative Industrial Area

Mathura Road, New Delhi 110 044

India

SAGE Publications Asia-Pacific Pte. Ltd.

3 Church Street

#10-04 Samsung Hub

Singapore 049483

Printed in Canada

Library of Congress Cataloging-in-Publication Data

Names: Vanover, Charles, editor. | Mihas, Paul, editor. | Saldaña, Johnny, editor.

Title: Analyzing and interpreting qualitative research: after the interview / edited by Charles Vanover, Paul Mihas, Johnny Saldaña.

Description: First Edition. | Thousand Oaks : SAGE Publications, Inc, 2021 | Includes bibliographical references and index.

Identifiers: LCCN 2021011026 | ISBN 9781544395876 (paperback) | ISBN 9781544395883 (adobe pdf) | ISBN 9781544395890 (epub) | ISBN 9781544395906 (epub)

Subjects: LCSH: Qualitative research. | Social sciences—Research.

Classification: LCC H62 .A58134 2021 | DDC 001.4/2—dc23

LC record available at https://lccn.loc.gov/2021011026

This book is printed on acid-free paper.

Acquisitions Editor: Helen Salmon

Production Editor: Preethi Agnes Thomas

Copy Editor: Christobel Colleen Hopman

Typesetter: TNQ Technologies

Proofreader: Benny Willy Stephen

Indexer: TNQ Technologies

Cover Designer: Karine Hovsepian

Marketing Manager: Victoria Velasquez

MIX
Paper from
responsible sources
FSC® C103567

21 22 23 24 25 10 9 8 7 6 5 4 3 2 1

• Contents •

• Acknowledgments •

The editors and chapter authors are grateful for feedback from the following reviewers during the development of this text:

Barbara Andersen, University of Idaho

derria byrd, Marquette University

Yiting Chu, University of Louisiana, Monroe

Dawne Clarke, St. Thomas University

Marcus Crawford, Fresno State University

Robin Grenier, University of Connecticut

Jacalyn M. Griffen, Fresno Pacific University

Anne M. Hornak, Central Michigan University

Kirk Leach, University of Arkansas at Little Rock

Jacquelyn Mallette, East Carolina University

Robert T. Palmer, Howard University

Heidi Paquette, Marquette University

Peggy Shannon-Baker, Georgia Southern University

Chareen Snelson, Boise State University

Jeanne Surface, University of Nebraska Omaha

Jane West, Mercer University

• About the Editors •

Charles Vanover is Associate Professor in Educational Leadership at the University of South Florida. He entered the field of qualitative studies working as a qualitative data analyst at the University of Michigan on the Study of Instructional Improvement. He met Johnny Saldaña at a session at AERA and together they developed Charles' first ethnodrama, "Chalkboard Concerto," a monologue about Charles' experience teaching in the Chicago Public Schools. Charles's 10 ethnodramas have been performed more 60 times, including 25 peer-reviewed sessions. Beyond *Analyzing and Interpreting Qualitative Research,* Charles is co-editing a book on assessing performance-based research that examines "Chicago Butoh," a film and a set of live performances he developed with Bob Devin Jones.

Paul Mihas is Assistant Director of Education and Qualitative Research at the Odum Institute for Research in Social Science at the University of North Carolina at Chapel Hill. He teaches qualitative methods at the Global School in Empirical Research Methods (GSERM) at the University of St. Gallen, Switzerland, the BI Norwegian Business School, and the University of Ljubljana, Slovenia. He also serves as faculty at the ICPSR Summer Program in Quantitative Methods of Social Research and the annual Qualitative Research Summer Intensive. Recent publications include chapters on qualitative data analysis in the *Oxford Encyclopedia of Qualitative Research Methods in Education* (2019) and in *Research Design and Methods: An Applied Guide for the Scholar-Practitioner* (SAGE, 2019)

Johnny Saldaña is Professor Emeritus from Arizona State University's School of Film, Dance, and Theatre. He is the author of *Longitudinal Qualitative Research: Analyzing Change through Time, Fundamentals of Qualitative Research, The Coding Manual for Qualitative Researchers, Thinking Qualitatively: Methods of Mind, Ethnotheatre: Research from Page to Stage, Writing Qualitatively: The Selected Works of Johnny Saldaña,* co-author with the late Miles and Huberman for *Qualitative Data Analysis: A Methods Sourcebook,* and co-author with Matt Omasta for *Qualitative Research: Analyzing Life.* Saldaña's qualitative methods works have been cited and referenced in more than 18,000 research studies conducted in over 130 countries.

Introduction

Charles Vanover, Paul Mihas, and Johnny Saldaña

*A*nalyzing and Interpreting Qualitative Research: After the Interview provides readers with practices and strategies for transcribing, analyzing, and interpreting interview data, whether from individual one-on-one sessions, focus groups, or secondary sources. Our goal is to provide a versatile how-to guide on these phases of the qualitative research life cycle. We offer a rich assortment of approaches to guide readers from the conclusion of substantial fieldwork to formal research writing.

Rather than sharing a single, unitary perspective on how to move from a recorded set of interviews to dissertation chapters, articles, and books, we have asked some of the leaders in the field of qualitative research to provide step-by-step accounts of their efforts to engage in different forms of data analysis. Our contributors' perspectives are as diverse as the field of qualitative studies, but one commonality runs through each text: Every chapter in this book celebrates the role researcher decision-making plays in skilled inquiry. Because every research question is unique and each set of interviews may be interpreted in multiple ways, there is no established pathway that will lead from a set of recorded conversations to a finished qualitative study. Researchers have provided guidance on how to engage in data analysis (e.g., Bernard, Wutich, & Ryan, 2016; Braun, Clarke, & Weate, 2016; Galman, 2016; Gee, 2014; Miles, Huberman, & Saldaña, 2020; Rubin & Rubin, 2011; Silverman, 2000), but there is no indisputable protocol that will lead to an optimal result.

Qualitative researchers must use and refine their judgment during each phase of the qualitative research life cycle. The goals we attempt to achieve and the questions we ask shape the practices we use to transform copious data into formal research writing. The decision to use a particular epistemological frame or theoretical lens shapes the questions we ask and the insights gained from their inquiry. Different theories generate different questions, and original questions can produce unexpected findings and unanticipated approaches to getting there.

Analysis and interpretation are, to some degree, separable. Analyzing data refers to a close reading of data, an examination of the component parts, listening and relistening to what we have gathered, and using practices, such as coding and memo writing, to systematically discern what we are reading, based on a priori knowledge or what one might call "emergent" discernment. Interpreting data refers to conceptualizing or making larger meaning of what we have examined. Here, we tell the meta-story, or build themes that tie together the seemingly disparate threads across data. Though the lines between analysis and interpretation can be blurred, we point to their differences to better understand the incremental shifts in the qualitative research life cycle, how we move from fragments to wholes.

The meaning of a set of interviews is constructed through care and practice—through the researcher's decisions and practices, which can be emergent as options for analysis become evident in early data review. Researchers arguably make meaning early in the research life cycle. As Charles Vanover, in Chapter 4, describes, a researcher's decision to use a particular set of transcription practices shapes their moment-to-moment understanding as they engage with prepared interview text during subsequent phases of inquiry. Some transcription practices may highlight participants' gestures and tones of voice while others erase these dimensions (Bartesaghi, Chapter 5). As data analysis progresses, different practices focus researchers' attention on distinct aspects of the interview content. No piece of recorded dialogue has an innate meaning. Discovering what matters most within a particular data set may be a complex and nonlinear process. Kakali Bhattacharya, Chapter 21, describes her efforts to use a set of contemplative and arts-based practices to bring "forward multiple elements of the interview that had a strong pull" and to investigate the "reasons for this pull."

Reflexive planning and decision making are critical during each stage of the qualitative research life cycle (Lincoln & Denzin, 2003; Saldaña & Omasta, 2018). Sometimes it is best to follow the original research design and perform each step of the analysis in the order the research efforts were planned. In other situations, the best choice may be to modify the original questions or choose to engage in forms of analysis that better fit the collected data (Bingham & Witkowsky, Chapter 8; Blanco & Rossman, Chapter 1). Such decision points cannot always be specified in advance. Skilled qualitative researchers perform their work with a profound understanding of the goals of their inquiry and a deep knowledge of the potential methods and range of practices they might apply.

Qualitative research is a democratic practice. Diversity in methods and approaches adds to the analytical richness of our field. There are numerous points of departure for data analysis and ways to organize interviews, videos, and research memos. Some of the authors in this volume argue for the careful use of qualitative data analysis software to organize and structure researchers' interactions with interview data (di Gregorio, Chapter 6; Larbi-Cherif, Egan, & Glazer, Chapter 17; Lester & Paulus, Chapter 2; Turner, Chapter 7). Other contributors emphasize the benefits of taking the time to develop insights through the use of writing practices such as memos and note cards (Fiddler, Chapter 16; Keane, Chapter 15; Mihas, Chapter 14). Transcription may be understood as a critical step in the analytic process (Bartesaghi, Chapter 5; Vanover, Chapter 4), or a practice that might be disregarded in favor of direct interaction with audio and video files (Bernauer, Chapter 10). Many of the contributors to *Analyzing and Interpreting Qualitative Research* describe the worth and challenges of different coding practices. Janet Richards, in Chapter 9, describes the use of thematic analysis to find commonality and diversity within a set of field notes. Andrea Bingham and Patricia Witkowsky, in Chapter 8, discuss combining theory-based and inductive approaches to coding. Their chapter provides examples of how to use deductive practices to sort and organize data and how to move to inductive practices to identify unanticipated topics, themes, and meaningful findings that connect data to theory and other concepts from the research literature. Adrian Larbi-Cherif, Cori Egan, and Joshua L. Glazer, in Chapter 17, describe their research team's efforts to investigate a school district reform process by coding 157 interviews taken over multiple waves of data collection. Elsa M. Gonzalez and Yvonna S. Lincoln, in Chapter 12, describe the challenges of coding interview data across languages and cultures.

Decision-making does not end at the conclusion of analytic work. Interpretation, synthesis, and write up require careful planning and further decision making. Some qualitative studies might be better rendered as collages, plays, films, and/or poems than as formal research reports. Arts-based practices might be engaged to interpret the data and communicate the study's meanings in moving and expressive ways (Bhattacharya, Chapter 21; Campbell Galman, Chapter 22; Saldaña, Chapter 19; Shenfield & Prendergast, Chapter 20). The insights produced by the use of arts-based practices might enrich the study's findings even if the researcher's poems, plays, comics, and/or drawings are never published. When arts-based practices are used skillfully to produce a provocative work of art, researchers gain the power to strike the imagination and speak directly to the public. A piece of art or performance of "high aesthetic quality has the potential to engage audiences emotionally and communally" (Saldaña, 2018, p. 374). Such is rarely the case with academic journal articles.

Qualitative researchers may choose to use a wide range of write-up practices. Tim Huffman, in Chapter 18, discusses how to develop claims from a qualitative analysis and how to use these assertions to create arguments about the issues that motivated the investigation. Jessica Smartt Gullion, in Chapter 24, discusses the practices and strategies researchers might use to engage in formal and informal forms of research writing such as concept papers and blog posts. Mitchell Allen, in Chapter 25, draws on his years of experience in publishing to discuss the choices and trade-offs researchers face when developing book-length manuscripts.

The meanings communicated by a set of qualitative data are not innate to the original recorded interaction. Meaning must be constructed through patient hours of practical work. This labor opens researchers' minds and hearts and allows them to communicate what they have learned to various audiences.

Finding One's Way Through Qualitative Inquiry

Each of the editors comes to this work through years of commitment to qualitative inquiry. Charles Vanover entered the field of qualitative studies at the beginning of the twenty-first century by working as a graduate researcher on a set of mixed methods studies similar to those described in Larbi-Cherif et al. (Chapter 17). What turned out to be most influential in his development, however, was Charles's membership in The Rackham Graduate School's Narrative Institute, a group of graduate students and faculty who established a set of monthly talks on narrative research. As these talks and meetings progressed, core members of the Narrative Institute made it a point to ask each presenter the same set of questions: "What did you do with the box of stuff you collected in the field? How did you transform the recordings, notebooks, and other items you produced during data collection into the completed book or set of articles we are discussing today?" The field of qualitative studies was just becoming digitized; researchers really did return from the field carrying boxes and suitcases filled with cassette tapes, rolls of film, stacks of note cards, and other materials.

Among graduate students at Michigan, it was common knowledge that the transition from fieldwork to data analysis was a perilous moment in the research process. Some of the richest conversations on method at the Narrative Institute revolved around the practical details of organizing and engaging with field material. Many of the researchers who presented their work had never been asked to share the particulars of how they transcribed their interviews or to discuss the techniques they used to interpret and write up their data. Many a cautionary tale was told, both at the Narrative Institute's formal sessions, and then at off-campus coffee shops and bars, about researchers who had returned from the field with high hopes and boxes filled with material, only to become lost in the data and to never find their way. It was said there were graduate students and senior faculty who completed their fieldwork, but who spent the rest of their careers circling through their data. Ideas might flow and descriptions grow thick, but chapters were never written, articles never submitted, and insights never disseminated.

Digital methods of data collection make this problem more complex by increasing the kinds of data available for analysis. Twentieth-century qualitative researchers were limited by the amount of field material they could carry or ship. Twenty-first century researchers have the resources to generate hour upon hour of digital audio and video files and to collect thousands of photographs, emails, and social media posts. Making informed decisions about how to organize and engage with this material and transform it into a completed research product is one of qualitative researchers' core competencies.

The second editor of this volume, Paul Mihas, first entered the realm of qualitative thinking when he taught a creative nonfiction writing course at Duke University Continuing Education in the 1990s. As the managing editor of a sociology journal, he was struck by how nonfiction could convey lived experience in evocative ways that were more memorable and more resonant than traditional academic writing. Survival stories and memoirs of crisis, in particular, caught his attention. He began collecting interview data on cancer survivors and focused on identities in transition, how survivors had their own way of making sense of their health challenges and retrieving suppressed selves. Metaphors—such as "cancer graduate" and "cancer veteran"—taught him what "data driven" meant before he had even heard the term. As he moved into the role of qualitative research consultant at the Odum Institute for Research in Social Science, he met with countless graduate students struggling through data collection and analysis. Whenever he embarks on a new study, he is reminded of the unpredictable nature of the qualitative odyssey and, in a world pushing for data acceleration, how much we have to learn by slowing down and listening to the moment—language that provides glimpses into lived experience and sense-making.

Johnny Saldaña's qualitative research coursework started in spring 1995 and came from Arizona State University professors Tom Barone (introductory methods) and Mary Lee Smith (advanced methods). Barone lectured on the fundamentals of the paradigm then ventured into arts-based approaches such as narrative inquiry and performance ethnography. Smith focused on methodologies such as grounded theory and assertion development with an emphasis on ethnographic fieldwork. Later in his career Saldaña took additional coursework in communication and qualitative research with Sarah Amira De la Garza (intercultural ethnography) and Sarah J. Tracy (advanced qualitative data analysis). An eclectic array of course experiences developed an eclectic researcher. He experienced a range of approaches to inquiry from systematic data analysis to evocative arts-based approaches. He attests to this day that qualitative researchers should not pigeon-hole themselves into one methodology for their careers, but should instead be well-versed in *multiple* methods of inquiry and analytic practices. This knowledge base serves the researcher well, providing a cultivated repertoire of problem-solving heuristics.

Assumptions About Qualitative Research and the Qualitative Research Life Cycle

The editors have organized this book around a set of assumptions about the goals and practices of qualitative research. As with all assumptions, some people may disagree with our views, including the contributors to this volume. Transparency and clarity are core virtues in qualitative inquiry. By sharing our assumptions, we hope to encourage researchers to approach the text from a reflexive perspective (Berger, 2015) and help those who question our perspectives to calibrate the editors' possible errors against the richness of the contributors' work.

Two primary assumptions guide our efforts. First, we believe qualitative research matters; asking people questions and disseminating the findings is a powerful engine for social change (Flyvbjerg, 2001). Second, we believe the skills necessary to do this work well can be learned through study and practice. What individuals say and do has value, whether those individuals are people who spend their days leading corporations, schools, or clinical care units (Benner, Hooper-Kyriakidis, & Stannard, 2011; Jackall, 1988; Wolcott, 1973) or whether they live and work in the margins (Behar, 2014; Bourgois, 2003; Finley, 2000; Ladson-Billings, 1994). The editors acknowledge people's speech and actions can be recorded and studied, and engaging these data allows researchers to gain insight into experiences, worlds, and minds—knowledge that is usable by academicians, clinicians, practitioners, and others. There is never a best way to interpret an interview, but researchers can do a better or worse job of understanding and communicating content and layers of meaning.

It is the editors' hope that one route researchers might take to do better is to refine their judgment as they skillfully deploy the methods and practices described in this book. However, technique is not the sole foundation of beneficial qualitative inquiry. Qualitative research is an ethical and emancipatory practice; the values displayed in and communicated by the work matter. Racist, homophobic, and sexist work, whether intentional or unconscious, cannot be described as successful, regardless of how careful the transcriptions or meticulous the coding system. Qualitative research must serve a politics of hope (Charmaz, 2017; Denzin & Giardina, 2009). There is no separate chapter on research ethics in this book, because all research decisions must follow from ethical principles regarding trustworthiness, diversity, equity, and inclusion (Christians, 2000).

Throughout the book we use the term the *qualitative research life cycle* to express the idea that qualitative research tends to have distinct and evolving stages. There is typically a research design stage where we consult literature, develop a conceptual framework, refine research questions, plan fieldwork, and develop interview and observation instruments (see Creswell & Poth, 2018; Leavy, 2017; Saldaña, 2014; Smith, Flowers, & Larkin, 2009 for descriptions of this work).

Once the design is in place, the grant is funded, the committee signs off, and the local internal review board accepts the data collection plan, the study moves from planning to action. Fieldwork begins. Researchers travel to another country, city, or their local neighborhood and observe what people say and do and take notes on these activities. They set up face-to-face interviews or they arrange for virtual encounters. Researchers take photographs, observe, or join in arts events, investigate community members' efforts to respond to a crisis, or partner with other people to change their corner of the world.

Eventually, the work changes as researchers return to their homes or spend more time at their favorite coffee shops. They begin to focus their efforts on analyzing data rather than collecting new information. During this stage of the qualitative research life cycle, researchers prepare transcripts, write memos, code data, or engage in other practices that help them organize and understand the material they have collected. Sometimes the researcher does most of this work on their own. Sometimes analysis and writing are organized around participatory, community-based practices. The end product might be a book, a play, or a project website, but the hope is findings will be shared and people will learn through and from the inquiry and the knowledge the study builds will be transformational, not simply transactional. Qualitative research is not navel gazing; it is active intervention into an unjust world.

TABLE 1 ● Project Glossary

The Qualitative Research Life Cycle

The Qualitative Research Life Cycle begins with a design stage, which can incorporate a theoretical or conceptual framework, then moves to data collection, analysis, interpretation, research products, and dissemination. In some cases, the process is iterative, circular, and emergent, with data collection and analysis informing another stage of data collection. Thus, questions that arise in analysis might lead to another round of interviews, and research products developed earlier in the investigation might be reanalyzed or reinterpreted.

Theory: A theory presents linked concepts that explain types, structures, conditions, processes, outcomes, or other abstractions based on previous research or constructed during the course of analysis and interpretation. Qualitative research can begin with theory and/or contribute to theory development. Some theories are explicit and may be learned or demonstrated through instruction; other theories are implicit and are particularly subject to interrogation (see Milner, 2007; Scheurich & Young, 1997).

Analysis: Analysis refers to the detailed examination of data, both at the micro-level of textual excerpts and the holistic level of transcripts (e.g., coding text segments, writing memos on transcripts). Analysis is comprised of, most often, methodical and systematic practices, yet can also consist of intuitive and creative approaches.

Interpretation: Interpretation refers to making meaning of data based on analysis. It can include conceptualizing, thematizing, or other forms of synthesis presenting a condensed understanding across data sources.

Theme: A theme is an often-abstract characteristic or pattern of the phenomena or topic of investigation. Themes are constructed or identified during analysis and interpretation using codes, categories, data, memos, and demographic characteristics. That is, themes synthesize pieces of the analysis into a more presentable and meaningful whole.

Levels of Inquiry: Levels of inquiry (Vagle, 2018) refer to the layers of investigation that researchers knowingly or unknowingly activate in their work. These include assumptions about the nature of reality and knowledge acquisition as well as research traditions and methods that align with these onto-epistemological paradigms. Aligning these levels of inquiry means ensuring that the research approach fits the larger paradigm and the methods that follow will provide the data best suited to answer the research question.

> **World views/Paradigms:** World views or paradigms refer to ontological/epistemological philosophies and assumptions that underpin qualitative traditions (e.g., constructivism, critical social theory).

> **Approaches/Traditions:** Qualitative approaches or traditions refer to established sets of data collection and analytical practices and strategies that form a coherent system of study (e.g., grounded theory, ethnography).

> **Methods:** Methods refer to specific tools for data collection (e.g., interviews, focus groups, participant observation).

> **Practices:** Practices refer to specific analytical or data-engagement tasks (e.g., in vivo coding, constructing themes).

> **Strategies:** Strategies refer to practices used for a particular analytic purpose (e.g., using codes and memos to construct themes, using key quotations to develop poems).

In the glossary in Table 1, the editors present their understanding of particular definitions of key terms used across chapters, though they have allowed authors to use their own perspective regarding these terms.

Blurred Boundaries and Informed Decisions

The stages of the qualitative research life cycle are not always distinct. Fieldwork, analysis, and interpretive meaning making may follow a reverberative rather than linear logic, and one stage may merge with another. Blurred boundaries may produce powerful research. Aishath Nasheeda, Haslinda Binti Abdullah, Steven Eric Krauss, and Nobaya Binti Ahmed, in Chapter 23, describe how questions about the meaning of research participants' interviews might be resolved, not through the use of various analytic and interpretive strategies, but by reinterviewing participants and asking them to comment on issues raised by their interview narrative. Craig M. McGill, Drew Puroway, and Mark Duslak, in Chapter 13, describe how recordings of data analysis meetings may become data to be analyzed. Sheryl L. Chatfield, in Chapter 3, describes how questions and research designs can be developed after the interview was conducted when researchers choose to use archived qualitative data. Alyson Welker and George Kamberelis, in Chapter 11, emphasize that data analysis may always remain incomplete. There are always new linkages and connections researchers might use to enrich the maps they create from their data.

Such blurred boundaries and nonlinear processes highlight the importance of researchers' ability to envision the end in mind and to organize inquiry to support the project's goals. One of the primary purposes of this book is to help readers increase their methodological literacy. We hope each chapter will help readers deepen the frames they use to guide their investigations or give them guidance on how to change their perspectives (see Bhattacharya, Chapter 21; Blanco & Rossman, Chapter 1). The section on transcription is intended to help readers decide how to best transcribe their interviews while the chapters by Jaime Fiddler (Chapter 16) and James A. Bernauer (Chapter 10) might support readers who decide to work directly from the recorded data. The range of coding practices we present (Bingham & Witkowsky, Chapter 8; Gonzalez & Lincoln, Chapter 12; Larbi-Cherif et al., Chapter 17; Turner, Chapter 7) can help readers compare research participants' experiences and develop analytic products that might be published in later phases of inquiry. We hope the discussions on memoing and other writing strategies (Fiddler, Chapter 16; Keane, Chapter 15; Mihas, Chapter 14; Welker & Kamberelis, Chapter 11) inspire readers to develop a system for recording their musings and make analytic connections within and across interviews. The sections on arts- and text-based communications practices are intended to broaden the range of strategies researchers use to interpret data and disseminate findings.

Qualitative research is a big tent with many performers (Tracy, 2010). We hope our book will inspire readers to step out of the audience and walk the tight rope and leap for the trapeze.

Charles Vanover
Paul Mihas
Johnny Saldaña

References

Allen, M. (2022). Sophie's choices: The social act of publishing a qualitative study. In C. Vanover, P. Mihas, & J. Saldaña (Eds.), *Analyzing and interpreting qualitative research: After the interview*. SAGE.

Bartesaghi, M. (2022). Theories and practices of transcription from discourse analysis. In C. Vanover, P. Mihas, & J. Saldaña (Eds.), *Analyzing and interpreting qualitative research: After the interview*. SAGE.

Behar, R. (2014). *Translated woman: Crossing the border with Esperanza's story*. Beacon.

Benner, P. E., Hooper-Kyriakidis, P. L., & Stannard, D. (2011). *Clinical wisdom and interventions in acute and critical care: A thinking-in-action approach* (2nd ed.). Springer.

Berger, R. (2015). Now I see it, now I don't: Researcher's position and reflexivity in qualitative research. *Qualitative Research, 15*(2), 219–234. https://doi.org/10.1177/1468794112468475

Bernard, H. R., Wutich, A., & Ryan, G. W. (2016). *Analyzing qualitative data: Systematic approaches* (2nd ed.). SAGE.

Bernauer, J. A. (2022). Oral coding: An alternative way to make sense of interview data. In C. Vanover, P. Mihas, & J. Saldaña (Eds.), *Analyzing and interpreting qualitative research: After the interview*. SAGE.

Bhattacharya, K. (2022). Embedding critical, creative, and contemplative data analysis in interview studies. In C. Vanover, P. Mihas, & J. Saldaña (Eds.), *Analyzing and interpreting qualitative research: After the interview*. SAGE.

Bingham, A. J., & Witkowsky, P. (2022). Deductive and inductive approaches to qualitative data analysis. In C. Vanover, P. Mihas, & J. Saldaña (Eds.), *Analyzing and interpreting qualitative research: After the interview*. SAGE.

Blanco, G. L., & Rossman, G. (2022). As a qualitative study unfolds: Shifts in design and analysis. In C. Vanover, P. Mihas, & J. Saldaña (Eds.), *Analyzing and interpreting qualitative research: After the interview*. SAGE.

Bourgois, P. (2003). *In search of respect: Selling crack in El Barrio* (2nd ed.). Cambridge University Press.

Braun, V., Clarke, V., & Weate, P. (2016). Using thematic analysis in sport and exercise research. In B. Smith & A. C. Sparkes (Eds.), *Routledge handbook of qualitative research in sport and exercise* (pp. 213–227). Routledge.

Charmaz, K. (2017). The power of constructivist grounded theory for critical inquiry. *Qualitative Inquiry, 23*(1), 34–45. https://doi.org/10.1177/1077800416657105

Chatfield, S. L. (2022). After someone else's interview. In C. Vanover, P. Mihas, & J. Saldaña (Eds.), *Analyzing and interpreting qualitative research: After the interview*. SAGE.

Christians, C. G. (2000). Ethics and politics in qualitative research. In N. K. Denzin, & Y. S. Lincoln (Eds.), *The Sage handbook of qualitative research* (4th ed.). SAGE.

Creswell, J. W., & Poth, C. N. (2018). *Qualitative inquiry and research design: Choosing among five approaches* (4th ed.). SAGE.

Denzin, N. K., & Giardina, M. D. (2009). *Qualitative inquiry and social justice: Toward a politics of hope*. Routledge.

di Gregorio, S. (2022). Voice to text: Automating transcription. In C. Vanover, P. Mihas, & J. Saldaña (Eds.), *Analyzing and interpreting qualitative research: After the interview*. SAGE.

Fiddler, J. L. (2022). Listening deeply: Indexing research conversations in a narrative inquiry. In C. Vanover, P. Mihas, & J. Saldaña (Eds.), *Analyzing and interpreting qualitative research: After the interview*. SAGE.

Finley, M. (2000). *Street rat*. Greenroom Press and the University of Detroit Mercy.

Flyvbjerg, B. (2001). *Making social science matter: Why social inquiry fails and how it can succeed again* (S. Sampson, Trans.). Cambridge University Press.

Galman, S. C. (2016). *The good, the bad, and the data: Shane the Lone Ethnographer's basic guide to qualitative data analysis*. Routledge.

Galman, S. C. (2022). Follow the headlights: On comics-based data analysis. In C. Vanover, P. Mihas, & J. Saldaña (Eds.), *Analyzing and interpreting qualitative research: After the interview*. SAGE.

Gee, J. P. (2014). *How to do discourse analysis: A toolkit* (3rd ed.). Routledge.

Gonzalez, E. M., & Lincoln, Y. S. (2022). Analyzing and coding interviews and focus groups considering cross-cultural and cross-language data. In C. Vanover, P. Mihas, & J. Saldaña (Eds.), *Analyzing and interpreting qualitative research: After the interview*. SAGE.

Gullion, J. S. (2022). Writing for a broad audience: Concept papers, blogs, and OpEds. In C. Vanover, P. Mihas, & J. Saldaña (Eds.), *Analyzing and interpreting qualitative research: After the interview*. SAGE.

Huffman, T. (2022). Making claims using qualitative data. In C. Vanover, P. Mihas, & J. Saldaña (Eds.), *Analyzing and interpreting qualitative research: After the interview*. SAGE.

Jackall, R. (1988). *Moral mazes: The world of corporate managers*. Oxford University Press.

Keane, E. (2022). Critical analytic memoing. In C. Vanover, P. Mihas, & J. Saldaña (Eds.), *Analyzing and interpreting qualitative research: After the interview*. SAGE.

Ladson-Billings, G. (1994). *The dreamkeepers: Successful teachers of African American children*. Jossey-Bass.

Larbi-Cherif, A., Egan, C., & Glazer, J. L. (2022). Emergent analysis: Strategies for making sense of an evolving longitudinal study. In C. Vanover, P. Mihas, & J. Saldaña (Eds.), *Analyzing and interpreting qualitative research: After the interview*. SAGE.

Leavy, P. (2017). *Research design: Quantitative, qualitative, mixed methods, arts-based, and community-based participatory research approaches*. Guilford.

Lester, J. N., & Paulus, T. M. (2022). Using qualitative data analysis software to manage the research process. In C. Vanover, P. Mihas, & J. Saldaña (Eds.), *Analyzing and interpreting qualitative research: After the interview*. SAGE.

° Lincoln, Y. S., & Denzin, N. K. (2003). *Turning points in qualitative research: Tying knots in a handkerchief.* Rowman/AltaMira.

McGill, C. M., Puroway, D., & Duslak, M. (2022). On being a researcher-participant: Challenges with the iterative process of data production, analysis, and (re)production. In C. Vanover, P. Mihas, & J. Saldaña (Eds.), *Analyzing and interpreting qualitative research: After the interview.* SAGE.

Mihas, P. (2022). Memo writing strategies: Analyzing the parts and the whole. In C. Vanover, P. Mihas, & J. Saldaña (Eds.), *Analyzing and interpreting qualitative research: After the interview.* SAGE.

Miles, M. B., Huberman, A. M., & Saldaña, J. (2020). *Qualitative data analysis: A methods sourcebook* (4th ed.). SAGE.

° Milner, H. R. (2007). Race, culture, and researcher positionality: Working through dangers seen, unseen, and unforeseen. *Educational Researcher, 36*(7), 388–400. https://doi.org/10.3102/0013189X07309471

Nasheeda, A., Abdullah, H. B., Krauss, S. E., & Ahmed, N. B. (2022). Turning transcripts into stories. In C. Vanover, P. Mihas, & J. Saldaña (Eds.), *Analyzing and interpreting qualitative research: After the interview.* SAGE.

Richards, J. (2022). Coding, categorizing, and theming the data: A reflexive search for meaning. In C. Vanover, P. Mihas, & J. Saldaña (Eds.), *Analyzing and interpreting qualitative research: After the interview.* SAGE.

Rubin, H. J., & Rubin, I. S. (2011). *Qualitative interviewing: The art of hearing data.* SAGE.

Saldaña, J. (2014). *Thinking qualitatively: Methods of mind.* SAGE.

Saldaña, J. (2018). Ethnodrama and ethnotheatre: Research as performance. In N. Denzin, & Y. S. Lincoln (Eds.), *The Sage handbook of qualitative research* (5th ed., pp. 377–394). SAGE.

Saldaña, J. (2022). Dramatizing interviews. In C. Vanover, P. Mihas, & J. Saldaña (Eds.), *Analyzing and interpreting qualitative research: After the interview.* SAGE.

Saldaña, J., & Omasta, M. (2018). *Qualitative research: Analyzing life.* SAGE.

° Scheurich, J. J., & Young, M. D. (1997). Coloring epistemologies: Are our research epistemologies racially biased? *Educational Researcher, 26*(4), 4–16. https://doi.org/10.3102/0013189X026004004

Shenfield, R., & Prendergast, M. (2022). What makes an effective teacher? Revealing good teaching practice through interview poetic transcription. In C. Vanover, P. Mihas, & J. Saldaña (Eds.), *Analyzing and interpreting qualitative research: After the interview.* SAGE.

Silverman, D. (2000). Analyzing talk and text. In N. K. Denzin, & Y. S. Lincoln (Eds.), *Handbook of qualitative research* (2nd ed., pp. 821–834). SAGE.

Smith, J. A., Flowers, P., & Larkin, M. (2009). *Interpretative phenomenological analysis: Theory, method and research.* SAGE.

° Tracy, S. J. (2010). Qualitative quality: Eight "big-tent" criteria for excellent qualitative research. *Qualitative Inquiry, 16*(10), 837–851. https://doi.org/10.1177%2F1077800410383121

Turner, D. (2022). Coding system design and management. In C. Vanover, P. Mihas, & J. Saldaña (Eds.), *Analyzing and interpreting qualitative research: After the interview.* SAGE.

Vagle, M. (2018). Learning from lived experience: How we can study the world as it is lived. Course at the qualitative research Summer Intensive. ResearchTalk, Inc.

Vanover, C. (2022). Transcription as a form of qualitative inquiry. In C. Vanover, P. Mihas, & J. Saldaña (Eds.), *Analyzing and interpreting qualitative research: After the interview.* SAGE.

Welker, A. P., & Kamberelis, G. (2022). Mapping trajectories: Analyzing focus group data rhizomatically. In C. Vanover, P. Mihas, & J. Saldaña (Eds.), *Analyzing and interpreting qualitative research: After the interview.* SAGE.

Wolcott, H. F. (1973). *The man in the principal's office.* Holt, Rinehart, & Winston.

Data and Conceptual Options

Charles Vanover and Paul Mihas

Introduction

The first section of this volume invites us to consider points of departure for a study and to be attentive to our decisions as researchers. What options for data collection and for analysis will we consider as we begin to map out our plan for data analysis? Qualitative research is a creative practice as well as an analytical one. Design and analysis are not governed by algorithms or the predetermined logic of a computer program. The hundreds of minor and consequential decisions necessary to transform a set of interviews into a complete study are not made on impulse but through careful and intentional decision-making. When qualitative researchers code, sift through, dig out, transform, and embody the data, they evaluate their progress according to a single set of guideposts. Research questions—not protocols, equations, or computer software—shape this progress.

Research questions shape the design of interview instruments and how researchers construct meanings from the participants' discourse. These questions guide decisions researchers make as they choose the dialogue they will analyze and their strategies for transcription and data management. Research questions are both unique to an individual research effort and shaped by the knowledge community that shapes what we already know or what we think we know. When we depart on the qualitative journey and begin to conduct interviews and review transcripts, we must ask ourselves whether our study is an opportunity to unlearn or unknow the assumptions and prior knowledge that produced the questions we carry into the field. That is, we may be faced with other ways of looking through a diverse and complex world based on our participants' lenses. Hence, we may need to document our *a priori* concepts and to what degree they will drive the study. We must ask whether these ideas are "sensitizing concepts"—topics that we are aware of—or whether they will be concepts that more formally direct our inquiry? (Charmaz, 2014, p. 30). In this way, points of departure are met with points of redeparture as we begin again with an ever-closer understanding of the participants' world and a better grasp of methods we will employ in knowledge production and dissemination.

Qualitative research's emergent character means that even the questions that guide the inquiry may change. Relevance is not determined by hard and fast rules; it is determined by the content of the data and the analyst's skill and judgment. This flexibility is a strength as qualitative researchers strive to understand lives and social worlds in flux. Research agendas must be adjusted to account for these emerging complexities. It may turn out the original questions and research design become less suitable as researchers enter and reenter the field. Similarly, once researchers have moved to the next phase of the qualitative life cycle and have made data analysis their central focus, the meanings produced by coding, memo writing, or artistic practices might refine the questions that guide the investigation. Researchers may discover the data tell a different or deeper story from the story they first envisioned when they conducted their literature reviews or first heard from participants in the field (Locke, Golden-Biddle, & Feldman, 2008).

The chapters by Gerardo L. Blanco and Gretchen B. Rossman (Chapter 1), Jessica N. Lester and Trena M. Paulus (Chapter 2), and Sheryl L. Chatfield (Chapter 3) that constitute this section provide rich accounts of the decision-making that guides qualitative inquiry. The authors tell different stories about their design and points of departure, but each chapter communicates the same core message—the qualitative research life cycle is both creative and analytical. Blanco and Rossman's chapter emphasizes that shifts in research questions must be made cautiously and intentionally. A new question may create a ripple effect of significant changes in the data analysis plan and necessitate new transcripts, new coding schemes, and new memos. In some cases, the data might remain the same, but the meanings researchers foreground might alter as researchers work with a focus more closely aligned with participants' stories and other field material. As Chatfield discusses in depth, qualitative researchers guided by different questions may construct different meanings from the same interview transcript.

Chatfield reminds us researchers are not required to go into the field. They have the choice of collecting new data or analyzing existing data. Secondary data might be archived, text-based or audio-visual recordings of oral history data and other records. Paulus and Lester remind us some of the most important decisions in the analysis might be made early in the qualitative research life cycle and might include numerous critical choices regarding managing data through software, such as taking the time to synchronize transcripts with transcribed data. Making informed decisions regarding how we intend to use sophisticated tools allow us to more effectively manage the data we collect. Qualitative data analysis software can give us immediate access to participant voices, sometimes literally allowing us to return to their audio voices as we read transcribed words.

A Tool for Beginning the Beginning of Data Analysis and Completing the Work

In the introduction to this volume, Charles Vanover described how he and his colleagues at the University of Michigan's Narrative Institute asked speakers to describe how they transformed the boxes of cassette tapes, notebooks, photographs, and floppy disks they produced during fieldwork into completed qualitative studies. The editors have crafted the following tool to help emerging researchers conceptualize and manage this work. The tool is designed to support research design and help researchers create detailed and realistic plans. The tool is also intended to be used after fieldwork and during data analysis to keep the project on track and to coordinate multiple efforts. Many of the initial questions are technical, and these prompts focus on the nuts-and-bolts details of the analytic process.

Planning and organization are the foundations for successful qualitative inquiry. Every qualitative study is a journey to the unknown. To make the journey successful, researchers must have the right tools for the job and the skill to use them well. Yes, plans may change, tools may be discarded, and unexpected landscapes might change the route of the journey, but preparation and planning make a difference when time is limited and the pressure is on.

We invite readers to fill out this tool as they contemplate their data analysis plan and as they enter the increasingly analytic stages of their inquiry.

Data Analysis and Interpretation Questions

1. What are your questions and assumptions?

    a. List your research questions at the top of the document you create from this tool and refer to them often.

    b. Briefly list any key assumptions that drive the inquiry.

2. What are your data?

    a. If you have not yet designed your study, refer to books on qualitative research to conceptualize your research design (e.g., Charmaz, 2014; Galman, 2007; Gullion, 2016; Leavy, 2017; Rossman & Rallis, 2011; Saldaña & Omasta, 2018).

    b. List the data you intend to collect or the material you have collected.

3. Where is your data?

    a. Create a set of computer and physical files where you might place interviews, photographs, observations, and other text and materials you will collect in the field or check to make sure the data you collected are in their place.

    i. Try to anticipate important filing dilemmas. For example, do the notes you wrote during an interview go in the folder for that interview, the folder where you place observations, or in a separate folder?

  b. Create a set of labels and time stamps that list key attributes of the data or check to make sure the data are labeled and filed correctly.

  c. How have you backed up your content?

4. Have you processed and stored the data in accordance with the policies of your Institutional Review Board (IRB)?

  a. Did your data collection efforts follow the procedures outlined in your IRB agreement, and are you giving research participants the level of confidentiality you promised?

5. How much time and money do you have to do the work?

  a. When is the book, paper, report, or dissertation due? What progress reports need to be sent to whom?

    i. Dissertation researchers should figure out their committee members' timelines and procedures as well as their university's policies. Time-to-degree requirements and dissertation credit hour registration deadlines may become important hoops to jump.

    ii. Early career, tenure-track researchers should figure out when progress reports are due for their annual reviews. They might also check when published and in press studies are due for their three-year evaluations and when portfolios are due for external letters and other steps in the process.

6. What are the procedures for filing amendments when one of your submitted papers does go into press?

  a. Did your fieldwork run on schedule? What are the consequences if things take longer than anticipated?

    i. The editors recommend putting all relevant due dates into an online calendar.

    ii. Does this schedule look realistic?

Reflection and Activities

1. Take your outline and look over the table of contents for this book. Write a memo that describes the most important sections and chapters you may

need for your study. Do you anticipate needing any other professional development?

2. Outline a written data analysis plan using a bulleted list or planning software. Emphasize what you know as well as any gaps you will fill by reading this book and engaging in other professional development. Examine your questions and assumptions. Do they match the current analysis plan? Write a brief summary that describes the alignment between questions, assumptions, data, and analysis. Develop this plan further based on the information shared in the upcoming chapters by Blanco and Rossman, Lester and Paulus, and Chatfield. What are some of the most important steps you might take in the next few weeks to firm up your inquiry?

3. Create a plan to revise this plan after you read this book and once you return from the field.

References

Blanco, G. L., & Rossman, G. B. (2022). As a qualitative study unfolds: Shifts in design and analysis. In C. Vanover, P. Mihas, & J. Saldaña (Eds.), *Analyzing and interpreting qualitative research: After the interview*. SAGE.

Charmaz, K. (2014). *Constructing grounded theory*. SAGE.

Chatfield, S. L. (2022). After someone else's interview. In C. Vanover, P. Mihas, & J. Saldaña (Eds.), *Analyzing and interpreting qualitative research: After the interview*. SAGE.

Galman, S. C. (2007). *Shane, the Lone Ethnographer: A beginner's guide to ethnography*. Rowman Altamira.

Gullion, J. S. (2016). *Writing ethnography*. Brill Sense.

Leavy, P. (2017). *Research design: Quantitative, qualitative, mixed methods, arts-based, and community-based participatory research approaches*. Guilford.

Lester, J. N., & Paulus, T. M. (2022). Using qualitative data analysis software to manage the research process. In C. Vanover, P. Mihas, & J. Saldaña (Eds.), *Analyzing and interpreting qualitative research: After the interview*. SAGE.

Locke, K., Golden-Biddle, K., & Feldman, M. S. (2008). Making doubt generative: Rethinking the role of doubt in the research process. *Organization Science, 19*(6), 907–918. https://doi.org/10.1287/orsc.1080.0398

Rossman, G. B., & Rallis, S. F. (2011). *Learning in the field: An introduction to qualitative research*. SAGE.

Saldaña, J., & Omasta, M. (2018). *Qualitative research: Analyzing life*. SAGE.

Vanover, C., Mihas, P., & Saldaña, J. (2022). Introduction. In C. Vanover, P. Mihas, & J. Saldaña (Eds.), *Analyzing and interpreting qualitative research: After the interview*. SAGE.

As a Qualitative Study Unfolds: Shifts in Design and Analysis

Gerardo L. Blanco and Gretchen B. Rossman

Abstract

Research design does not follow a linear trajectory. Researchers go back and forth between their original plan and the realities and limitations that data collection and analysis impose. This process is not always restrictive; new opportunities emerge, and new potential collaborators appear. Research is what happens as a result of this interactive process. The complex decision making processes involved in redesign do not take place in a vacuum. In this chapter, we discuss communities of practice and critical friends as crucial elements that guide what happens *after the interview*. The proposal defense and the research prospectus provide opportunities to reevaluate research designs, but they are not the only opportunities of this type. We provide examples from our own and our students' experiences. We argue that rather than seeing redesign as a shortcoming, researchers must be prepared to embrace the many twists and turns involved in thoughtful and responsible research.

Keywords: Critical friends; communities of practice; qualitative research; research design

Introduction and Overview of Relevant Literature

A central tenet of qualitative inquiry is that many studies are, at least in part, "emergent" (Creswell & Poth, 2017; Denzin, 2009). This emphasis on emergence stems from core assumptions about knowledge and inquiry, including the role of interpretation, empathy, and contextualization/embodiment in knowledge construction (Stake, 2010). Though studies begin with well-thought-out conceptual frameworks, guiding questions, and a solid analytic framework, the messiness of fieldwork often demands modest changes to this early design, which is typically encoded in the proposal and the pathways through data analysis. With our students, we stress that a proposal is just that—*proposed* actions that the researcher plans to undertake when conducting the study. Conceptualizing the proposal as a plan, rather than a contract, opens up space for the researcher to be responsive to developments while conducting fieldwork and subsequent analysis, making ethical, empathetic changes. Modest redesign and shifts in data analysis plans for the study become legitimate and, we argue, necessary to embody the flexible nature of qualitative inquiry. Thus, we argue, "emergence" may shift the original design plan as well as the focused analysis stage of many studies.

Though many major texts on qualitative inquiry (e.g., Merriam & Tisdell, 2015; Pailthorpe, 2017; Ravitch & Carl, 2016; Rossman & Rallis, 2016; Silverman, 2011) herald the emergent nature of qualitative inquiry, there are few examples that depict how modest changes in design and new pathways for analysis occur, under what circumstances, and why. In this chapter, we develop a set of situations often encountered that lead to decisions to redesign or shift an analytic framework of a study. We then offer an example from the work of Gerardo Blanco and provide a few specifics from the work of our students. We conclude with practical suggestions for systematically recording and justifying decisions in these emergent processes. The examples illustrate the dialectical nature of qualitative inquiry and the need to attend to relationships in the field and the ever-changing contexts where research is situated.

The specific practice that we focus on in this chapter is *collaboration*. We argue that shifts in design, data collection (either methods or sources), and analysis are best accomplished through deep, thoughtful discussions with others. This is frequently referred to in the literature as building *a community of practice* and relying on *critical friends*. Though related, these have somewhat different emphases.

Communities of Practice

Articulated by Lave and Wenger (1991) and Wenger (1998), communities of practice are groups of individuals who have the following characteristics:

1. they share a *domain of interest*, in this case, research;

2. they form *a community* where members participate in shared activities and conversations, are available to provide support and help to one another, and relate experiences and insights;

3. they are *practitioners*; that is, they have a "shared repertoire of resources—experiences, stories, tools, ways of addressing recurring problems—in short a shared practice" (Wenger-Trayner & Wenger-Trayner, 2015).

Crucial to an effective community of practice is trust: members feel empowered to share fears, worries, and fuzzy problems that have arisen in their research practice. They, in turn, are open to gentle critical feedback from other members, listen to and ponder questions that expand the scope of their thinking, and consider recommendations for ways through these thorny methodological issues. In short, in our field, a community of practice is a learning community engaged in helping members improve their research practice.

Critical Friends

Within the literature on qualitative methods, use of a critical friend is quite regularly listed as a way to guard against researcher bias (see, for example, Creswell & Poth, 2017; Marshall & Rossman, 2016; Merriam & Tisdell, 2015; Rossman & Rallis, 2016). The idea is that the critical friend can raise tough questions, encouraging the researcher to recognize—and move beyond—their own pre-conceptions. This is similar to the role that members can play in a community of practice: pushing one another to rethink their practice and move in new, perhaps creative and expansive, directions. However, rather than being situated in a community with a shared domain, critical friendships are often dyadic relationships between the researcher and an Other. They are, thus, perhaps more intimate. However, as with a community of practice, a generative critical friend relationship asks tough questions of the researcher, questions that may be difficult to truly hear.

Both forms of collaborative engagement are grounded in the notion of dialogue and built on trust. Etymologically, dialogue comes from the Greek *dialogos* meaning "conversation, discourse, valuable or constructive communication" (Brown, 1993, p. 661). "Dialogue, therefore, is a fundamentally interactive process of authentic thinking together. It is generative. It moves beyond any single individual's understanding to produce new knowledge" (Rallis & Rossman, 2000, p. 83).

We argue that collaborative practice—whether communities of practice or critical friendships—deepens the richness of a study. The work gets better when people work together in considering a thoughtful modification in design and subsequent shifts in data gathering or in enriching the depth of insights during analysis. We next present an example from research conducted by Gerardo Blanco. As we depict, he relied on collaborative relationships throughout this study.

More Is Not Always Better: An Example

Our experience directing and supervising student research informs our perspective on research design and redesign. Graduate students and novice researchers sometimes assume that shifts in design are the result of mistakes they have made or that these changes constitute a failure. Instead, we see shifts in design merely as the way qualitative research unfolds, opening new possibilities for analysis. It is common for significant changes to take place, for example, during dissertation proposal defenses and occasionally after the research proposal has been approved. As mentioned in the introduction, we do not see the proposal as a contract, but rather as an organized and detailed record of decisions that have been taken, and that are subject to change. Graduate students are sometimes shocked when committee members propose significant modifications to their study's structure—and even to the purpose of the study. We have learned that it is necessary to have open and intentional conversations with students about what can be expected from a dissertation proposal defense. The example we discuss takes us back to 2012, when Gerardo, one of the authors of this chapter, was getting ready to defend his dissertation proposal.

The Proposal Defense as Redesign Opportunity

Gerardo's dissertation explored the adoption of U.S. accreditation among private universities in Mexico, which is an emergent phenomenon of interest within the field of comparative and international higher education. He initially proposed a comparative case study where three different institutions in three different states in Mexico would be analyzed to identify similarities and differences. This multiple case study design (Stake, 2005) felt comprehensive enough to convey a sense of rigor and intentionality at the dissertation proposal defense. The reasoning supporting this initial approach was that there were four universities in Mexico holding U.S. accreditation, with a fifth being added at the time the research project was proposed. By studying the newly accredited institution in contrast with two already established institutions, a form of maximum variation (Patton, 2015) in case selection was expected. Gerardo thought that the "right way" to explore the unique characteristics of this newly accredited institutions was to compare and contrast it with previously accredited institutions.

The five eligible institutions are distributed in three regions of Mexico: two of them are located in central Mexico, two in north-central Mexico, and one in Mexico's northwest. All the institutions are private universities. Table 1.1 summarizes some characteristics of the institutions, using institution pseudonyms. NuevoTec, in boldface, was ultimately selected as the site for the research project.

However, the defense was different from what he had initially expected. Gerardo did not get through the carefully planned presentation slides. The defense turned quickly into a conversation among colleagues about what would be realistic to expect from a study conducted by a single researcher, and about the cost of visiting three different institutions in a different country, along with many other practical considerations. Considerations about the availability of resources are paramount when making decisions about the feasibility of a study (Rossman & Rallis, 2016).

As the conversation went on during the proposal defense, a committee member posed the following question: "Why don't you do a single case, but do it really well?" Initially, such a significant change in the study's design felt very threatening. Would a single case study meet the threshold required for earning a terminal degree in terms of making an original and significant contribution to the field? Would

	TABLE 1.1 ● Summary of Institutional Characteristics				
Institution	Location	Control	Accreditation		Initial accreditation
UniMex	Single campus, urban, central region	Private	Southern Association of Colleges and Schools (SACS)		1991
UPA	Single campus, urban, central region	Private	SACS		1959
Mex. I.T.	Multicampus, urban, northeast	Private	SACS		1950
UniNorte	Single campus, urban, northeast	Private	SACS		2001
NuevoTec	**Multicampus, urban, northwest**	**Private**	**Western Association of Schools and Colleges**		**2012**

anyone really care about what is happening in "just" one higher education institution? In addition, there was the feeling that somehow the work put into the research proposal had been misguided or off-target. In retrospect, these questions and feelings of struggle were not surprising, but neither were they warranted. This was just how qualitative research takes place. The purpose of the study and research questions could still be pursued through a single case.

Rather than the study "falling apart," the theoretical idea of *emergent design* was operating in a specific context as a result of engaging with critical friends and one's community of practice. Moreover, the way the committee member phrased the question was important. Implied in the phrase "but do it really well" was a statement about how difficult it would be to do a high-quality study with the proposed scope given the resources available at the time. Most importantly, implied in the question was a sense of care and investment in the success of the study and an interest in setting the student up for success. This dissertation committee member was, of course, being critical but most importantly they were acting as a friend—demonstrating care and legitimate interest. This is of paramount importance in our work mentoring students.

Group deliberation within a community of practice is crucial for making decisions about research redesign and for the research steps that take place after data collection. The significance of group deliberation is evident within dissertation committees, where experienced researchers guide graduate students. However, many other research settings provide opportunities for group discussion and decision-making. The idea of the lone qualitative researcher has been questioned over the course of the last few decades (Bresler, Wasser, Hertzog, & Lemons, 1996). Even single-author research studies involve a dialogue, and often compromise, between the researcher and the field—embodied by such gatekeepers as journal and book editors and reviewers.

Redesign and Data Analysis

Shifts in design continue after the scope of the study has been agreed upon and the proposal is approved. By narrowing the site selection from three cases to one, new opportunities for data collection and analysis became possible. At the time of the proposal defense, only traditional strategies for data analysis had been contemplated. With three research sites and multiple participants in each, it was possible to anticipate only a traditional open and focused coding of interview transcripts (Saldaña, 2016). The shift to a single case opened up new possibilities for analysis. Brinkmann (2012) argues that qualitative research has experienced "a certain inflation ... with more and more participants" (p. 1). The multiple case study initially proposed can be seen as an example of this trend.

As a result of the revised scope of a single instrumental case study, data collection and analysis expanded to include more than traditional interviews to be recorded, transcribed, and coded. Everyday artifacts, such as posters and banners displayed around campus, were added to the data collection strategies through researcher-generated images (Blanco Ramírez, 2015b). This opened up new avenues for visual analysis strategies of situated and everyday life data sources (Brinkmann, 2012; Pink, 2012). What started as a compensatory strategy to make up for a reduced research scope resulted in a more robust dataset and a more interesting study in the end, as the committee member had suggested during the proposal defense. The initial proposal did not contemplate any of these possibilities. Even though we will never know what the initial study could have become, it is likely that the pressure of collecting data in three sites involving international travel would have constrained the possibilities of engaging with alternative data forms in addition to the traditional recorded/transcribed interviews. It is also worth mentioning that redesign did not take place only at the proposal defense. It was the result of many conversations between the student and each member of the dissertation committee, as well as extensive e-mail correspondence among the group.

Shifting Design Is Not Correcting Errors

The example we have shared had multiple happy endings. After revising the scope to a single instrumental case study, Gerardo completed his dissertation and graduated the following year. Not only did the single case allow him to complete his graduate program, but it was also well-received in conferences and was published in one of the top journals in the field (Blanco Ramírez, 2015a). When data collection started, the revised design with a single case study approach still felt like a deficit despite all the advice and reassurance by the dissertation committee. This forced Gerardo to take an expansive approach to data collection: rather than focusing exclusively on the interviews, he paid attention to the physical environment and the material culture. For example, he had to wait outside faculty and administrators' offices and interact with multiple assistants. He focused on those waiting areas, the materials on the walls and the pamphlets on coffee tables. He was more mindful of his walk from the parking lot to the campus buildings (see Figure 1.1). Of course, these are all good research practices, but at the time they were the consequence of trying to fill the void that eliminating research sites had left.

In addition to the initial study, with the help of a coauthor and with funding from a research grant, Gerardo conducted a multiple case study in three universities in Canada exploring the same phenomenon (Blanco Ramírez & Luu, 2018). This study in the Canadian context was similar to the initial dissertation design, involving three cases, but it also incorporated a focus on visual elements. What is salient about this study was the increased availability of resources, as well as more experience conducting research. Moreover, a team of three researchers built upon

FIGURE 1.1 ● "With WASC, We Continue Striving for Educational Excellence." Researcher-Generated Image Photographed During Data Collection

the original single case study in Mexico and studied the phenomenon through a case study of three institutions (Barrett, Fernandez, & Gonzalez, 2019).

Perhaps more importantly, the visual data collected as a result of the narrower scope led to its own publication (Blanco Ramírez, 2015b), and visual analysis has become a central component in Gerardo's research agenda. The examples of successful publications presented above illustrate that design in qualitative research constitutes a cascading process in which one decision alters the course of subsequent decisions. From this perspective, we can hardly speak of mistakes when shifts in design occur. Instead, new possibilities unfold as we make decisions that alter the direction of a study. These changes that can be at times framed as failures can lead to entirely new ways of thinking about not only the study at hand, but more broadly, about one's approach to research and inquiry.

The Practice of Collaboration in Qualitative Research

As noted above in the brief literature review, opportunities for collaboration abound in any study. Redesign, with implications for data gathering (sources and methods) and new directions for analysis frequently emerge with collaborative partners who are committed to the high quality of the research. These opportunities for collaboration can take place early on, before commencing the empirical stage of the study, as well as during and after data collection. These changes, as discussed in Gerardo's dissertation example, may focus on redesign to simplify the study. In other instances, we find opportunities to reframe the design to focus on a different set of theories or a different conceptual framework. Sometimes redesign comes in the form of seizing an opportunity or an unexpected development in the field or the researcher acquiring a new set of skills.

Collaboration and Shifting Designs Before Data Collection

The example we discussed in the previous section illustrates how proposal defenses constitute a setting in which collaboration among researchers can take place in a structured setting. Collaboration does not always take such a structured form, with scheduled meetings and assigned roles, such as chairs and readers. More often than not, qualitative research is collaborative from the beginning: an interesting topic comes to mind as a result of an interesting conversation with a colleague at a conference, or we come together with colleagues who have different expertise to develop a grant proposal. Regardless of the level of structure and formality, it is important to attend to power differences in the collaborative process. A suggestion from a faculty member to a graduate student, or from a senior scholar to an early-career one, may feel as a nonnegotiable directive. We believe, however, that collaboration is a skill that can be learned and that practice goes a long way in becoming better at and more comfortable with the communicative process collaboration demands.

At a more recent dissertation proposal defense, in which Gerardo was no longer the student-researcher but a member, a student initially proposed a multiple case study approach. The proposed dissertation looks at underrepresented students who participate in living-learning communities on campus. As the discussion progressed, it became clear that the boundaries around the case were difficult to establish. Was each learning community a case? Was each participant a case? Was the institution, which also has several regional campuses, the case? The student was proposing aggregating all the interviews for analytical purposes and conducting a generic thematic analysis. With this information, the committee—in dialogue with the student—suggested to shift the design to either a narrative inquiry or phenomenological approach. After discussing different design options and their implications, the student-researcher opted for a phenomenological approach given her proximity to the research setting—as she works on campus as an adviser. The student-researcher was concerned that a narrative approach would require such level of detail that the identity of the participants could be easily identified. After the proposal defense, Gerardo shared how his own dissertation had shifted significantly and encouraged the students to see this as an opportunity, or as a blessing in disguise.

Recommending major changes to someone's research design or recognizing that our initial plan of action needs changes is not an easy process. However, we contend that a true collaborative process fosters trust and communication. From this perspective, the goal is to identify opportunities rather than finding errors to fix, and this approach makes shifts in design easier to accept.

Shifts in Design as Reframing Ongoing Work

Additional examples of collaboration in qualitative research include circulating a manuscript among colleagues before sending it out for review or presenting work in progress at a conference. In other cases, collaboration may not feel as such and take a more argumentative form where compromise is required. This is particularly the case with journal editors and, especially, when working with the proverbial "Reviewer 2" who thinks the study explores an important topic, but who also thinks that the study should include a different set of participants, take place in another setting, and include an entirely different set of data collection and analysis strategies. Rather than abandoning the project and starting again, researchers would benefit from reframing some of their methodological choices, keeping a particular audience, or community of practice, in mind.

In the example we discussed, Gerardo's dissertation, shifts in design were agreed upon collectively by the student-researcher and members of the dissertation committee before data were collected. In other cases, shifts in design result from collaboration while work is ongoing, and even after the empirical stage has concluded and researchers move to *write up* the study (Wolcott, 2009). Some of these shifts are about how the research is being framed. Going back to our example, the revised study scope, with a single institution, could be framed as an instrumental case study, according to a long-accepted typology of case studies (Stake, 2005). However, case studies emphasize eclecticism and the boundaries around the case (Yin, 2018), rather than the emphasis on an agreed-upon set of data collection and analysis strategies that are taken as a wholesale decision. As a result, researchers conducting case studies often borrow from other genres to describe their methodological choices.

After revising the study scope, Gerardo's dissertation was framed as an ethnographic case study, given its focus on actions and interactions, and the purposes of seeking shared meaning among the members of a group, namely the faculty and administration of a Mexican university. However, the same study—as Gretchen suggested when Gerardo was turning the dissertation into manuscripts for publication in journals—could be framed along the lines of compressed ethnography (LeCompte & Schensul, 2010). This distinction, it is worth noting, did not involve changes to how the study would be conducted but rather shifted how the study would be presented to a different audience. With the changes in scope that led to a more prominent role of visual data, it simply made sense to reframe the study retrospectively within the language of the ethnographic genre and given the long tradition of visual and public ethnography (Pink, 2007).

An example of redesign mid-data collection comes from Jenn Flemming, one of Gretchen's students, in her study of refugees on Lesvos Island, Greece. Lesvos has been—and continues to be—a destination for refugees from many countries (Syria, Iraq, Afghanistan, Congo, and Somalia, among others) departing from Turkey (under horrific circumstances) to reach Greece and, through Greece, hopefully to other European countries. The student designed a participatory ethnographic study focusing on two major refugee camps on the island. When she was in the midst of data collection, she learned that photography (and the PhotoVoice method) could be especially evocative for depicting refugees' experiences and also empowering as refugees of all ages took photos and narrated their meaning to her. She had not anticipated this in her original design but was fortunate to be invited to attend a summer seminar at the University of the Aegean on migration. This seminar was designed for graduate students conducting ethnographic research at many of the refugee camps in Greece and it was attended by Greek and other international scholars. This seminar proved a true community of practice and fostered the development of a handful of valued critical friendships. This community of practice encouraged Jenn to focus quite explicitly on the visual imagery.

The visual images, interpreted by her participants, told of the pain, loss, and hope that many of the refugees experienced. For example, an image of a young woman gazing out across the Mediterranean Sea toward the origin of her refugee journey elicited emotional reactions that went well beyond just words. The young woman narrated some of her feelings to the student (see Figure 1.2): "One of the women—Yusra—came to sit and speak with me. 'This is where our boat landed,' she explained. 'We haven't been back here until now. We arrived nearly 3 months ago'."

FIGURE 1.2 ● Woman on the Shores of the Aegean Sea. Researcher-Generated Image Photographed During Data Collection

Source: Republished with kind permission from Jennifer Flemming.

Jenn had been doing preliminary analysis on interview and observation data. As she moved into analysis more intentionally, and drawing on her community of practice's support, she realized that the photos and their accompanying narratives were quite powerful, in many ways more evocative than the interview transcripts. As noted above, she had not anticipated this and wanted to shift her data collection plan to emphasize the photographs and their narratives. While continuing to gather "traditional" interview and observation data, she argued, persuasively, that the visual images carried profound meaning. She discussed this possible new focus of the data collection and analysis extensively with Gretchen, her committee chair (and critical friend). The resulting presentation is deeply moving (Flemming, 2018), as refugees from many countries shared their viewpoints (photos) and their attendant meanings.

Sometimes the design shifts along the way and the researcher needs simply to catch up with those changes and update the language used in the proposal to reflect decisions that have already taken place. Both Gerardo's extended example and the example from Lesvos show how dialogue with a trusted community of practice and/or trusted critical friends moved design, subsequent data gathering, and analysis in creative, generative ways. Building trusting relationships takes time. We encourage students—and research teams—to practice giving helpful critical feedback.

Giving and receiving feedback are skills that can be learned (for the most part) and enhance the dialogues that occur. A recent example comes from a funded study of computational thinking among children and their families living in challenging economic circumstances. The multidisciplinary research team represented various theoretical and methodological persuasions; true collaboration was going to be challenging. However, one member of the research team, having learned about communities of practice and critical friendships in a course with Gretchen, brought these ideas to the full team. Given the respect this member held and how they modeled collaborative practice, others listened. Then they practiced these new skills by raising tough questions, all the while being supportive of the shared goal: a successful multisite, multiresearcher, multidiscipline study. The study is only now beginning, but reports of the dialogues that occur in team meetings are promising.

Conclusion

Central to our argument in this chapter is the idea that redesign is as much part of the qualitative research process as initial design. Redesign is what happens when researchers encounter unexpected challenges and opportunities that emerge in the field. Openness to these experiences in the field is crucial. These ideas would stand in tension with providing a prescriptive roadmap of steps to follow for redesigning a study. Instead, we recommend paying attention to moments that may lead to changes in our approach or perspective. This can be a conversation with colleagues, an unexpected artifact in the field, or a surprising theoretical connection. In our experience, successful redesign requires making space for changes or for new elements to be added. This is similar to the notion of "active waiting" offered by Hunt (2010) where they argue for the "need for the researcher to achieve a balance throughout a research project between moving forward and advancing the research process, and on the other hand allowing adequate space and time for the full development of each aspect of the research" (p. 72).

Resisting design inflation in the form of adding more participants—and more data collection approaches and more approaches to coding simply for the sake of "more"—is crucial to allow space for redesign to take place. At the same time, in order to remain focused, we need to mention that redesign will not necessarily lead to a more successful study. This cautionary note is not meant to stop us from redesigning a study. To the contrary: the worst that can happen is going back to the original design, but with a clearer conviction and renewed enthusiasm about that original plan (see Figure 1.3).

We have argued that intentional collaboration enriches a study. The ideas of others, shared with thoughtfulness and care, provide guidance that can well make a study stronger. However, finding and nurturing collaborative partners is not easily

FIGURE 1.3 ● Elements to Consider When Contemplating Redesign

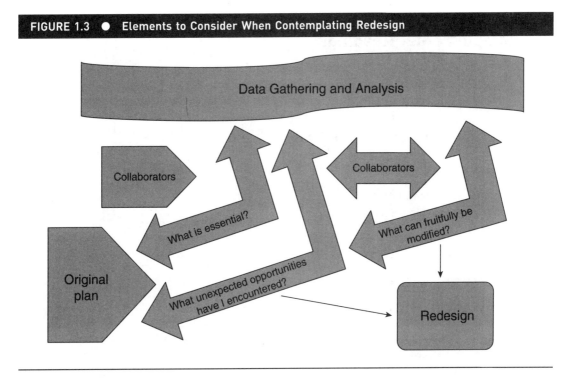

done. All too frequently, we learn of doctoral advisors imposing theoretical or ideological frameworks on mature students who are confounded—and often upset—that their advisors are not supportive. Such are, alas, part and parcel of the power dynamics of the academy. Given this, finding and trusting in critical friends and communities of practice can be challenging. The same holds true, we argue, for more established researchers. Think about the critical feedback provided by anonymous reviewers of manuscripts, as discussed earlier. Some provide excellent, thoughtful insights for how to improve the paper; others, not so much. The seasoned researcher weighs these comments with other trusted colleagues, seeking to find a balance between what a reviewer suggests and what the researcher holds as inviolable.

As we have illustrated throughout this chapter, relationships are fundamental at all stages of a research undertaking. Time, trust, and commitment to a shared goal are crucial.

Supplemental Readings

Appleton, C. (2011). "Critical friends," feminism and integrity: A reflection on the use of critical friends as a research tool to support researcher integrity and reflexivity in qualitative research studies. *Women in Welfare Education, 10*, 1–13. http://hdl.handle.net/2292/14443

Mazzei, L. A., & Smithers, L. E. (2020). Qualitative inquiry in the making: A minor pedagogy. *Qualitative Inquiry, 26*(1), 99–108. https://doi.org/10.1177/1077800419869966

Olan, E. L., & Edge, C. (2019). Collaborative meaning-making and dialogic interactions in critical friends as co-authors. *Studying Teacher Education, 15*(1), 31–43. https://doi.org/10.1080/17425964.2019.1580011

Reflection and Activities

1. In this class, how might we encourage open critical feedback? What guidelines do we want to follow?

2. Identify further readings that focus on communities of practice, critical friendships, and giving and receiving critical feedback.

3. Develop a fairly detailed memo-in-process (3–5 pp.) regarding the current design of your study. Describe the key elements of the design—overall approach (auto-ethnography, case study, phenomenological study, visual methods, hybrid). Describe the current plan for gathering data (method, target number of participants, location). Critically examine this plan, searching for assumptions (hidden or not) about its implementation. For example, what assumptions are you making regarding ease of access? Participants' willingness to engage via a certain method? If using virtual methods, assumptions about access to technology and the internet? Approval from "gatekeepers"? Value of the proposed data collection for responding to your research questions? Given these assumptions, what elements of the plan are essential and which are more modifiable? You may not know, fully, the answers to these questions until you are in the midst of data collection, but pondering them beforehand (and then again during) helps you locate the malleable borders of your plan and engage in intentional reconsideration of the design. (See Chapter 15, this volume, on memo writing.)

References

Barrett, B., Fernandez, F., & Gonzalez, E. M. (2019). Why universities voluntarily pursue US accreditation: The case of Mexico. *Higher Education*, 1–17. https://link.springer.com/article/10.1007/s10734-019-00427-y

Blanco Ramírez, G. (2015a). International accreditation as global position taking: An empirical exploration of U.S. accreditation in Mexico. *Higher Education*, *69*(3), 361–374. https://doi.org/10.1007/s10734-014-9780-7

Blanco Ramírez, G. (2015b). U.S. accreditation in Mexico: Quality in higher education as symbol, performance and translation. *Discourse: Studies in the Cultural Politics of Education*, *36*(3), 329–342. https://doi.org/10.1080/01596306.2013.871236

Blanco Ramírez, G., & Luu, D. H. (2018). A qualitative exploration of US institutional accreditation in three Canadian universities. *Studies in Higher Education*, *43*(6), 989–1001. https://doi.org/10.1080/03075079.2016.1203891

Bresler, L., Wasser, J. D., Hertzog, N. B., & Lemons, M. (1996). Beyond the lone ranger researcher: Team work in qualitative research. *Research Studies in Music Education*, *7*(1), 13–27.

Brinkmann, S. (2012). *Qualitative inquiry in everyday life: Working with everyday life materials*. SAGE.

Brown, L. (1993). (Ed.). *The new shorter Oxford English dictionary on historical principles* (Vol. I). Clarendon Press.

Creswell, J., & Poth, C. N. (2017). *Qualitative inquiry and research design: Choosing among five approaches* (4th ed.). SAGE.

Denzin, N. K. (2009). *Qualitative research under fire: Toward a new paradigm dialogue*. Left Coast Press.

Flemming, J. (2018). Unpublished manuscript. University of Massachusetts Amherst.

Hunt, M. R. (2010). "Active waiting": Habits and the practice of conducting qualitative research. *International Journal of Qualitative Methods*, *9*(1), 69–76. https://doi.org/10.1177/160940691000900107

Lave, J., & Wenger, E. (1991). *Legitimate peripheral participation in communities of practice*. Cambridge University Press.

LeCompte, M. D., & Schensul, J. J. (2010). *Designing and conducting ethnographic research: An introduction*. AltaMira.

Marshall, C., & Rossman, G. B. (2016). *Designing qualitative research* (6th ed.). SAGE.

Merriam, S. B., & Tisdell, E. J. (2015). *Qualitative research: A guide to design and implementation*. Jossey-Bass.

Pailthorpe, B. C. (2017). Emergent design. *International encyclopedia of communication research methods*. Wiley Online Library. https://doi.org/10.1002/9781118901731.iecrm0081

Patton, M. Q. (2015). *Qualitative research and evaluation methods: Integrating theory and practice* (4th ed.). SAGE.

Pink, S. (2007). *Doing visual ethnography*. SAGE.

Pink, S. (2012). *Situating everyday life*. SAGE.

Rallis, S. F., & Rossman, G. B. (2000). Dialogue for learning: Evaluator as critical friend. *New Directions for Evaluation, 2000*(86), 81–92. https://doi.org/10.1002/ev.1174

Ravitch, S. M., & Carl, N. M. (2016). *Qualitative research: Bridging the conceptual, theoretical, and methodological.* SAGE.

Rossman, G. B., & Rallis, S. F. (2016). *An introduction to qualitative research: Learning in the field.* SAGE.

Saldaña, J. (2016). *The coding manual for qualitative researchers* (3rd ed.). SAGE.

Silverman, D. (2011). *Interpreting qualitative data: A guide to the principles of qualitative research.* SAGE.

Stake, R. E. (2005). Qualitative case studies. In N. K. Denzin & Y. S. Lincoln (Eds.), *The Sage handbook of qualitative research* (pp. 443–466). SAGE.

Stake, R. E. (2010). *Qualitative Inquiry: How things work.* Guilford Press.

Wenger, E. (1998). *Communities of practice: Learning, meaning, and identity.* Cambridge University Press.

Wenger-Trayner, E., & Wenger-Trayner, B. (2015). *Introduction to communities of practice: A brief overview of the concept and its uses.* https://wenger-trayner.com/introduction-to-communities-of-practice/

Wolcott, H. F. (2009). *Writing up qualitative research.* SAGE.

Yin, R. K. (2018). *Case study research and applications: Design and methods* (6th ed.). SAGE.

Using Qualitative Data Analysis Software to Manage the Research Process

Jessica N. Lester and Trena M. Paulus

Abstract

This chapter illustrates how qualitative data analysis software (QDAS) can be used to manage an interview-based research study. Drawing upon an exemplar study that used ATLAS.ti, a QDAS package, we demonstrate how six particular software tactics might be used, including: (1) developing transcripts within and/or outside of a software package; (2) formatting and organizing interview data; (3) synchronizing transcripts with the recording; (4) creating quotations and directly coding and/or memoing media files; (5) comparing participant perceptions across cases; and (6) generating a description of the use of QDAS within a research report. To ground this discussion, we begin the chapter by introducing the Five-Level Qualitative Data Analysis (QDA) method and offering a brief overview of the current state of QDAS.

Keywords: ATLAS.ti; five-level QDA method; qualitative data analysis software (QDAS)

Introduction

Qualitative data analysis software[1] (QDAS) packages, such as MAXQDA, ATLAS.ti, or NVivo,[2] can be used by researchers to manage their entire interview study from start to finish (Paulus & Lester, 2022). From conducting a literature review (Lubke et al., 2017; O'Neill et al., 2018; Pope, 2016) to collecting a variety of data types (e.g., capturing Twitter data) to carrying out transcription (Lester, 2015), QDAS packages provide a suite of management and analysis tools. Significantly, these packages are not to be conflated with statistical software packages, such as SPSS or STATA, which are generally positioned as *doing analysis automatically*; rather, QDAS packages are best conceived of as "textual laboratories" (Konopasek, 2008) or workbenches (Muhr, 1997) within which a researcher can manage, organize, store, and/or structure their (unstructured) qualitative data in a systematic and methodologically informed manner. Notably, the way in which a qualitative researcher uses a QDAS package should be inextricably linked to the methodology guiding the study and thus it is perhaps unsurprising that two qualitative studies are unlikely to involve the same combination of tools. For example, Paulus and Lester (2016) illustrated how particular features within a QDAS package, specifically ATLAS.ti, can be leveraged when conducting a conversation analysis or discourse analysis study. They described how analytic strategies that are particular to conversation analysis and discourse analysis can be pursued when using features within ATLAS.ti, thereby highlighting how a particular qualitative methodology shapes the uptake and use of QDAS.

Though there is a long-standing body of scholarship around how to design and carry out interview-based qualitative studies (e.g., Brinkmann & Kvale, 2015), there has been little consideration of the place of digital tools, specifically QDAS packages, when planning such a study. In fact, relatively few researchers have been found to describe with much detail how they use QDAS tools (Woods et al., 2016). Thus, in this chapter, we aim to bring together considerations related to using QDAS when designing a study in which interviews are the primary data source. More particularly, we describe how to plan for an interview study in a way in which the use of QDAS package might be leveraged to manage the *entirety* of the research process.

We begin the chapter by briefly providing a contextual understanding of the place and potential of using QDAS. Within this section, we introduce Woolf and Silver's (2017) Five-Level QDA method as a way to plan for the effective use of QDAS features. We position the Five-level QDA method as an important framework for situating decisions around how to use QDAS in a methodologically grounded way. We then describe in detail the use of QDAS in an example interview-based study. The researchers involved in this study used ATLAS.ti version 7 and thus

---

[1]In the literature, it is also common to use the term computer-assisted qualitative data analysis or CAQDAS when referring to software that supports the qualitative data research process.
[2]The earliest version of NVivo was referred to as NUD*IST.

throughout the discussion we focus on describing strategies particular to ATLAS.ti (although there is certainly overlap with other packages). Notably, we are most familiar with ATLAS.ti, as we are long-time ATLAS.ti users and one of us (Paulus) is also a certified professional trainer for this software package. Since this particular study was completed, ATLAS.ti has released version 8; thus, the screenshots we include in the chapter have been updated to display version 8 (Windows version). Specifically, we highlight how software tactics were used to carry out the analytic strategies of:

1. Developing Transcripts Within and/or Outside of a Package

2. Formatting and Organizing the Interview Data

3. Synchronizing Transcripts with Recorded Data

4. Creating Quotations and Directly Coding and/or Memoing Media Files

5. Comparing Participant Perceptions Across Cases

6. Generating a Description of the Use of QDAS in a Research Report

In focusing on these six practices, we seek to highlight how a researcher might think about the use of QDAS when designing their study rather than coming to use QDAS *after* data collection or simply as an *afterthought*. We conclude the chapter by offering guidance for researchers planning to invest in learning and using a QDAS package to support their interview-based research.

Current State of QDAS in Qualitative Research

QDAS packages first emerged in the 1980s with the development of both Ethnograph and Non-numerical Unstructured Data Indexing Searching and Theorising (NUD*IST, now called NVivo). These packages were not initially developed with commercial intent; rather, they were designed to meet the needs of individual researchers. Nonetheless, with a rise in desktop computing in the 1980s, the use of QDAS packages increased substantially (Fielding, 2008). In the early 1990s, the Computer Assisted Qualitative Data Analysis (CAQDAS) Networking Project, located at the University of Surrey, functioned as a primary site for spurring conversation related to the use of QDAS. Over the last 15 years, a strong consortium of QDAS developers and users have emerged as evidenced in a proliferation of training, conferences, and scholarly publications. Today, there are a wide range of QDAS packages available, ranging from longstanding packages such as ATLAS.ti, NVivo, and MAXQDA to relative newcomers such as Quirkos to open source packages such as RQDA.

Though the availability of QDAS has increased, the relationship between QDAS and the qualitative research community has remained somewhat tenuous

(Davidson & di Gregorio, 2011). Indeed, qualitative researchers have long used tools when carrying out their research; yet, the use of QDAS in particular has given rise to debate regarding its place in the research process, particularly as related to QDA (Paulus & Lester, 2021). We have argued that this debate and its related concerns are often a result of misconceptions about the purpose and function of QDAS. Specifically, a commonly cited, and, we suggest, mistaken claim is that QDAS packages *do* analysis *for* a researcher—a claim that certainly is at odds with the very practice of doing qualitative research. Like Gibbs et al. (2002), we recognize that QDAS is "just a tool for analysis, and good qualitative analysis still relies on good analytic work by a careful human researcher" (p. 9).

Drawing upon Konopasek's (2008) notion of "textual laboratories," QDAS packages can be thought of as the site wherein a researcher reads, listens/views, writes, and manages the entirety of the process (Paulus et al., 2014). Di Gregorio and Davidson (2008), for instance, described how to build an *entire* research project in a software package, providing a useful exemplar of how to think about the use of QDAS *while* designing a study versus as an *afterthought*. Notably, Woods, Paulus, Atkins, & Macklin (2016) content analysis of 763 empirical articles that reported using NVivo or ATLAS.ti found that few researchers used QDAS packages for anything but data management and analysis. Yet, we argue that from the literature review to relevant files (e.g., IRB protocols) to data sources, a QDAS project file can be the "one-stop shop" for working through and carefully documenting decisions related to a given research study.

Importantly, how a researcher uses a QDAS package is inextricably shaped by both the study's methodology, methods, and a researcher's positionality and familiarity with a given package's features. Woolf and Silver's (2017) Five-Level QDA method is a particularly useful approach for carefully considering how to use software in a methodologically grounded way. They suggested distinguishing between analytic *strategies* and software *tactics*, offering five levels to support researcher use of QDAS. These levels highlight the following:

1. It is important to make the purpose of a study explicit; that is, it is critical for a researcher to clarify what they want to do with a particular dataset as this should drive how QDAS is leveraged.

2. It is critical to describe analytic plans for a given study.

3. A cyclical approach should be pursued wherein the analytic tasks should be translated to software tools, with the tools being mapped on to the analytic plans.

4. After the available tools have been mapped on to the analytic plans, the individual software tools can be engaged.

5. The software operations should all be engaged in a way that is specific and customized to a given study.

To illustrate how Woolf and Silver's approach might work, one might imagine a researcher interested in studying resource allocation and the implementation of a particular curriculum by interviewing school administrators, first, about their budgets and then about the curriculum, and inviting the administrators to describe the materials and facilities wherein curriculum use is supported. The researcher may ultimately seek to examine the potential connections or disconnections between the recurrent codes related to how resources are allocated and the recurrent codes related to the curriculum implementation process. In doing so, they might next examine potential links between the descriptions of the necessary resources and the ways in which the resources were accessible or inaccessible (e.g., ascertained via observations). This analytic strategy could be supported by using ATLAS.ti's network view as a software tactic to graphically conceptualize how program implementation and resource allocation may (or may not) go hand in hand.

Following the Five-Level QDA method (Woolf & Silver, 2017) is one way by which to make a researcher's aim(s) clear at the start of a project, with the methodological and analytic goals clarified long before engaging with a QDAS package. Notably, determining the analytic *strategies* that are going to be employed in a study must be considered regardless of whether a researcher has a predetermined research question/purpose or uses a more emergent qualitative research design. Such an approach allows for the use of QDAS to be methodologically driven and increases the potential to use QDAS features in innovative and powerful ways.

Context of the Exemplar Study

From September 2013 to July 2014, a research team (Lester & Lochmiller, 2014; hereafter referred to as "we") was contracted with the International Baccalaureate (IB) to study four K-12 private schools in Colombia, South America, that used IB's Primary Years Programme (PYP). The PYP is an inquiry-based program designed for children aged three to 12 that is "based on a constructivist view of learning and is concept-led" (Eaude, 2013, p. 11). The purpose of the study was to examine the perceptions of students, teachers, and administrators working in IB-PYP schools in Colombia, South America, particularly given the dearth of research about education in Colombia generally and IB-PYP in Colombia specifically. Thus, we explored these perceptions, taking note of how those working and learning within IB-PYP schools in Colombia made sense of their daily work life and learning experiences.

The study was designed as a case study (Yin, 2009) with the four schools positioned as the bounded systems (see descriptions below). This methodology was particularly useful as we sought to explore the contextual differences in the IB-PYP at the four school sites, as well as the perceptions of the students, teachers, and administrators. Further, this multisite case design allowed us to complete a cross-case analysis.

We conducted an intensive two-week field visit, during which time we collected numerous individual interviews and focus groups with teachers, PYP coordinators, school directors, and students. We also conducted observations across the school sites and collected relevant teaching, administrative, and student learning documents for analysis.

The primary data were the interviews and focus groups, with the other sources of data (i.e., observational data and documents/artifacts) serving to contextualize and deepen the interpretation. Given this chapter's focus, we next offer more detail related to the interviews themselves.

Interviews and Focus Groups

Across all of the interviews and focus groups, a Spanish translator was present, with only three of the interviewees requesting translation of questions into Spanish and responses into English. When conducting the interviews with teachers and administrators and focus groups with students, we used semi-structured protocols and digital recording devices.

All the PYP coordinators participated in multiple interviews. Each PYP coordinator participated in a sit-down interview, during which we asked questions listed in the protocol, and in a series of walking interviews, during which we "walked and talked." Walking interviews are particularly useful when researchers seek to make sense of participants' everyday practices in context (Clark & Emmel, 2009). Clark and Emmel (2010) noted this particular method affords "participants a greater degree of control over the research process, deciding where to take the research" and that the environment itself "can be used in an elicitation process to prompt more discussion or encourage further questioning that may not occur in room-based" interviews (p. 2). Thus, as the coordinators showed us the school space, we followed their lead, allowing them to make relevant those spaces and places that were of significance to their work. For instance, at School C, the PYP coordinator wanted to show us the "special needs department," stating:

> Okay, so let me show you, this is our special needs department. So what we do here is we help students that have any special needs. Teachers either pull them out or they walk into the classroom and help them out, so we have—they provide help for math, Spanish and English...we're very proud of our—we like to call it learning support more than special education.

We asked follow-up questions related to how students were identified for special education and how the program was funded. As such, the walking interviews provided information that was not elicited via the semi-structured protocols, but was essential to the everyday workings of the school.

Data Analysis

We conducted a thematic analysis (Braun & Clarke, 2006) of the qualitative dataset, carrying out eleven broad iterative phases of data analysis, during which we: (1) intensively listened to the recorded interviews and focus groups and directly memoed and coded the audio files; (2) had the interviews and focus groups professionally transcribed and reviewed the transcripts for accuracy, with the three interviews conducted in Spanish also being checked for translation accuracy; (3) engaged in multiple rounds of readings of the transcripts and observational notes; (4) identified key patterns across the data through multiple rounds of memoing; (5) coded the data in multiple rounds of patterns using in vivo and sociologically constructed codes; (6) developed themes for individual school sites; (7) developed descriptive reports of individual school cases; (8) conducted comparative analysis of themes across school sites; (9) shared initial interpretations with some of the participants for the purposes of member-checking; and (10) developed the description of thematic findings.

Using ATLAS.ti to Manage the Research Process

Within this exemplar study, ATLAS.ti was used from the earliest stages of the literature review process to the later stages of writing up the findings. Though we used ATLAS.ti to support the entirety of the research process, we describe here six practices that were most useful for this particular interview study.

Practice 1: Developing Transcripts Within and/or Outside of a Package

In all interview studies, important decisions regarding the type of transcript (e.g., verbatim, Jeffersonian, etc.) and how to produce it must be made. These decisions should be methodologically driven and involve a range of considerations (Hammersley, 2010), from how much data to transcribe (e.g., only transcribing selected segments of a dataset) to the degree of detail to transcribe (e.g., should pauses be transcribed). Thus, when carrying out the IB-PYP study, we decided where and how to produce our transcripts long before we even collected data. For the purpose of this study, we determined that verbatim transcripts were sufficient for our purposes, particularly given we were interested in what was being said but not necessarily how. Another important consideration was *where* to produce the transcripts. From hiring a professional transcriptionist to utilizing manual transcription software tools such as InqScribe or automated tools such as Temi, there are now a range of possibilities. Given our own preferences to do as much as possible within QDAS, we also considered producing the transcripts ourselves within ATLAS.ti version 7.[3] Because this study was a funded project with a tight timeline, we ultimately determined to request funding to use a professional transcription service. This service allowed us to generate a "first draft" verbatim transcript relatively

---

[3]As of this writing, ATLAS.ti version 8 does not support transcription.

quickly. Once these first draft verbatim transcripts were generated, we further formatted, organized, and prepared that data for importing into ATLAS.ti.

Practice 2: Formatting and Organizing the Interview Data

Upon receiving the transcripts, we anonymized the data, while further developing an accurate transcript. We felt anonymizing the data was an important step to take *prior* to importing the data into the ATLAS.ti, as it served to build ethical protections into the analytic process. We thus maintained a master list of the 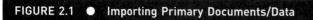 names and pseudonyms in a separate spreadsheet, which lived outside of our ATLAS.ti project file. Once we anonymized the entire dataset, we imported all the data into the project file, as illustrated in Figure 2.1.

Given we planned to conduct a cross-case analysis, we organized the data in relation to the school (e.g., School A, School B, School C, and School D) and the participant's role (e.g., teacher, student, administrator, coordinator, etc.). Our intent was to eventually compare across schools and participant roles at various stages of our analysis. This analytic strategy was part of our study's design and thus we engaged ATLAS.ti's software tactics to support our analytic intent. Specifically, after importing all of the data, we organized our data into groups. In ATLAS.ti, "document groups" can be used to organize the data sources in relation to attributes that may be relevant for analysis. For example, in the IB-PYP study, the school

---

FIGURE 2.1   ●   Importing Primary Documents/Data

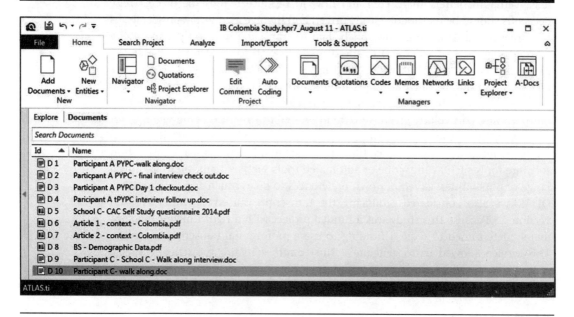

was a relevant attribute and thus we created document groups for School A, School B, etc. Given that one document can be a member of more than one group, we assigned data documents to groups related to a particular role (e.g., teacher). Our organizing scheme for the dataset is highlighted in Figure 2.2.

Though it was certainly tempting to immediately jump to memoing or coding our data, we viewed the process of first organizing data source into document groups as essential to our goal of completing a rich and insightful cross-case analysis. Ultimately, by doing this we knew we would be able to query our memoed and coded data throughout our analysis process—not just after completing multiple cycles of coding and memoing. We were thus able to explore questions such as *what did students at School A report about the PYP program in comparison to students at School B, School C,* etc. Contreras (2014) argues that "A good [document group] system [in ATLAS.ti] will allow you to set the stage for effective data exploration and analysis." Indeed, we found this to be true in this study.

Practice 3: Synchronizing Transcripts With Recorded Data

Qualitative researchers commonly move quickly to reading their transcribed interviews as a first phase of analysis. Though reading is generally more efficient

FIGURE 2.2 ● Document Group Manager

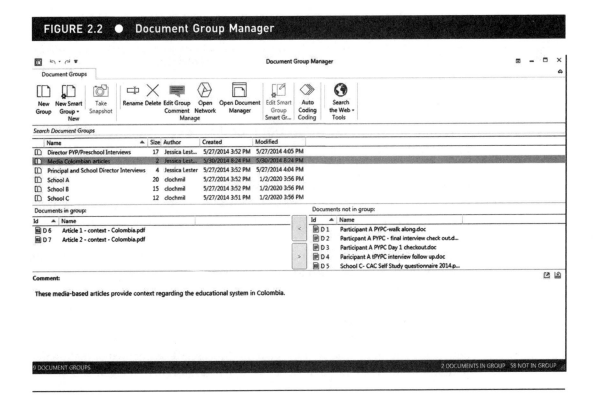

than listening/viewing a recorded interview, any decision to move quickly to transcripts risks losing out on "sitting with" the context found when repeatedly reviewing detailed recordings. A key advantage of using the transcription feature within a QDAS package is the ability to create a synchronized transcript. A synchronized transcript associates (via time stamps inserted by a researcher) a media file/recording with the representation/transcript of the recording (Paulus et al., 2014). Creating this kind of transcript allows for a researcher to easily navigate to various points in a media file and/or transcript. Further, the time stamps allow a researcher to create segments of an audio or video file that are particularly useful for analysis. Thus, rather than fast-forwarding the audio file to the most relevant portions of an interview, a researcher can simply click to navigate to the relevant segments of data.

In the IB-PYP study, we did not synchronize our transcripts, but we certainly could have. We offer here one example of where it might have been analytically relevant. Creating synchronized transcripts would have been particularly useful for studying the segments of the teacher interviews in which teachers shared about the challenges of implementing PYP within bilingual classrooms. After importing the data and engaging in multiple rounds of coding and memoing, we noted that all the participating teachers shared about the challenges they experienced. Ultimately, we returned to the audio recordings to listen to these segments of the interviews in greater detail, taking note of what was emphasized (e.g., attending to rising intonation, increases in volume) in the teacher's description to better ground our interpretation. Arguably, it would have been useful to have these audio segments directly linked/synchronized to the transcripts wherein we could generate more detailed transcripts in relation to what we were hearing. Had we synchronized our audio files to the verbatim transcripts this could have been done with greater ease and also been linked to the coded and memoed segments of the dataset.

Practice 4: Creating Quotations and Directly Coding and/or Memoing Media Files

Initial reviews of interview data are common in qualitative research, serving to familiarize a researcher with potential analytic pathways. In the IB-PYP study, our first phase of analysis involved intensive listening—wherein we spent time independently listening to the interview and focus group data. This intensive listening took place within ATLAS.ti prior to transcribing the data, thereby allowing us to stay close to the nuanced nature of the recorded conversations. When designing our analytic plan, we intended to take notes about things that were standing out to us as we listened to the data and then shared this with one another. Given we intended to use ATLAS.ti to support our research process, we leveraged the tool within ATLAS that allows a researcher to directly create quotations (or segments) of their media files. Creating quotations is similar to highlighting a transcript to note potentially relevant portions of the data. In this case, we segmented or highlighted portions of the audio files that stood out to us, as illustrated in Figure 2.3.

FIGURE 2.3 ● Interview Audio File With Quotations

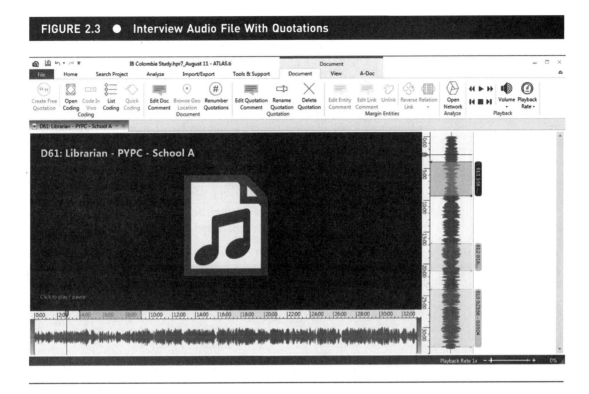

After creating a quotation, we then wrote a comment/memo to capture our initial musings and/or hunches about the data. We shared these comments/memos with one another and allowed these early musings to inform our analysis moving forward. Eventually, we coded the transcript files, creating quotations of relevant data segments, attaching analytic and theoretical memos to these segments, and applying codes to the segments during multiple rounds of coding. As noted above, we could have synchronized our audio files with the transcripts, thereby directly linking our initial musing with the transcript files that were ultimately memoed and coded.

A particular advantage of directly memoing media files is that this practice kept us close to the data and also allowed us to return to particular segments of the interview or focus group data again and again—even as our analysis moved to more abstract levels of interpretation. Notably, researchers can also directly code media files. Directly coded media files are a particularly useful resource for staying close to audio and/or visual/video data, and this coding supports a researcher in more selectively determining which data segments to transcribe (rather than transcribing the entire dataset).

Practice 5: Comparing Participant Perceptions Across Cases

After multiple rounds of coding the data, we were particularly interested in querying the data to begin to make sense of similarities and differences across the schools sites (i.e., School A versus School B, etc.), as well as among the participants themselves (i.e., teachers vs. directors, etc.). Silver and Lewins (2014) described this process as "interrogating the dataset." In the broadest sense, querying the coded dataset allows a researcher to examine potential relationships and patterns between key attributes of the data (e.g., school site, participant roles) and the outcomes of coding.

In our study, after coding the data, we queried the data to gain a general sense of the distribution of the codes across the different school sites (analytic strategy) by using the codes-document table in ATLAS.ti (tactic). The code-document table, as illustrated in Figure 2.4, allowed us to examine the similar and dissimilar ways in which the individual school sites implemented the IB-PYP program. We were also

FIGURE 2.4 ● ATLAS.ti Codes-Document Table

		22: Pilar PYP...) 15	23: Preschoo... 0	24: PYP Teac... 26	25: PYP Teac... 19	26: PYP Teac... 11	27: PYP Teac... 17	28: PYP Teac... 12	29: PYP Teac... 23
◇ administrator descriptions (teacher per...	20			3	1		2		1
◇ balanced	3								
◇ becoming an ib school	2								
◇ Bilingual instruction	27				3		1		1
◇ budgeting	13								
◇ caring	11					1	1		
◇ classroom tools or resources	30			2	1	3	2	2	
◇ collaboration amongst teachers	8			1					2
◇ Colombian context influences	6								
◇ Colombian educational policy	3								
◇ Colombian educational traditions	2								
◇ Colombian teacher training	2								
◇ communicators	2								
◇ comparing two PYP programs (teache...	4								
◇ curiosity	2								
◇ definition of learning	0								
◇ description of changes since adopting...	26	1		1		2		1	2
◇ Description of IB organization	1			1					
◇ description of 'successful learner'	3								
◇ equity	0								
◇ family descriptions	2								
◇ Good quote	54			2			1	1	1
◇ implementation challenges	54			1	2		4	2	4

able to organize our data in a way where we could explore variation between how teachers, school directors, and students perceived the IB-PYP program. Broadly, then, QDAS querying tools can help researchers identify patterns in the coding across meaningful attributes.

Practice 6: Generating a Description of the Use of QDAS in a Research Report

A frequently overlooked aspect of using a QDAS package to support the research process is reporting how it was used when generating a final research report. Paulus et al. (2017) advocated for researchers reporting in detail their use of QDAS. First, they argued for indicating which version of the software is being used given that the features available may be radically different from one version to the next. Second, they highlighted the importance of writing in an active voice when describing the use of the QDAS package to avoid implying that the software *did* the analysis *for* the researcher. Third, Paulus et al. (2017) argued that it was useful to introduce which QDAS package was used, why it was selected, and the features that were used, recognizing that many readers may be unfamiliar with QDAS packages generally. Finally, they noted that if a researcher is claiming that QDAS increased the rigor or veracity of their findings, it is critical to substantiate such claims with details of how particular QDAS tools were used to increase the study's quality.

In the two outputs associated with the PYP-IB study, two different descriptions were used to describe the use of ATLAS.ti. First, in the longer, more detailed report for the funding body, the research team wrote:

> Throughout our qualitative analysis processes, we used ATLAS.ti 7 (Muhr, 2004), a software package commonly used to the support the analysis of qualitative data. Taking advantage of the features available within ATLAS.ti 7, we systematically annotated the data, constructing detailed theoretical and analytical memos as we worked across the data set and used the coding features and coding families to move to more abstract levels of analysis. (Lester & Lochmiller, 2014, p. 19)

Notably, in the above description, the type and version of the QDAS package was shared (ATLAS.ti 7, not just "qualitative data analysis software"), and specific tools (memos, codes, and code families) were mentioned alongside their function (annotating, theorizing and analyzing, and moving to abstract levels of analysis). In this way, the level of detail regarding the selection of this package and the use of particular tools could provide guidance to other researchers.

Strikingly, in a journal publication related to this study, a much more abbreviated description of the use of ATLAS.ti was included.

> Throughout our qualitative analysis processes, we used ATLAS.ti 7 (Muhr, 2004), a software package commonly used to support the analysis of qualitative data. (Lochmiller et al., 2016, p. 162)

The above description, while in the active voice, offered no detail regarding what features were used and why. In retrospect, more detail could have served to substantiate the robust ways in which ATLAS.ti supported the research team in generating their interpretations.

Conclusion

When choosing a QDAS package, it is probably best to start with one supported by the institution (if there is one). Often this will be ATLAS.ti, NVivo, and/or MAXQDA. In the absence of institutional support, it can be helpful to, at minimum, find out which software colleagues are using and explore that package with their support.

If there is no institutional access to the software and no colleagues using QDAS, it may be worth exploring free trial versions. While most of the QDAS packages are cross-platform, not all were developed as natively Mac or Linux programs, so it is important to confirm that the software tactics needed are offered on the platform that will be used. This information should be available on the package's website or in the user manual. The CAQDAS network offers reviews of many packages which can assist in the decision-making process: https://www.surrey.ac.uk/computer-assisted-qualitative-data-analysis/support/choosing.

It is important also to check whether the software package provides the software tactics that will be needed. For example:

- Does the software support the needed transcription characters (e.g., Jeffersonian symbols)?

- Can it time-stamp and/or synchronize the media file with the transcript?

- Does it support direct coding of media files?

- Does it provide waveform or timeline representations?

- How many media files and/or transcripts can be supported per project file?

- What annotation methods are supported?

Reading articles comparing researcher experience with different software packages can provide invaluable guidance around adoption. We recommend Cypress (2019), Estrada and Koolen (2018), and Sotiriadou, Brouwers, and Le (2014) as a starting point. Reviewing such studies can inform decisions around which package to use and provide real-world examples of what worked and what did not. Learning new software can be a challenging task, and often learners opt to figure it out on their own (Freitas, Ribeiro, Brandão, Azevedo de Almeida, Neri de Souza, & Costa, 2019). We recommend watching the free webinars offered by the companies. These typically illustrate the main features of the programs. Next, investigate any in-person training workshops being offered nearby, or sign up for an online training. For just-in-time assistance, watch the video tutorials on the company website or shared by other users on YouTube. Before working with research data, use the sample project files included with the software to practice using a variety of features.

Finally, reading Woolf and Silver's Five-Level QDA books for ATLAS.ti, NVivo, or MAXQDA can provide guidance for selecting the appropriate software tool for the intended strategy. Using software to manage the qualitative research process is even more important now that most if not all our data sources are generated and exist in electronic formats from the start. Being able to organize and navigate all research study documents and media files in one "textual laboratory" (Konopasek, 2008) results in a more transparent and systematic analytic process. Organizing the data by key characteristics of interest makes it possible to ask in-depth questions about differences and similarities in findings that would be close to impossible without the use of software.

Supplemental Readings

Paulus, T. (2018). ATLAS.ti qualitative data analysis software. In B. Frey (Ed.), *The SAGE encyclopedia of educational research, measurement and evaluation.* SAGE. http://dx.doi.org/10.4135/9781506326139.n57

Paulus, T. M., & Lester, J. N. (2021). *Doing qualitative research in a digital world.* SAGE.

Paulus, T., & Lester, J. (2020). Using software to support qualitative data analysis. In S. Delamont & M. Ward (Eds.), *Handbook of qualitative research in education* (2nd ed., pp. 420–429). Edward Elgar Publishers.

Reflection and Activities

1. Think about the interview study you would like to conduct. What demographic or other variables (e.g., geographic location, institution size, participant ages, etc.) are present in your interview data that might be useful to help you interpret the findings? How can QDAS be used to help you make these interpretations?

2. How might you use QDAS to "manage, organize, store, and/or structure [your] (unstructured) qualitative data in a systematic and methodologically informed manner?"

3. Which data analysis method might be useful to help you analyze your interview data? Identify a methodological source to learn more about this method and map out the strategies that you will use to conduct this analysis.

4. Using the guidance provided in the conclusion, select one QDAS package and download the free trial version. View relevant YouTube or company-provided online tutorials and upload some video files and text-based transcription files. Practice the following software tactics:

    a. Create a memo that includes the research question, analytic plan/strategies, and describes the sources of data

    b. Create "groups" of data sources based on variables of analytic interest

    c. If possible, synchronize the media file with the transcript

    d. Select some interesting portions of the media file to transcribe and create an annotation (e.g., create a quotation, attached memo, and/or coded segment of data)

    e. Create another memo reflecting on the learning process of the above and generate a list of next steps.

References

Braun, V., & Clarke, V. (2006). Using thematic analysis in psychology. *Qualitative Research in Psychology, 3*(2), 77–101. https://doi.org/10.1191/1478088706qp063oa

Brinkmann, S., & Kvale, S. (2015). *Interviews: Learning the craft of qualitative research interviewing* (3rd ed.). SAGE.

Clark, A., & Emmel, N. (2009). Connected lives: Methodological challenges for researching networks, neighbourhoods and communities. *Qualitative Researcher, 11*, 9–11. http://usir.salford.ac.uk/id/eprint/10434

Clark, A., & Emmel, N. (2010). Using walking interviews. Realities Toolkit #3, ESRC National Centre for Research Methods. http://eprints.ncrm.ac.uk/1323/1/13-toolkit-walking-interviews.pdf

Contreras, R. (2014). Primary document families: An essential procedure for data exploration and analysis. https://atlasti.com/2014/11/09/primary-document-families-an-essential-procedure-for-data-exploration-and-analysis

Cypress, B. (2019). Data analysis software in qualitative research: Preconceptions, expectations and adoption. *Dimensions of Critical Care Nursing, 38*(4), 213–220. http://doi.org/10.1097/DCC.0000000000000363

Davidson, J., & di Gregorio, S. (2011). Qualitative research and technology: In the midst of a revolution. In N. K. Denzin & Y. S. Lincoln (Eds.), *The SAGE handbook of qualitative research* (4th ed.). SAGE.

Di Gregorio, S., & Davidson, J. (2008). *Qualitative research design for software users.* McGraw-Hill.

Eaude, T. (2013). *Primary education: A literature review.* International Baccalaureate Organization.

Estrada, M. L., & Koolen, M. (2018). Audiovisual media annotation using qualitative data analysis software: A comparative analysis. *The Qualitative Report, 23*(13), 40–60. https://nsuworks.nova.edu/tqr/vol23/iss13/4

Fielding, N. (2008). The role of computer-assisted qualitative data analysis: Impact on emergent methods in qualitative research. In S. Hesse-Biber & P. Leavy (Eds.), *Handbook of emergent methods* (pp. 644–673). Guilford Press.

Freitas, F., Ribeiro, J., Brandão, C., Azevedo de Almeida, C., Neri de Souza, F., & Costa, A. P. (2019). How do we like to learn qualitative data analysis software? *The Qualitative Report, 24*(13), 88–106. https://nsuworks.nova.edu/tqr/vol24/iss13/8

Gibbs, G. R., Friese, S., & Mangabeira, W. C. (2002, May). The use of new technology in qualitative research. *Forum Qualitative Sozialforschung/Forum: Qualitative Social Research, 3*(2), Article 8.

Hammersley, M. (2010). Reproducing or constructing? Some questions about transcription in social research. *Qualitative Research, 10*(5), 553–569. https://doi.org/10.1177/1468794110375230

Konopasek, Z. (2008). Making thinking visible with ATLAS.ti: Computer-assisted qualitative analysis as textual practices. *Forum Qualitative Sozialforschung/Forum: Qualitative Social Research, 9*(2), Article 12.

Lester, J. N. (2015). Leveraging two computer-assisted qualitative data analysis software packages to support discourse analysis. In S. Hai-Jew (Ed.), *Enhancing qualitative and mixed methods research with technology* (pp. 194–209). IGI Global.

Lester, J. N., & Lochmiller, C. R. (2014). *A mixed method case study of International Baccalaureate Primary Year Programmes in four Colombian schools.* Center for Evaluation & Education Policy.

Lochmiller, C. R., Lucero, A., & Lester, J. N. (2016). Challenges for a new bilingual program: Implementing the International Baccalaureate Primary Years Programme in four Colombian schools. *Journal of Research in International Education, 15*(2), 155–174. https://doi.org/10.1177/1475240916660803

Lubke, J., Britt, G., Paulus, T., & Atkins, D. (2017). Hacking the literature review: Opportunities and innovations to improve the research process. *Reference & User Services Quarterly, 56*(4), 285–295. https://doi.org/10.5860/rusq.56.4.285

Muhr, T. (1997). *ATLAS.ti 5: The knowledge workbench.* Scientific Software Development.

Muhr, T. (2004). User's manual for ATLAS.ti 5.0. ATLAS.ti Scientific Software Development GmbH.

O'Neill, M. M., Booth, S. R., & Lamb, J. T. (2018). Using NVivo™ for literature reviews: The eight step pedagogy (N7+1). *The Qualitative Report, 23*(13), 21–39. https://nsuworks.nova.edu/tqr/vol23/iss13/3

Paulus, T. M., & Lester, J. N. (2016). ATLAS.ti for conversation and discourse analysis studies. *International Journal of Social Research Methodology, 19*(4), 405–428. https://doi.org/10.1080/13645579.2015.1021949

Paulus, T. M, & Lester, J. N. (2022). *Doing qualitative research in a digital world.* SAGE.

Paulus, T., Lester, J., & Dempster, P. (2014). *Digital tools for qualitative research.* SAGE.

Paulus, T., Woods, M., Atkins, D., & Macklin, R. (2017). The discourse of QDAS: Reporting practices of ATLAS.ti and NVivo users with implications for best practices. *International Journal of Social Research Methodology 20*(1), 35–47. https://doi.org/10.1080/13645579.2015.1102454

Pope, L. (2016). On conducting a literature review with ATLAS.ti. *ATLAS.ti Research Blog.* http://atlasti.com/2016/09/01/litreview/

Silver, C., & Lewins, A. (2014). *Using software in qualitative research: A step by step guide* (2nd ed.). SAGE.

Sotiriadou, P., Brouwers, J., & Le, T. (2014). Choosing a qualitative data analysis tool: A comparison of NVivo and Leximancer. *Annals of Leisure Research, 17*(2), 218–234. https://doi.org/10.1080/11745398.2014.902292

Woods, M., Paulus, T., Atkins, D., & Macklin, R. (2016). Advancing qualitative research using qualitative data analysis software? Reviewing potential vs. practice in published studies using ATLAS.ti and NVivo, 1994–2013. *Social Science Computing Review, 34*(5), 597–617. https://doi.org/10.1177/0894439315596311

Woolf, N., & Silver, C. (2017). *Qualitative analysis using ATLAS.ti: The five level QDA method.* SAGE.

Yin, R. K. (2009). *Case study research: Design and methods* (4th ed.). SAGE.

After Someone Else's Interview

Sheryl L. Chatfield

Abstract

Qualitative secondary data are increasingly available via digitized, online collections, but they are used infrequently in published research studies. This chapter offers strategies for secondary analysis of interview data with particular emphasis on the use of archived oral history interviews. Data from the Kent State University May 4 Archives illustrate stages in data analysis and processing. Materials from this archive are used in a phenomenological research project exploring the lived experience of adolescents who were present when the Ohio National Guard fired into a crowd of unarmed university student protestors. The chapter considers ethical challenges related to consent, confidentiality, and context. Strategies are provided for matching existing data to researchers' interest. Advantages of secondary analysis of archived data include reduction of participant burden, ability to contribute to the body of knowledge in a given research area, and efficient use of an existing resource.

Keywords: Qualitative secondary analysis; archived data; oral histories; cross-case analysis; phenomenological research methods

Sustainability is an increasing priority for business but is less often associated with the process of research. Typical sustainable business practices include reducing of waste and maximizing use of existing resources. In this chapter, I describe application of these sustainable practices to research, through analysis of existing archived data. Qualitative secondary analysis reduces time, labor, and resources involved in data gathering and processing and helps maximize value from existing data.

The purpose of this chapter is to offer strategies for secondary analysis of qualitative interview data, with particular emphasis on the use of archived oral history interviews as data sources. Though qualitative secondary analysis is routinely incorporated into research instruction, published research studies based on someone else's data continue to be relatively rare. Key benefits of qualitative secondary analysis include the efficient reuse of data to maximize the value of participants' contributions and the potential to refine or provide new insights into historical, current, and emerging issues.

I begin with a definition and description of the contributions of select qualitative secondary analysis studies. Next, I consider scholars' responses to challenges associated with consent, confidentiality, and context of projects that use secondary data. I then refer to a published study to illustrate the processes and decisions that informed development of this example project. In the latter part, I provide additional thoughts to encourage thoughtful and useful research using data from "someone else's interview," and describe available resources. I conclude this chapter by advocating for increasing use of archived data for qualitative secondary analyses.

Definition of Qualitative Secondary Analysis

Boslaugh (2007) asserted primary analysis involves data collected and analyzed by the same researcher(s), whereas secondary analyses are conducted by different scholars. Heaton (2008) provided a data-driven definition and asserted qualitative secondary analysis only applies to "data derived from previous research studies" (p. 34), whereas she viewed analysis of "'found' materials" (p. 34) such as diaries and other documents, as primary. Hammersley (2010) asserted that any reuse of data by the original researchers constitutes primary analysis and, like Heaton, considered document analysis of data not generated for research as primary, rather than secondary. However, according to Hammersley, the initial analysis of someone else's research data is "a genuine borderline case between use and re-use" (para. 2.2).

My definition, inspired by yet distinct from these, is simple and broad. I assert: *secondary analysis refers to any analysis process researchers use instead of, or in addition to, the stated purpose that guided the original data collection.* My intent is to include reanalysis, regardless of who conducts the reanalysis, and to include initial analysis of archived, text-based or audiovisual recordings of oral history interviews and other archived records. The most common purposes for data archives include preserving records of events, memories, and experiences; therefore, I consider application of a systematic qualitative analysis process to be something "in addition to the stated purpose that guided the original data collection."

My definition applies to forms of qualitative data generated in the field or produced during other phases of the qualitative life cycle (see the discussion of the qualitative life cycle in the introduction to this volume and examples of the production of some of these different forms of data in chapters by Mihas, Keane, and Galman, among others). Field notes, memos, and other records are not my focus in this chapter, although I acknowledge the value of this information for providing contextual clues to support analysis of archived interviews. Multiple other applications are possible but are beyond the range of this chapter.

Contributions of Qualitative Secondary Analysis Studies

One important contribution of qualitative secondary analysis suggested by my own definition is demonstrated when authors conduct the initial systematic analysis of an available qualitative dataset to address a lingering or emergent purpose. For example, Bloor (2000) used 1970s oral history interviews with Welsh miners to explore lay knowledge about occupational safety, and to describe the critical role of the South Wales Miners' Federation in securing compensation for Miners' lung. Bloor described how he was "diverted by the rich oral history archive" that "describe[s] events from the partisan history of lived experience" (pp. 127–128). Bloor also argued for the ongoing relevance of his historical research report, asserting: "the success of the [South Wales Miners' Federation] has something to teach those contemporary social movements that seek to democratize medical science and technology" (p. 136).

According to Long-Sutehall, Sque, and Addington-Hall (2010), reduction of participant burden is another important contribution of qualitative secondary analysis. Fielding and Fielding's (2008) study of inmates in a maximum security prison is a clear example of this contribution, and these authors characterized secondary analysis as "an important way to exploit more fully research on sensitive topics and hard-to-reach populations" (p. 92).

Fielding and Fielding additionally described the role of qualitative secondary analysis as one of multiple "collective and incremental endeavor[s]" (2008, p. 92) to be integrated into the knowledge base along with findings from primary studies, to improve understanding of issues of interest over time. Thompson (2000) referred to this use of qualitative secondary analysis as a "seedbed" (para. 31) for a new research project.

Heaton (2004) identified reanalysis for verification of original findings as an essential contribution made by qualitative secondary analysis. In contrast, Savage (2007) saw little value in trying to "validate or disprove the arguments made by qualitative social scientists by going back to their data and showing if they misinterpreted their own work" (para. 2.3) and instead advocated for qualitative secondary analysis to better understand "historical patterns of change" (para. 1.1). Fielding and Fielding (2008) also argued against verification and suggested more meaningful contributions of qualitative secondary analysis include development of additional themes from existing data. Savage (2005, 2007) asserted additional insight about the primary study might be gleaned via encouraged use of researcher-created data, such as field notes and researcher journals.

Ethical Considerations

The primary ethical challenges in secondary qualitative analysis issues can be categorized as those relating to consent, confidentiality, and context. The first refers to the extent to which the informed consent process used when participants originally contributed data is adequate to address secondary analyses. When the scope of original consent is ambiguous, Bishop (2009) asserted researchers should consider their ethical duty to "avoid unnecessary duplicative data collection and to assure that participants' data are fully utilized for the public good" (p. 267) in deciding whether or not data can be appropriately used in secondary analyses. Bishop also described several current efforts to broaden applications of informed consent, including disclosure of intent to archive data, use of blanket consent forms, and efforts to recontact former participants.

For any research there is a continual need to respect participants' rights to confidentiality, especially when disclosure of identity associated with data is uncomfortable or otherwise undesirable. Typical research ethical board recommendations include keeping participant identities confidential through use of pseudonyms or altered details, or through development of composite cases, especially when information might be damaging or embarrassing. However, Thompson (2000) cautioned that in changing too many details there is risk that findings "lose their intrinsic validity as evidence" (para. 22).

The contrast between context of initial data gathering and circumstances of secondary analysis seems initially to be a design challenge, due to the analyst's lack of direct influence over the original research design and direct interaction with participants. However, there is a related ethical issue in that design challenges might complicate researchers' responsibility to participants to use their contributions to produce methodologically sound research that can be disseminated for the benefit of other interested individuals. Other issues of context or design that might be considered in secondary qualitative analysis include adequacy of data to address research questions and the appropriateness of data for a given qualitative approach or analysis strategy. Moore (2012) suggested researchers refer to Savage's (2007) work as a potential role model, as his method of using the "details of the research process itself as data" (p. 130) provides a potentially effective strategy to help researchers engage with a study.

In Bishop's (2007) "reflexive account" (para 1.1.) of her study informed by two sets of archived live history interviews, she concluded that qualitative secondary analysis was frequently "very similar to working with primary data" (para. 11.1). Bishop acknowledged minor modification of her project aims to ensure better fit with available data but suggested that multiple factors outside of the researchers' direct control, such as available funding opportunities, disciplinary affiliations, and research trends, typically exert similar influence over elements of primary research.

Reflections on Trauma After May 4, 1970: An Example of Qualitative Secondary Analysis

In this section, I describe key processes and decision points associated with a published qualitative secondary analysis project (Chatfield, DeBois, & Orlins, 2020) based on a series of oral history interviews from the Kent State University May 4 archive (Kent State University Libraries, 2019). On May 4, 1970, students at Kent State University in Kent, Ohio, gathered on campus to protest escalation in the Vietnam War. National Guard troops were sent to Kent beginning on May 2, following destruction of property in days leading up to the protest. During the May 4 gathering, guard members fired into the crowd of students, killing four and injuring several others (Lewis & Hensley, 1998/2019).

The permanent May 4 archive was established in 1990, and the extensive but well-organized online open access digital collection includes text, photographs, and audio recordings and typed transcripts from oral history interviews. A link on the main page (https://www.library.kent.edu/special-collections-and-archives/kent-state-shootings-oral-history-project) opens the "Oral history project" page which provides a link to existing sources and information for potential contributors. Available interviews were primarily conducted in person to capture and preserve experiences of witnesses to this historical event and are searchable by name, role, or an extensive subject list.

Reflections on Trauma After May 4, 1970: Purpose, Sample, and Ethical Approval for Secondary Analysis

The coauthors of this manuscript had previously investigated potential triggers that may precipitate youth and adolescent suicide, through secondary analysis of a case-based national dataset (Orlins, DeBois, & Chatfield, 2020). I was familiar with the May 4 collection from exposure during a qualitative research class, so I knew the archive contained interviews conducted with individuals who were adolescents in 1970. Given potential overlap with our existing interest in adolescent mental health, we decided to explore the May 4 data as a possible source of related information.

Because coherent qualitative research practice follows a clearly understood purpose or question (or transparently adjusts to an emergent one), having a purpose or question in mind at the beginning of the process is critical. When working with secondary data, often one of two other things occurs: either a researcher comes upon the dataset, finds the data appealing, and tries to come up with a meaningful way to use the data (I call this "backing into the research question"), or, as happened in this instance, we had a purpose in mind and the data overlapped but did not precisely fit our interests. To accommodate these data and still be consistent with our general research agenda, we determined it was appropriate to narrow the focus for this study to the impact of violent trauma on adolescent mental health.

As we refined the research question, we engaged in simultaneous processes of reviewing the data and reading published research, to further ensure the secondary analysis was doable and would make a meaningful contribution. We found other researchers (Leiner et al., 2018) identified a lack of comprehensive understanding of the long-term impact of exposure to violent trauma; this gap in the literature supported the merit of our investigation of the May 4 archive. Our final research question was: "What was the lived experience of the Kent State Shootings on May 4, 1970, for an adolescent living in Kent?"

We identified our sample interviews with adolescents by searching the archive interviews by role. We reviewed many transcripts to ensure fit and as a double-check in the event of misclassification. Eventually, we identified seven individuals who were adolescents in 1970 and were present in Kent on May 4, 1970. The interviews were primarily conducted on or around May 4 of various years, during the annual university commemoration of the incident. One was conducted in 1990; one in 2000; two in 2007; one in 2010; one in 2015; and one in 2018, so individuals were recalling an event that took place between 20 and 48 years earlier. Library staff and graduate students conducted the interviews using a standardized interview schedule.

After we identified our sample, it was necessary to secure institutional board approval for our study. Variations in aims, dissemination plan, data sources, and institutional policies mean that secondary analysis might or might not be subject to institutional review board review and oversight. My institution's board uses an expedited process for publicly available or deidentified secondary data, whether qualitative or quantitative. I suggest secondary scholars err on the side of caution and always consult with the governing research review board. Many journals require evidence of approval or exemption, so review board documentation is especially important when your intent is to disseminate findings from qualitative secondary analyses.

Reflections on Trauma After May 4, 1970: Design, Data Processing, and Steps in Qualitative Secondary Analysis

Research coherence includes matching purpose to data and matching approach to purpose. As our question shows, we were interested in how individuals made sense of a critical life experience. This suggested a phenomenological research method. I recommended to my coauthors we follow the transcendental approach to phenomenological research described by Moustakas (1994) for several reasons. Moustakas recommends individual interviews as the primary data gathering method, and as long as data can inform the desired outcome—a composite description of the experience—there are no prescribed interview questions. Also, because this work involved multiple analysts, I felt that a clear process description, provided by Moustakas, would help ensure consistent work. Most importantly, this approach is used "to reveal more fully the essences and meanings in human experiences" (Moustakas, 1994, p. 105), making it highly consistent with our stated purpose.

The interviews were stored as website text, so we exported the files to editable word processing software. We used a series of word processing functions including find and replace commands, and paragraph reformatting, to produce clean files for analysis. When datasets include audio recordings, as these do, researchers might make efficient use of their time by performing transcript clean-up operations and a final accuracy check, while simultaneously listening to the audio recording. As Bartesaghi, di Gregorio, and Vanover argue in chapters in this volume, such work also has an interpretive function and helps researchers get to know their data.

Prior to immersing ourselves in analysis, we followed guidance from Moustakas (1994) to engage in epoché, a process of identifying judgments, expectations, and existing knowledge. To do this, we spent time in independent reflection to identify current knowledge and personal context, then shared this information with coauthors. Throughout the analysis, we challenged ourselves and each other to ensure our impressions and interpretations were supported by the data.

We followed Moustakas's (1994) description of the Modified Van Kaam method which comprises an 8-stage analysis process combining intense individual case-by-case deconstructive stages of analysis with cross-case analysis. Rather than attempt to illustrate these steps, I present the transformation of the data related to key findings. We identified two triggers which encouraged retraumatization following exposure to this trauma: (a) unpredictable responses from others following the event and (b) living through other violent events, including those that occurred many years later. I first show related segments of raw data, identified as relevant expressions in the initial stage of "horizontalization" (Moustakas, 1994, p. 120) that contributed to our ability to understand and describe the lived experience of May 4 from the view of these adolescents in interviews they shared as adults.

Responses from others following the event

Student at Kent University School in 1970 interviewed in 2000

People would ask us every time we'd go anywhere as a family. We went to Canada that summer to visit friends … the first thing they asked us: "Where are we from?" and when we told them they said, "Well, are they still shooting students down there?" We went to Washington, DC, went in to the White House—took a tour of the White House—asked where we were from, said the same thing. And I lived in California for a few years, five years, every time they would ask me where I was from, same thing. So, I guess I'm kind of like the rest of us—branded.

Student at Kent Roosevelt High School in 1970 interviewed in 2007

By the time I got to college, with "Four Dead in Ohio" being a big tune and Woodstock and all that, all of a sudden if you said "Kent" then people looked at you funny, but at least they knew where you were from.

Student at Kent Roosevelt High School in 1970 interviewed in 2018

When people ask me … "What is the biggest thing that happened in your life?" Well, I say that. The Kent State massacre. And they go—people that remember go, "Wow, you were there," and I go, "Yeah," I mean, I ran the other way. Definitely when people ask, and then a lot of people want to know the details, you know the Q&A of it, and the outcome, the aftermath. . .

Comparisons with other events

Student at Kent Roosevelt High School in 1970 interviewed in 2007

With Virginia Tech happening just a couple weeks ago, it's just eerie that the reality that nobody's ever really safe and that nobody can keep you safe.

Student at Kent Roosevelt High School in 1970 interviewed in 2007

When the tragedy happened on 9/11 … those people had that same look. It was eerie and that was the feeling that you had on May 4th, it was that void, eerie feeling of those people's faces

Student at Davey Junior High School in 1970 interviewed in 2015

I remember then feeling probably the most incredible sensation of fear I had ever felt in my life and the only thing that I can compare it to now is watching the TV on 9/11 and watching the second plane hit the tower and then hearing about the Pentagon and not knowing what was going on and being out of control—and but that was on TV, this was like reality and I remember being scared to death.

The two passages below show how this information was aggregated to become part of a composite description of the adolescent lived experience.

Responses from others following the event

Kent, Ohio, a small town minimally known outside of the region prior to May 4, 1970, became notorious after the event and identifying as a Kent resident tended to inspire an emotional reaction from others—either in favor of the protestors or in defense of the violence.

Comparisons with other events

Various ensuing violent events, including the Virginia Tech University mass shooting perpetrated by a student, and the terrorist destruction in the US on September 11, 2001, revived feelings of sadness and loss in those who had direct or proximate experiences of May 4, 1970.

Reflections on Trauma After May 4, 1970: Reflections on This Qualitative Secondary Analysis Study

We found the major process differences between a secondary analysis, and our experiences with similar studies conducted as primary analyses occurred mostly in the beginning of the study. Differences between a secondary and primary approach included refinement of purpose to ensure the research question was meaningful and the secondary data were sufficient. In practical terms, extra time spent formatting the data was minimal for this specific study but might be more involved when researchers need to convert audio recordings to text-based transcripts. Once we began active data analysis, we found, as Bishop (2007) noted, more similarities than differences in analysis of secondary as opposed to primary data.

My perception is that I experienced similar depth of emotion when I engaged with the archived interviews as when I worked with my own primary data. Admittedly, it helped that I have an ongoing personal connection with this incident. While I was too young to understand what happened on May 4, 1970, my present office window has a clear view of the area where the protest took place, and I walk past the field and markers in honor of the four dead students on a regular basis. I do have a clear memory of September 11, 2001, and I found participants' comparisons between the two incidents provided me with a better ability to understand the impact of May 4, 1970. Along with this, May 4 is a part of the institutional history of Kent State University and is commemorated annually by events and suspension of classes for part of the day. However, my coauthors and I were also struck by the vivid recall and clear emotions participants conveyed through words and tone of voice, 30, 40, and nearly 50 years after the incident, and we felt this contributed to our ability to engage with the data in this secondary analysis. The overall experience suggested to me that it is quite possible to engage with qualitative secondary data, but also that it is helpful when researchers have some point of identification with the context or subject matter of the study.

One method-specific exception in this study was our inability to engage with participants to ensure they felt our presentation of the experience was accurate, as Moustakas (1994) recommends. This limitation is acknowledged in our report. One added value of this work is that our findings may be useful for others investigating the aftermath of adolescent trauma. Our inquiry thus adds value to the participants' contributions to the archive without risking additional retraumatization.

Qualitative Secondary Analysis

Qualitative secondary analysis has the potential to make meaningful contributions to human science research. As with primary research, qualitative secondary analysis is not without challenges, and, as with any approach, it is not the best method to address every research purpose. In this section, I provide additional thoughts about broad and specific elements of data fit. I also describe online sources of qualitative secondary data.

Paradigmatic Compatibility

The extent to which a certain lens, paradigm, or qualitative approach (e.g., critical, feminist) drives participant selection and interview questions will impact the suitability of qualitative secondary analysis in general, and specific datasets in particular, to address a given purpose. I echo Thompson's (2000) recommendation to look toward use of general, less structured interviews, such as oral histories, because qualitative data gathered using minimal and broad prompts may lend themselves more readily to secondary analysis.

Although archived interview transcripts are likely to be most associated with qualitative inquiry and the associated subjective, individual, constructivist framework (Saldaña & Omasta, 2018), there is nothing inherent in the data themselves that prevents a researcher from approaching analysis from a different orientation. For example, scholars using qualitative secondary data may opt to use strategies that disregard the subjective nature of the data, including converting qualitative data into quantitative or numerical data. As with any secondary or any primary work, it is contingent on researchers to justify their approaches to the data in a way that persuades others of its value and contribution.

Navigating the Fit Between Existing Data and Current Research Interests

I previously described the process I call "backing into the research question" and suggested that this is not an ideal way to approach scholarly research. Although it is generally preferred to begin with a good question rather than to begin with interesting data, it is not my intent to discourage all data-driven qualitative secondary analysis. Though data-driven questions can be challenging to develop and to rationalize as the focus of a research report, a logical and meaningful argument might be made to support efforts to condense and transform a mass of archived data into an alternative form, such as a description of a common experience, or a hierarchical list of themes and subthemes, that may be more accessible and therefore more likely to be used by others. This work is especially important when diverse and less heard voices are represented in the archive.

Because follow-up interviews or requests to clarify responses are unlikely if not impossible when working with archived data, available data need to be sufficient to address the purpose of the research. The character of the interview data may make one archive better suited for some qualitative approaches than others. I personally believe that descriptive and experience-based questions may be easiest to address through secondary analysis because archived interviews tend to focus on descriptions of experiences. If archived data are to be integrated with other data sources, other designs, such as case study research or grounded theory approaches, may additionally be appropriate. Braun and Clarke's (2006) guidelines for the family of approaches that comprise thematic analysis may present another useful source to frame some secondary analysis questions.

Available Resources

There are a growing number of online archives that include qualitative data; I present a list of US-based resources in the appendix. Many are oral or life history collections and, happily, these tend to be associated with ample consent processes to facilitate research use. Although locations for archived data in the United States include public libraries, professional interest groups, and project websites, I primarily provided links to collections held by academic libraries because web addresses for universities are typically stable, facilitating continual access to resources. Other attributes of academic library holdings include ongoing efforts to digitize collections and availability of a broad range of resources from a topical standpoint.

Although I did not include the UK Data Archive (n.d.) on my list, this resource, housed at the University of Essex, provides repository and data access services for researchers, with emphasis on storage of funded research results. Access to archives varies depending on project and requestor role. At present there is no central repository for funded US-based research, and policies and guidelines vary by repository and funder (Antes et al., 2018). Fortunately, much data housed in US-based digital archives were gathered from participants who consented that their information and their identities would be made available on an open access basis. Any other specific conditions of use are typically specified on archive websites.

Conclusion

In this chapter, I defined qualitative secondary analysis to emphasize analysis of archived interview data from oral histories or other projects. These data are increasingly available via digitized, online collections, but are still used infrequently in published research studies. Advantages of the use of these data include reduction of participant burden, ability to contribute to the body of knowledge in a given area, and efficient use of an existing resource. Primary concerns preventing greater use of archived data include limitations in participants' original informed consent and challenges in the sufficiency and context of existing data to fit researcher questions. Though I argue for purpose-driven rather than data-driven qualitative secondary analysis, I see value in the latter, especially when it facilitates dissemination of studies that reflect the views or experiences of those who have traditionally been underrepresented.

The worked example provided in this chapter shows the value of secondary analysis. The use of these archived data adds to the body of knowledge about adolescent trauma without exposing participants to additional retraumatization. While I was unable to personally connect with participants, I believe my emotional experiences were similar to what I have experienced when working with my own primary data.

One critical challenge that limits use of secondary qualitative analysis in the United States is lack of a comprehensive effort to gather, archive, and share these data. Qualitative datasets are a minority when compared to quantitative data available in a central repository such as the University of Michigan's Interuniversity Consortium for Political and Social Research (ICPSR, 2020). Although data sharing is increasingly encouraged by funders and publishers (DuBois et al., 2018), funders such as the National Institutes of Health and the National Science Foundation in the United States do not presently sponsor a central repository for open access archiving of qualitative data.

Additional work is needed in this area to encourage development and eventual use of extensive archives. DuBois et al. suggest a good initial step is for all researchers to integrate the expectation of data sharing and archiving into the initial stages of research planning. Thompson (2000) described development of data archives as a cyclical process, and encouraged researchers to draw from archives and to archive their own data, to "strikingly multiply the outcomes from your research through the publications of others from the same materials you have created" (para. 41). The advantages of qualitative secondary analyses facilitated by data archiving are clear; expanding available archives will increase the number and quality of contributions.

Supplemental Readings

Corti, L., Kluge, S., Mruck, K., & Opitz, D. (Eds.). (2000). Text. Archive. Re-analysis [special issue]. *Forum Qualitative Sozialforschung/Forum: Qualitative Social Research, 1*(3). https://www.qualitative-research.net/index.php/fqs/issue/view/27

Heaton, J. (2004). *Reworking qualitative data.* Thousand Oaks, CA: SAGE.

UK Data Service Qualitative Data. (2020). https://www.ukdataservice.ac.uk/get-data/other-providers/qualitative/uk-archives.aspx

Reflection and Activities

1. Imagine that you are a student in an introductory qualitative research class, and you have been asked to contribute an interview that will be housed as an audio and text file on an online archive about learning qualitative analysis. Describe your likely response to this request ("yes" or "no"), and the considerations that might impact your response. (Optional)—Would your response be different if the interview was about a different topic, for instance, a current or prior relationship, or your political views?

2. Disadvantages of using archived interview data for current research include that the researcher did not gather the data so does not have a good sense of all of the circumstances, or context of the research.

    What strategies, other than reviewing primary researchers' data (e.g., field notes, memos), might help a researcher get a better sense of the original study?

3. Use the list of archives developed for this chapter to locate an online archive for interview data that includes individuals who represent current or formerly underrepresented voices due to race/ethnicity, sex, age, disability, or other political or social factors. Use one of the chapters in this book to develop a data-driven research question or purpose that might be used to frame a study using at minimum two interviews from the archive. There is a list of these archives in the electronic material connected to this book in the Appendix to this chapter.

References

Antes, A. L., Walsh, H. A., Strait, M., Hudson-Vitalie, C. R., & DuBois, J. M. (2018). Examining data repository guidelines for qualitative data sharing. *Journal of Empirical Research on Human Research Ethics, 13*(1), 61–73. https://doi.org/10.1177/1556264617744121

Bishop, L. (2007). A reflexive account of reusing qualitative data: Beyond primary/secondary dualism. *Sociological Research Online, 12*(3), 43–56. https://doi.org/10.5153/sro.1553

Bishop, L. (2009). Ethical sharing and re-use of qualitative data. *Australian Journal of Social Issues, 44*(3), 255–272. https://doi.org/10.1002/j.1839-4655.2009.tb00145.x

Bloor, M. (2000). The South Wales Miners' Federation, miners' lung and the instrumental use of expertise, 1900–1950. *Social Studies of Science, 31*(1), 125–140. https://doi.org/10.1177/030631200030001005

Boslaugh, S. (2007). *Secondary data sources for public health: A practical guide.* Cambridge University Press.

Braun, V., & Clarke, V. (2006). Using thematic analysis in psychology. *Qualitative Research in Psychology, 3*(2), 77–101. https://doi.org/10.1191/1478088706qp063oa

Chatfield, S. L., DeBois, K., & Orlins, E. (2020). Reflections on trauma: A phenomenological qualitative secondary analysis of archived interviews about adolescent experiences during the 1970 Kent State student shootings. *Advance.* Preprint. https://doi.org/10.31124/advance.13477755.v1

DuBois, J. M., Strait, M., & Walsh, H. (2018). Is it time to share qualitative research data? *Qualitative Psychology, 5*(3), 380–393. https://doi.org/10.1037/qup0000076

Fielding, N. G., & Fielding, J. L. (2008). Resistance and adaptation to criminal identify: Using secondary analysis to evaluate classic studies of crime and deviance. *Historical Social Research, 33*(3), 75–93. https://doi.org/10.1177/S0038038500000419

Hammersley, M. (2010). Can we re-use qualitative data via secondary analysis? Notes on some terminological and substantive issues. *Sociological Research Online, 15*(1), 47–53. https://doi.org/10.5153/sro.2076

Heaton, J. (2004). *Reworking qualitative data.* SAGE.

Heaton, J. (2008). Secondary analysis of qualitative data: An overview. *Historical Social Research, 33*(3), 33–45. https://doi.org/10.12759/hsr.33.2008.3.33-45

Inter-university Consortium for Political and Social Research (ICPSR, 2020). https://www.icpsr.umich.edu/icpsrweb/

Kent State University Libraries. (2019). Kent state shootings: May 4 collection. *Special collections and* archives. https://www.library.kent.edu/special-collections-and-archives/kent-state-shootings-may-4-collection

Leiner, M., De la Vega, I., & Johansson, B. (2018). Deadly mass shootings, mental health, and policies and regulations: What we are obligated to do! *Frontiers in Pediatrics, 6,* Article 99. https://doi.org/10.3389/fped.2018.00099

Lewis, J. M., & Hensley, T. R. (1998/2019). The May 4 shootings at Kent State University: The search for historical accuracy. *University history.* https://www.kent.edu/may-4-historical-accuracy

Long-Sutehall, T., Sque, M., & Addington-Hall, J. (2010). Secondary analysis of qualitative data: A valuable method for exploring sensitive issues with an elusive population? *Journal of Research in Nursing, 16*(4), 335–344. https://doi.org/10.1177/1744987110381553

Moore, N. (2012). (Re)using qualitative data? In J. Goodwin (Ed.), *SAGE secondary data analysis, vol III: The secondary analysis of qualitative data* (pp. 121–139). SAGE.

Moutsakas, C. (1994). *Phenomenological research methods.* SAGE.

Orlins, E., DeBois, K., & Chatfield, S. L. (2020). Characteristics of interpersonal conflicts preceding youth suicide: Analysis of data from the 2017 National Violent Death Reporting System. *Child and Adolescent Mental Health*. https://doi.org/10.1111/camh.12439

Saldaña, J., & Omasta, M. (2018). *Qualitative research: Analyzing life*. SAGE.

Savage, M. (2005). Revisiting classic qualitative studies [43 paragraphs]. *Forum Qualitative Sozialforschung/Forum: Qualitative Social Research, 6*(1), Article 31. https://doi.org/10.17169/fqs-6.1.502

Savage, M. (2007). Changing social class identifies in post-war Britain: Perspectives from mass-observation. *Sociological Research Online, 12*(3), 14–26. https://doi.org/10.5153/sro.1459

Thompson, P. (2000). Re-using qualitative research data: A personal account. *Forum Qualitative Sozialforschung/Forum: Qualitative Social Research, 1*(3), Article 27. https://doi.org/10.17169/fqs-1.3.1044

UK Data Archive. (n.d.). https://www.data-archive.ac.uk/

Appendix

A Sample of US-Based Online Resources for Archived Oral Histories and Other Interviews

University of South Florida Libraries: "Oral history Program"—includes an extensive collection of audio files grouped by topic area. http://guides.lib. usf.edu/c.php?g=5770&p=25630

Kent State University: "Kent State shootings: Oral histories"—includes audio recordings and transcripts for interviews with individuals who reflect on the Kent State shootings. http://www.library.kent.edu/special-collections-and-archives/kent-state-shootings-oral-histories-0

Northern Arizona University: "Traders oral history"—includes audio recordings and transcripts from individuals who were involved with the United Indian Traders Association. http://library.nau.edu/speccoll/ exhibits/traders/oralhistories/oralhist.html

University of Michigan at Dearborn: "Voice/Vision Holocaust survivor oral history archive"—includes audio recording and transcripts from Holocaust survivors. http://holocaust.umd.umich.edu/interviews.php

United States Library of Congress: "civil rights history project"—includes video recordings and transcripts of interviews with individuals who share recollections of the civil rights movement during the 1960s in the United States. http://www.loc.gov/collection/civil-rights-history-project/abou.t- this-collection/

University of North Carolina at Chapel Hill: "Documenting the American South: Oral histories of the American South"—includes recordings and transcripts, subdivided into six categories. http://docsouth.unc.edu/sohp/

Harvard University Schlesinger Library: "Black women oral history project"—includes audio files and typed transcripts of interviews conducted between 1976 and 1981 with Black women born in the late nineteenth and early twentieth centuries. https://guides.library.harvard. edu/schlesinger_bwohp

University of California, Berkeley, The Bancroft Library Oral History Center: "Disability rights and independent living movement"—includes interview transcripts with individuals observing or participating in the US disability rights movement of the 1960s and 1970s. https://www.lib.berkeley.edu/ libraries/bancroft-library/oral-history-center/projects/drilm

Qualitative Data Repository (QDR): The QDR is hosted by the Center for Qualitative and Multi-Method Inquiry, a unit of the Maxwell School of

Citizenship and Public Affairs at Syracuse University. QDR curates, stores, preserves, publishes, and enables the download of digital data generated through qualitative and multi-method research in the social sciences. https://qdr.syr.edu/

UNC Dataverse: This repository, managed by the Odum Institute for Research in Social Science, enables individual scientists, research teams, scholarly journals, and other members of the research community to archive and publish their own datasets, including a growing number of qualitative datasets. https://dataverse.unc.edu/

Interview Transcription Strategies

Charles Vanover

Introduction

Qualitative researchers learn continuously from their data, a well to which they return for increasingly deeper understanding and insight (Charmaz, 2014; deMarrais & Lapan, 2003; Rossman & Rallis, 2011; Saldaña & Omasta, 2018). Starting with data collection, what they see, hear, and feel during inquiry is carried with them throughout the research life cycle. Entering the field and conducting a set of interviews is an emotionally demanding experience that creates opportunities for personal and professional growth as well as knowledge production (Clifford, 1983; Mienczakowski, 1995).

The practices of transcribing, analyzing, and interpreting interviews all provide opportunities to build knowledge. Insight may come in a flash or in slow waves. The direction of the entire qualitative research design might be altered by the experience of participating in a single interview session, transcribing an evocative piece of dialogue, or attentively reviewing the associated transcript. Intuition may also grow from careful attention across each stage of the qualitative research life cycle—from research design to write-up—and may flourish in memos and formal research writing.

This fluidity and evolution distinguish qualitative research from traditional forms of investigation. Research questions do not change in the middle of an experiment. Surveys are frequently submitted electronically, and researchers who use this method may have no face-to-face contact with their respondents and face few personal challenges during data collection. For the qualitative researcher, in contrast, transcription can introduce complications that are theoretical, interpretive, and representational and that require the researcher to make critical decisions about what their data will look like in textual form (Davidson, 2009).

Conducting interviews and other forms of fieldwork can be extremely stressful experiences. When researchers review their audio recordings of these events, they frequently discover they have forgotten large portions of what was said and done. They may also discover their initial understanding was incorrect and that they had misinterpreted critical pieces of dialogue. By taking the time to listen and physically transform recordings into written transcripts, researchers deepen their under-standing of these research episodes and build the connections that create insight. Transcription is an act of professional listening, one that develops with experience and with intentionality. Capturing in writing what one has experienced aurally is not a simple act but one that requires us to decide whether to consider dimensions such as silences, performativity, and linguistic competence.

The three chapters in this section discuss how transcription contributes to this learning process. Each author discusses the labor required to engage in rendering the data in different ways and describes the use of these texts during later stages of the qualitative research life cycle. All the authors in this section are united in the view that the products of this method of qualitative inquiry—transcripts—are integral to the work that follows. The decision to use a particular set of transcription practices to transform a round of interviews into texts with specific and intentional character-istics may be one of the most critical choices in the qualitative research life cycle. The stakes are high. What is transcribed shapes what is analyzed and interpreted (Cowan, 2014; Hepburn, 2004; Lapadat & Lindsay, 1999). By using a consistent set of tran-scription practices, researchers focus future investigators' attention on specific dimensions of discourse, from the nonverbal to involuntary vocalizations (Bezemer & Mavers, 2011; Davidson, 2009; Ochs, 1979; ten Have, 2007). Alternate sets of transcription practices may remove the same interactions from view. The choice to highlight or ignore different speech acts—such as gestures, accents, and tones of voice—may reverberate unexpectedly across the inquiry.

Taking the time to use transcription as an intentional method of qualitative inquiry comes with a price. Researchers' efforts significantly increase when they consider critical aspects of the audio or video recordings that may be lost as the interview is transformed into text (Bernauer, Chapter 10; Markle, West, & Rich, 2011). Intentional transcribers must create a strategy to select what matters, while avoiding the loss of important aspects of discourse.

It is also challenging to balance the benefits derived from doing transcription with the demands of managing other aspects of the research project. Fieldwork may take longer than expected; time in the field almost always consumes more resources and energy than researchers originally allocate. Dissertation researchers frequently find themselves held to committee schedules and due dates that do not provide adequate time for deep analysis and interpretation. When the pressure to start writing builds, an easy response is to transcribe atheoretically, without an informed strategy, and simply pay someone to do the work and then code directly from that material.

Intentional qualitative research requires complex choices and careful decision-making. There is no gold standard for deciding how long one should spend immersed in the details of the collected interviews, and how much time one should devote to more focused analytic practices such as coding and memo writing. Transcribing by hand allows researchers to physically embody their interviews and creates time for deep reflection on the data; transcribing by hand also takes time. Each of the chapters in this section provides clear descriptions of practices and strategies for doing transcription and discussions of how these choices add value to the analysis. Each of the chapters also provides strategies for avoiding some of the most laborious aspects of the transcription process while continuing to gain the benefits of physically transforming the recorded data.

Refining one's approaches during data collection and transcription in a way that more closely aligns with the lived reality of the participants or community lays the groundwork for high-quality blog posts, formal publications, and ethnodramatic performances. In this section, we consider approaches to transcription that bring us closer to what we have witnessed in the field and closer to participants' layered meanings. Charles Vanover, in Chapter 4, describes the use of a set of simple Microsoft Word formatting techniques to enhance the meanings communicated in transcripts. Mariaelena Bartesaghi, in Chapter 5, describes the use of transcription strategies from discourse analysis to create fine-grained renderings of interview data and discusses the benefits of group transcription sessions for making meaning from recordings and text. Silvana di Gregorio, in Chapter 6, describes the intentional use of online transcription programs to create rough transcripts that might then be refined by hand to develop richer visual and textual representations of discourse.

Each of the chapters is intended to help the reader conceptualize this important work and envision the use of transcription as an intentional method of qualitative inquiry.

Reflection and Activities

1. Secure a 5–10-minute audio interview from YouTube or another online site. Look over the automatic transcription of that segment if it is available.

2. After reading Chapters 4 and 5, consider formatting techniques to enhance the meaning of the interview. Begin transcribing the interview by hand based on these techniques. Transcribe two or three critical segments.

3. Revisit the same portion of the interview and consider alternative techniques to enhance different aspects of the audio file (e.g., tone, pauses). How does this version of the transcription compare to the automatic transcription and your initial effort?

References

Bartesaghi, M. (2022). Theories and practices of transcription from discourse analysis. In C. Vanover, P. Mihas, & J. Saldaña (Eds.), *Analyzing and interpreting qualitative research: After the interview*. SAGE.

Bernauer, J. A. (2022). Oral coding: An alternative way to make sense of interview data. In C. Vanover, P. Mihas, & J. Saldaña (Eds.), *Analyzing and interpreting qualitative research: After the interview*. SAGE.

Bezemer, J., & Mavers, D. (2011). Multimodal transcription as academic practice: A social semiotic perspective. *International Journal of Social Research Methodology, 14*(3), 191–206. https://doi.org/10.1080/13645579.2011.563616

Charmaz, K. (2014). *Constructing grounded theory*. SAGE.

Clifford, J. (1983). On ethnographic authority. *Representations, 2*, 118–146.

Cowan, K. (2014). Multimodal transcription of video: Examining interaction in Early Years classrooms. *Classroom Discourse, 5*(1), 6–21. https://doi.org/10.1080/19463014.2013.859846

Davidson, C. (2009). Transcription: Imperatives for qualitative research. *International Journal of Qualitative Methods, 8*(2), 35–52. https://doi.org/10.1177/160940690900800206

deMarrais, K. B., & Lapan, S. D. (2003). Qualitative interview studies: Learning through experience. In Kathleen B. deMarrais & Stephen D. Lapan (Eds.), *Foundations for research* (pp. 67–84). Routledge.

di Gregorio, S. (2022). Voice to text: Automating transcription. In C. Vanover, P. Mihas, & J. Saldaña (Eds.), *Analyzing and interpreting qualitative research: After the interview*. SAGE.

ten Have, P. (2007). *Doing conversation analysis*. SAGE.

Hepburn, A. (2004). Crying: Notes on description, transcription, and interaction. *Research on Language and Social Interaction, 37*(3), 251–290. https://doi.org/10.1207/s15327973rlsi3703_1

Lapadat, J. C., & Lindsay, A. C. (1999). Transcription in research and practice: From standardization of technique to interpretive positionings. *Qualitative Inquiry, 5*(1), 64–86. https://doi.org/10.1177/107780049900500104

Markle, D. T., West, R. E., & Rich, P. J. (2011). Beyond transcription: Technology, change, and refinement of method. *Forum Qualitative Sozialforschung/Forum: Qualitative Social Research, 12*(3). http://www.qualitative-research.net/index.php/fqs/article/view/1564

Mienczakowski, J. (1995). The theater of ethnography: The reconstruction of ethnography into theater with emancipatory potential. *Qualitative Inquiry, 1*(3), 360–375. https://doi.org/10.1177/107780049500100306

Ochs, E. (1979). Transcription as theory. In E. Ochs & B. Schieffelin (Eds.), *Developmental pragmatics* (pp. 43–72). Academic Press.

Rossman, G. B., & Rallis, S. F. (2011). *Learning in the field: An introduction to qualitative research*. SAGE.

Saldaña, J., & Omasta, M. (2018). *Qualitative research: Analyzing life*. SAGE.

Vanover, C. (2022). Transcription as a form of qualitative inquiry. In C. Vanover, P. Mihas, & J. Saldaña (Eds.), *Analyzing and interpreting qualitative research: After the interview*. SAGE.

Transcription as a Form of Qualitative Inquiry

Charles Vanover

Abstract

The choice of a transcription strategy reverberates across the qualitative research life cycle to influence the meanings people derive from transcribed interviews and other parts of the research project. This chapter describes how and why transcription matters and discusses important decision points and strategies for transforming recorded speech. It publishes multiple transcriptions of the same interview segments to convey meanings generated by different forms of transcription. Atheoretical transcription practices that render participants' discourse with shallow streams of meaning are contrasted to intentional transcription strategies that encourage understanding and theory building. These choices make a difference. The author discusses how his decision to use a simple set of Microsoft Word formatting commands to construct intentional transcripts that narrativized participants' speech altered the course of his research project. The chapter concludes by discussing the costs of engaging in intentional transcription practice and shares strategies for minimizing laborious aspects of the work.

Keywords: Transcription strategies; narrative interviews; reflexive qualitative research practice

Transcription is a method of transforming what people say and do into forms of text. Audio and video recordings are changed into words and images that allow researchers to analyze and interpret aspects of those research events. Transcription selects and condenses the complex series of interactions produced by interviews; it renders the big booming buzzing confusion of raw conversation into forms that support inquiry.

Transcription is more than a means to an end. The work of transcription provides occasions for researchers to immerse themselves in their data and develop insight. By seeing and hearing recordings of their interviews and building text from that content, researchers deepen their comprehension of the materials they study. The work of building these meanings and insights lies at the heart of the analytic work for qualitative inquiry (Charmaz, 2014, 2017; Locke, Golden-Biddle, & Feldman, 2004).

In this chapter, I review the research on transcription and discuss the symbols and Microsoft Word formatting commands I used to transcribe a set of narrative interviews for my dissertation research. I share the results of two different transcription strategies for two interview segments from this narrative dataset. The first examples provide atheoretical transcriptions of the segments—what the verbal data might look if the transcript was produced by a paid transcriber. The same interview segments are then transformed by a set of naturalized transcription practices intended to enhance readability and comprehension. My dissertation research evolved into arts-based inquiry. I conclude the chapter by briefly discussing how my transcription strategies supported this aspect of my work.

Literature Review: Transcription as Method

Using transcription as an intentional practice requires careful planning and decision-making. Different research designs and study goals necessitate different transcription strategies (Greenwood, Kendrick, Davies, & Gill, 2017; Lapadat & Lindsay, 1999). Conversational analysis does not use the same transcription practices as grounded theory. Transcripts of interviews recorded on video may demand different strategies than interviews recorded on audiotape (Heath, Hindmarsh, & Luff, 2010; Mondada, 2018).

The first step in transcribing all forms of data is to assess how the raw data look and sound. It may be worthwhile to review the recordings and test out possible forms of transcription. Researchers must evaluate whether a transcription strategy provides rich material for the deployment of the analytic practices specified by the research design. They may also investigate whether the transcribed text supports the future coding system and/or decide whether the transcripts complement their chosen arts-based practices.

An important step is to figure out how much of the data should be transcribed. It is always possible, and sometimes even desirable, to transcribe every interview in the same standardized fashion—see McLellan, MacQueen, and Neidig (2003) for rules and procedures to achieve such a goal. However, such standardization is not necessary for all research questions and study designs (Eaton, Stritzke, & Ohan,

2019; Halcomb & Davidson, 2006). Conversation analysts tend to transcribe small portions of their transcriptions in order to investigate the speech acts that are the focus of their inquiry (Bartesaghi, Chapter 5; ten Have, 2007). Grounded theory and narrative researchers might create verbatim transcriptions of the material related to their research questions while taking notes that describe less relevant parts of the interview. These notes might have time stamps or links to the recorded data that guide future users back to specific passages if they wish to investigate in more detail.

A wide array of published systems, practices, and strategies are available to guide researchers' efforts to transcribe their chosen interview segments (Bucholtz, 2007; Davidson, 2009; Lapadat & Lindsay, 1999). Dressler and Kreuz (2000) provide a model system of transcription based on a five-year study of articles published in the journal, *Discourse Processes*. The article provides what Dressler and Kreuz hope to be a standardized and universal set of symbols for 21 dimensions of oral discourse ranging from intonation to pauses, speech speeds, and breath. Crow (1988) uses ethnomethodology to create a framework of 17 performance acts such as playful deceits and code switching. Rather than sharing recommendations for a standardized system, Davidson (2009) provides a guide to choosing from different approaches to transcription. Davidson discusses the conduct of transcription during qualitative research and describes important decision points within the transcription process.

The use of specific transcription strategies may have important ethical and political implications. Oliver, Serovich, and Mason (2005) discuss the challenges confronting their research team as they transcribed and analyzed a set of interviews designed to study the disclosure decisions of HIV-positive men who have sex with men. The research team interviewed men from a wide range of ethnic backgrounds and were able to collect rich accounts of the men's decisions to disclose their HIV status to their sexual partners and, a felony offense in many states, the men's decisions not to disclose. Oliver et al.'s article shares examples of the complex decision-making the research team engaged in to produce renderings of the interviews for their analytic and interpretive work while protecting confidentiality.

A major focus of recent research on transcription is the challenge of rendering gestures, speech, and other aspects of discourse in interviews and observations recorded on video. Flewitt (2011) provides a discussion of key issues in the development of transcripts from video recordings and the use of these dynamic texts during inquiry. Cowan (2014) applies different sets of transcription conventions to the same video segment to show how these conventions draw attention to alternate dimensions of the recorded discourse. Markle, West, and Rich (2011) describe the many weaknesses of transcription as a research method. Markel et al. argue that coding video data directly from the digital recording provides more meaningful material for analysis than expending the time and resources required to develop potentially inaccurate and untrustworthy transcripts. Bernauer (Chapter 10) discusses the benefits and challenges of engaging in this form of transcriptionless coding.

Transcribing by hand and cleaning raw transcripts are ways of getting to know the data. Regardless of the specific analytic choices made to develop the text, time spent doing transcription may lay the grounds for abduction, insight, and theory-building (Alvesson & Karreman, 2011; Charmaz, 2011; Saldaña & Omasta, 2018). Careful transcription is also an ethical imperative. A core expectation of qualitative research is that interview participants' discourse is rendered with appropriate levels of accuracy.

Positioning Statement and Study Description

I am a White man who grew up in the Chicago suburbs and worked in the Chicago Public Schools (CPS) for eight years before I won a fellowship to study educational policy at an out-of-state research university. When I returned to Chicago to do the fieldwork for my dissertation, I conducted four rounds of semi-structured narrative interviews with five first-year teachers and seven veteran and accomplished educators working in the CPS (see Vanover, 2014 for interview guides and other study materials). At the time, my practice as an interviewer and qualitative analyst was immersed in the work of two writers. The first was Patricia Benner, whose focus groups and narrative interview methods generated rich streams of stories about nurses' courage and agency (Benner, Hooper-Kyriakidis, & Stannard 1999; Benner, Tanner, & Chelsea, 1996). The second writer was Robert Weiss, whose work provided the primary guidance for my research design. Weiss (1995) developed tools and strategies for semi-structured interview sessions that give participants control over what they say during their interviews and help participants share what they learn from experience.

While it may be a wonderful feeling to engage in a data collection effort that produced 48, ninety-minute interviews, I experienced something close to panic once I came back to my university. I carried my bags to my apartment, checked the messages on my answering machine, and then sat at my desk and tried to figure out what to do with the hundreds of photographs and 80 hours of audio recorded stories I had collected in Chicago.

During the time when I developed my research design, I was part of an interdisciplinary seminar of narrative researchers. Our discussions inspired me to transcribe the first round of interviews by hand. The graduate students and faculty in my research seminar viewed hand transcription as a best practice: transcription slowed the process down and created time for reflexivity and theory-building. Instead of listening to the stories the teachers shared, I decided to embody them by physically reproducing the teachers' words.

I will never be able to calculate the relationship between the time I spent transcribing the data and the quality of the final products I produced. However, one thing is certain: The work took a great deal of time. Transcribing 12 ninety-minute interviews is a labor-intensive task. The effort grows large if the goal is to reflexively engage with participants' storytelling, rather than to type out the words. I loved listening to the interviews, but many weeks did pass as I transcribed by hand from the original cassette tapes using a pedal transcription player.

Narrativizing the Interview Text and Other Transcription Strategies

The first problem I confronted when I transcribed the teachers' interviews was to create a meaningful document out of the thousands of words and other discourse produced by my interview methods. I conducted most of the first round of interviews in June, within two weeks of the end of the school year. During those sessions, there were times when the teachers fell so deep into their storytelling, five minutes or more might pass without any need for me to ask a follow-up question. The teachers shared so many words during their interviews, I found it challenging to transcribe what was spoken. Stories that fascinated me during the interview session became flat rows of words on a computer screen.

Table 4.1 illustrates the stakes of the work. The table's first row publishes an atheoretical transcription from my interview with Halsted Hoyne (pseudonym), the first recorded interview I transcribed for my dissertation. This row shares the type of text that might be produced if my intention had been to transcribe Halsted's interview quickly and record the spoken words without reference to overriding theories or goals—i.e., it renders the teacher's speech as if I was paid to transcribe the interview by someone I did not know for a project I did not understand. The transcript also has some inaccuracies; it does not transcribe every single word. A quick glance at Table 4.1 shows that such atheoretical transcriptions are not fertile ground for pondering, musing, and engaging in other analytic and interpretive practices. The text is exhausting and difficult to read.

Given Halsted spoke more than 26,000 words during her first interview, one can imagine the importance of developing a worthwhile transcription strategy. To organize these verbal data, I decided to engage in what I now describe as a form of naturalized transcription practice (see Bucholtz, 2000; Davidson, 2009; Oliver, Serovich, & Mason, 2005). I created a set of strategies to *narrativize* the text: I transcribed the teacher's stories using transcription techniques that enhanced readability and helped the text read like a story. I believe the decision to develop these strategies and narrativize the interviews changed the course of my research project.

The text in the second row of Table 4.1 is an example of my transcription strategy. Every time Halsted and the other teachers revoiced their speech and spoke in the voices of students, parents, colleagues, principals, or themselves, I hit the return key and used different Microsoft Word fonts to differentiate such speech from the teacher's more general narrative voice. After the usual time spent in trial and error learning, I decided what made the most sense was to use one font for

TABLE 4.1 ● Two Version of the Same Interview Segment From Pseudonymous Teacher, Halsted Hoyne

Version 1: An Atheoretical Transcription

And the reading special came in and just said you can't be in here. You have to go to your class. And that it was like she started sort of getting real direct with him. Telling him no, you are going to your class. You cannot stay in here. And I said and I sort of pulled her aside and I said you know his dad just passed away this morning. He's really calm. I don't mind him being in here. And she was like No, you are being very nice. But that's ridiculous. He has to go to his other class. Whipped him into a frenzy. Just you're going to this class. I'm not going to that class. You're going to this class. I'm not going to that class I mean just really and I stepped back because honestly I did not know what to do.

Version 2: A Narrativized Transcription of the Same Interview Segment

And the reading special came in and just said
You can't be in here. You have to go to your class.
And that, it was like, she started sort of getting real direct with him. Telling him,
No, you are going to your class. You cannot stay in here.
And I said—and I sort of pulled her aside and I said
You know, his dad just passed away this morning. He's really calm. I don't mind him being in here.
And she was like
No, you are being very nice. But that's ridiculous. He has to go to his other class
Whipped him into a frenzy. Just
You're going to this class.
I'm not going to that class
You're going to this class
I'm not going to that class
I mean, just really. And I stepped back because honestly I did not know what to do.

---

student voices, another font for adult voices, and then a different font for teachers' revoicing of their own speech. I did not need to mark the speech of each type of school professional with a different font or designate one font for Kid A and another font for Kid B. I could use NVivo software coding commands to make such comparisons if they were important later in the analysis.

The results of my transcription strategy can be seen by glancing between the two renderings of Halsted's story in Table 4.1. The narrativized text in Row 2 is much easier to read and more meaningful. I was able to achieve this goal not by altering or rearranging what the teacher said, but by changing how Halsted's words appear on the page and then adding some rough punctuation to highlight her speech. I also attempted to write down every word she uttered, without attempting to fix her grammar.

I do not have records of the decision-making process that produced this transcription strategy. I do know Halsted's interview was the first session I transcribed for my dissertation and that I developed most of my transcription strategy doing the work for that interview. If I had saved a Microsoft Word copy of the transcript each day after I transcribed, it might be possible—if perhaps not desirable—for me to publish my initial renderings of her stories. I could then analyze the changes to particular interview segments as my transcription strategy developed by hand and foot pedal.

Marking the Interviewer's Affirmations

In the next three sections, I use the term "interviewer" and the pronoun "he" for clarity in order to emphasize that I am no longer the person who sat in the offices of the Chicago Teacher's Union and the University of Chicago Alumni Association and conducted the interviews. Instead, I am the person who is analyzing the interviewer's work.

One of the goals for my research was to compare the stories of the first-year teachers, such as Halsted, with those of the more experienced veteran educators. In order for this comparison to make sense, however, it was necessary to show that the interviewer was not attempting to lead the interviews. Thus, I thought it important to transcribe the interviewer's exact words in the same verbatim stream I used to record the teachers' speech. I believed it was important for readers to see the questions the teachers responded to during the flow of the interview. I also decided to mark the moments when the interviewer responded to the teachers' stories and, as Weiss (1995) recommends, affirmed their discourse, mostly by muttering in agreement.

I eventually realized that I did not need to record every "'uh-uh," "nnhuh," and "yeah nnnmmhhmmm" the interviewer muttered. For my study goals, what mattered was the interviewer had affirmed the teacher's story. I decided to mark all of the interviewer's many grunts of agreement with two asterisks. This strategy broke the transcript into more easily readable units, while keeping the focus of the text on the teachers, rather than the interviewer. These marks can be seen in the text in Table 4.2, Row 2.

Marking the Teachers' Pauses

Halsted Hoyne told me she spoke about her teaching every morning of her first year in the Chicago Public Schools when she and one of her friends drove to work, and every afternoon when the two teachers drove home. Halsted spent her evenings talking about her classroom to her husband and to friends from her teacher education program. When I interviewed Halsted in the offices of the Chicago Teacher's Union in June 2004, she had a lot to say. Halsted leaped from story to story and she shared more words than any other teacher I interviewed. My initial transcription strategy was developed to make such material meaningful.

In contrast, Indiana Ingleside (pseudonym), the teacher whose interview segment is transcribed in Table 4.2, told me she spoke to almost no one about her

TABLE 4.2 ● Two Versions of the Same Interview Segment From Pseudonymous Teacher, Indiana Ingleside

Version 1: An Atheoretical Transcription

Interviewer
Okay great. Could you talk about moments during the year when you felt that you had really learned something new about your teaching or your students?
Indiana
Everyday. I learned so much from the kids this year. It's hard to pick one, but
Interviewer
Just pick a bunch, that's fine.
Indiana
A lot of what I learned is just how kids react to their environment and how they react to how people treat them. Before this year I did a year on the East Side as part of my Master's program and then this was my first year with my own classroom. I had never worked with kids this closely as this year. So it was a really a learning experience on a lot of levels. Just the psychology behind interacting with them and their interacting with each other

Version 2: A Narrativized Transcription

Interviewer
Okay great. Could you talk about moments during the year when you felt that you had really learned something new about your teaching or your students?
Indiana
Everyday. (LAUGHS). Um (10 SECOND PAUSE) I learned so much from the kids this year. I—it's hard to pick one, but
Interviewer
Just pick a bunch, that's fine.
Indiana
A lot of what I learned is just how (5 SECOND PAUSE) like how kids react to their environment and how they react to how people treat them and (6 SECOND PAUSE) before this year I just—I had
**

I did a year on the East Side as part of my Master's program and then this was my first year with my own classroom. I had never worked with kids this closely (LAUGHS) as this year. So it was a really a learning experience on a lot of levels. Just
**

(4 SECOND PAUSE) Uhhh Just the psychology behind interacting with them and and and their interacting with each other

teaching and rarely talked to anyone in her school besides her students. During her interview, Indiana paused frequently, mostly I believe, to search for words. As I transcribed Indiana's interview, I decided to document those significant pauses. I felt they added meaning to her transcript.

Some conversation analysts decide to mark pauses down to a 10th of a second, but after the usual amount of trial and error learning, I realized I did not need to transcribe in such fine detail. What worked best was to mark all pauses that seemed to be meaningful interruptions in the flow of speech, and I decided to measure, by the second, all pauses that lasted 3 seconds or more. The two versions of Indiana's interview in Table 4.2 show the changes produced by this strategy—I strongly recommend the reader time each pause to hear the full meanings of those speech acts. The transcripts also show the benefits of my decision to transcribe the teachers' exact words and mark important forms of discourse such as laughter.

Quantifying Transcription Symbols

I applied my chosen transcription strategies in a standardized fashion across each of the 12 interviews in the first round. I wrote each full word that was spoken in each interview and I formatted every piece of revoiced dialogue. I decided that if I was going to compare the interviews of the beginning and veteran teachers, their transcripts should all read in the same way. During the analysis, I often went back to the original interview tape; this labor helped me fix inaccuracies in the transcription and ensured my initial transcription choices made sense. Because I did not transcribe the pauses in the first two interviews, for instance, I had to relisten to those cassette tapes to add that notation.

This standardization provided an unexpected analytic benefit. When I was writing my methods chapter, I discovered I could use the formatted text and symbols I had created to quantify the transcriptions. I learned I could use commands in Microsoft Word to count the number of revoicings, pauses, and interviewer affirmations in each interview. I also summed up the number of words shared by the teacher and the interviewer in each session and calculated the ratio between the interviewer's and the teacher's recorded words. Table 4.3 shows the results for Halsted and Indiana's interviews. (The full set of results for the first round of interviews is discussed on pp. 106–116 of Vanover, 2009.)

I used this evidence to support my claim that while the conduct of each interview varied, there was no intentional variation in the interviewer's work. The interviewer did not use one style of interviewing for the beginning teachers and engage in a different style for the accomplished, veteran educators. Such findings, of course, cannot be used to claim that the interviews were conducted without bias. My status as a White, male, former CPS teacher, and out-of-state PhD student mattered. I am certain a different interviewer with other personal characteristics would inspire a different set of stories, even if they used the same interview guide.

Transcripts as Ethnodramatic Scripts

There were many strengths in the work I engaged in transcribing the teachers' stories. I was committed to doing the work and I felt it mattered that I took the time

TABLE 4.3 ● Quantifying Transcription Symbols							
Teacher	Student voice-speaking as a student	Adult voice-speaking as another adult	Classroom voice—speaking as herself, teaching	# of Interviewer Affirmations per Interview	Ratio of Interviewer Words to Respondent words	Percent Teacher Words	# of Respondent Generated Pauses per Interview
Halsted Hoyne	64	79	288	384	755/26,715	97%	4
Indiana Ingleside	18	1	48	100	644/11,315	94%	50

to listen to what the teachers said. There were also many problems with my approach. Time is not cheap. By spending time, I was also falling behind. I believed I benefited by transcribing the first few interviews by hand, but once I figured out my transcription strategy, it would have been reasonable to pay a transcriber to produce the raw transcript—as I did for the second, third, and fourth round of interviews. I could have then cleaned that material and used my transcription strategies to prepare the data with little loss of engagement.

It was also the case I was working alone through the entire process and, as the previous section implies, I did not produce a regular set of memos to record my progress. My lack of memo writing hid a bigger problem: I was a good writer, but I had not developed a voice to communicate what I had learned from the interviews. Likely as a result, when I finished my dissertation and it came time to develop papers from my research in Chicago, I had trouble pulling the material together.

As I have written elsewhere (Vanover, 2016a, 2017), what worked for me was to transform the transcripts into what are now six ethnodramatic scripts. It was challenging to figure out an ethnodramatic approach for the teachers' interviews (see Saldaña, Chapter 19), but once I figured one out, script writing came easily. Because I had narrativized the data, I saw the voices on the page when I reread the transcripts and began to develop the scripts. I was able to edit the boring parts out of the teachers' transcripts and condense the interviews for performance because I already knew what the exciting parts were. The scripted versions of the interview segments published in this chapter can be found in Vanover (2019, p. 26) and Vanover (2016b, p. 182). Saldaña (2003, 2011) provides suggestions for developing ethnodrama from data and examples of theatrical script writing conventions.

FIGURE 4.1 ● Jennifer J. Smith Playing Halsted Hoyne at the Performance of *System Failure* at the Gerald R. School of Public Policy, University of Michigan, Ann Arbor

Conclusion

Decisions made during the process of transcription shape the meanings researchers develop as they engage with the text during the subsequent stages of the qualitative research life cycle. All transcription is political (Bucholtz, 2000; Ochs, 1979). Words, gestures, and other aspects of discourse are always rendered from a particular set of biases and beliefs. Transcribers' articulated and inarticulated theories shape the words and symbols they use to render recorded speech acts. Such theories also shape machine learning. Automatic coding systems vary in their ability to render types of speech (di Gregorio, Chapter 6). Rigorous qualitative data analysis requires intentional and careful transcription.

A major theme of the chapter is that research questions and study goals shape researchers' choice of transcription strategies and practices. An intentional transcription strategy takes into account the characteristics of the data and the analytic framework the research team applies to this material. Time spent early in the analysis engaging with the recorded data and drafts of the transcribed text may

FIGURE 4.2 ● Bob Devin Jones and Lisa Tricomi Performing *Listening to the Silences* at the Studio@620 in St Petersburg, Florida

build the foundation for unexpected insights and deepen researchers' understanding of the content of the interview.

The simple Microsoft Word formatting commands used in this chapter illustrate how different transcription practices might guide the research team's attention. As I discussed, my decision as a dissertation researcher to narrativize my transcripts enriched the possibilities for analysis and interpretation available during later stages of the project life cycle. This transcription strategy shaped the flow of meanings and images I experienced as I read the teachers' stories.

Time is a precious resource. Qualitative researchers must find a balance between time spent engaging with the recorded interviews and time spent doing all the other work required to construct a finished study. In my view, rigorous qualitative work is not built from the unreflexive markings of paid transcribers and automatic coding systems. In my view, it is not necessary for researchers to transcribe each and every recording they make by hand. As di Gregorio (Chapter 6) discusses, it is worthwhile for researchers to outsource the more laborious aspects of the transcription process to paid transcribers and automatic coding systems if researchers then listen to the recording and engage with the unfinished transcript and organize the data to support their study goals.

The future of qualitative research is video (see Harris, 2016; Pink, 2013). As I discussed in the literature review for this chapter, almost all current, cutting-edge work on transcription focuses on this media. In my view, what holds the field back is the same thing that advances it forward: technology. Technology has yet to democratize video production in the way technology has democratized print, but the day is coming.

I no longer record my interviews onto cassette tape, but there are occasions when I take out my digital transcription pedal and transcribe by hand. I find that these transcription sessions bring me back to the joys of storytelling that first brought me to qualitative inquiry. These transcriptions are emerging as an important area of research (Langtiw & Vanover, under submission; Vanover, Knobloch, Salaam, & Agosto, under submission), and I now find it easier to justify the time to engage in this work. My work as a transcriber has been labor-intensive, but I treasure the memories.

Supplemental Readings

Cowan, K. (2014). Multimodal transcription of video: Examining interaction in Early Years classrooms. *Classroom Discourse, 5*(1), 6–21. https://doi.org/10.1080/19463014.2013.859846

Lapadat, J. C., & Lindsay, A. C. (1999). Transcription in research and practice: From standardization of technique to interpretive positionings. *Qualitative Inquiry, 5*(1), 64–86. https://doi.org/10.1177%2F107780049900500104

Oliver, D. G., Serovich, J. M., & Mason, T. L. (2005). Constraints and opportunities with interview transcription: Towards reflection in qualitative research. *Social Forces, 84*(2), 1273–1289. https://doi.org/10.1353/sof.2006.0023

Reflection and Activities

1. Compare and contrast conceptions and practices related to transcription as a method of inquiry, with practices that unreflexively use transcription as an atheoretical medium for analysis.

2. Discuss how alternative sets of research questions and study goals might require different transcription strategies.

3. The ethnodrama built from the transcript in Table 4.1, Halsted's interview, was performed as part of a series of talks on educational disparities at the Gerald R. Ford School of Public Policy: http://fordschool.umich.edu/video/2014/what-does-it-mean-work-system-fails-you-and-your-kids-beginning-teachers-journey-through-. Go to the start of the scripted performance in that video—41:30 minutes—and ask the class to develop a transcription strategy to render the first five minutes of the play. Students might have the option of building this text from the Ford's School's machine transcription. What aspects of the video should be selected and what aspects ignored?

References

Alvesson, M., & Karreman, D. (2011). *Qualitative research and theory development: Mystery as method.* SAGE.

Bartesaghi, M. (2022). Theories and practices of transcription from discourse analysis. In C. Vanover, P. Mihas, & J. Saldaña (Eds.), *Analyzing and interpreting qualitative research: After the interview.* SAGE.

Benner, P. E., Hooper-Kyriakidis, P. L., & Stannard, S. (1999). *Clinical wisdom and interventions in critical care: A thinking-in-action approach.* Springer.

Benner, P. E., Tanner, C. A., & Chelsea, C. (1996). *Expertise in nursing practice: Caring, clinical judgment, and ethics.* Springer.

Bernauer, J. A. (2022). Oral coding: An alternative way to make sense of interview data. In C. Vanover, P. Mihas, & J. Saldaña (Eds.), *Analyzing and interpreting qualitative research: After the interview.* SAGE.

Bucholtz, M. (2000). The politics of transcription. *Journal of Pragmatics, 32*(10), 1439–1465. https://doi.org/10.1016/S0378-2166(99)00094-6

Bucholtz, M. (2007). Variation in transcription. *Discourse Studies, 9*(6), 784–808. https://doi.org/10.1177/1461445607082580

Charmaz, K. (2011). Grounded theory methods in social justice research. In N. K. Denzin & Y. Lincoln (Eds.), *The Sage handbook of qualitative research* (Vol. 4, pp. 359–380). SAGE.

Charmaz, K. (2014). *Constructing grounded theory.* SAGE.

Charmaz, K. (2017). The power of constructivist grounded theory for critical inquiry. *Qualitative Inquiry, 23*(1), 34–45. https://doi.org/10.1177%2F1077800416657105

Cowan, K. (2014). Multimodal transcription of video: Examining interaction in Early Years classrooms. *Classroom Discourse, 5*(1), 6–21. https://doi.org/10.1080/19463014.2013.859846

Crow, B. K. (1988). Conversational performance and the performance of conversation. *TDR (1988-), 32*(3), 23–54. https://doi.org/https://doi.org/10.2307/1145905

Davidson, C. (2009). Transcription: Imperatives for qualitative research. *International Journal of Qualitative Methods, 8*(2), 35–52. https://doi.org/10.1177/160940690900800206

Dressler, R. A., & Kreuz, R. J. (2000). Transcribing oral discourse: A survey and a model system. *Discourse Processes, 29*(1), 25–36. https://doi.org/10.1207/S15326950dp2901_2

Eaton, K., Stritzke, W. G., & Ohan, J. L. (2019). Using scribes in qualitative research as an alternative to transcription. *The Qualitative Report, 24*(3), 586–605. https://nsuworks.nova.edu/tqr/vol24/iss3/12

Flewitt, R. (2011). Bringing ethnography to a multimodal investigation of early literacy in a digital age. *Qualitative Research, 11*(3), 293–310. https://doi.org/10.1177/1468794111399838

Greenwood, M., Kendrick, T., Davies, H., & Gill, F. J. (2017). Hearing voices: Comparing two methods for analysis of focus group data. *Applied Nursing Research, 35*, 90–93. https://doi.org/10.1016/j.apnr.2017.02.024

di Gregorio, S. (2022). Voice to text: Automating transcription. In C. Vanover, P. Mihas, & J. Saldaña (Eds.), *Analyzing and interpreting qualitative research: After the interview.* SAGE.

Halcomb, E. J., & Davidson, P. M. (2006). Is verbatim transcription of interview data always necessary? *Applied Nursing Research, 19*(1), 38–42. https://doi.org/10.1016/j.apnr.2005.06.001

Harris, A. M. (2016). *Video as method.* Oxford University Press.

Heath, C., Hindmarsh, J., & Luff, P. (2010). *Video in qualitative research.* SAGE.

Langtiw, C. L., & Vanover, C. (under submission). Sitting with: An interview with Cynthia Lubin Langtiw. *The Qualitative Report.*

Lapadat, J. C., & Lindsay, A. C. (1999). Transcription in research and practice: From standardization of technique to interpretive positionings. *Qualitative Inquiry, 5*(1), 64–86. https://doi.org/10.1177%2F107780049900500104

Locke, K., Golden-Biddle, K., & Feldman, M. S. (August 1, 2004). Imaginative theorizing in interpretive organizational research. *Academy of Management Proceedings, 2004*(1), B1–B6. https://doi.org/10.5465/ambpp.2004.13857425

Markle, D. T., West, R. E., & Rich, P. J. (2011). Beyond transcription: Technology, change, and refinement of method. *Forum Qualitative Sozialforschung/Forum: Qualitative Social Research, 12*(3). http://www.qualitative-research.net/index.php/fqs/article/view/1564

McLellan, E., MacQueen, K. M., & Neidig, J. L. (2003). Beyond the qualitative interview: Data preparation and transcription. *Field Methods, 15*(1), 63–84. https://doi.org/10.1177/1525822X02239573

Mondada, L. (2018). Multiple temporalities of language and body in interaction: Challenges for transcribing multimodality. *Research on Language and Social Interaction, 51*(1), 85–106. https://doi.org/10.1080/08351813.2018.1413878

Ochs, E. (1979). Transcription as theory. In E. Ochs & B. B. Schieffelin (Eds.), *Developmental pragmatics* (pp. 43–72). Academic Press.

Oliver, D. G., Serovich, J. M., & Mason, T. L. (2005). Constraints and opportunities with interview transcription: Towards reflection in qualitative research. *Social Forces, 84*(2), 1273–1289. https://doi.org/10.1353/sof.2006.0023

Pink, S. (2013). *Doing visual ethnography.* SAGE.

Saldaña, J. (2003). Dramatizing data: A primer. *Qualitative Inquiry, 9*(2), 218–236. https://doi.org/10.1177/1077800402250932

Saldaña, J. (2011). *Ethnotheatre: Research from page to stage.* Left Coast.

Saldaña, J. (2022). Dramatizing interviews. In C. Vanover, P. Mihas, & J. Saldaña (Eds.), *Analyzing and interpreting qualitative research: After the interview.* SAGE.

Saldaña, J., & Omasta, M. (2018). *Qualitative research: Analyzing life.* SAGE.

ten Have, P. (2007). *Doing conversation analysis.* SAGE.

Vanover, C. (2009). *The expertise in urban teaching project: A theory-based study* (dissertation), University of Michigan. Deep Blue. http://deepblue.lib.umich.edu/handle/2027.42/62224

Vanover, C. (2014). *The Expertise in Urban Teaching Project: Interview instruments, recruitment letters, and other materials.* USFSP Digital Archive. University of South Florida St. Petersburg. https://digital.usfsp.edu/fac_publications/2881/

Vanover, C. (2016a). Inquiry theatre. *Qualitative Inquiry, 22*(4), 238–248. https://doi.org/10.1177%2F1077800415572395

Vanover, C. (2016b). Listening to the silences: A teacher's first year in words and music. *Art/Research International: A Transdisciplinary Journal 1*(1), 174–207. https://ejournals.library.ualberta.ca/index.php/ari/article/view/24952

Vanover, C. (2017). From connection to distance: Using the practice of arts-based research to interpret field work. *Journal of Contemporary Ethnography, 46*(1), 51–80. https://doi.org/10.1177/0891241615598201

Vanover, C. (2019). What does it mean to work in a system that fails you and your kids?: A teacher's first year in the Chicago Pubic Schools. *International Journal of Education & The Arts, 20*(4), 1–56. http://doi.org/10.18113/P8ijea20n4

Vanover, C., Knobloch, K. T., Salaam, O., & Agosto, V. (under submission). Act 2: inquiry and discussion on "Goodbye to All That!" at the 7th Annual the Qualitative Report Conference. *The Qualitative Report.*

Weiss, R. S. (1995). *Learning from strangers: The art and method of qualitative interview studies.* Free Press.

5

Theories and Practices of Transcription from Discourse Analysis

Mariaelena Bartesaghi

Abstract

In this chapter, I consider transcription in discourse analysis as a critical practice of transparency, academic currency, and analytical reflection. Even basic transcription notations such as the volume and speed of speech, symbols that indicate if speech between two speakers overlaps as well as numbers that indicate the timing of pauses are key resources for the analyst. These notations point to how everyday performances fit in larger social discourses of gender, race, and other power asymmetries. By focusing on one example from a data session in a graduate seminar and how a pause was first transcribed and subsequently retranscribed by way of careful listening, I argue that careful transcripts of microinteractional features of conversation are essential to the interpretation of the constitution of social life.

Keywords: Discourse analysis; data session; pause; transcription; listening

Transcription: A Brief Introduction

In his studies of the orderly nature of social interaction, the way everyday mundane exchanges like telephone calls, how we say hello to each other, and the rituals of service encounters (see Merritt, in Aston, 1988) make up what we call "society," sociologist Harvey Sacks told his students in the mid-1960s,

> I started to work with tape-recorded conversations, for the single virtue that I could replay them; that I could transcribe them somewhat and study them extendedly. [O]ther things, to be sure, happened, but at least what was on the tape *had happened*. I could study [them] again and again and also, consequentially, others could look at what I had studied and make of it what they could, for example, if they wanted to disagree with me (Sacks, 1984, p. 26, my italics).

Sacks's (1992) proposal for "close looking at the world" (p. 420) entreated qualitative researchers to produce transparency and accountability in a way that ethnographic field notes could never have. From the inception of what I discuss here as discourse analysis (DA),[1] the move toward the labor-intensive, painstaking, and, most importantly, generative practice of recording and transcribing speech changed the study of everyday life, institutions, social problems, and even the practice of doing qualitative research.

In 1974, when the first study of conversation appeared in an academic journal (Sacks et al., 1974), five years had passed since the moon landing, and yet no researcher had put forth insights about how turn-taking and the ways in which speakers manage the conversational "floor" comprise the "simplest systematics" (Sacks, Schegloff, & Jefferson, 1974) by which social identities, asymmetries, and power are constituted each time we are *doing* talk.

For discourse analysts like me, who endeavor to connect talk to the broader contexts and societal discourses at our disposal to make and authorize claims of knowledge, for example, transcripts create and circumscribe the universe we wish to capture. As recordings of the "transient, highly multidimensional, and often overlapping events of an interaction" (Edwards, 2006, p. 321), transcripts are two important things. They are both records and analyst accounts of recording that claim to distill the features of an interaction and recontextualize it across time and space (as I illustrate later). Transcripts are also methodological necessities. They are a way for analysts to communicate by a *lingua franca* (shared, common language) of conventions and advance arguments about what they study. As artefacts of reflexive practice, transcripts are themselves highly theorized epistemological texts, inasmuch as the arguments we generate from transcripts are ultimately ontological. Transcriptions bring forth possible universes for the speakers we study to inhabit, including ourselves. In this sense, they are liminal texts (Turner, 1967), for transcripts involve a continuous and ongoing change of state from the ephemeral and

---

[1] I define DA as an umbrella term for the interdisciplinary approach to spoken discourse (see Stubbe et al., 2003; Tracy & Mirivel, 2009).

experiential of in-the-moment experiences to a fixed record of "what happened" for analysis. Each state only makes sense in relation to what it is not.

In the sections that follow, I discuss how, if doing DA is the study of talk in its social context (Tracy, 2006), then how discourse analysts go about establishing a ratified version of "what happened" in a transcript is highly consequential; without a transcript, there could not be a DA. Without a good transcript, there would not be a valid and compelling theoretical argument. I begin a brief review of the literature on transcribing in DA. Then, I introduce the practice of data sessions and describe how a particular session taught me and the students in a graduate DA seminar about how transcribing a pause in speech can make all the difference in understanding the meaning of an interaction and what we can claim about it. I conclude with a reflection on the importance of and possibilities afforded by DA as a methodology and as a metatheoretical approach to transcribing and analyzing data.

Transcription Notation

Most discourse analysts use the Jeffersonian transcription system (Sacks et al., 1974, see this chapter's Appendix and Gee, 1999 for a well-known variant of this system), developed from the very first forays of studies of conversation. This notation provides guidance for transcribing words as pronounced, and not "cleaning" speech such as imposing contractions when they are not uttered by speakers, as in the case of "wanna" and "gonna." The Jeffersonian transcription system has specific symbols and written conventions for restarts and repetition, nonlexical sounds (such as umm, mmm, uh huh, which can serve several purposes in the course of talk), the volume of speech, prolonging or stressing of syllables, length of pauses in seconds, and other forms of vocal quality. Scholars—and I am one of them—often use simplified versions of this transcription system, depending on the goals of the analysis. Longer stretches of talk, where the analyst's aim is to analyze how talk acts in a broader context, may not require as much notation as do microanalyses of utterances in their immediate context (also known as adjacency pairs as, for example, the sequence by which we accept or deflect an invitation).

Ochs (1979) notes—and I agree—that a selective transcript is more useful than a transcript filled with detail that is not attended to and thus irrelevant to the analysis. For this reason, one of the critical decision points researchers face when they engage in all forms of transcription is selecting the particular features of talk to transcribe. Making these choices is a process that reflects the "theoretical goals and definitions" (p. 44) that make us accountable to other scholars reading our work. We must be intentional about the decision to select and the decision to exclude.

Once produced, a transcription may appear to be a text that is removed from its context; this separation is true of any written record. Transcripts are also, however, very much embodied. They are entangled in how we listen and capture what we hear, which is itself inextricable from our cultural understandings of how to represent speech and how micro-discourse is done. Consider the Western assumption transcripts should be read top to bottom, which allows discourse analysts to understand speakers' utterances as sequential and contingent upon one another, with each contribution opening a slot for the next speaker to take a turn (Ochs, 1979; see Sacks et al., 1974 for this understanding). Ochs (1979) calls attention to the fact that while adults do conversation this way, children do not. Their speech is often not in response to the immediate previous utterance and may not attend to their conversational partners' utterances at all.

As researchers, we are therefore obligated to understand our own biases in constructing and generating a record of "what happened." We must stay open to alternative logics of how talk is done. Developing a reflexive transcription practice requires the discourse analyst to be in a constant state of awareness and acknowledgment of the affordances of specific transcription choices. To me, reflexivity emerges from transparency—that is, from making clear to our readers (and therefore ourselves) exactly why we have chosen to do what we are doing and let readers judge for themselves. This reflexivity can be as simple as offering a brief account of our process, which I do here in a qualitative study about psychotherapy as social interaction (Bartesaghi, 2009):

> I transcribe at an intermediate level of detail, which is minimal compared to conversation analysis (Sacks et al., 1974; see Ochs, 1979 for a reflection on transcription itself). I leave punctuation marks (Labov & Fanshel, 1977, p. 41). Additionally, I code for false starts and vocalizations, overlaps, latched utterances, emphases on words, and increased volume. Due to space constraints, I omit lines in excerpts that do not offer additional data salient to the analysis. In these cases, I account for what is being said and for the number of lines omitted. In discussing each example, I refer to therapists with gendered pronouns, as I am aware of their gender.(p. 17)

Accountable Records of Recordings: Variation in Transcription

Like Ochs (1979), Bucholtz (2000) argues that transcripts "serve as politicized tools of linguistic representation" (p. 1439). As technologies of talk (Jones, 2006), transcripts mediate experience so they cannot but be political, but this is true of embodied and not just linguistic experience. They exist in an ongoing reflexive trialectic between our bodies that produce them, the data they produce, and the shifts in positioning the data require for different interpretations we may wish to advance (Ashcraft et al., 2017). Transcripts afford certain interpretations, unwittingly privilege specific speakers, and advance particular ideologies. Thus, Bucholtz characterizes "responsible transcription" as transcription where analysts invest in open and reflexive attention to their role in the creation of a transcript and the resultant ideological implications (see above for my attempt at doing so). An example of political stakes in transcription is Bucholtz's comparison of her own transcription of a police interrogation versus the transcript provided by the police.

Neither transcript is "objective"—in the sense that there is only one possible rendering of the dynamic—and yet, both index the transcribers' interpretive universe. The police, aiming to convict, transcribe several instances as "unintelligible," whereas Bucholtz (2000) transcribes those instances as moments in which the police actively collaborate in making a deal with the suspect.

Bucholtz (2007) identifies four types of variations in transcription. These are as follows:

1. global format choices based on an analytic focus on content versus form (or the level of detail chosen by the analyst)

2. variation in the details of transcription format in reproducing one's own or others' transcripts (we will see this below, in the decision of where to transcribe a pause)

3. orthographic variation in a single transcript

4. variation in translation, where the original language of the speakers is converted to another by the transcriber.

This variation is why discourse analysts will always provide an account of which interactional features (which some DA scholars refer to as "little-d" discourse) they analyze, the mutually constitutive relationship between these and (what is also known as the "Big-D" Discourse) of social action, and the analysts' goals in doing so. As Bucholtz notes, significantly reframing Ochs's critique, it is this practice of transparency that allows for multiple analytical uptakes of the same data by other scholars, each working within a set of possible valid interpretations. Though space does not permit to properly delve into the issue of validity of an analysis, not all possible interpretations of an interaction are equally valid. Hopefully the exemplar will shed light on this.

Discourse analysts put forth versions of how best to transcribe as well as what words, utterances, and longer stretches of talk mean in context (and the two cannot but inform each other) in the course of "data sessions." Whether in person or virtually, DA researchers get together for the purpose of "repeatedly looking/listening and then trying out arguments on equally observant others" (Tracy & Mirivel, 2009, p. 157). Stubbe et al. (2003) exemplify the benefits of this collaborative listening by examining how five different approaches to DA can be used to interpret the same data. Using conversation analysis, interactional sociolinguistics, politeness theory, critical DA, and discursive psychology, these authors analyze an interaction between two people in a New Zealand workplace. Stubbe et al. attribute the variations and similarities in their findings to the methodological and ontological commitments of the five different DA approaches brought to bear on the data. In the sections that follow, we turn to examining our own experience in a particularly memorable and heated data session.

Practicing Transcription in Discourse Analysis: An Exemplar

The interaction in Extract 1, transcribed by Nivethitha Ketheeswaran (2018) (henceforth, Niv) for the graduate seminar *Doing Research with Discourse Analysis* taught by me, is excerpted from an audio recording posted on YouTube by a declared pickup artist (yes, there is such a discourse genre) as part of his channel advising men on how to emulate his craft. The title: "PUA Audio In-Field - Bantering with Indian Girl 2 Set in Vegas," which after a brief Google search Niv identified as an unscripted recording of a "public interaction,"[2] in this case, between the PUA and two ethnically, Indian "girls" in Vegas (one of whom speaks in the transcribed extract). Though it would make sense from the exchange that the male is ethnically Caucasian, there is actually no evidence of this from the data alone. What we do know, however, is that the two speakers in the extract—and this is important—are Standard American English (SAE) speakers. The transcript that follows occurs after the PUA (M) has heard the "girl's" (W) name.

When presented with data, the main empirical questions for a discourse analyst are always meta-questions: "What are they doing?" and "How does this particular doing signify in the context of other interaction and(re)produce social/institutional/ideological doings?" By closely attending to the first question, examining what Goffman (1964) called "the greasy parts of speech" (p. 133), we focus on the way participants in a particular situation make sense and, reflexively, reproduce the social order. As a result, the transcriber's choices are the "difference that makes a difference" (Bateson, 1972/2000, p. 318). These decisions have big implications for us as much as those who may disagree with our analysis. Notice how a discourse analyst's

EXTRACT 1 ● Doing Banter, First Transcription		
1	M:	((fake Indian accent)) My name is Dorothy I live in Kansas
2	W:	It's Jyothi
3	M:	Oh hey my best friend is Sruti
4	W:	(2.0) That's not the [same] thing
5	M:	[Sruti] (.) I don't know but it sounds similar

---

[2]I distance myself from the politics and ethics of this categorization by the " ", but this is what IRBs are for.

simple choice of numbering talk by different speakers in terms of "turns" already makes a big difference. This choice allows us to take in how meaning is dynamic and intersubjective, and how much can happen in as little as five turns. Niv transcribed the interaction at the level of detail sufficient for her analysis (she transcribed phonological features, as opposed to an actual phonemic transcription of the accent (line 1)), pauses and overlapping speech. In line 4, the (2.0) notation marks a times pause of two seconds (see the Appendix). In line 5, Niv placed the square brackets to signal the beginning ([ ) and the endpoint ( ]) of a brief stretch of talk where W and M are talking at the same time. Once transcribed, the question of whether this is an interruption or a rapport-building (known as cooperative) overlap (see Nordquist, 2019) may become part of an accountable interpretation.

Briefly, Niv's argument (Ketheeswaran, 2018) was that what the PUA branded on YouTube in terms of "banter" was racially fraught from the very beginning. In line 1, M uses an Indian accent in his reference to *The Wizard of Oz*, calling attention to the irony of W's name being the Anglo "Dorothy" when her appearance (by the PUA's classification in the title) said otherwise. The next question might be: is this a sincere or purposeful mishearing of W's name? Discourse analysts answer that question by staying close to their transcript data; unlike other qualitative researchers, we eschew interpretations about "cognition," "intention," or things "behind" discourse. So, what we have to go on is W's correction by her actual name and, ironically, M's grounds for the humor (line 2). The fact that M now accounts for his poor judgment (line 3) is evidence of his awareness of "interactional trouble" (see, for example, Sidnell, 2016). He attempts to repair this by offering the somewhat ambiguous, multifunctional gloss that should prove he does know about ethnically Indian names. And M's familiar comeback "Oh hey" allows him to extend the argument that the context for the exchange is one of "all in good fun." Lines 4 and 5 are therefore crucial to participants' and analysts' meaning-making about what M and W are up to. As their speech overlaps (is this what is called a cooperative overlap? And if not, what does M and W talking at the same time mean?), the two speakers could be very engaged in talking to each other or the PUA could be talking on top of Jyothi briefly in line 5, indicating he is not listening. By claiming that W was "resisting a racialized identity," and that therefore the conversation was not cooperative, Niv advanced the latter interpretation.

...and What Happened Next

Once Niv presented her analysis to the class in these terms, the data session became very heated. The class split down the middle. The first group argued that Niv was wrong, inasmuch as what was transcribed was no more than an exchange of names, in the course of playful flirtation. It was Niv, rather, who was imposing her own ideas of racialization on the exchange because there was simply not enough evidence on the transcript to support her version of the situation. Others vehemently disagreed. To them, the fake accent (line 1) racialized the incongruity between Dorothy's *Wizard of Oz*, all-American Kansas origin and W's suggested name and appearance. In addition, members of this group argued that M's attempts to maintain face by the dismissive, all too familiar (and absurd) strategy of excusing the "joke" by "but-I-have-a-friend-just-like____," suggested M was doing something more than flirting.

During class, data session participants argued about two apparently incommensurable versions of how the interaction should be analyzed. Personal racial and sexual politics in the exchange, clashing with my insistence to stay close to the data, likely raised the stakes of one choice over the other. The participants in the data session fought about how things were as if their lives depended on it (they were putting the body back into the liminal text). Participants raised their volume, quickened their speech, used emphasis (by way of boosters such as "very," and "absolutely"), repeated what they were saying verbatim and in different ways, by supporting their own side (and here is where we would see latched utterances and the cooperative overlaps of engaged speech) and, conversely, by overlapping talk that competed for the floor.

In order to diffuse the conflict, I called attention to the (2.0) pause transcribed in line 4. Because most four syllable words take a second to say, with each syllable equivalent to a quarter of a second pause (Levinson, 1983, p. 320), a (2.0) second pause is therefore meaningful both to the analyst and the speakers. In fact, Niv could have chosen to transcribe it in its own line. Notice how Levinson (p. 320) does just this in Extract 2 below.

EXTRACT 2 ● Client to Therapist (All Notation Removed Except Line 3)		
1	C:	So I was wondering would you be in your office on Monday by
2		any chance?
3		(2.0)
4	C:	Probably not.

According to the dynamics of conversation (first set forth in Sacks et al., 1974), speakers understand utterances in sequential fashion. Each speaker's contribution opens a slot for the next speaker to take a turn (or not). Thus, the therapist's silence in line 3 speaks volumes. The (2.0) pause is not only the withholding of an answer, but an answer in itself, which the client interprets (correctly) and responds to in line 4.

The exchange between M and Jyothi is not bound by the same professional expectations as that between client and therapist (e.g., Bartesaghi, 2009); nonetheless, it involves several asymmetries. The notion of an asymmetry is little understood outside of an empirical analysis and transcription of conversation (see Marková & Foppa, 1991), for it means something as simple that for one of us to speak, another should be silent. In going back to our example in Extract 1, we can see from the transcript that when Jyothi's answers for M, her (2.0) requires that M wait for her to speak. In DA, pauses are strategies for withholding a response, giving the next utterance consideration, and taking time to produce a formulation. In this case, I suggested during the data session, that Jyothi's "That's not the same thing" (line 4) is a reasoned response, and supported the claim that she may be, in fact, offering an alternative to her interlocutor's version and, if you will, resisting the ascribed racialization of the joke in line 1.

As soon as I suggested this, two things happened. Though some were persuaded, not all participants to the data session found my proposition satisfactory (and good for them). The second thing is this: I finally realized that, all along, we had not been—quite literally—*doing transcription!* So, instead of going by the transcript that Niv had created, we took the time and actually *listened* to the recording. Once we listened, everything changed. What Niv did not transcribe on the reasonable grounds that it would not be necessary for her "resistance to racialization" argument, turned out to be the features of interaction we *needed* to transcribe. Most importantly, once we generated a shared version of "what happened" by actually listening together, it became possible for us to put forth a valid analysis. And the argument we could make from the transcript became more compelling.

The revised transcription looked like this:

EXTRACT 3 ● Doing Banter: Re-transcribed		
1	M:	((fake Indian accent)) > My name is Dorothy I live in Kansas<
2	W:	It's Jyothi↑ =
3	M:	= >Oh hey my best friend is Sruti<
4	W:	(.) >That's not the [same] thing↑<
5	M:	[Sruti] (.) > I don't know but it sounds similar<

Notice how elements like the fast pacing of talk (lines 1, 3, 4, 5), rising intonation (i.e., pitch changes in lines 2, 4, latched utterances (lines 2 and 3), and overlapping speech (lines 4, 5; both indicating high involvement/cooperation (Tannen, 2000)) give the interaction a very different feel as to what the participants are doing. Most importantly, notice how we retranscribed the pause in line 4, which we now heard as Jyothi taking a breath. This told us that her response to M (in line 5) came near immediately; it suggested that "banter" may in fact have been an appropriate characterization of the exchange.

Reworking the Analysis

Like many other qualitative researchers, discourse analysts recognize the laminated character of social activities, or the in situ negotiation of orientations to "what is happening" by those engaged in an ongoing interaction (Goffman, 1983). The difference between DA and other approaches is that we study this empirically and stay close to the data. Our transcripts allow us to track how, with each utterance, speakers are able to invoke Big-D discourses (e.g., racialization, gender) moving in and out of contexts of social order (e.g., how we do banter), as well as the contingent and shifting positions they occupy within these contexts. For example, Jyothi is at once a woman, of Indian descent, a native speaker of English, competent in "banter," a traveler to Las Vegas, engaged in talk with M, familiar with *The Wizard of Oz* (and we encourage you to think of more to add to this list). A dynamic understanding of the relationship between identities and contexts allows us to theorize about the greater scheme of the interaction or social order. This scheme includes the way authority and power are done. Discourse analysts (those affiliated with critical approaches excepted) avoid cognitive notions of intention, but rather look for how a situation is constituted by all who participate in it by way of the discursive strategies and resources speakers deploy.

The transcript in Extract 3 allows us to examine the shifting contexts called into play by M and W as they work through definitions of the situation, but "also definitions of themselves as certain kinds of people...who are qualified to engage in the social practice being indexed" (Jones, 2006, p. 94). Remember that "banter" is the definition of the situation assigned by the PUA (M), who is also producing it for consumption, using Jyothi as his unwitting coparticipant (bait?), but participant nonetheless. What is useful about M's definition is that it allows us to examine the complexities involved in the production of banter/pickup strategies (and ratified production at that, since M has his own YouTube channel, and there are many more like it), and shifting in and out of contexts/identities that may occur. And what is crucial about upping the level of detail in our transcription is that it tells us that Jyothi's speech matches the PUA's. As well, from an interactional perspective, they each take turns and maintain cooperation (in lines 4 and 5) and at no point does Jyothi disengage, though she could. This little-d analysis opens the door to Big-D critiques of social asymmetries and how we produce them together.

Concluding Reflection on the Data Session

Peräkylä (2004) notes that the ear of the transcriber develops through experience. We teach ourselves to listen to what was originally inaudible, learn how to time pauses to a fraction of a second, and notice the speed or intonation of talk or how speakers can overlap (like M and W do briefly in lines 4 and 5) over multiple turns. This is why a DA transcript will go through several revisions, with notation (including the acknowledgment of additional speakers or reassignment of speaker contributions) added or subtracted as a result (Rapley, 2018). By our hearing, we generate and make real what was not previously there. Transcription may begin as a solo enterprise, but it should, when possible, be done with others and practiced in data sessions, so as to attune our hearing and check for our own deafness. In the data session I discussed here, we learned something that I had (thankfully, only briefly) forgotten: hearing and listening are not the same thing. Often, we hear what we may want to hear because we have already theorized what the situation is.

Our ears are never neutral, which is why what they tell our fingers to produce and our eyes to see is up for discussion, disagreement, and revision. But hearing and sight are not the only senses we engage in transcribing. A claim to how people practice social life is a claim that positions them, and this claim includes our own activities and position(s) within that life.

Transcripts are records that say much about us, as Ochs and Bucholtz have noted, and the data session we participated in brought this home loud and clear. The argument that erupted showed how invested the class was in their claims, that is, their interpretations of the situation, of social life and identities, of the possibilities for things to be and to be otherwise. And this, we believe, happens utterance by utterance.

Conclusion: On Transcription in Qualitative Research

As the authors in this volume demonstrate, qualitative researchers choose their craft and pursue it with passion. In my training as a traditional social scientist,

> I became familiar with hypotheses, different sorts of variables...SPSS, the desirable value of p for what was deemed statistically significant, validity, and reliability. In short, I learned how to look for and dis-cover (literally, as in removing a cover) what, if I could only find the right tools for the task, were answers to the enigmas of the data—or, etymologically, givens, as in properties already there. It was not as easy as it sounds... The quantitative researcher, it seemed, was plagued by hermeneutics of suspicion—a perceived lacuna between truth and method. This meant a constant need for alertness, sharpening measurements, strategizing ways to recruit and obtain subjects' compliance, worrying about what subjects' language might not reveal, and how to find entry into what was hidden (Bartesaghi, 2013, p. 108).

Transcripts are tools, sure. But producing accurate transcripts (where accuracy itself is a process of social interaction) and recontextualizing them in our analyses does allow us to understand the social world and open ourselves to how we examine its workings in a way I would not wish to give up. Notation, while not always possible (for we may be inheriting finished transcripts) is nonetheless the best we can do to faithfully capture how the social is built, as a web of interaction.

Because we listen, transcribe, and therefore theorize with our bodies, discourse analysts embody their transcriptions. Yes, this is difficult, tiring, time-consuming, but it is *the work*. If someone else is doing the work by listening for us, and typing up a transcript, then what we get is another ear, another rendition, but what we miss is the value of understanding, in an embodied way, what we can do with our data and what, reflexively, our data do to us and our passion for qualitative inquiry.

Supplemental Readings

Jones, R. (2006). *Spoken discourse*. Bloomsbury.

Muñoz, K. L. (2014). *Transcribing silence: Culture, relationships, and communication.* Left Coast Press.

Stubbe, M., Lane, C., Hilder, J., Vine, E., Vine, B., Marra, M., Vine, B. Weatherall, A. (2003).

Multiple discourse analyses of a workplace interaction. *Discourse Studies, 5*(3), 351–388. https://doi.org/10.1177/14614456030053004

Reflection and Activities

1. Try your hand with this YouTube post, "You Have A GREAT Body." that is very similar to the one we analyzed: https://www.youtube.com/watch?v=Cpr92IEIx78. Which part of the video would you choose to transcribe and why? How much context (for example, that the man produced the exchange, that it acts as a "tutorial" for other would-be pickup artists, that it is posted on YouTube and therefore presuming a wide appeal to a discourse community of consumers, that it reconstitutes understandings of banter, flirtatious, and heteronormative identities, etc.)? What sorts of contextual choices would illuminate certain features instead of others? What level of transcription detail would you choose? Notice the fact that there are comments under the clip as well: should those be analyzed as part of what gives meaning to the interaction?

2. Two readings will prove indispensable to inform your practice and reflection for Question 1. The first is Emmanuel Schegloff's (2000) *On Granularity*, which will allow you to consider how delineating your analytical focus in a transcript will afford you to see very different aspects of an interaction. The second is Rodney Jones's (2006) *Spoken Discourse*, which teaches us how focusing in and out on context (utterances, speakers, gendering, YouTube as mediation and technology, genre, social practice, etc.) means advancing very different theoretical arguments about identities, relationships, power, and mediation.

Acknowledgments

I want to thank Nivethitha for her generosity in providing the transcript for this chapter, and for the invaluable insights about her process and the data session. I am also grateful to the students of SPC 6934 *Doing Research with Discourse Analysis* in Fall 2018, without whom this chapter would not have been possible.

References

Ashcraft, K., Kuhn, T., & Cooren, F. (2017). *The work of communication: Relational perspectives on working and organizing in contemporary capitalism.* Routledge.

Aston, G. (1988) (Ed.), *Negotiating service. Studies in the discourse of bookshop of Encounters.* CLUEB.

Bartesaghi, M. (2009). How the therapist does authority: Six strategies for substituting accounts in the session. *Communication & Medicine, 6*(1), 15–25. https://doi.10.1558.cam.v5i2.15

Bartesaghi, M. (2013). Qualitative research: Mapping an ongoing journey. *Journal of Medicine and the Person, 11*(3), 108–112. https://doi.10.1007/s12682-013-0160-3

Bateson, G. (1972/2000). *Steps to an ecology of mind: Collected essays in anthropology, psychiatry, evolution, and epistemology.* Chandler.

Bucholtz, M. (2000). The politics of transcription. *Journal of Pragmatics, 32,* 1439–1465. https://doi.org/10.1016/S0378-2166(99)00094-6

Bucholtz, M. (2007). Variation in transcription. *Discourse Studies, 9*(6), 784–808. https://doi.org/10.1177/1461445607082580

Edwards, J. (2006). The transcription of discourse. In D. Schiffrin, D. Tannen, & H. E. Hamilton (Eds.), *The handbook of discourse analysis* (pp. 321–348). Blackwell.

Gee, J. P. (1999). *An introduction to discourse analysis: Theory and method* (4th ed., 2014). Routledge.

Goffman, E. (1964). The neglected situation. *American Anthropologist, 66,* 133–136. https://doi.org/10.1525/aa.1964.66.suppl_3.02a00090

Goffman, E. (1983). The interaction order: American Sociological Association, 1982 Presidential Address. *American Sociological Review, 48*(1), 1–17. https://www.jstor.org/stable/2095141

Jones, R. (2006). *Spoken discourse.* Bloomsbury.

Ketheeswaran, N. (2018). *A discourse analysis of a pickup artist interaction: Techniques to resist imposed racial identities.* [Unpublished Manuscript]. The University of South Florida.

Levinson, S. C. (1983). *Pragmatics.* Cambridge University Press.

Marková, I., & Foppa, K. (1991). *Asymmetries in dialogue.* Harvester Wheatsheaf.

Nordquist, R. (2019). *Cooperative overlap in conversation.* ThoughtCo. https://www.thoughtco.com/cooperative-overlap-conversation-1689927

Ochs, E. (1979). Transcription as theory. In E. Ochs & B. Schieffelin, (Eds.), *Developmental pragmatics* (pp. 43–72). Academic Press.

Peräkylä, A. (2004). Conversation analysis. In C. Seale, D. Silverman, J. Gubrium, & G. Gobo (Eds.), *Qualitative research practice* (pp. 165–179). SAGE.

Rapley, T. (2018). *Doing conversation, discourse and document analysis.* SAGE.

Sacks, H. (1984). Notes on methodology. In J. Heritage & J. Maxwell Atkinson (Eds.), *Structures of social action: Studies in conversation analysis* (pp. 2–27). Cambridge University Press.

Sacks, H. (1992). Lectures on Conversation, Vols. 1–2. G. Jefferson, Ed. Cambridge, USA: Blackwell.

Sacks, H., Schegloff, E. A., & Jefferson, G. (1974). A simplest systematics for turn-taking for conversation. *Language Learning, 50*(4), 696–735. https://doi.org/10.1016/B978-0-12-623550-0.50008-2

Schegloff, E. (2000). On granularity. *Annual Review of Sociology, 26,* 715–720. https://doi.org/10.1146/annurev.soc.26.1.715

Sidnell, J. (2016). Interactional trouble and the ecology of meaning. *Psychology of Language and Communication, 20*(2), 98–111. https://doi.org/10.1515/plc-2016-0006

Stubbe, M., Lane, C., Hilder, J., Vine, E., Vine, B., Marra, M., & Weatherall, A. (2003). Multiple discourse analyses of a workplace interaction. *Discourse Studies, 5*(3), 351–388. https://doi.org/10.1177/14614456030053004

Tannen, D. (2000). Language and culture. In R. W. Fasold & J. Connor-Linton (Eds.), *An introduction to language and linguistics* (pp. 353–382). Cambridge University Press.

Tracy, K. (2006). Discourse analysis in communication. In D. Schiffrin, D. Tannen, & H. E. Hamilton (Eds.), *The handbook of discourse analysis* (pp. 725–749). Blackwell.

Tracy, K., & Mirivel, J. (2009). Discourse analysis: The practice and practical value of taping, transcribing, and analyzing talk. In L. R. Frey & K. N. Cissna (Eds.), *Routledge handbook of applied communication research* (pp. 153–177). Routledge.

Turner, V. (1967). Betwixt and between: The liminal period in rites of passage. In *The forest of symbols: Aspects of Ndembu ritual* (pp. 93–111). Cornell University Press.

Appendix

Jeffersonian Transcription Symbols

(.)	A full stop inside brackets denotes a micro pause, a notable pause but of no significant length.
(0.2)	A number inside brackets denotes a timed pause. This is a pause long enough to time and subsequently show in transcription.
[ ]	Square brackets denote a point where overlapping speech occurs.
> <	Arrows surrounding talk like these show that the pace of the speech has quickened
< >	Arrows in this direction show that the pace of the speech has slowed down
( )	Where there is space between brackets denotes that the words spoken here were too unclear to transcribe
(( ))	Where double brackets appear with a description inserted denotes some contextual information where no symbol of representation was available.
Underline	When a word or part of a word is underlined it denotes a raise in volume or emphasis
↑	When an upward arrow appears it means there is a rise in intonation
↓	When a downward arrow appears it means there is a drop in intonation
→	An arrow like this denotes a particular sentence of interest to the analyst
CAPITALS	Where capital letters appear it denotes that something was said loudly or even shouted
Hum(h)our	When a bracketed 'h' appears it means that there was laughter within the talk
=	The equal sign represents latched speech, a continuation of talk
::	Colons appear to represent elongated speech, a stretched sound

Voice to Text: Automating Transcription

Silvana di Gregorio

Abstract

This chapter begins with a concise review of technological developments in the collection and analysis of voice-based data—in particular, interviews in social science research. The problematic nature of producing transcripts is explored. The chapter's major focus is on how automating transcription will enhance qualitative data analysis by enabling more time for reflection and interpretation. The author's experience of managing the transcription issues she encountered with an interview-based research project in 2008 is compared with her experience recently revisiting that project using an automated transcription service. The chapter ends with guidance on using automated transcription services and the need for researchers to rethink the workflow between data collection, transcription, and analysis.

Keywords: Transcription; automatic speech recognition; technology; analysis process; NVivo

The literature on the use of tools or technology in the social sciences is thin compared to that of the natural sciences (Lee, 2004; Platt, 2002). Ray Lee (2004) cites the importance of labs in the natural sciences as one explanation. But he also quotes Ravetz (1971) that research tools have "low status" as they are associated with the craft aspect of social science. The development of tools for transcription is linked with the development of the voice recorder. Lee (2004) has pointed out that within qualitative research "the tape recorder is not seen as a device for recording sound but for producing text" (p. 880).

Brief History of Development of Transcription Tools

Evers (2011) lists the development of tools for transcription. When recordings were produced with analogue devices, the transcriptionist would use a typewriter, carbon paper (for multiple copies), Tipp-Ex for corrections, and a headset for listening to the tape recorder. Transcription machines were the next development and became a more effective way of transcribing. With digital files, it became possible to play the recording on a PC's media player while typing in the word processor. During the 1990s, transcription software—such as F4, Express Scribe, and Transcribe came on the scene. This software combined the word processor and media player in one window. The software also allowed the synchronization of the audio and the words and incorporated timestamps. This synchronization between the spoken word and text allowed for more nuanced interpretations—as the tone, hesitations, and emotions in the voice could be linked to the text.

Evers also points out that Computer Assisted Qualitative Data Analysis (CAQDAS) software such as ATLAS.ti, MAXqda, NVivo, and Transana allow for direct coding on an audio or video file without the need for transcription. However, in an exercise with her own students working with just the audio/video file, she found that while they initially were enthusiastic about doing away with transcripts, they were frustrated with losing contact with parts of the audio they hadn't coded, and that their rephrasing of the respondents' words were sloppy. In addition, the visual nature of transcripts makes it easier to scan and to track the analysis process. Being able to search for text in the transcript was seen as a key benefit over coding on the audio file.

Developments in automatic speech recognition led to researchers starting to apply dictation software to their recordings through programs such as Dragon and MacSpeech. These packages could only be trained in one voice, so the researcher had to train the application by reading set speeches such as the Gettysburg Address. Researchers would then revoice their audio files in order to produce transcriptions. Matheson (2007) describes this process of "listening and repeat"—listening to the recording and then repeating it for the voice recognition software. She describes in detail the technology she used—a digital voice recorder, voice recognition software (Dragon Naturally Speaking), transcription software (which came with the voice recorder), and a headphone/microphone set. Fletcher and Shaw (2011) describe a similar technique except they used the voice recognition software (MacSpeech) with NVivo 8. However, by revoicing audio files, researchers are losing the original intonation and hesitations of the interviewee, and this loss of nuanced meaning can have an impact on the analysis.

Automated Transcription Services

Automated transcription services are a recent development and there is not much literature at the time of writing about their value for the research process. Moore (2015) discusses the value of automated transcription for conversational analysts. Moore used an automated transcription server internal to IBM powered by IBM's "Attila" speech recognition engine which is used to produce subtitles for videos. The raw data were unreadable as a transcript and had to be transformed by a Python script to make it readable. There was a high error rate of 36% (Moore's second set of recordings had slightly better error rates of 29%, 19%, and 2%) and other problems in the transcript including that speaker turns had to be transcribed manually, overlapping talk led to errors, and the transcript was not phonetic. Nonetheless, Moore still found automated transcripts to be a "good enough" first pass through the recording. The automated transcripts reduce the transcriptionist's time in capturing words and timing silences. In addition, Moore found that transcripts with time stamps enable analysts to work in an iterative way—moving between the auto-transcript, the auto-index (timestamps), and the recording. This transcription process supports "collections," which is a method in conversation analysis where a recurring pattern in talk is identified and the analyst searches the corpus for more examples. In addition, Moore argues that auto-transcription can increase the scale of conversation analysis in the era of big data.

Bolden (2015), in her reply to Moore's article, raises three issues cautioning about the use of auto-transcription in conversation analysis. Transcribing is a crucial research activity for conversation analysts, not a first step toward analysis. Bolden feels that there is a danger that adoption of automatic transcription could replace good research practice and have a negative effect on the training of new researchers. She also points out that automated transcription relies on high-quality recordings where there are no overlaps in conversation and everyone speaks in a standard accent. She fears that researchers could be steered away from studying (a) ordinary conversations, (b) interactions among people who have various dialects and lesser known languages, and (c) complex interaction situations. In addition, she also feels that analysts might be encouraged to use a limited set of analytical techniques, focused mainly on lexical searching. Bolden's final point is that automated transcription appears to encourage researchers to work with large corpora of unfamiliar data. She is not sure if this trend should be encouraged.

Bokhove and Downey (2018) conducted a proof-of-concept exploration of automating transcriptions using YouTube's automated captioning facility to transcribe three types of audio file—an interview, a public hearing, and a classroom setting. They used Turnitin, a plagiarism detection software program, to compare for accuracy with manual transcriptions. They conclude that transcription involves a trade-off between time or means and the quality of the transcript. They see automated transcription as a good enough first draft to form the foundation of successive rounds of engaging with the audio to capture all the elements from the raw file.

The technology involved in creating automated transcripts has developed substantially since Bokhove and Downey (2018), Bolden (2015), and Moore (2015) wrote their articles. A number of companies have developed automatic transcription software that can recognize multiple voices and produce transcripts with punctuation and indications for different speakers. Some packages include an editor which links the audio to text to enable easy corrections (di Gregorio, 2019; Duca, 2019). NVivo transcription is one such software and its application is the subject of the rest of this chapter. But other applications include Happy Scribe, Trint, Temi, Zoom, and Descript. Companies at the forefront of developing the algorithms for these applications include Amazon Transcription, Google Cloud Speech to Text, and Speechmatics. Improvements in the accuracy of these packages are constantly happening through algorithms being trained in large datasets of speech (Saon, Kurata, Sercu, Audhkhasi, Thomas, Dimitriadis, Cui, Ramabhadran, Picheny, Lim, Roomi, & Hall, 2017). The number of languages supported is growing. In addition, in some of these packages, English language recognition includes understanding a wide variety of English dialects.

Why Automation Is Valuable

As is evident in the above discussion of the history of transcription, researchers have been searching for ways to make their recordings accessible so they can spend more time on analysis. Without any automation, the transcription process is a laborious and time-consuming process (Vanover, Chapter 4). While transcription is part of the analysis process and offers the opportunity to reflect on the data and gain insights, the reality is that the focus on getting down all the words can become a chore and deadens the mind from analytic thoughts.

Positioning Statement and Study Description

I am a sociologist and have worked as a consultant on analyzing qualitative data using QDA software. Since 2013, I have worked at one of the companies that developed such software—QSR International, the developers of NVivo.

In 2008, QSR brought out NVivo 8, software which supported, for the first time, audio and video files. I developed my own training project in NVivo 8 to illustrate how researchers could transcribe and analyze media files in the software. To do that, I conducted a small piece of research. The aim was to look at how Year 11 students (in the UK, these would be high school juniors in the US) who plan to attend university respond to materials for prospective applicants on university websites. Each student (four boys and three girls) initially viewed two university websites following a Talk-Aloud protocol which was videoed using the screen-recording software, Camtasia. After all the students viewed the websites, I conducted two focus groups—one with the boys and the other with the girls—which I recorded their perceptions of the two universities.

As this was a project to be used to train new NVivo users, I kept detailed memos on the data collection, transcription, and analysis process. In this exemplar, I contrast my experience of transcribing within NVivo 8 back in 2008 with using the same audio and video files using an automatic transcription service—NVivo Transcription.

Transcribing Within a Qualitative Data Analysis Package—NVivo

In my research journal, I started to reflect on the focus groups immediately after I conducted them and before I transcribed them.

There was quite an interesting discussion about the colour scheme of the two sites and the kind of impressions that gave. This was led by (I think) Zidane and Russell who are Art and Humanities oriented. There was a lot of discussion about the photo of the tree covered in snow on the Manchester web-site—how it was a ridiculous filler—how it had nothing to do with the university and the impression it gave.

They all liked the photos and statements from students. They preferred those with a caption which gave some context to the student, e.g., where they're from, what subject they're studying. Also for the statements to include specific information—such as when talking about the city—which clubs they frequent as opposed to general statements. The specifics make you feel that the statements are genuine and not made up.

It is important to remember that reflection and analysis happens both during and immediately after collecting data. The above memo highlights my immediate impressions after the focus group. The students talked at length about the color scheme, what different colors meant to them, and the importance of photos as long as they were relevant. These were the issues that they talked passionately about over and above the content. They also could relate to the student statements as long as they had enough context about them. These reflections started me on thinking that the visual image of the university was an important consideration for these high school students. These reflections directed my initial coding of website appearance.

My journal also notes how I hadn't anticipated how long it would take to transcribe the focus groups within NVivo. But I also noted how as I transcribed within NVivo, I could comment and use links to the parts of the website they were talking about.

I just finished early this morning transcribing the focus group in NVivo. It took longer than I thought it would. I don't normally transcribe so I don't have foot pedals which I think you can use with NVIVO and would have made it a bit faster, I think. But I got used to using F7 to start/pause and F9 to go back 5 seconds and F8 to indicate a turn. I was annotating and adding See-Also links as I went along. That worked quite well—it was easy to do. They were referring a lot to different parts of the home page, so I could use the See-Also links to identify the parts of web-page they were referring to. It is nice so that when you double click on the See-Also link the photo opens up with the part of the photo they are referring to, in this case, the web homepage (see Figure 6.1).

The other thing I did—was I had a column for Speaker and indicated the speaker as I transcribed. This worked well. After I finished transcribing, I added a second column called Topic and put in the broad topic areas. I could do this quite quickly.

However, I still had to listen and transcribe word for word. The length of time it took to transcribe led me to reconsider the design of the project. I noted in my journal:

> Given the time it takes to transcribe, I will have to alter my plans and not do the selective grammar school students at this stage. I think that is fine for the NVivo training project. As there is quite enough data to play with.

And:

> I would like to finish transcribing Zidane's Bristol Talk Aloud and transcribe one of Holly's Talk Aloud but don't think I have time at the moment. I will have to move on to coding and writing the course handbook.

The result was that I only transcribed and coded the two focus groups. I only transcribed one of the Talk Aloud Videos so I never analyzed the Camtasia video data.

FIGURE 6.1 ● See-Also Links in NVivo Referring to an Image on a Web Page Mentioned in a Focus Group Transcript

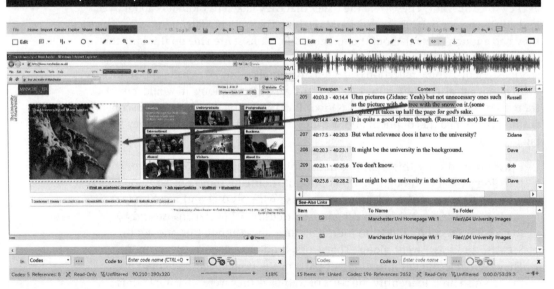

Eleven Years Later

QSR International launched their online automatic transcription service—NVivo Transcription—in 2018. I decided I would revisit the University Website project as I never had the time to transcribe the 14 Talk-Aloud videos.

I uploaded the Talk-Aloud video Russell made about his experience on the University of Bristol's website. At the time of writing, the NVivo Transcription service supports only direct importation of audio files.[1] To transcribe the video, I had to import the video into NVivo and access the transcription service from within NVivo. The audio portion of the video was then uploaded to the transcription service as an .mp3 file. This video is just over 17 minutes long. It took eight minutes for NVivo Transcription to provide a draft. Figure 6.2 shows the

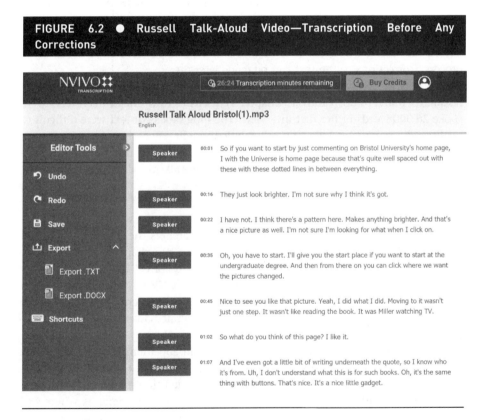

FIGURE 6.2 ● Russell Talk-Aloud Video—Transcription Before Any Corrections

---

[1]NVivo Transcription supports the following audio file formats: MP3, M4A, WAV, AAC, AIFF, AMR, ASF, AU, CAF, FLAC, RA.

beginning of the transcript in NVivo Transcription's editor before I reviewed it and made any corrections.

Automatic transcription is a new tool for researchers. As with any new tool, researchers need to consider its affordances and how to leverage them for their purpose. The quick turnaround in getting a draft of the transcript (half the time of the length of the audio/video file) is a real bonus. It means that researchers can get a draft of the transcript on the same day they conducted the interview. Transcription and analysis can begin shortly after the interview while it is still fresh in the mind of the interviewer. That is one affordance of automated transcription.

There can be an expectation that the transcription is word perfect. If the audio file is of a high standard, it can be nearly word perfect. As a first step, the temptation is to go through the draft to make it word perfect. However, that is losing sight of the purpose of a transcript. A transcript is an aid to support the analysis. The words themselves are just part of the interview/group discussion/observation or whatever event was recorded. In addition to the words is the setting or context where the words were uttered, the body language involved, the tone of the voice, hesitations, and so on. Going through the draft to make it word perfect delays the analysis process. Corrections to the text can be made later on.

It is better to consider how the transcript can support the kind of analysis the researcher wants to do. Vanover (Chapter 4) discusses how one of his interviewees spoke 26,000 words in her first interview. The long blocks of text were difficult to read and did not enable reflection or analytic thought. He designed a transcription strategy that *narrativized* the text. Bartesaghi (Chapter 5) discuss transcription conventions for Discourse Analysis. In my case, the Talk-Aloud protocol was linked to the areas in the webpages the student was exploring. So I had an additional layer to consider—the video.

A second affordance of automated transcription is that the words in the draft are linked to the audio file. This affordance gives researchers the opportunity to not only easily make corrections but also to structure the shape of the transcript according to their purpose. I wanted to structure and correct the transcript before importing it into NVivo. So I continued to work in the NVivo Transcription editor.

In the transcription editor, I was focusing on how to structure the shape of the transcript. As shown in Figure 6.2, the automatic draft had already put in punctuation and broke up the text. It couldn't identify speakers by name (only Speaker 1, Speaker 2, etc.) but had a column where I could add them. As this was a Talk Aloud protocol, most of the time the speaker was the student (Russell) with occasional prompts by myself. The transcript also included timestamps for each paragraph. In my initial pass through the draft, I made new paragraphs wherever I heard a pause in the audio. Shorter pauses were indicated with a dash. I also made some key corrections as I was trying to understand the meaning of the text as well as identifying the speakers.

In my second pass, I replayed the audio. As I went through the transcript, I created new empty paragraphs for silences over a few seconds and labeled the speaker name "Exploring"—as that was when the student was exploring the website (Figure 6.3). NVivo Transcription only supports (at the time of writing) the audio portion of a video. I was leaving blank spaces in the editor where I could write comments later about what was happening in the video. The transcript, audio, and video were reunited when I imported the transcript back into my NVivo analytic software.

I imported the transcript in NVivo and reviewed it with the synchronized video—adjusting the timespans for the silent bits where necessary. I also reviewed the videos of the silent bits and wrote descriptions in ***bold italics*** of what was happening in the video in the cells that I left empty and the cells where Russell is talking (Figure 6.4).

The description of what was happening in the video gave fuller meaning to the Talk-Aloud commentary. It was easy to review as the video was automatically synchronized. As I was reviewing, I was starting to comment and reflect in memos. As I was reflecting on Russell's comments on the Bristol website, I recalled and then reviewed his comments in the focus group which I had previously analyzed.

FIGURE 6.3 ● Russell Talk-Aloud Video Transcript—Transcription After Preparation in NVivo Transcription Editor

Exploring	09:17	
Russell	09:19	Can we go back to courses and online prospectus.
Russell	09:23	This is different. I thought it was going to that list of course it again but it's not.
Exploring	09:33	
Russell	09:36	All the pictures have disappeared. I don't know where they've gone to.
Exploring	09:43	
Russell	09:46	I'm not so sure what this page is about. I'll click on disabled students. Because if I were a disabled student that is where I would go.
Exploring	10:00	
Russell	10:03	I don't know if that picture is supposed to be depicting someone disabled. Oh it's sign language.

FIGURE 6.4 ● **Russell Talk-Aloud Video Transcript—With Synchronized Video and Descriptions of the Screencast in NVivo**

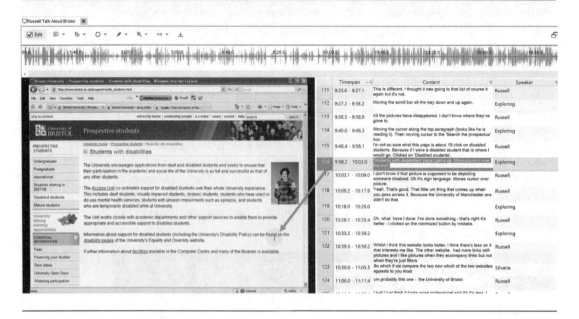

Russell's Talk-Aloud provided more context on the views he expressed during the focus group and why he was arguing strongly for the superiority of the Bristol website. I could link his comments on the color scheme, on the use of pictures, the type of layout, and navigability. When I also transcribed and viewed Russell's other Talk-Aloud on the Manchester University website, I could clearly see that Russell's initial (negative) reaction to a picture on the home page set his views about that website and focused his subsequent attention on pictures.

Working initially from the automated draft provided a time-saving boost to the analysis process. While the ability to transcribe with synchronized audio/video was possible in the earlier version of NVivo, there was no automation. I had to play, listen, and type word for word. Not only was this transcription process time consuming but it was also analytically numbing. Working from a synchronized automated draft is different—as long as researchers recognize its affordances. If automatic transcription had been available back in 2008 when I conducted this project, I would have had the time to analyze the Talk-Aloud website screencasts and integrate their analysis with the focus groups analysis I had done. This broader analysis would have produced a richer study and I would have been able to give useful feedback to the two universities who had given me permission to do the inquiry. Instead, I had to limit my study to my primary purpose, which was as a training project on how to use the NVivo software.

Guidance on Using Speech Recognition Transcription Services

Researchers need to understand the affordances speech recognition software offers and align them with their approach to the data collection and analysis process. Transcription is often seen as a stand-alone one-off task which can be outsourced to professional transcribers (if funding is available) or to research assistants. Even if the researcher or team do their own transcription, it often appears as a task separate from data collection or analysis. This is because of the time-consuming nature of transcription. A typical nonautomated work plan can be quite linear. Figure 6.5 illustrates a typical simple workflow.

As mentioned earlier, speech recognition technology is a recent innovation and not much has been written on how to use it in practice (Bokhove & Downey, 2018; di Gregorio, 2019; Duca, 2019; Moore, 2015). The focus in its development has been to increase the accuracy of word recognition (Juang & Rabiner, 2004). As a result, there is disappointment when these systems produce transcripts that are less than 100% word perfect. While accuracy is obviously important for qualitative analysis, transcripts need to be reviewed and mulled upon. Transcription is not a one-off task. The digital files need to be played and reviewed several times to gain meaning. Synchronization with the audio/video enhances the analysis process. Working from a good-enough automated first draft speeds up the process to get to reflection and analysis.

With speech recognition software, the first draft of the audio/video can be available the same day of the interview or the event recorded. This allows for a more iterative approach between data collection, transcription, and analysis. The research team's work plan can be reconfigured in new ways. If the team is working using a grounded theory approach (Charmaz, 2014; Corbin & Strauss, 2015; Glaser & Strauss, 1967), Table 6.1 illustrates a potential workflow.

Working from an initial interview guide and an initial sample, the researcher can conduct the first interview and immediately upload the audio file to the online automated transcription service. While reviewing the draft transcript, they can reflect on the transcript itself as well as writing up reflections in a memo. The reflections can

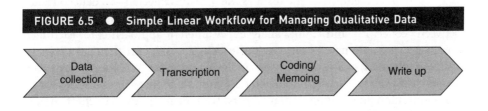

FIGURE 6.5 ● Simple Linear Workflow for Managing Qualitative Data

Data collection → Transcription → Coding/ Memoing → Write up

TABLE 6.1 ● Example Workflow for a Grounded Theory Study

DESIGN	xxxxxxxxxx	xxxxx		xxxxxxxxxxx		
	Interview Guide	Revise Guide		Revise sample		
SAMPLING	xxxxxxxxxx			xxxxxxxx		
	Initial sample			New criteria		
DATA COLLECTION	xxxxxxxxxx		xxxxxx		xxxxxxxx	
	Interview 1		Interview 2		Interview 3	
TRANSCRIPTION		xxxxxx	xxxxxxxx			xxxxxxxx
		Interview 1	Interview 2			Interview 3
REVIEW/REFLECT		xxxxxxxxx	xxxxxxxxxx			xxxxxxxxxx
		Interview 1	Interview 2			Interview 3
CODING						xxxxx
						Initial coding
MEMOING		xxxxxxxxx	xxxxxxxxxxx	xxxxxxxxxxx		xxxxxxx
		Interview 1	Interview 2	Review memo		Interview 3
WRITING UP						

lead to revising the interview guide for the second interview. Interview 2 would follow the same cycle. However, after reviewing both interviews in a memo, the researcher may decide they need to change the criteria for the sample to get a different perspective. The point is that transcription is not a bottleneck in the workflow of the study. Transcription can be easily incorporated into the analysis process.

Even if researchers are not using a grounded theory approach, the work plan can be adjusted so that transcription is integrated with analysis. If working in a team, the work plan can be adjusted across the team. Interviewers might hand over analysis to other members of the team as the data are collected—so data collection and analysis are happening simultaneously with team members divided initially between "collectors" and "initial analysts." A different approach is for each team member to use automated transcription to be responsible for their own iterative cycles of interview, analysis, interview, analysis, and so on. Whichever way a team adapts their work flow using automated transcription, there are implications for the communication flow among team members. Team members need to check in more frequently to share what they are learning. This can be done using regular online sessions using Zoom, Microsoft Teams, or Skype. These systems allow for screen sharing where transcripts, coding structures, and interpreting passages of text can be discussed. Analysis usually requires focused work on one's own but connecting with team members online at a set time during the day can ensure that everyone is learning from one another.

Adjustments in the work plan are linked to the second affordance that speech recognition software has—the ability to review the initial draft with the words linked to the original media file. This affordance allows a multimedia focus on the draft. Researchers can hear changes in the tone of voice, hesitations, and so on. Researchers have developed the Jeffersonian Transcription system to capture this content. This system was developed before it was possible to link text to media. Now that text can be linked to audio/video, it is much easier to transcribe with this system, and if the transcript is combined with a CAQDAS package that maintains this relationship, technology greatly eases the analysis process. In my example, conversation analysis was not the focus of my analytic approach. If it was, I could have indicated changes in tone, for example, by using capital letters when the tone of voice was raised. For the long silences in the recording, I did create empty cells to add descriptions later in NVivo when viewing the synchronized video of what Russell was exploring on the website.

Table 6.2 summarizes the affordances of speech recognition transcription and how they can enhance and develop qualitative research practices. As speech

TABLE 6.2 ● Affordances of Speech Recognition Software and Implications for Qualitative Research Practice

Affordance	Implication	Practice
Writing Up		
Cloud upload and first draft in half the time of the length of the digital file.	Can start analysis same day of recording interview/event.	Rethink process—data collection can be integrated with data analysis.
Link between draft and media—word for word.	Can focus on more than the words.	Begin analysis in transcription editor on tone of voice, hesitations, etc.—if that is relevant to your approach.
Automatic timestamps for link to media when exported out of the transcription editor.	Can import into qualitative data analysis software with links to media maintained.	Can code both transcript and media file, if relevant, for deeper analysis.

recognition transcription services continue to develop, new affordances may emerge. It is important for researchers to reflect critically on how they can take advantage of these new affordances. A temptation would be to keep their current practice of, for example, outsourcing the transcription and sticking to a linear work flow of data collection > transcription > coding/memoing > writing up. Speech recognition transcription offers so much more.

Conclusion

Automated transcription is a new tool for researchers and will continue to develop. As with any new tool, researchers need to consider how best to incorporate it within their working practices. Transcription is part of the analysis process and should never be seen as a technical preliminary before the analysis. In fact, during the initial stages of transcription/analysis, it can be important to maintain the link between the original media and the transcript as the words alone may not make sense without the link to their audio/video context. In addition, researchers need to be aware of how privacy and security are managed by whatever platform or transcription service they use. Transcription also comes with a cost—whether it is the researcher's time, if they decide to do it all by themselves or whether they outsource it to a professional transcriptionist or an automated platform.

The discussion of workflow issues that concludes the chapter asks researchers to envision new strategies and practices for qualitative research not constrained by the technologies of the past. What type of studies might we conduct, and how might we manage the work of interpretation and analysis, if we received the first draft of our transcripts almost instantaneously by using an automatic coding system? I believe there would remain much work to be done to ensure even the most accurate automatic transcript reflected study goals, however the flexibility provided by the new technology might have enormous benefits for qualitative inquiry. Respondents might be queried the next day to clear up any concerns in their interviews. Research designs might change flexibly and organically as result of fast, but rigorous, analysis of the transcribed data. High-quality transcription will always require careful and thoughtful work, but the ease and speed of automatic transcription may support new questions, research goals, and research designs.

Supplemental Readings

Bokhove, C., & Downey, C. (2018). Automated generation of 'good enough' transcripts as a first step to transcription of audio-recorded data. *Methodological Innovations, 11*(2). https://doi.org/10.1177/2059799118790743

di Gregorio, S. (2019). *Transcription: More than just words.* https://www.qsrinternational.com/nvivo-qualitative-data-analysis-software/resources/blog/transcription-more-than-just-words

Evers, J. C. (2011). From the past into the future. How technological developments change our ways of data collection, transcription and analysis. *Forum Qualitative Sozialforschung/Forum: Qualitative Social Research, 12*(1). http://dx.doi.org/10.17169/fqs-12.1.1636

Reflection and Activities

1. Reflect on current types of transcription practices and how their workflow might change when adopting a speech recognition transcription service.

2. When using any cloud-based service it is important to check their security and privacy policies and the geographical location of their servers. There are national, regional, and subject area compliance issues—such as GDPR, HIPAA, FEDRAMP, and FERPA. Look up these compliance issues and then check out some automated transcription services to learn whether they comply. Examples of automatic transcription services include https://trint.com; https://www.temi.com; https://www.happyscribe.co; https://www.qsrinternational.com/nvivo-qualitative-data-analysis-software/about/nvivo/modules/transcription. As this is a new technology which is developing rapidly, extend your search to see if you find others.

3. Select or create a 15-minute audio recording of an interview or an event. Have half the class transcribe it listening to the audio and typing in Word. The other half will upload it to NVivo Transcription—https://www.qsrinternational.com/nvivo-qualitative-data-analysis-software/try-nvivo. (The first 15 minutes of using this service are free of charge for new users.) Both groups are to review the transcription and decide how best to structure it in the transcription editor or Word. Try focusing on how to break up the words in the transcription editor or Word. Note silences, hesitations, and the tone of voice. Ask the class to write up thoughts on the codes emerging. Allow both groups only 30 minutes to do this exercise and have them stop where they are when the 30 minutes are up. Facilitate a discussion between the two groups on their experience. If you do not have any audio files, you can download audio files from the Library of Congress. One interesting collection is the Occupational Folklife Project—https://www.loc.gov/collections/occupational-folklife-project/about-this-collection/

References

Bartesaghi, M. (2022). Theories and practices of transcription from discourse analysis. In C.Vanover, P. Mihas, & J. Saldaña (Eds.), *Analyzing and interpreting qualitative data: After the interview*. SAGE.

Bokhove, C., & Downey, C. (2018). Automated generation of 'good enough' transcripts as a first step to transcription of audio-recorded data. *Methodological Innovations, 11*(2). http://dx.doi.org/10.1177/2059799118790743

Bolden, G. B. (2015). Transcribing as research: "Manual" transcription and conversation analysis. *Research on Language and Social Interaction, 48*(3), 276–280. http://dx.doi.org/10.1080/08351813.2015.1058603

Charmaz, K. (2014). *Constructing grounded theory* (2nd ed.). SAGE.

Corbin, J. M., & Strauss, A. L. (2015). *Basics of qualitative research: Techniques and procedures for developing grounded theory* (4th ed.). SAGE.

di Gregorio, S. (2019). *Transcription: More than just words.* https://www.qsrinternational.com/nvivo-qualitative-data-analysis-software/resources/blog/transcription-more-than-just-words

Duca, D. (2019). *Who's disrupting transcription in academia?* https://ocean.sagepub.com/blog/whos-disrupting-transcription-in-academia

Evers, J. C. (2011). From the past into the future. How technological developments change our ways of data collection, transcription and analysis. *Forum Qualitative Sozialforschung/Forum: Qualitative Social Research, 12*(1). http://dx.doi.org/10.17169/fqs-12.1.1636

Fletcher, A. K., & Shaw, G. (2011). How voice-recognition software presents a useful transcription tool for qualitative and mixed methods researchers. *International Journal of Multiple Research Approaches, 5*(2), 200–206. http://dx.doi.org/10.5172/mra.2011.5.2.200

Glaser, B. G., & Strauss, A. L. (1967). *The discovery of grounded theory; strategies for qualitative research*. Aldine Publishing Company.

Juang, B. H., & Rabiner, L. R. (2004). *Automatic speech recognition – A brief history of the technology development.* https://www.ece.ucsb.edu/Faculty/Rabiner/ece259/Reprints/354_LALI-ASRHistory-final-10-8.pdf

Lee, R. M. (2004). Recording technologies and the interview in sociology, 1920-2000. *Sociology, 38*(5), 869–889. http://dx.doi.org/10.1177/0038038504047177

Matheson, J. L. (2007). The voice transcription technique: Use of voice recognition software to transcribe digital interview data in qualitative research. *Qualitative Report, 12*(4), 13. https://nsuworks.nova.edu/tqr/vol12/iss4/1/

Moore, R. J. (2015). Automated transcription and conversation analysis. *Research on Language and Social Interaction, 48*(3), 253–270. http://dx.doi.org/10.1080/08351813.2015.1058600

Platt, J. (2002). The history of the interview. In J. F. Gubrium, & J. A. Holstein (Eds.), *Handbook of interview research: Context and method*. SAGE.

Ravetz, J. R. (1971). *Scientific knowledge and its social problems*. Oxford University Press.

Saon, G., Kurata, G., Sercu, T., Audhkhasi, K., Thomas, S., Dimitriadis, D., Cui, X., Ramabhadran, B., Picheny, M., Lim, L., Roomi, B., & Hall, P. (2017). *English conversational telephone speech recognition by humans and machines.* https://arxiv.org/pdf/1703.02136.pdf

Vanover, C. (2022). Transcription as a form of qualitative inquiry. In C. Vanover, P. Mihas, & J. Saldaña (Eds.), *Analyzing and interpreting qualitative data: After the interview*. SAGE.

Strategies for Coding and Categorizing Data

Paul Mihas

Introduction

Many methodologists have addressed what it means to code textual data (Auerbach & Silverstein, 2003; Blair, 2015; Charmaz, 2014; Miles, Huberman, & Saldaña, 2020; Saldaña, 2016). Coding is a way of focusing our attention on what matters—incidents, emotions, perceptions, actions, reactions, events, phenomena, and subtext. As an attentive practice, coding is part of the researcher's ongoing attempt to identify or construct *meaning*—reading through what might seem chaotic and inconsistent yet finding repeating narrative signals and identifying patterns that give shape and *coherence* across stories, individuals, or settings. "Humans are pattern-seeking story-telling animals," Michael Shermer (2000) reminds us, "and we are quite adept at telling stories about patterns, whether they exist or not" (para. 1). We must be careful to be rigorous and systematic, to question our emerging insights and approach our interview data not with certitude, but with wonder. One of the strengths of coding is that it sustains this period of wonder, of checking and rechecking, naming and renaming, and "diving in and stepping back" (Maietta, Hamilton, Swartout, & Petruzzelli, 2019). Coding creates a conceptual foreground against the larger canvas of copious data.

Fiction writer Robert Olen Butler (2005) sees the single sentence as the unit of consciousness. In coding, we see into this consciousness—words, lines, sentences, and other units—which become an entry into the participant's experiential world. Dwelling in the data means that we are, for a time, inhabiting the participant's life world to the extent that we are able to do so.

Marine biologists have discovered that we can tell where a whale has travelled from the themes in its song. "The sharing of whale song is a kind of cultural transmission that can give clues about where a whale has travelled on its migration, and where it started out" (Whyte, 2019, para. 2). More specifically, "we can pinpoint a population a whale has likely come from by what they are singing" (Whyte, 2019, para. 2). Biologists code their data just as we code ours. Qualitative researchers, too, are interested in a kind of cultural transmission—what makes participants' stories seem similar or dissimilar. What do the stories suggest about where participants have been—physically and psychologically? Interviews activate language that gradually reveals a participant's life course and meaning making. Participants, too, are trying to make sense of what they are saying.

Whether our work is applied (e.g., addressing whether a particular health intervention is feasible) or social scientific (e.g., building theory regarding a phenomenon such as negotiation), coding compels us to look at data moment by moment—the unit of consciousness can be profoundly illuminating—and to carefully name what we see.

We should note that this section does not specifically address established qualitative research traditions such as grounded theory, narrative analysis, or ethnography. These traditions have their own approaches to coding that are outside the scope of this book (Charmaz, 2014; Creswell & Poth, 2018; Daiute, 2014; Riessman, 1993; Strauss & Corbin, 2008). This section instead presents approaches that are relevant to a range of descriptive and interpretive inquiry. However, the chapters herein can still be useful for researchers guided by established traditions.

More specifically, this section provides strategies for coding data and managing these codes. In Chapter 7, Daniel Turner walks us through managing a coding framework from the early stages of engaging the data. A coding system provides researchers with scaffolding for naming what they already know and building upon this knowledge to discern and identify critical topics that surface. Managing codes also means structuring these topics, perhaps hierarchically or thematically, *decisions* to which the researcher must be accountable. In Chapter 8, Andrea Bingham and Patricia Witkowsky present distinctions between deductive and inductive approaches to coding and how these can be integrated. Their chapter addresses the tensions between the strength of qualitative research—investing in its "emergent nature"—and applying previously existing theories and communities of knowledge. The practice of coding brings to the surface this tension—exactly when do we bring our literature review into our coding strategy? Janet Richards, in Chapter 9, clarifies how coding is part of a larger reflexive search for meaning. Coding is a matter of judgment and what we find depends, on some degree, on who we are. Richards reinforces that coding cannot be separated from the epistemological and ontological lens of the researcher. Engaging in practices of researcher reflexivity means that we will be more attentive to our lens. James Bernauer, in Chapter 10, offers oral coding as an alternative to traditional coding, inviting us to be inventive in our practices, to ask ourselves what we can do differently in service to knowledge production. Oral coding invites us to invest time listening and relistening to audio files, moving closer to the participant's aural voice, not simply to the transcribed words on the page. In Chapter 12, Elsa M. Gonzalez and Yvonna S. Lincoln remind us that coding becomes even more challenging when bridging cultures and languages, such as coding in English when the data are in a native language.

Each of these chapters is intended to help the reader make decisions about how and what to code; to consider how central coding will be to the larger analysis; and to monitor researcher positionality as we "listen" to data and track our unfolding ideas using an intentional practice of coding.

Reflection and Activities

1. For each chapter in this section, discuss how coding slows us down to look at data moment by moment. What are the particular benefits of dwelling in the data?

2. Code a paragraph of text in your (or a colleague's) transcripts with several codes. You might also use one of the interview excerpts in the transcription section. Which codes seem to best represent the participant's own voice and experience? What did you learn from performing this analysis?

3. What are the advantages and disadvantages of both written and oral coding?

References

Auerbach, C., & Silverstein, L. B. (2003). *Qualitative data: An introduction to coding and analysis.* New York University Press.

Bernauer, J. A. (2022). Oral coding: An alternative way to make sense of interview data. In C. Vanover, P. Mihas, & J. Saldaña (Eds.), *Analyzing and interpreting qualitative research: After the interview.* SAGE.

Bingham, A., & Witkowsky, P. (2022). Deductive and inductive approaches to qualitative data analysis. In C. Vanover, P. Mihas, & J. Saldaña (Eds.), *Analyzing and interpreting qualitative research: After the interview.* SAGE.

Blair, E. (2015). A reflexive exploration of two qualitative data coding techniques. *Journal of Methods and Measurement in the Social Sciences, 6*(1), 14–29. https://doi.org/10.2458/v6i1.18772

Butler, R. O. (2005). *From where you dream.* Grove Press.

Charmaz, K. (2014). *Constructing grounded theory* (2nd ed.). SAGE.

Creswell, J., & Poth, C. (2018). *Qualitative inquiry and research design: Choosing among five approaches* (3rd ed.). SAGE.

Daiute, C. (2014). *Narrative inquiry: A dynamic approach.* SAGE.

Gonzalez, E. M., & Lincoln, Y. S. (2022). Analyzing and coding interviews and focus groups considering cross-cultural and cross-language data. In C. Vanover, P. Mihas, & J. Saldaña (Eds.), *Analyzing and interpreting qualitative research: After the interview*. SAGE.

Maietta, R., Hamilton, A., Swartout, K., & Petruzzelli, J. (2019). *ResearchTalk's qualitative data analysis camp* (Short course conducted by ResearchTalk, Inc.). ResearchTalk.

Miles, M. B., Huberman, A. M., & Saldaña, J. (2020). *Qualitative data analysis: A methods sourcebook* (4th ed.). SAGE.

Richards, J. (2022). Coding, categorizing, and theming the data: A reflexive search for meaning. In C. Vanover, P. Mihas, & J. Saldaña (Eds.), *Analyzing and interpreting qualitative research: After the interview*. SAGE.

Riessman, C. K. (1993). *Narrative analysis*. Qualitative research methods Series, Vol. 30. SAGE.

Saldaña, J. (2016). *The coding manual for qualitative researchers* (3rd ed.). SAGE.

Shermer, M. (2000). Chicken soup for the evolutionist's soul. https://michaelshermer.com/articles/chicken-soup-for-the-evolutions-soul

Strauss, A., & Corbin, J. (2008). *Basics of qualitative research: Techniques and procedures for developing grounded theory*. SAGE.

Turner, D. (2022). Coding system design and management. In C. Vanover, P. Mihas, & J. Saldaña (Eds.), *Analyzing and interpreting qualitative research: After the interview*. SAGE.

Whyte, C. (2019, September 4). We can tell where a whale has travelled from the themes in its song. *New Scientist*. https://www.newscientist.com/article/2215121-we-can-tell-where-a-whale-has-travelled-from-the-themes-in-its-song/

Coding System Design and Management

Daniel Turner

Abstract

Analyzing qualitative data is a complex and time consuming process, but coding can help to structure interview data, making interpretation easier. However, the analysis process and coding framework can themselves become overwhelming without a system to keep track of the stages of analysis and many codes used. This chapter outlines several important considerations in the design of a system for analyzing and exploring qualitative data, with examples and practical advice for applying a system in a real-world context. Qualitative data analysis software is discussed as a useful, but not essential tool for managing qualitative coding. This chapter will also discuss the benefits and challenges of coordinating qualitative analysis with groups and teams of coders and setting rules and procedures to manage and explore differences in interpretation.

Keywords: Qualitative data management; system design; qualitative data analysis software

Coding qualitative data is a useful and important way to manage, sort, and bring structure to unstructured data (Miles et al., 2020, Chapter 4). Coding allows for more than just categorization; it also helps researchers find new and unexpected categories and different ways to read qualitative data.

Ironically, coding can itself become a large and unstructured system, and without appropriate structure and management, poor coding choices may hinder qualitative analysis. Many students attempting coding for the first time struggle with defining codes, having too many codes, or being unsure how to draw their coding together to find deeper meaning. Many new principal investigators struggle with managing the coding process between multiple members of a research team. Often there is a great desire to begin analysis as soon as data are available. Interviews can reveal and capture exciting and nuanced data and jumping into analysis immediately is tempting. However, coding is only a part of the analysis process, albeit one that serves to address the research questions and help write up results.

There is a need to step back and plan the coding and analysis process (see Chapter 1) to make sure that the whole process of creating and using codes is recorded. Valuable time must not be lost because of insufficient information on why early work was done.

Managing a coding framework is essentially an analytic process in itself, and coding works best when the coding process is well documented. Keeping records of what codes mean, why they were created, as well as annotations or analytic memos (see Chapter 15) that explain why data are being coded in a certain way are essential elements of well-managed qualitative analysis (Savin-Baden & Major, 2013, Chapter 27). Though qualitative interview research typically involves small sample sizes compared to quantitative data collection, the depth of data from each participant, as well as the dozens or hundreds of codes sometimes used, means that the analysis is always a cognitively intensive process.

Thus, qualitative researchers must develop a system for working not just with the data, but for tracking the development of the codes themselves to prevent the process from becoming messy. An untidy coding system may hide the rich insights the researcher set out to uncover. This chapter takes the reader through an example project, illustrating how a coding framework was created and managed, and shares a series of widely applicable techniques to manage parts of the analysis. We begin by discussing coding issues that will be applicable for individual researchers and then describe how to lead and manage the work of an analysis team.

Tools for Data Management and Their Use

Systems are required to manage codes and the extracted sections of text in a qualitative analysis project. A system can be as simple as using colored highlighter pens to identify sections of text that match a topic, or Post-It notes on printed interview transcripts. The system may also utilize the comments or colored text features in a word-processor, or columns that list text, code, and source in a spreadsheet.

There are specially designed software tools for analyzing qualitative data, including ATLAS.ti, MAXQDA, NVivo, and Quirkos, but these are not systems in themselves. These tools each enable many different ways to work with and structure data, so in effect, researchers still need to choose a coding management system and approach to use within the software. At the basic level, the major qualitative packages, sometimes called qualitative data analysis software (QDAS),[1] have the same basic features that allow users to code, annotate, retrieve, and explore qualitative data. From the point of view of a coding management system, there are few significant differences between tools, and such a great variety of ways that each software package can be utilized, that it is rarely the case that one software package is a better tool for coding than another. Much comes down to personal preference, or if there are specific desired ways of working with the data that have better support in one tool. The Five-Level QDA (qualitative data analysis) approach designed by Woolf and Silver (2018) stresses that the strategies and tactics for interpreting qualitative data should be independent from the software tool, not driven by what features a particular tool promotes. The University of Surrey CAQDAS Network has independent reviews of all the major packages (CAQDAS Network, 2019) and Chapter 2 of this book provides an overview of some their capabilities.

Whichever tool is chosen, the QDAS should let the research team record and find data and metadata for all the questions they will want to ask of the dataset once it has been coded. The software should also allow the team to quickly and easily work with codes and sections of data. Metadata is the "extra" information above and beyond the data themselves that describes the data and their purpose, and this information should also be easily entered and analyzed. This chapter will look at types of metadata later.

Exemplar

In the example I am using for this chapter, I describe the work that my company, Quirkos, engaged in for a complex project that was difficult to structure: trying to understand people's shift in allegiances to different political parties in Scotland. The setting was the aftermath of a 2014 divisive referendum on Scottish Independence from the United Kingdom that cut across traditional party lines. As with many qualitative research projects, the reasons driving peoples' behavior were complex and varied, so there were few preconceived plans for how the coding framework would look.

We conducted interviews with a small sample of 12 people who had voted in the referendum and were based in Edinburgh, aiming to have a representative sample of age, gender, and how people voted (Turner, 2015).

Complete verbatim transcripts were created from these one-on-one interview recordings and anonymized so they could be made publicly available for teaching with the consent of the participants. The text files of the transcripts were brought

---

[1]In the literature, it is also common to use the term computer-assisted qualitative data analysis or CAQDAS when referring to software that supports the qualitative data research process.

into a qualitative software package, Quirkos, which was used to structure and manage the coding process. The raw transcripts as well as coded project files can be downloaded from https://www.quirkos.com/workshops/referendum/.

The dataset is fairly typical for a small qualitative research project: 12 short semi-structured interviews transcribed as 58,000 words. This is nearly equivalent to a master's level thesis, and while the number of interviews is not large, the work required to code such documents should be planned and managed with care. Using a basic descriptive coding framework, 75 codes were created and a total of 3,100 highlights or coded text units. This coding provided only a starting point for thematic analysis; the descriptive codes provided the genesis for more nuanced research questions.

Descriptive and Interpretive Coding

The first step was basic descriptive coding (Saldaña, 2016). All source documents were coded to identify the most common elements across the interviews and to allow for initial comparisons across participants. A basic first approach like this also helps researchers familiarize themselves with the data. This part of the analysis was done using simultaneous coding (Saldaña, 2016), where one piece of text was coded to several single-concept codes. This is an approach that can be used with any coding technique (highlighters, Excel, cut and paste), but is most useful with digital methods that can help manage many different codes on a single piece of text. Breaking down text into basic common codes allows the researcher to later assess connections between them, showing how often certain topics occur together.

The example text below was coded with several simultaneous and overlapping codes, including: "Scottish identity," "Emotions," "Impact," and "Edinburgh":

> I had one friend who I didn't want to talk to the day after [the referendum] because I knew he would be really hung-over and miserable because he was such a staunch "Yes" campaigner. I think that's some kind of soothing of troubled waters. So, I go to church and there were, like prayers for making sure people could still get on with their friends and neighbours even though they voted differently, and some people said that wasn't necessary, and I think I would rather that was in place and it not be necessary than no one thinking about it at all. I actually saw three of my friends wearing kilts the Sunday after the referendum because they voted "No" but they were still proud to be Scottish and they wanted people to know that they were still proud to be Scottish even though they voted "No," so they were wearing their national dress and I thought that was kind of cool. I mean, Edinburgh feels like its 90% tourist most of the time and there are still people crowding round Holyrood. It just felt like life was normal. –June

Also, because the researchers adopted a simultaneous coding process where multiple codes were attached to most text segments, we took advantage of software tools that showed us where and how often codes overlap in the text. Figure 7.1 illustrates this analysis for the code "Negative," with codes closest to the center of the figure showing the largest number of co-occurrences. The close proximity in the visualization shows that participants were very "Negative" about "General Politics," and then overwhelmingly negative about the "Labour" party in this context.

Broadly speaking, there were two different types of codes that were developed. The first was basic coding of the people, parties, and topical areas mentioned. "Edinburgh" is an example of one of these codes. Coding these text segments made

FIGURE 7.1 ● An Analysis for the Code "Negative"

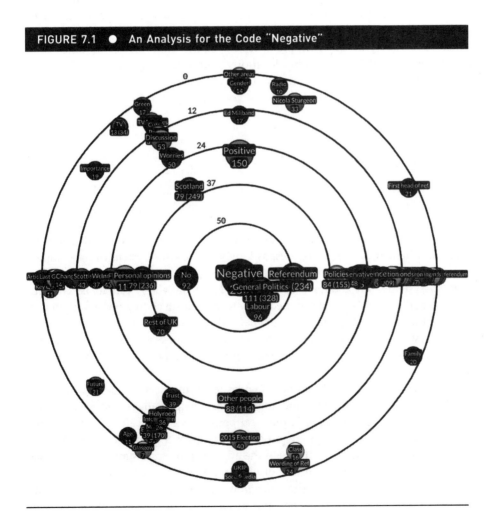

it easier to later identify everything participants said about a particular political figure or city. These simple descriptive codes were relatively nonsubjective and would allow a research team to structure the data without requiring elaborate code descriptions.

The second stage was a complete reanalysis of the data using interpretive coding, whereby deeper messages and topics that were important to the participants were identified. For example, many of these interpretive codes were independence-related policy lines, debates, or arguments about topics such as health care and the economy, along with more abstract concepts such as "Scottish pride" and "Scottish identity." Though it was easy enough to put text units in these codes, sometimes there were ambiguities. Text was sometimes coded to seemingly contradictory codes (for instance, some statements by participants were coded for both "Positive" and "Negative sentiments" about independence) or new codes were created for specific concepts that often ended up merged with other codes later. In the example text above, the code for "Edinburgh" was eventually merged with the other locations mentioned (e.g., Glasgow, London, EU) which had been coded separately. The team decided that these locations did not reveal a particular trend and hence could be merged into a broader code, "Location."

Hierarchy and Groups of Codes

In the research exemplar above, there are many examples of subcodes. For example, the code "Location" had the subcodes of "Edinburgh," "Glasgow," etc. In analysis, this allows the author to quickly compare opinions on one specific media type, as well as review all content about media in general. This dual level of depth is an important benefit to using subcodes, as long as the coding system can accommodate it. Most qualitative analysis software packages allow for these hierarchies. Manual systems and coding with Word or Excel, however, can make creating subcodes difficult. It is not always necessary to structure a coding framework in this way, and some researchers may prefer a flat coding system with no subcodes. A flat coding system can make it easier to see all the codes or discourage the researcher from prematurely starting to group codes into themes before they have finished coding.

However, once a certain number of codes (even just several dozen) have been reached, a hierarchy of codes and subcodes can help manage and group codes under a common theme. From a practical point of view, it can be easier to find codes if there is a subcode system, especially as top-level themes can be collapsed when not needed. But it can also help the analysis process to start grouping codes together, leading to the recognition of higher-level conceptual themes.

Codes were also created in the Referendum project to note where participants had discussed factors of age, gender, and social class. These codes could have been grouped together under a general code, "Demographics," where participants discussed these characteristics as factors in their opinions. However, if there was a clear trend showing their thoughts about particular groups being disadvantaged by the prospect of Scottish independence—for example, older people, women, and people of lower socioeconomic status—then this overarching code could have been called "Discrimination" or "Privilege." This coding could lead to a significant finding or interpretation that might otherwise remain hidden if references to particular demographic groupings were not reassessed and the codes applied to them carefully titled.

This also illustrates a risk of using hierarchies: a temptation to group codes together too early, cementing connections as implied hierarchies of concept that may not be represented in all the sources or that could have been structured differently. Researchers may be hesitant to start creating subcodes because they are not sure there are clear exclusive connections between a code and subcode. However, as long as researchers remain conscious of the way that hierarchies can shape and narrow thinking and interpretation, it is possible to group codes early. In all software packages, it is possible to ungroup and restructure codes without losing the data assigned to them. Reviewing and restructuring codes in this way is an important part of an iterative coding process.

There are situations where creating hierarchies or subcodes is unlikely to be problematic—in our project, the large number of political parties are grouped under a "Parties" code. This basic coding has little impact on interpretation but reflects an already existing real-world grouping. There are also situations where codes can be grouped but are not hierarchical. For example, the "Positive" and "Negative" codes are kept close to each other on the coding canvas in Quirkos, as they are opposite feelings, but could be grouped as "Sentiment."

Figure 7.2 shows the final list and structure of codes as shown in Quirkos. Some codes are major themes without subcodes; others are positioned close to each other if they have similar thematic meaning, and the size shows the number of extracts in each code.

Both the structure and the content of the codes themselves may be revealing. Figure 7.2 shows the dominant topics shown by the size of the code and the number of codes assigned to them but also how hierarchies have been created. These hierarchies give structure to the coding framework.

Voices of Participants and Others

For in-depth qualitative research, it could be argued that there are many different types of voices present in the data. First, participants may be considered to voice their opinions as representatives of the many different facets of their identity. These facets could be based on their age, gender, race, etc. Researchers may wish to look at a group of voices together that represents one such facet.

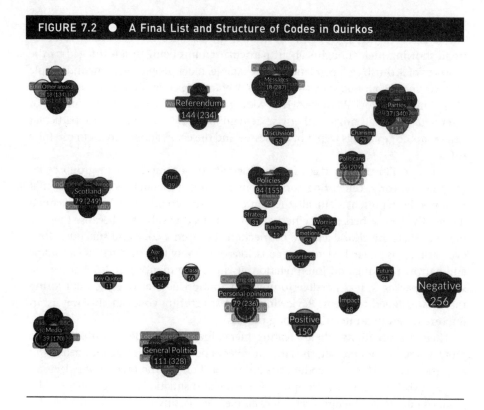

FIGURE 7.2 ● A Final List and Structure of Codes in Quirkos

Secondly, participants often discuss not only their own options but also their interpretation or representation of others (e.g., discussing how they believe a friend or partner might think about or express something). Finally, the interviewer's own voice is often present in interview transcripts and should not always be discounted. If an interviewer asks a leading question, participants echo the terminology of a question posed by the interviewer, or if the participant gives a one-word answer to a question, then the voice of the interviewer is an important part of the data. All these types of voices should be labeled and captured in the coding management system.

In the Referendum research project, much personal information was collected for each participant, but analysis focused on three particular characteristics: occupation, gender, and how participants voted in the referendum. In Quirkos, these formed the properties of each of the sources (also known as attributes). Ensuring that the coding management system can draw from these groups of voices is important for later stratifying the data.

In the example dataset for this chapter, the voice of the interviewer is denoted by "Q:" and the participant by "A:" (as in question and answer). Interviewer/ participant could also have been used. Because all sources have been marked up in the same way, it is always clear across sources when the interviewer or partici-pant is speaking. In focus groups where there are multiple voices, identifying contributions by each person within a source is especially important.

Another common management issue in qualitative data is keeping track of when people are talking about their own opinions, or when they are interpreting or describing other peoples' sentiments. The extract below illustrates this issue:

> I think there was a lot of people who had a fixed point of view right from the start and they, like myself, it was never changing. I think a lot of people for a lot of valid reasons, maybe a lot of invalid reasons, there was never going to be any movement. I think there is always fear around change. People's natural default isn't really-, like change is a bit scary and there was a lot of things thrown up that, you know, you could lose your job. –Simon

The section above could be coded in many different ways. There are parts when the participant is talking about their own opinion, the opinion of others, and also how the participant believes people behave in general. Our research team coded the different parts of the text as such. All these opinions provide valuable insights into the beliefs of the participant, but we do not always want to take a participants' perspective of other people at face value. Thus, by coding a section of text to make clear that an extract is showing a third-person perspective, we can make sure it is always identified in this way. In the example, this is done by assigning sections of text to a code for Personal opinions as well as a code for Other people.

To look at how a group of users responds, the system must be able to identify sources with particular characteristics and an ability to assign that data to a source. To manage the first, a database, table, or spreadsheet of participants is usually maintained, started before the recruitment process begins to keep track of partici-pants' real names and pseudonyms, contact details, demographics, consent, and planned dates for interviews. While often collected in a separate file or folder, these variables can easily be included in the properties or characteristics function in qualitative software (even before data have been collected). For the second process, the variables are associated to a source such as a particular interview. This system allows the researcher to quickly see sources and coded extracts from participants of a particular gender identity, role, or any other characteristic that has been collected. This coding is also easy to implement if data are being analyzed in spreadsheet data but more difficult to manage with paper-based methods.

Figure 7.3 provides an example of a side-by-side comparison of the coded responses from female and male participants that has been generated in Quirkos. This analysis allows us to see demographic differences in the data; for example, the figure shows how much more men discussed the Scottish National Party (SNP) compared to the women but also the difference in opinion: women were much more skeptical than men. Illustrating this is only possible because the different types of voices have been recorded in the management system.

FIGURE 7.3 ●   A Side-by-side Comparison of Coded Responses in Quirkos

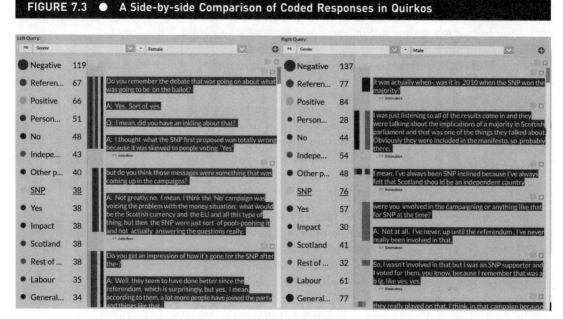

Meta-Codes

Any coding process can also be used for more than just coding of data segments. It can also be used to identify text specifically for the meta-process of writing up and managing the data process itself.

For example, while reading through the data, other useful things can be tagged. In the example project we have a code called Key quotes, used to identify the most illustrative text in the hundreds of quotations coded—those that are the most likely to be used in the report or that best illustrate a category or trend. Having meta-coded extracts in this way makes it easy to find, for instance, all the best quotes about TV debates when we come to write up that section.

Other examples of effective meta-codes include identifying quotes that are contradictory, ones that the researcher does not understand and wants to come back to, or even a ranking system for quotes. A star rating can be used to rank the best quotes should we need to resort to 4- or 3-star quality quotes to illustrate a particular point. A good coding management system can then be used to assist with the review and writing up of the data.

Leading and Managing a Multistage Coding Process

Data are not always coded in a linear process. A multistage or cyclical analytical process is often used for qualitative data as it is rare that all the codes and trends of the data will become clear with a single read-through of data. One of the challenges in managing coding frameworks is recording and identifying which codes were created at what stage of the analytic process—for example, if they were part of descriptive or thematic analysis, or open or axial coding (Saldaña, 2016). These records are important because researchers will often want to draw from different stages of the analysis during the writing-up process. For example, an introductory research section might want to draw quotes from descriptive coding to show how people talked about a simple topic like how they describe their home city. For later sections, researchers are likely to draw from more abstract codes like "Identity" or "Shifting allegiances." Using a software tool is advantageous here as the software logs the user and time each code and piece of coding were created. Metadata for codes can be used to identify which ones belong to different analytic approaches.

Capturing previous attempts is important since there is not always a linear progression. A new analytical approach may actually work worse than the previous iteration or fail to capture something that worked well before. So, when starting a new process, it is important to make sure that the old coding system is retained and with enough information to identify it if required in the future. Once again, this is simple when using any software package, as the old file can be saved with a descriptive name, such as "Descriptive Coding Attempt 2 Full Data – 11-11-2021 DT." This label makes it easy to identify what analysis was done, what dataset was used, when the system was last modified, and who did the coding.

Any new work should be created in a separate file with a descriptive name, making sure that the old work is not overwritten. It is often advantageous to create new files, capturing the process at certain time intervals, even when the researcher is not intending to embark on a new process. These backups mean that if the research team discovers their work over the last few days did not add value, there is always a preexisting foundation to work from rather than having to start from scratch.

Usually, descriptive filenames or subdirectories are enough. However, different versions could also be detailed in a research diary, giving more context such as the reason a particular approach was not working and the aims of a new method of interpretation. If using a paper-based method, iterations are more difficult to manage but new folders (with fresh transcript printouts) of different colored paper, or even a different text color, can help distinguish different physical versions, especially if they get accidentally mixed up by well-meaning cats or toddlers.

However, it's also possible to use features within the software to manage different versions of the nonlinear process. For example, codes can have longer descriptions as they evolve, clarifying their definition but also their history.

Memoing can also be used to document changes in the process, all without creating new files at major milestones.

Leading and Managing an Analysis Team

In the Referendum research project, there were multiple people who created codes, applied codes, and interpreted text. In addition to the primary researcher, several participants who had been interviewed for the project were also invited to analyze their own and others' data. Though involving participants in analysis is somewhat unusual (cf. Chapter 13), many projects have more than one coder to either share the burden of work or to check the validity of coding. In these cases, managing the team and bringing their contributions together is a major administrative hurdle.

In the example, separate project files were created for each coder to work on, and later merged to compare their interpretations. In Quirkos, multiple files can be merged simultaneously, or collaborators can work on one project stored on Quirkos Cloud and see their changes in real time on their own computer. The latter greatly eases the management of the data because the lead researcher does not have to be responsible for tracking different file versions and merging them at certain times during the process. In any case, it is again important to create and maintain an analytical system that will log work by different users. Software tools can make enacting this process easier, but a manual system can also be effective.

Regardless, it is very important to have a written set of guidelines for anyone contributing to the analysis. These guidelines might describe what the process will be, what the expectations are, and how inevitable discussions about the work will be facilitated, leading to decision-making. For example, the team will either want to agree upon a code list before coding begins, or have a process for deciding which codes created during the process will be kept or merged. They will also want to have detailed definitions for every code used. In the example project, the lead researcher created a long description of each code name. For example, "Scottish identity" was given a brief description such as: "When people describe feeling, or being, 'Scottish'" so that other coders would understand when to apply the code. Annotations to the text (using the memo system in Quirkos) could also be used to explain the rationale behind categorizing difficult interpretations of the data.

In the Referendum project, there was no attempt to use statistical tools to calculate interrater reliability such as Cohen's Kappa or Krippendorff's Alpha. Since these methods are quantitative, they do not give a detailed picture into what is being agreed or disagreed upon between interpretations. In qualitative research it is important to understand the differences between participants, but it is also important to understand why each difference in coding application and interpretation of a text segment is present. An average figure of, say, 95% agreement might sound impressive but belie the fact that, on one important code, coders disagreed every time. Even with a statistical measure, manual checks of coding agreement are needed.

On a practical level, a management plan should also clearly show who is expected to code which sources, the deadlines for completing the work, and when everyone should be available for a team review. Team leaders should also have space to hear from coders about their overall insights into the data, and make sure that their opinions and contributions are considered in the research outputs.

Once coding has been completed across all sources, and possibly for multiple iterations of the coding, researchers are able to read not just by interview source but by code across all the sources and voices in the project. In our project, the data and the coding showed commonalities and differences in opinions on a particular topic and allowed us to integrate content across transcripts and develop a consistent narrative.

Conclusion

There is not a single, superior way to manage and design a coding system, but the examples above illustrate the variety of options available. As in most parts of qualitative research, flexibility is key: letting the research questions, data, and the researcher suggest the best way to structure the data and the coding system. However, the basic discipline of creating detailed labels, notes on the process, tagging voices of participants and researchers, producing guidance for team members and techniques such as meta-coding are likely to greatly increase the efficiency and rigor of the writing-up process. These may all seem like extra work at the time, especially when confronted with exciting interview data, but managing the process of analysis is as important as writing up the interpretation.

As with analysis itself, practice and familiarization with qualitative datasets can help researchers understand the challenges and steps necessary to manage these data. The examples used in this chapter (as well as those from other chapters) can all be downloaded and used for practice. However, researchers can also experiment with public archives of qualitative data, borrowing data from colleagues or supervisors, or analyzing their own data as they are collected (Silverman, 2013).

The one overarching piece of guidance from this chapter is to consider not just the coding but what other information the research team needs to turn the data into a meaningful narrative. This care and precision are also about rigor and trusting the process. By identifying how data were coded and creating records about how the code framework was structured, we become more confident in our interpretations. At other times, this work is about knowing who said what, and understanding why different participants have differing views. Getting lost in the data or process can cost a lot of time for a single researcher, but this loss multiplies with large research teams, possibly causing the project to miss key deadlines and go over budget.

All these processes and steps are designed to help researchers discover what matters in their data, turning snatches of insight into stories (see Chapter 23) that let us write and communicate with others (see Chapter 24). While there are many coding processes that can help us get to these later stages, in the next chapter Bingham and Witkowsky will look at the two different major ways of structuring coding, *a priori* and *inductive approaches*.

Supplemental Readings

Miles, M. B., Huberman, A. M., & Saldaña, J. (2020). *Qualitative data analysis: A methods sourcebook* (4th ed.). SAGE.

Saldaña, J. (2016). *The coding manual for qualitative researchers* (3rd ed.). SAGE.

Reflection and Activities

1. Make a list of what you might want to know about your data and the coding process. This could be information about the participants, who and when and why codes were created, the quality or relevance of quotations, and all the other metadata listed in the chapter. Then think of how you could record and work with these metadata.

2. Take the coding framework from the example coding project for this chapter and try to restructure the codes. The raw transcripts as well as coded project files can be downloaded from https://www.quirkos.com/workshops/referendum/

a. Create a set of descriptive and interpretive codes.

b. Code first without any hierarchy, then regroup codes in a way that makes sense to you. Do you need to relabel any of the codes to make this work? How does this change your understanding of each code?

c. Are there any meta-codes that might support your analysis?

d. Create a written set of guidelines for a coding management plan for this project. What might you do as an individual or as a team to create a successful analysis?

References

CAQDAS Network. (2019). *Choosing an appropriate CAQDAS package.* https://www.surrey.ac.uk/computer-assisted-qualitative-data-analysis/resources/choosing-appropriate-caqdas-package

Miles, M. B., Huberman, A. M., & Saldaña, J. (2020). *Qualitative data analysis: A methods sourcebook* (4th ed.). SAGE.

Saldaña, J. (2016). *The coding manual for qualitative researchers* (3rd ed.). SAGE.

Savin-Baden, M., & Major, C. H. (2013). *Qualitative research: The essential guide to theory and practice.* Routledge.

Silverman, D. (2013). *Doing qualitative research*. SAGE.

Turner, D. (2015). *Overview of a qualitative study on the impact of the 2014 referendum for Scottish independence in Edinburgh, and views of the political process*. Quirkos. https://www.quirkos.com/workshops/referendum

Woolf, N., & Silver, C. (2018). *Qualitative analysis using ATLAS.ti*. Routledge.

Deductive and Inductive Approaches to Qualitative Data Analysis

Andrea J. Bingham and Patricia Witkowsky

Abstract

This chapter outlines and provides examples for how deductive and inductive analysis practices strengthen qualitative analysis. We discuss how deductive practices can be used to: (1) sort data into organizational categories, such as data type, participant, or time period; (2) organize data into categories to maintain alignment with research questions; and (3) apply theoretical or conceptual frameworks. We outline how inductive practices can be used to: (1) make meaning from the data; (2) develop codes, themes, and findings; (3) identify representative data to support findings; and (4) explain findings using theory and literature. We argue that using deductive and inductive analytic practices iteratively provide the deductive tools to organize the data and bound the inquiry, the inductive tools to allow findings to emerge from the data, and the understanding to apply existing knowledge and theory to interpret and explain findings.

Keywords: Data analysis; coding; inductive strategies; deductive strategies

Introduction

Qualitative analysis can generally be divided into two categories: deductive and inductive approaches. Deductive, or *a priori*, practices are part of an analytic strategy in which the researcher applies predetermined codes to the data (Saldaña & Omasta, 2018). Inductive analysis practices are part of a strategy in which the researcher reads through the data and allows codes to emerge (Miles, Huberman, & Saldaña, 2020).

Many qualitative researchers encounter difficulties in choosing the appropriate type of analysis that allows for balance among data organization, focus on the study purpose, theoretical and conceptual concerns, and the emergent nature of qualitative analysis. As Miles and Huberman (1994) note,

> The challenge is to be explicitly mindful of the purposes of your study and of the conceptual lenses you are training on it—while allowing yourself to be open and reeducated by things you didn't know about or expect to find. (p. 56)

Qualitative researchers must embrace the strength of qualitative research—its emergent nature and capacity to generate theory. Simultaneously, they must focus on organizational practices, including organizing by data type, keeping track of transcriptions, and categorizing representative data excerpts while focusing on their research questions, coding schemes, and emergent theories and concepts.

In this chapter, we outline how deductive and inductive practices can be used to strengthen qualitative analysis. We discuss how deductive practices can be used to:

1. Sort data into organizational categories, such as data type, participant, or time period.

2. Organize data into categories to maintain alignment with research questions.

3. Apply theoretical or conceptual frameworks.

We outline how inductive practices can be used to:

1. Make meaning from the data.

2. Develop codes, themes, and findings.

3. Identify representative data to support findings.

4. Explain findings using theory and literature.

We argue that using deductive and inductive analytic practices iteratively provides the deductive tools to organize the data and bound the inquiry, the inductive tools to allow themes and findings to emerge from the data or to construct themes based on emerging topics, and the understanding to apply existing knowledge and theory to interpret and explain findings. A data analysis process that draws on both deductive and inductive practices supports a more organized, rigorous, and analytically sound qualitative study.

Deductive and Inductive Analysis

Deductive analysis is a process of working "from the 'top down', from a theory to hypotheses to data to add to or contradict the theory" (Creswell & Plano Clark, 2007, p. 23). Applications of deductive analysis vary, but can include data organization, applying theory, and setting the stage for inductive analysis. Coding is a key part of deductive analysis. In the practice of deductive coding, codes are developed prior to analysis, and the researcher reads through the data to determine whether and how the data fit within those codes.

Deductive practices help to organize the data, identify relevant data, and maintain focus on the research questions. Miles, Huberman, and Saldaña (2020), for example, recommend "attribute coding" as a means of organizing the data by type and source (e.g., interview, observation). Deductive strategies can also be used to apply theory and set the stage for developing interpretations and explanations for the findings. Crabtree and Miller (1999) recommend a template approach to deductive analysis, where codes from a codebook are applied as a first round of coding to organize the data for subsequent inductive analysis, wherein inductive codes emerge as subcodes of the deductive codes. For example, Bingham, Pane, Steiner, and Hamilton (2018) used an iterative coding process, in which deductive macro-coding was first used to sort data into broad categories, after which inductive analysis—termed inductive micro-coding—was conducted within each category to identify common experiences and themes. Similarly, in their study of self-assessment practices in nursing, Fereday and Muir-Cochrane (2006) created a template *a priori*, based on their research questions and their theoretical framework, and then assigned inductive codes to segments of deductively coded data. Deductive approaches are appropriate when structures, conceptual frameworks, and theories are present to guide the analysis (e.g., Milkie & Warner, 2011; Ravitch & Riggan, 2017).

Inductive analysis is the process of reading through the data and allowing codes, categories, patterns, and themes to emerge (Miles, Huberman, & Saldaña, 2020). Some qualitative scholars argue that rather than "emerging from the data," codes and themes are identified in the data (e.g., Sandelowski, Barroso, & Voils, 2007). However, we use the idea of "emergent" codes and themes to characterize inductive analysis. The steps of inductive analysis include applying codes to describe the data and seeking patterns to develop categories, themes, or theories that demonstrate commonalities and variance across the data.

As with deductive practices, inductive analysis relies on coding; however, codes are developed as the researcher makes sense of the data. The inductive approach is especially useful in research of emerging topics (Hsieh & Shannon, 2005). Qualitative analysis practices foundational to inductive analysis include open coding, the constant comparative method, and in vivo coding. Open coding is the practice of attaching codes to the data to label the concepts and phenomena (Glaser & Strauss, 1967). The constant comparative method involves examining the data, assigning codes, comparing data points, and coding until all data fit into a higher-level category (Glaser, 1965). In vivo coding involves using words from the data as codes (Saldaña, 2016).

Deductive and inductive analysis practices can be utilized to answer the same research questions. Employed together, these approaches provide a more complete perspective of the phenomenon being investigated (Blackstone, 2014; Hyde, 2000). In this chapter, we engage both deductive and inductive analysis strategies. Our data analysis process involves sorting the data into deductive categories aligned to the research questions, open coding for emerging concepts and ideas, identifying patterns across those codes, condensing those pattern codes into themes, and explicating the findings represented by those themes. In a final cycle of analysis, theory is applied to explain the findings.

Study Description

From 2012 to 2015, I (the first author of this chapter) conducted a qualitative case study of a personalized learning school (see Bingham, 2016; Bingham, 2017; Bingham, 2019; Bingham & Ogunbowo Dimandja, 2017). The research questions were as follows:

1. How does a high-tech personalized learning charter school develop as an organization from its inception through its first several years of operation?

2. Why does it evolve as it does?

3. What are the implications of this school's development and evolution for other schools implementing a personalized learning school model?

This study, as with most qualitative studies, produced *a lot* of data in three years. I used a single case study approach with embedded cases, meaning I engaged in within-case analysis for the school as a whole, and cross-case analysis for the embedded cases—teachers. The data collection yielded 37 interviews, four focus groups, 76 observations, and hundreds of documents. To engage in an iterative process of data collection and analysis, and to keep a record of analytic decisions and processes, I used NVivo qualitative data analysis software to organize my data, code, and write memos.

My theoretical framework, Activity Theory, played a key role in the analysis process. Activity Theory is a complex theory of individual and organizational learning that involves many mediating and interacting components (Engeström, 1999). In order to apply such a complicated theoretical framework, I developed a plan for analysis that allowed findings to emerge and guided the application of the theory to explain and situate those findings.

Saldaña (2016) divides coding into two primary stages: first-cycle coding and second-cycle coding. First-cycle codes are those initially applied to the data, and second-cycle codes can be applied to the data within the generated first cycle codes.

In other words, the researcher can inductively analyze the coded text of the first cycle, adding a second layer of coding to the initial first-cycle codes. I took a similar approach to coding, dividing my coding process into deductive and inductive approaches, and operating in cycles within each of those approaches for a total of five analysis cycles. These cycles included first using deductive practices to organize the data and bound the inquiry; then using inductive practices to allow codes, patterns, and then themes to emerge, and to develop findings from those themes; and finally using deductive and inductive processes together to examine the findings using deductive codes developed from the theoretical framework, in order to apply the theoretical framework and explain the findings.

Taken together, deductive and inductive approaches support sorting and categorizing data, identifying findings and representative data, and interpreting and explaining those findings in order to make recommendations. Using a theoretical framework in the final cycle of coding facilitated moving between deductive analysis and more granular inductive strategies through the lens of *a priori* codes developed from the theoretical framework. This last deductive coding cycle helped me think with theory.

Applying Inductive and Deductive Analytic Strategies

Here, I use excerpts from the study data to illustrate my analysis process and discuss the decision-making process. I also provide reflections, detailing key decision points and analytical strategies. Engaging in both inductive and deductive processes of analysis allowed me to manage large amounts of data, maintain focus on my research questions, develop findings, and apply theory. For each cycle, I have included tables of example data, codes aligned to that data, and reflections about the connections and conclusions that were facilitated by the coding cycle. I have included two figures demonstrating the analysis process visually. See Figure 8.1 for an overview of the analysis process and Figure 8.2 for an example of how the coding cycles were applied toward developing and explaining findings.

Deductive Coding Processes (Cycles 1 and 2)

Deductive or *a priori* coding involves a process of creating codes prior to data analysis and applying those codes to the data as one reads. What should a researcher base these codes on? Existing theory? Hypotheses? Topics of interest? The answer is all these and more.

With a large amount of data, it is critical to have strong organizational practices in place. Thus, my first step was to organize the data using categories such as data type, participant, and time period, which made it easier to keep track of the data and identify the sources of my evidence. In the first cycle of coding, I reviewed the interview data and then the observational data and used attribute coding (Miles, Huberman, & Saldaña, 2020) to sort the data into purely organizational categories (e.g., "Interview, Ms. L, 2013"), in order to develop an organizational schema in NVivo.

FIGURE 8.1: ● Overview of Analysis Process

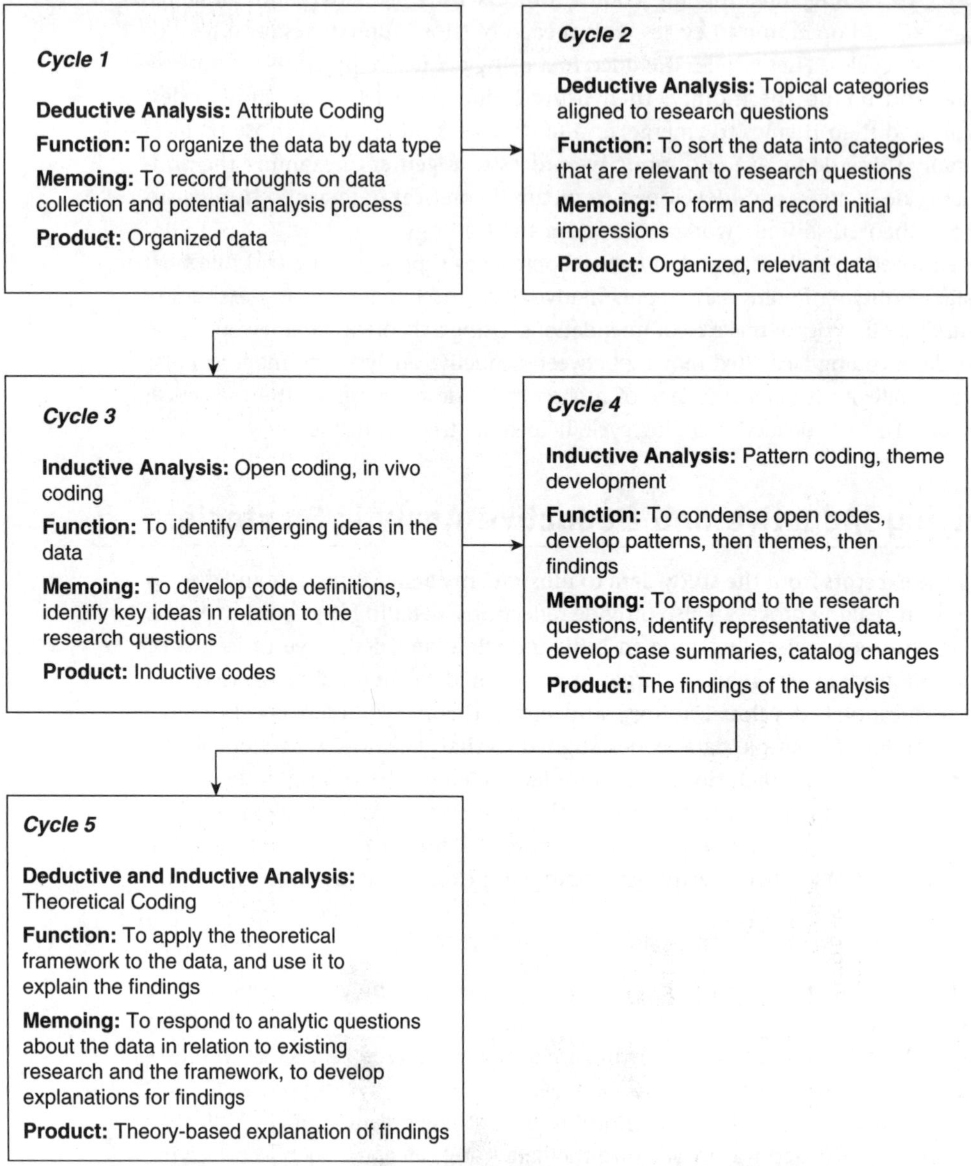

Cycle 1

Deductive Analysis: Attribute Coding

Function: To organize the data by data type

Memoing: To record thoughts on data collection and potential analysis process

Product: Organized data

Cycle 2

Deductive Analysis: Topical categories aligned to research questions

Function: To sort the data into categories that are relevant to research questions

Memoing: To form and record initial impressions

Product: Organized, relevant data

Cycle 3

Inductive Analysis: Open coding, in vivo coding

Function: To identify emerging ideas in the data

Memoing: To develop code definitions, identify key ideas in relation to the research questions

Product: Inductive codes

Cycle 4

Inductive Analysis: Pattern coding, theme development

Function: To condense open codes, develop patterns, then themes, then findings

Memoing: To respond to the research questions, identify representative data, develop case summaries, catalog changes

Product: The findings of the analysis

Cycle 5

Deductive and Inductive Analysis: Theoretical Coding

Function: To apply the theoretical framework to the data, and use it to explain the findings

Memoing: To respond to analytic questions about the data in relation to existing research and the framework, to develop explanations for findings

Product: Theory-based explanation of findings

FIGURE 8.2: ● Coding and Analysis Process, Cycles 1-5

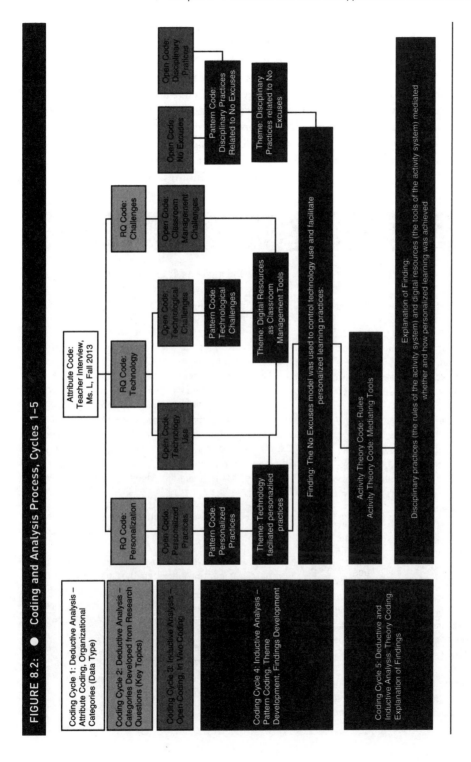

Coding Cycle 1: Deductive Analysis – Attribute Coding, Organizational Categories (Data Type)

Coding Cycle 2: Deductive Analysis – Categories Developed from Research Questions (Key Topics)

Coding Cycle 3: Inductive Analysis – Open Coding, In Vivo Coding

Coding Cycle 4: Inductive Analysis – Pattern Coding, Theme Development, Findings Development

Coding Cycle 5: Deductive and Inductive Analysis: Theory Coding, Explanation of Findings

Attribute Code: Teacher Interview, Ms. L, Fall 2013

RQ Code: Personalization
RQ Code: Technology
RQ Code: Challenges

Open Code: Personalized Practices
Open Code: Technology Use
Open Code: Technological Challenges
Open Code: Classroom Management Challenges
Open Code: No Excuses
Open Code: Disciplinary Practices

Pattern Code: Personalized Practices
Pattern Code: Technological Challenges
Pattern Code: Disciplinary Practices Related to No Excuses

Theme: Technology facilitated personalized practices
Theme: Digital Resources as Classroom Management Tools
Theme: Disciplinary Practices related to No Excuses

Finding: The No Excuses model was used to control technology use and facilitate personalized learning practices:

Activity Theory Code: Rules
Activity Theory Code: Mediating Tools

Explanation of Finding:
Disciplinary practices (the rules of the activity system) and digital resources (the tools of the activity system) mediated whether and how personalized learning was achieved

In the second cycle of coding, I read through the data more carefully and sorted the data into *a priori* codes aligned to broad topical categories of interest based on my research questions (such as "personalization," "technology," "change," etc.). I created these codes to maintain focus on my research questions, and to identify pertinent data and facilitate the next stage of inductive analysis.

Below are two excerpts from the study's data: an excerpt of a field note from a classroom observation and an excerpt from an interview. For each excerpt, I have provided the associated *a priori* organizational codes and research question codes (RQ code) in italicized brackets next to the relevant data. I then offer reflections on how this cycle of coding facilitated my analysis, findings, and written report.

Data Excerpt: Field Notes from Classroom Observation

[Organizational Attribute Code: Classroom observation, Ms. L, Fall 2014]

At the beginning of class, Ms. L plays "Rosie the Riveter" and other World War II songs while students work on their Do Now. There are more than 8 different Do Now activities with students' names listed next to each. *[RQ code: Personalization] [RQ code: Change]*

During the Do Now, Ms. L announces, "If your Do Now is not in yet, then you earn 1 demerit for taking too long on that. I updated the name board...if your name is there you owe me 2 hours of tutoring. You need to figure when you're going to pay me your hours." *[RQ code: Classroom-level change] [RQ code: Change]*

Students begin to work on their objectives. Some students are sitting alone, while some are in groups. There are students working silently on their computers, and some are working on worksheets. Some students are doing both. A few have their headphones on and some are talking in groups quietly. *[RQ code: Personalization]* The room is fairly quiet and students seem to get to work pretty quickly. Ms. L moves a few students to other tables to have a small group lesson. *[RQ code: Personalization]*

Ms. L has checked the scoreboard (digital report of student progress) and is keeping real-time tabs on their progress. *[RQ code: Technology]*

She tells the students at the table, "We're all here because we're all struggling a little bit." She gives them a new handout and walks them through an activity. This is a group of 6 students. She helps students to define some of the words and reads some of the questions and passages aloud. *[RQ code: Personalization]*

Ms. L carries around her computer with the scoreboard, and checks in with other students. *[RQ code: Technology]* She navigates through some of the questions with students as they struggle. To the small group she was working with, she says "I'm going to step away for a minute and I want you guys to answer numbers 5–7. At the end of class, you can turn those in. Explain what you're thinking."

Data Excerpt: Participant Interview

[Organizational Attribute Code: Administrator interview, Mr. O, Fall 2014]

"I think what we'll see over the next few years is that we'll continue to shed the structures that don't allow for complete personalized learning. What that means is, time structures and core structures. *[RQ code: Change]* Those are the two systems that don't allow for it because they force people to move out of a certain phase...Next year we're going to take away a lot of the periods and have more open, flexible working times. *[RQ code: Change] [RQ code: Personalization]* Then you'll see a lot of our design be more student-focused."

These cycles of coding offered a few benefits. First, I used this round of coding as an opportunity to organize myself, (re)familiarize myself with the data, and begin to form some overall impressions. Though applying attribute codes can sometimes be tedious, that process helped me track where my eventual evidence came from.

Using NVivo was especially useful during these cycles as it ultimately allowed me to examine the data that were cross-coded (e.g., data coded as both "Personalization" and "Technology"), when I was interested in conceptual intersections. Similarly, I was able to examine data that were cross-coded as "Change" and "Personalization," which, in later rounds of analysis, helped me to see how practices evolved.

It may be tempting to integrate an inductive analysis process into this cycle, but doing too many things at once can cause researchers to miss something. If ideas about potential themes begin to develop, or overall patterns are noticed, creating a memo to record these thoughts is useful. Then, in the third round of coding—inductive coding—the researcher can determine whether those ideas emerge during coding.

Inductive Coding Processes (Cycles 3 and 4)

Inductive analysis is the kind of analysis that appears in most qualitative studies—and it should! Inductive analysis can be used for meaning-making, developing findings, and evidence generation (pulling out representative quotes in support of findings). Inductive analysis is messier than deductive analysis because inductive practices go beyond sorting and require the researcher to pull out what is happening in the data and allow the data to speak to them.

In the third and fourth cycles of coding, I followed an inductive process. Having sorted the data into categories aligned to my research questions in the previous round of coding, I maintained focus on those research questions by inductively analyzing the data by category. I began the third cycle with a process of open coding, in which I reviewed the data within the categories applied in the first and second cycles of coding. In this third coding cycle, I read through the data in each category, creating and applying codes and identifying emerging topics or concepts as I read. For example, the in vivo codes "time structures" and "student-focused" emerged in this process, as did the codes "disciplinary practices," "technological challenges," "classroom management issues," and "No Excuses."

In the fourth cycle, I reviewed the coded data, looking for patterns across and within data sources. I used pattern coding, a process of condensing the codes created during open coding to chunk the data into fewer analytic concepts (Miles, Huberman, & Saldaña, 2020; Saldaña, 2016). The codes "disciplinary practices" and "No Excuses," for example, were condensed into the pattern code "disciplinary practices related to No Excuses." This process of condensing the codes developed during open coding into patterns helped me to summarize what I saw in the data. I memoed throughout this process to identify themes from the pattern codes. The themes emerged from condensing the patterns I had identified in the data into a series of key concepts. For example, the open code "personalized practices" also became a pattern code, as it was a both a pattern seen throughout the data and the conceptual glue that helped tie together incidents across data. When I looked at data coded as both "personalized practices" and "technology use," I was able to see the theme "technology facilitated personalized practices." I then developed findings from the themes by condensing and rewording the themes into short phrases that clearly answered the research questions. The themes "technology facilitated personalized practices," "disciplinary practices related to No Excuses," and "digital resources as classroom management tools," became the finding "The No Excuses model was used to control technology use and facilitate personalized learning practices." This analysis cycle allowed me to distill the codes and patterns into themes and then findings. Throughout this process, I memoed in response to my research questions, identifying representative quotes and excerpts from field notes to support my findings.

The table below includes the excerpts from field notes and interviews illustrated earlier as well as inductive codes that emerged from the data, which appear in brackets.

Because I had already sorted data into the relevant categories developed from the *a priori* codes aligned to my research questions, I used the inductive coding cycles to generate findings and identify representative data to support those findings. For example, one of my findings was that the school reprioritized personalization in its third year. I was able to develop that finding from reviewing data that were coded inductively as "time structures," "design changes," and "reprioritizing personalized learning."

The third and fourth cycles of coding were more involved than the first two cycles because they required me to engage in within-case analysis (the school), cross-case analysis (the teachers), and cross-time analysis (each year). I identified what was happening in each classroom, and memoed to summarize each classroom as a case. I then had to figure out what was happening across the cases, memo to summarize commonalities and identify pertinent evidence, and finally memo to summarize how the school had changed over time. I created a memo that served as a running log of different types of evidence relevant to my research questions that included participant quotes and field note excerpts. Though coding formed the crux of this cycle of analysis, the memos helped me organize the patterns, themes, and findings from the inductive analysis into a written report.

In summary, the third and fourth cycles allowed me to do the following. First, I read through each broad category of data (those codes that were developed in alignment with the research questions) and engaged in open coding. Then I condensed open codes into patterns, identified themes across patterns, and developed findings from those themes. For example, I read through all of the data cross-coded as "personalization" and "change," and let the data "speak for itself" to identify patterns in how the school evolved. I then condensed those patterns into themes. "Reprioritizing personalized learning," was a theme that emerged from this

Data Excerpt: Field Notes from Classroom Observation

At the beginning of class, Ms. L plays "Rosie the Riveter" and other World War II songs while students work on their Do Now. There are more than 8 different Do Now activities with students' names listed next to each *[Open code: Instructional changes]*.

During the Do Now, Ms. L announces, "If your Do Now is not in yet, then you earn 1 demerit for taking too long on that. I updated the name board...if your name is there you owe me 2 hours of tutoring. You need to figure when you're going to pay me your hours." *[Pattern Code: Disciplinary practices related to "No Excuses" schooling]*

Students begin to work on their objectives. Some students are sitting alone, while some are in groups *[Open code: Personalized practices]*. There are students working silently on their computers *[Open code: Technology use]*, and some are working on worksheets. Some students are doing both. A few have their headphones in and some are talking in groups quietly. The room is fairly quiet and students seem to get to work pretty quickly. Ms. L moves a few students to other tables to have a small group lesson.

Ms. L has checked the scoreboard (digital report of student progress) and is keeping real-time tabs on their progress. *[Open code: Technology use] [Open/pattern code: Personalized practices] [Theme: Technology facilitated personalized practice] [Theme: Digital resources as classroom management tools]* She tells the students at the table, "We're all here because we're all struggling a little bit." *[Open/pattern code: Personalized practices]* She gives them a new handout and walks them through an activity. This is a group of 6 students. She helps students to define some of the words and reads some of the questions and passages aloud.

Ms. L carries around her computer with the scoreboard, and checks in with other students. *[Open code: Technology use] [Open/pattern code: Personalized practices] [Theme: Digital resources as classroom management tools] [Open code: No excuses]* She navigates through some of the questions with students as they struggle. To the small group she was working with, she says "I'm going to step away for a minute and I want you guys to answer numbers 5–7. At the end of class, you can turn those in. Explain what you're thinking."

Data Excerpt: Participant Interview

"I think what we'll see over the next few years is that we'll continue to shed the structures that don't allow for complete personalized learning. *[Open code/Pattern code/Theme: Reprioritizing personalized learning][Open code/Pattern code: School-level change]* What that means is, time structures *[In Vivo code: "Time structures"]* and core structures. Those are the two systems that don't allow for it because they force people to move out of a certain phase *[Open code: No Excuses] [Open/pattern code: Technological challenges]*...Next year we're going to take away a lot of the periods and have more open, flexible working times. *[Open code: Design change] [Open code/pattern code: School-level change] [Open code/pattern code: Personalized practices]* Then you'll see a lot of our design be more student-focused *[In Vivo code: "Student-focused"]*."

process. To develop findings, I then turned themes into sentences or phrases that directly responded to my research questions. "Reprioritizing personalized learning" became "The school reprioritized personalized learning in its third year." This is how I identified findings organized by research question; I took significant themes and formed them into statements of key, pervasive points in the data.

Integrating Deductive and Inductive Approaches (Cycle 5)

Finally, I engaged in one last cycle of coding, where I combined deductive and inductive processes. In this coding cycle, I reanalyzed the data, as they were sorted from my round of inductive analysis. I applied codes aligned to concepts from my theoretical framework and codes aligned to the existing literature to the inductively coded data, sorted by finding. I reanalyzed all the data that aligned with the emergent findings, using codes developed from the theoretical framework and literature. However, this round of coding was not purely deductive. While I read, I also developed short phrases that connected my inductive findings with theory and existing literature. For example, the code/phrase "Disciplinary practices mediated whether and how personalized learning was achieved" emerged as a theory-based explanation for my finding: "The No Excuses model was used to control technology use and facilitate personalized learning practices." This code was created by sorting the inductively developed findings into theory-aligned *a priori* codes/categories ("Activity theory: Rules" and "Activity Theory: Mediating tools/artifacts"), and then making sense of the findings through the lens of the theory.

Sorting the data into theory-aligned categories was helpful in identifying relevant pieces of data for analysis. However, situating findings in the literature and using the theoretical framework analytically required additional work. To facilitate this, I engaged in analytic questioning—a process that involved memoing in response to deeper questions about the data in relation to existing research and the framework. Questions I asked myself in these memos included: What do the teacher interviews tell me about how the school evolved? What do these findings mean in context? How are they related to the larger existing literature base? What can we learn from these findings? This final cycle of analysis pushed my thinking around what my findings meant in the larger sense.

In the data excerpts presented below, I included the associated theoretical codes developed *a priori* from the theoretical framework, as a well as a reflection that outlines how I made connections between the theory and the findings to support the discussion and implications of the study. Figure 8.2 provides an example of how I funneled from codes to patterns to themes to findings, and how I applied theory to explain those findings.

This cycle was the most difficult part of the analysis process. It involved applying theoretical concepts and interpreting how my findings exemplified and diverged from those concepts. However, this part of the analysis facilitated explaining *why* events were happening as they did. I was able to answer my second research question and to expand upon my findings to discuss implications of the school's development and evolution for other schools implementing a personalized learning school model (my third research question). Though a researcher could certainly justify using theory-based deductive coding earlier in the process, I found that I was better able to engage in the inductive process of analysis without first imposing theoretical concepts on the data.

Data Excerpt: Field Notes from Classroom Observation

At the beginning of class, Ms. L plays "Rosie the Riveter" and other World War II songs while students work on their Do Now. There are more than 8 different Do Now activities with students' names listed next to each. *[Activity theory: Division of labor]*

During the Do Now, Ms. L announces, "If your Do Now is not in yet, then you earn 1 demerit for taking too long on that. I updated the name board...if your name is there you owe me 2 hours of tutoring. You need to figure when you're going to pay me your hours." *[Activity theory: Rules]*

Students begin to work on their objectives. Some students are sitting alone, while some are in groups. There are students working silently on their computers, and some are working on worksheets. Some students are doing both. A few have their headphones in and some are talking in groups quietly. The room is fairly quiet and students seem to get to work pretty quickly. Ms. L moves a few students to other tables to have a small group lesson.

Ms. L has checked the scoreboard (digital report of student progress), and is keeping real-time tabs on their progress. *[Activity theory: Tools]* She tells the students at the table, "We're all here because we're all struggling a little bit." She gives them a new handout and walks them through an activity. This is a group of 6 students. She helps students to define some of the words and reads some of the questions and passages aloud.

Ms. L carries around her computer with the scoreboard and checks in with other students. *[Activity theory: Tools]* She navigates through some of the questions with students as they struggle. To the small group she was working with, she says "I'm going to step away for a minute and I want you guys to answer numbers 5–7. At the end of class, you can turn those in. Explain what you're thinking." *[Activity theory: Division of labor]*

Data Excerpt: Participant Interview

"I think what we'll see over the next few years is that we'll continue to shed the structures that don't allow for complete personalized learning. *[Activity theory: Rules]* What that means is, time structures and core structures. Those are the two systems that don't allow for it because they force people to move out of a certain phase...Next year we're going to take away a lot of the periods and have more open, flexible working times. Then you'll see a lot of our design be more student-focused." *[Activity theory: Object]*

Though coding formed the basis for this round of analysis, memoing helped me understand what all of it meant and why anyone should care about it. The combination of deductive and inductive coding and memoing supported me in developing my discussion and implications. This cycle helped me to understand my findings in relation to existing research, examine how my theoretical framework explained my findings (and where it didn't), and provide actionable, meaningful implications and recommendations. For example, the idea that disciplinary practices were key to how the school enacted personalized learning emerged from this cycle of coding and led directly to a discussion of the implications of highly structured disciplinary models for personalization, particularly for traditionally underserved students.

Summary

The five-cycle analysis process outlined above impacted the findings that emerged from the study and how I made sense of them within the context of the research questions and the theoretical framework. This process allowed me to identify findings to answer my research questions and explain those findings using my theoretical framework. For example, one of the primary findings was that teachers used a "No Excuses" disciplinary model to control technology use and facilitate personalized learning. This was a finding that emerged during inductive analysis. By applying the theoretical framework during the final analysis cycle, I was able to identify *why* this "No Excuses" model emerged. I would not have been able to produce theoretically grounded work without engaging iterative inductive and deductive coding. This process also supported my discussion and implications section by facilitating clear connections between the findings and the theory and between the findings and the literature.

Conclusion

Drawing on and balancing appropriate analysis practices is critical to conducting rigorous qualitative research. Integrating deductive and inductive approaches can help the researcher focus on the research purpose as well as paradigmatic, theoretical, and conceptual lenses. We argue that deductive practices can help with organization and focus. However, the purpose of qualitative research is to understand experiences and perceptions of phenomena in context. If researchers do not allow the data to speak to them through inductive approaches, they risk imposing their own experiences and perceptions on the data and the participants, rather than allowing the answers to emerge from the participants' words and actions.

Our recommendation is for researchers to use both deductive and inductive analysis practices, but to ensure that there is clarity around how and why these practices are being used. Analytic clarity may be produced by using clearly defined *a priori* codes, employing consistent inductive analysis within and across *a priori* codes and categories, and engaging in a systematic process of memoing. These practices allow qualitative researchers to organize the data, maintain focus on the research questions, allow themes to emerge, engage in theoretical analyses, and ensure trustworthiness. Ultimately, qualitative researchers should draw on the strengths of deductive analytic practices and lean into the opportunities provided by inductive analytic strategies.

Supplemental Readings

Miles, M., Huberman, M., & Saldaña, J. (2020). *Qualitative data analysis: A methods sourcebook* (4th ed.). SAGE.

Saldaña, J. (2016). *The coding manual for qualitative researchers.* (3rd ed.). SAGE.

Saldaña, J., & Omasta, M. (2018). *Qualitative research: Analyzing life.* SAGE.

Reflection and Activities

1. Consider a theoretical framework to apply to your study or a theoretical framework with which you have knowledge. What deductive (*a priori*) codes could be useful to apply to data in an analysis phase?

2. In what research scenarios might it be challenging to apply deductive and inductive coding as described in this chapter?

3. How can the use of deductive and inductive coding together strengthen analysis for a study you are conducting or considering?

References

Bingham, A. J. (2016). Drowning digitally? How disequilibrium shapes practice in a blended learning charter school. *Teachers College Record, 118*(1), 1–30.

Bingham, A. J. (2017). Personalized learning in high technology charter schools. *Journal of Educational Change, 18*(4), 521–549. https://doi.org/10.1007/s10833-017-9305-0

Bingham, A.J. (2019). A look at personalized learning: Lessons learned. *Kappa Delta Pi Record, 55*(3), 124–129. https://doi.org/10.1080/00228958.2019.1622383

Bingham, A. J., & Ogunbowo Dimandja, O. (2017). Staying on track: Examining teachers' experiences in a personalized learning model. *Journal of Ethnographic and Qualitative Research, 12*(2), 75–96.

Bingham, A. J., Pane, J., Steiner, E., & Hamilton, L. (2018). Ahead of the curve: Implementation challenges in the personalized learning movement. *Educational Policy, 32*(3), 454–489. https://doi.org/10.1177/0895904816637688

Blackstone, A. (2014). *Principles of sociological inquiry: Qualitative and quantitative methods.* The Saylor Foundation https://resources.saylor.org/wwwresources/archived/site/textbooks/Principles%20of%20Sociological%20Inquiry.pdf

Crabtree, B. F., & Miller, W. L. (1999). Using codes and code manuals: A template organizing style of interpretation. In B. F. Crabtree & W. L. Miller (Eds.), *Doing qualitative research* (2nd ed., pp. 163–177).

Creswell, J. W., & Plano Clark, V. L. (2007). *Designing and conducting mixed methods research.* SAGE.

Engeström, Y. (1999). Activity theory and individual and social transformation. In Engeström, Y., Miettinen, R., & Punamäki, R.-L. (Eds.). *Perspectives on activity theory* (pp. 19–38). Cambridge University Press.

Fereday, J., & Muir-Cochrane, E. (2006). Demonstrating rigor using thematic analysis: A hybrid approach of inductive and deductive coding and theme development. *International Journal of Qualitative Methods, 5*(1), 80–92. https://doi.org/10.1177/160940690600500107

Glaser, B. G. (1965). The constant comparative method of qualitative analysis. *Social Problems, 12*(4), 436–445. https://doi.org/10.2307/798843

Glaser, B., & Strauss, A. (1967). *The discovery of grounded theory.* Aldine.

Hsieh, H. F., & Shannon, S. E. (2005). Three approaches to qualitative content analysis. *Qualitative Health Research, 15*(9), 1277–1288. https://doi.org/10.1177/1049732305276687

Hyde, K. F. (2000). Recognising deductive processes in qualitative research. *Qualitative Market Research: An International Journal, 3*(2), 82–89. https://doi.org//10.1108/13522750010322089

Miles, M. B., & Huberman, M. A. (1994). *Qualitative data analysis: An expanded sourcebook.* SAGE.

Miles, M., Huberman, M., & Saldaña, J. (2020). *Qualitative data analysis: A methods sourcebook* (4th ed.). SAGE.

Milkie, M. A., & Warner, C. H. (2011). Classroom learning environments and the mental health of first grade children. *Journal of Health and Social Behavior, 52*, 4–22. https://doi.org//10.1177/0022146510394952

Ravitch, S. M., & Riggan, M. (2017). *Reason & rigor: How conceptual frameworks guide research* (2nd ed.). SAGE.

Saldaña, J. (2016). *The coding manual for qualitative researchers* (3rd ed.). SAGE.

Saldaña, J., & Omasta, M. (2018). *Qualitative research: Analyzing life.* SAGE.

Sandelowski, M., Barroso, J., & Voils, C. I. (2007). Using qualitative metasummary to synthesize qualitative and quantitative descriptive findings. *Research in Nursing & Health, 30*(1), 99–111. https://doi.org//10.1002/nur.20176

Coding, Categorizing, and Theming the Data: A Reflexive Search for Meaning

Janet C. Richards

Abstract

In this chapter, I provide an overview of reflexive thematic analysis and the phases of identifying, analyzing, and interpreting patterns of meaning within qualitative data. I offer examples of analysis of data for each of these steps and provide data flow diagram segments that illustrate researchers' recursive patterns as they work to reduce data yet maintain meaning. Throughout the chapter, I pose queries to encourage researchers' reflexivity and promote discussions. I list thought-provoking questions researchers might ask themselves as they initiate and proceed through data analysis and interpretation, and I accompany these questions with suggested responses. In the conclusion, I emphasize the reflexive nature of the decision-making that guides thematic analysis.

Keywords: Data coding and analysis; data flow diagrams; researcher reflexivity; teaching qualitative research

There are many ways to analyze and interpret qualitative data, depending upon the type of study, the researchers' goals, and epistemological and ontological assumptions (Adu, 2019). In this chapter, I position my ideas through reflexive thematic analysis since this method is theoretically flexible, straightforward, intuitive, and compatible with many, although not all, types of inquiries. In their well-received conceptualization of reflexive thematic analysis, Braun and Clarke (2006) and Clarke and Braun (2013b) conclude themes do not spontaneously emerge from coding and categorizing data. Rather, researchers engage in active, decision-making processes to generate themes.

Learning From a Course Evaluation

To begin my work on this chapter, I first considered my own positionality. I am a professor of literacy and qualitative research. I hold an interpretivist position (i.e., epistemology) and therefore seek to explore and consider study participants' views. However, I am also aware my own biases influence my research efforts from start to finish. Moreover, my positionality has influenced my data interpretations shared later in this chapter.

I asked doctoral students in my Qualitative Research Methods #2 class to respond in writing to this question: "What should qualitative researchers consider as they plan and proceed through data analysis and interpretation?" I share three of my students' responses below with salient ideas bolded:

Response #1

Researchers should think about how to **organize** the information **in the most appropriate way**. Once the information is **organized,** read, reread, ensure it is **organized.** Begin **circling common reoccurring words, concepts, thoughts—find ways to see how these common words are connected.**

Response #2

Re-read the data to **reflect** on the data collection experience on that particular day—Keep a **researcher journal** to **record initial impressions—thoughts, reactions, initial interpretations**, **questions, etc.** **Reflect** on the data collected to consider to what extent the **data help answer research question(s)**. **Read or re-read the literature on the topic to continue to view the data collection process through the lens of the body of related literature on my topic.**

Response #3

Reflect on the entire data collection experience. **Write down your ideas, experiences, etc. that occurred when you collected data.** Look at the data in its raw form (again). Then, transcribe the data, looking at/analyzing the data as it is transcribed. Then you want to **review/analyze the transcribed data inductively**. Then you want to conduct **thematic analysis** to discover themes. Once you **establish themes**, re-analyze the data for accuracy. **Themes should be tied to the theoretical framework**. The **themes should also answer the a priori questions.**

The bolded ideas in the responses above indicate my students have assimilated some apropos terminology and concepts into their analysis schemas, such as *organize data, common themes, related literature, a priori questions, review data, common words, constant comparative analysis, establish themes,* and *reflect*. However, I learned from their feedback I have much more work to do as the instructor of the class because their replies were vague and the statements did not directly answer the question I posed. Their indefinite responses and omissions indicate the students did not know precisely what to consider as they planned and progressed through data analysis and interpretation. More to the point, their answers indicate—mea culpa—I did not do a good job to help my students understand the essential steps recommended in thematic analysis and recognize the importance of researcher reflexivity.

I had supported my students as they transmediated textbook chapter content through the visual and performing arts; critiqued published traditional qualitative genre inquiries; interacted with me in "student/instructor qualitative conversations"; engaged in collaborative, group simulations in which they devised an inquiry based upon given scenarios; attended weekend discussion meetings with me focused on qualitative research processes; and presented an individual end-of-semester authentic inquiry. But I had neglected to adequately help them as they learned the systematic steps appropriate for qualitative reflexive thematic analysis. Accordingly, the students were unclear about what to do as they prepared and worked to transform raw/primary data into a concise summary of themes and ultimately: meaning. In fact, Erlingsson and Brysiewicz (2017) note novice researchers often struggle to understand how to engage in qualitative data analysis.

Teaching Theming and Reflexibility

In an effort to help clarify these processes, I begin with a brief overview of reflexive thematic analysis and then explain the phases of identifying, analyzing, and interpreting patterns of meaning (or themes) within qualitative data. I also offer examples of analysis of data for each of these steps. In addition, at all stages of the progression, I provide data flow diagrams (DFDs) (Woodman, 1988) that illustrate researchers' recursive patterns as they work to reduce data yet maintain meaning.

At various points throughout the chapter, I pose queries to encourage researchers' reflexivity. In addition, as a summary to my explanation of reflexive thematic analysis, I list nine questions researchers might ask themselves as they initiate and proceed through qualitative data analysis and interpretation. I accompany these questions with suggested responses. I conclude the chapter with some final points to remember and also list three questions to promote discussion in classrooms and study groups.

Reflexive Thematic Analysis: An Art and a Challenge

Analyzing data refers to the process of converting collected information into interconnected unified categories (Adu, 2019; also see Hesse-Biber, 2017). Ultimately, all data analysis is about data reduction achieved by thoughtfully coalescing like patterns and themes. Themes synthesize pieces of the analysis into a more presentable and meaningful whole. Patterns help the researcher with the process of identifying or constructing themes.

However, it is vital the progressively abbreviated forms continue to represent the raw/primary data. No intractable rules exist to convert or group qualitative data to achieve the goals of discovering, making meaning, and building new knowledge (Patton, 2015). But there are recommended guidelines researchers follow, along with necessary, recursive actions, to check and recheck their assumptions as they analyze data (see Miles, Huberman, & Saldaña, 2020).

The qualitative analytic process is subjective and, therefore, interpretive. Accordingly, at every step of the process, researchers need to examine and consciously acknowledge the assumptions and biases they bring to their inquiries that impact their decisions and interpretations. To that end, Patton (2015) cautions researchers to be mindful as they progress through data analysis. Skillful data analysis, the work of grouping codes into patterns and themes in order to reduce the data while not losing meaning, "is a matter of judgment, and it all depends on who is doing the judging with what criteria and for what purpose" (p. 520). Patton also observes, "data analysis ultimately depends upon the skill, intellect, training, and insight of the analyst" (p. 522).

An Explanation of Reflexive Thematic Analysis Illuminated Through DFD Segments

In the next sections, Christy Bebeau, a geology doctoral student, provides DFDs she created to illustrate how researchers' iterative, or repeated, looping analysis of their data represents reflexive thematic analysis. The DFD segments also help identify and trace researchers' thinking and actions during the analysis process in which they transform raw data to codes, categories, and themes (Bebeau, 2020). For example, each DFD shows how researchers' reflexive decisions might either redirect them back to previously explored and documented processes or might direct them forward to the next step in the data analysis process. Note the DFDs pinpoint researchers' presence directly in the center of analysis. Rectangles in the DFD represent researchers who access data, reflect, analyze, and decide to keep the data as is, or augment or edit the data. The ovals represent each of the steps. Open-ended rectangles represent places where researchers have stored data. Labeled arrows represent the type of data transferred and how data are transformed through the processes (see Figure 9.1).

FIGURE 9.1 ● Data Flow Diagram Symbols

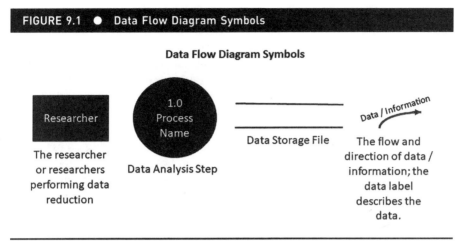

Data Flow Diagram Symbols

Source: Modified from DeMarco (1979). Graphic by Christy Bebeau, 2020.

Steps in Reflexive Thematic Analysis

Data analysis is a looping, iterative process. The steps described in the following reflexive thematic analysis paradigm "should not be viewed as a linear model where one cannot proceed to the next phase without completing the prior phase (correctly); rather analysis is a recursive process" (Clarke & Braun, 2013b, p. 120).

In the following section I show how I code data and then create categories and generate themes using data from my researcher's notebook.

An Extract from my Researcher's Notebook

As I walked into the classroom to meet my new students in qualitative research, I hoped I would see happy students. But instead, I saw some students frowning. Some were looking down at their desks. As I sat down, one of the students said, "Dr. Richards, I'm worried about the long syllabus." Another student added, "This is making us nervous."

I was confident of my syllabus content. I had used it before. So, I said, "I can see you are concerned, but I'll help you with the syllabus and the course. You will love qualitative research. It will all work out."

Step 1: Know the Data

In reality, data analysis actually begins when researchers initiate data collection from: (1) observations; (2) face-to face interviews; (3) study participants' weekly journal entries; (4) focus groups; (5) visual and performing arts representations, etc. In other words, qualitative data collection and analysis are not linear. "They usually proceed simultaneously" (Patton, 2002, p. 514). As researchers collect data, they read through and inspect the data they have collected to identify problems and revise data collection methods if necessary (Patton, 2015). After transcribing the data (if transcribing is needed), researchers continue to return to their interviews (see discussions in di Gregorio, Chapter 6, and Bernauer, Chapter 10; this beginning step takes considerable time and mental expenditure but is well worth the effort.

In this initial phase (Figure 9.2), researchers take notes in their journal in which they record their suppositions and ideas (i.e., memo writing). Taking notes during data collection and immediately after interviews and observations "promotes new discoveries, helps keep track of one's thought processes, aids in categorizing codes, and facilitates detailing an account of the coding process" (Adu, 2019, pp. 85 and 86). Memo writing also proves useful when researchers appropriately include their notes in their final report. In these notes, researchers return to their a priori questions, and they continue to reflect on these questions throughout the research process to determine if the data answer these queries; if not, they edit them. In addition, researchers review the theoretical perspectives (i.e., theories) they chose to support the study to consider if these frameworks are still appropriate or if they should change, exclude, or add one or more theories.

FIGURE 9.2 ● Data Flow Diagram of Step 1: Know the Data

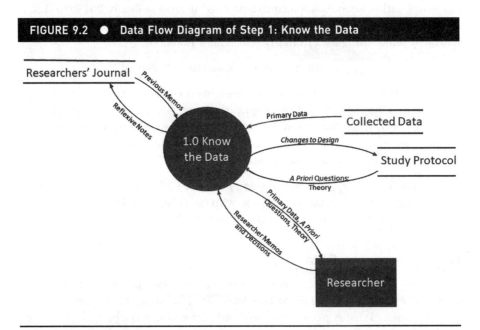

Graphic by Christy Bebeau, 2020.

Step 2: Code the Data

In the next step, researchers code (i.e., assign labels to) the data. Researchers look over text they have gotten to know and they look for content for their inquiry. The following extract shows the text segments I marked using the codes and categories shown in Table 9.1:

The Coded and Categorized Extract

As I walked into the classroom to meet my new students in qualitative research, **I hoped I would see happy students**. But instead, I saw some students frowning. Some were looking down at their desks. As I sat down, one of the students said, "Dr. Richards, I'm worried about the long syllabus." Another student added, "This is making us nervous."

I was confident of my syllabus content. I had used it before. So I said, "I can see you are concerned, but I'll help you with the syllabus and the course. **You will love qualitative research. It will all work out.**"

In this extract, I formated pertinent text segments in different fonts corresponding to important ideas in my analysis. I included everything I thought was relevant because I knew I could always delete some of the ideas and codes and, later on, I could always add more codes if I thought it was appropriate.

TABLE 9.1 ● Coding and Categorizing the Data

Text Segments	Codes	Categories
hoped I would see happy students	My Expectations for Students' Happiness	
students frowning	Concerned Students	Apprehensive Students
looking down at their desks	Apprehensive Students	Apprehensive Students
worried about the long syllabus."	Worried Students	Apprehensive Students
This is making us nervous	Nervous Students	Apprehensive Students
Confident of my syllabus content.	My Confidence	
I can see you are concerned	My Acknowledgement of Student Concerns	
You will love qualitative research. It will all work out."	My Expectation for Students' Happiness	

Table 9.1, above, shows the codes for the text segments I marked in the excerpt. Note how I used the same code, *My Expectations for Students' Happiness* for two text segments. If I was doing a longer analysis, I might then use these codes to mark other parts of my researcher's notebook as well as other data from my study. As shown in Figure 9.3, I might go back over a piece of text a few times to figure out how best to connect it to my coding system.

Coding is the heart of data analysis. "Coding is not something you do to get the data ready for analysis" (Miles, Huberman, & Saldaña, 2020, p. 86). Rather, as Anselm Strauss (1987) writes, "the excellence of the research rests in a large part on the excellence of the coding" (p. 27). Coding refers to the systematic identification of topics, issues similarities and differences in data researchers consider relevant. This relevance connects to the researchers' a priori questions and the theoretical perspectives they chose to support the inquiry (Spickard, 2017; see Figure 9.3).

FIGURE 9.3 ● Data Flow Diagram of Step 2: Code the Data

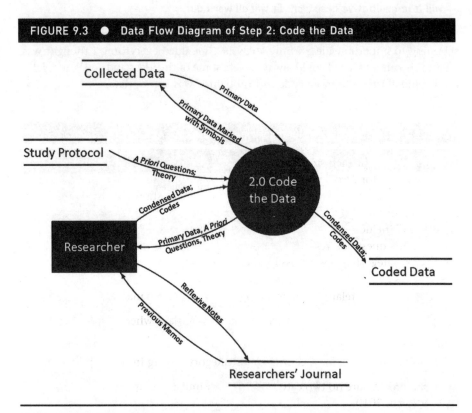

Graphic by Christy Bebeau, 2020.

In Saldaña's (2016) words,

A code in qualitative inquiry is most often a word or short phrase that symbolically assigns a summative, salient, essence-capturing and/or evocative attribute for a portion of language-based or visual data. (p. 4)

Researchers use symbols such as underlining, highlighting, or circling words, phrases, or sentences to mark raw/primary data. The coding phase helps to condense the data, which allows researchers to make sense of it and consider what topics might go together (Patton, 2015). As researchers code, they continue to jot down reflective comments or questions in their journal (i.e., memo writing), and they assiduously remember, "The perspective or position of the researcher shapes all research" (Briggs, 2019, para. 2). They remain focused on their research questions and the data they plan to analyze (Adu, 2019). They continuously check their previous decisions. Then, they collate all the data into groups identified by their codes. These shorthand codes allow researchers "to gain a condensed overview of the main points and common meanings that recur throughout the data" (Caulfield, 2019, para. 5).

Step 3: Categorize the Data

As I mark my data, I might also begin to combine and elevate several of these codes into categories. Researchers create "categories by chunking together groups of previously coded data" (Chenail, 2008, p. 72). Then they label these categories. As shown in Table 9.1, I decided a few the codes I had created about students had a similar meaning, and I combined those codes into a single category, *Apprehensive Students*.

As we can see, at each step of analysis, the concepts become more abstract, and this holds true for *Step 3: Categorize the Data*. Yet, despite this abstraction, it is essential researchers maintain meaning. As Figure 9.4 shows, most of this data condensing occurs when I take the time to examine my memos and other parts of my analysis, including the text I have labeled in my coding system.

Important questions researchers might ask themselves as they engage in the coding and categorization process are:

1. Do my codes relate to the meanings of the text they mark?

2. Did I maintain meaning despite condensing data when I moved from codes to categories?

3. Do all units under a specific code or category belong in that grouping?

4. Did I make sure no two categories are too similar? (Adapted from Bernard & Ryan, 2010)

5. Does this coding system make sense given my questions and assumptions, or do I need to go in a new direction?

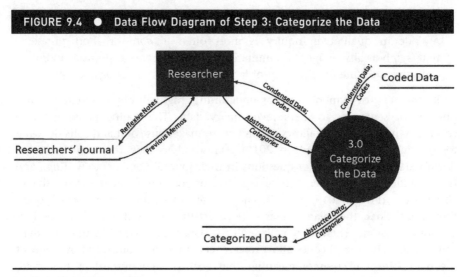

FIGURE 9.4 ● Data Flow Diagram of Step 3: Categorize the Data

Graphic by Christy Bebeau, 2020.

Step 4: Create Themes

Yet, despite its importance, generating themes is often a mysterious task for emerging qualitative researchers (Bernard & Ryan, 2010). "A theme may be initially generated *inductively* from the raw data or generated *deductively* from theory and prior research" (Nowell, Norris, White, & Moules, 2017; also see Boyatsis, 1998 for additional information on generating themes inductively or deductively). A theme encompasses numerous discernments organized around a central concept or idea (Braun & Clarke, 2006) and "is an extended phrase or sentence that identifies what a unit of data is about and/or what it means" (Saldaña, 2016, p. 199). Themes are broader than categories because researchers often combine several categories into themes. As Figure 9.5 illustrates, themes might be developed by engaging with many different parts of the analysis.

In order to create themes, researchers inspect the codes and categories they have created and identify patterns among them (see Figure 9.5). Not every code needs to become part of the analysis. Researchers must use their judgment about what to keep, what to combine, and what to delete. As Caulfield (2019) notes, "codes might become themes in their own right. I always keep in mind that what I decide to keep must connect to what I am trying to discover" (n.p.). In Table 9.2, I made sure to remain true to the purpose of my study and not to lose meaning as I condensed the data to more refined concepts.

The reader might also note boundaries between codes, categories, and themes are fuzzy. In Table 9.2, below, I thought the category *Apprehensive Students* was broad enough I could use it as a theme. Nonetheless, the number of themes should

FIGURE 9.5 ● Data Flow Diagram of Step 4: Generate Themes

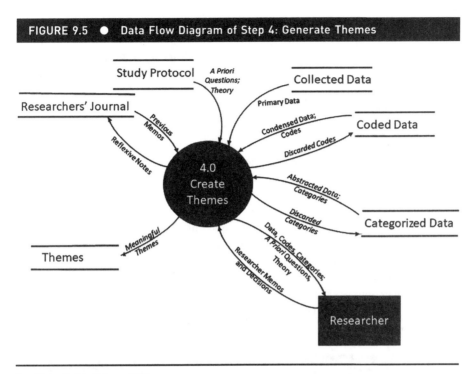

Graphic by Christy Bebeau, 2020.

TABLE 9.2 ● Creating Themes

Codes and Categories	Themes
Janet (professor)	**Janet (professor)**
My expectation of students' attitudes My expectation of student happiness My acknowledgement of student worries My confidence in the syllabus My concern for students My expectation for students' happiness	Attitude and expectations for students Pedagogical caring Trust in the qualitative journey
Students	**Students**
Apprehensive Students Apprehensive Students Apprehensive Students	Apprehensive Students

be limited to the most important concepts in the data. Here again, concepts become more abstract but meaning must not disintegrate. As we can see in these reduction phases, researchers must use their "skill, intellect, training, and insight" (Patton, 2015, p. 522).

Step 5: Interpret the Data (i.e., Interpret Themes)

After once again checking their assumptions, the researcher's next step is to make meaning (i.e., interpret the themes). Throughout all of these processes, researchers' reflexivity efforts are paramount to the quality of theme interpretation (see Figure 9.6). Ultimately, reflexivity at all levels of qualitative life cycle (advancing from data analysis, to codes, to categories, generating themes, and interpreting the data) allows researchers to reach greater levels of abstraction (see Erlingsson & Brysiewicz, 2017). In our example, my reflexive understanding of my position and the students' responses shapes the choices I make as I code different text segments. This understanding then guides my efforts to create categories and themes. It is only by moving thoughtfully through the phases of reflexive thematic analysis researchers are able to interpret and make meaning, and thus create knowledge. As the DFD figures emphasize, however, phases are not strict sequences. I may move back and forth between data and analyses as I construct meaning.

FIGURE 9.6 ● Data Flow Diagram of Step 5: Interpret the Data

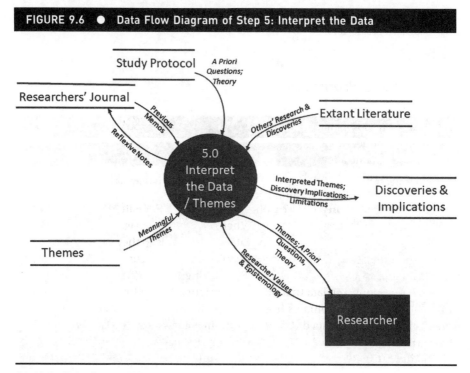

Graphic by Christy Bebeau, 2020.

Interpretation of the data will depend on the theoretical standpoint taken by researchers. What might help researchers interpret themes? One way is to review the literature because those who review the literature produce more themes (Ryan & Bernard, 2004). Other theme interpretation stems from researchers' values, theoretical orientations, personal experiences with the subject matter, and knowledge of the subject matter (Maxwell, 1996). For example, a researcher who has personal experiences with and knowledge of the subject matter, such as serving as a USAID scholar on literacy projects in the jungles between Myanmar and Thailand, as I have, would have considerable pertinent schema that would influence and aid their theme interpretations. I also suggest researchers turn to their thesaurus to help extend their vocabulary.

Reflexively Engaging in Active, Decision-Making Processes

After reading this chapter, readers will likely have a good understanding of the importance of qualitative researchers' reflexivity as they think about and proceed through data analysis. To assist emerging qualitative researchers and others who conduct qualitative inquiries to explicitly reflect upon what they should consider prior to and during data analysis and interpretation, I have developed a list of nine questions to stimulate their reflexivity. By no means is this list finite. Qualitative researchers might add their own questions to this list to stimulate their thoughtfulness as data analysts.

Questions to Prompt Qualitative Researchers' Reflexivity

In what form are my data? (e.g., visual, poetic, and performing arts representations; responses to questionnaires; observation notes; field notes; video recordings; autoethnographic accounts; narrative inquiry; responses to specific questions, to name a few [Spickard, 2017]). The type of data influences researchers' coding schemes (see Miles, Huberman, & Saldaña, 2020, Chapter 4, for an extensive listing and description of coding possibilities).

How do I code my data? Codes mark/signify/designate the smallest unit of text that conveys the same meaning. When researchers engage in coding data, they mark areas of interest of raw/primary data with symbols so they can go back to their codes and group similar ideas together (Spickard, 2017). For example, a researcher might choose to identify and code: (1) recurring topics, (2) data that answer the research questions, (3) data that offer new insights about a topic; (4) in vivo coding that employs words or phrases from study participants' own language. Researchers might manually code data directly on printouts of raw/primary data and then use a table they create to track themes by using a separate sheet for each question (Spickard, 2017). Researchers might also use qualitative data analysis software such as, NVivo, ATLAS.ti, MAXQDA, Quirkos, Dedoose, Provalis Research's QDA Miner, and webQDA.

What analysis procedure(s) would be best to code my data? Consider the type(s) of data the team has collected. There are many ways to analyze and code data (Saldaña, 2016). For example, reflexive thematic analysis is the process of identifying patterns and generating themes within qualitative data. Braun and Clarke (2006) suggest thematic analysis is the first qualitative method students should master because "it provides core skills that will be useful for conducting many other kinds of analysis" (p. 78). Also read Chapter 4 in Miles, Huberman, and Saldaña (2020).

Why are my theoretical frameworks/perspectives (theories) and *a priori* research questions that support my inquiries important? The theoretical perspective(s) relate to information researchers hope to discover in an inquiry (i.e., what will be studied in an inquiry) (Miles, Huberman, & Saldaña, 2020). Theoretical perspectives are theories, a set of assumptions, or frameworks that inform a study and connect to researchers' *a priori* questions. For example, consider the following research question: "In what ways do four preservice teachers incorporate social justice and equity issues in their lessons over the course of a semester?" Having devised this question, researchers would search the literature for theories that inform what they plan to explore. The study would be impossible to conduct without knowledge of social justice and equity issues. Researchers might also engage in empirical data collection and might observe the preservice teachers' lessons and lesson plans, conduct interviews with the four preservice teachers and, in all probability, attempt to answer the research questions by looking for words, terms, and phrases in the dataset that pertain to the phenomena of social justice and equity issues (see Braun & Clarke, 2006).

In what ways might my epistemological and ontological perspectives influence my data analysis and interpretation? Researchers must ask themselves this question: What are my epistemological and ontological assumptions? Do you, the researcher, believe there is one truth or multiple realities? (see Adu, 2019, Chapter 1) Adu (2019) emphasizes qualitative researchers need to reflect on, acknowledge, and bracket their preconceived notions (i.e., "preventing one's perspective and preconceptions from influencing the qualitative analysis process" (p. 72)). Understandably, qualitative researchers hold diverse philosophical views and assumptions about the nature of inquiry they may not recognize or acknowledge. Epistemology is concerned with all aspects of the validity, scope, and methods of acquiring knowledge such as: (1) what constitutes a knowledge claim; (2) how can knowledge be acquired or produced; and (3) how the extent of its transferability can be assessed. Epistemology is important because it influences how researchers frame their research in their attempts to discover knowledge (Moon & Blackman, 2017) and epistemology guides researchers' perspectives about how knowledge can be acquired (Ormston, Spencer, Barnard, & Snape, 2014). Some researchers lean toward a postpositivist view (Lincoln & Guba, 1985), others hold a postmodern stance (Merriam, 2002), while others may adhere to a mainstream typology.

In what ways did I keep good records of my data analysis and interpretations? Good qualitative researchers always take the time to record their thinking and actions. Writing in a journal to document a significant incident and also writing daily as they move through data analysis and interpretation are effective ways to record thoughts and questions so researchers can fuel their memories. An added plus is researchers' responses to this question can be included in their final report.

What is missing from the data that might be just as important as what is in the data? Take some time and ask, "What is missing in the data and what might I have missed?" as opposed to just looking for what is there. "Researchers have long recognized that much can be learned from qualitative data by what is not mentioned" (Ryan & Bernard, 2004, n.p.). In fact, more than fifty years ago, Bogdan and Taylor (1975) suggested researchers must be "attentive to topics that study participants avoid" (p. 82). Also consider ideas from poststructural tenets that emphasize the meanings of silences and ellipses (see Jackson & Mazzei, 2012).

How might I establish credibility for my data analysis procedures? One way to establish the credibility of data analysis procedures is to ask an exemplary qualitative researcher to serve as a "critical friend" and code, categorize, theme, and interpret their raw/primary data. The two of you can discuss similarities and differences in the two analyses. This procedure may lead to new awareness of what is in the data or the process may confirm your thinking.

In what ways can I contribute to the honesty and accuracy of my research report? Consider the responsibilities researchers have to their participants and their profession. Obtain informed consent from study participants. Maintain confidentiality and anonymity of study participants. Do not misinterpret the data. Guard against plagiarism and if you are using someone else's coding system please cite and acknowledge their work. Be true to yourself and to the discipline of qualitative research. Write well (Richards, 2019).

Conclusion

I am optimistic my framing of reflexive thematic analysis in this chapter will not be viewed as a lasagna or eggplant parmesan recipe researchers must follow step-by-step. In this chapter, due to space constraints, I portray one way to employ reflexive thematic analysis. Yet, as Braun and Clarke (2019) note, reflexive thematic analysis is flexible in process and procedures. I list important takeaways below:

- There are recommended steps that guide reflexive qualitative researchers as they move from raw/primary data to themes, discoveries, and interpretations (i.e., making meaning), but there are no strict rules.

- Researchers generate themes. Themes do not emerge like magic.

- Researchers' reflexive decisions might redirect them back to previously explored and documented processes, or these decisions might move them forward to the next step in the data analysis process.

- Researchers must strive to preserve the meaning of the data throughout all phases of data analysis.

- With reflexive thematic analysis in mind, no longer can researchers write, "Themes emerged," as if themes are independent, mystical entities that develop spontaneously. Rather, Braun and Clarke's work (2019) places researchers' thinking central to the data coding and analysis process.

- The qualitative analytic process is subjective. Therefore, at every step of the process, researchers need to examine and consciously acknowledge the assumptions and biases they bring to their inquiries and understand how these biases impact their decisions and interpretations.

- This central positioning of researchers in the analytic process puts researchers in charge of their decisions and requires them to be introspective and reflexive (i.e., take actions that direct attention back to themselves and to make their coding and analysis transparent as portrayed in the DFDs interspersed throughout this chapter). "Reflexivity offers us a way to turn the problem of subjectivity in research into an opportunity. Without reflexivity the validity of the research could be undermined" (Finley, 1998).

- Reflexive thematic analysis can reflect researchers' different philosophical epistemological assumptions and positionalities relevant to their research.

- Clarke and Braun (2013a) believe their current views of reflexive thematic analysis may continue to evolve organically. My views on the subject also continue to evolve.

Supplemental Readings

Boyatzis, R. (1998). *Transforming qualitative information: Thematic analysis and code development.* SAGE.

Gibbs, G. (2007). Thematic coding and categorizing. In *Analyzing qualitative data* (pp. 38–55). SAGE.

Miles, M. B., Huberman, A. M., & Saldaña, J. (2020). *Qualitative data analysis: A methods sourcebook* (4th ed.). SAGE.

Reflection and Activities

1. Why do Braun and Clarke (2012) view reflexive thematic analysis as theoretically flexible?

2. How might researchers demonstrate they have conducted data analysis in a rigorous and methodical manner? (see Nowell et al., 2017)

3. Take a small piece of data, then code and theme it following the practices described in this chapter. Use the DFD segments to organize your discussion and explain the different steps of your analysis to a critical friend. If you don't have data of your own, you might use the three pieces of data and my commentary in the section in this chapter, Learning from a Course Evaluation.

References

Adu, P. (2019). *A step-by-step guide to qualitative data coding.* Routledge.

Bebeau, C. (January 2020). *Data flow diagrams as audit of qualitative data analysis methods.* Presented at The Qualitative Report 11th Annual Conference "Contemporary Qualitative Research." Fort Lauderdale, FL.

Bernard, H., & Ryan, G. (2010). *Analyzing qualitative data: Systematic approaches.* SAGE.

Bernauer, J. A. (2022). Oral coding: An alternative way to make sense of interview data. In C. Vanover, P. Mihas, & J. Saldaña (Eds.), *Analyzing and interpreting qualitative research: After the interview.* SAGE.

Bogdan, R., & Taylor, S. (1975). *Introduction to qualitative research methods.* Wiley.

Boyatzis, R. (1998). *Transforming qualitative information: Thematic analysis and code development.* SAGE.

Braun, V., & Clarke, V. (2006). Using thematic analysis in psychology. *Qualitative Research in Psychology, 3*(2), 77–101. https://doi.org/10.1191/1478088706qp063oa

Braun, V., & Clarke, V. (2012). Thematic analysis. In H. Cooper, (Ed.), *APA handbook of research methods in psychology. Vol. 2: Research designs* (pp. 57–71). American Psychological Association. https://doi.org/10.1037/13620-004

Braun, V., & Clarke, V. (2019). Reflecting on reflexive thematic analysis. *Qualitative Research in Sport, Exercise, and Health, 11*(4), 589–597. https://doi.org/10.1080/2159676X.2019.1628806

Briggs, K. (May 22, 2019). *Reflection and Reflexivity* [web log]. http://kathrynbriggs.weebly.com/blog/reflection-reflexivity

Caulfield, J. (September 9, 2019). *How to do thematic analysis.* Scribbr. https://www.scribbr.com/methodology/thematic-analysis/

Chenail, R. (2008). Categorization. In L. M. Given (Ed.), *The SAGE encyclopedia of qualitative research methods* (Vol. 1, pp. 72–73). SAGE. https://methods.sagepub.com/reference/sage-encyc-qualitative-research-methods/n41.xml

Clarke, V., & Braun, V. (2013a). *Successful qualitative research.* SAGE.

Clarke, V., & Braun, V. (2013b). Teaching thematic analysis: Overcoming challenges and developing strategies for effective learning. *The Psychologist, 26*(2), 120–123. https://thepsychologist.bps.org.uk/volume-26/edition-2/methods-teaching-thematic-analysis

DeMarco, T. (1979). Structure analysis and system specification. In M. Broy, & E. Denert (Eds.), *Pioneers and their contributions to software engineering* (pp. 255–288). Springer. https://doi.org/10.1007/978-3-642-48354-7_9

di Gregorio, S. (2022). Voice to text: Automating transcription. In C. Vanover, P. Mihas, & J. Saldaña (Eds.), *Analyzing and interpreting qualitative research: After the interview.* SAGE.

Erlingsson, C., & Brysiewicz, P. (2017). A hands-on guide to doing content analysis. *African Journal of Emergency Medicine, 7*(3), 93–98. https://doi.org/10.1016/j.afjem.2017.08.001

Finley, L. (1998). Reflexivity: A reflexive component for all research? *British Journal of Occupational Therapy, 61*(10), 453–456. https://journals.sagepub.com/doi/10.1177/030802269806101005

Hesse-Biber, S. (2017). *The practice of qualitative research* (3rd ed.). SAGE.

Jackson, A., & Mazzei, L. (2012). *Thinking with theory in qualitative research: Viewing data across multiple perspectives.* Routledge.

Lincoln, Y., & Guba, E. (1985). *Naturalistic inquiry.* SAGE.

Maxwell, J. (1996). *Qualitative research design: An interactive approach.* SAGE.

Merriam, S. (2002). *Qualitative research in practice: Examples for discussion and analysis.* Josey-Bass.

Miles, M. B., Huberman, A. M., & Saldaña, J. (2020). *Qualitative data analysis: A methods sourcebook* (4th ed.). SAGE.

Moon, K., & Blackman, D. (2017). *A guide to ontology, epistemology, and philosophical perspectives for interdisciplinary researchers.* Integration and Implementation Insights: Research Resources for Understanding and Acting on Complex Real-World Problems. https://i2insights.org/2017/05/02/philosophy-for-interdisciplinarity/

Nowell, L., Norris, J., White, D., & Moules, N. (2017). Thematic analysis: Striving to meet the trustworthiness criteria. *International Journal of Qualitative Methods, 16*(1). https://doi.org/10.1177/1609406917733847

Ormston, R., Spencer, L., Barnard, M., & Snape, D. (2014). The foundations of qualitative research. In J. Ritchie, J. Lewis, C. Nicholls, & R. Ormston (Eds.), *Qualitative research practice: A guide for social science students and researchers* (pp. 1–25). SAGE.

Patton, M. (2002). *Qualitative research and evaluation methods* (3rd ed.). SAGE.

Patton, M. (2015). *Qualitative evaluation and research methods* (4th ed.). SAGE.

Richards, J. C. (2019). Empowering students of qualitative research to take charge of their academic writing. In J. C. Richards & W.-M. Roth (Eds.), *Empowering students as self-directed learners of qualitative research methods: Transformational practices for instructors and students.* Brill.

Ryan, G. & Bernard, H. (2004). *Techniques to identify themes in qualitative data.* Analytic Technologies. http://www.analytictech.com/mb870/readings/ryan-bernard_techniques_to_iden tify_themes_in.htm

Saldaña, J. (2016). *The coding manual for qualitative researchers* (3rd ed.). SAGE.

Spickard, J. (2017). *Research basics: Design to data analysis in 6 steps.* SAGE.

Strauss, A. L. (1987). *Qualitative analysis for social scientists.* Cambridge University Press.

Woodman, M. (1988). Yourdon dataflow diagrams: A tool for disciplined requirements analysis. *Information and Software Technology, 30*(9), 515–533. https://doi.org/10.1016/0950-5849(88)90131-0

Oral Coding: An Alternative Way to Make Sense of Interview Data

James A. Bernauer

Abstract

This chapter describes the development of oral coding as a method for analyzing and interpreting interview data. Oral coding is viewed as a way to more fully capture aural–oral data from recorded interviews compared to traditional transcription methods. The step-by-step process of oral coding is explained and illustrated using an example of how it has been used in actual practice. Both the benefits and possible drawbacks of oral coding as an alternative to traditional transcription methods are offered since it is recognized that this method may not meet the requirements or predilections of all researchers. It is also pointed out that, while the criterion of validity is not directly addressed, written accounts using oral coding may be perceived as more authentic because of extended immersion in the aural–oral encounter with participants.

Keywords: Oral coding; CAQDAS; mixed methods; validity

Introduction and Brief Literature Review

While coding is generally accepted as the way to make sense of qualitative data, Saldaña (2016) forcefully puts things into perspective when he writes, "Coding is just *one* way of analyzing qualitative data, not *the* way. Be cautious of those who demonize the method outright. And be equally cautious of those who swear unyielding affinity to codes, or what has been colloquially labeled 'coding fetishism'" (p. 3). It was with this perspective in mind that I developed a hybrid method I label oral coding (Bernauer, 2015a).

I admit that, while my primary motivation for developing oral coding was to capture interview data in a more authentic and naturalistic manner, I also felt I was expending too much time and energy on transcribing. I like to think that a happy confluence occurred between these two reasons, but I also wonder sometimes to what degree my feelings about transcribing influenced my decision to move forward with developing oral coding. However, I can also honestly say that I have found oral coding has greatly increased my understanding of participants and phenomena and that, even given continuing improvements in software transcription and automated coding, my personal choice for interviews is oral coding since it provides me a more authentic way to represent participants in my accounts.

As a teacher of both quantitative and qualitative inquiry (see O'Dwyer & Bernauer, 2014), I typically draw a comparison for my students between using statistical procedures for making sense of quantitative data and using coding to make sense of qualitative data. I also make a corresponding connection between SPSS and NVivo since these are two software packages we use at my university for quantitative and qualitative data analysis. While statistical software like SPSS allows individuals to analyze and make sense of numerical data, even if they do not fully understand the rationale or assumptions underlying statistical tests, I don't think that this same line of reasoning can be used for CAQDAS (Computer Assisted Qualitative Data Analysis Software). CAQDAS, such as NVivo, does not claim to produce anything comparable to statistically significant findings based on probability. Rather, the oft-voiced maxim that the researcher is the principal instrument and all that this implies signals a chasm in analytical methods between quantitative and qualitative data that cannot (and hopefully never will) be bridged. As the principal instrument, inquirers are tasked with mustering all that they have in terms of experience and insights in conjunction with CAQDAS or other noncomputer methods of analysis in order to try and make sense of qualitative data and to interpret findings in light of stated research questions.

Notwithstanding this seemingly less powerful role of qualitative software versus quantitative software, CAQDAS does offer an increasing number of creative ways to make sense of data. However, when it comes to interview data, whether we use manual methods, general software such as Microsoft Word, or specialized software such as NVivo, it still comes down to identifying and analyzing segments of textual data that coalesce around important concepts and themes that inform our research questions. We achieve this task of identification and analysis with the help of coding in order to "transform what we see and hear into intelligible accounts" (Agar, 1980, p. 189).

Illustrating the differences between transforming qualitative data versus quantitative data into intelligible accounts by juxtaposing NVivo and SPSS highlights the fact that we are working with two different paradigms. As Guba (1981, pp. 77–78) states, and later amplified by Lincoln and Guba (1985, pp. 14–46), there are three major assumptions that differentiate the qualitative and quantitative paradigms: (1) the nature of reality, (2) the nature of the inquirer–researcher relationship, and (3) the nature of "truth statements." While Guba maintains that the *methods* of quantitative and qualitative inquiry can be used interchangeably, I have found this contention to be difficult to put into practice. In today's research milieu, it is quite fashionable to think of mixed methods as the pinnacle of inquiry, and I regularly see doctoral students who decide early on that such an approach is sure to please their doctoral committees. However, too often mixing methods results in a fragmented dissertation where the pieces have not been quite pieced together in a way that paints a portrait but rather looks like two different snapshots.

Let me hasten to say that I am not against mixed methods—in fact, I support the use of mixed methods when the study's purpose, research questions, and the research context make their use appropriate. The real challenge lies in the validity and the interpretation of findings where quantitative data have been analyzed using statistical procedures and qualitative data have been analyzed using some type of coding procedures (see Creswell & Plano-Clark, 2011; Onwuegbuzie & Johnson, 2006; Poth, 2018). I cannot help but think that we sometimes go too far trying to replicate the tenets of science in order to gain legitimacy for qualitative inquiry, including how we analyze and interpret findings.

The Development of Oral Coding

I have used the steps I originally developed in 2015 for two studies that have been published and one that I am in the process of completing. In this section, I will reference the two published studies and will discuss the article in progress in the next section.

A critical element in this method is the strategic use of listening and writing. For me personally (and I assume many others), the art of active listening has unfortunately fallen victim to more frenetic communication modes such as email, texting, Twitter, and social media in general. Conversely, Socratic questioning invites active listening and, while I certainly do not place myself even remotely at the same level as described by Plato, the spirit of such questioning provides us with a model for designing questions that invite not simply a replay of existing perceptions and knowledge, but rather the dynamic creation of new discoveries as the dialogic interview unfolds. Such questions and resulting new discoveries energize participants since they, perhaps for the first time, are presented the opportunity to reconstruct their experiences using fresh perspectives as they converse which, in turn, energizes researchers to listen and simultaneously construct their own emerging understanding of phenomena. Oral coding capitalizes on this kind of listening by using it as the principal way to analyze and interpret participant data.

Writing also facilitates reflection and the discovery of new insights. As Thomas Mann (1981) said through his character Settembrini, "for writing well was almost the same as thinking well, and thinking well was the next best thing to acting well" (p. 164). Wolcott (2009) makes the connection between writing and thinking even clearer by arguing that "the conventional wisdom is that writing reflects thinking. I am attracted to a stronger position: that writing *is* thinking" (p. 18, emphasis in original) which means that, although writing is the final step in the research act, it is not merely a simple report of what has been learned but rather part of the continuing creative effort to analyze and interpret the original aural/oral data.

The Steps of Oral Coding

I outline the seven steps of oral coding as they were first codified (adapted from Bernauer, 2015a, pp. 7–8). To use this method, researchers should:

1. Conduct and record interviews.

2. As soon as possible after recording the interviews, listen carefully to them in order to get a feeling or gestalt of the data. As one listens, carefully and critically reflect on what one hears and does not hear. Do not take written notes; rather, make "mental notes" in relation to participant pauses and emphases, and be sensitive to one's own awareness of both propositional and tacit understandings that emerge from the data.

3. In the days that follow, listen again to the tapes in relation to the research questions and identify and document those terms, codes, themes, and concepts that begin to emerge. This step constitutes first-round coding.

4. Based on steps 1–3, listen once again to the original recordings but stop and rerecord salient segments from participants on a second recording device, as well as reflections and observations as they pertain to the research questions. So, turn on a second device, play the original interview, and then talk about what was said. This step in the coding process not only helps to identify initial themes across participants but also facilitates the simultaneous interplay of analysis, interpretation, and reflexivity. This step constitutes second-round coding.

5. Based on steps 1–4, write an initial abstract that describes the purpose of the study, what the researcher was trying to discover, how she went about trying to make these discoveries, what was found, and what these findings mean in relation to the research questions. This step may be somewhat difficult since neither findings nor interpretations have been completed. However, at this point in the coding process, researchers know more than they think they know. And even though there may be changes based on

further analysis, writing an abstract helps the researcher begin to harmonize the report in terms of purpose, procedures, results, and interpretations.

6. 'Using the condensed recording completed in Step 4, transcribe participant responses based on oral–aural immersion using a combination of keyboarding and perhaps voice recognition software (such as temi.com). Create a consolidated file where each salient participant response and researcher comment is listed under each research question and its corresponding interview question or conversation prompt. This step constitutes the third and final round of coding using the oral coding process.

7. Finally, using the consolidated file, begin writing the final report by comparing, contrasting, and critically analyzing participant data and researcher comments both within and across research questions. This process exemplifies data analysis and synthesis as critical thinking (see Bernauer, Lichtman, Jacobs, & Robertson, 2013a). It should also be noted that extending these steps over a period of several days (or weeks) allows the researcher to incorporate the serendipitous insights that sometimes arise prior to and concurrent with writing up the final report.

Before these steps were codified in 2015, I tested oral coding in a study that investigated how research methodologies were taught in a doctoral program (Bernauer, Semich, Klentzin, & Holdan, 2013b). In this study, a focus group comprised of the authors served as the primary data collection source since three members of this group (Bernauer, Holdan, & Semich) were faculty members who taught different methodology courses in the doctoral program, while the other member (Klentzin) was a graduate of the program. Although the major goal of this study was to investigate the most effective ways to prepare doctoral students to learn about research methodologies in an accelerated, cohort-based doctoral program, a secondary purpose was to try and validate the process of oral coding. This was done by me using oral coding to analyze the interview data while Klentzin used a modified version of a data analysis procedure described by Moustakas (1994) for analyzing phenomenological data. Although the seven steps in oral coding noted above were not codified as such in this first study, these were the steps I used to analyze these same data. In this study, I was designated "QUAL" since I taught qualitative methodology, while Klentzin was designated "PG" [post-graduate] since she was a graduate of the program:

As one of the final steps in the analysis process, QUAL and the PG used peer checking to compare, contrast, discuss, and synthesize their separate analyses. This final step served to not only foster trustworthiness of data, but also afforded each participant-researcher the opportunity to explain her and his "take" on the data. It was found that QUAL and PG identified very similar themes with little variability in interpretation. This was encouraging not only because two different researchers were drawn to the same findings (and ultimate conclusions), but it also provided some assurance that oral coding yielded similar results as the transcription approach—a kind of concurrent validation. (Bernauer et al., 2013b, p. 182)

These findings were quite gratifying to me because, while very similar themes were identified, I was also able to experience a greater immersion in the actual vocal dialogue that took place in the interviews compared to my coresearcher, especially using steps 2–4 of oral coding. I assert that the elimination of word-for-word transcription did not reduce the trustworthiness or interpretations of the study compared to a traditional approach such as the ones used in phenomenological inquiry. In fact, I found that oral coding resulted in a greater sense of authenticity to me as the writer and also hopefully to my readers.

I also conducted a second study with oral coding (Bernauer, 2015b) just prior to its codification into seven steps. In this study, I interviewed ten graduates of Catholic schools across generations to inquire about their remembrances and reflections of their schooling experiences. These ten participants graduated from Catholic high schools between 1954 and 2000. This rather large range of graduation dates resulted, not surprisingly, in some quite diverse views. However, there were also poignant themes that were identified across generations including academics, faith, and why (or why not) they sent their own children to Catholic schools or planned (or not) to do so in the future.

I found that, because of the extended time listening to the recordings of these ten participants, I came to share deeply in their remembrances and reflections about Catholic schooling. Due to my immersion in the recorded interviews as described in the seven steps above, I was able to experience what seemed like an ongoing continuation of the original conversation with participants, and I was becoming more comfortable with oral coding. It is again the extended connection of researcher to participants through continued intimacy with the original voices of participants that I believe is the essence of this coding method.

Exemplar

I recently had an opportunity to use oral coding to analyze data from interviews with faculty regarding their perceptions of their primary motivation to remain in higher education. Because this study is being completed just prior to writing this chapter, I think it offers a "real-time" examination of oral coding. There are four research questions in this study but the primary one is, "What motivators are the most important to faculty for continuing in their roles as university professors?" The eight faculty members I interviewed were purposely selected for this study to represent different academic disciplines as well as years of teaching experience. Although there are some disciplines (such as business, communication, and other areas in the social sciences) not currently represented in this study, I may decide later to interview professors in these disciplines to expand the current data base.

The data that I analyzed from interviews with two professors (ANTHRO and CHEM as their pseudonyms) using oral coding helped me understand faculty motivation based on both overlapping and nonoverlapping responses to the prompts I used to answer my research questions. It is also important to point out that analysis began concurrently with the interviews since the flexibility of qualitative inquiry allows us to avoid the rigidity of the traditional "siloing" of data collection, analysis, and interpretation practiced under the traditional quantitative paradigm. That is, as I use oral coding, I have begun to construct meanings and understandings built upon what I discerned during the actual interviews.

It is also important to note that, while research questions represent what we want to discover, interviews provide a way to go about that discovery. As such, I like to transform or unpack research questions into what I call "conversation prompts" that serve as a bridge between what we want to discover and the individuals from whom we learn things. While I developed conversation prompts based on four research questions, I have listed below only a subset that has connections to the research questions:

1. Now that we have begun this conversation and you have begun to think about motivation, what comes to mind as being important to you in terms of motivating you to continue to grow as a teacher and scholar?

2. Looking back, how would you describe how your motivation may have changed in terms of teaching and scholarly inquiry from the time you started teaching until now? What do you think were the major factors that may have influenced these changes?

3. If you had to identify the three most important factors that motivate you to continue to grow and to remain in teaching, what are they?

Prompts 1 and 2 were designed to elicit the kind of data needed so that I can include context and "thick description" (Geertz, 1973) in the final report. These initial prompts were also designed to set the tone for a *conversation* rather than a formal interview. Although in actual practice, I viewed all eight conversations as more of a gestalt using the seven steps in oral coding, I focus here on the anthropology faculty member (ANTHRO) for exposition and clarity.

Professor ANTHRO is a seasoned instructor and also has a significant publishing résumé. I was reminded again as I began this interview that analysis is concurrent with data collection, and steps 1 and 2 of the oral coding process should probably be amended to underscore this understanding.

Step 1

As I sat listening to Professor ANTHRO and recording his responses to the conversation prompts using GarageBand on my Mac laptop, it was apparent that here was a faculty member whose motivation emanated almost completely from a desire to continue to learn by engaging in individual and collaborative scholarly inquiry. One of the most salient responses by Professor ANTHRO when asked what he finds to be most motivating is, "What I find to be most interesting about things." He went on to say,

> I discovered that I probably had a research agenda about ten years after I started working in higher education. I do not go in search of publications for my latest article but I have what you might say is a continuum of research that I've been doing for a long time and when I go to conferences it is still a continuation of that. I find that any individual is indeed an information system and therefore is connected to computers broadly conceived.

Step 2

The initial understanding gleaned in step 1 was deepened as I listened to the recorded conversation the day following the interview. While I try to listen attentively to my informants as they respond to my questions, I have also found that the element of time allows for the fermentation of insights much like it makes for more mellow and refined wine. While listening again to the voice of ANTHRO, Maslow's Hierarchy of Needs came to mind and I mentally placed this informant on the highest level (Self-Actualization) of the original taxonomy (Maslow, 1968) as well as the highest level (creating) on the revised taxonomy (Anderson & Krathwohl, 2001). I also reflected that while I, like Professor ANTHRO, am a tenured professor and therefore have more latitude to pursue my scholarly and pedagogical interests, we soon forget that our nontenured colleagues are still very much concerned with promotion. Promotion entails accomplishing those things that will, one hopes, be looked upon favorably in relation to teaching, scholarship, and service (the triumvirate of tenure) that will presumably get them also to academic nirvana. "Publish or perish" is still a fairly accurate mantra. By listening deeply and over an extended period of time, I have found that self-reflexivity becomes more integrated with empirical data which I find akin to what happens after watching a favorite movie several times.

Step 3

Approximately five days after I finished the interviews, having completed steps 1 and 2, codes and concepts began to emerge in relation to the four research questions. I identified codes including SCHOLAR, TENURE, and FREEDOM, based on my immersion in the recorded conversations. These codes are certainly more inductive than deductive and probably arose due to a confluence of experience, values, and the voices of the informants themselves. While we as qualitative researchers must strive for accurate portrayals of our coresearchers (and I found that as this study progressed that the term "coresearcher" was more valid than either "participant" or "informant"), we must embrace that the comingling of objective data with subjective interpretation of these data is necessary since we as humans simply cannot admit inquiry that is "scientific" as capturing the essence of either ourselves or the phenomena we are investigating. These codes also led quite naturally to concepts and a deeper understanding of ANTHRO and his responses to each research question. They also began to shape the context for later interviews.

Step 4

I listened once again to all the interviews originally recorded on my laptop. When I got to ANTHRO's interview, I used my mobile phone recorder (QuickVoicePro) to rerecord those segments that struck me as especially descriptive of his responses to the conversation prompts. I suspect that I will identify both in vivo codes from this rerecording as well as quotes that I think will further illuminate this participant's perspectives. Listening yet again to my informant was in some ways like hearing it for the first time because, just like reading the same novel or seeing the same movie several times, this subsequent oral–aural encounter seemed to invite me to explore additional nuances. In this case, I noticed that the informant not only continued to describe his passion for scholarly inquiry in propositional terms but the very tone and cadence of his speech conveyed this same passion. Consequently, the code SCHOLAR now came to convey to me not only propositional language meaning but also a more tacit understanding intuited from voice and inflection (see Polanyi, 1958, 1966). I also recorded my own reflections on the mobile phone recorder directly following these rerecorded participant segments in order to further facilitate the process of interpretation, meshing empirical data with my growing understanding of these data. For example, in response to conversation prompt 3, regarding motivation in relation to professional growth, ANTHRO responded that his major motivator was "what I find to be interesting about things." After recording this segment, I commented that "His response is consistent with his focus on learning and scholarship with no concern for advancement or other rewards—of course, having attained tenure, such 'need' motivators are notably muted which contrasts with the responses of some of the newer faculty." After I complete this process for all eight interviewees, I will have finished second-round coding.

Step 5

I began to write an abstract as the step suggests and this is what I have developed thus far:

The purpose of this case study was to investigate what motivates higher education faculty to continue in their chosen profession at a doctoral-granting, medium-sized university located in the mid-Atlantic region of the US. In-depth interviews were conducted with eight faculty members from different academic disciplines and with varying years of experience. It was learned that, while extrinsic motivators such as salary and promotions are indeed important, the primary motivating factor cited by faculty is their continuing intrinsic desire to strive for excellence in teaching and scholarship.

It is important to note that the finding regarding the role of extrinsic motivators is an emerging one and this may change as I move forward. However, I do believe that researchers know more than they think they know, and I have learned to trust my own instincts as I move along in trying to understand a study. I also think that by writing early drafts of the abstract, it serves as a reciprocating influence on my interpretive thinking as I am writing up the final article. That is, repeated listening to informants serves to shape and reshape the abstract which, in turn, shapes and reshapes my writing.

Step 6

I created a consolidated file, a Word document where research questions serve as the major headings and where the text under each of these research questions is obtained from the reduced recording produced in step 4. As a reminder, the reduced oral file in step 4 resides on my mobile phone recorder and contains both selected participant responses to each conversation prompt (which in turn reflects a specific research question), as well as my reflections about those responses. If we view the entire process as a funnel, the whole process from step 1 to step 6 is designed to both reduce and distill the data that were collected in response to each research question into a continuum, culminating in findings and interpretations as well as simultaneously refining the abstract. These steps were also designed to keep the aural–oral component active throughout these steps to more authentically capture what participants said and how they said it.

Step 6 of the oral coding process leads directly to writing the final report because the "consolidated file" incorporates and reflects the intimacy that was nurtured by an immersion in participant voices. I used Dragon Dictate to "listen" to my reduced file on my mobile phone recorder and to transcribe from voice to text. While I have found voice recognition software to be helpful, it is not an error-free process and transcriptions must be closely monitored and corrected (using such software is optional).

Along with highlighting the responses of ANTHRO, I have tentatively written the following as part of his response to a primary research question:

ANTHRO strongly voiced his desire to "connect my teaching with scholarly inquiry." It is becoming apparent that for him (and possibly some others), teaching and research go hand-in-hand and that he simply could not conceive of doing one without the other. There does not seem to be any bifurcation in terms of teaching and scholarly inquiry, but rather teaching is seen as an opportunity to share his research with students and also as an opportunity to discover new ideas for his research from his students.

I have found that, just like a great movie or novel that engages us to the point where we feel ourselves to be a part of the story and perhaps identify with a particular character, deep repetitive listening at this stage serves to create a shared "lived experience" with informants. In the case of ANTHRO, I found myself understanding him in a way that I don't think I would have attained using traditional transcription and coding techniques. It has also become apparent to me upon reflection that, as I listened to him, I could sense that he too found himself understanding things about himself that, while he may have known tacitly, now became clearer to him as he articulated some of his deepest-held values and passions. I intend to continue this same process for each research question and participant drawing heavily on each of their consolidated files.

Step 7

While following steps 1–6 does not result in the final report writing itself, I am finding that as I continue to mine the consolidated file in step 6 in concert with modifying the abstract, I can begin to see the emerging themes and important findings from the study. Regarding the abstract, at the time of this writing this is what I have thus far:

> The purpose of this case study was to investigate how faculty across schools within a doctoral-granting medium-sized university in the Northeast describe their motivation for continuing to teach and conduct scholarly inquiry and what universities can do to sustain this motivation. This case study is based on in-depth interviews with eight faculty across nine disciplines with differing years of teaching experience. The most important finding is that faculty are overwhelmingly motivated to excel in teaching and scholarship due to intrinsic rather than extrinsic motivating factors and that there exists a deep passion among faculty to make a difference. While salary and promotions are appreciated, the primary motivating factor cited by faculty is their desire to continue to strive for excellence in teaching and scholarship. While all faculty valued scholarly inquiry, some felt that it was weighted too heavily in promotion decisions in relation to teaching and service. One particularly relevant suggestion is to provide faculty with a teaching or research path to tenure since trying to do both well is seen by some participants as extremely challenging, and for universities to provide ongoing mechanisms to support collegial teaching and scholarship.

My first draft of this abstract (Step 5), while containing some elements of this more current rendition (such as the purpose, demographics, methodology, and even my guess that intrinsic motivation would outweigh extrinsic motivation), one of the most important additions is the term "passion" came especially to the fore based on deep listening to ANTHRO. As I think about it now, writing an abstract early on in the research endeavor is akin to using a kind of "deductive coding" that has been drawn from our own experiences and insights, while revisions to the abstract arise from a kind of "inductive coding" based on both what our informants have shared with us as well as our own coconstruction of what they have revealed during the interview. I have also found that as data analysis based on oral coding continues, it becomes paired with data synthesis. The creative process continues as we write, while writing continues to reveal new insights.

Hopefully this authentic example has demonstrated the process of oral coding. I do not view the seven steps as "cast in concrete" or rigid, but rather as a malleable medium, sensitive and responsive to the ideas and insights of others who try this process.

Conclusion

Oral coding offers both potential benefits as well as challenges to individuals who decide to use it. Let's begin by first looking at the potential benefits.

I developed oral coding because I felt a simultaneous desire to capture and retain the aural–oral nature of interviews as long as possible, as well as to reduce the need for word-for-word transcription. I have found that extended exposure to the actual voices of participants as incorporated into the oral coding process conveys inflections, pauses, distastes, and even humor to me more authentically than transcribed text. It also recreates a mental picture in my mind of the actual interview as it took place, something like a video and audio rerun of the interview event. I am certain that researchers who rely on written transcriptions also experience such multimedia moments but, for me, the oral coding process is more powerful. The entire process has helped me connect research questions to both findings and interpretations in a more seamless manner. Finally, I have discovered that the seven steps also help me to craft a final report that seems more alive because it echoes the voices of participants more clearly and authentically.

As with most approaches to coding, there are some drawbacks and challenges to consider. Oral coding needs to be thought of as malleable so that users can customize the process to fit their own unique ways of transforming data into written accounts. I have found that using oral coding lends vibrancy to the act of transforming data into accounts and that, while we who engage in qualitative inquiry do not rely on statistical methods to assess validity, I have found that oral coding results in accounts that are more *authentic* because of deep listening which I personally find to be a more satisfying criterion than any statistical measure. Wolcott (1990) advises to "talk little, listen a lot" as his first criterion for seeking validity (pp. 126–128), and I believe that this captures the essence of oral coding.

Supplemental Readings

Bernauer, J. A., Bernauer, M. P., & Bernauer, P. J. (2017). A family affair: Caring in teaching and implications for teacher and researcher preparation. *Brock Education Journal, 26*(2), 4–15.

Paulus, T., Lester, J. N., & Dempster, P. (2014). *Digital tools for qualitative research.* SAGE.

Wolcott, H. F. (1994). *Transforming qualitative data: Description, analysis, interpretation.* SAGE.

Reflection and Activities

1. After reading this chapter, how would you compare oral coding to other approaches for analyzing and interpreting interview data in terms of its potential to yield credible and trustworthy findings? Consult other sources to provide additional context. Two possible sources include:

    a. Kvale, S., & Brinkmann, S. (2014). *InterViews: Learning the craft of qualitative research interviewing* (3rd ed.). SAGE.

    b. Saldaña, J. (2016). *The coding manual for qualitative researchers* (3rd ed.). SAGE.

2. Identify a topic and a related field site, then discuss how you might integrate observational data with interview data using oral coding.

3. With a team of 3–4 members, identify a phenomenon of mutual interest and three possible research questions. Next, identify a participant who is "in the know" regarding the phenomenon and who might be willing to be recorded for a 20–30 minute interview. After the interview is completed, ask several members of your team to analyze the data using the seven steps of oral coding while the other members analyze the data with a different method. Write a brief report using an agreed-upon format. Finally, discuss and compare your findings. What are the benefits of the deep listening required by oral coding?

References

Agar, M. H. (1980). *The professional stranger: An informal introduction to ethnography.* Academic Press.

Anderson, L. W., & Krathwohl, D. R. (Eds.). (2001). *A taxonomy for learning, teaching, and assessing: A revision of Bloom's taxonomy of educational objectives.* Longman.

Bernauer, J. A. (2015a). Opening the ears that science closed: Transforming qualitative data using oral coding. *The Qualitative Report, 20*(4), 406–416. https://nsuworks.nova.edu/tqr/vol20/iss4/3

Bernauer, J. A. (2015b). Reflections on Catholic education in the USA: A dialogue across generations from the 1950s to the 2000s. *International Studies in Catholic Education*, 1–20. https://doi.org/10.1080/19422539.2014.998500

Bernauer, J. A., Lichtman, M., Jacobs, C., & Robertson, S. (2013a). Blending the old and the new: Qualitative data analysis as critical thinking and using NVivo with a generic approach. *The Qualitative Report, 18*, 1–10. http://www.nova.edu/ssss/QR/QR18/bernauer2.pdf

Bernauer, J. A., Semich, G., Klentzin, J. C., & Holdan, E. G. (2013b). Themes of tension surrounding research methodologies education in an accelerated, cohort-based doctoral program. *International Journal of Doctoral Studies, 8*, 173–193. http://ijds.org/Volume8/IJDSv8p173-193Bernauer0397.pdf

Creswell, J. W., & Plano-Clark, V. L. (2011). *Designing and conducting mixed methods research* (2nd ed.). SAGE.

Geertz, C. (1973). Thick description. Toward an interpretive theory of culture. In C. Geertz (Ed.), *The interpretation of cultures* (pp. 3–30). Basic Books.

Guba, E. G. (1981). Criteria for assessing the trustworthiness of naturalistic inquiries. *Eric/ECTJ Annual Review Paper, 29*(2), 75–91.

Lincoln, Y. S., & Guba, E. G. (1985). *Naturalistic inquiry*. SAGE.

Mann, T. (1924; 1981). *The magic mountain*. The Franklin Library.

Maslow, A. H. (1968). *Toward a psychology of being* (2nd ed.). Van Nostrand.

Moustakas, C. E. (1994). *Phenomenological research methods* (6th ed.). SAGE.

O'Dwyer, L. M., & Bernauer, J. A. (2014). *Quantitative research for the qualitative researcher*. SAGE.

Onwuegbuzie, A. J., & Johnson, R. B. (2006). The validity issue in mixed research. *Research in the Schools, 13*(1), 48–63.

Polanyi, M. (1958). *Personal knowledge: Towards a post-critical philosophy*. University of Chicago Press.

Polanyi, M. (1966). *The tacit dimension*. University of Chicago Press.

Poth, C. N. (2018). *Innovation in mixed methods research*. SAGE.

Saldaña, J. (2016). *The coding manual for qualitative researchers* (3rd ed.). SAGE.

Wolcott, H. F. (1990). On seeking—and rejecting—validity in qualitative research. In E. W. Eisner, & A. Peshkin (Eds.), *Qualitative inquiry in education: The continuing debate* (pp. 121–152). Teachers College Press.

Wolcott, H. F. (2009). *Writing up qualitative research* (3rd ed.). SAGE.

Mapping Trajectories: Analyzing Focus Group Data Rhizomatically

Alyson Welker and George Kamberelis

Abstract

This chapter analyzes focus group data rhizomatically, a process designed to surface intra-actions and relations among intra-actions that constitute assemblages that come close to capturing the becomings of complex objects of study. Using the construct of "answerability," we explain why focus groups are especially useful for understanding relations between individuals and the social formations to which they belong. The quasi-unique affordances of focus groups as data collection tools inform our brief introduction to "postqualitative" inquiry, the ethico-onto-epistemology within which we situate our work. Operating within this theory–method assemblage, we subsequently provide an introduction to the new materialist philosophies of Gilles Deleuze and Felix Guattari and Karen Barad coupled with a description of "mapping," which is the primary theoretically-informed strategy we deploy in our work. Our chapter offers guidance to readers who may wish to use this "mapping" antimethod to analyze and interpret focus group data and relevant theoretical constructs.

Keywords: Rhizomatic networks; intra-actions; data mapping; thinking with theory; assemblages

In their infancy, "focus groups were simply extensions of interviews meant to elicit individual opinions" (Kamberelis & Dimitriadis, 2013, p. 3). As notions of focus groups, interviews, and qualitative inquiry continued to push the boundaries of ontological reasoning, so too did the need for the dense interpretive work that often accompanies such modes of inquiry:

> Let us not forget that focus groups can and have encompassed a wide range of discursive practices—from formal structured interviews with particular people assembled around clearly delimited topics to less formal, more open-ended conversations with large and small groups that can unfold in myriad and unpredictable ways. (Kamberelis & Dimitriadis, 2013, p. 4)

Indeed, because of their quasi-unique affordances, focus group conversations generate exciting material for expanding modes of inquiry beyond traditional notions of qualitative inquiry, or what is now commonly called postqualitative inquiry (e.g., St. Pierre, 2014). Key among these quasi-unique affordances is "indexicality" (or the possible relational connections between/among data), thus "pointing to" the unsaid (and even the unlived) that might be identified and produced. Additionally, focus groups elicit "breakdowns" (or conscious interruptions to the common autopilot mode that characterizes typical human activity) which, as Heidegger taught us, are crucial to human understanding and interpretation. Focus groups also instigate "memory synergy" among participants, disclosing the richness, complexities, and nuances of the phenomena under study. Memory synergy occurs when a group of people who have a shared common experience recall it together to more fully understand the nature of the experience collectively. Focus groups also promote "political" synergy among participants, thus becoming tools for advocacy and social change efforts.

To understand the generative affordances of focus group data requires mapping multiple and various vectors of force. Thinking metaphorically, we use the mathematical concept of the vector here quite intentionally (though not exactly as mathematicians or physicists use it). Vectors have both directionality and intensity (strength). Imagine multidimensional space filled with an ever-emerging set of vectors of varying intensities moving in various directions. As these ever-emerging vectors traverse the space and interact with each other, these interactions continuously produce new realities. In Karen Barad's (2007) lexicon, vectors are more or less the same as "agents of intra-action" (see below), and the ways they affect each other as they interact are similar too.

Interlude: Postqualitative Inquiry

There are many books (e.g., Jackson & Mazzei, 2011; Thomas, Bellingham, & Murphy, 2020) and many articles (e.g., Lather & St. Pierre, 2013) devoted to explaining what postqualitative research is about, and we encourage our readers to explore some of them. Still, it seems important here to outline key elements of this form of inquiry because it informs our analyses and interpretations. Postqualitative inquiry is an expanded mode of inquiry predicated on becoming rather than being.

As such, it resists closure; it invites us to think, feel, and act differently during every moment of the inquiry process. Postqualitative inquiry does not privilege objective knowledge and truth, but instead embraces the inseparability of ethics, ontology, and epistemology or what Barad (2007, p. 409) has called "ethico-onto-episte-mology." Postqualitative inquiry rejects predefined or prefigured methods, and it is opposed to the idea that faithful adherence to specific coding and analysis procedures ensures trustworthy findings. Because reality and human understanding are ever-becoming, postqualitative inquiry is unfinalizable and nontotalizing; thus Deleuze and Guattari (1987) referred to such inquiry as "antimethod" and Lather called it "a thousand tiny methodologies" (2013, p. 635). The researcher's task is to produce new understandings of reality rather than simply to represent it with language or other semiotic systems. This expanded mode of inquiry involves resisting the "habitual reading of data" (Lather & St. Pierre, 2013, p. 639); it involves generating readings from multiple perspectives and thinking with data and theory simultaneously to produce new insights, even new realties. Given these characteristics, postqualitative inquiry encourages us to experiment and to look for transformative potentials; it urges us to imagine and enact new ways of being and produce new discursive and material realities.

Answerability and Focus Group Work

The work in this chapter builds on previous focus group work (e.g., Kamberelis & Dimitriadis, 2013; Kamberelis, Dimitriadis, & Welker, 2017). Previous conceptions of focus group affordances help us to outline the ways in which we have collected and analyzed data, as well as acknowledge the embedded historical experiences and connections of this work to previous times, authors, and projects. Focus groups, for example, embody Bakhtin's (1993) concept of answerability, which foregrounds the social fact that being and becoming are essential to understanding the realities we inhabit with others. In other words, our ideas change when we respond to one another as opposed to just thinking with and for ourselves. Considering collective risks and rewards as opposed to individual risks and rewards becomes an important aspect of focus groups because "only within relationships of answerability can individuals (with others) embrace or resist the historical or cultural realities in which they find themselves" (Kamberelis & Dimitriadis, 2013, pp. 92–93). This is an important part of any research project as well as any educational enterprise. Focus groups also help keep the focus on the whole rather than its parts because they are predicated on the social fact that, as Bourdieu (1977) taught us, individuals are deeply rooted in the social fields to which they belong and are constructed within the discourses and practices of those fields:

> The self is a particular configuration of discursive and material practices that is constantly working on itself—constructing, deconstructing, and reconstructing itself in and by multiple discourses and social practices, their

effects, and the ways they intersect, transverse, and challenge one another. (Kamberelis & Scott, 1992, p. 5)

Because the self is always already imbricated in the social and its discursive and material practices, focusing on the group is crucially important.

Conceptual Framework

Focus group data are indexical; their full meanings depend upon contextual information. Therefore, the more data the better. According to Barad "[context] presumes there is an object that exists apart from its environment or surroundings and that this environmental context matters in some way" (Barad, 2007, p. 459). The focus group we discuss in this chapter does not stand alone but instead is situated within a larger set of data that include, among other things, the histories of the individual persons involved, the genres of art/writing/creation consumed and produced, the concept of place, the university/city/state where the work occurred, and the participants' notions of time/current events/known and unknown histories. Figure 11.1 can be used to understand how we (the researchers) framed and reframed the meanings and meaning potentials of focus group data throughout the mapping process; as such, it is a model for imagining how other researchers might engage in similar processes.

Utilizing tools from Barad and Deleuze and Guattari (or other theorists), data analysis and interpretation becomes a matter of mapping. For this project, the data were almost limitless and required a layering or topographical approach to generating understandings. Whereas other forms of data may be linearly placed or categorized into clear boxes, focus group data are typically messy and defy boundaries—bubbling over with potential connections and meanings, and indexing all kinds of other data that must be chased down and considered.

Mapping as/is Thinking/Understanding Rhizomatically

Mapping (or rhizomatic analysis) is a sociological, postqualitative approach to generating understanding that involves creating layered maps from focus group transcripts and the phenomena they index. These maps make visible the interactions among varying forces at play. Interactions as Foucault has taught us, produce social realities in unpredictable but specific ways that may be understood after the fact (i.e., historically). Like most postqualitative approaches, mapping rhizomatic formations has no prefigured set of procedures for interpretation and knowledge production. Similarly, one need not read this chapter linearly from beginning to end. Instead one may begin with any section, read the sections in any order, and read the sections in a different order at another time. Indeed, the chapter was organized to be read rhizomatically.

FIGURE 11.1 ● Conceptual Framework

Conceptual Framework

When thinking post-qualitatively, researchers deploy the concepts below as they "think with theory" to understand and interpret the data before them. Turning and returning to these terms can help create trustworthy, though unfinalizable, interpretations.

- **Becoming**, as opposed to being, focuses on unique connections among data (especially intra-actions) that make visible the continuous production of reality (e.g., self, social formations, world, etc.).

- **Lines of flight** occur from within the map when rhizomes explode into new possible realities that are both disconnected to but also always connected to what came before. The construct of the **rhizome** is one of connection, which includes both close, overlapping clusters and far-reaching leaps and lines. Unlike a root structure, a rhizome can shoot up and spread out into new shapes or forms at any given time. To think rhizomatically is to think productively rather than representationally. . . to think about how connections produce new realties rather than representing what was and is already "there."

- **Mapping** is the process of understanding data in non-linear and largely visual (spatial) ways. Maps can have depth and peaks; maps can expand in all directions. Similar to roads that connect faraway places to one another, the various lines that constitute maps can reach across far distances and connect with each other to create new realities with new meanings . . . infinitely. Think, for example, of how the production of geographic maps creates new nations and relations among existing nations. Think also about how different nations produce different maps of the same basic geographical spaces, thus producing different realties with different social, political, and economic effects.

- The concept of **intra-actions** arises out of Karen Barad's ontological notion of **agential realism**, which assumes that matter-in-the-process-of-becoming creates inexhaustible, dynamic agencies that allow for on-going reconfigurations of the world (Barad, 2007, p. 170). Barad's "intra-actions" thus function like Deleuze and Guattari's "rhizomes."

The overall goal of this type of mapping is to make visible as many intra-actions as possible that contribute to understanding how social phenomena came to be organized (and often naturalized) historically. Mapping is thus a socio-cultural-historical-linguistic "antimethod" that encourages researchers to "think with theory" to identify what Deleuze and Guattari (1987) have called molar lines (lines of rigid segmentarity; elements that embody and support taken-for-granted or received perspectives and are thus very durable), molecular lines (lines of supple segmentarity; elements of majority perspectives that are not totally sedimented and can shift or change as they interact with other lines or vectors), and lines of flight (lines of potential change; or those that break free from what's expected or assumed to produce reality in new ways) revealed in talk, social interaction, and relevant cultural artifacts indexed in participants' discursive and material practices.

Additionally, as an analytic strategy, mapping invites researchers to construct constellations of unpredictable, ceaseless, and ever-changing connections among these various "lines" to provide accounts or readings of social phenomena and social formations both as they exist in the present and how they have changed (or not changed) over time. Finally, mapping encourages researchers to write up research findings in nonlinear ways to foreground the contingent, self-organizing nature of the phenomena under study. The overall goal of this postqualitative approach is to imagine and produce new ways of being, new social formations, and new versions of reality.

Our decision to use mapping (or rhizomatic analysis) for this project was largely motivated by the nature of our *exemplar* study and the data it yielded. Figure 11.2 represents a summary of the most important takeaways we learned from engaging in this type of analysis.

In the remainder of this chapter we walk readers through the processes of our nonlinear analysis of a focus group we conducted (and other data indexed by the event). We hope this "walk-through" will help motivate researchers to play with their data in new and insightful ways as they embrace this uncommon paradigm (e.g., new materialism, postqualitative inquiry). Thus, we intentionally communicate the processes and the decisions we made along the way. We hope others may generate similar strategies to understand their data with new eyes and in new ways to produce new knowledge, while understanding most (maybe all) knowledge is contextual, contingent, partial, perspectival, and dynamic.

Exemplar

In the remainder of this chapter we unpack our analyses and interpretations of focus group data from a museum-based study of college students in an honors course exploring the relations between consuming and producing art and exploring cultural identity. We have data from four iterations of this course. However, to

FIGURE 11.2 ● Plan of Action

Plan of Action

This figure describes our research process. Although discursive accounts suggest that such processes are linear, they are not. These "steps" may occur in any order (some are iterative, some occur simultaneously, some might not have happened had we made different choices); there are always multiple entry points and multiple pathways that might be pursued.

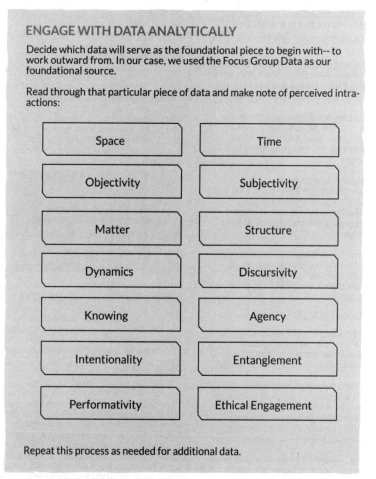

ENGAGE WITH DATA ANALYTICALLY

Decide which data will serve as the foundational piece to begin with-- to work outward from. In our case, we used the Focus Group Data as our foundational source.

Read through that particular piece of data and make note of perceived intra-actions:

Space	Time
Objectivity	Subjectivity
Matter	Structure
Dynamics	Discursivity
Knowing	Agency
Intentionality	Entanglement
Performativity	Ethical Engagement

Repeat this process as needed for additional data.

(Continued)

FIGURE 11.2 ● (Continued)

BUILD MAP FOUNDATION

- Pull intra-actions out of the data and situate them onto a plane to begin the creation of a map-of-becoming. These foundational data serve as the base-layer of the map.

- After laying the foundation, layer the intra-actions from all other data that intersect, oppose, call into question, or emerge to create new meanings in relation to the foundational layer.

(RE)MAPPING THE LAYERS

- Leave and return to the intra-actions with fresh eyes. Draw or create various types of lines across and between the intra-action locations on the map.

- Create layers of intra-actions as you return to the full data set to look for smaller, less obvious intra-actions. Notice the rhizomes beginning to emerge.

- Leave the data and return again. Where are intra-actions layered thickly? Where are intra-actions webbed heavily with connectivity? Engage with the rhizomes that have emerged.

- Know that this process could repeat indefinitely, but that once learned insight and new knowledge are produced, syntheses can arise organically.

RHIZOMATIC REFLECTION

- Reflect upon the entanglements of data (in our case, the authors, artists, classmates, facilitators, personal experiences and memories).

- Create a coherent (but never finalized) set of findings to share with others by interpreting the new knowledge(s) produced, the new meanings made, and the continual becomings indexed in/by the data.

- Move beyond description and identify thematic and synthesized insights.

THINKING WITH THEORY

Throughout the research process, it is important to remember that maps have multiple entryways (Deleuze & Guattari, 1987) and that there is not one right place to start.

It may be helpful to imagine a natural plant when embarking upon the thinking with theory process. "One will bolster oneself directly on a line of flight enabling one to blow apart strata, cut roots, and make new connections . . . a tree branch or root division may begin to burgeon into a rhizome" (Deleuze & Guattari, 1987, p. 15).

This burgeoning or rapid development occurs as all data are related to the foundational data of the focus group. Using this mapping strategy, the data burgeon into an entirely new plural phenomenon that allows for actions of material and non-material agencies to be applied, where possible, to any and all connecting agencies in relation to the focus group data.

The above image is one example of this burgeoning as it occurred in our exemplar. This portion of our map helps to illustrate the idea that "the coordinates are determined not by theoretical analysis implying universals but by a pragmatics composing multiplicities or aggregates of intensities" (Deleuze & Guattari, 1987, p. 15).

There are infinite ways in which a map can be composed as long as it continues to serve the purpose of locating new places and spaces within the data landscape so they may be returned to again and again. Think about the ways in which this process could have unfolded differently and/or could continue indefinitely. Notice how once learned insights and new knowledges are produced, possible syntheses emerge organically.

demonstrate the depth and detail that is typically produced through rhizomatic analytic work, and given the limited space of this chapter, we have chosen to focus on one particular student (Marcella) from one focus group from one iteration of the course. This single focus group was conducted near the end of the semester and included a facilitator, Marcella (our focal student), and two other students.

Our analytic goal for this particular study was to understand the process of identity transformation or becomings, given the set of opportunities provided by the layers of intra-actions that became embedded within varying plateaus embodied in and indexed by the focus group conversation. We began our analytic work looking at the focus group conversation; those data compelled us to look at other data including artwork in the museum where the class was held, art talks, students' written reflections on exhibits in the museum, students' art journaling, student-produced artwork, and whole-class discussions about each students' artwork. Because the course asked students to reflect upon their cultural identities in the context of art making and art viewing, most (probably all) students developed more complex and less tacit ways of understanding who they were and who they were becoming. Among other things, we found that focus group data are especially useful for understanding "how the self develops in and through its relationships with other selves" (Kamberelis & Dimitriadis, 2013, p. 92), as well as in and through relationships with other materials (texts, settings, artwork, etc.).

Connecting Theory/Strategy/Practice

Thinking with theory affords the opportunity to make visible that which cannot be seen when data are forced into naturalized categories and false continuities. In *Cinema II*, Deleuze (1989) describes the challenges associated with "situations which we no longer know how to react to, in spaces we no longer know how to describe" (p. xi). Mapping focus group data is an approach that allows for uncertainty and even expects it. Mapping focus group data is a complex process that draws on both arts-based methods and writing as thinking. The map is created by the need to build an apparatus from which to look for intra-actions (see Figures 11.3 and 11.5); in our case, the map facilitated the process of looking for how agencies intra-acted with how participant(s) chose to act and intra-act within the focus group, the course itself, and beyond.

As we worked our way out from mapping focus group content, we began to see intensities that appeared to be talking to one another across time and space. For example, Marcella seemed confident in her position regarding what the course had taught her about art and identity when she responded to the facilitator's questions during the focus group conversation. However, going back through her class journal (which she began nearly four months earlier), Marcella had very different ideas about identity and art that contradicted her focus group statements. This led us to chase down further assigned readings, artist/gallery visit field notes, and class

FIGURE 11.3 ● Rhizomatic Mapping Exemplar

Rhizomatic Mapping Exemplar

For this project, we focused our research on data collected from a focus group conversation that took place toward the end of the experimental course. The focus group transcripts served as the base layer, or the foundation, of our created map; we then worked through our other data (especially art journals and students' final projects). This process allowed us to see what actions and activities might have intra-acted within and among the individual students as they worked to present their selves-as-becomings to others within focus group interactions.

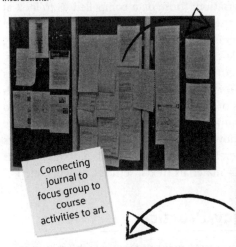

This is the beginning of our map that was created with focus group transcripts only (what we call our base layer or foundation). Many constellations were formed as pieces of the transcript were re-printed and overlapped in various locations as intra-actions emerged.

Connecting journal to focus group to course activities to art.

The map expands as other data (such as the student journals, lectures, and activities) are layered rhizomatically onto focus group data, thus creating molar lines, molecular lines, and lines of flight.

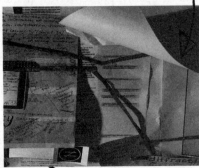

A thickening of the layers in the map indicates a rhizome of intra-actions. These thick phenomena often lead to rich insights where new knowledge is produced. In our study, these thick rhizomes marked space for the continual becomings of the participants to be indexed.

(Continued)

FIGURE 11.3   ●   (Continued)

Facilitator: [...]In what ways do think visual art has the power to evoke memories, meanings and emotions that language, talk and text, do not?[...]

Hallie: I'm kind of the opinion that visual, that an effective use of literary expression and an effective use of visual art that can both express the exact same thing and neither one is necessarily better but just as far as me personally I'm more effective at expressing things visually than I am with words. Even when I use words because I write poetry, uhm, I really heavily on images and so it's one of those things that like where I don't necessarily think that visual art has anything that it can communicate <u>better</u> or more effectively than the written word can but they just do it in completely different way, but that whole like Burtynsky versus the short story thing, like both had very heavy thoughts and both get you really into the depth of the matter, but they do it in different ways. Obviously it would be really difficult to have a story, and a photograph that expressed the <u>exact</u> same thing, but for what they're both trying to express I don't that either one does it necessarily better, they just do it completely differently.

Hazy: That makes a lot of sense, and I think that people probably will say, visual, definitely 100%, and you're going to find people that say literary works are the way to go, and it's just a preference.

Marcella: Yeah, I was thinking about that question, I'm thinking okay, well, with words, there's like a finite number of meanings to what you're saying, like words have double meanings, you can be very sarcastic or something but there's a finite number of <u>things</u> that this sentence can mean, and I think about visual art and it can mean anything to anybody, every single person's going to come up to it with a different set of experiences and look at it differently, but I think that people can approach the written word like that as well, but again, like even though words, they have a specific definition and how they are arranged can mean a certain thing, I still think like visual art every person who approaches it will think of it differently and will interpret it differently and understand it differently.

Intra-actions reaching across these two focus group conversations (left and below):

Facilitator: [Tell me] how have the experiences in this class affected you or changed how you think about yourself. So you started out, knowing you were a scientist, I would imagine [addressing Marcella who laughs] pretty black and white as you just said, so how has this changed you?"

Marcella: Uhm, yeah, I try and think more, maybe openly, and pick up more on what people in art are expecting of me, not just when they concretely say, I want you to do this, not even just in classes but in social situations, the social expectations, I pick up more on what they want me to do about it than what they actually say, and I think it's helping me read beyond their expectations for me as a person better and helping me figure out things in a way, that not everything is explicitly put in front of me [...] Going back to the thinking about the world thing, another thing this class has shown me or has helped me think about is truly how interconnected everything is, like nothing stands by itself, nothing at all, like nothing is the sole reason for this or the sole cause, or the sole result of this, like everything has so many confounding factors in it that you can't really separate anything, there's too much that goes into building everything.

Answerability intra-acts across multiple planes to complete ideas.

Brian Dickerson's campus visit and artist talk became an intra-action of experience for Marcella. This experience intra-acted with Marcella's previous attitudes toward art, class, and identity. Interestingly, Marcella's response to the facilitator (above) seems to intra-act with Marcella's previous experiences. This is demonstrated in her journal entry (below) where she considers her intra-action with art (material), artist talk (discursive), and the artist (human) agencies as an assemblage to her previous previously conceived self.

Artist Brian Dickerson

Marcella's Journal: "Our discussion with Brian Dickerson made me thing of how an artist takes their piece, something incredibly personal and close to the artists' heart, and release[s] it to the masses. I'm not sure I would be comfortable putting this thing I've created into the hands of strangers. You have no idea what they'll do with it, if your piece will be abused. The only thing one can be sure of is that they won't interpret it exactly the way one intended. There is too much room for interpretation, so the artist must take a leap of faith and put themselves, through their art, out into the world."

Artwork by
Brian Dickerson

"Bone grinds upon bone
Hanging in the air
Like a misshapen
windsock
Mocking me
...
More. More.
There's always more to
amputate
More that I can go
without
For the purpose of having
less."

--Marcella's Poem

transcripts to assemble, as best we could, the ways in which this multiplicity of layered experiences allowed for transformations of Marcella's understanding of art and identity.

When mapping focus group data, one cannot part with any data until after final (for now) interpretations are made. And even then, it is likely that researchers will not part with data and interpretations of data even if these do not end up in published accounts. In our case, we had difficulty parting with many journal entries and drawings Marcella had made about the power of art even though we do not include them here. The map in the researcher's mind can almost never fully be shared or explained; it is too large and too complex to be conveyed in linear (or even layered) text on a page.

The map itself becomes a work of art, an artifact with meanings and meaning potentials regarding the phenomenon under study. The researcher can share their material map, can place it in a gallery for others to view and make sense of, but unless viewers explore the data themselves and create their own maps, they will not fully understand the meanings (and surpluses of meaning) disclosed in and through the research process.

Engaging in Data and Theory-Informed Decision-Making

Engaging in intentional decision-making thus becomes an important part of the research process. Researchers must make decisions at every turn and return to data as they work to understand the stories they tell. For our project, we first had to decide to use the focus group transcript as our entry point for understanding the effects of the course we studied. This decision led us to understand the indexical nature of these transcripts—the other data they pointed to that we needed also to study. In other words, our focus group data formed a solid foundation for the work of chasing down and analyzing other data relevant to our research goal.

Antimethods and Antistrategies

In making the first and important decision to start with focus group data, theory played a central role. Because the course we collected data from was designed to help students reconsider their understanding of self through art, and because the focus group conversations were where students made pivotal transformations public, we decided to work backward to find as many possible "intra-actions" as we could that may have played a role in "identity becoming" processes. Moreover, focusing on material connected to one student (Marcella), we began to see how identity as an assemblage was coming into view based on all kinds of intra-actions. As we continued our analytic and interpretive work, we began to see how maplike assemblages evolved into rhizomic entanglements, which are nonhierarchical, social, and seemingly endless intra-actions of becoming. This process galvanized for us the fact that rhizomatic analysis was a most fitting strategy for our project.

In this regard, the ways in which Barad's work overlaps with the affordances of focus group research are many. Focus groups themselves resemble and simulate natural interactions among human (and sometimes nonhuman) agents; however, because focus group research leans toward the postqualitative end of the epistemological–ontological inquiry spectrum, it considers and incorporates the infinite inter- and intra-active potentials afforded by focus group data and the other data they index. As focus groups tend to shift the control of the research out of the hands of the researcher, modes of inquiry no longer drive the study, but rather unfold in the comfort/discomfort of the unknown:

> There are no solutions; there is only the ongoing practice of being open and live to each meeting, each intra-action, so that we might use our ability to respond, our responsibility, to help awaken, to breathe life into ever new possibilities. (Barad, 2007, p. x)

In relation to these issues, and as shown in Figure 11.4, we found it helpful to chart Barad's list of intra-actions to serve as a guide for looking at and across our

---

FIGURE 11.4 ● Intra-actions

Intra-actions

All elements in Barad's list of intra-actions may not be relevant to any given study. Thus, researchers need to figure out which intra-actions are present in their data set, as well as how these intra-actions function together to create a rhizomatic assemblage with unique affordances and constraints.

BARAD'S LIST OF INTRA-ACTIONS	OUR LIST OF INTRA-ACTIONS USED IN THE EXEMPLAR
• Space	• Space
• Time	• Time
• Matter	• Dynamics
• Dynamics	• Agency
• Agency	• Discursivity
• Structure	• Performativity
• Subjectivity	• Entanglement
• Objectivity	
• Knowing	
• Intentionality	
• Discursivity	
• Performativity	
• Entanglement	

specific constellations of data. We believe this practice would be useful in any focus group study (and some other kinds of studies as well).

Although these steps and the list of intra-actions appear linear, no one intra-action was more important than another when we created this figure. Further, the relations between intra-actions could not be prefigured. This "antimethod" of mapping is appropriate to use when focus group data are just one parcel of collected data (which is almost always the case in most social science research) and when these data index and are thus connected to other data necessary to capture the depth and complexity of the object of study. As we continued our interpretive work, each intra-action was almost never sectioned off or separate from other intra-actions. Intra-actions come together in the end and may or may not include all 14 types of intra-actions, listed above. Some intra-actions may be more powerful than other intra-actions, and deciding on the relative power of each intra-action and the relations among intra-actions is data-driven but also up to the researcher. Decisions are always unique to each project and require the researcher's insight and judgment; if they were not, we would be back to method as procedure (as in grounded theory or conversational analysis).

As we explored our data, we began to see how Marcella was diffractively becoming/practicing various selves in her journal entries, in conversations with others, and in relation to readings in the class, the artists' presentations, and the artists' works. Her answers, ideas, and perceptions shifted/diffracted as she listened to and reflected on the various voices, ideas, spaces, and materials with which/whom she intra-acted. For example, Marcella expressed her distaste for what she termed "dense metaphors" in one of her earliest journal entries. More specifically, when responding on an assigned reading that referred to the nervous system as "the organ of the mind" Marcella remarked, "Uh, you mean the brain? [...] The sensory system does not need culture to function. How dare you try to force your metaphysical theories on the laws of science!" Later on, however, Marcella composed another journal entry in which she embraced the use of metaphors for understanding:

> In a very abstract sense, I began to think about art as a sort of Russian doll. The object, or what the art depicts, in its most basic sense, is like a mask or a shell over the idea it represents. Although the object obscures what's underneath until you can remove it and see past it to the idea.

Finally, within the focus group conversation, Marcella took this shift in perspective even further when she claimed:

> ... with words, there's like a finite number of meanings to what you're saying, you know, like words have double meanings, you can be sarcastic or something but there's a finite number of things that this sentence can mean, and you know, I think about like, visual art and it can really mean anything to anybody, every single person's going to come

up to that with a different set of experiences and make them look at that [particular work] differently, but I think that people can approach the written word like that as well, but again, like even though words, they have a specific definition and how they are arranged can mean a certain thing…

This focus group reply combined both Marcella's frustration from earlier in the semester with her new understanding of words and their meaning potentials and is a brilliant and beautiful example of identity becomings. She wrestled with this idea out loud and seemed to work her way back through her previous journal entries in a way that assembled lines of flight reaching back and forth, talking to one another on the page in her journal, on the page of the transcript, and across her various experiences in the class.

Interestingly, all three students in the focus group had very different ideas written in their journals than what they expressed to one another in the focus group. As differences in opinions and ideas from these students (but specifically from Marcella) were chased down across the data, one could easily come to some conclusions about how other participant responses and facilitator questions/tones may have influenced the shifting perspectives and understandings that evolved through the conversation. For example, as a science major, Marcella seemed frustrated at times with the nature of this "artsy" course. Marcella's tone signaled annoyance in some of her first journal entries, as she asked questions of the authors and artists and wished their ideas could be conveyed more concretely and simply. However, after Marcella encountered another student's frustration with the facilitator's queries, she seemed to shift her attitudes and begin to see the benefits of complex, even ambiguous, renderings. It is likely that these shifts were working their way into Marcella's consciousness throughout the semester, but her participation in the focus group seemed to provide her with opportunities to play with these new understandings and to solidify some of them for herself and for others in ways that further affected the perspectives and understandings of the other participants and also the flow of the focus group conversation.

Strategies/Tactics for Postqualitative/Rhizomatic Analysis

As with more traditional analytic work (e.g., grounded theory, conversational analysis), memoing is a useful activity. More specifically, memos become key elements of maps. Memo writing begins upon the first read-through of data. Additionally, it is important to read through and create memos for data in the same order they will be mapped. In our case, we first read the transcripts of the focus group once without making any comments. In the second read, we made comments using the "review" function in MS Word.

Next, we printed transcripts and laid them out as the base layer or foundation of our map (recall Figure 11.3; see Figure 11.5). We found it useful to envision this base layer (metaphorically) as land at sea level. From this level, we could then add

FIGURE 11.5 ● Rhizomatic Mapping Redux

Rhizomatic Mapping Redux

As the theory suggests, "the rhizome pertains to a map that must be produced, constructed, a map that is always detachable, connectable, reversible, modifiable, and has multiple entryways and exits and its own lines of flight" (Deleuze & Guattari, 1987, p. 21). This means that the mapping process can start anywhere and can be revised, returned to, and/or renewed at any point during the construction phase.

When analyzing rhizomatic data, it can be helpful to consider the following:

- "The rhizome is composed not of units but of dimensions, or rather directions in motion." Try not to separate sections or paragraphs at this stage but to capture the stream of consciousness that is afforded by this thinking with theory process.

- "The rhizome has neither beginning nor end, but always a middle (millieu from which it grows and which it overspills)." Begin by considering interpretations of data with a continual flow of thought without interruptions, definitions, sense-making schema, or boundaries.

- Developing interpretations should and will undergo metamorphoses once they are returned to after the initial stream of consciousness process ends. This step can then be repeated until [unfinalizable] 'saturation' is reached or the researcher begins to make necessary interruptions that provide additional layers of context.

- "The rhizome connects any point to any other point." This means that researchers can play with the organization of interpretations in order to see additional connections between and among the intra-actions.

- A rhizome is: "all manner of 'becomings'"

(Deleuze & Guattari, 1987, p. 21)

(Continued)

FIGURE 11.5   ●   (Continued)

As we (the researchers) noticed these things happening, our understanding of the focus group conversations changed--often radically. For example:

Marcella created photography, drawing, writing, and poetry in the studio to translate her ideas, questions, and current understandings into material artifacts, from which emerged yet new understandings, new learning. Artwork became materiality that gave Marcella agency. Her material practices led to or were part of her continual becoming.

The various spaces of the course were also part of this process. The studio, the classroom, the galleries, the presentations/campus talks, the focus group rooms, etc. were all spaces that were above sea level on our map-of-becoming and can be viewed as sediments that formed the foundation for the work of both the individuals in the class and the class as a dynamic social formation.

Tangible materials used both by students and us as researchers included journals, final projects, images of the artwork/artists, lectures and discussions. Tangible intra-actions realized or indexed in focus group conversations connected art in the galleries, student artwork, course readings, student journals, etc.

The stories shared by students regarding their ancestors, their histories, their experiences, their expressed understanding of their identities, etc. each intra-acted in ways that contributed to the students' processes of becoming and new forms of agency.

Additionally, discursive intra-actions involving authors and readings (both in this class and in others) informed what individuals found significant, which contributed to transformations in the work they produced and the ways they thought about themselves. These intra-actions were agentic in that they formed and (re)formed students' beliefs and attitudes about art, about self, and about the purpose of the course.

The human agents (teachers, the researchers, the authors, the artists, and the other students) were intra-actions that exerted known and unknown effects on the thinking and doing of individual students and the class as a dynamic social formation. All individuals' goals, personal interests, time constraints, art-making, journal writing, rethinking assumptions, life histories (shared and not shared), and a host of other attributes and practices were intra-actions that contributed to the ever-expanding agencies of all parties involved.

Further, Marcella's own human intra-actions with herself continue to shift and shaped her identity by creating a space to name parts of herself . In her journal she wrote, "I love to get lost in thought, hold conversations with myself. I also leap at any chance to explore the sensory world in a new way, from a new perspective."

We used these characteristics of the rhizome to create a map of "exploring identity through the production and consumption of art."

To create this map we began with focus group transcriptions and connected all other data to them. We worked intentionally yet fluidly to create a rhizomatic assemblage that seemed to capture key becomings indexed in the focus groups and visible within other kinds of data. Importantly, we had to work hard not to categorize or constrain the potentials for becoming embodied in the data. With this in mind, neither the parts nor the connections of this rhizomatic assemblage are necessary or permanent; we might have foregrounded different parts of the data set, and we might have organized those parts differently because any assemblage is always already dynamic and changing.

or chart other data below and above sea level (i.e., that occurred before or after the focus group took place) as the map began to grow three-dimensionally. As hard copies of transcripts and related memos were layered onto a physical space, high-lighters, sticky notes, string, and paper clips served as modes of becoming related to interesting insights, questions, similarities, contradictory statements/moments, etc. As this analytic and interpretive work unfolded, the map grew as more connections were made with other data from the study being layered on top of, below, or perpendicular to certain parts of the transcripts—a process that sparked us to revisit and reconsider the focus group transcript many times. We engaged in this process of reading and mapping/remapping repeatedly—often adding typed memos, often printing out other data which had been collected and scanned onto two 128GB flash drives, such as handwritten notes and artifacts from Marcella's Art Journal, her final project, significant artists and artwork, significant readings and presentations, and conceptual ideas, including ones from the work of Barad and Deleuze & Guattari. In other words, this process of analysis and interpretation was iterative as analysis continued to inform analysis, and interpretation continued to inform interpretation as we continually revised our map and constructed our written account. We only stopped this process when we felt we had arrived at a point of cogent saturation: cogent because we felt we had captured our object of study reasonably and reasonably well; saturated because, like all deconstructive work, one needs to stop the analytic process at some point, despite knowing that the process is ultimately unfinalizable.

Literal lines of flight can be made with writing utensils, color-coordinated sticky notes, or even the detective-style yarn or cord. Sometimes the lines are left invisible but are verbally or visually noted across two of the plateaus that have formed. Plateaus are formed when layers occur in the charting of the map; these layers can be thin or thick, and a thicker layer does not necessarily mean a more important plateau. Sometimes, just three layers of sediment can form an important plateau to excavate. One important thing to note about the first step of laying the foundation of a focus group map is that rather than having the focus group transcript be the very bottom layer, it is helpful to have a blank layer accessible underneath the transcript or another way to hang or place layers before or behind the base layer of data. This helps to visualize what is at sea level (the base layer of data: the focus group transcript) while also allowing for there to be things below (before: in this study actions and activities that occurred prior to the focus group), beside (next to, or happening at the same time), or above (actions and activities that occurred after the focus group). The more layers, the denser the plateau is, as each memo or other data artifact acts as a metaphorically layer of sediment deposited over time.

The physical process of mapping printed, written, and visual data with other mapping artifacts (sticky notes, paper clips, tape, glue, etc.) was an important activity for this particular research endeavor—affording new meanings and phys-ical lines of flight to be detailed and processed in ways that would not have been possible with more linear or constricting materials and processes. (Layering documents on a computer, for example, does not allow for the rhizomes to visually burgeon into existence.)

Once a map is initially constructed (it is never "finished"), researchers typically look at their data for new ways of seeing the object of study. Because maps have multiple entryways, "one will bolster oneself directly on a line of flight enabling one to blow apart strata, cut roots, and make new connections […] a tree branch or root division may begin to burgeon into a rhizome" (Deleuze & Guattari, 1987, p. 15). This burgeoning occurs as all data are brought together and constructed relationally with focus group data. Using the mapping technique, the object under study often shape-shifts into something quite new because it now includes actions of material and nonmaterial agencies previously unseen. (If omniscience were possible, any and all agencies embodied in focus group transcripts and all other indexed data would be included.) Importantly, the process of analysis and interpretation involves returning to data many times.

Analyzing focus group data by mapping various intra-actions can lead to trajectories, ruptures, and appendages as researchers work through the meaning-making process of data interpretation. For this paper, we will focus primarily on trajectories.

Trajectories: Intra-actions Within Focus Group Conversations

Trajectories are vehicles for further analyzing and interpreting data being mapped. Trajectories for focus group data begin with focus group transcripts and move outward to other data indexed in the transcripts. As this happens, transcription meanings often change as additional data allow researchers to see their initial meanings in a different light. In our case, the path we hoped to follow involved understanding how student identities and cultural conceptions undertook transformative becomings as they intra-acted with one another in the focus group setting. However, when we added additional data to the mix, we had to consider additional pathways and alternative meanings. For example, Marcella participated in a focus group with two other students and a facilitator. The consistent actions (and concomitant forces/effects of those actions) involved the setting of the focus group, including the open-ended questions the facilitator asked. By projecting these actions onto the study/participants, we began to see how and where the purposes of the research and the needs of the participants intersected and acted upon one another.

Marcella's personal transformation was one trajectory visible within the focus group transcript. Further, intra-actions we noticed indexed related intra-actions in the larger dataset. For example, Mary, the facilitator, asked: "How have the experiences in this class affected you or changed how you think about yourself. So you started out, knowing you were a scientist, I would imagine [addressing Marcella who laughs] pretty black and white as you just said, so how has this changed you?" Marcella responded:

> This class has shown me or has helped me think about is, like, truly how interconnected *everything* is, like nothing stands by itself, nothing at all, like nothing is like the sole reason for this or the sole cause, or the sole result of this, you know, like everything has so many confounding factors in it that you can't really separate *anything* that has to stand alone, there's too much that goes into building everything.

This response demonstrates clear intra-actions with other experiences in the class that needed to be mapped and considered further within the overall interpretive process. Additionally, Marcella's response underscored the fact that focus group data cannot be viewed alone but must be considered in relation to other data they index.

Honoring Diverse Perspectives and Readings

The prior experiences the researcher/s bring to any dataset are limitless, and often consciously and subconsciously guide their thoughts and actions regarding data analyses and interpretations. In this regard, prior experiences rooted in unique life histories will likely lead different researchers in different directions, and these experiences need to be taken into consideration when looking at, interpreting, and constructing findings. In other words, researchers need to acknowledge their "experiential intelligence" and the enablements and constraints it imposes upon their positionalities, as well as their analyses and interpretations. In this regard, Barad (2007) argues for the importance of transparency on the part of the researcher—both to acknowledge and frame their work for others as entangled practices, and to acknowledge that "entangled practices matter: different intra-actions produce different phenomena" (p. 58).

Concluding Comments: Guidance of Sorts

As we have said several times, focus group content cannot be viewed alone (unless no other data were collected, which is usually not the case); it must be analyzed and interpreted in relation to the various intra-actions that occur across the numerous appendages of any given dataset. Additionally, "thinking with theory" adds content that may be included in the maps researchers construct. Paying attention to intra-actions that become visible as rhizomes develop can help push interpretations into new interdependent realms of possibility.

In our case, we had a focus group that took place toward the end of a semester-long course. Although the focus group transcript was our starting point and the main focus of our analytic work, we had to also acknowledge and chase down the many intra-actions it indexed and that were at play within the experiences of the students in the course: art materials, art journals, artwork, artists, teachers, other individuals, family histories, and more. Mapping these kinds of intra-actions allows researchers to effectively take many (though never all) moving parts into consideration. Again, the analytic and interpretive processes really could go on forever.

In this regard, Marcella wrote the following in her art journal: "I've always held the idea that I'll know where I belong when I arrive there." The process of mapping focus group intra-actions we have described in this chapter allowed us to view data repeatedly, and they looked somewhat different each time we return to our map(s). These kinds of returns and the differences they reveal often provide researchers with hints about which data are more important and which data are less important in constructing arguable yet unfinalizable accounts to be shared with others. There is almost never one clear route to take, but researchers come to know when they have arrived even though they also know that the end is never really the end (saturation's "new look").

"Thinking with theory" can be a challenging activity for novice social science researchers and researchers not well-versed in theory. We hope our presentation of postqualitative analytic and interpretive processes as largely a matter of thinking with theory provides inspiration for our readers to engage in some exciting and enlightening research endeavors. Our final piece of advice:

> Forget how research is 'supposed' to be.
>
> If you're moving toward closure (saturation),
>
> you're heading in the wrong direction.
>
> Turn around,
>
> but not before making forecasts;
>
> keep them as warning of overcrowded trails.
>
> Take time to follow more paths than necessary.
>
> Follow the rabbit down its deepest hole.
>
> This journey will take you to places you have not been,
>
> to places that didn't even exist before.

Supplemental Readings

Kamberelis, G., Dimitriadis, G., & Welker, A. (2018). Focus group research and/in figured worlds. In N. K. Denzin, & Y. S. Lincoln (Eds.), *The SAGE handbook of qualitative research* (5th ed., pp. 692–716). SAGE.

Hordvik, M., MacPhail, A., & Ronglan, L. T. (2019). Negotiating the complexity of teaching: A rhizomatic consideration of pre-service teachers' school placement experiences. *Physical Education and Sport Pedagogy, 24*(5), 447–462. https://doi.org/10.1080/17408989.2019.1623189

St. Pierre, E. A. (2019). Post qualitative inquiry in an ontology of immanence. *Qualitative Inquiry, 25*(1), 3–16. https://doi.org/10.1177/1077800418772634

Reflection and Activities

1. Print out a small portion of transcribed data and share it with multiple students. Ask them to create their own preliminary map of the data (students will likely need scissors, tape, and markers). Share maps with others when finished and note how any student's map can connect to any other student's map to create new rhizomatic networks of becoming. You will likely see that no map is better or worse than any other; any map can overlap another to undergo a metamorphosis of meaning to provide new and insightful revelations.

2. Read Chapter 7 from Jackson and Mazzei's (2011), *Thinking with Theory in Qualitative Research* to consider Barad's concept of intra-action as it is applied from another perspective. Explore your dataset for the intra-actions embodied within it.

References

Bakhtin, M. M. (1993). *Toward a philosophy of the act* (M. Holquist, Ed., V. Liapunov, Trans.). University of Texas Press.

Barad, K. (2007). *Meeting the universe halfway: Quantum physics and the entanglement of matter and meaning.* Duke University Press.

Bourdieu, P. (1977). *Outline of a theory of practice.* Cambridge University Press.

Deleuze, G. (1989). *Cinema II* (H. Tomlinson, & R. Galeta, Trans.). University of Minnesota Press.

Deleuze, G., & Guattari, F. (1987). *A thousand plateaus: Capitalism and schizophrenia* (B. Massumi, Trans.). University of Minnesota Press.

Jackson, A. Y., & Mazzei, L. (2011). Barad: Thinking with intra-action. In *Thinking with theory in qualitative research: Viewing data across multiple perspectives* (pp. 118–136). Routledge.

Kamberelis, G., & Dimitriadis, G. (2013). *Focus groups: From structured interviews to collective conversations.* Routledge.

Kamberelis, G., Dimitriadis, G., & Welker, A. (2017). Focus group research and/in figured worlds. In N. Denzin, & Y. Lincon (Eds.), *The SAGE handbook of qualitative research* (5th ed., pp. 692–716). SAGE.

Kamberelis, G., & Scott, K. D. (1992). Other people's voices: The coarticulation of texts and subjectivities. *Linguistics and Education, 4,* 359–402. https://doi.org/10.1016/0898-5898(92)90008-K

Lather, P., & St. Pierre, E. A. (2013). Post-qualitative research. *International Journal of Qualitative Studies in Education, 26*(6), 629–633. https://doi.org/10.1080/09518398.2013.788752

St. Pierre, E. A. (2014). A brief and personal history of post qualitative research: Toward "post inquiry." *Journal of Curriculum Theorizing, 30*(2), 2–19.

Thomas, M., Bellingham, R., & Murphy, M. (Eds.). (2020). *Post-qualitative research and innovative methodologies.* Bloomsbury Academic.

Analyzing and Coding Interviews and Focus Groups Considering Cross-Cultural and Cross-Language Data

Elsa M. Gonzalez and Yvonna S. Lincoln

Abstract

Considering the premise that there is no formula to translating culture—collecting data in the native language, and then presenting the analysis in a second language (primarily English)—this cross-cultural work becomes an important, if complex, issue to unpack. Analyzing data and presenting findings are a huge endeavor for any researcher who hopes to make certain that the local reader understands and makes sense of the data from local participants and foreign researchers. The process involves a translation of the language with a deep understanding of the context which will help the researcher and ultimately the reader to understand better the phenomenon. This chapter looks to present strategies to address the analysis of data with a cross-cultural and cross-language origin using content analysis and constant comparative analysis as analytic practices.

Keywords: Cross-language data; cross-cultural data; decolonizing methodologies

Introduction and Brief Literature Review

In the past, qualitative researchers have assumed that cross-cultural work required deep understanding of the culture being reported on. Earlier, cross-cultural work focused on "receiving contexts" and on end-users who were primarily Western and English-speaking. The utility of such studies is severely limited, however, in a globalized world, and studies undertaken now must serve the interests of not only western and English-speaking scholars, but also the needs of nationals and locals (or indigenous peoples). Research conducted in different languages, non-Western contexts, and different cultures becomes more problematic and understanding intrinsic issues more urgent with the increasing number of reports (such as dissertations) conducted by scholars outside the U.S., and thus bear potential for decolonizing the academy. (González y González & Lincoln, 2006, p. 193)

Considering the premise that there is no formula to translating culture; collecting data in the native language, and then presenting of the analysis in a second language (primarily English); this cross-cultural work becomes an important, if complex, issue to unpack. The analysis of data and the presentation of the findings are a huge endeavor for any researcher who hopes to make certain that the reader understands and makes sense of the data from both local participants and foreign researchers (and their cocreated realities). The process involves a translation of the language with a deep understanding of the context that will help the researcher and ultimately the reader to understand better the phenomenon, ensuring throughout the process that there is no loss and misinterpretation of valuable data (Temple, 1997).

Coding interview and focus group data is consistently both a methodical and an intuitive task, reliant not only on the shared reality cocreated by interview participant(s) and interviewer but also upon the propositional and tacit knowledge stored from earlier work in the mind of the researcher/coder. However, working cross-culturally and cross-linguistically poses four additional and extraordinary problems. First, there is the issue of "translating" field notes, often taken in the native language, into another language, frequently English. This creates two sets of field notes which may have to be coded. This labor is particularly challenging if the interviewer is working in the native language but must be responsible to an English-competent audience. Second, working across cultures and languages signifies working across constructed realities, both cultural and linguistic. The implication, in its simplest form, is that idioms, dialects, colloquialisms, and peculiar locutions do not "travel well" and may consequently need "unpacking" for a nonnative audience. Though these speech patterns may fit smoothly and seamlessly within their native culture, frequently some sort of shared parlance may have to be sought or created in the English version. These meaning transfers will mandate a partially bilingual text, without exception (González y González &

Lincoln, 2006). Third, the search for some sort of shared resonance between a native proverb, colloquialism, or idiom and some reasonably close English translation (if such is to be found) may necessitate working with an individual who is conversant with both cultures as peer debriefer (Lincoln & González y González, 2008). And fourth, the identity of the coder, the consideration of the language that the coder speaks, understands, and dreams; the positionality of the coder; and finally, the cultural background of the coder (González y González & Lincoln, 2007) are all critical to understanding how well any narrative approaches some kind of representation that research participants would or could agree is a fair "portrait" of themselves and their context. Such a test would be considered a reasonable approximation of internal validity, or plausibility, in qualitative, constructivist inquiry (Lincoln & Guba, 1985, 2013).

The implications for coding are enormous because these problems imply that coding is neither straightforward nor it is a one-to-one dataset-to-text-unit creation (unitizing process). English-to-English coding may be a one-to-one process, but cross-cultural and linguistic coding may mandate several index cards (coming from text units or units of meaning) be coded for the same phrase or data unit (the use of index card process is described by González y González, 2004). Not only is the task made more complex via the cultural and linguistic barriers, but the work is often more extensive and requires working into a narrative structure with multiple reality constructions and their "fit" in two or more languages. Examples of how this was done in one of the authors' studies will be demonstrated in this chapter, with suggestions for aiding in cultural transitions more broadly in similar cases. Reasons to favor not only the use and presentation of bilingual texts but also the analysis of cross-language and cross-cultural texts is explained by Ryen (2002):

> Social reality and how we talk about reality are intertwined. Reality varies according to the context of its articulation, and this by implication presents a challenge especially for cross-cultural research. In low-context languages, for example, the interactional context has little impact upon the meaning of what is said; the message, in effect, is in the words. In the high-context Latin languages, in contrast, messages cannot be interpreted literally, but have to be linked to performances. Moving from a low-context to a high-context language can be interactionally complicated. (p. 342)

Our earlier work (González y González & Lincoln, 2006) supported this type of cross-cultural and cross-language data analysis, outlining five ways in which Western scholars might aid in decolonizing methodology and research through the analysis of cross-cultural and cross language data:

1. addressing working bilingual data and the consideration of translation and translators (Temple & Edwards, 2002)

2. considering non-Western cultural traditions

3. considering multiple perspectives in texts from the locals to the readers

4. including multivocal and multilingual texts

5. including rich discussions of technical issues to ensure accessibility in publications (Lincoln & Gonzalez, 2008).

At this moment in time, we would add another step toward decolonization, and that is a frank and full discussion of ethical issues encountered in such cross-cultural or cross-linguistic work, including, perhaps, issues around negotiations with publication outlets, some of which may find such texts daunting or even unpublishable.

In this chapter we present additional strategies to address the analysis of data with a cross-cultural and cross-language origin using methods of data analysis, content analysis, and constant comparative analyses the authors have practiced in the past (González y González, 2004).

Exemplar

A dissertation where the authors served as the main researcher and advisor is the source of exemplars for this chapter. Twenty-years ago, we, the authors, sat to have conversations about what researchers do when they have data in another language that is not English, in that case Spanish. We conducted interviews in 20 different higher education institutions in Mexico, searching for answers around the definition of competencies that leaders in those institutions needed to take their universities to a successful future. Data were rich and deep, but as researchers we faced the challenge of translating and understanding what the participants told us so that we could share it with the readers. The challenges were great, as the data were collected in a different language and culture to the one where the data would be initially presented. Through this process we arrived at several methodological decisions that support a more authentic presentation of the findings to the multiple audiences for this research: an academic and policy audience, a local audience, and an audience back in the locales where data were collected. In particular, these locals included a cadre of senior administrators in the 20 most prestigious institutions in-country, administrators who were themselves deeply concerned about issues of succession and ensuring their institutions' strong future.

Data analyses interacted continuously with data collection: after the first interview was collected and analyzed, preliminary findings were used to guide the collection of data from the next participant. During the development of this study the perception and experience of each participant was crucial in detecting and building future scenarios that allowed the researcher to organize competencies by different criteria. Therefore, the use of content analysis and constant comparison of the findings were necessary (Holsti, 1969).

First, interview data in Spanish were transcribed from audiotapes into computer files. Second, the transcripts were broken into "units" of data, or the smallest fragment of data from which meaning could be obtained. Unitizing data is the crucial step in transforming interview data "into the smallest pieces of information that may stand alone as independent thoughts in the absence of additional information other than broad understanding of the context" (Erlandson, Harris, Skipper, & Allen, 1993, p. 117). Third, the units were identified by source of information, site, participant, date, and gender. Then, text units on the transcripts were printed to cards in two different colors relating to the type of institution, private or public (see Figure 12.1).

Units were kept in Spanish, in order to maintain the original language and continuity in each narrative made by the participants. Additionally, this procedure was used with the purpose of keeping the richness of the data in Spanish. For the presentation of the data, units are, in several cases, presented in both languages. This procedure supports the idea that the Spanish-speaking reader understands the exact meaning of the unit and its context.

Anzaldúa (1987), in her social studies about the Mexico–US border, insists on presenting her analyses in Spanish, in English, and in many cases as a mix of both languages. This conveys the social phenomenon of two cultures bordering each other and invites the reader to understand the "language of the border" where bilingual texts (and the social constructions they represent) exhibit great power. The influence that language can have in the analysis of data had to be considered because the "primary function of human language would be to scaffold human affiliation within cultures and social groups and institutions" (Gee, 1999, p. 1). In this study, the researcher had to consider the presence of multiple audiences with different data needs. This situation created the need for the researcher to make special considerations regarding language in order to ensure that the audiences would be able to make correct interpretations of the data and ultimately of the findings.

The objective of coding is "to bring together into provisional categories those cards that apparently relate to the same content" (Lincoln & Guba, 1985, p. 347). The process of coding and discovering patterns included the following steps: the researcher selects the first index card, studies it, and places it into a pile to be created using cards with similar data, thus forming categories. Then, the researcher selects the second card, studies it, and if it contains similar relevant information, places it with the first card or starts a new stack if the relevant information differs. Eventually, each card is analyzed so that piles of similar information are created under different categories. A name in English is given to each code to identify the "essence" of the properties that connects the cards contained within it; these properties are combined into a decision rule (Lincoln & Guba, 1985). In this instance, we used English in all codes' names since the first audience of this work was an only-English speaker doctoral committee; language used in the codes is based on the receiving first audience.

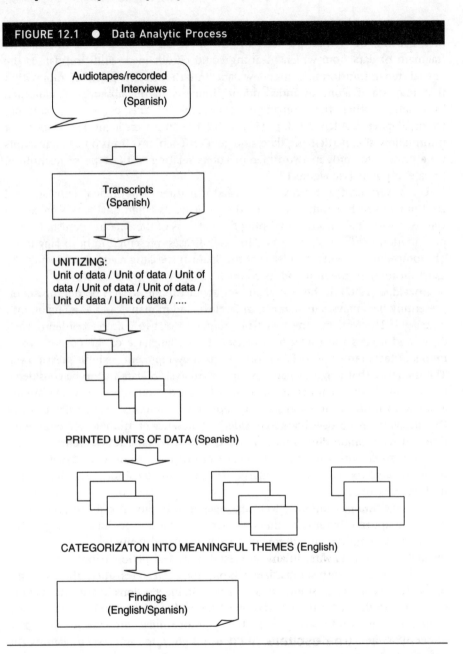

FIGURE 12.1 ● Data Analytic Process

The researcher, based on the analysis of the data and the contributions of the peer debriefer (a bilingual colleague), identified relevant themes and patterns uncovered during the unitizing process. Beginning at this point, the analysis of data started being presented in English. At this point, the names of the codes and then the identified themes were defined in English, and research memos that included interpretation, findings, and conclusions were presented in English along with the units of meaning, in Spanish, that supported the findings. Those units were introduced into the text in English and Spanish, as we considered further audiences, who are other critical stakeholders from the local country where data were collected.

Examples of portions of data in this dissertation where findings are introduced in English and Spanish are below. Cultural familiarity, cultural sensitivity, and cultural understanding serve as a framework for the analysis of cross-language and cross-cultural data; interpretation of these data and the presentation of findings are shown in each of these examples. The five examples include translations that are not literal. All of them had to first have an interpretation (i.e., a reading between the lines) and then a translation to English that captures the meaning from the original unit of data in Spanish.

Five Cross-Cultural and Cross-Language Units of Data

Example 1: "A ton y son"

"Some years ago, licenses were given for the right to open universities [State or national] without control ... where the academic level was not as good as could be ... generating in some ways more unemployment." (Hace unos años se dieron licencias para abrir universidades a "ton y son." Donde el nivel académico deja mucho que desear ... generando de una forma mas desempleo) (González y González, 2004, p. 101). This quote supports the findings under the code "Present situation of higher education in Mexico" where the participant explains what happened with some of the opening of small private universities in the past and how it is affecting the current institutions: "universities were opened a 'ton y son'." In Mexico these small private institutions do not fall under State or accreditation guidelines and therefore their decision-making was different. This is the interpretation of "a ton y son": institutions emerged without any control. A literal translation will not present this interpretation. In short, the relationship of private institutions to the state are very different in Mexico than the relationships of such institutions in the United States, and the process of how they are approved is different, too.

Example 2: "Una escuela dura"

"In some ways, the education market in Mexico is not giving value to a solid education, as they should." (De alguna forma el mercado de educación en México, no está valorando una educación sólida, todo lo que debería). "In the United States, a stronger social value and recognition is given to someone who graduated from a recognized school. The labor market recognizes it as well." (En Estados Unidos, se dá un valor social muy fuerte en sueldo y reconocimiento de alguien que es egresado de una *escuela dura*, el mercado de trabajo lo reconoce suficientemente) (González y González, 2004, p. 107). During the original analysis process, these units are part of the code "social context" which is part of the theme "Context of higher education in Mexico."

Example 3: "La revolución tecnológica"

Senior administrators are sure that technological changes affect and will affect higher education institutions and ultimately how they will perform their roles, but the impact of these changes is still not very clear for them. "The technological revolution still has unknown impacts ..." (Toda la revolución tecnológica tiene impactos todavía desconocidos...). "We still do not know well the implications that it is going to have, it is a new paradigm to learn and we are just kind of waiting ..." (todavía no sabemos bien que implicaciones va a tener, es una nueva forma de aprender y estamos un tanto a la expectativa ...), "all this is a motive to study." (todo esto es motivo de estudio) (González y González, 2004, p. 112). These examples illustrated the technological context of higher education in Mexico and how it is understood for university leaders.

Example 4: Diversity Competencies

For one of the senior administrators from a private institution, the competency of being aware of diversity is implied because of their position. He stated that "this job is a task of working with diversity." (El trabajo es así, es un trabajo de trabajar con la diversidad). This can be explained and understood in the context of private universities, particularly in Mexico. Private universities in Mexico are more diverse than public institutions in terms of gender, age, and even socioeconomic status of their students, staff, and faculty (González y González, 2004, p. 119).

Example 5: "En su casa las conocen"

Senior administrators from public institutions recognized that the well-known private higher education institutions in Mexico are growing, but at the same time, they expressed their concern about the academic quality of those private institutions that are just emerging: "But look at those institutions that nobody knows. There are many, and they have a great market but with doubtful, very doubtful academic quality." (Pero "hechale una mirada" a las instituciones que "en su casa las conocen" y si las sumas, te "vas para atrás" del crecimiento de mercado que están atendiendo con una dudosa, muy dudosa calidad académica). This concern is shared also by senior administrators of recognized private institutions (González y González, 2004, p. 141). This quote was organized under the code "present perceptions," where the term "hechale una mirada" introduces a phrase that doesn't have literal translation; the presentation of a literal translation would lose the meaning of the quote.

These examples show how administrators from public and private universities see themselves within the national context and for the foreseeable future. The five examples also give some flavor as to the very strong differences between the two kinds of institutions in this particular country, differences that are a result of a variety of cultural, social, and even historical development of the higher education institutional ecology in Mexico. Although some of the differences represented in the five examples are subtle, the nuances become clearer both with the translation and with the original words of speakers. The participants' original framing of their answers demonstrates clearly why a bilingual text can be critical to understanding a study's deep context.

Methods/Practices and Their Use

In our previous work (Lincoln & Gonzalez, 2008), we explored a variety of practices to approach cross-language and cross-cultural research, presenting with this approach further strategies for liberatory and democratic inquiry and examples such as the previous ones. These strategies evolved from our research exploring the decisions that several authors of these texts have taken. Those strategies include:

1. Engaging in a thoughtful decision-making process around when, how, and why one would choose to produce bilingual research reports, dissertations, and journal articles

2. Deciding to develop true bilingual texts, providing rich contextual translations throughout the text

3. Understanding the investigator as a living part of the study, identifying how the researcher and how the interactions and participants influence both the shape and form of the bilingual text and the decisions that are made as the research progresses

4. Engaging in partnerships between the researcher and a local/native partner when the researcher is not a local speaker, and assessing the value and effects that this decision produces

5. Deciding to pursue studies with the indirect influence or the presence of non-English language in the collected data

6. Choosing not to present bilingual texts by bilingual researchers with non-English data when the pressure for the final reader is to present and publish these research projects in English.

These strategies engage some of the decisions that scholars with cross-cultural and cross-language data have decided to use as they approach their readerships, audience, collaborators, local partners, translators, and other stakeholders.

The number of English-speaking scholars in different fields that do cross language-cross cultural research is increasing. We identified issues that they wanted to raise, such as working with an inexperienced translator, using a professional translator, expressing oneself as an author, and the role of the translator. In order to address analyzing data that were to be presented in English, our research indicated, as part of a reflexive process, strategies to consider and those that researchers reflexively realized they wish they had followed.

Transcription and Dataset Creation

The researcher used three data sources: audiotapes of the interviews, transcripts, and content analyzed. Unitized data were transferred to index cards for ease of sorting and code creation. In retrospect, a second dataset, all in English, might have proven equally useful. We noticed as senior administrators grappled with fore-casting changes that they saw approaching their institutions, they occasionally created contradictions in the statements they made. These would have been more readily noted had one dataset been in English. Consequently, our recommendation is that, however time-consuming, a dataset in the language which is projected to be the primary receiving context also be created. This methodological strategy is somewhat more sophisticated and complicated than doing it all in the local lan-guage solely, but acts as a cross-check for meaning, and a tactic for trying to grasp nuance from the original language. If the researcher is fully bilingual (in this case, she was), this would have proven time-consuming but readily accomplished. If one were working with a translator, however, this might prove more difficult, and depending on the skill and facility of the translator, nuance could be lost.

Multiple language datasets can also facilitate the work of any peer debriefer with whom the researcher might work. This is especially the case if a debriefer is not thoroughly conversant with the sending language. Data units translated into the receiving language (in most cases, this would be English) can aid a peer debriefer to understand where data have arisen and why inferences are made from those data.

Local Versus Global Meaning-Making

As we considered different meanings, we found we had to balance data that could prove interesting but hardly useful to nonlocal audiences, although such data might carry enormous significance for *local or indigenous consumers* of the research. That is, the statements participants made could prove powerful to local consumers simply because the words might tie into larger events, circumstances, customs, issues, problems, or relationships. Consequently, we realized coders have to look deeply into data as they connect to local, regional, or national events which could or will prove useful or locally meaningful, and which might provide fodder for positive social change. That is, coders cannot rely on the words alone. As Krippendorf (1980) has pointed out, data have not only *manifest* meanings, they may also carry *latent* significance, particularly to participants. This is so because data may also reference tacit knowledge on the part of interviewees and participants, data of which the researcher might not be aware, but which may have powerful local history and meaning.

Peer Debriefer or Peer Consultant?

For this research project, a peer debriefer was not chosen, largely because of the paucity of such individuals who might know both sending and receiving contexts. Rather, a deliberate methodological decision was made to rely on someone we termed a *consultant*. This individual was raised in Mexico, the son of missionaries, and consequently was not only fully bilingual, but comfortably bicultural as well. He traveled often back to the homestead in Mexico and spent many family holidays down there. When at our institution, he was frequently called upon to write or check the technical language of grants, contracts, memoranda of understanding, study abroad agreements, scholarly visits, research cooperatives, and the like on behalf of the institution because of his fluency in Spanish. He proved invaluable in, for instance, idioms, local usages peculiar to Mexico (not shared with any other Spanish-language country), and general academic circumstances. As a result, when the bilingual research narrative was created, occasionally no word-for-word translations were possible; rather, idioms with similar meanings from English were substituted for the Spanish idioms. This bicultural, bilinguistic fluency enabled the creation of a text meaningful to both research participants and to English users of the work.

It may not always be possible to arrange for such a serendipitous or felicitous collegial arrangement; however, informants with access to and familiarity with both cultures prove extraordinarily useful. We were delighted he agreed to work with us in the assembly of a text with layered meanings embedded for several different audiences. It may be useful to invite the services of what sociologists term a *key informant*, especially if this participant is able to unpack for the researcher the intent, analogy, or wisdom behind local colloquialisms, idioms, or figures of speech if a consultant such as ours is not available.

Structuring the Text

In data analyses, coders will frequently use as a sign of salience the size of a code (i.e., the amount of text coded to a code), and this is one useful way to proceed. The researcher, however, was searching for deeper meaning when she explored chief academic administrators' ideas of competencies to manage the twenty-first century institutions of Mexico. This meant following a deeper and further analysis that organizes the findings beyond the projections of these administrators, including, in addition, their expressed and otherwise communicated anxieties, particularly regarding whether or not individuals with needed competencies for the next generation were being prepared for such tasks. For this reason, the largest number of text units may not be the code of highest salience. Researchers have to ask themselves whether there are other issues, concerns, anxieties, worries, and the like that are shaping interview responses (an insight not always readily recognized initially during interviews). Key informants and consultants (such as the fortuitous colleague we were fortunate enough to work with), as well as peer debriefers, can help to identify such issues that frequently lie "between the lines." Reflexive journals, too, can provide strategic help as researchers puzzle out what they have heard and what interviews mean.

The Importance of Local Users

Nonlocal consumers of the research cannot know what kind of actions will be triggered via the original language, or what social action may be prompted. Only local users can understand what the words, especially untranslatable, idiomatic terminologies, might mean, or what positive forces might be enabled, moving them to a different dimension as the "real reader" of those studies.

Through recognizing and giving voice to these scholars and the actors around this process, we present their hope of obviating some of those hidden cultural assumptions that they found in the eye of different readers and instead expressing a full and deep understanding of the context and showing the richness of each culture and richness of this experience.

Bringing together across time, space, and language local and nonlocal consumers of the research, we have intended to move people to a moral dimension, making them more able to present a critique that moves the reader and spectator toward social justice (González y González & Lincoln, 2010).

Conclusion

During our continuous search for emerging decolonizing methodologies, we encountered a repeated sympathy around the use of bilingual texts for the presentation of research carried out in cross-cultural and cross-language contexts (González y González & Lincoln, 2006). Authors of this kind of work expressed the need for the opening of academic spaces for the presentation and publication of such research. However, it was not clear to us the intentions and expectations of the authors of these bilingual texts, nor has it been clear what the intended role of the readers might be, as well as their response to this kind of text. The responses from monolingual versus bilingual readers may differ considering the nature of language, understanding this as a way of thinking, and a form of life (Fish, 1980). As texts are "decolonized," we suggest companion case studies to document and explore the catalytic and tactical effects (Guba & Lincoln, 1989)—on both authors and readers—as well as the uses to which such text are directed.

Scholars in cross-cultural studies, mainly international doctoral students, have increasingly favored the use of bilingual texts. Interest in ethics in the social sciences suggests that research done internationally should serve the communities in which the research was conducted as well as serving Western academic knowledge communities and universities (González y González & Lincoln, 2006, 2007, 2010). Faculty and researchers aware of these situations have presented different possibilities for those texts and the analysis of this research (Robinson-Pant, 2005) and its linguistical and cultural equivalence (Peña, 2007). Authors of cross-cultural texts with language proficiency in the native language report that the use of the native language was not a question, but rather an intuitive decision (Lincoln, Gonzalez, & Aroztegui, 2016). On the other hand, English-speaking authors of cross-language studies expressed their decision to conduct these studies in order to present rich and in-depth data, but also as a way for their participants to experience a level of comfort and a means for them to express their ideas more effectively. One of these authors explains: "We had to take a bilingual approach to the [study] and also to the analysis; without that we will have superficial interpretations" (Diego Garcia, personal communication, 2016).

Supplemental Readings

González y González, E. M., & Lincoln, Y. S. (2006). Decolonizing qualitative research: Non-traditional reporting forms in the academy. In N. K. Denzin & M. Gardina (Eds.), *Qualitative inquiry and the conservative challenge.* Left Coast Press.

Lincoln, Y. S., Gonzalez, E., & Aroztegui, C. (2016). "Spanish is a loving tongue ...": Performing qualitative research across languages—A performance piece for two readers. *Qualitative Inquiry, 22*(7), 531–540. https://doi.org/10.1177/1077800416636148.

Lincoln, Y. S., & González y González, E. M. (2008). The search for emerging decolonizing methodologies in qualitative research: Further strategies for liberatory and democratic inquiry. *Qualitative Inquiry, 14*(5), 784–805. https://doi.org/10.1177/1077800408318304.

Reflection and Activities

1. Some discussion questions to consider in order to present and include a crisis of representation and crisis of authority are as follows:

   a. What are the special responsibilities when English-speaking researchers are working with international students who are concerned about and working with local problems?

   b. How can authors legitimatize their findings with local communities and diverse audiences?

   c. How can we reference the academic responsibility in a globalized world when we try to bring marginalized people to the center of the research context?

2. Create a plan to interview and analyze the perspectives of English and non-English speakers on the same issue. How might the ideas and strategies discussed in this chapter influence the following?

   a. the research questions and interview guide

   b. the sampling strategy and the selection of interviewers and other members of the research team

   c. transcription and coding strategies

   d. interpretive and write-up strategies

References

Anzaldúa, G. (1987). *Borderlands/la frontera: The new mestiza.* Aunt Lute Book Company.

Erlandson, D., Harris, E., Skipper, B., & Allen, S. (1993). *Doing naturalistic inquiry: A guide to methods.* SAGE.

Fish, S. (1980). *Is there a text in this class? The authority of interpretive communities*. Harvard University Press.

Gee, J. P. (1999). *An introduction to discourse analysis: Theory and method*. Routledge.

González y González, E. M. (2004). *Perceptions of selected senior administrators of higher education institutions in Mexico regarding needed administrative competencies* (Doctoral dissertation). ProQuest Dissertations Publishing. (Order No. 3157028).

González y González, E. M., & Lincoln, Y. S. (2006). Decolonizing qualitative research: Non-traditional reporting forms in the academy [41 paragraphs]. *Forum Qualitative Sozialforschung/Forum: Qualitative Social Research, 7*(4), Article 1. http://www.qualitative-research.net/fqs-texte/4-06/06-4-1-e.htm

González y González, E. M., & Lincoln, Y. S. (May 2007). *Decolonizing methodologies further: Authorial intentions, reader response, and the uses of qualitative research*. Paper presented at the 2007 Third International Congress of Qualitative Inquiry, Urbana-Champaign, IL.

González y González, E. M., & Lincoln, Y. S. (May 2010). *Voices on voice: Decisions to engage cross-cultural and cross-language research*. 2010 Fifth International Congress of Qualitative Inquiry, Urbana-Champaign, IL.

Guba, E. G., & Lincoln, Y. S. (1989). *Fourth generation evaluation*. SAGE.

Holsti, O. R. (1969). *Content analysis for the social sciences and humanities*. Addison-Wesley.

Krippendorf, K. (1980). *Content analysis: An introduction to its methodology*. SAGE.

Lincoln, Y. S., Gonzalez, E., & Aroztegui, C. (2016). "Spanish is a loving tongue …": Performing qualitative research across languages—A performance piece for two readers. *Qualitative Inquiry, 22*(7), 531–540. https://doi.org/10.1177/1077800416636148

Lincoln, Y. S., & González y González, E. M. (2008). The search for emerging decolonizing methodologies in qualitative research: Further strategies for liberatory and democratic inquiry. *Qualitative Inquiry, 14*(5), 784–805. https://doi.org/10.1177/1077800408318304

Lincoln, Y. S., & Guba, E. G. (1985). *Naturalistic inquiry*. SAGE.

Lincoln, Y. S., & Guba, E. G. (2013). *The constructivists' credo*. Left Coast Press.

Peña, E. D. (2007). Lost in translation: Methodological considerations in cross-cultural research. *Child Development, 78*(4), 1255–1264. https://doi.org/10.1111/j.1467-8624.2007.01064.x

Robinson-Pant, A. (2005). *Cross-cultural perspective on educational research*. Open University Press.

Ryen, A. (2002). Cross-cultural interviewing. In J. F. Gubrium & J. A. Holstein (Eds.), *Handbook of interview research: Context and method* (pp. 335–354). SAGE.

Temple, B. (1997). Watch your tongue: Issues in translation and cross-cultural research. *Sociology, 31*(3), 607–618. https://doi.org/10.1177/0038038597031003016

Temple, B., & Edwards, R. (2002). Interpreters/translators and cross-language research: Reflexivity and border crossing. *International Journal of Qualitative Methods, 1*(2), Article 1. http://www.ualberta.ca/~ijqm

Reflection and Analytic Memoing Strategies

Paul Mihas

Introduction

Memo writing, and the reflection it is intended to capture, is a tool that often remains mysterious, misunderstood, or continuously postponed in qualitative research. For researchers already burdened with copious amounts of data, it may seem unwieldy or laborious to generate, in effect, another layer of textual data. Some researchers suspend writing until they are *sure* about what a quotation or interview means, but memo writing works far better when we start with unknowns and intangibles. We write toward and through our suspended questions, moving closer to the participant's world-framing as well as to our own wisdom.

We celebrate in this section the many advantages of memo writing (Birks, Chapman, & Francis, 2008; Corbin & Strauss, 2015; Richardson, 2000; Saldaña, 2016). Rather than coding based on what we think we already know, memo writing can sharpen our interpretive acumen and lead to a potentially new language for codes. Because writing is recorded thinking, memo writing also forces us to see what is unclear in our own minds and to work toward understanding and insight.

Memo writing is a practice that documents our understanding—our incremental awareness as well as "aha" moments—along the qualitative research life cycle. In the early stages of design, memo writing can help us form and reform research questions, decide upon whom to interview, and shape our plans for an appropriately targeted literature review. As we are about to enter the field, we can also write a memo regarding what we are connected to and disconnected from in our work (Vagle, 2019). That is, we can write about how we see ourselves as listeners before we enter the participant's world and put our listening to the test.

After the interview, memo writing moves us closer to the participant's story. "While we're reading, we listen harder and we feel we can talk back" (Hickey, 1993, p. 2). That is, *we begin a private conversation with the data.* Reflection becomes an act of listening and responding. In incorporating participant quotations in our memos, we reactivate the speaking personality of the participant and show how this voice moves our thinking. Memo writing opens up the data and invites us to have a documented conversation with a world that is perhaps unfamiliar or downright confusing. One of the audiences of memos is our future selves. When we revisit the memo—in many weeks or months—we will identify seeds that were planted and nascent insights that have developed into crystalized insight. In this way, we become our own best colleagues. Our collection of memos can serve as an audit trail, establishing "what we know so far" (Maietta, Hamilton, Swartout, & Petruzzelli, 2019).

In the practice of writing memos, we develop our writing voice for a particular study. Every project comes with its own lexicon and unwieldy thoughts—contradictions and mysteries—that we work through in writing. In developing the practice of memo writing, as we have singular perceptions, we are ready to document them in writing, rather than waiting until the eleventh hour to "write up" our results. Patricia Goodson calls this the "write habit" (Goodson, 2013, p. 15). If we do not write down our thoughts, our sagacity disappears like fog.

Memo writing functions alongside coding (and, for some researchers, in place of it) to elucidate data and make connections between codes and data. In this conversation with data, we are saying, "let me tell you why this matters" and why the participant's words—distinctive to them—illustrate a condensed code—distinctive to the study. Coding can, at times, become arduous, and condensed code names can seem too abridged. Memo writing, as its analytical companion, is a way of expanding upon what coding is intended to capture. It helps us acknowledge what our process is doing for us, what the code is doing for us, or how the participant's language has opened up a new world of comprehension. Just as coding is a way of condensing, memo writing is a way of expanding.

Writing can be a way of describing data, of bringing our assumptions down a notch as we take inventory of the textured world of data. The opposite is also true; we might use memos to move up the conceptual ladder, as we do in grounded theory when we think of raising our work to the level of a category. Hence, memo writing is an approach for working through both the tangible and the more abstract. In this section, Elaine Keane, Chapter 15, addresses this very topic—how we use different kinds of memos at various junctures in the research process, from using memos as a way to just start "somewhere" to using them as a form of critical analysis. She addresses moving from storying toward conceptualizing and asking analytic questions of our data. As Kathy Charmaz reminds us, memos are a place to sustain inquiry (Charmaz, 2014), like a shelf where we can place our thoughts and return to them. Eventually, we have a whole library or, as Adele Clarke calls it, a "project bank," with our memos functioning as "intellectual capital" (Clarke, 2005, p. 107).

In my chapter on writing about parts and the whole, Chapter 14, I remind researchers of the wide-angle lens, of stepping back to address the contiguity of an interview, as well as zooming in on a particular quotation and writing about how a fragment functions within the contiguous whole. In Chapter 13, Craig McGill, Drew Puroway, and Mark Duslak's walk us through their use of memo writing in a collaborative autoethnography process. These research practices allow for unique access to "internal mental events" and layers of collaborative memo writing. At first, McGill et al. reflect individually then share their written responses among other team members, then return to their individual responses to expand upon points of commonality. In this way, memos, once shared, activate another round of refinement and deeper, shared understanding and collective intelligence. When the researcher is also the participant, the intricacies of analysis are especially well suited to documentation via memos.

Reflection and Activities

1. Brainstorm a list of what an analytic memo's topics might consist of—e.g., categories in progress, related theory, ethical issues.

2. Secure a 30- to 60-minute verbatim interview transcript document. Acquaint yourself with the transcript by reading it several times.

   a. After reading Chapter 14 on memo writing strategies, compose a "first impression" document reflection memo about the transcript.

   b. After reading Chapter 15 on critical analytic memo writing, compose an analytic memo that addresses your researcher positionality and standpoint in relation to the transcript's contents.

   c. After reading Chapter 13 on autoethnography, imagine you could dialogue with the interviewed participant. Select a passage from the transcript that motivates you to respond, and compose a first-person, autoethnographic passage/memo to the participant.

3. Discuss how each chapter in this section addresses how to use memos as a way to sustain inquiry.

References

Birks, M., Chapman, Y., & Francis, K. (2008). Memoing in qualitative research: Probing data and processes. *Journal of Nursing Research*, 13(1), 68–75.

Charmaz, K. (2014). *Constructing grounded theory* (2nd ed.). SAGE.

Clarke, A. (2005). *Situational analysis: Grounded theory after the postmodern turn*. SAGE.

Corbin, J., & Strauss, A. (2015). *Basics of qualitative research: Techniques and procedures for developing grounded theory* (4th ed.). SAGE.

Goodson, P. (2013). *Becoming an academic writer: 50 exercises for paced, productive, and powerful writing.* SAGE.

Hickey, D. (1993). *Developing a written voice.* Mayfield.

Keane, E. (2022). Critical analytic memoing. In C. Vanover, P. Mihas, & J. Saldaña (Eds.), *Analyzing and interpreting qualitative research: After the interview.* SAGE.

Maietta, R., Hamilton, A., Swartout, K., & Petruzzelli, J. (2019). *Qualitative data analysis camp.* ResearchTalk, Inc.

McGill, C. M., Puroway, D., & Duslak, M. (2022). On being a researcher-participant: Challenges with the iterative process of data production, analysis, and (re)production. In C. Vanover, P. Mihas, & J. Saldaña (Eds.), *Analyzing and interpreting qualitative research: After the interview.* SAGE.

Mihas, P. (2022). Memo writing strategies: Analyzing the parts and the whole. In C. Vanover, P. Mihas, & J. Saldaña (Eds.), *Analyzing and interpreting qualitative research: After the interview.* SAGE.

Richardson, L. (2000). Writing: A method of inquiry. In N. K. Denzin, & Y. S. Lincoln (Eds.), *Handbook of qualitative research* (2nd ed., pp. 923–948). SAGE.

Saldaña, J. (2016). *The coding manual for qualitative researchers* (3rd ed.). SAGE.

Vagle, M. (2019). *Learning from lived experience: How we can study the world as it is lived.* Course at the qualitative research Summer Intensive. ResearchTalk, Inc.

On Being a Researcher-Participant: Challenges With the Iterative Process of Data Production, Analysis, and (Re)Production

Craig M. McGill, Drew Puroway, and Mark Duslak

Abstract

For the past four years, our research team has been exploring our professional socialization to the emerging profession of academic advising through collaborative autoethnography (CAE). Using CAE, a group of individuals draw upon their own lives and experiences to explore an issue. The researchers, therefore, are also the participants. CAE is similar to other forms of qualitative research involving self-exploration, allowing unique access to internal mental events with the added layers of collaborative critical questioning and support. The method changes the relationship between researcher and participant found in traditional social science studies. Our process involved six overlapping phases: designing and team-building, initial writing, conversing and note-taking, coding and analysis, theory building, and research writing, submitting for publication, and responding to feedback. In this chapter, we explore the intersection of writing, analysis, interpretation, and the inherent challenges when working in autobiographical methods.

Keywords: Collaborative autoethnography; critical reflection; higher education; researcher-participant; professional socialization

In this chapter we explore the intersection of writing, analysis, interpretation, and
the inherent challenges when working with autobiographical methods. For the past
four years, our research team has explored our professional socialization to the
emerging profession of academic advising through collaborative autoethnography
(CAE). CAE is a research method in which researchers "use data from their own life
stories as situated in sociocultural contexts in order to gain an understanding of
society through the unique lens of self" (Chang, Hernandez, & Ngunjiri, 2012, p. 18).
In other words, using CAE, a group of individuals draw upon their own lives and
experiences to explore an issue. The researchers, therefore, are also the participants.

Before going further, it is important to distinguish CAE from other similar
methodologies: ethnography, autoethnography, and duoethnography. CAE builds
on autoethnography, in which a person explores their own unique experiences in
the context of their environment (Ellis, 2007). Autoethnography emerged from
ethnography, the study of people or a cultural group. "Ethnographic inquiry takes
as its central and guiding assumption that any human group of people interacting
together for a period of time will evolve a culture" (Patton, 2015, p. 100). While
ethnographers seek to understand the "other," autoethnography acknowledges the
role of the self within the environmental context. The focus on the self is obviously
a feature of biography, but autoethnography is distinguished from autobiography
because the study of the self is oftentimes connected to the social science literature.

A third related method is duoethnography, in which two or more researchers
explore contrasts between their lived experiences. When utilizing duoethnography,
researchers endeavor to "work in tandem to dialogically critique and question the
meanings [we] give to social issues and epistemological constructs" (Sawyer & Norris,
2013, p. 2). Our work meets certain goals of duoethnography: it is a collaborative
qualitative methodology and our experience as research-participants was polyvocal
and dialogic. However, our goal was not juxtaposition of differences (indeed, we did
not intentionally explore differences between each of us), and we did not specifically
question held beliefs. We, therefore, arrived at CAE, the focus of this chapter.

CAE is similar to other forms of qualitative research involving self-exploration,
allowing unique access to internal mental events with the added layers of collaborative critical questioning and support. As a method bordering on social science
and humanistic inquiry, CAE allows research teams to reflect on critical issues and
challenges on a particular issue. CAE also provides a way to extend autoethnographic approaches to be more inclusive of a wide swath of readers, such as graduate students, community members, professionals, and organizational leaders,
therefore addressing the restriction of scope issue (Lapadat, 2017). The method
changes the relationship between researcher and researched found in traditional
social science studies: CAE "flattens power dynamics in the team because all the
co-researchers are vulnerable in sharing their stories. In this way, it supports team

building and the development of trust" (Lapadat, 2017, p. 599). As the experience of practitioners is almost entirely absent from the literature (McGill, 2019), we found CAE to be a useful starting point for understanding professional academic advisors' professional socialization by exploring the convergences and divergences of our own experiences. We discuss challenges and what we learned about conducting a CAE project.

Exemplar

Our process included individual reflections on 25 questions and weekly phone calls (most of which were recorded) from 2014 to the present. We discuss our process in six overlapping phases: 2014: designing and team-building; 2015: initial writing; 2015–present: conversing and note-taking; 2016–2018: coding and analysis; 2017–2019: theory building; 2018–present: research writing, submitting for publication, and responding to feedback. To emphasize the collaborative nature of our process, we end each phase with individual reflections, though, for brevity, some sections feature just two of us.

2014: Designing and Team-Building

In 2014, Craig, the first author of this piece, chatted with three other advising colleagues at his previous institution about exploring their professional roles through the literature of professional identity. The group presented concepts from the literature at a local advising conference. Prompted by audience response, they began designing a collaborative study to further explore these issues through 25 reflection questions (McGill et al, 2020b). At this point, Mark was invited to the project. The five participants discussed the questions and rephrased them until consensus was reached. Prior to finalizing the questions, three participants realized the project would be a major multiyear undertaking and dropped out of the study due to time commitment. Craig and Mark were prepared to go forward as a pair, but when Craig saw Drew present on critically reflective advising at a conference, he wanted to invite Drew. Mark agreed and the invitation was extended. Upon accepting the invitation, Drew reviewed the questions and provided minor edits about the questions and study design. The 25 questions were organized around four broad areas: knowledge of advising history/theory/philosophy, professional experience and academic preparation prior to entering the field, perceptions of advising/culture of the organization, and personal characteristics and reflections on practice. Although we initially struggled to articulate our exact research question, our broad research goals were to explore primary-role advisors' professional socialization experiences to the field of academic advising. We tried out several and feature two below:

1. How do three white midwestern men describe their experience of professional socialization within the field of advising?

2. What characteristics of professional socialization were experienced by three white men?

From the onset, the research team grappled with the ethics of human subject research and whether or not we needed to obtain permission from each of our institutions' review boards (IRBs). We consulted an expert on reflective writing practices who told us an IRB submission was unnecessary for the work we wished to do: "It's your narrative that comprises the study's data—not other people's opinions or perceptions..." (Personal Communication, November 2, 2015). Based on this advice, we concurred IRB approval was unnecessary. We reread *Collaborative Autoethnography* (Chang, Hernandez, & Ngunjiri, 2012) and decided to follow the set of ethical standards from the American Educational Research Association: freely consenting, avoiding harm, and respecting confidentiality of one another as collaborators and those we write about (AERA, 2011). We created an agreement delineating a pledge of ethicality and confidentiality among all participant-researchers and outlined the process for leaving the research team and retracting said team member's data from the data corpus.

> *Mark:* Craig and I had just published an article, so I was excited to be invited to another project. As a new advisor, I was eager to be involved, even though I had no idea what CAE was. Up to this point, I had only conducted quantitative research. When the three other participants dropped out, I relied on Craig's judgement as a justification for their departure. This faith in Craig extended to his recommendation to include Drew in our group. I was too naïve to be apprehensive about any of these changes, and because I knew so little, these challenges did not worry me much. In retrospect, I see how critical these decisions were, and I am grateful this all worked out.

> *Craig:* After losing three participants, two of whom were women of color, the prospect of inviting another white man was uneasy. But Drew was so perfect for this project and he was very self-aware and intentionally thought about his privilege (as we did). The more we talked, the more we realized we could go forward as three white men, provided we constantly reflected on privilege.

> *Drew:* I was taken in by Craig's earnestness and Mark's kindness. I had some trepidation about our shared privileged identities, but the ground we were trying to cover was open enough I thought I would just see where the collaboration would lead.

2015: Initial Writing

The primary data collection consisted of written responses to 25 questions. Several rounds of reflection and revision produced our initial dataset. In the first round, we reflected and responded to the questions individually over the course of six weeks. We did not share written responses among one another until the individual responses were complete. When each member felt satisfied with his initial responses, we each read the other responses. We then revisited our own responses to note similarities and expand upon points of commonality or places where the reflections of collaborators inspired further response. Each of us made notes using the track changes function in Microsoft Word in reaction to the others' responses, which also served as the points of conversation in the second phase. This was not dissimilar to the process of open coding in which an analyst makes general remarks. It differs, though, because we posed questions to clarify meaning or to further develop the ideas/events in the initial reflections. Thus, we did not conduct formal coding of the first reading but made notes that served to further develop the data and begin preliminary analysis.

> *Mark:* The questions were straightforward and the task unambiguous. But it forced me to think critically about my advising role, and, in retrospect, I am struck by how these beliefs persisted or changed over time.

> *Drew:* I needed to tap into something authentic and check myself for honesty. There was a temptation to pontificate on what was good and bad about our emerging profession, which was not out of bounds but which I felt needed to be tempered. That all came after getting myself to believe I had something to say worth saying.

2015-Present: Conversing and Note-Taking

We continually held weekly, hour-long, mostly unstructured phone conversations (on occasion, semi-structured). After updating each other on our lives, we moved onto the business of the task at hand, usually a manuscript or conference presentation. In the beginning of the project, we discussed each written response. This included expressions of surprise at others' writing, comments of validation about each other's reflections, questions for clarification, and questions to challenge reflections. We discussed convergences and divergences of our individual written responses and critically engaged with one another's stories. Based on these conversations, we added notes to the initial response documents to capture reflections from our conversations as useable data. These notes became the seeds of codes, but not necessarily in a direct or systematic way. We laid out hunches and biases about the situation of advising (i.e., we all come from these different tributaries of other professional experience) and so it was good data for unpacking hunches/intuition/logical observations. For example, a discussion regarding the different ways Mark's two master's degrees shaped his academic advising approach led to a conversation about what transferable skills were valued in the practice of academic advising. This point prompted a larger discussion about how our backgrounds provided transferable skills, a concept that became more fully formed with further analysis and eventually incorporated into our final model of advisor professional socialization.

Mark: The unstructured nature of our conversations was a very different experience from my quantitative projects. As our relationships developed, the role switching between friend/colleague/researcher/participant became more fluid. Having my writing analyzed by others was equally intriguing and terrifying. It led to insights about my own experiences as an advisor and helped me grow professionally.

Drew: I enjoy my colleagues and am passionate about the work we are doing, but generally dislike talking on the phone. Even after years on this project, it is still a challenge for me to maintain my concentration and focus. The conversations take all sorts of interesting turns, and I relish the moments when some nugget of revelation or wisdom is catalyzed. Sometimes this was captured formally in a memo, other times it was a thread of conversation carried over to another week and became part of our analysis.

2016–2018: Coding and Analysis

Due to the iterative nature of CAE and the dual role of researcher-participant, our phone conversations produced not only analysis of the issues we were exploring but also more data. Our weekly recordings produced an ever-expanding data corpus, and after a few years it became a bit overwhelming. How would we manage all the data? How would we continue to do analysis focused on a particular slice of the data when the data kept growing?

We engaged in multiple rounds of collaborative coding from our initial writing phase. Our coding practices were not predetermined and evolved frequently through the process. We read books and articles on autoethnography (Chang, 2008; Chang, Hernandez, & Ngunjiri, 2012; Pace, 2012) and qualitative coding more generally (Saldaña, 2015), but analyzing our work—with a buffet of analysis options—was daunting and still unclear. Though we understood what was driving our desire to do this study, what was our research purpose? What research questions were we seeking to answer? What contributions did we wish to make? Even after we began, we questioned if we were doing it correctly. We reasoned the best way forward was to just keep pushing through and learn by doing.

We began coding reflections paragraph by paragraph using a combination of open and in vivo coding, in which participants' exact words are used to shape codes (Saldaña, 2015). Each paragraph was pasted into Google Sheet cells with potential codes entered by all of us in adjacent rows and columns. This allowed for sorting and basic descriptive analysis of each code's location and frequency. We developed a coding naming system to track back a given code to its parent paragraph(s). Each of us reviewed each other's codes and added our own. We thoroughly discussed each code and, as we began recognizing common patterns through weeks of discussion, we identified focused codes illustrating key features of our socialization experiences to the field. Through these discussions, we began collapsing initial codes into more focused codes, a process not unlike the constant comparative method used in grounded theory. Examples included "misconceptions" eventually becoming part of the "ambiguity" concept and "working conditions" adding nuance to our "opportunity" concept. These focused codes then became a de facto, a priori coding structure moving forward.

We then considered the chronology of these focused codes in the data: What part of our stories did "opportunity" emerge? When did things become "ambiguous" in our socialization experiences? When did the "community of practice" matter? Through these discussions, we further refined these focused codes, at which point we began referring to them as concepts. In refining these concepts, we began looking for supporting evidence in both our written reflections and in our memory banks. When there was initial disagreement about the application of a focused code, we returned to the original data. Importantly, we did not restrict ourselves to the reflective data alone. For example, it was not uncommon for one of us to say, "Remember when you spoke about experience A? That connects codes B and C. Would you agree?" These conversations yielded nuances and clearer definitions of the concepts and led to more data creation. We did not systematically revisit all previously coded data and recode in light of these discussions. Unlike other qualitative methods in which participants and researchers are different people with clearly defined roles, we could conduct an instant focus group on the refinement of concepts and had license to run with them.

There was a tentativeness when we began coding, in part because this practice required criticality of a collaborator that could not be rendered with the anonymity of more traditional methods. As participant-researchers, we had to assign a code to the reflective writing of our collaborators, they were going to read it, and the team was going to discuss it. This added a layer of complexity, but once we began working together, the method brings nearly absolute interrater reliability.

> *Mark:* This was difficult. I wanted to quantify the codes and learned a great deal about the coding process from this exercise. I recall lengthy discussions over coding semantics and I now appreciate the power of finding the right descriptive word.

> *Drew:* At its best, coding on a CAE team was a fascinating exercise in falling deeply into the data: the care and tentativeness of open coding leading to the hairsplitting agony of focused coding. At its worst, it felt like world-class over-thinking. The deep and shared experience of coding connected me to this project in ways unique to CAE.

2017–2019: Theory Building

Through ongoing conversations and revisitation of the original data, we refined and settled on nine interconnected concepts:

1. Life Events

2. Opportunity

3. Transferable Skills

4. Idealism

5. Competency

6. Ambiguity

7. Struggle

8. Communities of Practice

9. Habits of Practice

We probed the data for elements of the emergent theory, but also reviewed recordings of prior conversations for additional clarity. This is not dissimilar to theoretical sampling (Glaser & Strauss, 1967). In this case, we had the added dimension of immediate reflections in those conversations serving as accessible data for analysis. We began thinking axially about our concepts and the emerging relationships (Charmaz, 2014). We played with several visual diagrams with all kinds of relationships proposed between the nine concepts. After several proposed and discarded diagrams outlining relationships between the nine concepts in conveying the story/process of our socialization to the field (i.e., conditions that brought us to advising), we tentatively settled on a model (see Figure 13.1). Over the course of a year and a few conference presentations, we received feedback on the model, though no major adjustments were made.

The current model (McGill et al., 2020a) is presently our best conceptualization of our socialization. The search for dis/connections in our experiences was an engaging part of the project. Though the model emerged through our three stories, in the uncovering of the dis/connections, we wondered: Does this content resonate? What part of this is our story as participant-researchers and what part of this is ours alone? What part of the theory is perhaps a dis/connection for the general story of people in our emerging profession? Will the model inform additional research on professional socialization among our colleagues?

We, as three privileged white men, readily accept that this model might look different if constructed from data collected from a wider and more diverse swath of advisors. Still, it is a product we brought into the world: first at conferences to gauge how it resonated with others and eventually for publication in a new journal in our field.

Mark: This process was the most ambiguous and required the most critical thinking and creativity. Working as a group allowed much more complexity

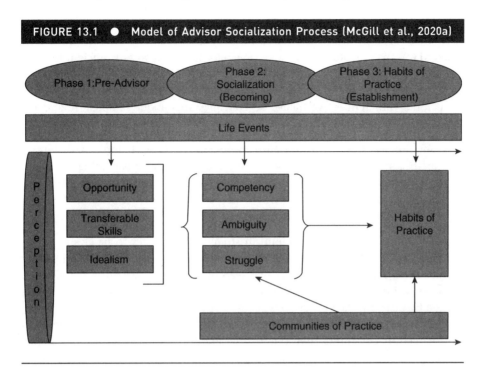

FIGURE 13.1 ● Model of Advisor Socialization Process (McGill et al., 2020a)

of theory building and resulted in a more accurate model than had I developed it on my own.

Craig: Experimenting with how these concepts related to each other—and perhaps more importantly, ensuring they accurately captured our collective experiences—was hugely rewarding.

2018-Present: Research Writing, Submitting for Publication, and Responding to Feedback

After we had coded and organized our analysis, we engaged in a prolonged period of collaborative scholarly writing. In some ways, this was an extension of analysis as the process of writing caused us to sharpen our ideas. However, like any writing project, writer's block is a reality in collaborative writing. Some challenges stemmed from our efforts to refine the analysis, as we would have long discussions wherein we second-guessed initial analyses. At the same time, we set our sights on publication venues that would care about our work and be open to autoethnographic methods.

Our first attempt at publication did not go well. We submitted to an advising journal, the article was rejected outright without panel review, and the feedback we received was that our study could serve as a pilot study but was insufficient to stand alone as a valid contribution to the field. We frequently encountered misunderstandings about the nature and purpose of our research. When we presented at national conferences, we fielded several questions about sample size and the generalizability of our findings. A reviewer from a different submission wrote:

> I am not as sure about the auto-ethnography paper. I don't have any expertise in ethnography [*sic*] so I don't know what its epistemology is, i.e. what kind of argumentation/evidence needs to be presented to substantiate claims...Using "data" isn't sufficient in itself to mark the work as being scientific. (Anonymous editor/reviewer feedback)

This type of feedback was helpful in stretching ourselves to be clearer in our descriptions, specifically for audience members with postpositivistic lenses. But admittedly, it was frustrating when reviewers or conference attendees framed their critiques within a foreign methodological paradigm (e.g., suggesting the work was invalid because it lacked other participants outside of the research team).

Still, we believed our work would extend conversations in the field. The rejection helped us determine that, due to the amount of data (e.g., several original reflections and years of subsequent phone calls not yet analyzed), there was more than a single paper. In regrouping after our first rejection, we sought advice from a methodological expert on publication venues open to autoethnographic work. Responding to this expert's advice required several recalibration sessions wherein we reviewed and discussed the merits of various publication venues before breaking and rebuilding our first manuscript.

Most of the data we coded, discussed, and wrote about thus far illuminated our experiences of professional socialization. For our first paper (McGill et al., 2020a), we stripped much of the rich descriptions of our experiences of the nine concepts in the model to meet journal word limits. We reasoned we should get our model into the knowledge base first, and the evocative and emotional passages illustrating our lived experiences could be better explored in another article (in development), framed around our felt tensions between individual professional identity and the establishment (organizational) identity.

> *Craig:* It is interesting to look back on our process five years out. I remember being so enthused about conducting this different sort of research that seemed strange and even somewhat dangerous. Many of the changes we faced early on had less to do with using this method and more to do with simply being novice researchers.

> *Drew:* Putting our model out there in the world is an exciting and extremely vulnerable act.

Methods/Practices and Their Use

CAE is an appealing method for practitioner-scholars due to the flexibility the iterative process provides (Chang, Hernandez, & Ngunjiri, 2012). Our process evolved from a highly structured, individual, and sequential data collection to a free-flowing, collective, concurrent, and iterative process.

Like any other study, the basic process of conducting a CAE study involves data collection, data analysis and interpretation, and report writing. The primary differences lie in the cyclical relationship between data collection, analysis, and interpretation. CAE allows for a variety of data types: personal memory/recollection, archival materials (e.g., our audio recordings), self-observation (e.g., Drew's memos), self-reflection (e.g., the initial question set), self-analysis (e.g., our second and third drafts of answers to the initial questions after discussion and reflection), and interviews (e.g., weekly phone conversations) (Chang, Hernandez, & Ngunjiri, 2012). There are several data strategies which require the group to balance thinking ahead with flexibility. These include individual versus collective data collection and sequential, concurrent, and/or iterative rounds of coding. Due to the unique symbiotic relationship between data collection, analysis, and interpretation, CAE is both process and product (Chang, 2008).

Conducting a CAE project involves forming a research team, deciding upon a research focus, selecting a collaboration model, and defining group member roles and boundaries. Forming a collaborative group can sometimes present a chicken and egg question (Chang, Hernandez, & Ngunjiri, 2012, p. 62): Does the group come together and then decide to explore something together or does the research question determine who should might be invited to the team to participate? The number of participants in a CAE can be varied and may be related to the topic, type of project, convenience, and group dynamics. Any team undertaking a CAE project should thoughtfully set expectations for time investment on the front end. As such, those taking up collaborative autoethnographic research projects often find ways to fit the work into myriad other personal and professional demands. Pressure and motivation to move projects forward may come from the expectation of collaborators, deadlines to submit manuscripts or scholarly presentations, and the publication pressures typical of academic life. Based on our experience, a consistent weekly meeting time has been an effective way to keep projects moving forward. Participant-researchers should be honest with collaborators on the time available to them for completing project work. There will be times when collaborators need to hold one another accountable to completing the work and to show grace when demands of work and life preclude progress toward completing projects.

Conducting a CAE project may require a learning curve as participant-researchers begin to understand and navigate a dual role of researcher and participant. Some may have worked as researchers in the past, but others may not. Either case requires a researcher to adjust to this new role that participates and contributes both to the generation of autobiographical data and to analysis. The role of researcher-participant afforded the opportunity to study our subjective experiences from two distinct positions. As participants, we understood our experiences first-hand. As researchers, we placed our experiences in the context of the experiences of the other two participants and the relevant literatures. This interpretive work is illustrative of an important difference between CAE work and more traditional forms of qualitative research: In a more traditional setting, emphasis is placed on the participant's comfort and the researcher should be aware of the power dynamics of their role and guard how much they reveal about the mundane activities of their life. All of us were participant-researchers, so the relationships and role boundaries were permeable. Most of our meetings begin with discussing what is happening in our lives, which an outsider might regard as wasted time. However, for the three of us, it is an essential checkpoint into our inner worlds, allowing our team to offer empathy and support.

When done well, CAE should bring dissonance and discomfort. This is in part due to the level of disclosure and the relationships necessary to carry forward the work of autoethnography. Relational ethics come into play and, though consent might seem implicit, it is a grave concern (Ellis, 2007). There is a level of necessary vulnerability and self-disclosure that poses risks. At times, we deliberated about whether to attach a specific name to a quote or to preserve anonymity through thoughtfully omitting an attribution. For instance, on one occasion, one of us did not wish to attach his name to a critique of our professional association. However, the other members thought the critique to be essential in explaining a concept, and more valid and authentic with the name. In this scenario, we engaged an organic process of discussion to reach an agreement.

CAE requires participant researchers to set a deep intention to proceed with humility, genuineness, and vulnerability. Empathy and support are foundational to establishing trust, necessary to carry forward one another's stories and experiences in the research. When we use autobiographical methods, there are risks of over-generalizing our own experiences and our own contexts within socially constructed identities. In our project, our professional role identity and like-minded interest in further probing that identity brought us together. However, we had to challenge one another to recognize our experiences and perceptions of them did not occur in isolation from our social identities (some shared and some not; some of privilege and some not). At the same time, the purpose of the research is to uncover deep meanings, both positive and negative. Without genuineness, there is no truth in the data. Without a sense of vulnerability, there are walls around the data.

One of the most beneficial outcomes of this method was the relationships we have formed with one another. Like a qualitative interviewer seeks to develop rapport with participants, collaborative autoethnographers develop rapport with one another both organically and by intentionally establishing rituals. In a typical qualitative project, researchers might come back to their participants/subjects a number of times and a relationship between a researcher and participant might deepen. There is an intake of that person's world and inner contemplation of that data, then some checking by an expert and member checking of that data. As qualitative researchers who carry out work with more traditional methodologies, we frequently feel close to our participants' stories. But this connection is not necessarily reciprocated as it is in CAE. Throughout our project, we have dealt with all the stuff of life (e.g., painful break-ups, births of children, deaths of parents) that become part of the iterative meaning-making of the method. Frankly, there have been meetings in which the events of one of our lives took precedence over the project work. During those meetings, it was more important for the other team members to listen and support him than it was for us to accomplish a specific analytical or writing task. Though we maintain this policy to this day, we are equally committed to ensuring the project moves forward.

Conclusion

Using CAE, we drew upon our experiences to explore professional socialization to an emerging profession. Our process involved six overlapping phases: designing and team-building, initial writing, conversing and note-taking, coding and analysis, theory building, and research writing, submitting for publication, and responding to feedback. Given the intersection of writing, analysis, and interpretation involved in CAE research, we experienced many of the challenges unique to autobiographical methods. However, for us, CAE has been an immensely personal and professionally rewarding method. We began the project as novice qualitative researchers. Through the years, all of us have pursued or are pursuing terminal degrees. We are all active with our families and friends and have high professional aspirations. Holding weekly conversations is ambitious and it is remarkable that we are able to meet as often as we do. Our process is time consuming, frustrating, and the path forward is (still, after five years) unclear. We navigate these challenges with trust, consideration, and compassion for each other. We were fortunate to be a group of three individuals who had a similar work ethic, standards of quality, expectations, and vision. The collaborative aspect of CAE should not be underestimated. Our work created friendships, collegial relationships, and deep professional learning.

Supplemental Readings

Chang, H., Ngunjiri, F., & Hernandez, K. A. C. (2016). *Collaborative autoethnography*. Routledge.

Jones, S. H., Adams, T. E., & Ellis, C. (Eds.). (2016). *Handbook of autoethnography*. Routledge.

Bochner, A. P., & Ellis, C. (Eds.). (2002). *Ethnographically speaking: Autoethnography, literature, and aesthetics*. Rowman/Altamira.

Reflection and Activities

When deciding whether CAE is a viable method for a given study, we suggest considering the following questions:

1. Will the topic or question(s) and current state of literature benefit from participant-researcher's autobiographical perspective? (e.g., there is some aspect of the study that will broaden understanding of a culture, process, phenomenon, etc.)

2. Does the goal of the study lend itself to a collaborative, qualitative approach?

3. Are you and your fellow researchers willing to dig deep, become vulnerable, and to challenge each other? How much of the stuff of your life are you willing to have out there in the world?

4. How much time do you have?

References

AERA code of ethics: American Educational Research Association approved by the AERA council February 2011. (2011). *Educational Researcher, 40*(3), 145–156. https://doi.org/10.3102/0013189X11410403

Chang, H. (2008). *Autoethnography as method*. Left Coast Press.

Chang, H., Hernandez, K.-A. C., & Ngunjiri, F. W. (2012). *Collaborative autoethnography*. Routledge.

Charmaz, K. (2014). *Constructing grounded theory*. SAGE

Ellis, C. (2007). Telling secrets, revealing lives: Relational ethics in research with intimate others. *Qualitative Inquiry, 13*, 3–29. https://doi.org/10.1177/1077800406294947

Glaser, B., & Strauss, A. (1967). *The Discovery of grounded theory: Strategies for qualitative research*. Sociology Press.

Lapadat, J. C. (2017). Ethics in autoethnography and collaborative autoethnography. *Qualitative Inquiry, 23*(8), 589–603. https://doi.org/10.1177/1077800417704462

McGill, C. M. (2019). The professionalization of academic advising: A structured literature review. *NACADA Journal, 39*(1), 89–100. https://doi.org/10.12930/NACADA-18-015

McGill, C. M., Duslak, M., & Puroway, A. (2020a). Entering academic advising: Theorizing professional socialization. *Journal of Academic Advising, 2*, 3–10. Semantic Scholar. https://pdfs.semanticscholar.org/22ff/65cfa829dd7bae207aed860ec2b367d8e22e.pdf

McGill, C. M., Puroway, A. & Duslak, M. (2020b). *Primary-role academic advising professional socialization/identity autoethnographic reflection protocol.* K-State Research Exchange. Handle System. https://hdl.handle.net/2097/40864

Pace, S. (2012). Writing the self into research using grounded theory analytic strategies in autoethnography. *TEXT: Journal of Writing and Writing Courses, 13*(4). https://www.text-journal.com.au/speciss/issue13/Pace.pdf

Patton, M. Q. (2015). *Qualitative evaluation and research methods.* (4th ed.). SAGE.

Saldaña, J. (2015). *The coding manual for qualitative researchers.* SAGE.

Sawyer, R. D., & Norris, J. (2013). *Duoethnography.* Oxford University Press.

Memo Writing Strategies: Analyzing the Parts and the Whole

Paul Mihas

Abstract

Memo writing, an integral tool in qualitative analysis, invites researchers to think holistically about interviews as well as home in on specific text segments to make sense of the parts in relation to the whole. Document reflection memos provide a tool for condensing the narrative trajectory of a transcript. In contrast, key quotation memos unlock a participant's insight evident in a particular piece of text. Memos are the result of a close reading and can be a precursor to coding or can be used alongside coding as tools for comparison and synthesis. Memos comparing quotations from the same transcript or across transcripts are another means to promote discovery, providing a systematic way for researchers to approach data from both a wide-angle lens and a close-up view of pieces of data.

Keywords: Memo writing; key quotation; holistic memo; constant comparison

The purpose of this chapter is to describe how memo writing plays a critical role in qualitative data analysis. Analyzing textual data requires paying close attention to language, to how participants reveal what matters most to them. Memos are a vehicle for this attention, and as such, they are a complement to coding. Memos have been an instrumental component of established traditions such as grounded theory and ethnography but can be used in all genres of qualitative research.

Overview

Memo writing incorporates various investigative lenses, including an exploratory lens as well as a more strategically analytical one. Memos develop a researcher's conversation with the data and can serve as a precursor, a companion, or a follow-up to coding (Birks, Chapman, & Francis, 2008; Charmaz, 2014; Corbin & Strauss, 2008; Lofland & Lofland, 1999). As a method of inquiry, memo writing moves us closer to reportable knowledge production. A question guiding memo writing is: "What does this quotation or transcript teach me about my research question?" (Maietta, Hamilton, Swartout, & Petruzzelli, 2019). Initially, our thoughts may be speculative; we write through our doubt. As a precursor to coding, memos on key quotations—those segments that are especially meaningful—capture our close reading of text. A "close reading" suggests "empirical intimacy"—dwelling in data and moving closer to the research problem and textured language of participants (Truzzi, 1974).

Rather than starting with coding, and perhaps applying topics within easy reach based on our *a priori* assumptions, memo writing invites us to first notice complexities in the nuanced discourse itself. Goodall invites us to "describe before you evaluate or analyze" (Goodall, 2008, p. 30). By writing about a quotation—not just reading it—we document our thoughts and see how participant narratives can activate an intersection of values, beliefs, behavior, and emotions; these are sometimes competing discourses, revealing intricate layers of a participant's life-world (Richardson, 2000). Memo writing helps us write through these complexities to a deeper understanding of the participant voice or voices. Early memos can then be mined for initial codes—topics that are based on our having developed greater "cognitive empathy" with the participants, an understanding of how the participant makes meaning (Small, 2018). Saldaña (2016) reminds us that codes, categories, and concepts can be "embedded *within* analytic memos" (p. 54) and in this way memos can serve as channels for more condensed topics. Early memos can also be material for memos written later in the qualitative analysis life cycle that document how the researcher's understanding of the data has changed over time, thereby capturing the data-driven nature of the analysis. Charmaz's (2014) work in grounded theory similarly invests in memo writing as a tool for comparison of data and data, data and codes, codes and codes, and codes and higher-level categories.

Though memo writing is often associated with grounded theory and ethnography, this chapter focuses on using memos productively for any genre of qualitative research. In particular, I investigate the use of different lenses for seeing the contiguous whole, the transcript, as well as the similarity across the parts, the quotations. As a pragmatic practice, memo writing allows us to gradually discover both the voice of the participant and our own researcher voice. Seasoned qualitative researchers emphasize the importance of finding one's voice as a writer (Sandelowski, 1998; Thorne, 2008) as well as the participant voice. Our goal is to speak *with* participants, not for them. For this reason, memos often incorporate quotations so that researchers do not interpret beyond the data; rather, their reflections are grounded in the interview's textured language.

Researchers' strategies for memo writing can develop organically over the length of the project or be specified in advance. Grounded theorists make their memos "increasingly analytic" (Charmaz, 2014, p. 165) and refer to them as "intellectual capital" in the bank (Clarke, 2005). Charmaz encourages researchers to title their memos for more effective retrieval and organization. (For suggestions on how to write early and advanced memos, see Charmaz, 2014, pp. 169–170.)

Different types of memos address particular study goals. The *document reflection memo*, for example, is a holistic memo designed to highlight threads that run through a single interview. It captures the narrative trajectory of a document—turning points, patterns, and episodic flow. At this point, our analysis is "vertical"—we review a transcript from beginning to end (Maietta, Hamilton, Swartout, & Petruzzelli, 2019); we first assess a single transcript, rather than looking across data, allowing us to step back from the fragmented review of quotations. *Key quotation memos*, in contrast, are memos at the level of a text segment, the "most telling quotes in your data" (Hesse-Biber & Leavy, 2011, p. 305). This memo allows a researcher to consider implications and meanings at the microlevel. Even a short quotation can unlock insight that addresses the research question.

As a companion to coding, memo writing allows us to elaborate on why we apply particular topics to textual fragments, helping us "stay true to the data and data context" (Naghmeh, Mahboobeh, & Mahvash, 2015). That is, it is a way of engaging constant comparison (Corbin & Strauss, 2008, pp. 73–74). Rather than waiting until after we have coded data to begin thinking more analytically, writing memos during coding affords a place to sustain inquiry, allowing us to make meaning along the way. Researchers might attend to the growing range of content coded to a code and begin writing a memo comparing quotations (addressed further below), or they might refine the code definition as surfacing data calls into question their initial understanding of the topic. As a follow-up to coding, memo writing allows us to compare codes, to assess conceptual overlaps between topics, and to provide a place to track patterns across transcripts. When it comes time to write a paper or dissertation chapter, the intellectual capital of memos is invaluable.

Study Description

The memo examples in this chapter come from a study using oral history data collected by the Southern Oral History Program at the University of North Carolina at Chapel Hill and written accounts by students attending East Carolina University. The purpose of the study, conducted in 2018, was to understand how survivors make sense of their circumstances during and after a natural disaster (Mihas, 2019a, 2019b, 2019c).

To investigate our research questions, I engaged in a strategy of intentional memo writing and used several forms of memos. The first set of memos I describe below illustrates practices for writing memos from individual transcriptions. My scope then widens, and I discuss memos that compare transcripts and then memos that synthesize insights from having coded and reviewed quotations across transcripts.

Practices for Writing Memos on Single Transcripts

Making meaning requires the intentional use of research practices—such as transcribing and coding—during the qualitative research life cycle. Memo writing strategies discussed in this section provide practices for preserving researchers' discernment into data and developing these ideas while collecting and coding further data.

Document Reflection Memo

An especially pragmatic memo is the document reflection memo, a record of the researcher's initial understanding of a transcript that may be examined later in the project when looking across participants. In a document reflection memo, we are more likely to notice participant assumptions redolent in a transcript or a way of speaking or thinking that inhabits an entire interview. Here, we attempt to hold in our mind the interview *context*. Repetitions and patterns lead us to meaning, interpretive insights based on evidence contextualized within the document as a whole. Put another way, document reflection memos capture "contiguity as a source of coherence" (Maxwell, 2012, p. 67). Rather than immediately fragmenting the data into text segments, contiguity privileges the holistic view of a single transcript. Even in a semi-structured interview, there is an unfolding logic as the participant works their way through the topics and reveals a perspective, what Maxwell (2012) might call a "local connection," rather than a general one (p. 67). Here, we are not summarizing across narratives, we are simply casting a net around a particular transcript to see it as holistic account of a single lifeworld. In this way, we are attentive to the "flow of logic" (Thorne, 2008, p. 182) evident in the transcript, rather than "interrupting" the story by pulling out quotation fragments.

Below is an example of a document summary memo based on a 15,000-word transcript of Jenny, a white woman who lived through Hurricane Floyd in North Carolina. Notice how the memo condenses a long transcript but also addresses the research question: How do individuals experience living through a hurricane? A similar memo was written for each interview in the study.

Writing prompt: What does this one transcript teach me about the research question?

"Mind Is Working Faster Than Your Hands"

Document Reflection Memo on Jenny, a Hurricane Survivor

Based on Transcript K-0281

"Voices After the Deluge," Southern Oral History Program, 1999

In the interview with Jenny and her husband, Aaron, the couple describe their initial reaction to the flooding and its aftermath. Jenny and Aaron run a turkey farm as well as an antique business. Before Hurricane Floyd, Jenny relied on certain indicators to predict flooding, but Hurricane Floyd "broke the rules," disrupting her regular process of decision making. She leaves her house on a rescue truck wearing only a nightgown, feeling like a "refugee." This identity statement casts the moment that she is forced out of her home as a turning point.

The aftermath of flooding leaves Jenny and Aaron with seemingly never-ending tasks—ultimately throwing out a hundred thousand dollars worth of pieces of damaged furniture. Central to Jenny's story is that when she starts the day, nothing "you're planning to do or want to do is what you do." With limited agency, she is focused on the physical state of her farm and house, doing whatever she can to make the house livable, to keep it feeling like *home*. After discovering mold under the sub-floor, she and Aaron cut out the walls and pull out insulation. This is part of minimizing uncertainties. Rather than accepting the assessment of the walls by the Federal Energy Emergency Management Agency (FEMA), she finds out for herself. FEMA indicated that they didn't have to take out walls, but their own exploration suggests otherwise. She frequently uses the word "we" because her goals are so closely tied to Aaron's. The "mess" is a shared one. Friends, neighbors, and family all volunteer to help them, but their assistance is largely task-based, rather than psychosocial. "Hands have been the biggest asset that anybody—if you've ever been flooded, hands are what a person needs. They need financial stuff, too. But in the very beginning those hands—." Volunteers bring physical labor—their "hands"—which in the early days matters even more to Jenny than financial assistance which is still an abstraction.

When Jenny says that her "mind is working faster than your hands," it captures her overwhelm. She is conscious of what needs to be done but cannot physically keep up with the tasks, large and small. Aaron spends four days trying to clean out 60,000 dead turkeys while Jenny cleans every crevice of the refrigerator with a Q-tip and Clorox. "Of course I was so strained at that time I didn't even know who I was. I didn't think. But without their hands we could have never gotten it done, just never." Jenny's statement, that she didn't know who she was, harks back to her statement about feeling like a refugee. Not only are her circumstances different; her identity seems different.

In inhabiting this emerging identity, Jenny feels a sudden bond with those who share similar circumstances, but these are the very people who do not have time for a simple conversation. Victims live parallel lives, rather than intersecting ones. Jenny and Aaron experience a sustained limbo—they have to wait before being paid and they don't know when they'll open the antique business again. They have a "two-fold problem" in that they have no one they can trust to take care of the farm if they go antique hunting. Furthermore, the money they received from FEMA is not commensurate with their loss.

Throughout the aftermath of the flooding, Jenny and Aaron do things their way, such as questioning the safety measures pushed by FEMA. "I thought I had to get rid of my shoes. But I didn't." Rather than heeding the authorities, they do what the two of them think is right, but their locus of control is narrow. In the weeks that follow, Jenny lives off retirement. "What else can you do, you know?" This rhetorical question encapsulates Jenny's limited agency. "And too the flooding washed out roads. That's just some of the things that were problems that we had no control over. There was nothing we could do." Not only does Jenny have to face these environmental constraints, she also lacks a working phone during this time. Nor does she have significant legal leverage to make requests or claims to those in power, such as the company that owned the turkeys on her farm. In her interaction with government authorities, such as FEMA, which loans her and Aaron a trailer but does not give them adequate funds for recovery, Jenny exhibits both overwhelm and lack of faith in the system. "I've not had time to appeal or do anything other than keep our head above the water."

In regard to the research question, *How do individuals experience living through a natural disaster?*, this transcript suggests that survivors are consumed by physical logistics, finding reliable transportation, and finding comfortable shelter or making their home habitable. Psychosocial needs, such as seeking out neighbors and friends, are especially difficult to address. Though Jenny feels a bond with those in similar circumstances, she does not find time to reach out to them. Instead, she relies on the physical assistance offered by others and works daily until her home and farm are habitable. Stability in one's housing becomes central and all-consuming. Though Jenny senses the collective stress of her community, she does not have resources to offer assistance in the face of her own overwhelm.

Writing a document reflection memo on each transcript is a way to work vertically through each participant's experience using a wide-angle lens. Such memos provide a condensed, yet comprehensive account of the narrative trajectory of each interview—pivotal moments, takeaways, and governing perspectives that give shape to the transcript as a whole. In analysis, these memos, along with codes, help the researcher avoid getting lost in copious amounts of data. As we engage in coding smaller textual segments as a more microlevel analytical practice, the document reflection memo reinforces the holistic nature of the data collection episode—the context of the narrative's emotional and psychological landscape.

Key Quotation Memo

In contrast to a document reflection memo, a key quotation memo, also called a "pulse" or "power quote" memo, focuses on a quotation that is especially illustrative in its content or tone (Maietta, Hamilton, Swartout, & Petruzzelli, 2019; Walsh, 2019). By focusing on the participant's language, researchers have a window into rationale—the story individuals are telling themselves—moving closer to seeing the world as participants see it. Key quotation memos can describe the quotation or go beyond description to reflection, offering conceptual reflection of nascent meanings.

Below is a quotation from Jenny's transcript. I singled it out was because it elucidates her shifting relationship with her neighbors during the aftermath of the flooding.

Excerpt: Jenny's Reflections on Neighbors

Jenny: There's something about when I am around when I meet somebody down at the center. Or if somebody—if you do get together and talk. I had a neighbor stop by and talk this morning. It's like there is a closeness and you share the same things. Our lives are somewhat the same right now because everybody's got the same problems. She doesn't have the income problem. I have the income problem but we both have the house that we're working as a goal. I think there probably is more closeness. And other people might have more time to socialize but I don't think so. I don't think so.... You know some people could go to their jobs and they came home and they were through. We were never through. We're still not through. But ours was—we worked seven days a week up until this past weekend. And I'm serious—seven days a week. (Transcript K-0281, "Voices After the Deluge," Southern Oral History Program, 1999, p. 33)

The function of the key quotation memo, presented below, is to open up the quotation and to attempt to make sense of the participant's own insights. Below is also a writing prompt to help activate this type of memo.

Writing prompt: Why does this particular text segment capture my attention? How does this single quotation help me better understand the participant's lifeworld?

Recognizing a New Intimacy

Key Quotation Memo on Jenny, A Hurricane Survivor

Jenny tries to explain a sense of newfound "closeness" that she suddenly feels with those whom she recognizes are experiencing similar circumstances, despite the fact that there are few opportunities for extended conversation. This intimacy is based on sensing something that was perhaps not there before ("there's something about when I'm around" them), a sense that she is now living parallel lives with others. Jenny is aware of not only what is the same between them but of what is different. Her neighbor "doesn't have the income problem." She cannot seem to help but compare her circumstances with others. She guesses that others, like her, probably do not have time to socialize either. The sudden intimacy with others seems palpable, even though her energy is focused on working all day, everyday. It becomes part of her peripheral vision, noticing when others are now mirroring her life.

Key quotation memos can focus on a process, behavior, or an implicit or explicit action—how participants act, react, or interact. This memo can later be developed into a more encompassing memo on a process identifiable across data. A memo on *recognizing a new intimacy* captures a cognitive shift in survivors when they can articulate an awareness that they share increasing similarities with others who they might otherwise see as different. In writing about this process, I was able to later analyze what activated it, what destabilized it, and what kept it in place. This initial memo became a seed for formal writing once I had reviewed additional transcripts.

In writing a key quotation memo, a researcher has identified a power paragraph, an especially evocative excerpt that is not simply a quotation of interest itself; it is a quotation that also serves as a story's "fuse box," elucidating different parts and conceptual levels of an interview, a window into how we might read other parts of the transcript. The power quotation can also serve as a "hinge" in the middle of an interview, looking forward and backward, to the future and the past (Walsh, 2019). Power quotes can also help researchers revisit the transcript as a whole. For another example of a key quotation memo, called an "early memo," see Charmaz (2014, p. 163).

Memos Comparing Quotations From the Same Transcript

Reviewing two or more quotations from the same transcript and writing about how they echo, contradict, or complicate each other is a way of assessing the inscribed meaning between pieces of text. Inscribed meaning points to the arc of meaning surfacing between parts of a transcript. We do not read a quotation in isolation; we read it in light of earlier quotations, as if there is a subtextual arc connecting them. Inscribed meaning is the connective tissue that holds those quotations together in our minds, each quotation unlocking unknowns about the other. For example, in the first quotation below, Jenny discusses how time as a resource has diminished.

Excerpt: Jenny's Reflection on Time

Jenny: And there's been no time. We've worked so hard. We've not had time to talk to our neighbors to find out really what happened with each one. I think it would be so interesting to know what went on in that house and that house and with us because we've not had any time. We have worked around the clock. (Transcript K-0281 from *"Voices After the Deluge,"* Southern Oral History Program, 1999, p. 8)

Later in the interview, when Jenny refers to a FEMA agent as arrogant, the interviewer asks for clarification.

Excerpt: Jenny's Reflection on FEMA

Interviewer: How was [the FEMA agent] arrogant?

Jenny: Just didn't have time. It was like he walked through and walked right back out. And he punched some numbers on a little handheld computer. And anything—. I remember asking a couple of questions. Right now I can't remember what they were. And it was like, "What does it matter to you?"... And I think I even asked him where he was from and he said he was from California. He went right over to one of our neighbor's and he was the same way there. (Transcript K-0281 from *"Voices After the Deluge,"* Southern Oral History Program, 1999, p. 41)

The first quotation addresses time as a barrier, whereas the second quotation addresses time within the realm of authority. In analyzing these quotations side by side—holding them in suspended inquiry—I see that Jenny, due to stress, experiences time as a depleted resource. Finding time for a conversation with a neighbor is now a luxury, something she must postpone. In the second quotation, she comments on the FEMA employee being arrogant because he did not make time for her. As researchers, we might use the following prompt to engage these two quotations in concert.

Writing prompt: How do these separate quotations inform each other? What do they reveal together that may not be otherwise evident?

Based on this prompt, a memo on these two quotations might focus on an apparent contradiction regarding time. Assessing similarity (and difference) between quotations is another source of coherence, as is contiguity. Jenny understands her own lack of time but seems to assume that the FEMA representative, an outsider, has control over time. The inscribed meaning between these quotations invites us to look into the tension between these two assumptions. The connective tissue here brings to the surface a meaning that might otherwise be lost, that time is a kind of capital in the aftermath of a natural disaster. While Jenny is at the mercy of time, she presents authority figures as having control over time. For example, they can decide how many days Jenny has access to the loaner trailer; hence, they seem arrogant when they are not generous with their time, whereas Jenny sees her own lack of time as insurmountable. Time as a commodity divides the haves and the have-nots.

Compositional Ellipses: Connecting the Parts of a Transcript to the Whole

Researchers can take advantage of the connection between a key quotation memo and the holistic document in a *parts–whole memo*. In art composition, the relationship between the part and the whole is sometimes referred to as "compositional ellipses." A shape in a painting, such as an oval, can encapsulate or be encapsulated by a similarly implied shape. "Ellipses ... connect and tie together specific elements to create a sense of unity" (Cowman, 2019). In this type of memo, the researcher addresses what the key memo suggests about the larger contextual unit—how the "DNA" of the whole is contained in the part. A survivor's statement, "it was a curse and a blessing," might illuminate apparent contradictions in the transcript as a whole. Similarly, a key quotation memo can shed light on the larger narrative territory of the transcript. Below is a writing prompt to generate this type of memo.

Writing prompt: How does this particular quotation mirror or contradict the holistic message of the transcript itself?

To engage this prompt—to use a quote as a flashlight to illuminate the whole—I reviewed an interview with a hurricane survivor, Kurt. In it, I found a pulse quotation that illustrates several layers of interaction between Kurt and his world—with the media, with the environment, with other actors, and with himself. In one short paragraph, Kurt describes his growing realization that he is experiencing a hurricane. First, he notices the water, then the weather report on TV, then his gut feeling, and then noticing water rising before his eyes, and finally seeing his neighbor trying to get his attention. At the end of the paragraph, Kurt concludes, "I knew we were in bad shape." This is not an instantaneous reaction to a single moment. It is a conclusion based on incremental awareness, layers of evidence received through multiple sources before he reaches this certitude.

I next considered the document reflection memo I wrote on Kurt which addresses how he rescued 17 people but did not see himself as a hero while he was doing so. This label only occurs to him later in his interview after he absorbs several layers of information. Though people comment on his bravery as he goes from flooded house to house, "it just didn't sink in until later on" (Transcript K-0604, "*Voices After the Deluge*," Southern Oral History Program, 2002, p. 9).

In writing the parts–whole memo, I attempted to make deeper sense of a process or structure, in this case, the process of cumulative awareness. In this memo, I was able to describe how Kurt made sense of his heroism during the storm. I described how just as it takes multiple sources of information for Kurt to acknowledge that he is, in fact, experiencing a hurricane, it takes multiple rescues and cumulative awareness for him to acknowledge (in the interview as a whole) his larger-than-life, heroic actions, and in fact, a new identity as hero. These are what fiction writer Charles Baxter (1997) might call "rhyming" actions, actions that are not identical but that "sound" the same, that share similar characteristics at their core. In other words, *cumulative awareness* is not simply a code to be applied to a single quotation; it characterizes the structure of the interview itself, one in which the participant takes on a new identity. A *parts–whole memo* can highlight the participant's process of meaning-making and document two levels of evidence, the fragmented quotation and the larger content and structure of the narrative taking shape in the contiguous interview.

Using Memos to Synthesize Patterns Across the Data

One of the primary challenges of qualitative analysis is synthesis—making sense of data across participants who may demonstrate different attitudes, experiences, and outcomes. In addition to coding across these incidents, systematic memo writing can help the researcher with this analytic integration. Memos, at the level of quotations and single documents, are initially self-contained analytic products, but as we look across data, we use them as tools for synthesis. This means that researchers assess meaning across memos by reviewing them for commonalities and paradoxes. Memo writing puts researchers in the position to write a final chapter, report, or results section. Comparative memos, in particular, are scaffolding for this kind of integrative reporting. This kind of memo is especially relevant in grounded theory (see Charmaz, 2014, pp. 176–177).

Memos Comparing Transcripts

After completing document reflection memos on each transcript, the next step would be to compare these memos and perhaps develop a typology—for example, identifying different types of survival stories. Comparing participant transcripts via the holistic document reflection memos allows researchers to look for patterns and differences across participant experiences. Using the holistic memos as stand-ins for the transcripts themselves, the researcher looks for configurations across the memos, identifiable clusters across the larger dataset. In the hurricane study, one identifiable pattern was that people who played active roles as heroes or rescuers had fewer conflicted emotions about the hurricane. Those who saw themselves as recipients of misfortune were more reflective about the dimensions of the hurricane and had more conflicted emotions, including anxiety, luck, guilt, and gratitude (Mihas 2019a, 2019b, 2019c).

Writing prompt: Is there an identifiable pattern across document reflection memos? Do certain participants cluster together based on similar accounts and perspectives?

In the hurricane study, the memo I wrote on Kurt highlights his physical skills to help people, whereas the memo on another survivor, Bruce, emphasizes his counseling skills. Despite these differences, the memos' evaluative conclusions are similar. "We knew everybody, and we were real proud of the neighborhood we had, and the flood just devastated that neighborhood, and it never recovered" (Transcript K-0604, *"Voices After the Deluge,"* Southern Oral History Program, 2002, p. 8).

This sentence could have come from either Kurt or Bruce's transcript. It shows that despite differences in personal motivations and skill sets, the "helpers" framed the hurricane as an event that generated pride and collective devastation.

Another helper, a nurse, amplifies this sentiment, mentioning how the hurricane could flatten everyone in a community equally: "It forged a stronger bond in our community, black, white, low income, middle income, upper class, because it didn't matter what you had, you could very easily lose it" (Transcript K-0606, "*Voices After the Deluge*," Southern Oral History Program, 2002, p. 12). A major contrast to this collective framing comes from participants who understood themselves as casualties, like Jenny, who were more focused on the overwhelm of recovery.

In this way, comparing document reflection memos can be used to develop a *typology* in a study—to construct identifiable types of participants based on their behavior, perspectives, or values: reluctant rescuers, shell-shocked observers, tapped-out survivors, and so on. We might further discern that witnesses, who did not suffer major negative consequences, tend to move from disbelief to altruism while those affected directly by the storm are so overwhelmed that they inhabit a longer phase of grief and recovery.

Memos Comparing Quotations Across Transcripts

Memos may also be used to promote discovery during other phases of the qualitative life cycle. This section discusses comparison memos. This form of writing invites us to look across data using a *code* as a lens.

After coding data, researchers review quotations to assess the variation of quotations coded to a particular code. They can discern patterns among the range of voices and make sense of quotations that might not fit the pattern. Rather than treating all quotations as simply illustrative of a code and presenting them as such, a *comparison memo* is intended to show how a topic takes on different shape in different circumstances or for different types of people. In other words, researchers can discern aspects or dimensions of the code, such as varying degrees of intensity. In the hurricane study, the text coded for *luck* for three narrators—Mitchell, Hannah, and Luke—shows us the range of circumstances in which luck is activated.

Mitchell: It really felt great to know I had been able to help out others who had not been as lucky as me and my family.

Hannah: Luckily I had the most wonderful friends who took me under their wing…. Even though I had so little on this birthday I never felt so lucky.

Luke: It made me very appreciative of how well I fared and very humble concerning my damage, which in comparison was trivial. (East Carolina University, 1999)

Writing prompt: Aside from the code, what is similar in these quotations? How do these segments on luck suggest the different forms luck can take on? That is, despite their similarity, what is different across them?

Given this prompt, I wrote a memo about these data to develop the code, to dimensionalize luck, not simply note its prevalence. I looked across further narratives and identified more accounts of people comparing themselves with others or comparing themselves with what could have happened, suggesting that experiencing luck is based on "evidence" both real and imagined. This comparison helped me understand that Mitchell's thoughts about luck are framed in what he gave others, whereas Hannah's are embedded in what she tangibly received. In a more intellectualized tone, Luke expresses the same sentiment regarding feeling lucky. Though luck is the connecting thread across the quotations, it is characterized differently across them. For participants, claiming luck depends on identifying a lesser comparative state, which might be evident from what is real or what is imagined. The comparative memo is a place to work through the "evidence" on how luck is not simply a static "one note" code; it is activated in different ways depending on one's role in the natural disaster.

Conclusion

Coding textual data creates a strategic focus, and as a companion, memo writing throughout analysis can strengthen researchers' understanding of the codes they are using, making what is ponderable more tangible. By having a documented conversation with data, a researcher can more easily identify topics that are surfacing—making coding more engaging—notice how quotations support a priori codes or a conceptual framework, and develop empirical intimacy with data.

Memo writing is a form of rigor. From the beginning of data review, memo writing invites researchers to make claims from data and to learn how participants see and frame their experience, rather than treating coding and writing as artificially separate phases of analysis. Memos provide a systematic space to track cumulative illustrative "evidence" into the participants' decision-making, actions, and the foregrounding of particular values.

Researchers will develop their own writing style, and memos will become more complex as one's study evolves. Revisiting memos or appending new content to them can track a researcher's growing knowledge and attendant evidence. Later memos may clarify or call into question earlier memos. This is part of an audit trail showing how a researcher investigated data and made claims grounded in evidence.

Supplemental Readings

Birks, M., Chapman, Y., & Francis, K. (2008). Memos in qualitative research: Probing data and process. *Journal of Research in Nursing, 13*(10), 68–75. https://doi.org/10.1177/1744987107081254

Charmaz, K. (2014). Memo-writing. In *Constructing grounded theory* (2nd ed., pp. 162–191). SAGE.

Corbin, J., & Strauss, A. (2008). *Basics of qualitative research* (3rd ed.). SAGE.

Reflection and Activities

1. Select an interview transcript and write a document reflection memo. Consider the larger shape of the document, the narrative trajectory it suggests.

2. Select one quotation from that interview and write about what it suggests in regard to a process, actor, or structure.

3. Next, select 3–5 quotations that are especially provoking and write about how they relate to each other—narratively and conceptually. These quotations might come from a single transcript or, if the study is far enough along, a set of transcripts or coded data.

References

Baxter, C. (1997). *Burning down the house: Essays on fiction*. Graywolf Press.

Birks, M., Chapman, Y., & Francis, K. (2008). Memos in qualitative research: Probing data and process. *Journal of Research in Nursing, 13*(10), 68–75. https://doi.org/10.1177/1744987107081254

Charmaz, K. (2014). *Constructing grounded theory* (2nd ed.). SAGE.

Clarke, A. (2005). *Situational analysis: Grounded theory after the postmodern turn*. SAGE.

Corbin, J., & Strauss, A. (2008). *Basics of qualitative research* (3rd ed.). SAGE.

Cowman, J. W. (2019). *Dynamic symmetry art*. https://www.dynamicsymmetryart.com/ellipses.html

East Carolina University. (1999). *Listening to history: Telling our stories about the flooding of 1999*. History 5135 special collections.

Goodall, H. L. (2008). *Writing qualitative inquiry: Self, stories, and academic life*. Left Coast Press.

Hesse-Biber, S. N., & Leavy, P. (2011). *The practice of qualitative research*. SAGE.

Lofland, J., & Lofland, L. H. (1999). Data logging in observation: Fieldnotes. In A. Bryman, & R. G. Burgess (Eds.), *Qualitative research* (Vol. 3). SAGE.

Maietta, R., Hamilton, A., Swartout, K., & Petruzzelli, J. (2019). *ResearchTalk's qualitative data analysis camp (short course conducted by ResearchTalk, Inc.)*. ResearchTalk.

Maxwell, J. (2012). *A realist approach to qualitative research*. SAGE.

Mihas, P. (2019a). *Learn to build a codebook for a generic qualitative study*. SAGE Research Methods Datasets. http://methods.sagepub.com/Datasets

Mihas, P. (2019b). *Learn to analyze written text using discourse analysis*. SAGE Research Methods Datasets. http://methods.sagepub.com/Datasets

Mihas, P. (2019c). *Learn to use narrative analysis to analyze written narratives*. SAGE Research Methods Datasets. http://methods.sagepub.com/Datasets

Naghmeh, R., Mahboobeh, A., & Mahvash, S. (2015). Memo and memoing in qualitative research. *Journal of Qualitative Health Science, 4*(2), 206–217.

Richardson, L. (2000). Writing: A method of inquiry. In N. K. Denzin, & Y. S. Lincoln (Eds.), *The SAGE handbook of qualitative research* (2nd ed., pp. 923–948). SAGE.

Saldaña, J. (2016). *The coding manual for qualitative researchers* (3rd ed.). SAGE.

Sandelowski, M. (1998). Writing a good read: Strategies for re-presenting qualitative data. *Research in Nursing & Health, 23*, 334–340. https://doi.org/10.1002/(SICI)1098-240X(199808)21:4<375::AID-NUR9>3.0.CO;2-C

Small, M. (March 1, 2018). Rhetoric and evidence in a polarized society. In *Harvard University public lecture, coming to terms with a polarized society lecture series, ISERP, Columbia University*.

Southern Oral History Program. (1999–2002). *Collection #4007, voices after the deluge*. Southern Historical Collection, Wilson Library, University of North Carolina at Chapel Hill.

Thorne, S. (2008). *Interpretive description*. Left Coast Press.

Truzzi, M. (1974). *Verstehen: Subjective understanding in the social sciences*. Addison-Wesley.

Walsh, C. (June 17, 2019). *The power paragraph. Fiction writers review*. https://fiction-writersreview.com/essay/the-power-paragraph/

Critical Analytic Memoing*

Elaine Keane

Abstract

This chapter examines critical analytic memoing as a core generative tool for all qualitative researchers. The chapter commences with an exploration of how memos are defined and used, and of the different types of memos that are generated during the research process, particularly (but not only) from a constructivist grounded theory (CGT) perspective. After outlining contextual details about a CGT study of social class in higher education in Ireland, the next section presents excerpts from preparatory and more advanced, conceptual memos, demonstrating how memos can be employed to move from "storying" a code, concept, or category towards more abstract conceptualizing. In the final section, further memoing-related practices are discussed, including diagramming which aids thinking more conceptually, and using journaling and memoing to assist researchers in being critically reflexive about their positionalities as coparticipants in the research process.

Keywords: Memoing; analytic memoing; critical reflexivity; researcher positionality; constructivist grounded theory

Memos constitute a significant part of constructivist grounded theory (CGT) studies, but as shown in Chapter 14 by Mihas, memo writing can be used in *all* qualitative inquiry. Building on the strategies examined in the previous chapter, this chapter focuses on how memos can be employed to raise the analytic level of,

---

*This chapter is dedicated to the memory of Kathy Charmaz, an incredible scholar, mentor, and friend, who died on July 26, 2020.

and to inject criticality about researcher positionalities into, one's developing qualitative analysis. I share a set of memos that illuminate the conceptual development within my analyses and the critical awareness I experienced with regard to my positionalities.

Overview and Literature Review

Memo writing is a core feature of grounded theory studies. While memos are written throughout the research process, a core function is to bridge the gap between coding, conceptual development, and drafts of writing. Memoing enables the researcher to ask: "What is going on here?" and "How can I make sense of it?" (Thornberg & Charmaz, 2014, p. 163). In memoing, we stop and write ideas about our codes whenever they occur to us (Charmaz, 2014; Glaser, 1978, 1998). Indeed, Glaser (1978, p. 83) states that "the *prime rule* is to *stop and memo*—no matter what he [the analyst] interrupts." Glaser (1978, 1998) and other grounded theorists (e.g., Charmaz, 2006, 2014) emphasize *freedom* in memo writing, freedom from consideration about "correct" writing, and freedom to write in a private dialogue with oneself about one's ideas in whatever way one wishes. As Glaser (1998, p. 180) emphasizes, "A memo is whatever the writing happens to be at the moment capture of an idea so it is not lost." Along with freedom, Lempert (2007, p. 249) also stresses the private dialogic nature of memo writing, commenting that "Whatever works is just fine in a memo: a memo need only be the account of a researcher talking to him/herself." Likewise, Charmaz (2014, p. 162) highlights that memos are "interactive" and "for conversing with yourself about your data, codes, ideas and hunches."

At heart, memo writing is a *generative* enterprise. As Glaser (1998, p. 178) notes, "writing memos is the vehicle by which concepts and ideas pour out, are saved and *grow*." Thus while memos record, they also *produce*; the process of writing encourages, clarifies, and helps us to articulate our thinking in the creative theorizing process. Memoing is an excellent focusing tool, and it encourages us to put pen to paper (or text on a screen) about our ideas early in the research process. Indeed, in the context of ethnography, Hammersley and Atkinson (2007, p. 151) note that constructing "analytic memoranda" forces the researcher to engage in "a process of explication" through which one must ascertain "what one knows, how such knowledge has been acquired, the degree of certainty of such knowledge, and what further lines of inquiry are implied."

Qualitative researchers in general, as well as grounded theorists specifically, compose different types of memos throughout the research process. While in grounded theory[1] we aim to develop a theoretical analysis, and therefore our

---

[1]Note that analytic memos are used and are very useful in qualitative research more generally; you do not have to be doing grounded theory to engage in memoing.

memos aim to raise the analytic level of our writing, we may *initially* "story a category" (Glaser, 1998, p. 181) during the process of constant comparison (Glaser, 1965). Storying a category can involve some description of the data on a particular issue—participant by participant or otherwise—to summarize the data. Charmaz (2014, p. 163) gives an example of an early memo which performs this story-ing function, describing how one of her participants ("Teresa") portrayed losing her voice. Charmaz brings Teresa's words directly into the memo, and explores her codes and thinking in relation to Teresa's statements. Similarly, Thornberg's early memo from his 2015 study on school bullying (cf. Charmaz et al., 2017, p. 430) presents summary information, reflections and questions regarding his participants' explanations about bullying, and he also brings participant quotes into the memo.

In later memos, we focus on raising the analytic level of our writing, moving from "storying" toward conceptualization. While we can still bring data-based examples, including quotations, into analytic memos, we think—and write—on a more abstract, conceptual level. Engaging in the constant comparative method facilitates conceptualization (Glaser, 1998); hence, an important part of analytic memoing is making comparisons, comparing data with data, data with codes, codes with codes, and codes with categories (Charmaz, 1995, 2014). In analytic memos, we *define* core aspects of our codes, concepts and categories, and *articulate relationships* therein. A key tool in doing this conceptual work is *asking analytic questions of our data*, a Strauss mantra (Charmaz, 2014). Very helpful here are Glaser's (1978) theoretical coding families and, in particular, the 6 Cs (causes, contexts, contingencies, consequences, covariances, and conditions). Researchers tend to use theoretical codes quite naturally (consciously or unconsciously) in asking questions about their data in order to relate, organize, and integrate their categories (Charmaz et al., 2017). Examining the various aspects of a particular category, we may ask:

- What is going on here?
- What seems to have led to this happening?
- What are the conditions under which this occurs?
- What seems to have happened as a result of this?

Of course, asking questions of our data implies providing—even tentative—answers. A key feature of this process is its iterative nature; going back and forth between memoing and our data and coding to follow up on hunches, to address our questions, and to ascertain linkages, using abductive reasoning (Bryant & Charmaz, 2007). Abductive reasoning involves considering all possible theoretical explanations for a puzzling finding from our analysis, forming a question about this finding, and exploring (or "testing") the question with data (Charmaz et al., 2017). In this way, memo writing also enables us to see gaps in our analyses—and our data—thus facilitating the design of a theoretical sampling entrée into the field to fill conceptual gaps in—or between—categories. We may make conjectures in our memos, but we go back to the field to check them (Charmaz, 2014).

Thornberg's memo on "Identity Struggling" is an example of a memo from later in the research process (cf. Charmaz et al., 2017, p. 428) which accomplishes important conceptual work; it defines the main category being examined, and explores relationships between this and other categories. In Charmaz's (2014, pp. 176–177) example of an analytic memo, she defines "suffering as a moral status," considers what codes the category subsumed, and examines the conditions under which "moral status" rises or falls. Both Thornberg and Charmaz bring examples and participant quotes into their analytic memos but do so in an illustrative rather than descriptive fashion. In this illustrative role, the quotes provide data-based examples of the more abstract elements of one's developing analysis.

A related and useful tool to use in conjunction with memoing in CGT, and qualitative research more generally, is *diagramming*, which can be employed before, during, and following memo writing (Charmaz, 2014). Within analytic memos, we also pay attention to the potential applicability of "sensitizing" concepts from our substantive fields. Where relevant, we may compare an aspect of our emerging analysis to an extant concept, specifying *how* it may apply rather than overlaying it on our analysis (Charmaz, 2014). A memo can also be *critically* analytic in its interrogation of researcher positionalities and relationships with the research process (Charmaz et al., 2017; Keane, 2009, 2015). These tools and foci—diagramming, the use of sensitizing concepts, and researcher positionalities—will be examined later in the chapter.

The Study

The memo examples in this chapter are drawn from a study about widening participation and social class in higher education (HE) Ireland. The purpose of the research was to explore and compare the academic and social experiences of students from different social class backgrounds at undergraduate level in university (cf. Keane, 2009, 2011a, 2011b, 2012, 2015). The study employed CGT and involved one or two in-depth semi-structured interviews with 45 students over a three-year period. There were two groups of student participants: (1) School-leaver Access (SLA) students, who had progressed to university via a preentry Access course, having met criteria related to socioeconomic disadvantage, and having not achieved the required results in the Leaving Certificate (Ireland's terminal school examination) for progression to university through the "traditional" route; and (2) Traditional-Entry (TE) students, who were from higher socioeconomic backgrounds and had achieved the required results in the Leaving Certificate for progression to university through the traditional route.

In line with (constructivist) grounded theory procedures, coding commenced early during the data collection process and involved line-by-line initial coding, focused coding, and categorizing (Charmaz, 2006, 2014). Memos of various types were written throughout the study to explore, summarize, synthesize, and conceptualize the data, as well as to explicate and problematize researcher positionalities. The material included in this section was developed at a mid-late stage in the study, and after initial and focused coding had been conducted.

Memoing Practices and Their Use

In this section, we explore the different types of memos I wrote at various junctures of the research process, commencing with preparatory memos, which I used to "story" the data, as previously described, and moving on to more conceptual memos, through which the conceptual level of the analysis was raised.

Preparatory Memos: Storying the Data

As previously noted, similar to Mihas (2022), we use different types of memos at various junctures in the research process. Despite emphasizing conceptual development in grounded theory, it can be helpful to "story" the emerging category initially. In my study about widening participation in HE, I first wrote preparatory memos on key codes, concepts, or provisional categories, which were, in part, descriptive in nature. These preparatory memos gave me confidence to just start *somewhere* in my writing, and they captured in summary form participants' experiences in relation to the particular code, concept, or category through the use of the constant comparative method. In this way, all the data relating to a particular aspect were summarized, participant by participant. Importantly, along the way, connections, conceptual possibilities, and questions were raised as they occurred to me, *and preparatory conceptual work was conducted* through which the properties or dimensions of the code, concept, or category were explored. This consisted of a review of the elements of the memo and free writing (cf. Charmaz, 2014) about the emerging category to identify its properties and raise its analytic level within this preparatory memo. This early analytic work can be seen in the second half of the preparatory memo, below.

Excerpt from a Preparatory Memo

In this memo, I summarized how HE progression was differentially conceived by my participants, as line-by-line initial and focused coding had identified this as a significant potential category. In this example, I have included memo entries relating to just six of the 45 participants, for space reasons.

Compiling the preparatory memos was an important and helpful first step on the way to developing more analytic memos. As illustrated in the example below, the concept of consciously vs. unconsciously progressing was first devised *during* the preparatory memoing process, having first "storied" the relevant data.

PREPARATORY MEMO: HIGHER EDUCATION PROGRESSION BEING "THE DONE THING" VS. A SIGNIFICANT STEP

Glenda (1st SLA) talked about students generally being in college because they don't know what else to do. She felt this was a moral and ethical issue, commenting that such students who were wasting time and doing nothing were taking places from "other students who really deserved a place and couldn't get one." She advised asking students to consider if they really wanted to be there—again, this idea of *really wanting*—and recounted how her friend had eventually dropped out after having lots of problems in college but emphasized how she wasn't really sure if she wanted to be there or not. She compared this friend to herself and noted that she was completely certain that she wanted to be there.

Jamie (1st SLA), who left school at 15, represents a case in point in terms of the starkness of difference between the two groups. He saw college as a different lifestyle and career choice having been an early school leaver (age 15). While at school he wanted to "get out now and get a trade like everybody else in the household"—like his family. He claimed college "wasn't even a thought at the back of my mind" or a thought in his family. He strongly linked the thought of college to having the idea in the family. He claimed it was more sensible and "more *normal or accepted* to go and start working." Like the TEs talking about college progression like it was the totally normal, acceptable, and indeed the expected thing to do, for Jamie, it was the opposite.

Carolyn (3rd SLA), like Glenda (1st SLA), also contrasted herself with other students who she felt were in college because of parental pressure and the sense that they had to progress to HE after school. She emphasized how she was different to them, noting how she wanted to be there, she always wanted to do this, and that she wasn't pushed by anyone.

Alva (1st TE) noted that she always knew she'd go. So we have *always wanting* vs. *always knowing*. Here she links always knowing she'd go to parental emphasis on importance of education. She also noted that you now need a degree in order to get a good job, and noted that everyone has a degree.

Elizabeth (1st TE) said "it was the done thing where I was from ... It was *never really on the agenda not to*" and she noted all her family members and classmates had progressed to HE. Her parents always said she was going and she never questioned it. She noted her parents said university was what you do after school then get a job, and that it was never on the agenda not to go. Unquestioning ....

David (2nd TE) talked about college as a kind of traditional route that he had to follow, that it was expected, that it was the logical conclusion, that it was assumed that you would go on. He felt you wouldn't be very sure of yourself if you didn't go to university. He also noted that it was the route everyone else around him was taking, and one his parents had taken—again we have this family link—and so it seemed to him to be the way to go.

This is a significant underlying process, which determines, or at least strongly influences, the pathway of the experience for both groups in terms of both the academic and the social, particularly the latter, once at college. The original question related to how they decided to go to university in the first place. There is a clear difference between SLA and TE groups.

The vast majority of TEs reported that progressing to university was just the done thing, a logical next step, a natural progression, never considered not going, wondered what else one would do, etc. They were *unconsciously progressing*. In contrast, for the SLAs, progression to university was not taken for granted at all. Many talked about *always wanting to go*, and hoping they would as they had an interest in particular areas/learning generally, but not expecting it to happen for various reasons. Conscious ...

Unconscious vs. conscious progression ...

Unconsciously progressing due to:

- Feeling have to do it/parental pressure/keeping others happy, not necessarily wanting it themselves

- Not knowing what else/what want to do

- Needing it for jobs—to get a "good" job

- Just to get **a** degree

- Everyone has a degree these days, everyone else doing it (family/friends)

Not assuming, but wanting to go:

- Always *wanting* to go

- Thinking not able for it while at school, lacking points and/or hated school

- Not the usual/normal thing to do

- Being interested in a subject (**genuinely**, *not* for status)

The category: Un/consciously progressing (consciously vs. unconsciously progressing to HE)

Properties: 1. Consciously progressing
            2. Unconsciously progressing

Conceptual Memos

For each preparatory memo compiled, a more advanced conceptual memo was also developed in which key points from the former were summarized, and raised to a more conceptual level. Possibilities were explored and questions were developed with regard to potential relationships between properties of a category, and also between categories. Questions typically asked of the data within these more analytically oriented memos were: "what factor(s) may have led to this happening?" and "what seems to have happened as a result of this?" Such questions initially focused on possible cause and effect type conceptualizations, including Glaser's (1978) "6 Cs" (causes, contexts, contingencies, consequences, covariances, and conditions) theoretical coding family. During this process, and in order to address these questions, the raw data and my coding were revisited in an iterative fashion to examine possibilities in response to these questions. Importantly, in conceptual memos, I frequently employed diagramming to elucidate the relationships I was seeing in the data (e.g., see Figure 15.1). Diagramming was an invaluable aid to thinking more conceptually.

In the example of a conceptual memo below, I am concerned with defining the category of un/conscious progression through a delineation of its properties, identifying the conditions under which such progression occurs, and considering its genesis (or antecedents) and implications (or consequences). My thinking involves asking questions of the data about the genesis, the essence, and the implications of such an approach to HE progression. In line with abductive reasoning (Bryant & Charmaz, 2007; Charmaz, 2014), when questions suggested certain possibilities, I returned to the data and previous coding stages to ascertain linkages and explanations.

As I explore the various aspects of this category, I note similarities between what I am interpreting and conceptualizing in my data and previous research and scholarship. For example, the sensitizing concept of the "normal biography" (Du Bois-Reymond, 1998) and related work, from my substantive field, seemed to fit what I was explicating on a conceptual level. Rather than just noting its applicability, however, in this memo I start to specify *how* it applies, for example, what such a "biography" might lead to, based on my data. I also included a reminder (a warning?) to myself toward the end of the memo to not be dogmatic or "demonizing" in my conceptualization of certain approaches to HE. In my memos, I was beginning to identify my sense of alignment with the SLAs' approach due to my positionalities and past experiences, which made me realize the potential for being overcritical of "other" approaches.

My conceptual memos were heavily used in preparing drafts of writing for publication. They were further developed, formalized in tone and style, and participant quotes were incorporated to illuminate the analysis.

Further Memoing Practices

A number of other practices are used *during* memoing. Diagramming is useful in thinking more conceptually and helps to further raise the analytic level of one's writing. Including a focus on researcher positionalities in memos contributes to a *critically* analytic approach.

Diagramming

Diagramming enables the researcher to explore and chart the various aspects of the particular code, concept, or category *in visual form*. Diagramming is an excellent aid in creating and refining more abstract conceptual analyses due to its ability to assist the researcher in *visualizing* core concepts, and relationships therein, in their work. Charmaz (2014, p. 218) notes that diagrams help us to "tease out relationships" and allow us to see the "relative power, scope, and direction of the categories in your analysis as well as the connections among them." In my study of widening participation, I regularly diagrammed to explore conceptual relationships and their directionality. In agreement with Charmaz (2006, 2014), I found this to be an

EXCERPT FROM A CONCEPTUAL MEMO

Un/consciously Progressing to Higher Education

The category: un/consciously progressing to HE (consciously vs. unconsciously progressing to HE)

There was a difference between the SLAs and TEs in their reasons for going on to university. For the former, it was a conscious, planned, carefully taken step. For the latter, it was a largely unconscious movement, like being carried along by the crest of a wave, an un-thought-about, not-decided-upon movement.

Properties:

1. Consciously Progressing

Consciously progressing involves active, conscious, planned thinking about an action that has heretofore been abnormal in terms of one's background. The pros and cons, and implications, are considered and it is viewed as an active and significant step forward. It is an actual decision—made based on really wanting to go as opposed to just drifting along; there is no assumption of inevitability, it's not expected, not something taken for granted; rather it is accorded high value. It's conscious decision-making because the lack of family history of HE participation makes progressing to HE something different, nonnormal/usual, not expected, not assumed. Because it's outside the norm, one has to actively and consciously consider it. While no expectation, there is a real desire, an active always-wanting-to do this evident in those who consciously progressed. Really wanting to be in HE is a core feature of conscious progression.

However, one could consciously progress without a true desire to do so .... So, in what way is "the always wanting to" related to consciously progressing? The true desire to progress provides an impetus, the drive to consciously progress. Progressing when it's not part of one's "normal biography" (Du Bois-Reymond, 1998), see also Ball et al. (2002)... may lead to anxiety—it is outside one's comfort zone. So, in order for it to happen, a strong desire needs to be there—to "better" oneself, get out of poverty, make a better life.

Because HE is outside the norm and not expected, it is valued/appreciated more, and therefore progression is seen as a privilege. The resulting feeling of being lucky and grateful gives rise to a more focused and effortful approach to HE; the stakes are high, hence the need to be focused on the end result.

2. Unconsciously Progressing

Unconsciously progressing to HE is passive. It happens to you. You are drifting along, on the crest of the wave, almost without even getting into the water, being moved along by the current. Unconsciously progressing involves an expectation/assumption about it happening—it's just what you do after school, the next logical step, a natural progression, the done thing, a given, taken for granted, a certitude. It is a nondecision, in that progressing is not decided upon, it just happens—perhaps even a nonchoice.

As part of unconscious progression, one is always knowing (rather than—but not ruling out—always wanting) about progression. It's unquestioned. It's being in the cycle of things. Unconscious progression occurs due to family history of HE; it's the natural thing to do as others did; the normal thing to do after school, an inevitable course of (non?) action—never thinking of not going due to family expectation and assumption—even pressure. Almost being programmed into progressing—being indoctrinated into the assumption that the normal and inevitable life pathway is HE after school. The high level of expectation can mean HE is less valued and seen just as progression (vs. as a privilege) (TEs, for example, didn't talk about feeling lucky or grateful), resulting in an approach to HE that is less focused on the academic and more on the overall "experience." Unconscious progression also occurs as a result of not knowing what else to do; HE is seen as a safe bet of sorts, especially in a societal context of increasing credentialism (see Collins on this, and also Dore (1970s), with "everyone having a degree nowadays." Progression is seen as necessary to get a "decent" job; a sense of having to go to keep up with others.

Need to be careful not to demonize going on to HE for no (apparent) particular reason. This action which seems meaningless and feckless needs to be seen in the wider social and economic context. Doing what everyone else is doing in order not to be at a disadvantage is a logical thing to do really …

excellent aid in thinking and writing more conceptually. Memoing and diagramming essentially bridged the gap between coding and conceptual development. In relation to the concepts and category discussed in the previous section, I developed many diagrams, including the example in Figure 15.1 in which I focused on sketching out the relationships between concepts in the data, actively considering the antecedents of "conscious"/"unconscious" progression to HE, and implications for students' approach (considered in detail elsewhere).

Allow oneself the same freedom in diagramming a code, concept, or category—particularly in early sketches—that is advised with respect to memoing per se; in other words, follow your instincts and then check and refine. Analytic memoing and diagramming are intrinsically connected and are, in fact, embroiled in a rather symbiotic relationship, with each contributing to and benefiting from the other. These are *not* elements in a linear process; rather, as Lempert (2007, p. 258) attests, these practices are "conjoined; both are necessary and simultaneous." Sometimes it will feel right to start by diagramming an aspect of our analysis because it can capture very quickly what's "in our head," and subsequently we follow up with a detailed articulation of that which we have presented in visual form, focusing on specifying in words the properties of, or the relationships between, the code, concept, or category. At other times, a diagram will *follow* the written memo, when we try to capture in visual form what we have articulated in words. It is very much an iterative process, similar to the back-and-forth process of posing questions in early memos and revisiting our raw data and coding to check something before returning to the memo to refine our articulation. Of course, diagrams themselves go through various stages of development; they evolve over time as we return to them to refine earlier versions and/or create new versions as our thinking and writing develop. Whilst being free and spontaneous in our early diagrams (and memos) is key, ensure that they are as comprehensible as possible and date and title them.

FIGURE 15.1 ● Antecedents and Implications of Conscious Versus Unconscious Progression to Higher Education

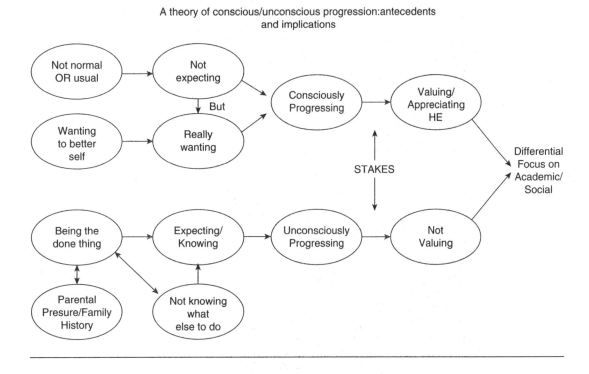

A theory of conscious/unconscious progression:antecedents and implications

Developing Critical Reflexivity About Researcher Positionalities

Analyses of the social world are constructed and inevitably influenced by researcher historicality and autobiography (Lather, 1991); indeed, for Reay (1998), "all research is in one way or another autobiographical or else the avoidance of autobiography" (p. 2). The social locations/positions of the knower (class, race, gender, and sexual orientation, histories, social standing, and cultural background) are brought to bear on our research (Rhoads, 1997). From a CGT perspective, researcher positionalities and impact on data and theory construction are vital considerations (Charmaz et al., 2017; Keane, 2009, 2015; Lempert, 2007), requiring deep reflexivity and "methodological self-consciousness" (Charmaz, 2017, p. 35). This reflexivity involves critically interrogating our personal history, biography, and sociodemographic positionalities, to *identify* our preconceptions (especially those "taken-for-granted," Charmaz, 2017), perspectives, and standpoints in relation to our research, and put this information "on the table" (Clarke, 2005, p. 12).

Maintaining a reflective journal assists in recording a researcher's thoughts and experiences, including in relation to our positionalities. Analytic memo writing is, however, facilitative and generative of *reflexivity* in this regard, pushing us to interrogate who we are, who we think we are, and *how these* identity/ies and positionalities *relate to and influence* the research process, relationships, and outcomes. For these experiences, perspectives, and positionalities, we trace their likely *provenance* (or "source") but also their *implications* or consequences for how we approach and engage in the research process (Charmaz, 2017; Keane, 2009, 2015). This includes our interactions and relationships with participants, especially given that the researcher and "the researched" frequently hold unequal positions of power and privilege (Charmaz et al., 2017; Lempert, 2007). In critical analytic memo writing, we ask if and in what way(s) our position impacts on the data we collect, and what we "see" and interpret in the data.

In my study, I included a critical autobiographical reflection (cf. Keane, 2009, pp. 5–10, 2015) based on numerous memos—at developing levels of criticality—composed throughout the research process. This served to "lay my cards on the table" and positioned myself, my background, motivations, prior engagement in area, and my perspectives within the study. Memos had examined my social class identity, experiences growing up and in education, and my professional experiences. While early memos were somewhat descriptive and focused on recollections, later memos became more critical and analytic by helping me to understand connections between my prior experiences and my research focus, and my *engagement in* the research process. From a constructivist perspective, I began to see and articulate myself as a coparticipant in the research process. It was through critical analytic memoing about my past that I realized the provenance of my interest in social class, and how my personal history oriented me to the problematization of issues of inequality and privilege (Keane, 2009, 2015). It also helped me to recognize and problematize similarities between my emerging findings and my own past experiences.

Writing about personal positionalities and experiences is challenging. As academics we are often unused to such a focus, and articulating on paper views and memories, which previously inhabited only perhaps the background of our mind, and connecting them to our academic work, is demanding and can result in a sense of vulnerability (Keane, 2009, 2015). Critical analytic memos, however, facilitate a *private* conversation between me-as-person and me-as-researcher, as we navigate the terrain of the personal to the theoretical and back again. Certainly this vulnerability again arises when one considers making public (for example, through publications) one's writing, particularly in academic work which still has the veneer of the "abstract supposedly universal speaker" (Grumet, 2001, p. 171). As I have argued previously, however, (cf. Keane, 2015), as a coparticipant in a constructivist research endeavor, offering of oneself in this way adds a layer of authenticity and reciprocity to a study, particularly when research participants give so much of themselves to researchers.

CRITICAL ANALYTIC MEMO EXCERPT

In recent months, however, my mind has begun to harp back to specific incidents, fleeting moments, and powerful feelings, and I clearly remember refusing to engage in any process in which I felt I might be "found out" and thus rejected. Whilst it is indeed obvious to me now, it was with genuine surprise that I began to see the similarity between some of what I have found in this study and my own personal experiences as an undergraduate. I have realized the provenance of my interest in social class, the student experience, peer relationships, and social integration. On a personal level, this study has, I suppose, been somewhat cathartic: it has allowed me to better understand myself as a person, as a student, as a lecturer, and as a social actor caught up in and performing a somewhat confused class identity. And so, I have come to agree with Professor Reay: my research has been somewhat autobiographical. I feel that my personal experiences of feeling strangely "between worlds" oriented me towards the problematization of issues of equality, disadvantage, and privilege in my academic work. Further, my professional experiences as a postprimary teacher (in both "designated disadvantaged" and "middle-class" schools), my work designing and implementing access programs nationally and my former role as a university researcher on student diversity in HE, all constitute converging paths to this doctoral research study.

Source: Keane, E. (2015) Considering the practical implementation of constructivist grounded theory in a study of widening participation in Irish higher education. *International Journal of Social Research Methodology*, *18*(4), 415–431. Reprinted by permission of Informa UK Limited, trading as Taylor & Francis Group, www.tandfonline.com

Conclusion

Critical analytic memoing is a core tool for all qualitative researchers, not just for those doing grounded theory. As well as helping us to record our ideas, memos (and diagrams) are *generative* of our thinking. The different types of memos encourage us to "start somewhere" in our writing, facilitate constant comparison and the summarizing of large datasets, and assist in working toward conceptualization. Diagrams and memos interact symbiotically. Critically analytic memos recognize and support our roles as coparticipants in the research process, enabling us to be reflexive about our positionalities and related impact on the research process.

Supplemental Readings

Charmaz, K. (2014). *Constructing grounded theory* (2nd ed.). SAGE.

Keane, E. (2015). Considering the practical implementation of constructivist grounded theory in a study of widening participation in Irish higher education. *International*

Journal of Social Research Methodology, 18(4), 415–431.

Lempert, L. (2007). Asking questions of the data: Memo writing in the grounded theory tradition. In A. Bryant & K. Charmaz (Eds.), *The SAGE handbook of grounded theory* (pp. 245–264). SAGE.

Reflection and Activities

1. Take a code in your data and write a preparatory memo. "Story" the specific element in focus, by using the constant comparative method to summarize what is happening in your data. Begin to identify relevant properties and interrelationships and diagram these.

2. Based on the preparatory memo in no. 1, revisit the raw data and coding as necessary. Then develop a more analytic memo, more fully explicating the concept or category's properties, and relationships therein, using Glaser's 6 Cs (causes, contexts, contingencies, consequences, covariances, and conditions). Diagram the work.

3. Write a critically analytic memo about your positionalities in relation to your research. Consider:

   a. sociodemographic positionalities (race/ethnicity, class, gender, disability, sexual orientation, etc.)

   b. personal history and biography

   c. personal and professional interest in and experiences of the area

   d. motivations and beliefs

   e. standpoints and perspectives

   f. taken-for-granted preconceptions

   g. how the above impact upon your research process

References

Ball, S. J., Davies, J., David, M., & Reay, D. (2002) "Classification" and "judgement": Social class and the "cognitive structures" of choice of higher education, *British Journal of Sociology of Education, 23*(1), 51–72. https:///doi.org/10.1080/01425690120102854

Bryant, A., & Charmaz, K. (2007). Grounded theory research: Methods and practices. In A. Bryant & K. Charmaz (Eds.), *The SAGE handbook of grounded theory* (pp. 1–28). SAGE.

Charmaz, K. (1995). Grounded theory. In J. A. Smith, R. Harre, & L. Van Langenhove (Eds.), *Rethinking methods in psychology* (pp. 27–49). SAGE.

Charmaz, K. (2006). *Constructing grounded theory: A practical guide through qualitative analysis.* SAGE.

Charmaz, K. (2014). *Constructing grounded theory* (2nd ed.). SAGE.

Charmaz, K. (2017). The power of constructivist grounded theory for critical inquiry. *Qualitative Inquiry, 23*(1), 34–45. https://doi.org/10.1177/1077800416657105

Charmaz, K., Thornberg, R., & Keane, E. (2017) Grounded theory in the 21st century: A qualitative method for advancing social justice research. In N. Denzin & Y. Lincoln (Eds.), *Handbook of qualitative research* (5th ed., pp. 411–443). SAGE.

Clarke, A. (2005). *Situational analysis: Grounded theory after the postmodern turn.* SAGE.

Du Bois-Reymond, M. (1998). "I don't want to commit myself yet": Young people's life concepts. *Journal of Youth Studies, 1*, 63–79. https://doi.org/10.1080/13676261.1998.10592995

Glaser, B. (1965). The constant comparative method of qualitative analysis. *Social Problems, 12*, 436–445. https://doi.org/10.2307/798843

Glaser, B. (1978). *Theoretical sensitivity.* Sociology Press.

Glaser, B. (1998). *Doing grounded theory: Issues and discussions.* Sociology Press.

Grumet, M. (2001). Autobiography: The mixed genre of public and private. In D. Holdstein & D. Bleich (Eds.), *Personal effects: The social character of scholarly writing* (pp. 165–177). Utah State University Press.

Hammersley, M., & Atkinson, P. (2007). *Ethnography: Principles in practice* (3rd ed.). Routledge.

Keane, E. (2009). *"Widening participation" and "traditional-entry" students at an Irish University: Strategising to "make the most" of higher education* [Unpublished doctoral dissertation]. NUI Galway.

Keane, E. (2011a). Distancing to self-protect: The perpetuation of inequality in higher education through socio-relational dis/engagement. *British Journal of Sociology of Education, 32*(3), 449–466. https://doi.org/10.1080/01425692.2011.559343

Keane, E. (2011b). Dependence-deconstruction: Widening participation and traditional-entry students transitioning from school to higher education in Ireland. *Teaching in Higher Education, 16*(6), 707–718. https://doi.org/10.1080/13562517.2011.570437

Keane, E. (2012). Differential prioritising: Orientations to higher education and widening participation. *International Journal of Educational Research, 53*, 150–159. https://doi.org/10.1016/j.ijer.2012.03.005

Keane, E. (2015). Considering the practical implementation of constructivist grounded theory in a study of widening participation in Irish higher education. *International Journal of Social Research Methodology, 18*(4), 415–431. https://doi.org/10.1080/13645579.2014.923622

Lather, P. (1991). *Getting smart: Feminist research and pedagogy with/in the postmodern.* Routledge.

Lempert, L. (2007). Asking questions of the data: Memo writing in the grounded theory tradition. In A. Bryant & K. Charmaz (Eds.), *The SAGE handbook of grounded theory* (pp. 245–264). SAGE.

Mihas, P. (2022). Memo writing strategies: Analyzing the parts and the whole. In C. Vanover, P. Mihas, & J. Saldaña (Eds.), *Analyzing and interpreting qualitative research: After the interview*. SAGE.

Reay, D. (1998). "Always knowing" and "never being sure": Familial and institutional habituses and higher education choice. *Journal of Education Policy, 13*(4), 519–529. https://doi.org/10.1080/0268093980130405

Rhoads, R. (1997). Crossing sexual orientation borders: Collaborative strategies for dealing with issues of positionality and representation. *International Journal of Qualitative Studies in Education, 10*(1), 7–23. https://doi.org/10.1080/095183997237368

Thornberg, R., & Charmaz, K. (2014). Grounded theory and theoretical coding. In U. Flick (Ed.), *The SAGE handbook of qualitative data analysis* (pp. 153–169). SAGE.

Interpretive Strategies

Paul Mihas

Introduction

As we move along the qualitative research life cycle, we are faced with the task of interpreting textual data and codes, of identifying larger meaning lurking in the narratives. Inquiry might focus largely on description—such as a public health study describing barriers and facilitators to accessing health care—but even description requires low-level interpretation. This means we often need to hone our interpretive skills from the moment we begin interacting with data. In other words, interpretation can be considered a stage but it is also an ongoing process of perception that we heed and refine.

Interpretation requires conceptualizing data, sometimes moving up the conceptual ladder or synthesizing codes to construct a more evocative theme, an explanation that tells a larger story. We might say that a theme is a cure for the "common code." If we find our codes uninspiring, we can assess them together and see how they share meaning, how they say more together than they do on their own. In a study on refugees, the code *identity* together with *group memory* might inspire the theme *collective identity*, suggesting how participants see their identity as a communal one. In other words, instead of simply naming stars, we identify constellations, a pattern that tells a meta-story.

Interpretation addresses the question, "So what?" It gives us a takeaway that we could not have had with closed-ended surveys or strictly quantitative data. In a horizontal analysis (Maietta, Hamilton, Swartout, & Petruzzelli, 2019), we look across data for what holds stories together, for configurations that suggest meaningful coherence across multiple experiences and realities.

Anthropologist Clifford Geertz (1973) reminds us of the need to take account of how participants see their world, but that this in itself is not sufficient for analysis. The researcher builds an interpretation on top of the participants' stories. The challenge is to not read beyond the data, to not impose a framework that does not align with individual accounts, to not construct abstractions without textured evidence for doing so. This is one reason why we use cycles of coding (Saldaña, 2016). First-cycle coding invites us to attend to what topics dwell in the data—an inventory of sorts—and second-cycle coding allows us to go further in addressing what these topics mean across data.

In interpretation, we enter a dialogue of ideas; we think with codes, not just with data. In conceptualizing a phenomenon, we are "reaching up to construct abstractions and simultaneously reaching down to tie these abstractions to data" (Charmaz, 2014, p. 323). The tension of interpretation lies in this dual process, in the quest to privilege the participant's view to the extent possible while also constructing concepts that tie their stories to the individualistic accounts of others. Interpretation is a privileged act and one that we should not take lightly. Member checking—returning to the field to check in with participants regarding our interpretations—is not always feasible, nor will participants always understand academic knowledge production.

Interpretation is always tied to the contingencies of local understandings. Even if we are not doing grounded theory, our interpretive work must always be grounded in the nuanced accounts of participants who have lived unique lives. We must show readers how we legitimately synthesized multiple accounts, how we wove together a meta-story, or how we constructed a theme based on words on pages. This is why we might thread interpretation with quotations and palpable stories that have earned our attention. Interpretive logic is also inherently tied to our ontological and epistemological positioning. If we see knowledge as situational and constructivist, then we present our interpretations as coconstructions and our knowledge as locally situated.

In Chapter 16 of this section, Jaime L. Fiddler shares an inventive approach to interpretation. She uses practices that involve listening to audio data and making note cards, transcribing critical pieces of text that can be used later and out of sequence, and sharing this content to the participants in order to think more conceptually about connections. In Chapter 17, Adrian Larbi-Cherif, Cori Egan, and Joshua L. Glazer address emergent analysis, capturing the energy of an analysis that is in motion as they make meaning from more than 100 interviews conducted in a large, mixed-method study. Larbi-Cherif, Egan, and Glazer use their initial codebook to extract quotations and then recode within emerging domains, using an interpretive device called pattern coding, which combines knowledge from first-cycle coding into a kind of meta code (Saldaña, 2016). In Chapter 18, Tim Huffman discusses forms of reasoning that help us with the work of interpretation. Deductive reasoning focuses on drawing conclusions by applying general claims to data. Inductive reasoning involves making claims based on how much evidence is available in the data. And finally, abductive reasoning involves proposing possible explanations for why something is the case. All three of these logics can be integrally part of qualitative thinking.

All the chapters in this section invite us to stretch our understanding of what it means to interpret interviews in a way that condenses, clarifies, and calls forth explanation.

Reflection and Activities

1. Create a diagram of several codes you are using in a study. Draw links between codes and label the links to suggest the relationship among the codes. Give this diagram a name that suggests an interpretive concept tying together the codes and the named relationships.

2. Listen to a recorded interview, preferably in a small group, and code important information onto note cards as described by Jaime L. Fiddler in Chapter 16. After you have listened to the interview and written your codes, discuss your interpretations with your groupmates and record your conversation—try not to speak for too long. Please carry around your note cards for a couple of days and look them over between classes, at stores and coffee shops, and when you come home from work. When you next meet with your research group, discuss what you learned from looking over your note cards and then play the recording of the group's first impressions. How did your interpretation grow and develop over time? Yes, you might record this concluding discussion, edit or add to your note cards, and engage in the process again as discussed by McGill et al. (Chapter 13).

3. Using the techniques described by Tim Huffman in Chapter 18, discuss how each of the authors in this section, along with one or two more from other sections of the book, use qualitative evidence. What claims might the authors make and what are the different warrants for their assertions?

References

Charmaz, K. (2014). *Constructing grounded theory* (2nd ed.). SAGE.

Fiddler, J. L. (2022). Listening deeply: Indexing research conversations in a narrative inquiry. In C. Vanover, P. Mihas, & J. Saldaña (Eds.), *Analyzing and interpreting qualitative research: After the interview*. SAGE.

Geertz, C. (1973). *The Interpretation of cultures*. Basic Books.

Huffman, T. (2022). Making claims using qualitative data. In C. Vanover, P. Mihas, & J. Saldaña (Eds.), *Analyzing and interpreting qualitative research: After the interview*. SAGE.

Larbi-Cherif, A., Egan, C., & Glazer, J. (2022). Emergent analysis: Strategies for making sense of an evolving longitudinal study. In C. Vanover, P. Mihas, & J. Saldaña (Eds.), *Analyzing and interpreting qualitative research: After the interview*. SAGE.

Maietta, R., Hamilton, A., Swartout, K., & Petruzzelli, J. (2019). *Qualitative data analysis camp*. ResearchTalk, Inc.

Saldaña, J. (2016). *The coding manual for qualitative researchers* (3rd ed.). SAGE.

Listening Deeply: Indexing Research Conversations in a Narrative Inquiry

Jaime L. Fiddler

Abstract

In this chapter, readers will learn a method of analyzing group conversations in a narrative inquiry that has deep listening and "indexing" at its center. Many data analysis methods ask researchers to transcribe during the early steps of the analytic process, but the method presented here describes a process in which deeper methods of analysis and interpretation precede transcription that is partial and much more targeted. This chapter also presents an example of ontologically informed research choices, and therefore begins with a discussion of Dewey's philosophy of experience and the ways in which this ontology shapes narrative inquiry as a relational methodology. The analysis method is then deconstructed in detail for those interested in using or adapting this strategy.

Keywords: Narrative inquiry; ontology; listening deeply; indexing research conversations

In this chapter, readers will learn one method for working with group research conversations. This method, an alternative to traditional transcription, coding, and interpretive strategies, was inspired by my desire to ensure that every part of my research project aligned explicitly with the ontological underpinnings of the research, underpinnings that had implications for all aspects of the research, from ethics to methods. For those beginning their research experiences, the idea of an "ontology" may seem unfamiliar, and the idea of it shaping research even more so. Yet, it is an appropriate starting place, for an ontology has to do with what exists to be researched. In social science research, when we articulate a particular ontology, we are expressing a belief about what constitutes the human experience that we want to learn more about. In this particular case, I engaged in narrative inquiry (Clandinin & Connelly, 2000), a methodology grounded in a relational ethic and a Deweyan ontology of experience (Dewey, 1934/2005, 1938/1997), and I will discuss more about what that means in this chapter.

Aligning all aspects of the research in this way was not without challenges. Though qualitative research paradigms are now well established, it is still the case that postpositivist traditions remain normative in many ways. For example, institutional ethics forms are steeped in the language of postpositivist research and, as a beginning researcher, I found I had internalized many of the research norms associated with this dominant paradigm. I had to confront my own hidden assumptions about research and researchers in order to become the researcher I wanted to be, to maintain integrity in the research process, and to create knowledge that reflected the particular ontology within which I was working.

At present, as I work to support graduate students as they design their own research studies, I see many of them repeat my earlier struggles. For example, I see researchers wanting to work narratively but gravitating toward a large-scale survey as a data collection tool because it will allow them more objectivity. I understand the impulse and its source. It is my hope that, in addition to offering a practical way to work with qualitative data, this chapter also invites others to make methodological choices aligned with the philosophical assumptions to which their research is anchored.

Since this chapter presents an example of ontologically informed research choices, I will begin by sharing my understanding of Dewey's philosophy of experience and the ways in which this ontology shapes narrative inquiry as a relational methodology. Then, I will share my experiences of using this methodology in practice and describe the journey that led me to the "indexing" method of working with qualitative data. I will then deconstruct the method in detail for those interested in using or adapting this strategy. Many data analysis methods ask researchers to transcribe during the early steps of the analytic process (see, for instance, Chapters 4–6). This chapter describes a process in which deeper methods of analysis and interpretation precede transcription, transcription that is partial and much more targeted.

Dewey's Ontology of Experience and Narrative Inquiry

Dewey's philosophy of experience is described by Clandinin and Connelly (2000) as a constant "conceptual, imaginative backdrop" (p. 2) to narrative inquiry, a methodology that considers experience to be storied and story. Dewey (1934/2005) described experience as continuous, as transactional or as happening in interaction, and as having an inherent emotional quality. Narrative inquiry begins in this understanding of experience, and this understanding shapes the research process entirely.

To describe the continuity of experience Dewey offered the metaphor of a river and described how the river's "flow gives a definiteness and interest to its successive portions. In an experience, flow is from one thing to another ... one part carries on what went before" (p. 38). We can look at a waterfall for a stark example—if there is rushing water falling from height upstream, then what comes next is a deep pool of tumultuous water. Indeed, it is the only thing possible. Experiences are just like this—early experiences become part of the context for later experiences, setting parameters for what is possible. Therefore, in order to learn about experience through research, we need to look beyond a single moment in time; we must look back and understand the history a person brings, and we need to look forward as well, into an imagined future (Clandinin & Connelly, 2000).

Dewey's ontology also characterizes experience as "transactional," as happening in interaction, and in particular situations: "Life goes on in an environment; not merely *in* it but because of it, through interaction with it" (Dewey, 1934/2005, p. 12, emphasis in original). Narrative inquirers, then, understand that experience does not happen in a vacuum but is directly shaped by context. Dewey's philosophy directly shapes the "three-dimensional inquiry space" that frames narrative inquiry work. When studying experience, narrative inquirers look to "the *personal* and *social* (interaction); past, present, and future (continuity); combined with the notion of place (situation)" (Clandinin & Connelly, 2000, p. 50). Experience is storied, continuous, and constructed through the "confluence of social influences on a person's inner life, social influences on their environment, and their unique personal history" (Clandinin & Rosiek, 2007, p. 41).

Dewey's transactional ontology of experience has more than one implication for educational research. First, if experience always happens in interaction with the environment, then we must look to the environment or context, as well as to the individual, in order to learn more about experience. Methods of inquiry then must be those that include an inquiry into context. Second, if experience is always transactional, then to be an objective "observer" of experience is an impossibility: "Narrative inquirers are always in an inquiry relationship... they cannot subtract themselves from relationship... nor can they pretend to be free of contextual influences themselves" (Clandinin & Rosiek, 2007, pp. 69–70). For narrative inquirers, there is a relational ethic and that must be considered: "...narrative inquirers hold responsibilities and obligations for, and toward, the people whose stories are lived and told" (Caine, Estefan, & Clandinin, 2013, p. 576).

Dewey (1934/2005) also characterized experience as having an inherently emotional quality. He described an emotive or aesthetic component as the very part of a *single* experience that separates it from the *whole* of experience. He was careful to point out that we cannot separate emotions from an experience, as emotions are not as "simple and compact as are the words by which we name them: joy, sorrow, hope, fear" (p. 43). Rather, emotions are complex and evolving; they too need to be understood as continuous. Experience is intrinsically emotion-full, as it is always "a matter of people in relation contextually and temporally" (Clandinin & Connelly, 2000, p. 189). If we understand experience as being defined by an emotional quality for it to be *an* experience, then our approach to inquiry must consider understanding emotion as key to understanding experience.

The language of narrative inquiry, as defined by Clandinin and Connelly (2000), and others who take up their work (see, for example: Huber, Caine, Huber, & Steeves, 2013; Josselson, 2007; Lessard, Caine, & Clandinin, 2015; Swanson, 2014), reflects these foundational assumptions. For example, narrative inquirers do not posit "research questions" or gather "data" to present "findings." Rather, they wonder about "research puzzles" and work alongside people "in the midst" of experience to "compose or co-compose research texts." They do not "interview" people, but they engage in "research conversations" that are relational in nature. These choices of language reflect the ontological commitments that researchers take up when engaging in narrative inquiry (Caine, Estefan, & Clandinin, 2013). In the next section, I reflect on my own experience of living out these commitments.

Stories to Stay By: A Narrative Inquiry with Teachers Who Stay

This narrative inquiry began with a wonder about how the experiences teachers have in their induction years *continue* to influence teacher identity and practice. I placed emphasis on *continue* within this research puzzle to remind me of the nuances of meaning possible in this word. Viewing experience as continuous was, to me, essential to developing an understanding of the experiences of teachers. Leaving the classroom, or staying in school, or any other single event, is not "a thing happening at that moment, but [is] an expression of something happening over time" (Clandinin & Connelly, 2000, p. 29). I wondered: If beginning teacher experiences can be so challenging that some teachers leave, as I had explored in an earlier project (Beck, 2010), then how do beginning experiences shape the identity and practice of those who stay?

In order to study experience as defined by Dewey, my methodology addressed experience as continuous, transactional, and aesthetic. To explore a phenomenon that is continuous requires prolonged engagement rather than a "snapshot" approach. So, instead of a survey or a single interview with teachers, I engaged three teachers in research conversations over the course of a one-year period. Initially, we agreed to meet monthly, but the rhythms of our year enabled us to meet 6 times in total, for at least 2 hours per meeting. Learning about their experiences over a period of time meant that we could delve deeper: we could look back, look forward, or speak of present experiences as we talked over time. In order to understand experiences that are transactional, no part of a life can be disregarded. Our research conversations then, while focused on teaching experiences, also included discussions about other parts of our lives. I also acknowledged from the outset that every research project is "simultaneously a description of, and intervention into, human experience" (Clandinin & Rosiek, 2007, p. 45). There is no such thing as a narrative inquirer or a narrative inquiry that does not impact the lives of those engaged in the research.

Finally, to understand the aesthetic nature of experience, a narrative inquirer must be willing to deeply listen to the emotional landscape in research conversations. To include this landscape, I included some aesthetically oriented activities (such as a collage at our first meeting, and an "annals and chronicles" (Clandinin & Connelly, 2000, p. 112) activity at a later meeting) to help us unpack the emotional colors of the storied experiences we shared. I also prepared myself to make space for emotions that might arise in the conversations.

Though all of these decisions reflected both Dewey's ontology and the relational ethic of narrative inquiry, I still questioned everything. For example, I noticed that I felt uncomfortable in research founded on a relational ethic, calling the teachers that joined the inquiry "my participants." I chose instead to embrace the word "collaborators." This language was intended to remind me that inquiry based on a transactional ontology is always "a *collaboration* between researcher and participants" (Clandinin & Connelly, 2000, p. 20), and to communicate to those who might come alongside me for this inquiry, that this was not a research approach where they would be positioned as *my* participants or as "subject … but instead [as] collaborators" (Finley, 2005, p. 682). The word *collaborate* comes from the Latin *collaborare*: to labor together, and is defined as: to work together or to work with somebody else on a common project or with a common aim ("Collaborate," 2000).

Though I was satisfied with the meaning behind this term while speaking about my research as it unfolded, whether within my "relational response community" (Clandinin, 2013) or with my family while they watched me prepare meals for my research meetings, "collaborators" never felt quite right. What I eventually settled on to avoid the scientific paradigm evoked by "participants" was "research friends." Not only was anonymity assured, but the kind of relationship I was working so hard to create was reflected back to me each time it was spoken. It was also a term by which we could more easily address each other, both to each other and to outsiders. When meeting by chance one day in public, for example, Serena (the pseudonym of one of my collaborators) introduced me easily as her "research friend" and I could do the same.

Entering the Inquiry

As we enter into narrative inquiry relationships, we begin the ongoing negotiations that are part of engaging in a narrative inquiry. We negotiate relationships, research purposes, transitions, as well as how we are going to be useful in those relationships. These negotiations occur moment by moment, within each encounter, sometimes in ways that we are not awake to. The negotiations also occur in intentional, wide awake ways as we work with our participants throughout the inquiry. (Clandinin, 2006, p. 47)

I approached the first meeting of my narrative inquiry ready to surrender to the conversation that would emerge, hoping to create a relaxed and inviting space. I prepared a simple and healthy meal. This was part of how I hoped to "be useful" to my research friends: I wanted our meals and the conversations to nourish, to be healthy and generative, rather than heavy and difficult to digest. Regardless of my planning, thinking, or intentions, I worried the location was too far, that people would get lost. I worried that I was taking too much time out of everyone's Sunday, knowing that teachers often spend Sunday evenings planning for the week ahead. I worried that we would not "click" as a group and that this whole process would be a burden. I worried about when to turn on the audio-recorder and, after deciding to wait until after dinner, questioned that decision almost immediately as our conversation quickly found its way toward teaching. I remained relatively quiet; at times I wanted to jump in but I remembered my intention to let the discussion guide itself.

I also found, and noticed more explicitly as the weeks passed, that there remained an image of the "objective" social scientist in me, a part of me that was trying to stay "removed" lest I "influence" the conversation. After that first conversation, that same voice told me that our conversations were too shallow, we were not getting at anything "important." How could I call it research if all we were doing was sitting around chatting? These worries were unfounded, but I will not go so far as to say they were unnecessary. The worries drove a constant feedback loop of reflection and action, and this was a meaningful part of this relational research. Later, it was in reflection that I was able to shake off the "objective" researcher and embrace the relational one. In my field texts, I marked the shift that happened during our third research meeting, the meeting where I truly embraced my role as a narrative inquirer.

My drive to our research meetings was a long one, and that stretch of highway became an important space in the inquiry. During my drive to our third research meeting, this thoughtful stillness was set to music as I listened to Alt-J (2012) perform "Interlude 1." I thought about my research friends, how their school year was coming to an end, and how they were looking ahead to the next. Each of them had choices and challenges ahead, just as I did … just as *I* did. The thoughts of my own story prompted me to consider the notion that what had been missing from our first two meetings was not a more "objective" or "focused" researcher, but what was missing was *me*. I reflected on how I had participated in the conversations as minimally as possible. I was holding back. I was staying distant rather than being fully present and engaged. This realization surprised me because I *knew*, theoretically at least, I could not pretend that I was not there, that I was part of this relational research. Though in every formal way I had acknowledged and claimed to embrace the interactive, transactional ontology described earlier, I also knew, in that moment, I was holding fast to the image of the objective researcher. I let that image fade, and as it did I felt excited to be truly present with my research friends that evening and to embrace, rather than shy away from, the richness of our interactions. There was a shift in that meeting, and this marked the beginning of a very rich phase in the inquiry. I even received an email after the meeting from a research friend who noted that it was "our best one yet!"

Entering Analysis

Once I found more of an ease methodologically, I could focus more of my attention on analysis. In this inquiry, there were several spaces of interim analysis. I will speak to a few of these before looking in more detail at the indexing method specifically.

Interim analysis in conversation. In this group narrative inquiry setting, analysis began in conversation. The back and forth dialogue, the laying of individual experiences alongside those of others, was itself a process of analysis. At times we really sought to unpack an experience together. During that third meeting for example, the term "heavy hours" was coined and developed into a defining and misunderstood feature of the teaching life. This became the focus of one of the published works from this inquiry (Beck, 2017). Sometimes a topic or line of inquiry was marked as important by a firm statement from one of us indicating significance. Sometimes there was just a certain energy to our discussion, a generative feeling in the room, heightened interest from everyone, questioning, circling, laughing. I was drawn to these moments of generativity as I listened to our conversations in between meetings.

Interim analysis in listenings. The space between meetings was a second space of interim analysis. My rhythm of reflection and planning for each meeting continued, which meant that sometimes I shared a prompt or topic in advance, and sometimes I simply showed up ready to let the evening unfold. Sometimes I kept questions at the back of my mind in case certain topics arose again. For example, one of our early conversations about "choosing not to break" stood out to me, both because of the energy it created in discussion and because I had written about a similar topic in my narrative beginnings (which, in narrative inquiry, is initial writing done to situate yourself in the topic of inquiry). When the conversation circled around again, I wondered aloud over the things I had thought about while listening to our conversations between meetings. I engaged in much of this reflection as I was driving to and from our research conversations. At the time, I did not realize how significant those long drives were to be, but by the end of the inquiry I clearly saw their value.

As the value of listening to the recorded research conversations became clear to me, I became less and less convinced that transcribing the conversations was my next step. I had transcribed our first meeting and had produced, what seemed to me when compared with the recording, a rather lifeless stack of paper. I wondered if there was another way I could work with the recordings, a way I could make use of the flow of listening and engage in deeper analysis. My search for a useful way to organize the audio conversation became another space for analysis. In the next section, I will explore the indexes I created.

Listening to Research Conversations: Indexing Method Deconstructed

Our research conversations, held Sunday evenings over dinner, were often about the weather, television shows or, in the beginning, full of the kind of conversations people share as they get to know each other. I knew I did not need to have all of this word-for-word, but I did want to be reminded of all of our topics of conversation later on. I wanted to keep the stories as whole as I could. To me, bracketing out parts of our conversation meant bracketing out the context, which Dewey suggests is a key part of experience. For example, in May, part of the context for our conversation was the gorgeous day. There was something lighter about that warm, sunny weather, and about the end of the school year that seemed connected to the experience. I wanted to remember that part of our conversations. I also wanted to maintain the kind of listening I had been doing in my car, or while puttering around the house between meetings. While listening, I was present, I was in the conversation, I was thinking and reflecting. I wanted to find a way to maintain this presence and to guide myself back to whole pieces of conversation later.

As I engaged in these reflections, I remembered a method of indexing large amounts of data I learned in a methodology course in my master's program (Loutzenheiser, 2007, personal communication). I could not remember or find the details of the approach, but used the notes I had taken and adapted this strategy to my practice of listening on the go. As materials, I worked with two things I always had with me: my pack of coloured pens, and my notebook with perforated pages that could be torn out and used as index cards.

The next time I listened to the audio recordings of our conversations, I made notes about what was being said. I included the topics under discussion and who was (very generally) saying what. As I indexed the conversation, I periodically wrote down a time stamp so that I could easily find my way back to a specific part of the conversation. I labelled each card with the month of the conversation, the length of the audio recording (as this was how my audio-recorder labelled the conversations), and I also numbered the cards so that I could work with them out of sequence later on. The note cards were color-coded, one color for each person including me. In order to preserve anonymity should the worst happen and the cards be misplaced, I used pseudonyms or initials of pseudonyms for both names and places. Figures 16.1 and 16.2 present examples of what the index cards looked

FIGURE 16.1 ● Fictionalized Index Card Example

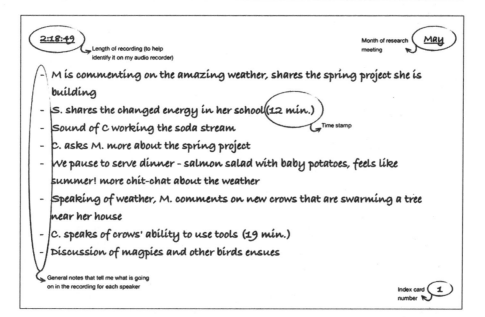

2:18:49 — Length of recording (to help identify it on my audio recorder)

Month of research meeting — **May**

- M is commenting on the amazing weather, shares the spring project she is building
- S. shares the changed energy in her school (12 min.) — Time stamp
- Sound of C working the soda stream
- C. asks M. more about the spring project
- We pause to serve dinner - salmon salad with baby potatoes, feels like summer! more chit-chat about the weather
- Speaking of weather, M. comments on new crows that are swarming a tree near her house
- C. speaks of crows' ability to use tools (19 min.)
- Discussion of magpies and other birds ensues

General notes that tell me what is going on in the recording for each speaker

Index card number — **1**

FIGURE 16.2 ● Fictionalized Index Card Example Highlighting a Researcher Note or "MOT" (My Own Thought)

2:18:49   **May**

- C. discusses the challenges of teaching a "one-off" course (24 min.)
- M. remembers the advice "don't reinvent the wheel" from BEd and reflects on how impossible that is
- S. remembers other impossible advice from BEd, segues into preparing to take on a student teacher (28 min.)
- M. is considering the same
- C. asks what I think, I share my student teacher experience, we discuss what an ideal student teacher experience will be. [MOT: How do these descriptions compare to the research?]

  A shorthand to let me know this is a thought not in the recording
- M. remembers the moments that were the most supportive for her in BEd (34 min.)

2

like. I have not included real data in them, but have obscured or fictionalized details so that I can share the structure of them here.

This way of indexing allowed me to do many things. I could jot down little "MOTs" (an abbreviation I began using long ago standing for "My Own Thought") to remind myself of ideas I was having without interrupting my listening. I could almost keep up with the flow of conversation as I created the indexes, pausing the recording only occasionally to keep up with particularly dense bits. I also realized I was creating a visual artifact I could work with in a number of ways. I could, for example, read through the orange bits at a glance to be reminded of Serena's story as it unfolded over the time of our inquiry, or read the brown bits for the MOTs I had left for myself. I could also select cards that spoke to heavy hours (for example) and lay them all out in front of me as I wrote (see Figure 16.3).

I carried these cards along with me, always ready for spontaneous writing sessions, held together by little bulldog clips and kept tucked within the safety of my notebook. I pulled them out to read through them often; it was nice to have them on hand to keep my mind focused on analysis. As I began to build research texts, I pulled threads together from the index cards and would return to the audio (guided by those bright green time stamps) to do a targeted relisten, or to transcribe the pieces I was calling forth.

Since nothing was left out, I could continue to include the contextual pieces in my analysis and later in my writing. As I began to draft interim texts, I was drawn to those generative moments of rich conversation of course, but I also found myself drawn to strong imagery, symbols, and metaphors during our discussions. The lingering sensation of a pulled tooth, for example, was one thing I found symbolic, though Carlos, my research friend who had an unfortunate trip to the dentist, did not intend it as such at the time. This "pulled tooth conversation" made its way

FIGURE 16.3 ● Index Cards Ready for Transport (Left) and for Work (Right)

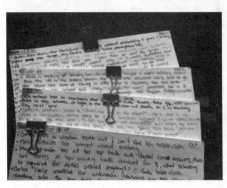 

into my research texts, perhaps because, as I listened, I heard there was more to this story. Carlos was not only recounting his experience of having a tooth pulled, but I could hear clearly on the audio that he was pacing, finding tablecloths, making coffee, opening and closing cupboards and doors, talking even more quickly than was his normal. I knew I had read these cues during the dinner because on the audio recording I heard myself check in with him about how he was feeling. In the relistening, these cues reminded me again that there was something important to attend to here. In the relistening, my attention was no longer split by the other things present, like keeping an eye on the time or wondering if everyone had everything they needed. The index cards allowed me to see these images at glance and to be guided back to them if needed. They allowed me to live my ontology as I engaged in the analysis.

Sharing the Inquiry: Moving to Research Texts

The next layer of analysis was in weaving together the resonant literature I had found and the pieces of conversations I had selected from our dinners—in other words, this was the beginning of writing texts that others outside of our research group would read. Writing is, I believe, another opportunity for us to create a space in which meaningful learning can happen. I wanted to invite readers into our conversations. I sought to present a dialogue that represented our experience and shared our understandings, but that was also open enough for readers to find a space in which to enter. I was aware that I was creating an experience for readers, one in which I hoped they would come to know the pedagogical space this narrative inquiry created (Huber, Caine, Huber, & Steeves, 2013).

Although I had other readers in mind as the key audience for final papers, I was also always writing with my research friends in mind. I held fast to the tenet of narrative inquiry that tells us "we owe our care first to research participants" (Clandinin, 2013, p. 205). Even if "there is no such thing as 'getting it right'" (Richardson, 1997, p. 91), I hoped the contours of what I was composing would feel familiar to them. All of these goals combined added up to a great deal of pressure. I felt a lot of tension during the writing process as a result.

Despite all of the goals I held in tension, the final stages of the writing process were also a vital space for analysis. As I explored the concept of heavy hours for example, I wrote in verse, I drew mind maps, I experimented with ways of explaining heavy hours until I found my way into the research text. During the process, I was open to including these other forms of writing within the academic papers, but in the end I found they were just a step in the writing inquiry, one that deepened my understandings and shaped the direction for the final research texts.

Once a clear direction emerged from this exploratory writing, I transcribed the pieces of conversations I was calling forth from the indexes, and began to draft the research conversations. While writing these I kept verbatim dialogue as much as possible, especially in attempting to capture each person's speaking rhythm and style. However, because I was composing conversations for readers not present during our conversations, readers who did not have the benefit of all the getting-to-know-each-other conversations my research friends and I shared, I edited the verbatim text to make understanding them easier. I hoped to make them flow together in written form. I reworked inside jokes or sarcasm used within our discussions as shorthand that someone outside our conversations might not understand. I omitted the "ummms" and "likes" common in conversation, and at times I added a rejoinder clause to link together pieces of conversation from different meetings but about the same topic. There were a few details I changed or omitted to ensure anonymity for each research friend, or to blur the identifying details of anyone outside the inquiry of whom we spoke. By engaging in these transcription strategies at the end of my analysis, I was able to perform those tasks with the deep knowledge of our conversations gained by listening and speaking with my research friends. My transcriptions were more sensitive to my friends' voices than those I produced when I attempted to transcribe our first conversation.

When I shared the manuscript drafts with my research friends, I explained my choices in this way:

> The goal is for the final papers to reflect your experience in a way that feels true for you, to invite the readers into these kinds of deeper discussions about teaching, and to share the experiences and understandings we came to during the inquiry in a way that is clear. Those goals are much more important than choices of single words or phrases which, while they are verbatim for the most part, have been edited with those other goals in mind.

I encouraged each research friend to remind me of anything key I had missed, to change any details they felt were inaccurate, or to expand anything they wanted explained more clearly. This step helped me confirm my understanding of their experiences and of our shared conversations.

Despite the opportunity to reflect on research texts with my research friends and with my relational response community, I still found the writing process challenging. I feel it is important to make the struggle of writing research visible, lest anyone think they are struggling alone. As Clandinin (2013) affirms:

> Holding [the] conceptual commitments of narrative inquiry mean that the kinds of interim and final research texts we create are difficult ones in at least two ways. They are difficult in the sense of composing texts that continue to honour these commitments, but they are also difficult because they challenge us to attend in multiple directions and toward multiple audiences. (p. 205)

As researchers, we are writing for so many audiences. It is easy to allow our minds to ponder over the faults these imagined critics will find in our writing before there is even a word on the page. For myself, in order for words to arrive, I had to temporarily distance myself from these audiences and even from my research goals. I had to trust the process. I wrote about some of the things my friends and I believed mattered the most and I found that other audiences were interested in our dialogue.

Conclusion

This chapter summarizes one researcher's journey with narrative inquiry. It describes my efforts to engage in research that reflected the Deweyan ontology framing my inquiry. In the midst of my experience, I found a way of working with and reflecting on research conversations aligned with the philosophical approach to the inquiry, one that practically helped me organize and easily access my field texts. The index cards were a way for me to creatively engage as I listened, and they helped me index a rather large set of audio recordings. They also encouraged me to keep listening, literally and figuratively, as I sought to understand the experiences of my research friends. I learned, and was able to share, a great deal about the identities and experiences of teachers who stay in the classroom.

For beginning researchers reading this, I would encourage you to reflect deeply on your beliefs about research. I ask all students I work with to begin to understand research by uncovering and confronting any unexamined beliefs about what researchers should do and what research is. If we can deeply consider and articulate the foundational beliefs that we bring to our research, then we can make methodological choices that reflect the paradigm within which we are working. We can then avoid methodological confusion and honor ways of knowing beyond those that have traditionally dominated the academy. For experienced researchers, I hope my analysis will provide a useful set of interpretive strategies. I believe that by listening to our conversations and using the index cards, I was able to engage in a deep analysis of the work of teaching.

Supplemental Readings

Beck, J. L. (2017). The weight of a heavy hour: Understanding teacher experiences of work intensification. *McGill Journal of Education, 52*(3), 617–638. https://mje.mcgill.ca/article/view/9352.

Clandinin, D. J. (2013). *Engaging in narrative inquiry.* Left Coast Press.

Lincoln, Y., Lynham, S., & Guba, E. (2011). Paradigmatic controversies, contradictions, and emerging confluences, revisited. In N. K. Denzin & Y. S. Lincoln (Eds.), *The Sage handbook of qualitative research* (4th ed., pp. 97–128). SAGE.

Reflection and Activities

1. What is your earliest memory of research? Or of researchers? You might be surprised by how young you were when you engaged in your first research project. Write about your early experiences in rich detail. Share them with a friend and, together, consider the philosophical assumptions that underpinned those early experiences. Consider how those early experiences shaped your ideas about what counts as research, or about what knowledge is or where knowledge resides.

2. Begin and commit to keeping a research journal. Through each step of your research, from idea to published paper, reflect on everything happening in and around your research—do not neglect the personal or contextual. Regardless of the methodology or data analysis methods you are using, explicitly reflecting on your experience of the research will help you to identify the ways in which you, the researcher, are a part of the knowledge created. The exercise above might make a great entry in a research journal. Once in the field, you might include:

   a. Details about the time, space, and place of your research.

   b. What you were feeling or thinking before, during, and immediately after engaging sessions in the field.

   c. What surprised you in the field? Or inspired you? Or puzzled you? (These moments of tension/richness are signposts—what do they mean?)

   d. What do you need to think more about?

   e. What is going well? Or, what happened that you are sure to laugh about later? (Always leave yourself some encouragement!)

   These are just examples; you will find your own way of reflecting, but do document your reflections. They will be useful to you as you engage in analysis and writing, and they will help you stay true to your own research methodology and goals.

3. Practice indexing an everyday conversation. With a willing partner or group (perhaps someone from a research methodology course), record a 20-minute conversation on an agreed-upon topic. Each of you should then, on your own, listen to the conversation once all the way through, then listen to it again while indexing the conversation. Regroup with your partner(s) and reflect—Was it easy to know what to write as you indexed? Could you keep pace with the flow of conversation? Did your understanding of the conversation change over multiple listenings?

References

Alt-J. (2012). *Interlude 1*. Atlantic Records.

Beck, J. L. (2010). *Breaking the silence: Beginning teachers share pathways out of the profession* (Unpublished masters thesis, University of British Columbia, Vancouver, BC). https://circle.ubc.ca/handle/2429/27689

Beck, J. L. (2017). The weight of a heavy hour: Understanding teacher experiences of work intensification. *McGill Journal of Education*, *52*(3), 617–638. https://mje.mcgill.ca/article/view/9352

Caine, V., Estefan, A., & Clandinin, D. J. (2013). A return to methodological commitment: Reflections on narrative inquiry. *Scandinavian Journal of Educational Research*, *57*(6), 574–586. https://doi.org/10.1080/00313831.2013.798833

Clandinin, D. J. (2006). Narrative inquiry: A methodology for studying lived experience. *Research Studies in Music Education*, *27*(1), 44–54. https://doi.org/10.1177/1321103X 060270010301

Clandinin, D. J. (2013). *Engaging in narrative inquiry*. Left Coast Press.

Clandinin, D. J., & Connelly, F. M. (2000). *Narrative inquiry: Experience and story in qualitative research*. Jossey-Bass.

Clandinin, D. J., & Rosiek, J. (2007). Mapping a landscape of narrative inquiry. In D. J. Clandinin (Ed.), *Handbook of narrative inquiry* (pp. 35–41). SAGE.

Collaborate. (2000). In R. Allen (Ed.), *New Penguin English Dictionary*. Penguin Books.

Dewey, J. (1934/2005). *Art as experience*. Perigee Trade.

Dewey, J. (1938/1997). *Experience and education*. Simon and Schuster.

Finley, S. (2005). Arts-based inquiry: Performing revolutionary pedagogy. In N. K. Denzin & Y. S. Lincoln (Eds.), *The Sage handbook of qualitative research* (3rd ed., pp. 681–694). SAGE.

Huber, J., Caine, V., Huber, M., & Steeves, P. (2013). Narrative inquiry as pedagogy in Education: The extraordinary potential of living, telling, retelling, and reliving stories of experience. *Review of Research in Education*, *37*(1), 212–242. https://doi.org/10.3102/0091732X12458885

Josselson, R. (2007). The ethical attitude in narrative research: Principles and practicalities. In D. J. Clandinin (Ed.), *Handbook of narrative inquiry: Mapping a methodology* (pp. 537–563). SAGE. http://srmo.sagepub.com/view/handbook-of-narrative-inquiry/n21.xml

Lessard, S., Caine, V., & Clandinin, D. J. (2015). A narrative inquiry into familial and school curriculum making: Attending to multiple worlds of Aboriginal youth and families. *Journal of Youth Studies, 18*(2), 197–214. https://doi.org/10.1080/13676261.2014.944121

Richardson, L. (1997). *Fields of play: Constructing an academic life.* Rutgers University Press.

Swanson, C. (2014). Unbundling stories: Encountering tensions between the familial and school curriculum-making worlds. *Learning Landscapes, 7*(2), 299–317. https://doi.org/10.36510/learnland.v7i2.667

Emergent Analysis: Strategies for Making Sense of an Evolving Longitudinal Study

Adrian Larbi-Cherif, Cori Egan, and Joshua L. Glazer

Abstract

When researchers are investigating multifaceted phenomena, such as instructional processes and systemic change, the inquiry process is likely to be complex. In such situations, researchers typically need to refine their research questions as their understanding of the phenomena under investigation evolves. In such circumstances, initial codes that represent preliminary working theories are no longer sufficient and require reconceptualization. These issues can be compounded when the number of data sources makes it infeasible to recode the entire dataset. In our chapter, we explore the analytical decisions and memoing strategies that we enacted as we analyzed more than 150 interviews from educators within a school turnaround system aiming to develop ambitious instructional practices in math. We document processes for large research teams to move from coded data to memos when grappling with a database that spans multiple role groups, system levels, and school years.

Keywords: Longitudinal qualitative analyses; analytic memo writing; instructional improvement

Introduction

Ideally, the links between research questions, interview protocols, and a codebook are unambiguous. The interview protocols translate the research questions into queries understandable by participants who, over the course of interviews, provide the data needed to address the question. The codebook—code names with definitions (MacQueen, McLellan, Kay, & Milstein, 1998; Saldaña, 2016)—allows the researcher to designate which parts of the transcript correspond to particular research questions, and then analysis entails "pulling" the relevant codes to construct a set of findings and interpretations.

Though this may sound like an idealized vision of qualitative research, there are situations in which this process can be applied in the linear and straightforward way just described. For example, studies posing unambiguous questions that address a limited conceptual terrain or that involve a small number of participants could potentially align data collection, coding and analysis, and memo writing without unanticipated issues arising.

For a great deal of social science research, though, circumstances are more complex and uncertain. Often, the research questions, or even the larger research topic, change over the course of the study. This occurred in our recent study of Tennessee's state takeover district, the Achievement School District (Glazer & Egan, 2018). Our initial questions concerned the technical elements of the improvement model meant to drive changes in teaching and learning (TAL; e.g., curriculum, school leadership). A year into the study, however, we discovered that these issues were overwhelmed by the political dimensions of the state takeover and the passionate response of local community members. It soon became apparent that we needed to adapt our research questions in accordance with events on the ground.

As a subject of inquiry develops increasingly complex theories, researchers require a second cycle of coding between the initial coding of transcripts and the final memo writing stage. In this second cycle, interview excerpts are systematically recoded in ways that assign them to conceptually salient categories previously unanticipated or otherwise not captured by the original codebook. This process aims to resolve the *emergent* unfolding of the qualitative research cycle, an experience familiar to qualitative researchers as they often cannot anticipate the nonlinear course of a complex study.

The process we describe here also serves as a useful check on researchers' tendency to formulate analyses and tentative claims prior to a thorough and systematic review of the data. Researchers typically engage in active sensemaking from the outset of the project, and, as the inquiry moves forward, they are continuously revising their working narratives (Helms Mills, Thurlow, & Mills, 2010). In many instances, this sensemaking is integral to good research. But what if the number of participants, the diversity of issues, and the size of the research team are all too extensive to reliably construct an empirically valid analysis through informal sensemaking processes? What if an informal sensemaking process among researchers inadvertently neglects large portions of data, misses the perspectives of certain role groups, or is subconsciously mediated by researchers' biases and pre-dispositions? The system we propose here is intended to mitigate against those possibilities by introducing a formal method by which the data are systematically analyzed subsequent to the initial coding process.

In the remainder of this chapter, we describe a process by which a second round of coding enables researchers to identify and conceptually classify previously coded excerpts in ways that take advantage of the initial coding scheme while also introducing a new set of codes unanticipated at the outset of the study. This second round of coding then informs a collective memo writing process that is organized around the study's emergent analytic themes and concepts. In this way, it combines the flexibility of informal sensemaking with the analytic rigor of formal coding and analysis.

Exemplar

The analytic method described in this chapter emerged in the context of a multiyear, mixed-methods study of Shelby County Schools' turnaround district, the iZone. The iZone represents an ambitious effort to dramatically improve TAL in 23 of the most underperforming schools in the state (Glazer, Massell, Lenhoff, Larbi-Cherif, Egan, Taylor, Deleveaux, Ison, & Millinton, 2020; Larbi-Cherif, Lehnoff, & Glazer, 2019). In addition to their consistently low test scores, these schools serve communities beset by intergenerational poverty, social isolation, and neglect. The iZone gained prominence across Tennessee and nationally when a research study showed it to be outperforming competing reform initiatives in its initial three years (Zimmer, Henry, & Kho, 2017). Our research, which began in the spring of 2017 and concluded in the winter of 2019, focused on understanding the iZone's improvement strategy and the key factors that shaped how teachers and leaders enacted the model.

Stage 1: Refining Research Questions, Analytical Domains, and Research Subquestions

We launched the study with five research questions that framed our inquiry:

1. What are the iZone's goals as they relate to improvement in TAL?

2. What is the iZone's strategy for realizing these goals?

3. How is the iZone's strategy interpreted and enacted by district staff, school leaders, and teachers?

4. What factors in the local and state environment mediate the design and implementation of the iZone strategy?

5. How, if at all, does the district learn to improve the design and implementation?

After a round of interviews in the Fall of 2017, we developed a codebook aligned with these initial questions. For the first question about iZone goals, we defined straightforward codes like "iZone Mission and Goals" to tag instances where participants described the iZone Mission. This code and additional ones were tightly linked to the initial research questions (e.g., "iZone Strategy and Theory of Action"). This first round of coding helped us describe the iZone's strategy and aspects of implementation in ways that were clearly aligned with our research questions. At this early juncture, the key research processes and stages of inquiry seemed well aligned. The research questions informed the interview protocols which, in turn, shaped the coding scheme.

However, after we conducted two additional data collection trips in the study's first year, our interpretation of the iZone strategy for school turnaround began to shift. Figure 17.1 illustrates both the timeline of our research project and how ongoing data collection, memo writing, and first-cycle coding shaped our research questions. Consequently, we found the need to revise our research questions at the conclusion of each study year.

At the conclusion of the first year, we homed in on a trio of intersecting challenges that included: the conceptual and pedagogical rigor of the iZone's vision of math instruction, the pressure of high-stakes accountability, and the weak

FIGURE 17.1 ● First- and Second-Cycle Coding and Analysis in the Shelby County iZone Project

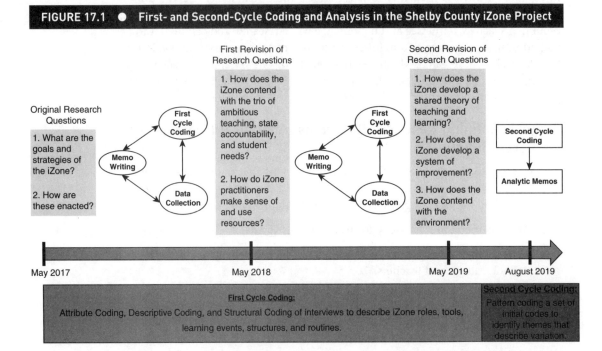

academic foundation and pressing social needs of iZone students. We reframed our research questions and interview protocol at the beginning of the second year to focus on the key problems of practice that emerged from the interaction of these challenges and the way in which iZone leaders attempted to address them through a combination of material resources, learning opportunities, and incentives. Our overarching topic of inquiry was the same, but our questions and analytic perspective were more focused and nuanced.

By the end of the second year of the study, we refined our theory by distinguishing between the iZone's theory of TAL and its theory of improvement. More specifically, we came to understand that the development of the iZone could be interpreted in terms of two systems: a system of TAL in classrooms, *and* a system of improvement that supported teachers and leaders in enacting these practices in their day-to-day work. We also observed that the iZone faced challenges in the environment that threatened to undermine a collective commitment to this vision. Such environmental challenges included pressure for continued improvement on state assessments and varying beliefs about how students should learn mathematics. The complexity of establishing and managing these systems, coupled with the demands of the environment, made it clear that success depended on the ability of the iZone to learn and improve over time. But how would this learning occur in the context of a large, bureaucratic urban district that was founded on norms of autonomy and teaching to the test? Moreover, how could we study this empirically?

The language and framing of the first and second iterations of the research questions, while not wrong, no longer adequately depicted the complexity of the enterprise we were observing. Consequently, as illustrated in Figure 17.1, we revised our research questions again to better represent our understanding of the iZone and to more explicitly inform our data analysis:

1. What factors foster and undermine the development of a shared theory of TAL across the iZone?

2. What factors foster and undermine a shared theory of improvement across the iZone?

3. What processes foster and undermine iZone leaders' ability to learn and improve the iZone design strategy?[1]

These questions directed our attention to the ways teachers understood and interpreted the iZone's vision for mathematics instruction, the extent to which it

---

[1]The remainder of the chapter focuses on our analytic procedures for the first two questions.

clashed with practitioners' pre-existing beliefs, and whether they thought it met the needs of their students. A similar line of inquiry applied to the question of improvement. We queried school and system leaders regarding whether the focus on curriculum fidelity made sense and how school and iZone systems supported teachers in their practice and other components that comprised the improvement strategy. We also sought to understand the extent to which various leaders articulated different improvement strategies and the extent to which these various strategies resulted in incoherence throughout the district.

Though these new questions were a more accurate representation of our research, they rendered some of the initial codes as less relevant and the overall codebook as incomplete. In other words, our codes that were defined from first-cycle coding did not house excerpts that could be connected to our most recent iteration of our theory. In a way, we thought of our task as uncovering the relevant codes hidden in our initial codebook.

Additionally, the fact that our dataset spanned multiple years and role groups, including teachers, principals, iZone district personnel, and state leaders, made it cumbersome to recode initial codes to start with our second-cycle coding process. For instance, the lesson planning code was applied to more than 500 excerpts from a variety of participants. Thus, we needed to devise methods to simplify our work conceptually as well as analytically. Moreover, many of our participants, particularly iZone level leaders, transitioned to new roles or out of the iZone altogether within the span of the study, which, in turn, brought new professionals into the iZone. This growing pool of participants—157 interviews across nine data collection trips—resulted in a large dataset and expanded codebook[2] that included 93 codes and subcodes, 4,800 coded excerpts, and more than 23,000 code applications. Suffice to say, recoding all our data was not an inviting option!

One strategy that simplified the recoding was specifying precise *analytical domains* that were nested under the first two research questions: *tools, problems of practice, professional learning,* and *incentives.* These analytical domains helped us refine theories on how the iZone developed a system of TAL and a system of improvement. For example, understanding how iZone practitioners used tools revealed the problems of practice that emerged from tool use. We then analyzed how iZone leaders contended with these problems of practice through a combination of professional learning events (e.g., professional development, one-on-one coaching) and incentives. For our purposes, we defined problems of practice as

---

[2]We used Dedoose, an online coding platform, to manage and code our dataset. The coding platform allows for multiple users to code concurrently, which was a feature well suited for our geographically dispersed research team.

fundamental dilemmas that practitioners encountered in their day-to-day work, particularly as they applied to the enactment of iZone strategies and tools.

However, the formation of the analytical domains did not provide a structure for how to analyze the data in these domains. Toward that end, we developed a more fine-grained set of research subquestions for each domain to structure our analysis. For example, when investigating the problems of practice domain, we sought to answer the following questions:

1. How are the key problems of instructional practice defined and experienced by practitioners across the iZone?

2. What factors contribute to the processes by which these problems are defined and experienced?

3. How do problems of instructional practice vary across contexts?

See Figure 17.2 for an illustration of how our analysis progressed from research questions to domains to subquestions. Throughout this chapter, we will focus on the "problems of practice" domain to illustrate our methods.

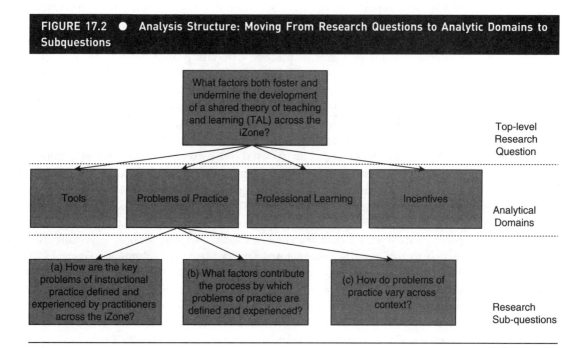

FIGURE 17.2 ● Analysis Structure: Moving From Research Questions to Analytic Domains to Subquestions

Stage 2: Analyzing Each Analytical Domain Systematically

With our analysis structure established, we divided ourselves into two teams, each of which was assigned to investigate one of the top-level research questions:

1. What factors both foster and undermine the development of a shared theory of TAL across the iZone?

2. What factors both foster and undermine a shared theory of improvement across the iZone?

Over the course of the next 10 weeks, both teams sorted and coded thousands of excerpts for each analytical domain. Importantly, we *used our original codebook to extract excerpts that we then recoded within our new domains*. This process, which we elaborate in depth below, included examining excerpts, using pattern coding to identify themes, and eventually documenting findings in an analytic memo for each domain (Miles, Huberman, & Saldaña, 2020; Saldaña, 2016). As defined in Saldaña (2016, p. 236), a pattern code pulls together first-cycle codes into a "more meaningful and parsimonious" meta-code (i.e., theme).

Step 1: Determining Which Codes to Pull for Each Analytical Domain. To address each analytical domain, we met in teams to first discuss which codes to pull from the original codebook and which role groups to consider. The team first read and discussed the subquestions associated with this domain to select a subset of codes from our original codebook, codes that we inferred as consequential for problems of practice. The task proved difficult because, even though the problems of practice domain seemed sufficiently constrained, many codes in our original codebook housed upwards of 1,000 excerpts—an amount that far surpassed our team's capacity to reanalyze for each analytical domain. Additionally, none of these initial codes were labeled "problems of practice," nor did one single code neatly house excerpts relevant only to problems of practice.

Our research team landed on 300–400 coded excerpts per domain as a number that was at once manageable for our team size and time constraints, yet provided enough data to address our research questions. For the problems of practice domain, we selected the initial codes "Tools for Instruction" and "Instructional Practice" because we discerned that these codes would contain data in which participants reported their teaching dilemmas in iZone schools, especially as it related to the recently implemented Eureka Math curriculum (see Figure 17.3). These two codes, though, still yielded more than 700 excerpts. To reduce this quantity to meet our target of 300–400 excerpts, we identified theoretically meaningful subcodes within the two larger codes. For example, we chose to include all excerpts from the initial "Instructional Practice" code that fell into both of its subcodes "Challenges and benefits of implementing the Eureka Curriculum" and "Supporting currently struggling students" because we found that the majority of iZone practitioners contended with supporting students and teaching content at

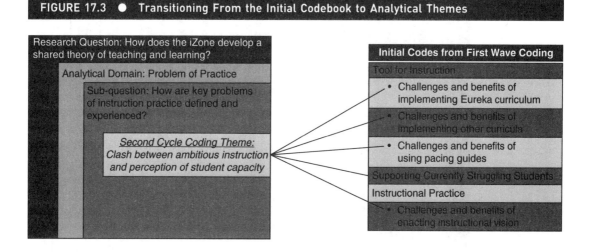

FIGURE 17.3 ● Transitioning From the Initial Codebook to Analytical Themes

grade level. From the "Tools for Instruction" code, we also pulled subcodes relating to pacing guides and using other curricula. These selections reduced the set of 700 excerpts to 300–400 excerpts. The main takeaway here is that it took some trial and error to select codes from the initial codebook that contained relevant excerpts and that constituted a manageable analytical task for the research team.

Step 2: The Second-Cycle Coding Process. Once we selected excerpts for each analytical domain, we had to analyze these still-large swaths of data in a systematic way. Whereas in the first-cycle coding we applied descriptive and structural codes, in the second-cycle coding we used pattern coding to represent theoretically salient themes for the research subquestions. Toward this end, we downloaded these selected excerpts from our data analysis software to a spreadsheet. We set up the columns in the spreadsheet to designate the excerpt and its identifying attributes (participant, year, role group, school, etc.). We also wrote a summary for each excerpt, noted whether and how the excerpt related to each subquestion, and added any additional analytic notes to help with the upcoming memo writing process. See Figure 17.4 for an illustration of how we wrote summaries for each excerpt, designated a problem of practice, and considered how it varied across contexts. From this spreadsheet, we were able to review the excerpts and define themes. For example, note this excerpt from a 5th grade math teacher: "The curriculum is not aligned with the problems students see on the end of year test." This excerpt highlights the theme *Clash between curriculum and state assessments*, which was noted by many teachers in the sample. The outcome of this spreadsheet was a set of themes that enabled us to conceptualize, categorize, and make claims about problems of practice in the iZone.

FIGURE 17.4 ● Screenshot of Analytical Spreadsheet

	B	C	D	E	F	G
A	Excerpt Copy	(a) How are the key problems of instructional practice defined and experienced by practitioners across the iZone?	(b) What factors contribute to the process by which POP are defined and experienced (e.g., tools, expectations, beliefs, and goals?)	(c) How do problems of instructional practice vary across context?	Quick Summary	Analytic Notes
Not Pictured: Qualifier columns (Respondant, Year, Role Group)	The challenge for me is that Eureka Math (EM) curriculum is not necessarily aligned to our state test. If we only do EM this year and we don't show it to them in different ways, when they get the test at the end of the year, they are going to struggle with it because it is going to look different. It is not that the content is a whole lot different. It is a challenge trying to make sure that we expose them to what they are going to see at the end of the year, as to what they are going to see at the end of the year, as well, while teaching the curriculum.	Curriculum format is not aligned to state test format	Clash between ambitious math instruction and state assessment	High level iZone leaders believe that if the curriculum is taught with fidelity, students will excel on the test despite differences in format.	Teacher feels that EM does not sufficiently prepare students to answer the questions on the end of year test because of formatting differences.	Belief that EM is insufficient for preparing students for assessment: high expectations and accountability contribute to pressure for teachers and students.
	Interviewee: A lot of times the way the curriculum is written, they want students to be conceptual first and then go to the procedural. But when you're working with children that are fragile learners, it doesn't always happen that way. Once they get the procedural part of it, they get confident and then they can make the connections to the conceptual. Interviewer 2: It sounds like some of your decisions are based on also like building up students' confidence -- Interviewee: Right, yes.	Students who are behind can't start with conceptual before procedural, but that's what EM wants teachers to do.	Clash between ambitious instruction and student capacity	Across respondents, beliefs about whether to teach procedures or concepts first vary widely.	T explains that fragile learners need to start with procedural first, and that as a teacher you first need to build their confidence before giving them more difficult material.	Poignant excerpt because T seems to really want to support students, but her theory of teaching and learning is that her students can't handle grade-level work.

Stage 3: Writing Memos for Each Analytical Dimension

The last step in our analytic process was to leverage our data, now coded by domain, to inform memos that transformed the problems of practice spreadsheet into a theoretically informed narrative.

Step 1: Using Themes to Formulate Claims for the Analytic Memo. Our team used the excerpt summaries, analytic notes, and themes to develop empirically based claims linked to our research questions. Each researcher read, analyzed, and synthesized a portion of the recoded data to draw connections between themes and relevant research subquestions.

We constructed claims by more deeply analyzing excerpts within a theme. For each theme, we sought to analyze commonalities across excerpts, posit initial hypotheses, note differences across contexts, and further refine initial claims. For the theme *Clash between ambitious instruction and perception of student capacity*, we observed that teachers generally struggled to teach rigorous math content at grade-level because they perceived that students had critical gaps in their background knowledge that prevented them from engaging with grade-level content. Consequently, teachers justified their decisions to teach below grade level by citing their perceptions of students' abilities. This phenomenon was more entrenched at the high school level because teachers perceived that students were even farther behind. By immersing ourselves in what was now a theoretically coherent subset of our data, we were able to formulate hypotheses that, in turn, informed fully formed narratives in our analytic memos.

Step 2: Revising Memos as a Team. Working together to check the validity of claims was an essential aspect of the memo writing process. As a team, we debated initial claims and used additional sources of data to test and refine these hypotheses. For example, an early claim was that iZone teachers and leaders consistently viewed Eureka as inappropriate for students behind grade level. Upon further examination, we uncovered evidence noting pockets of iZone teachers and leaders who believed that all students should be exposed to grade-level instruction, particularly given that many students are several grade levels behind. Importantly, these leaders framed this as an issue of equity and access. As this example illustrates, collaboration and collective revision of claims allowed the team to further refine findings, carefully construct responses to subquestions, and coconstruct memos that reflected the breadth and depth of our data. The rigor and multistage nature of this process enabled us to refine these identified themes, capture nuance, and highlight examples all explicitly linked to our research questions.

To build on the example above, our team-based process of memo writing helped us examine how teachers and school leaders adapted the Eureka curriculum to, in their words, better suit student needs. This stood in direct contrast to other leaders who implemented strategies to enable teachers to teach the curriculum at the rigor intended. Ultimately, our exploration of this single theme, *Clash between ambitious instruction and perception of student capacity*, helped us explore how problems of practice were defined and experienced within and across research sites. Both the TAL Team and the Improvement Team completed this process for each of the four domains, resulting in eight analytic memos that represented our understanding of the iZone's strategy for school turnaround.

General Methods for Coding and Writing Analytic Memos for Longitudinal Studies

In the sections below, we describe general methods for refining research questions, conducting second-cycle coding, and writing analytic memos in teams. Throughout, there is guidance for researchers to use the analytical and memo writing processes to revise their working theories. There is also some discussion of how to conduct qualitative analyses in teams.

Stage 1: Refining Research Questions, Analytical Domains, and Research Subquestions

After conducting a number of data collection trips, writing memos, and conducting a first-cycle coding, researchers may want to consider whether their understanding of the study has evolved to the point that the initial research questions no longer adequately represent the subject of inquiry. Consider the following questions to guide the process of redefining research questions:

1. Have initial analyses rendered the study more complex?

2. Have you introduced new concepts and frameworks into your thinking?

3. Has your understanding of what mediates change evolved?

4. Have changes in the research sites or the broader environment (e.g., turnover, new policies) surfaced new dilemmas?

In addition to refining research questions, it can be helpful to define analytical domains that help break down the analysis into smaller, conceptual chunks that reflect the working theory of the phenomena under investigation. Following this, research subquestions within each of these domains can further guide and specify inquiry. Researchers can include different types of questions, such as descriptive questions, synthesis questions, and inferential questions to guide the research process (Agee, 2009). Returning to our study, we used *descriptive questions* to identify key processes that practitioners engaged in, such as how tool use surfaced problems of practice. We then used *synthesis questions* to understand if problems of practice were common in multiple school contexts. Last, we used *inferential questions* to examine how tool use led to different problems of practice emerging in different school contexts. Researchers can leverage different kinds of research questions to make sense of and add conceptual layers to the analysis.

For researchers working in teams, this revision process requires time and consideration to collectively reconsider (and reconstruct) research questions and jointly make sense of emergent theories. While integrating multiple researcher perspectives and disciplines can add dimensions to working theories and break new research ground, it is also a time-consuming process that requires a risk-taking team culture founded on norms of listening, coconstructing meaning through dialogic processes, and constructive criticism. Although it takes time for researchers to develop shared frames of reference and may seem to not be directly related to the "study," researchers in teams should consider engaging in routines that help build consensus around goals as they enter each phase of the project. Additionally, we recommend the importance of engaging in routines that both surface disagreements and provide for the resolution of these disagreements.

Stage 2: Analyzing Each Analytical Domain Systematically

The next step is to determine which first-cycle codes fall under each analytical domain and how to engage in the second-cycle coding process. There are many coding techniques available for researchers for second-cycle coding (Saldaña, 2016), so researchers have to determine which technique is the most relevant to their study. We selected pattern coding because it helped us identify and structure themes (i.e., "super codes") that were germane to our investigation (Gibson & Brown, 2009).

Step 1: Determining Which Codes to Pull for Each Analytical Domain. After setting up the analytical domains and subquestions, the next step is to identify relevant data for second-cycle coding (Miles, Huberman, & Saldaña, 2020; Strauss & Corbin, 1990). Researchers have to select a set of codes from the initial codebook that contain conceptually relevant excerpts. When dealing with large datasets, it is important to consider what is a manageable coding and analytic task given time constraints and current resources. That is, if the dataset is large, research teams are unlikely to have the time or funding to recode the entire dataset. The following questions can help researchers select high-leverage codes for second-cycle coding:

1. Which codes are theoretically relevant for the revised research questions?

2. Which role groups' perspectives are critical and provide a more complete picture of the phenomenon of interest?

3. If your research is longitudinal, have your codes identified phenomena that change over time?

By addressing these questions, researchers can make clear connections between the codes and role groups selected and their revised research questions. At this juncture, it is vital that researchers take note of data that might not be accounted for by only recoding a subset of the data. Researchers can refer back to field notes, discussions, and preliminary memos to recollect important findings in their study and consider if they are omitting key sources of data.

Step 2: The Second-Cycle Coding Process. After determining which first-cycle codes will undergo a second round of coding, it helps to set up an analytical spreadsheet to structure the second-cycle process. Each coded excerpt can be organized by relevance to the dimensions of the sample (e.g., participant, year, role group, location, initial code, year, etc.). Additionally, it helps if researchers make explicit connections between these excerpts and the subquestions for that domain. As illustrated in Figure 17.4, our research team used subquestions, indicated in the first row, to analyze each excerpt. These analyses can identify important themes that describe the phenomena under investigation (e.g., *Clash between ambitious instruction and student capacity*).

The task here is to define a relatively small set of pattern codes that indicate central themes, thereby grouping first-wave codes into more condensed and theoretically salient topics. We recommend that researchers initially recode a small portion of excerpts (~10% of the selected excerpts) to identify a parsimonious set of themes. At this stage, we found that limiting the number of themes in second-cycle coding pressed our team to identify central concepts that could be used to describe our theory. Researchers can then reflect on these preliminary themes to understand if they have defined central aspects of their theory.

Researchers might identify additional themes as they progress in the second-cycle coding process. Here, you should consider if potential themes add conceptual depth to the analysis. If so, it is important that researchers recode data to ensure that excerpts are coded under the most apt theme as the additional codes may shape researchers' theories. Recoding can be greatly facilitated by coding software; however, in our case, we elected to recode excerpts in our analytical spreadsheet. The recoding process will improve the clarity of the analytic memos.

Stage 3: Writing Memos for Each Analytical Domain

After completing second-cycle coding, researchers are now ready to further analyze coded data and form initial claims. In this section, we focus on the process of writing analytic memos that can be used for research publications. We provide guidance on synthesizing data from the second-cycle coding and writing memos in teams.

Step 1: Formulating Claims for the Analytic Memo. At this stage in the research cycle, researchers are asked to examine their data to identify relationships between concepts, form if/then statements, and explain the phenomena that arise in the study (Birks, Chapman, & Francis, 2008; Miles, Huberman, & Saldaña, 2020; Saldaña, 2016). In our study, we formed claims by identifying commonalities in the data for each theme that explained participants' behavior. Recall how we identified the theme *Clash between ambitious instruction and perception of student* *capacity* by observing that teachers consistently justified teaching below grade level based on their perceptions of student capacity. We also analyzed data within each theme to understand the prevalence of these trends and to potentially identify exceptions. It is essential to keep in mind that this is an iterative process that involves testing initial claims with additional data to understand whether these claims, which comprise the working theory of the phenomena, need to be refined.

While developing initial claims, we advise that researchers ensure that data are representative of the various dimensions of the sample (e.g., by context, role groups, years, etc.). Doing so will help researchers understand if they are omitting consequential data. We recommend that researchers document data sources and the corresponding dimensions of their sample. In our study, for example, we considered if data adequately represented school context, role group, and study year. Documenting sources of data can help identify potential gaps in the data, thereby indicating which data sources might provide relevant information (Shenton, 2004). This can be especially important in longitudinal studies in which sampling data uniformly over different time periods can be challenging. However, sufficient sampling over multiple time periods can ensure that researchers develop robust hypotheses that explain how phenomena develop over time. Last, researchers can refer back to previous memos to vet the credibility of the claims and identify instances in which there are analytical gaps.

Step 2: Revising Memos as a Team. Throughout this process, researchers must maintain a degree of skepticism as to whether they have fully captured the phenomena in question. Toward this end, we suggest revising analytic memos in teams. Note that the collective revision of analytic memos involves multiple rounds of refining claims and supporting evidence. For each analytical domain, this revision process typically entailed cycles of reading analytic memos, commenting on and editing content, and discussing points of agreement and disagreement. We repeated this process until we reached conceptual saturation (Saunders, Sim, Kingstone, Baker, Waterfield, Bartlam, Burroughs, & Jinks, 2018). Two key indicators of saturation in our analysis were resolving major disagreements and incorporating additional data to address theoretical gaps. Here, collaborating as a team improved our analytic memos by identifying and challenging our various perceptions of field experiences and thus enhanced our confidence in the claims in the analytic memos.

Writing memos in teams, though more time-consuming, turns this into a collective learning process. Each team member can share their research expertise and experience in the field, a process that can enhance the inquiry by integrating multiple disciplinary perspectives. Researchers can leverage experience in the field and conceptual perspectives to more thoroughly interrogate claims, refine these claims, and further develop theories explaining the phenomena under investigation.

Conclusion

In this chapter, we discussed how the memo writing process can be *emergent* as the focus of your study and its corresponding theory develop across multiple site visits and over time. We have argued that for complex studies, first-cycle coding methods may not provide the desired conceptualization needed to write analytic memos. In such cases, second-cycle coding is required. And, if the dataset is extensive, it is likely that you will need to apply second-cycle coding to a subset of the data. Researchers, though, must be strategic when recoding a subset of data, making sure to select initial codes that contain theoretically meaningful data and diverse perspectives. We also advocated for writing analytic memos in teams when analyzing large datasets. Although time-consuming, this process can lead to more conceptually rigorous analytic memos and research products by integrating multiple field experiences and disciplinary perspectives.

Despite the multistage and deliberate nature of the analytic memo writing process, it is important to incorporate methods that enhance the validity of your findings. Researchers can enhance the confirmability and the credibility of their claims by thoroughly documenting the evidence used to write analytic memos. By carefully attending to sources of information, researchers can identify potential gaps in their analysis, which is especially relevant when you are recoding only a portion of the data. Additionally, in longitudinal studies, it is important to test your working theories across multiple time periods and sources of data. Taking the time to thoroughly vet the claims in analytic memos will help researchers refine their theories as they prepare meaningful manuscripts for publication.

Supplemental Readings

Glazer, J. L., Massell, D., Lenhoff, S., Larbi-Cherif, A., Egan, C., Taylor, J., Deleveaux, J. Ison, A., & Millinton, Z. (2020). *District-led turnaround at scale: Lessons from the Shelby County iZone*. George Washington University.

Saldaña, J. (2016). *The coding manual for qualitative researchers* (3rd ed.). SAGE.

Shenton, A. K. (2004). Strategies for ensuring trustworthiness in qualitative research projects. *Education for Information, 22*(2), 63–75. https://doi.org/10.3233/efi-2004-22201.

Reflection and Activities

1. Consider the extent to which your understanding and conceptualization of your topic has evolved. How might you reframe your original research questions, given what you now understand? Does this reframing have implications for future data collection, your codebook, and/or preliminary analyses?

2. In this chapter, we described applying second-cycle coding only to a subset of first-cycle codes. What are some affordances and constraints of this approach? How can researchers enhance the validity of the claims constructed from this approach?

3. Referring to Figure 17.3 of this chapter:

   a. Make connections between the theme *Clash between ambitious instruction and perception of student capacity* and the set of initial codes ("Challenges and benefits of implementing Eureka curriculum," "Challenges and benefits of implementing other curricula," "Challenges and benefits of using pacing guides," "Supporting Currently Struggling Students," and "Challenges and benefits of enacting instructional vision"). Draw connections between this initial set of codes and the theme. In your explanation, elaborate on why the theme is a higher-level, more abstract conceptualization of these initial codes.

   b. Given that qualitative research is inherently subjective, identify a theme that you can construct from the initial set of codes in part a. Then, explain how the initial codes connect to your constructed theme.

References

Agee, J. (2009). Developing qualitative research questions: A reflective process. *International Journal of Qualitative Studies in Education, 22*(4), 431–447. https://doi.org/10.1080/09518390902736512

Birks, M., Chapman, Y., & Francis, K. (2008). Memoing in qualitative research: Probing data and processes. *Journal of Research in Nursing, 13*(1), 68–75. https://doi.org/10.1177/1744987107081254

Gibson, W., & Brown, A. (2009). *Working with qualitative data*. SAGE. https://doi.org/10.4135/9780857029041

Glazer, J. L., & Egan, C. (2018). The ties that bind: Building civic capacity for the Tennessee achievement school district. *American Educational Research Journal, 55*(5), 928–964. https://doi.org/10.3102/0002831218763088

Glazer, J. L., Massell, D., Lenhoff, S., Larbi-Cherif, A., Egan, C., Taylor, J., Deleveaux, J., Ison, A., & Millinton, Z. (2020). *District-led turnaround at scale: Lessons from the Shelby County iZone*. George Washington University.

Helms Mills, J., Thurlow, A., & Mills, A. (2010). Making sense of sensemaking: The critical sensemaking approach. *Qualitative Research in Organizations and Management, 5*(2), 182–195. https://doi.org/10.1108/17465641011068857

Larbi-Cherif, A., Lehnoff, S. W., & Glazer, J. (2019). Where's the playbook? Common curriculum and high school turnaround. In C. Meyers & M. Darwin (Eds.), *School turnaround in secondary schools: Possibilities, complexities, and sustainability*. Information Age Publishing.

MacQueen, K. M., McLellan, E., Kay, K., & Milstein, B. (1998). Codebook development for team-based qualitative analysis. *CAM Journal, 10*(2), 31–36. https://doi.org/10.1177/1525822x980100020301

Miles, M., Huberman, M., & Saldaña, J. (2020). *Qualitative data analysis: A methods sourcebook* (4th ed.). SAGE.

Saldaña, J. (2016). *The coding manual for qualitative researchers* (3rd ed.). SAGE.

Saunders, B., Sim, J., Kingstone, T., Baker, S., Waterfield, J., Bartlam, B., Burroughs, H., & Jinks, C. (2018). Saturation in qualitative research: Exploring its conceptualization and operationalization. *Quality & Quantity, 52*(4), 1893–1907. https://doi.org/10.1007/s11135-017-0574-8

Shenton, A. K. (2004). Strategies for ensuring trustworthiness in qualitative research projects. *Education for Information, 22*(2), 63–75. https://doi.org/10.3233/efi-2004-22201

Strauss, A., & Corbin, J. (1990). *Basics of qualitative research*. SAGE.

Zimmer, R., Henry, G. T., & Kho, A. (2017). The effects of school turnaround in Tennessee's achievement school district and innovation zones. *Educational Evaluation and Policy Analysis, 39*(4), 670–696. https://doi.org/10.3102/0162373717705729

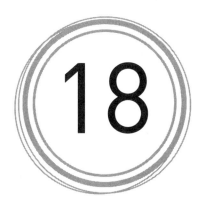

Making Claims Using Qualitative Data

Tim Huffman

Abstract

Claim making is an exercise that helps qualitative researchers move from data analysis to writing. By making claims, researchers can play with and test out possible directions for their projects. This chapter offers six heuristic devices which can be used to generate or deepen claims. These heuristics include: (1) conceptual cocktail parties for envisioning possible analytic directions; (2) abductive reasoning for postulating possible explanations; (3) *Jeopar*dy research questions for linking claims to questions; (4) phronetic claims for helping people make wise choices; (5) carrying claims for testing the fit and vibrancy of a claim; and (6) negative case analysis for throwing out or tightening claims. Taken together, this set of tools helps researchers creatively and effectively move from data analysis into the writing stage of the project.

Keywords: Claim making; abductive reasoning; heuristics; data analysis

Introduction and Brief Literature Review

It can be hard to transition from the rigors of analysis to the creative process of writing. It is challenging to teach the inventive leaps that move a person from patterns in data to the structure of an argument. Researchers can get lost in coding, unable to see how they get from the conceptual categories they have made to a full paper with a clear thesis. Sometimes, qualitative researchers get data and code and code and code, but we are not sure when we are done or what to do with our coded data.

Many stories I hear about qualitative analysis have "eureka" moments, breakthroughs in thinking, or periods of obstruction opening in sudden bursts of clarity. To be honest, it happens to me sometimes. I will have spent hours at my computer doing qualitative analysis by sifting, coding, and memoing. But later in the day, when I'm doing something else somewhere else, I'll suddenly realize a promising path ahead. But relying on eurekas is not a reliable strategy. What, then, should this chapter be about? "Make sure you talk to people while coding. You might make a sudden realization." Or perhaps, "When you get stuck, take a shower. Lots of people have 'aha' moments in the shower."

That's silly. Yes, researchers should keep showering and talking to other humans while doing qualitative analysis. But how to get from analytic practices to things worth saying is not a total mystery. While one cannot force creativity, there are practices that foster it. These practices are called heuristic devices. They are modes of thinking that create new forms of thinking (Abbott, 2004). Heuristic devices work because they lower the cognitive barriers to invention by offering generative frameworks.

Researchers can use heuristic devices to navigate the twilight zone between analysis and writing. I believe that in the middle ground between analysis and writing lies *claim making*. Claims are hybrid. They are analytic in that they explain and make sense of data. But claims are also a statement of an idea, which is the fundamental building block of writing. A well-made claim (or set of claims) can serve as the foundational thesis statement or theoretical contribution that can focus final analysis and undergird the rest of the writing.

Claim-making heuristics also help researchers get to transformative ideas. Since I take a pragmatic approach (in critical/social justice contexts; see Huffman, 2018), I want my ideas to be more than just summative statements about clusters of data. I want them to challenge and transform oppressive structures and discourses that disenfranchise and marginalize. I want my ideas to move people to action. I want them to speak to academics, professionals, policy makers, and citizens. As such, my claims must be made from the data, yes, but also speak to diverse stakeholders within broader contexts of scholarship and society. While some analytic strategies suit critical and justice-oriented scholarship (Charmaz, 2011), heuristic devices also help bridge this gap.

In this chapter I offer a set of heuristic devices to aid the inventive process. They are a set because different types of studies/data/claims require different types of invention. Also, different thinkers find some heuristic devices more or less helpful. Having various choices allows both artful and prudent development of ideas. I hope that this set of heuristic devices can serve the qualitative researcher or student as a toolkit, an herb garden, or a set of brushes (pick the metaphor that works best) that helps create space for eurekas.

I articulate two modes of thinking that move qualitative projects forward: *claim making* and *claim deepening*. Claim-making strategies help take the researcher from analyzing to developing a set of arguments, while claim deepening activities invite critical, theoretical, and community-based logics to nuance the nature of those budding claims. The activities are based on the thinking and writing of various scholars. Some are mainstays of qualitative research, like negative case analysis from grounded theory. Others are derived from the works of philosophers out of the tradition of American Pragmatism (such as William James, Charles Sanders Pierce, and Richard Rorty). Still others are drawn from current thinkers (like Bent Flyvbjerg). The heuristic devices presented here are assembled from these various writers' work and pertain to the creation or critique of ideas. I offer them as step-by-step processes to make them more accessible during data analysis. I have employed these strategies in my own research, used them in both undergraduate and graduate classes, and have used my own reflections and the feedback of others to amend the heuristic processes.

The purpose of these exercises is to create and deepen claims. Most academic articles and concept papers have a small number of claims that they ultimately argue. Sometimes it's as little as one claim. For instance, Matthew Desmond's work *Evicted* (2016) is driven by the single claim that it is more sensible to think of eviction as a cause of poverty rather than resulting from poverty. When writing about a project, of course, we make more claims than just the central one. But our additional claims are often in support of the central claim or thesis of the work. Claim making can help generate the central and supportive claims that build the skeleton of the broader writing.

To show how claim making works, I start by narrating an example of the process of claim making through a qualitative research project. Then I describe each claim-making heuristic device and explain how it works. The heuristics presented are the conceptual cocktail party, abductive reasoning, *Jeopardy* research questions, phronetic claims, carrying claims, and negative case analysis. Each offers a process for making or deepening claims from data. I conclude with a set of questions and activities to put the heuristics into practice.

Exemplar

In this section, I tell the story of a qualitative research project in which I used various claim-making activities. The project was a three-and-a-half year community-based qualitative research project focused on homeless young adults and the nonprofit organizations that served them. Specifically, my project became an effort to understand and improve how the young adults experienced care inside these organizations by looking at successful and failed acts of compassionate communication—that is, social interactions that make people feel cared for. Many of the details of this story are outlined in Huffman and Tracy (2018). It serves as a comprehensive example of all the heuristic devices outlined in this chapter.

The project started in fall 2009. I began by serving as a volunteer at a branch of StandUp For Kids in Phoenix, Arizona. My volunteering involved going on outreach (offering food, water, hygiene supplies, etc.), training volunteers, and running a weekend drop-in day center. By the end of the project, I stepped into the role of executive director of the local branch. On a scholarly level, for the first two years I worked on projects focused on nonprofit organizing, altruism, and positive communication in organizations. In 2011, I began conceptualizing a larger research project (my dissertation).

To focus my interpretation, I used *phronetic claim making* (explained in detail later) to generate ideas that would guide others in making wise choices in related contexts. I considered what directions the social situation was going by considering who was advantaged and disadvantaged by the status quo, if that was desirable, and what should be done about it. In the two years I had been involved, I had seen various aspects of communication in nonprofit organizations that were humanizing (like one-on-one relationships, processing conflicts) but also saw deeply dehumanizing ones (like projecting needs onto the young adults). When the young adults didn't feel cared for in an organization, they were less likely to use its services. Also, staff and homeless young adult conflict, at times, led to young adults being kicked out of the program. In all these cases, negative interactions were the cause of service failure. Such negative interactions were most detrimental for the youth, who were usually the most vulnerable in the social situation. One practice that could remedy the situation was to purposefully seek and draw on the experience of homeless young adults. By listening to their concerns, nonprofits could improve practice, training, and policy. This practical frame, oriented toward wise decision-making, focused my study on compassion and successful nonprofit organizing.

After I had done significant first-level coding (open-ended reading while noting observations) and second-level coding (systematic identification of emerging themes in the data) of my fieldwork data, I used a strategy called the *conceptual cocktail party* (Huffman & Tracy, 2018). It invites researchers to imagine their research project like a group of people talking, including the people they cite and participants in the field. In so doing, it helps researchers consider their expertise, the audiences they hope to reach, the literatures they could engage, and the sorts of claims they can make. At that time, I knew a few areas of scholarship that were relevant to the scene, namely: nonprofit/volunteer literature, emotion and compassion issues in organization, and various conceptualizations of homelessness. So I chose to learn more about the process theories of compassionate communication (Miller, 2007; Way & Tracy, 2012). I wanted the audience for my work to include social justice and communication scholars. I picked a few target journals that had published similar topics. I also identified the professional audiences I wanted to engage and strategized the ways I could best do that (e.g., presentations at regional conferences, trainings of nonprofit staff, and direct organizing). I also considered the kinds of knowledge and justification these communities used.

After I reviewed the related literature, identified my ideal audiences, and thought about what my different communities needed to consider me credible, I began to generate claims that accounted for what was happening in my data using *abductive reasoning*. This claim generating technique uses surprise to push explanation. For instance, I was surprised by how often homeless young adults referred to volunteers' physical presence and embodied acts when talking about care. Thus, I conjectured: "Physical presence communicates care." I thought that by physical presence and the use of bodies in service, volunteers and staff show that they care. I looked for more support and asked myself, "Are all instances of presence seen as caring and compassionate?" I also conjectured claims about dynamic boundary spanning, humor, and nontraditional problem-solving. But which one should I investigate further?

To decide this, I used a practice called *carrying claims*, where I would take a claim into the field and work to see how it moved me to action and helped me make choices. I labored and served within the nonprofit through outreach, training, and creating relationships with the young adults. I asked questions and observed processes. I reflected on my experiences and envisioned new models for theorizing and organizing. I gathered resources (including financial, human, and scholarly) and presented my work within and beyond the organization.

Two examples of claim carrying are as follows. Early on, I thought that nontraditional problem-solving was critical to positive interaction between volunteers and youth. I read more about leader–member exchange theory and dynamic boundary spanning (Lilius, Worline, Dutton, Kanov, & Maitlis, 2011), both of which articulate the importance of dynamic and nonroutine linkages between people. I carried the claim while I was in the field. I used it to try to make sense of social situations. But even with this claim close to mind, it did not change my activities or give me new directions. Ultimately, I dropped the claim. Since it never helped me make choices moving forward, I chose not to focus on nontraditional problem-solving.

To investigate the claim that "physical presence communicates care," I carried it into the field. This claim was extremely useful. It helped me be strategic about both my own nonverbal interaction and the structure of the environment. It gave me ideas for how to interact more compassionately.

My claim was rooted in my data and resonated in the field. The next step was *negative case analysis*. I looked both at the data I had and actively sought data in the field that disproved the claim. A complication arose: Physical presence did not always communicate care! Notably, the young adults critiqued staff who were "just there for the paycheck" or "just there clicking on their computers." They used the phrase "being there" to describe feeling cared for, but "just being there" wasn't caring. After more collection and analysis, I managed to figure out what was going on. It turns out there is an embodied enactment of care traceable through different nonverbal practices and acts of service. So, I revised the argument to suggest that what is considered compassionate is when people make their body *about* the other (as opposed to merely being present). Hence, a new claim arose: "Embodied 'aboutness' communicates care." That became the central argument of the project (Huffman, 2017).

Claim-making Methods/Practices and Their Use

Conceptual Cocktail Party

Imagine you are throwing a conceptual cocktail party and trying to invite the right people to make the most stimulating conversation.

Imagine you are throwing a party. What sort of party is it? Who do you invite? What preparation is needed to make the best possible conversation happen at the party? Should there be seat assignments or should people just mingle? Imagining a conceptual cocktail party is the first heuristic device for making claims. Huff (1999) suggests that papers can be best imagined as crowded rooms full of scholars. Burke (1973) describes it this way:

Imagine that you enter a parlor. You come late. When you arrive, others have long preceded you, and they are engaged in a heated discussion, a discussion too heated for them to pause and tell you exactly what it is about. In fact, the discussion had already begun long before any of them got there, so that no one present is qualified to retrace for you all the steps that had gone before. You listen for a while, until you decide that you have caught the tenor of the argument; then you put in your oar. (pp. 110–111)

This metaphor calls to mind the community-based nature of knowing. What we know isn't a static, isolated thing. It's a dynamic and relational construct, which means that who we know matters. When researchers move to interpretation of their analysis, it is helpful to think about audience, related literatures, and fundamental goals. This sets the stage for more targeted claim making.

The conceptual cocktail party heuristic involves considering (1) the scholarly literature related to the project (the scholarly writer guests at your party), (2) the data you've generated and analyzed (the data/participant guests), and (3) the potential audiences including professional, activist, and scholarly (the reader guests). Each of these spheres includes voices you want to "invite." In the case of scholarly literature, you are inviting scholars who have written things that bring important insights to your project. In the case of your data, you want to invite the voices and conversations that speak most powerfully about the realities of the social world of your research. In the case of your audience, you want to imagine your potential readers and what they consider important, interesting, and relevant. Use the conceptual cocktail party to set the stage for claims by asking:

1. What scholarly writers, data/participants, and readers should the project bring together?

2. What are the themes/arguments/ideas that emerge from each group? What are the questions that they raise?

3. How do the questions and arguments emerging from each sphere connect? Which are most fruitful for focusing on?

In a research project focused on permanent supportive housing for people without homes, I used the conceptual cocktail party activity to list out voices the project could draw on. The data spoke to health, architecture, and community. In reviewing the literature, I saw connections with trauma-informed care, definitions of community, and nonprofit organizing. I ultimately chose to write for a scholarly audience focused on homelessness. By combining these three spheres the conceptual direction of the paper was established. The ultimate thesis of the paper was that trauma-informed architecture created opportunities, though not without challenges, for fostering community among once homeless residents.

This strategy is most effective after at least two-thirds of data are collected and after a data immersion process. Ideally, the party is imaginatively "performed" inside the researcher's mind before the researcher is completely done with analysis. Answering these questions will either begin to generate claims or set the context you'll be making claims within.

Abductive Reasoning

I just asked Dad a simple question, and he freaked out!

He might not have eaten lunch. He's a grump when his blood sugar is low.

The next heuristic device is abductive reasoning. Abductive reasoning is one of (at least) three types of logical reasoning: deductive, inductive, and abductive. Deductive reasoning focuses on drawing true conclusions by applying general and specific claims. Inductive reasoning involves making claims that are likely, given how much evidence supports a particular claim. Abductive reasoning involves proposing possible explanations for why something is the case. All three of these logics play a role in qualitative research. For instance, inductive reasoning is the foundation of any observation-based theorizing. (Event B happens regularly after event A; therefore, there is a relationship between them.) Deductive logic can aid in many coding approaches, but induction is particularly helpful for making claims.

The following prompts are motivated by Charles Peirce's (1903) outline of abductive reasoning, or what he calls the logic of guessing. Abduction has four steps in qualitative research:

1. Identify a surprising instance (e.g., Dad freaked out after I asked him a simple question).

2. Conjecture a claim that, if it were true, the surprising fact would be a matter of course (e.g., It probably wasn't the question that freaked him out but because he didn't have lunch).

3. Try to articulate how the claim would actually lead to the surprising fact. If it does, there is reason to suspect that it is true.

4. Look for other support. (Let's ask Dad if he had lunch, wait until he eats, ask our question again, and see how he reacts.)

Example:

1. Identify a surprising instance: The participants in this therapeutic horticulture training draw emotional strength from plants.

2. Conjecture a claim: Nonhuman actors, such as plants and animals, can also be actors in a supportive community.

3. Articulate how the claim might lead to the mysterious or surprising instance: Through persistence, interaction, and familiarity, nonhuman actors participate in the emotional life of people in a community.

4. Look for evidentiary support that caring provides emotional resources. This could mean more coding, an added interview question, focused field observations, and/or looking to the literature.

This process of "surprise—conjecture—articulate—support" is best used following data immersion. It is valuable for two primary reasons. First, it helps shift the researcher's thinking into a creative space that is relatively unencumbered. Every conjectured claim is not going to make it into the paper. But generating explanations is productive for pushing the interpretive frame the researcher brings to the project. I encourage researchers to be bold when conjecturing claims. Make wild conjectures. Throw in a few silly ones. Make strong statements. Later parts of the process (namely, negative case analysis) are used to remove the claims not worth making. But as many creative people know, there is value to putting on the inventive hat and silencing the critic for a time. Critiquing ideas can stop the creative process. Later is the time for critique. Make some bold claims about why some surprising things in the data came to pass.

The second reason the heuristic is helpful is because creating an explanation for a surprising fact is generally considered necessary. As Pierce (1903) argues, the human mind seeks explanation following surprise. By focusing on surprise as the starting point, we orient ourselves to what our readers are most likely to consider interesting or newsworthy. Different audiences will be surprised by different things, so it can be valuable to use abduction to conjecture claims after a conceptual cocktail party.

Jeopardy Research Questions

In *Jeopardy*, the answer is worded in the form of a question. In fact, the show was originally called "What's the Question?" In many ways, qualitative analysis is similar. The transcript is a giant pile of data. It contains answers, and it is the researcher's job to figure out what questions it answers. This heuristic device inverts the question–answer dyad. Also, the heuristic aptly recognizes that part of the thought-work of interpretation is in formulating and reformulating questions. Many interpretive approaches to qualitative research do not have static research questions formulated before the study. They begin with hunches or formulations of possible questions, but researchers often withhold the final mental frame for later. This technique has many positives, but it does mean that the researcher can make it all the way to the interpretation phase of the project and be in serious need of thinking backward. The researchers may know what the data are saying, but they need to orient themselves to the sorts of questions the data could answer.

There are two basic steps:

1. What is a statement my data make?

2. What question(s) does that statement answer? (see Figure 18.1)

FIGURE 18.1 ● *Jeopardy* Research Question Table

Statement from the data	What question(s) does it answer?

Using *Jeopardy* research questions is best done after some form of data immersion (coding, multiple readings, etc.). It can also be helpful following abductive conjecture of claims by treating those claims as statements and imagining the kinds of questions they could answer. Also, it is important to remember that different kinds of questions have value to different people. Using this heuristic after the conceptual cocktail party activity can help because familiarity with related articles can give a sense of where another scholar's ideas are leading. This can be explicit in the case of "future research" sections. It can also be implicit in the case of theories that can be extended, or in new contexts that can be explored.

Research questions are best when they serve as logical links between the study and related works. Consider how they can incorporate the technical/theoretical language found in similar works into research questions. This signals to readers what they can expect, constitutes the audience linguistically, and honors prior work.

Phronetic Claims

Can you prove your account of this issue is true?

No, but I can provide detailed narratives of what is happening and some concrete examples of what the consequences are for whom. I suspect that sort of clarity will help us decide what to do next.

Aristotle teaches that there are various forms of knowing:

- *Episteme*—knowledge that is abstract, hypothetical, and always/very often true;

- *Techne*—technical assertions, processes, and know-how based on everyday contingencies; and

- *Phronesis*—practical wisdom that helps people make context-based judgments.

Qualitative research can make all three of these types of claims. It excels at revealing the episteme-knowing of interviewees/participants. Also, inductive arguments about the broad occurrence of particular phenomena undergird claims of episteme-style knowledge. Producing techne-based knowledge is best done by close attention to how processes actually happen and the outcomes of those processes. But phronetic knowing is perhaps qualitative data's strongest form of knowledge because it can, by paying close attention to context, help people make wise choices as they consider practical problems in related contexts.

Trying to make a phronetic claim does not require a researcher to prove his point beyond a reasonable doubt. Rather, it needs to help others make decisions about what can and should be done. There are four layers of phronetic claims (drawn from Flyvbjerg, 2004, see Figure 18.2).

By answering the questions in Figure 18.2, the researcher is making a series of claims about the social context studied. This includes claims that praise or critique the social issue/actors and considers possible action. Depending on the style of the paper, the claims that a researcher uses to frame the paper can emerge from any of these questions.

The idea of phronesis can also drive a more focused, microlevel analysis of choice making (see questions below). Any of these questions can generate the central claim of a written paper for an academic or professional audience. But as a set, they focus the researcher's attention on the pragmatic, choice-making space that occurs within the data:

1. Where in the social scene are the most meaningful outcomes?

2. What choices or enactments lead to those outcomes?

3. In the data, where are these choices being made and who is making them?

4. Given the data, what do wise choices look like? What does folly look like?

FIGURE 18.2 ● Phronetic Claim Making

Guiding Questions	Researcher Assessments
What direction is this social world going in?	
Who gains and who loses, and by which mechanisms of power?	
Is this development desirable?	
What, if anything, should we do about it?	

5. What are the most promising practices for leading to the best outcomes?

6. What does a person need to know to make wise choices in this context?

Each answer is a claim. Some might be clustered together to make a broader argument. Others might carry a whole paper or book. In my work with homeless young adults, I used these phronetic questions to generate a series of claims about how nonprofit organizations can consistently communicate care. These questions helped identify practices but, more importantly interpersonal approaches, which are interpreted by young people as caring.

Of course, not all claims are as useful as others. Using techniques like carrying claims and negative case analysis help figure out which are the most powerful and rigorous.

Carrying Claims

Theories become instruments, not answers to enigmas, in which we can rest. We don't lie back upon them, we move forward, and, on occasion, make nature over again by their aid. Pragmatism unstiffens all our theories, limbers them up and sets each one at work. (James, 1904, p. 42)

Carrying claims is a claim deepening practice where the researcher assesses the power and use of a claim by reflecting on it while they continue to engage in fieldwork. It is rooted in the pragmatic maxim, that is, the true value of an idea can be measured in its ability to lead to different actions and outcomes.

The first step to carrying claims is to clearly articulate a claim. Second, carry the claim (either by writing it on paper and carrying it in a pocket or mobile phone case, or by keeping it close to mind) while in the field. Third, and in no particular order,

- ask questions that allow people's voices and experiences to challenge and support the claim;

- observe everyday life using the claim as a framework for interpretation;

- serve people using the claim as a guide;

- labor on behalf of the community and pay attention to how the claim does or does not account for how things are organized;

- gather material and knowledge relevant to the community and see how the claim enables or constrains this effort;

- present the claim to knowledgeable others;

- reflect on past experiences using the claim as a focus of consideration; and

- envision how the organization/community considers the claim. (Huffman & Tracy, 2018)

Finally, the researcher considers if the claim they carried was helpful, motivating, or valuable to their action and interpretation of the scene. If it isn't, that doesn't doom the idea, but it might not be as valuable as other claims made by the process. Often, the process of carrying a claim changes the claim as new data/field experiences reshape the idea. In my project connected to homeless young adults, I had an early claim that I thought was very interesting about nonroutine problem-solving as a foundation for rapport between volunteers and young adults. However, after carrying the claim in the field, I decided that it wasn't that valuable. It was probably true, but it didn't help me see new things or move me in a particular way. The later claims about compassionate communication, however, were much more directive and ended up being the focus of my future papers.

The value of carrying claims is simple. It gives the researcher a chance to reflect on the pragmatic value of the idea. While, of course, different people find different ideas more or less helpful for moving them in a social space, the best claims are useful for people moving and acting in the world.

Negative Case Analysis

Your cheesecake was the best dessert at the party.

Are you sure? Are you just saying that to be nice?

Trust me. I ate three servings of every dessert there in an effort to find something better. It's still my favorite.

Some people have trouble making claims based on qualitative evidence because they worry that they are wrong. The good news is that there is a method for building rigor into claim making. After using techniques like abduction or *Jeopardy* research questions to make bold, creative claims, the researcher can use negative case analysis to do everything she can to disprove them. This technique builds from grounded theory's constant comparative method. The technique can help reject weak arguments and nuance strong ones. The process of negative case analysis is outlined below.

1. Clearly state a claim

2. What evidence in my data disproves my claim? Are there data I could collect that could disprove it?

3. Should I throw out my claim?

4. Or can I nuance or tighten it to incorporate the new data?

Negative case analysis is done after the researcher has claims and wants to consider their strength. The strongest version of negative case analysis is done when further fieldwork is still possible, as seeking contradictory data in the field helps the researcher challenge assumptions that might have influenced his initial data collection. That said, looking across well-collected data is sufficient for using the technique. Negative case analysis can be used multiple times in a row. The researcher can make a claim, run it through the process, make a new claim, and repeat the process. In this way, negative case analysis can evolve arguments so that they are tighter, more useful, and more revealing. Often original claims critiqued by negative case analysis become deeper insights.

Conclusion

In this chapter, I reviewed the generative heuristics of: the conceptual cocktail party, abductive reasoning, *Jeopardy* research questions, phronetic claims, carrying claims, and negative case analysis. Each offers a way to make claims—that is, clear statements that guide the conceptual course upon which a larger work is based.

How do we get from a giant pile of data to a coherent, well-written paper? To be frank, some people just start writing and keep revising until they have something beautiful. Writing itself can be analytic/interpretive. But many researchers struggle with that process, particularly new researchers. I hold up claim-making heuristics as stepping stones between analysis and writing—an imaginative, critical, and generative mind path.

Supplemental Readings

Abbott, A. (2004). *Methods of discovery: Heuristics for the social sciences*. W. W. Norton & Co.

Davis, M. S. (1971). That's interesting! Towards a phenomenology of sociology and a sociology of phenomenology. *Philosophy of the social sciences, 1*(2), 309–344. https://doi.org/10.1177/004839317100100211

Huffman, T. P. (2018). Paradigmatic tools for communication scholar-activists: Toward a pragmatic and relational epistemology. *Review of Communication, 18*, 19–36. https://doi.org/10.1080/15358593.2017.1405460

Reflection and Activities

1. Establish a conceptual cocktail party by asking:

    a. What published scholarly literature do I know (or should I know) that is relevant to the project?

    b. What are the main ideas/themes that are emerging from my data?

    c. Who are the people/audiences who will care about what this project has to say? Consider how the answers to these questions overlap to become the context for your future claim making.

2. Make some claims, then:

    a. Use abductive reasoning to establish some beginning claims. Find a surprising fact in your data. Then, conjecture a claim that would make the surprising fact a matter of course. If you can articulate how your conjectured claim explains the surprising fact, put a star by it.

    b. Use the phronetic questions to generate some claims about how power is operating and what might be done because of it. Review your claims in light of the audiences you established in the conceptual cocktail party activity. If you think the audience will find the claim relevant to decision-making, put a star by it.

    c. For every claim with a star by it, use the carrying claim and negative case analysis activity below.

3. Make sure the claims are good:

    a. Use negative case analysis with data you already have. With your claim in mind, read all your existing data with the aim of disproving it. If you find lots of countervailing evidence, consider throwing it out. If you find only some, consider tightening your claim and then carrying it into the field.

    b. Carry the claim into the field. Write it on a piece of paper and do fieldwork with it in mind. Take field notes. See if the claim shapes your interpretation or motivates your action. If it shapes an interpretation, there's reason to believe it has scholarly merit. If it moves you or provides a tool for action, then it is of practical merit. If it does both, you should consider writing a paper about it.

References

Abbott, A. (2004). *Methods of discovery: Heuristics for the social sciences*. W. W. Norton & Co.

Burke, K. (1973). *The philosophy of literary form: Studies in symbolic action* (3rd ed.). University of California Press.

Charmaz, K. (2011). Grounded theory methods in social justice research. In N. K. Denzin, & Y. S. Lincoln (Eds.), *The SAGE handbook of qualitative research* (4th ed., pp. 359–380). SAGE.

Desmond, M. (2016). *Evicted: Poverty and profit in the American city*. Crown.

Flyvbjerg, B. (2004). *Making organization research matter: Power, values and phronesis*. Department of Development and Planning, Aalborg University.

Huff, A. S. (1999). *Writing for scholarly publication*. SAGE.

Huffman, T. P. (2017). Compassionate communication, embodied aboutness, and homeless young adults. *Western Journal of Communication, 81*(2), 149–167. https://doi.org/10.1080/10570314.2016.1239272

Huffman, T. P. (2018). Paradigmatic tools for communication scholar-activists: Toward a pragmatic and relational epistemology. *Review of Communication, 18*, 19–36. https://doi.org/10.1080/15358593.2017.1405460

Huffman, T., & Tracy, S. J. (2018). Making claims that matter: Heuristics for theoretical and social impact in qualitative research. *Qualitative Inquiry, 24*(8), 558–570. https://doi.org/10.1177/1077800417742411

James, W. (1904). *What is pragmatism, from a series of eight lectures dedicated to the memory of John Stuart Mill, A new name for some old ways of thinking*.

Lilius, J. M., Worline, M. C., Dutton, J. E., Kanov, J. M., & Maitlis, S. (2011). Understanding compassion capability. *Human Relations, 64*, 873–899. https://doi.org/10.1177/0018726710396250

Miller, K. I. (2007). Compassionate communication in the workplace: Exploring processes of noticing, connecting, and responding. *Journal of Applied Communication Research, 35*, 223–245. https://doi.org/10.1080/00909880701434208

Peirce, C. S. (1903). Harvard lectures on pragmatism. In P. A. Turisi (Ed.), *Pragmatism as a principle and method of right thinking: The 1903 Harvard "lectures on pragmatism."* State University of New York Press.

Way, D., & Tracy, S. J. (2012). Conceptualizing compassion as recognizing, relating and (re) acting: An ethnographic study of compassionate communication at hospice. *Communication Monographs, 79*(3), 292–315. https://doi.org/10.1080/03637751.2012.697630

Arts-Based Practices

Johnny Saldaña

Introduction

It has been eye-opening, reading the research methods literature written by educators, social scientists, health-care professionals, and so on, and noticing that the very things they prescribe to others as important skills for qualitative inquiry are things that artists do virtually every day in their studios and venues. Artists are trained to think conceptually, symbolically, and metaphorically—essential attributes for the analysis of narrative and visual data—if not life itself. Whenever qualitative researchers construct codes, categories, themes, and other interpretive summations of interview transcripts, they condense naturalistic data into richer forms of meaning.

Artists are also taught to bring emotions to the forefront of their work. Art theorist Susanne K. Langer (1977) famously proposed that art is "significant form symbolic of human feeling." Little did she know at that time that her definition would also apply, decades later, to the qualitative research report.

The arts are unique languages. Their vocabularies and grammars form creative epistemologies—ways of knowing—that can insightfully inform researchers about the human condition (Barone & Eisner, 2012; Eisner, 1993). I assert that qualitative researchers with an arts background in music, visual art, dance, theatre, film, or poetry all share two things in common: (1) heightened, perceptive insight into social life and (2) innovative methods for studying it.

I was surprised to learn how some of the most prominent figures in ethnography such as anthropologist Claude Levi-Strauss dabbled in scenic design for the stage, and the prolific sociologist Patricia Leavy began her academic training as a theatre major. Famed ethnographer Harry F. Wolcott was a patron and aficionado of opera, while Elliot Eisner based his groundbreaking approaches to inquiry as a visual artist.

My own background is in theatre, so I "think theatrically" in virtually everything I do (Saldaña, 2015). But I've participated in all the art forms throughout my education and career, ranging from watercolor renderings to concert band, from

329

dance drama to poetry, and from film studies to stage directing. When I first learned about qualitative inquiry, I was surprised how much drama and theatre terminology such as *actor, scene, performance, dramaturgy,* and so on appeared in the academic research literature. And when I learned how eminent scholars such as Victor Turner, Dwight Conquergood, and D. Soyini Madison centered their fieldwork from a performance studies standpoint, I felt reassured that the arts held legitimate places in qualitative inquiry. Recently published handbooks in arts-based research (Cahnmann-Taylor & Siegesmund, 2018; Knowles & Cole, 2008; Leavy, 2018, 2020) testify to the validity of the genres and provide qualitative researchers accessible models for guidance.

Arts-based research also has strong connections to autoethnography, a recent genre of qualitative inquiry that asks researchers to turn a reflexive gaze toward themselves. Adams, Jones, and Ellis (2015) explain that the methodology is an "artistic and analytic demonstration of how we come to know, name, and interpret personal and cultural experience" (p. 1). Reflexivity—the introspective examination of one's positionality and standpoint as a researcher in relationship with the participants and the topic of study—is what artists are taught to do. They have been trained to look deep within in order to come to a richer understanding of what it means to be human and to realize those meanings through significant form. Film director Martin Scorsese himself proclaims, "The most personal is the most creative."

Arts-based research refers not only to the study of participation in and reception to the arts, but to *the use of artistic modes of expression for the analysis, interpretation, representation, and presentation of primarily qualitative data.* As examples:

- A researcher notices in an interview transcript a helpless and pessimistic tone to the participant's stories and voice. The researcher reflects on the type of music that might accompany or "soundtrack" the interview's audio recording. She selects Samuel Barber's *Adagio for Strings* because the piece's tempo, keys, phrases, etc. harmonize with the narrative. The researcher draws parallels between the somber music and the transcript to come to a deeper, empathic understanding of the participant's emotional worldview.

- An interview recording is played as a researcher, in an open space, moves her body in reaction and response to the participant's words, stories, and vocal tones. She is "dancing the data," using her body as an interpretive instrument, trusting her instincts to move in accordance with the narrative. This nonverbal analytic exercise informs her of possible insights about the participant. After she listens and moves to the recording, she composes several analytic memos about her learnings, stimulated by the dance.

- A former visual arts educator interviews fellow art teachers working in urban high schools about their pedagogy and careers. He transcribes the interviews verbatim for traditional qualitative data analysis, but he also renders a portrait of each participant in mixed media (water color and/or collage) to capture the phenomenological essences of their lived experiences. His strategic artistic choices of color, line, texture, and other design elements provide him visual symbols that represent the teachers' perspectives. The interview transcripts inform his art, while the art informs his interpretation of the transcripts. The portraits are included as figures in the final report's results section.

These three examples are just some of the possible approaches to arts-based research.

Using this analytic and interpretive methodology does not always have to result in artistic products such as a theatrical performance or written poem. The processes of artistic exploration in the researcher's private space—a *research studio*, if you will—can generate significant understandings about social life.

In my qualitative data analysis workshops with participants primarily from non-arts disciplines, I always include improvisational movement activities and opportunities for creative, poetic writing. I openly acknowledge with the group that they may feel uncomfortable, at first, participating in these exercises, but I encourage them to take a risk and to keep themselves open to new heuristics, or, methods of discovery. I have yet to see anyone decline to participate. In fact, the artistic experiences they undertake—for some of them, for the very first time in their careers—make them realize that their bodies, not just their minds, are analytic instruments, and that interview transcript data can be condensed and transformed from mundane prose into powerful verse. And all it took was a willingness to risk, the first step in the creation of any work of art.

Perhaps artists' greatest gift is their creativity—the ability to work as master craftspeople and artisans in order to elevate and transcend traditional scholarly work into rich, aesthetic shapes. The chapters in this section demonstrate how qualitative data analysis can be approached through novel methods in order to produce insightful representations and presentations of what it means to be human—the ultimate goal of art *and* qualitative inquiry.

In Chapter 19 I provide an overview of ethnodrama and ethnotheatre, the transformation of fieldwork data into performed accounts for the stage or screen. The guidelines focus on monologic adaptations of interview transcripts with an emphasis on artistic rigor.

Chapter 20, by Robyn Shenfield and Monica Prendergast, illustrates through riveting examples the transformation of interview and reflexive texts into poetic formats. The goal of poetry is to evoke meaning through elegant use of language. The coauthors demonstrate the techniques of found poetry and poetic transcription.

Chapter 21 showcases Kakali Bhattacharya's deeply contemplative and meditative approaches to analysis, and their rendering through visual representations. Her arresting illustrations exhibit the power of social interpretation through design.

The section concludes with illustrator Sally Campbell Galman's signature comic panels in Chapter 22. She provides a behind-the-scenes tour of her creative process through the artistic medium itself. Artists are rule breakers, and Galman encourages researchers to draw, not just write, their analyses.

Perhaps the most difficult perspective to change is the traditionally educated qualitative researcher who perceives the arts as incompatible with the rigorous goals of social science. All artists take risks in the execution and exhibition of their work. It takes tremendous courage to display original, creative ideas in front of audiences. So, I invite readers to explore these arts-based research chapters and experiment fearlessly with dramatizing, poeticizing, and illustrating their data. Arts-based practices are a way of knowing—that is, a way of analyzing and interpreting the social world. And *any* method that helps researchers achieve deep understanding of what it means to be human should be embraced and explored.

Reflection and Activities

1. After reading Chapter 19 on ethnodrama and ethnotheatre, adapt selected portions of an interview transcript into a one- to two-minute monologue for the stage.

2. After reading Chapter 20 on poetic inquiry, adapt selected portions of an interview transcript into found poetry.

3. After reading Chapter 21 on contemplative data analysis, render through pencil sketch, collage, or color media (markers, water color, colored pencil, etc.) a portrait of an interview transcript's participant.

4. After reading Chapter 22 on comics-based data analysis, draw a three- or four-panel comic strip that illustrates a vignette or story contained within an interview transcript.

References

Adams, T. E., Jones, S. H., & Ellis, C. (2015). *Autoethnography*. Oxford University Press.

Barone, T., & Eisner, E. W. (2012). *Arts based research*. SAGE.

Cahnmann-Taylor, M., & Siegesmund, R. (Eds.). (2018). *Arts-based research in education: Foundations for practice* (2nd ed.). Routledge.

Eisner, E. W. (1993). *The enlightened eye: Qualitative inquiry and the enhancement of educational practice*. Macmillan.

Knowles, J. G., & Cole, A. L. (Eds.). (2008). *Handbook of the arts in qualitative research: Perspectives, methodologies, examples, and issues.* SAGE.

Langer, S. K. (1977). *Feeling and form: A theory of art developed from philosophy in a new key.* Charles Scribner's Sons.

Leavy, P. (Ed.). (2018). *Handbook of arts-based research.* Guilford.

Leavy, P. (2020). *Method meets art: Arts-based research practice* (3rd ed.). Guilford.

Saldaña, J. (2015). *Thinking qualitatively: Methods of mind.* SAGE.

Dramatizing Interviews

Johnny Saldaña

Abstract

This chapter illustrates methods of adapting interview transcript data into dramatized accounts for scripted performance. An *ethnodrama* is a play script that artistically dramatizes for the stage or screen a research-based account of fieldwork. *Ethnotheatre* is the production and staging of an ethnodramatic play script utilizing the conventions of live theatre or media. The ethnodramatic adaptation process consists of (1) securing written permission from participants to adapt interview data for performance; (2) condensing the narrative to portions that hold dramatization potential; (3) considering whether verbatim excerpts and/or adaptation of the interview text would best serve the monologic narrative; (4) giving careful thought to the most effective beginning and ending lines and/or stage action; (5) rendering a three-dimensional portrait of the participant; (6) considering whether an "organic poetry" format for the monologue is appropriate; and (7) envisioning all the scenographic devices of theatre or digital video effects for the performance.

Keywords: Ethnodrama; ethnotheatre; monologue; dramatization; arts-based research

Introduction

The purpose of this chapter is to describe how interview transcript data can be transformed into dramatic and theatrical formats as arts-based representations of qualitative research.

Terms and Definitions

An *ethnodrama* (a compound word joining ethnography and drama) is a play script that artistically dramatizes for the stage or screen a research-based account of fieldwork. Sources for ethnodramas can originate from interviews, participation observation, written documents, and other empirical materials, though most writers adapt interview transcript data into monologue and dialogue formats. Ethnodramas are not necessarily documentaries (as they are conventionally labeled in video and film), but additional terms for the genre include *docudrama*, *nonfiction playwriting*, *ethnographic performance text*, and other variants.

Ethnotheatre is the production and staging of an ethnodramatic play script utilizing the conventions of live theatre or media (e.g., costumes, lighting, editing). The magnitude of the staging can range from seated actors reading aloud from a script, to a fully mounted formal production with a full complement of theatrical devices as might be seen on professional Broadway stages. Among the terms for this presentational form are *documentary theatre*, *performance ethnography*, *verbatim theatre*, and other variants.

Brief Example

Educational anthropologist Harry F. Wolcott conducted a series of interviews with "Brad," a 19-year old drifter who squatted unknowingly on Wolcott's expansive wooded property in Oregon in the 1980s. The researcher originally documented the interviews in an article and book chapter (Wolcott, 1983, 1987), and the near-verbatim excerpts were thematically organized in the reports through category subheadings (e.g., Formal Schooling, Welfare, "Getting My Life Together"). The 1983 article presented Brad's life story as an extended profile, while the 1987 chapter's quotes were interwoven with Wolcott's commentary and analysis.

Saldaña's arts-based project—an ethnodramatic adaptation of Harry and Brad's research and personal relationship titled *Finding My Place: The Brad Trilogy* (Wolcott, 2002)—took interview excerpts and arranged them in dramatic structures to simulate conversations between the ethnographer and his participant. In the scene below, Wolcott interviews Brad outdoors. Note the italicized stage directions—a literary convention of play scripts—which indicate key phrases from the monologue as slide projections, and suggested stage action for the actors:

(SLIDE: "a big difference")

BRAD: I saw a guy a few weeks ago who's the same age as me. He lived in a house behind us when I was in fifth grade. He still lives with his parents in the same place. I think about what he's been doing the last nine years and what I've been doing the last nine years and it's a big difference. He went to high school. Now he works in a gas station, has a motorcycle, and works on his truck. I guess that's all right for him, so long as he's mellow with his parents.

(SLIDE: "I've never really held a job.")

(crosses to HARRY, sits on the lawn chair)

I've worked for my dad for a while—helped him wire houses and do light construction. I scraped paint for one company. I worked for a graveyard for about eight months, for a plumber a while, planted trees for a while. Dishwashing. I've never really held a job. I wouldn't want to have to put up with a lot of people on a job that didn't make me much money. Like at a check-out counter—I don't want to be in front of that many people. I don't like a job where everyone sees you do it.

(SLIDE: "a loner")

I guess that I'm sorta a loner, maybe a hermit. I've had close friends, but I don't have any now.

(fighting back tears)

HARRY: *(to BRAD)* Shall I turn the tape recorder off for a while?

BRAD: *(shakes his head "no," tries to put up a brave front)* You've got what you've got. It doesn't make any difference what anybody else has. You can't wish you're somebody else, there's no point in it. Being by myself doesn't make all that much difference. No one knows who I am anyway.

(HARRY puts his hand comfortingly on BRAD's knee; BRAD remains still, looks as if he's about to reach for HARRY's hand, then pulls away, gets a wrench and starts working on his bike) (Wolcott, 2002, pp. 187–188)

Purposes of Ethnodrama and Ethnotheatre

Qualitative researchers might choose to dramatize interview transcript excerpts when an artistic rendering of the participant's experiences will offer readers or audiences the most credible, vivid, and persuasive representation of the research. "A traditional journal article in print may competently present the descriptive and analytic findings from fieldwork. But a performative approach of high aesthetic quality has the potential to engage audiences emotionally and communally through real-time theatrical immersion" (Saldaña, 2018a, p. 378).

Second, dramatizing an interview transcript into monologic form offers the qualitative researcher a more intriguing way to approach the analysis and interpretation of narrative data. Instead of coding or constructing themes, adapting an interview into a short play script provides a creative outlet for capturing the human dimensions of inquiry. Theatre artists label character monologues "portraits in miniature." Thus, the one-person ethnodramatic format serves as a self-standing vignette of a participant's experiences.

Third, dramatizing a transcript prioritizes the participant's voice. "Theatre and media are democratic forums for people from all walks of life to share their unique experiences and perceptions. In well-written ethnodramas, scholarly discourse is pushed aside to communicate both the everyday and exceptional through more authentic, accessible language" (Saldaña, 2018a, p. 379).

Key playwriting and production methods sources in this arts-based genre include Ackroyd and O'Toole (2010), Hammond and Steward (2008), Kaufman and McAdams (2018), Norris (2009), and Saldaña (2005, 2011, 2018a). Next, I present an extended case study as an exemplar to demonstrate how an interview transcript might develop into ethnodramatic form.

Exemplar

Below are excerpts from a verbatim interview transcript of a man in his late 50s with chronic obstructive pulmonary disease (COPD) who sleeps with a CPAP (continuous positive air pressure) machine, discussing his current health status with an interviewer:

[I: What medications are you taking for COPD?]

WILLIAM: I'm on Montekulast, Dulera, the gray thing, what's it called? Spiriva, and the ProAir rescue inhaler. And, if it matters, I sleep with a CPAP machine, but that was long before I was diagnosed with COPD.

[I: How are the medications working for you?]

WILLIAM: OK, I guess. My condition's constant but at least it's not getting worse.

[I: What's constant?]

WILLIAM: A shortness of breath, sometimes climbing upstairs, and sometimes just bending over to pick something up. There's a mild tightness in my chest, I have to take some deep breaths now and then to catch my breath. Sometimes I feel tired all day, but I think that's more my sleep than the COPD. I had a bout recently with atelectasis, I think it's called, and I had to go on antibiotics for that for, for a few weeks, had x-rays, it cleared up. No problems since then.

[I: How has COPD affected your daily life?]

WILLIAM: I'm not exercising as much as I should, but not because of the COPD, but just because I just tend to sit around a lot. I do notice that when I go outside sometimes my breathing gets more labored, so I guess that's stuff in the air that's affecting me. I try to stay indoors as much as possible. It hasn't really debilitated me in any way, but I know I'm not going to be running marathons, so.

[I: Has there-]

WILLIAM: Like, right now, there's a slight tightness in this part of my chest *(moves hands across upper chest area)*, but it's not painful, it's just noticeable. And I don't have as much air power as I used to have for speaking. My breath sometimes runs out at the end of a sentence. I have to breathe a little more air in to speak.

[I: How often do you use the rescue inhaler?]

WILLIAM: Not all that often, really, maybe just once every two weeks or so. That's when I feel my chest is real tight and I'm having some difficulty breathing and I need some relief. It really works, the ProAir, it's good.

[I: How does the CPAP machine work for you?]

WILLIAM: It's OK. Sometimes I feel like the pressure isn't strong enough, but I know what it's like to have a higher pressure than you need. There's always that adjusting when you first turn it on, you have to sync your breathing to the pressure, gasp in some deep breaths, get into a rhythm of breathing through your mouth or nose. I've been using it for years, maybe 15 years now, but it's still a nightly thing. I do know what it's like to not have the machine, so it works, for sure, and helps me feel better when I wake up in the morning.

[I: In what ways?]

WILLIAM: A clearer head, like I'm more alert. I got the machine for a snoring problem originally. I used to be a smoker and I snored loud, woke up really foggy. My doctor had me go through some sleep studies and they felt it best that I go on the machine. It really made a difference in the way I felt when I woke up in the morning. Not as muddled or drowsy. I used to be on prescription meds for sleep, but none of those worked or had weird side effects, so I just use over-the-counter sleep meds now from Walgreen's.

[I: What concerns, if any, do you have about your COPD?]

WILLIAM: Is it going to get worse, which from what I understand, it will. So far so good, it's not excellent but it's good. I worry if I'm ever going to have a really bad attack where I can't breathe at all. I worry about whether I'll ever need an oxygen tank. I just take it easy now, don't strain myself, but I can't control what happens inside my lungs. So, I've just gotta live with that. (Saldaña, 2018b, pp. 13–15)

After the interview, the goal of this study and its analysis was to transform health care-related interview excerpts into arts-based forms. Poetry was the first adaptation, and ethnodramatic monologue was the second. The study is unpublished to date but is part of an ongoing qualitative project in aging. Its intended audiences are primarily seniors and health care workers in gerontology and assisted living.

I approached the adaptation by "thinking theatrically" (Saldaña, 2015, pp. 129–131)—meaning, letting my imagination fueled by my theatrical training re-envision the interview transcript as a short, performed piece for the stage. Though verbatim monologue is possible and sometimes preferable, I decided to give William's story *aesthetic shape*—a retelling that uses an economy of words in a rearranged order that flows more coherently than the original transcript. Also, thinking theatrically means that the physical devices of theatrical production—costumes, lighting, hand props, scenery, sound effects, and so on—are considered in the adaptation and suggested in italicized stage directions.

William's earlier interview narrative includes 591 spoken words. The monologic adaptation below uses 281 of those words—approximately half the original length. The interviewer and his questions are purposely excluded from the adaptation to prioritize the participant's voice:

"I Worry"

(Setting: a bedroom, nighttime. Beside the bed is a nightstand with an inhaler, lamp, and CPAP [continuous positive air pressure] machine with a mask and hose attached. WILLIAM, a 50-ish man dressed in pajamas, enters slowly and out of breath; he sits on the bed, picks up an inhaler from the nightstand, shakes it and takes a deep puff; after a pause he takes a second deep puff and massages his chest; he speaks to the audience)

WILLIAM: When I'm having difficulty breathing, I need some relief.

(moves hands across upper chest area)

Like, right now, there's a slight tightness in this part of my chest—it's not painful, it's just noticeable. I used to be a smoker. I don't have as much air power as I used to for speaking. My breath sometimes runs out at the end of a sentence. I have to breathe a little more air in to speak.

(takes a deep breath, sets inhaler on nightstand, rises and prepares the bed for sleep)

I have to take some deep breaths now and then to catch my breath, climbing upstairs, sometimes just bending over to pick something up. I do notice that when I go outside my breathing gets more labored—that's stuff in the air affecting me. I try to stay indoors as much as possible. I feel tired all day, I'm not exercising as much as I should, I just tend to sit around a lot. *(chuckles)* I'm not going to be running marathons.

(sits on bed, picks up CPAP mask)

And I sleep with a CPAP machine, but that was long before I was diagnosed with COPD.

Sometimes I feel like the pressure isn't strong enough, There's always that adjusting when you first turn it on, you have to sync your breathing to the pressure, gasp in some deep breaths, get into a rhythm of breathing through your mouth or nose.

(pause; looks concerned)

My condition's not bad but, is it going to get worse? From what I understand, it will. I worry about whether I'll ever need an oxygen tank. I worry if I'm ever going to have a really bad attack where I can't breathe at all.

(he straps the CPAP mask over his face and speaks through it)

I just take it easy now, don't strain myself, but I can't control what happens inside my lungs. So, I've just gotta live with that.

(he turns the CPAP machine on and labors to sync his breath with the air pressure; he lies in bed and turns the lamp off; the CPAP machine sounds get louder then fade out slowly in the dark)

The next section will discuss the specific methods and options analysts have for adapting interview transcripts into ethnodramatic formats, with reference to William's monologue.

Ethnodramatic Methods and Their Use

Several methods decisions enter the researcher-playwright's mind for transforming interview transcript data into ethnodramatic form. Any one of these decisions can initiate the adaptation, but they are discussed in the order in which they may typically occur.

Before the Interview

All research with human participants must adhere to ethical guidelines, particularly those studies under the supervision of Institutional Review Boards (IRBs). Principal investigators may know at the conception of a project that dramatic representation and a theatrical presentation of the study are the intended outcomes. But it is also possible a researcher may not realize until later into a conventional study that an arts-based product, such as a play script, is a more suitable method for displaying the findings.

Regardless of when the decision occurs, ethnodramatic adaptation of a participant's interview transcript necessitates additional language in written consent forms. "The representation of a person on stage or in film creates exponentially heightened vulnerability than it does in mere print. Any agreements between parties must be negotiated on a case-by-case basis" (Saldaña, 2018a, p. 391). Individual researchers should consult with their IRBs for guidance with ethnodramatic projects. Some IRBs, in fact, may not even consider ethnodramatic work research, considering it "artistic work" instead and exempting it from necessary review.

New York University professor Joe Salvatore, director of the Steinhardt Verbatim Performance Lab, developed a participant consent form unique for ethnotheatrical productions. Excerpts from that document are included below for possible adoption by ethnodramatic researcher-playwrights.

The consent form also includes legal agreements regarding copyright ownership and production rights, along with standard consent topics such as assurances of confidentiality, possible risks, benefits, voluntary participation, withdrawal from the study, compensation, contact information, and signature lines. Ethnotheatrical playwrights and directors should customize the permissions processes and written agreements for each unique project.

As noted earlier, most arts-based researchers enter their studies knowing beforehand that the collected data will be adapted into ethnodramatic form. Other researchers may not realize until later that their interview transcripts hold dramatic potential. Regardless of when inspiration arises, always secure written permission from participants whose stories will be dramatized and staged for public view.

INTERVIEW RELEASE FORM

You have been invited to take part in a verbatim documentary theatre project, [title], that will explore [topic]. This project will be conceived and created by [playwright and director's names] with researcher-actors under their supervision and training.

If you agree to be part of this project, you will be asked to take part in an open-ended interview concerning your own experiences with [topic]. The outcome of these interviews will be a theatrical performance, and you, as an interview participant, may be played by one of the researcher-actors in the performance, using the words and actions from your interview verbatim.

Your interview will be audio recorded and transcribed and portions of your interview and the interviews of other participants will be arranged to create a script. That script will be rehearsed by the group of researcher-actors working on the project, the lines will be memorized, and then the script will be performed for an audience. Your characteristics, such as mannerisms, gestures, or appearance, may also influence the onstage presentation of the script that results from your interview and the interview of others.

It is also possible that your interview may not be used in the final version of the script due to the limitations of time or duplicative material....

Condensing the Narrative

The first adaptation decision is to consider which portions of the original transcript should remain and which ones seem unnecessary for the final monologue product. An experienced actor could perform William's complete interview transcript as is and present it effectively, but the narrative itself includes extraneous detail. Theatre performance relies on an economy of time, and thus the dramatic script should focus on key elements of the story and only the words essential for its telling. Approximately one third to one half of the transcript may hold the richest content for adaptation consideration, and it is possible that a 60-minute interview may yield no more than five minutes of rich dramatic narrative.

In William's story, I interpreted that his difficult breathing issues contained tension, an essential element of good drama. But the details of his medications and sleep studies, while interesting, were too factual in content and did not drive the action forward. Just as qualitative analysts focus on those portions of collected data that address the research questions of interest, ethnodramatists should focus on portions of the interview transcript that seem the most compelling and highlight the study's primary issues or the participant's central problem.

For studies that include separate interviews with multiple participants, dramatists may consider a series of brief monologues as the play script's structure if several of the transcripts contain thematically related yet unique perspectives on the research topic. Yet another option is to create a composite narrative, in which different participants' data are interwoven into a single piece, spoken by one "character" representing the collective. Remember that not every interviewee may provide material with dramatic potential. Select and adapt what is both relevant and intriguing for performance.

Verbatim and/or Adaptation

A second common decision is to consider whether the dramatization should include or consist entirely of verbatim passages from the transcript, or whether the researcher should adapt the participant's narrative into a more aesthetically shaped product. "Verbatim excerpts heighten the realism of the presentation and maintain the participant's 'voiceprint.' Edited adaptations eliminate the occasional verbal debris of everyday speech to create a more artistically rendered account" (Saldaña, 2018a, pp. 380–381). At times the natural false starts, repeated words, and stutters of everyday speech are intriguing and characterize an individual's distinct personality. But it takes a highly competent actor to deliver verbatim verbal debris naturalistically and believably.

I chose to include selected verbatim passages from William's story but rearranged their order. Each sentence in the transcript became a different puzzle piece that I literally cut-and-pasted on a text editing page to assess the best flow from one thought to another. Participants may not always share the elements of their stories fluently and in a coherent order. So, an ethnodramatic adaptation can reconstruct the narrative with a stronger, linear story-line. When necessary, a grammatical correction can be made for clarity or aesthetic purposes, but I am a firm believer in keeping children's and adolescents' narratives verbatim to provide keen insight into their ways of thinking.

Beginnings and Endings

One piece of advice I pass along to participants in my autoethnodrama workshops when they compose their original work is, "Carefully consider what your monologue's first line is—something that hooks your audience from the very start—and what your last line is—the final impression you want to leave that will have maximum impact. What happens in-between your starting and ending points is your personal journey from the first thought through the last."

Sometimes stage action rather than spoken lines provides intriguing bookends to the performed work. Breathing issues are the central tension for William. Thus, I began William's story with him using his inhaler, a central prop related to his life dilemma. The ending is an ironic, verbatim extract of the way he himself ended his interview: "So, I've just gotta live with that," followed by a sound effect in darkness of the CPAP machine's air flow.

The Participant's "Character"

Next, the researcher considers whether the monologue in progress maintains the general tone and integrity of the participant's perspective and experiences. Playwrights are taught to not just write a script but to voice it out loud to assess the language's flow, word choices, and performability. I advise the same technique for researchers adapting interview transcripts for ethnodrama. By speaking the text aloud, you take ownership and come to a greater understanding of the "character" of your work.

When I read aloud William's monologue in progress, I became aware of unconscious word repetition and extraneous passages that could be deleted. Informally performing the work (colloquially called an *informance*) also gave me a sense of whether there was believability to the text—a sense that qualitative researchers sometimes refer to as verisimilitude or fidelity.

By reading in role, playwrights also become aware of their characterizations. A faithful ethnodramatic representation of an actual participant is certainly not fictional, but selected aspects of dramatic character should be considered to better insure a more three-dimensional rendering. The first of these is *objectives*—what a character wants or wants others to do. Actors create action verbs which they keep in their minds to propel their vocal and physical performance. In William's monologue, his primary objective may be, quite simply, "to breathe easily."

A second characterization element is *conflict* or *tension*—the things or people keeping the character from achieving his or her objectives. William's COPD prevents him from breathing easily, and thus he generates *tactics*—actions that will help him overcome the conflict and achieve his objective, a third element of character. He himself describes several tactics throughout the monologue: "breathe a little more air in to speak," "take some deep breaths now and then to catch my breath," "stay indoors as much as possible," and so on.

The fourth element is *attitudes*—feelings and beliefs about self, other characters, the conflicts, etc. I heighten William's concern about his future health status by including and even titling the piece "I Worry." The fifth element is *emotions*—a universal of the human condition. Worry is a prominent emotion throughout the monologue, but I insert a glimmer of humor through the self-deprecating "*(chuckles)* I'm not going to be running marathons." The sixth element is *subtext*, what the reader or audience infers from the narrative and the actor's subtleties of performance. William, in both the interview transcript and monologue, seems directly honest and does not hide his perceptions. The final line, "So, I've just gotta live with that," does present the opportunity for irony—meaning, the actor saying the final sentence with a tinge of regret before he lies down.

Objectives, conflicts, and tactics are generally inherent elements of the play-writing. But attitudes, emotions, and subtext manifest themselves primarily through the actor's interpretation in performance. Nevertheless, researchers adapting a participant's story should consider whether these six major facets of character are realized in the script.

Poetic Formatting

One formatting option for ethnodramatists comes from the written work of performance ethnography pioneer Anna Deavere Smith (2000). Smith attests that people speak every day in forms of "organic poetry," and she listens attentively to when her audio recorded participants pause and parse their speech. Her early work formatted verbatim dialogue into poetic stanzas, which brings heightened awareness to literally every word in the script.

The first portion of William's monologue appears in prosaic form:

WILLIAM: When I'm having difficulty breathing, I need some relief.

(moves hands across upper chest area)

Like, right now, there's a slight tightness in this part of my chest—it's not painful, it's just noticeable. I used to be a smoker. I don't have as much air power as I used to for speaking. My breath sometimes runs out at the end of a sentence. I have to breathe a little more air in to speak.

Utilizing Smith's organic poetry formatting, the same passage now appears like this:

WILLIAM: When I'm having difficulty breathing,

I need some relief.

(moves hands across upper chest area)

Like, right now,
there's a slight tightness
in this part of my chest—
it's not painful, it's just
   noticeable.

I used to be a smoker.

I don't have as much
air power as I used to for speaking.

My breath sometimes runs out
   at the end of a sentence.

I have to breathe a little more air in
   to speak.

Poetic formatting is recommended to call the reader's attention to the phrases of a participant's story, and when verbatim interview excerpts will be chosen for performance.

Thinking Theatrically

The final method is to *think theatrically*—meaning, consideration of all the scenographic conventions and devices of theatre and how they incorporate into the monologue. Those not trained in theatre often default to a speaker's podium for scenery, the interviewer present on stage with the participant, and sitting down while the story is told. This is not thinking theatrically since these are conventions of research conferences, not performance. All production companies are limited by budgetary constraints, available time, and personnel expertise. But creativity is the theatre's capital, and researchers are strongly advised to *"Stop thinking like a social scientist and start thinking like an artist"* (Teman & Saldaña, 2019).

William describes several items for his health maintenance such as prescription drugs, inhalers, and a CPAP machine. These become a roster of ideas for hand properties he can use during the monologue. His interview also suggests particular environments: outdoors, a bedroom, an x-ray clinic, a drug store, a sleep study center, and a doctor's examination room. Any one of these places can become the physical setting with its accompanying scenic elements for the performance. I chose a bedroom since breathing during sleep was prominent in his narrative. Breathing issues are William's primary concern, and the sounds of difficult breathing and a CPAP machine can become powerful effects if intensified in some way. Most often the participant suggests in an interview the visual and aural elements needed for its adaptation for the stage or screen. It is the researcher's dramatic imagination that responds to these cues and envisions their realization in production. When possible, social science researchers can collaborate with theatre artists for guidance.

To summarize the ethnodramatic adaptation process:

1. *Before the interview:* Secure written permission from participants with their knowledge about how the interview data will be adapted for scripted performance.

2. *Condensing the narrative:* From the full interview transcript, consider which portions hold dramatization potential and relate directly to the goals of the study.

3. *Verbatim and/or adaptation:* Explore whether verbatim excerpts and/or adaptation of the original interview text would best serve the monologic narrative.

4. *Beginnings and endings:* Give careful thought to the most effective ways to begin and end the ethnodrama with impactful lines and/or stage action.

5. *The participant's "character":* Render a three-dimensional portrait of the participant by staying authentic to the representation, with consideration of the participant's objectives, conflicts, tactics, attitudes, emotions, and subtexts.

6. *Poetic formatting:* If appropriate, consider whether an "organic poetry" format for the monologue would provide heightened awareness of phrases for the reader and performer.

7. *Thinking theatrically:* Envision all the scenographic devices of theatre (costumes, props, sound, etc.) or digital video effects (editing, dissolves, close-ups, etc.) for potential staging of and action within the performed piece.

Conclusion

There are times when the analysis of interview data merits coding, categorization, and themeing to extract and construct insights about human experiences. But artistic dramatization of a participant's story prioritizes first-person narrative as the analytic medium. Ethnotheatrical representation of interview selections literally brings the data alive through onstage or mediated performance. Ethnodramatic plays in print can also make an impact on the reader, but the litmus test of a play script's efficacy is enacting it through the actor's body and voice for an audience.

Artistic quality in both the written script and its performance are critical for the ethnodramatic representation to succeed:

A researcher's criteria for excellent ethnography in article or book formats don't always harmonize with an artist's criteria for excellent theatre. This may be difficult for some to accept but, to me, theatre's primary goal is neither to educate nor to enlighten. *Theatre's primary goal is to entertain*—to *entertain ideas* as it *entertains its spectators*. With ethnographic performance, then, comes the responsibility to create an entertainingly informative experience for an audience, one that is aesthetically sound, intellectually rich, and emotionally evocative. (Saldaña, 2005, p. 14)

The most important criterion for an ethnodrama is that the play contains a sense of *artistic rigor*. A play script is not a journal article; therefore, the ethnodramatic script should not contain footnotes or citations of the academic literature. Let the participant speak for himself or herself. If well adapted and well staged, the ethnotheatrical performance can be an engaging, revelatory, and aesthetic experience for an audience.

Supplemental Readings

Maslon, L., Sankoff, I., & Hein, D. (2019). *Come from away: Welcome to the rock.* Hachette Books.

Saldaña, J. (2011). *Ethnotheatre: Research from page to stage.* Left Coast Press.

Teman, E. D., & Saldaña, J. (2019). "Stop thinking like a social scientist and start thinking like an artist": The research-based aesthetic product. *International Review of Qualitative Research, 12*(4), 453–475. https://doi.org/10.1525/irqr.2019.12.4.453

Reflection and Activities

1. What can an ethnodramatist do to better ensure that the play script (and production) possesses credibility and trustworthiness for audiences who may be skeptical of the scholarly legitimacy of arts-based qualitative research?

2. Read at least three monologic ethnodramas and discuss their efficacy as dramatic works and research representations. Recommended titles:

   a. *14* by José Casas (2018).

   b. *Ann* by Holland Taylor (2016).

   c. *Erma Bombeck: At Wit's End* by Allison Engel and Margaret Engel (2016).

   d. *The Gun Show* by E. M. Lewis (2019).

   e. *I Am My Own Wife* by Doug Wright (2004).

   f. *My Left Breast* by Susan Miller (2006).

   g. *Notes from the Field* by Anna Deavere Smith (2019).

   h. *Pretty Fire* by Charlayne Woodard (1992).

   i. *This Beautiful City* by The Civilians, written by Steven Cosson and Jim Lewis, music and lyrics by Michael Friedman, from interviews by The Company (2010).

   j. *The Vagina Monologues* by Eve Ensler (2001).

3. Select an interview transcript of an individual participant and adapt an excerpt into a self-standing monologue of approximately three to five minutes in length for the stage. Include italicized stage directions and recommendations for its production (e.g., scenic elements, actor movement, sound/music effects).

References

Ackroyd, J., & O'Toole, J. (2010). *Performing research: Tensions, triumphs and trade-offs of ethnodrama*. Trentham Books.

Casas, J. (2018). *14*. Dramatic Publishing.

Engel, A., & Engel, M. (2016). *Erma Bombeck: At wit's end*. Samuel French.

Ensler, E. (2001). *The vagina monologues*. Villard.

Hammond, W., & Steward, D. (Eds.). (2008). *Verbatim verbatim: Contemporary documentary theatre*. Oberon Books.

Kaufman, M., & McAdams, B. P. (2018). *Moment work: Tectonic theater project's process of devising theater*. Vintage Books.

Lewis, E. M. (2019). *The gun show*. Samuel French.

Miller, S. (2006). *My left breast*. Playscripts, Inc.

Norris, J. (2009). *Playbuilding as qualitative research: A participatory arts-based approach*. Left Coast Press.

Saldaña, J. (2005). *Ethnodrama: An anthology of reality theatre*. AltaMira Press.

Saldaña, J. (2011). *Ethnotheatre: Research from page to stage*. Left Coast Press.

Saldaña, J. (2015). *Thinking qualitatively: Methods of mind*. SAGE.

Saldaña, J. (2018a). Ethnodrama and ethnotheatre: Research as performance. In N. K. Denzin, & Y. S. Lincoln (Eds.), *The SAGE handbook of qualitative research* (5th ed.), (pp. 377–394). SAGE.

Saldaña, J. (2018b). *Writing qualitatively: The selected works of Johnny Saldaña*. Routledge.

Smith, A. D. (2000). *Talk to me: Listening between the lines*. Random House.

Smith, A. D. (2019). *Notes from the field*. Anchor Books.

Taylor, H. (2016). *Ann*. Dramatists Play Service.

Teman, E. D., & Saldaña, J. (2019). "Stop thinking like a social scientist and start thinking like an artist": The research-based aesthetic product. *International Review of Qualitative Research*, *12*(4), 453–475. https://doi.org/10.1525/irqr.2019.12.4.453

The Civilians, Cosson, S., Lewis, J., & Friedman, M. (2010). *This beautiful city*. Dramatists Play Service.

Wolcott, H. F. (1983). Adequate schools and inadequate education: The life history of a sneaky kid. *Anthropology and Education Quarterly*, *14*(1), 3–32.

Wolcott, H. F. (1987). Life's not working: Cultural alternatives to career alternatives. In G. W. Noblit, & W. T. Pink (Eds.), *Schooling in social context: Qualitative studies* (pp. 303–325). Ablex.

Wolcott, H. F. (2002). *Sneaky kid and its aftermath: Ethics and intimacy in fieldwork*. AltaMira Press.

Woodard, C. (1992). *Pretty fire*. Dramatists Play Service.

Wright, D. (2004). *I am my own wife*. Faber and Faber.

What Makes an Effective Teacher? Revealing Good Teaching Practice Through Interview Poetic Transcription

Robyn Shenfield and Monica Prendergast

Abstract

This chapter presents a collection of found poems crafted from interview data to engage in the poetic representation of a question posed in the interviews: What kinds of characteristics or qualities are required to be a "good" drama teacher? We chose this particular question to respond to due to the affective nature of these teachers' responses that lead to what we understand as the "poetic occasion" (Sullivan, 2009). In the chapter we discuss the burgeoning field of poetic inquiry, as well as approaches to working with interview data through poetry, including examples from the literature and our own work. We conclude with a call to qualitative researchers interested in exploring poetic approaches to data representation. This call includes consideration of poetic occasion, poetic language, and poetic form.

Keywords: Poetic transcription; arts-based research; poetic inquiry; teaching; drama

Introduction and Brief Literature Review

In the past decade, poetic inquiry has emerged as a vibrant arts-based research methodology that privileges the voices of both the participant and researcher. It is a form of arts-based research, a transdisciplinary approach to knowledge building that employs the principles of the creative arts in research contexts (Leavy, 2018). Arts-based research practices and methodological tools can be used by researchers across the disciplines during any or all phases of research including problem generation, data or content generation, analysis, interpretation, and representation.

Poetic inquiry rose in response to what Denzin and Lincoln (2011) referred to as a "crisis of representation" (p. 3), questioning how researchers sought to represent the complex social world within research documents. Poetry provides an alternative that showcases qualitative data in an evocative and aesthetically rich manner where voice is elevated to the fore. Writing poems from research data or analyzing through poems is represented in the literature as a way to "expand perspectives on human experience" (Vincent, 2018, p. 51), and its marked increase in adoption demonstrates what Leavy (2015) calls a "turn toward scientific artistic expression" (p. 66) within the qualitative research community. As a research methodology, poetic inquiry blends the creative and the analytical. It promotes criticality, can explicitly reveal the position of the researcher, and allows for a variety of voices, perspectives, and experiences to be examined through the aesthetic and expressive medium of poetry.

In her postdoctoral study, a survey of poetic inquiry praxis, Prendergast (2009) found more than 230 published, peer-reviewed, journal articles or book chapters that identified poetry as a major element of the research processes or research presentations. Though a number of terms were used synonymously with poetic inquiry, most studies could be placed into three categories:

1. Vox Autobiographia/Autoethnographia—Poems about the researcher's lived experience

2. Vox Participare—Poems crafted from interview, focus group or observational data, either by the researcher or between the researcher(s) and participant(s)

3. Vox Theoria—Poems created from preexisting theoretical, philosophical, or other kinds of texts.

Prendergast (2015) later expanded these voice forms to five more:

1. Vox Theoria/Vox Poetica—Poems about self, writing and poetry as method

2. Vox Justitia—Poems on equity, equality, social justice, class, freedom

3. Vox Identitatis—Poetry exploring, self/participants' gender, race, sexuality

4. Vox Custodia—Poetry of caring, nursing, caregivers'/patients' experience

5. Vox Procreator—Poems of parenting, family and/or religion. (p. 6)

Regarding poetic inquiry as a research methodology, Sullivan (2009) argues that some materials are more welcoming of poetic rendering than others, and that "most of us [poetic researchers] who do this work probably recognize these materials intuitively or by knowledge so deeply internalized it feels intuitive" (p. 111). As for when to look to poetic inquiry as an appropriate research methodology, she asks researchers to become "alert, attentive, and attuned" to the "poetic occasion":

> Higher level thinking (as we like to call it) demands connections, associations, linkages of conscious and unconscious elements, memory and emotion, past, present and future merging in the processes of making meaning, these are the very processes which poets actively seek to cultivate. Material in which these kinds of complexity inhere is material to catch a poet's eye and heart, sit him or her down to work. (Sullivan, 2009, p. 118)

Poetic inquiry is a versatile tool of qualitative research, appearing in a variety of forms across a multitude of fields, but is found particularly within the literature from health care, anthropology, sociology, and education. However, as a form of scholarly methodology, it is essential that poetic inquiry be done *well*, and demonstrates considered balance between the aesthetically pleasing art form and critical inquiry, lest its reputation become undermined (Barone, 2001; Faulkner, 2007). Correspondingly, we acknowledge that there remains resistance to poetic inquiry from scholars in certain fields, particularly those who most frequently practice quantitative and mixed methods research. Richardson (2000) has argued that art and inquiry do not need to be separate, and Eisner (1997) also sought ways of integrating the creative and analytical, contending that poetry could transcend language and possessed an "evocative presentation of data" (p. 5). We proclaim that poetic inquiry is a transdisciplinary methodology that can provide scholars with opportunities to liberate voice in a manner that both affectively captures a moment or feeling, and reveals the core of the data, should the poetic occasion arise.

Exemplar

Poetic inquiry emerged as a methodology in our research into drama education. One central and irreplaceable ingredient across all manifestations of drama education is the teacher who facilitates the class, and research demonstrates that the success of the work is dependent, at least in part, upon the artistry and pedagogy of the teacher (Dunn & Stinson, 2011; Gray, Wright, & Pascoe, 2017; Stinson, 2009). Neelands (2004) reminds us that "drama cannot, of course, of itself teach in any kind of way, nor can it, of itself, be powerful. It is what we do, through our own human agency, with drama that determines the specific pedagogy and specific powers" (p. 48). He argues elsewhere that drama "by itself does nothing. It is only what teachers do with drama that makes the difference" (Neelands, 2009, p. 11). Thus, in our attempt to uncover the essential elements of drama teaching practice, we decided to go directly to the source: drama teachers themselves.

In 2016–2017, we worked on a research project interviewing teachers within the Greater Victoria, British Columbia area in order to glean their thoughts surrounding the implementation of a new performance studies curriculum entitled *Web of Performance: An Ensemble Workbook* (Prendergast & Weigler, 2018). After receiving ethical approval from the University of Victoria, we selected seven teachers with significant drama teaching experience (15–30+ years) to participate in individual, semistructured interviews. These teachers were chosen to broadly represent the diversity of school types and districts in the local area; three teachers were from independent schools, and four were from local public school districts. In terms of gender, three participants were female and four male. Racially, all seven were of white European extraction, reflective of the majority white teacher population in this part of Canada. All interviews were audio recorded and then transcribed twice to ensure the accuracy of the transcriptions. This research produced a "trans/script" (Cahnmann-Taylor & Soutou-Manning, 2010, p. 38), whereby the teachers' voices were entwined into a scripted piece which sought to bring the disparate voices into an imagined professional space as a dramatic rendering of *overheard conversation* (Neelands & Goode, 2015, p. 49). We presented this work at IDIERI 9 (The 9th International Drama in Education Research Institute) in Auckland, New Zealand, in 2018, and it was subsequently published in *Research in Drama Education: The Journal of Applied Theatre and Performance* (Prendergast & Shenfield, 2019).

As part of these interviews, the teachers were also asked to share information about their educational and professional backgrounds, teacher identity, and pedagogical approaches. The first question they were asked was, "What does it mean to be an effective drama teacher?" These are the data we have chosen to focus on for the purpose of this chapter.

Using selected moments from the interview transcripts, we created two found poetry or poetic transcription pieces, one by Robyn and one by Monica, intended as a poetic representation of the *overheard conversation* dramatic convention (Neelands & Goode, 2015, p. 49). We are "dropping in" on the words spoken by these seven experienced drama educators. For anthropologist and poet Miles Richardson (1998), "[p]oetry, as a special language, is particularly suited for those special, strange, even mysterious moments when bits and pieces suddenly coalesce" (p. 451). Accordingly, when considering scholarly consensus surrounding the myriad contextual qualities of a drama educator, the particular methodology of poetic inquiry struck us as *apropos*.

After reading the transcripts several times, we began the creative process with a thematic coding approach, coding and sorting the data, and generating major themes (such as pedagogy, teacher-student relationships, and personal reflection) before arranging the text into a work of poetic transcription. Poetic transcription is "the creation of poemlike compositions from the transcribed words of interviewees, shaped by the researcher to give pleasure and truth" (Glesne, 1997, p. 213). It is a form which moves in the direction of poetry, but it is not poetry in the truest sense of the word. Truth(s) representing particular perspectives or experiences of the interviewees are filtered through the researcher, giving the piece a reflexive quality. Readers are made more aware of a researcher's relationship with participants, and the deliberate poeticized "staging" of the interviewees' responses ethically privileges their voices over the researcher's voice (Glesne, 1997; Richardson, 1992).

In this piece we have attempted to "crystallize" (Richardson, 2000) the seven teachers' thoughts surrounding the core requirements of good drama teaching practice in our own ways. This process involved careful reading and re-reaching of the interview transcripts and selecting particular moments of dialogue which stood out for their content and/or evocations. Robyn's longer poem is made up of words found across the seven participant interviews. After collating the selected pieces of dialogue into a document and sorting them into themes, Robyn arranged her poem into a piece of free verse, tumbling one piece of dialogue from a teacher into another to create a sense of rolling flow of conversation, experimenting with shifting cadence between voices and moments. Slicing the dialogue and making it "fit" inorganically into a more formal poetic structure would have felt contrived and the purity and richness of dialogue would have been compromised.

While the content of the poem is ordinary conversational dialogue, she worked to highlight some particularly salient moments from the transcripts and create some sense of poetic imagery and feeling in the piece though the physical placement of text and spacing. For instance, conveying the richness and grand history of theatre and theatrical tradition by the stacking of text:

> theatre
> as a
> global
> and
> universal
> and
> ancient
> art form.

the breadth of pedagogical, educational, and artistic possibilities by stretching it:

> our   art   form   can   be.

and moment-by-moment discoveries in the classroom by layering sections of text side-by-side:

holding on lightly
so that you can follow
        the emergent curriculum .
                 as it presents
                       itself

Monica chose to work with a single teacher's voice, one at a time. Her interpretive method was focused on privileging each teacher's voice, in contrast with Robyn's mashup/collage approach. There is no "better" method here; so for the purposes of this chapter we chose to work in contrasting ways. Monica's approach, like Robyn's, involved paying close attention to the data in order to find the rhythm and imagery within the participant's voice. In this way, she captured words and phrases that expressed what she interpreted as participants' meaning-making responses to the interview question: What does it mean to be a good drama teacher? The question posed is a philosophical one in that it reveals the values carried by a drama teacher into their daily practice and formed over time. This reflective stance lends itself well to poetic transcription; poetry is a contemplative and reflective practice, and so is philosophy. Monica makes use of poetic tools of repetition ("I think", for example, repeats many times, as spoken by participants) and imagery (for example when a participant describes themself as like a "salmon swimming upstream your entire life") in her poetic transcriptions. She also experiments with erasure poetry, wherein words are erased from a transcript and what is left behind becomes a prose poem.

The interest for the reader of this book is to "see" how the same data can lead to a wide variety of poetically transcribed responses. That said, in both cases we worked to create a sense of conversation and collegial dialogue via the selection of specific moments of text from the participants' responses. We also experimented with how to situate the text on the page in order to represent the themes and ideas common to many of the participants interviewed, as well as the flow of conversation with its natural lulls and silences. Perhaps the blank space upon the page serves to represent the countless other unspoken matters relevant to the topic of effective teaching and practice that may not have been revealed during the interviews. It is through these exemplars that we illustrate poetic inquiry's methods.

I. Robyn's Found Poem

What does it mean to be an effective drama teacher?
A poetic representation of overheard conversation

such an important question!

you have to have subject knowledge, strategies for communicating such knowledge, and relationship skills. that's just logic. if you have any of those missing, something just won't work.

a personality that lets the children know its ok to   be different,
and to take risks,
and to be adventurous,
and to play.

compassion and empathy.

you know *this*   and I know *this*   so let's meet in the middle.
that's that first thing.

the ability to stop driving the bus.
to engage listening.
to ask questions you didn't know the answer to.

I think you need to have some critical thinking skills and work cooperatively with other people.
I think you have to be really flexible.
I think you have to be patient.
I think you have to communicate really well, not just with your peers, but with your students, and try to see things from their point of view as well.

if you want to do this really well you'll have a lot of energy.
when I tell [people] I'm a drama teacher
their first response almost 80% of the time is:

"you must have so much fun!"

well the kids have a lot of fun, and I do have those
moments   [but]
just like any other job
it is a lot of work.

It is draining sometimes...   energy wise.

a breadth of understanding about what this art form is and can be.
theatre
as a
global
and
universal
and
ancient
art form.

a fine balance between theory and practice.
where you hopefully have a context of skill and technique and historical placement,
but also a freedom and willingness to play with what is at hand and available.

> I am concerned with the idea that someone can take one class in
> drama or theatre in the department of education and then become a
> high school drama teacher.
> that concerns me a lot.

> what do you learn in one class?

                                                    an arts teacher *is* the curriculum.

I'm very grateful for my personal experience.
I'm also grateful for those younger colleagues
who are doing some really cutting edge work
and redefining what it is that

                our   art   form   can   be.

I think you should be creative, and you need a sense of humor.
you have to have a strong work ethic

                        …it's easy to fall into doing not much at all.

                        you have to want to keep up on things that are
                        happening in the community in the theatre field.

I think you have to love theatre,
because if you don't love theatre
I don't know why you would be doing it.

                        I think that arts education should be dangerous.

maybe the science department is training new scientists,
and the math department is training new mathematicians,
but I'm not training new actors.

                        I'm giving people skills to go through life.

I always tell my students "I don't expect you to go into theatre."
                in fact…

                                                    a few of them do.

but I don't expect most...

> they're not going to be stars.
> but most
> of them
> will gain
> all these
>
> amazing
> qualities
> from the
> drama
> classroom.

hearing something in a classroom and allowing
    a moment of wonder about what someone had just said.
        you pause and
        you listen and
        you puzzle and
        you throw that out into the air
        and you let it

        sit.

holding on lightly
so that you can follow

    the emergent curriculum

        as it presents

           itself

    rather than have a laminated lesson plan
    that says we must be working on this part
    of the show or that part of the curriculum.

sometimes the really good stuff
is the stuff that happens

    here

and it doesn't allow you to get to

        there.

  sometimes chaos is the proper outcome of a situation.

you can have people doing a lot of different things
and they can still be a community;
                    they don't become isolated.

                         It keeps me inspired working with this age group
                         because of their unbridled ambition and curiosity.

I've learned that students really want to do different things.

        I think one of the first things we feel when we first get into a classroom in a
        practicum situation is that this   <MASS>
                    they all think
                    the same thing,
                    they all judge us
                    the same way,
                    they all want
                    the same thing,
                    they all dislike
                    the same things.

        After you spend time you appreciate that you have to
            create
                        different paths
                                    for
                                            different kids.

                        I want to
                        create
                        some sort
                        of a site
                        that
                        facilitates
                        self-expression,
                        unique and singular

                        to the individuals
                        that we're working with
                                            collectively.
        there's nothing more to it.

II. Monica's Found Poems

What makes an effective drama teacher?

I think
it's the same
for any teacher

You have to have
subject knowledge
strategies for communicating
and relationship skills.

That's just logic.

If you have any of those missing
something just won't work.

There's nothing more to it.
Is there more to it?
Of course there is
but those are the foundations.

I tried to have a career
and did theatre
before I became a teacher.
that is (I think) the beauty
that I bring to it as a teacher.

What in your view makes for an effective drama teacher, a good drama teacher?

A personality that
lets the children know
its ok to be different,
and to take risks,
and to be adventurous,
and to play.

I think I'm very lucky.
I do get a lot of people
coming up to me
saying what they learnt
from my program.

I've talked to my principal
about some of those emails.
I'm just overwhelmed because
some of the students have emailed me to say
"you helped me find a creative side."

I realized that my options
were much broader
than I ever thought
that I could dare
to do stuff.

That was great
and parents were
appreciative of that.

We (the arts) still tend to be sidelined.
Not so much in this school.
In other schools I've been in
the academics tend to be treasured…

                                    drama tends to be pushed to the side.

How important is it that you have the education and experience?

I think the education
is very important.
I can't stress that enough.
Just experiencing everything.

What do you need to bring to the work to be a good drama teacher? (Two found erasure prose poems)

my first response ▮▮▮▮ what it takes to be a good teacher ▮▮
▮▮▮ philosophy of Education ▮▮▮▮▮▮ theories and ▮▮ practices
▮▮▮▮ personal experience▮▮▮▮▮▮▮▮▮▮▮▮▮▮ teach by asking
questions ▮▮ inviting students to speak about ▮▮ reflect on ▮▮ understand
their own experiences ▮▮▮ anything that I have to offer them ▮▮ my
expertise ▮▮ my experience ▮▮▮▮▮▮ a connection ▮▮ I make with their
▮▮ experience▮▮▮▮ that's good teaching. That's the first step for a good
teacher. ▮▮▮▮▮▮▮ who are you ▮▮ where are you from ▮▮ what do
you know about this ▮▮ what do you think about this. Okay ▮▮ you know
this ▮▮ I know this ▮ let's meet in the middle. ▮▮▮▮▮▮▮▮▮▮ The
second thing ▮▮▮▮ connected to that ▮▮▮▮▮▮▮▮▮▮▮▮▮▮
▮▮▮ it's vital for everybody in this vocation ▮▮ the qualities of compassion
and empathy ▮▮▮▮ ▮▮▮▮▮▮▮▮▮▮ ▮▮▮▮▮▮▮▮▮ wanting every
one of your students to thrive to be their best selves ▮▮ to do their best
work. What else? To be a good drama teacher. ▮▮▮▮▮▮ ▮▮▮▮▮▮▮
from experience ▮ studying ▮ reading ▮ having been an audience in many
many different manifestations of theatre▮▮▮▮ a breadth of understanding
about what this art form is and can be. I'm saddened ▮▮▮ that many
students▮▮▮▮▮▮▮▮▮▮▮▮▮▮▮▮▮▮ mostly North American
students, who've had a background in drama in schools▮▮ their understanding
of drama is very very limited. They don't ▮▮▮ have ▮▮ any introduction
to theatre as a global ▮▮ universal ▮▮ ancient art form. ▮▮▮▮▮▮▮
▮▮▮▮▮▮▮▮▮▮▮▮▮▮▮▮▮▮▮▮▮▮▮▮ I'm not
▮▮▮▮ overly impressed with ▮▮▮▮▮▮▮▮▮▮▮▮ some drama

syllabuses ██████████ I hope that doesn't sound unkind or ungenerous ████████ a good drama teacher ████ needs to have reference points ████ ████ you can actually say oh yes that reminds me of Indonesian shadow puppetry right or yes, isn't that animated TV series that you like, you might want to see this thing about commedia dell'arte because there's a lot of overlap ████████████ having a breadth that allows ██████ ████████ students to have a root into what this art form is rather than having a very narrow sense of drama and theatre based on ██████████ western ████████████████████████████ sort of conventional ███ middle of the road sense of theatre. I'm very grateful for my personal experience ████████ a range of theatre ███ addressed social issues ████████████████████ I'm grateful for that experience. I regret ████████ our younger colleagues, that experience is not available to them. I'm also grateful for those younger colleagues ██████ doing some really cutting edge work ███ redefining what it is ███ our art form can be.

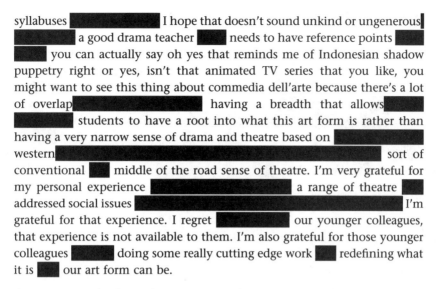

Can you speak about how you taught IB (International Baccalaureate)?

The IB theatre curriculum ████████████ ████████████████████████ this is my favourite iteration of the theatre syllabus, curriculum ██████ ███ components of it require ████ analysis ███ reflection ███ research ███ creative ███ practical ability. I would say those are the qualities that it looks for. ████████████████████ to create ████ ██ original theatre. One ██████ a solo piece or performance ███ another ████████ a collaborative piece ██████████ a long way for new theatre practices ████ the actor is seen as more than the actor. The actor is ███ creator or co-creator. ██████████ my way of teaching ██ to experiment ███ then reflect. ██████████████

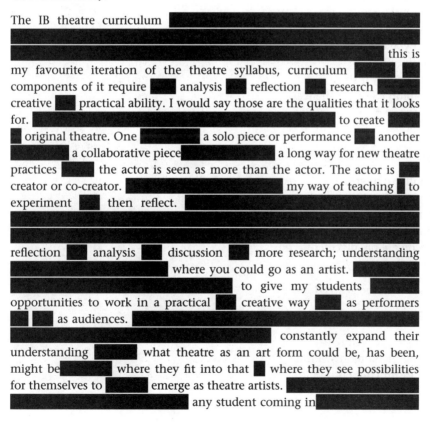

reflection ███ analysis ███ discussion ███ more research; understanding ████████████ where you could go as an artist. ████ ████████████ to give my students ██████ opportunities to work in a practical ███ creative way ████ as performers ███ ██ as audiences. ████████████ ████████████████ constantly expand their understanding ██████ what theatre as an art form could be, has been, might be ██████ where they fit into that ██ where they see possibilities for themselves to ██████ emerge as theatre artists. ████████ ████████████████ any student coming in ████████

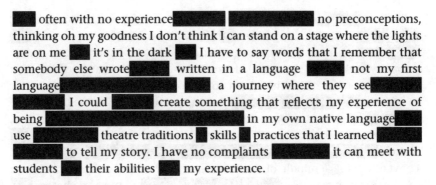

█ often with no experience ████ ████████ no preconceptions, thinking oh my goodness I don't think I can stand on a stage where the lights are on me █ it's in the dark █ I have to say words that I remember that somebody else wrote ████ written in a language ████ not my first language ████████████ █ a journey where they see ████████ ████████ I could ████ create something that reflects my experience of being █████████████████████ in my own native language ██ use █████████ theatre traditions █ skills █ practices that I learned ████ ██████ to tell my story. I have no complaints █████ it can meet with students █ their abilities █ my experience.

stop driving the bus

engage listening
ask questions (you didn't know the answer to)
have a moment of wonder
about what someone
had just said

You pause and
you listen and
you puzzle
and you throw that
out into the air
and you let it sit
(comfortable with silence)

sometimes chaos
is
the proper outcome

you have to create
different paths
for
different kids
become more divergent
be a community

don't become isolated

I know the feeling

I know the feeling of
being the salmon swimming
upstream your entire life

I think

you'll have a lot of energy

I always tell people
when I tell them
I'm a drama teacher
their first response
almost 80% of the time is
"you must have so much fun!"

Well the kids have a lot of fun
and I do have those moments
just like any other job
but it is a lot of work
(energy wise)

be creative
(you need
a sense of humour)

a strong work ethic
(it's easy to fall into
doing not much at all
really)

keep up on things
that are happening
     in the community
     in the theatre field

I think you have to love theatre
because if you don't love theatre
I don't know why
you would be doing it

I think you need to collaborate

I think you have to be really flexible
I think you have to be patient
I think you have to communicate really well

I think you need to be open
to new ideas
not be critical
but encouraging

arts education should be dangerous

an arts teacher *is* the curriculum

(I don't want students to pander to my tastes)

I want to create some sort of a site
that facilitates self-expression,
unique and singular to the individuals
that we're working with
                                                and collectively

(I recognize that that's improbable)

awareness of those ethical sensitivities is important

It keeps me inspired
working with this age group
because of their
unbridled ambition and curiosity.

That enables me to stay
artistically ambitious and curious.

I think that it's also about control
and holding on lightly

follow the emergent curriculum
as it presents itself

It's a fine balance between theory and practice.

have a context of skill and technique
and historical placement
but also a freedom and willingness
to play with what is at hand and available

I'm proud of the work that we've done

Making hard work fun.
Sacrifice.
Putting others' needs before your own.

Those are some of the first things that come to mind
that would be virtues of a good drama teacher.

Methods/Practices and Their Use

For support in developing the craft of poetic inquiry, we recommend Sandra Faulkner's (2019) book *Poetic Inquiry: Craft, Method and Practice*. Faulkner provides a wealth of exemplars and ways of working with data, including her own excellent poetry. The Poetic Inquiry website (www.poeticinquiry.ca) lists all the journal special issues and books published from the biennial International Symposium on Poetic Inquiry and is another good resource for readers who wish to know more about this qualitative arts-based methodology. The journal *Qualitative Inquiry* regularly publishes poetic inquiry, as does *Anthropology and Humanism*. In the continuing debate in arts-based research about researcher qualification, we suggest that some prior experience with poetry writing is ideal (such as an MFA in Creative Writing), but the willingness to explore and experiment with this genre may be sufficient to craft good poetic inquiry.

Conclusion

In this chapter we have provided an overview of the field of poetic inquiry and discussed approaches to working with interview data, examining the literature as well as demonstrating our approaches to crafting poems to represent the voices of interviewees. Carl Leggo (2012), a prominent poetic inquirer, wrote, "I no longer ask, 'Is this a good poem?' I ask, 'What is this poem good for?'" (p. 143). For any researcher intrigued with the possibilities of poetic inquiry, we suggest a deep immersion in literary poetry of all kinds. We also advocate for an openness to the creative process of "surrender-and-catch" (Wolff, 1972; see also Prendergast, 2015), a phenomenological approach to arts-based research in general and poetic inquiry in particular. In surrendering to interview data, in a full immersion that allows the voices of participants to wash over the researcher in waves of interpretation and meaning-making, a poem may (perhaps) be caught.

Supplemental Readings

Faulkner, S. L. (2019). *Poetic inquiry: Craft, method and practice* (2nd ed.). Routledge.

Glesne, C. (1997). That rare feeling: Re-presenting research through poetic transcription. *Qualitative Inquiry, 3*(2), 202–221. https://doi.org/10.1177/1077800 49700300204.

Sullivan, A. M. (2009). On poetic occasion in inquiry: concreteness, voice, ambiguity, tension, and associative logic. In M. Prendergast, C. Leggo, & P. Sameshima (Eds.), *Poetic inquiry: Vibrant voices in the social sciences* (pp. 111–126). Sense Publishers.

Reflection and Activities

1. What are the characteristics of the "poetic occasion" (Sullivan, 2009) and why might a researcher consider poetic approaches to data analysis?

2. Under what circumstances would poetic approaches to data analysis be an inappropriate choice?

3. Reread the examples of poetic transcription from the authors. What qualities do you notice about the work that seems to represent all the interviewees, and the work which privileges singular voices? What are the strengths and weaknesses of each approach?

References

Barone, T. (2001). Science, art, and the predispositions of educational researchers. *Educational Researcher, 30*(7), 24–28. https://doi.org/10.3102/0013189X030007024

Cahnmann-Taylor, M., & Soutou-Manning, M. (2010). *Teachers act up!: Creating multicultural learning communities through theatre.* Teachers College Press.

Denzin, N. K., & Lincoln, Y. S. (2011). Introduction: The discipline and practice of qualitative research. In N. K. Denzin, & Y. S. Lincoln (Eds.), *The SAGE handbook of qualitative research* (pp. 1–20). SAGE.

Dunn, J., & Stinson, M. (2011). Not without the art!! The importance of teacher artistry when applying drama as pedagogy for additional language learning. *Research in Drama Education: The Journal of Applied Theatre and Performance, 16*(4), 617–633. https://doi.org/10.1080/13569783.2011.617110

Eisner, E. W. (1997). The promise and perils of alternative forms of data representation. *Educational Researcher, 26*(6), 4–10. https://doi.org/10.2307/1176961

Faulkner, S. L. (2007). Concern with craft: Using arts poetica as criteria for reading research poetry. *Qualitative Inquiry, 13*(2), 218–234. https://doi.org/10.1177/107780040629563610.1177

Faulkner, S. L. (2019). *Poetic inquiry: Craft, method and practice* (2nd ed.). Routledge.

Glesne, C. (1997). That rare feeling: Re-presenting research through poetic transcription. *Qualitative Inquiry, 3*(2), 202–221. https://doi.org/10.1177/107780049700300204

Gray, C., Wright, P., & Pascoe, R. (2017). There's a lot to learn about being a drama teacher: Pre-service drama teachers' experience of stress and vulnerability during an extended practicum. *Teaching and Teacher Education, 67*, 270–277. https://doi.org/10.1016/j.tate.2017.06.015

Leavy, P. (2015). *Method meets art: Arts-based research practice* (2nd ed.). Guilford.

Leavy, P. (2018). Introduction to arts-based research. In P. Leavy (Ed.), *Handbook of arts-based research* (pp. 1–21). Guilford.

Leggo, C. (2012). Living language: What is a poem good for? *Journal of the Canadian Association for Curriculum Studies, 10*(2), 141–160. https://jcacs.journals.yorku.ca/index.php/jcacs/article/view/36281

Neelands, J. (2004). Miracles are happening: Beyond the rhetoric of transformation in the Western traditions of drama education. *Research in Drama Education: The Journal of Applied Theatre and Performance, 9*(1), 47–56. https://doi.org/10.1080/1356978042000185902

Neelands, J. (2009). Acting together: Ensemble as a democratic process in art and life. *Research in Drama Education: The Journal of Applied Theatre and Performance, 14*(2), 173–189. https://doi.org/10.1080/13569780902868713

Neelands, J., & Goode, T. (2015). *Structuring drama work* (3rd ed.). Cambridge University Press.

Prendergast, M. (2009). "Poem is what?" Poetic inquiry in qualitative social science research. *International Review of Qualitative Research, 1*(4), 541–568. https://www.jstor.org/stable/10.1525/irqr.2009.1.4.541

Prendergast, M. (2015). Poetic inquiry, 2007–2012: A surrender and catch found poem. *Qualitative Inquiry, 21*(8), 678–685. https://doi.org/10.1177/1077800414563806

Prendergast, M., & Shenfield, R. (2019). From theatre to performance studies: Collaborating on curriculum change with secondary level dramatic arts teachers. *Research in Drama Education: The Journal of Applied Theatre and Performance, 24*, 118–132. https://doi.org/10.1080/13569783.2018.1551127

Prendergast, M., & Weigler, W. (Eds.). (2018). *Web of performance: An ensemble workbook.* [eBook]. University of Victoria. https://dspace.library.uvic.ca/handle/1828/9426

Richardson, L. (1992). The consequences of poetic representation. In C. Ellis, & M. G. Flaherty (Eds.), *Investigating subjectivity: Research on lived experience* (pp. 125–137). SAGE.

Richardson, M. (1998). Poetics in the field and on the page. *Qualitative Inquiry, 4*(4), 451–462. https://doi.org/10.1177/107780049800400401

Richardson, L. (2000). Writing: A method of inquiry. In N. K. Denzin, & Y. S. Lincoln (Eds.), *Handbook of qualitative research* (2nd ed.). SAGE.

Stinson, M. (2009). 'Drama is like reversing everything': Intervention research as teacher professional development. *Research in Drama Education: The Journal of Applied Theatre and Performance, 14*(2), 225–243. https://doi.org/10.1080/13569780902868820

Sullivan, A. M. (2009). On poetic occasion in inquiry: Concreteness, voice, ambiguity, tension, and associative logic. In M. Prendergast, C. Leggo, & P. Sameshima (Eds.), *Poetic inquiry: Vibrant voices in the social sciences* (pp. 111–126). Sense Publishers.

Vincent, A. (2018). Is there a definition? Ruminating on poetic inquiry, strawberries and the continued growth of the field. *Art/Research International: A Transdisciplinary Journal, 3*(2), 48–76. https://doi.org/10.18432/ari29356

Wolff, K. H. (1972). Sociology, phenomenology, and surrender-and-catch. *Synthese, 24*(3–4), 439–471. https://doi.org/10.1007/BF00144932

Embedding Critical, Creative, and Contemplative Data Analysis in Interview Studies

Kakali Bhattacharya

Abstract

Grounded in an interview study of doctoral students in a qualitative research class, in this chapter I discuss the methodological moves I made toward enacting a critical, creative, and contemplative framing of design, data collection, and analysis. I argue that data analysis is an analysis of self, other, and an analysis of the outcome of the relationship we develop with the participants exceeding the transactional purpose of rapport and trust building. I detail a mixed-medium, arts-based analysis process that generated intuitive insights beyond verified transcribed text. Since relationships are recursive so is data analysis, yielding to a need to cultivate a presence without expectations. Such presence requires abandoning a will to know and enter the research relationship with humility to learn from the participant. Ultimately, I disrupt the whiteness-centered discursive nature of qualitative research to make space for culturally situated moves exceeding traditional and/or privileged boundaries of inquiry and analysis.

Keywords: Contemplative; critical; arts-based

Once, at the International Congress of Qualitative Inquiry's (ICQI) annual meeting, I suggested to a room full of scholars that data analysis is part self-analysis. People gasped, and one panelist, a white woman with whom I attended graduate school, quickly corrected me: "I don't think, Kakali, I'd go that far." In this chapter I will *go that far*, arguing that self-analysis is not only part, but one of the most critical parts, of understanding and executing data analysis.

I was trained as a qualitative methodologist and have worked in this field since 2005. I have supervised dissertations that incorporated interpretive, critical, deconstructive, and experimental approaches to qualitative inquiry. Consequently, I have met students who preferred a clearly defined path, or at least some broad set of guidelines, for data analysis, and others who felt limited by such standards. Still others vacillated between desiring a predetermined approach and wanting to remain open to engaging with the data to see what would unfold. The most successful and powerful work, regardless of approach, was executed by students who understood that the self is so intricately involved in sense-making that failing to account for the entanglements between researcher, participant, and data often renders analysis superficial, sterile, and falsely performative.

Despite emergent conversations in qualitative research informed by new materialism and posthumanism, I posit that one cannot fully decenter the human when conducting human inquiry. Human beings writing about anything, human or nonhuman, inescapably center human sensibility and interpretation. This belief is integral to my unapologetic stance on engaging in critical and de/colonial research, where I intentionally center people who have been traditionally erased or underrepresented. This centering is personal, political, and urgent. Qualitative research is rife with examples of xenophobia, ethnocentrism, patriarchy, and dehumanism (Smith, 1999/2002, 2005). Thus, data analysis is never value neutral, ahistorical, or acultural.

I situate myself in critical and de/colonial frameworks of qualitative inquiry (Bhattacharya, 2006, 2009, 2015, 2019). Since I have written extensively about these frameworks and my relationship with them elsewhere, here I offer only a brief orientation to my positionality. I am a woman of color, born in India, educated in India, Canada, and the United States. I pursued a BS in biochemistry as an undergraduate, eventually switching to psychology, and graduating with enough credits for a dual biochemistry and psychology major. Thus, when I meet scholars intent on arguing the "science" of qualitative research, I am comfortable dialoguing with them. I am uncomfortable when qualitative researchers reference scientific concepts metaphorically without properly understanding them.

I come from a background of caste, class, and religious privileges in India. When I came to the west those privileges were mostly erased until I earned back some class privilege through higher education. I am committed to doing justice work in my research and mentoring, to document the histories and materialities of those who are underrepresented and to leverage my academic position to make space for such narratives.

I do not view de/coloniality as limited to a fight for land in settler-colonial countries, but from a broader, globalized perspective that includes those who were once-colonized. From that perspective I view colonialism as a force of oppression and invasion that affects people and societies in myriad ways, even after the settler-colonialists' departure. Thus de/coloniality represents a hybridized form of existence, a constant flux between desiring a utopian future free of colonialism and negotiating one's current existence among various colonizing forces.

I bring to my work Anzaldúan notions of mestiza consciousness, nepantlera (one who moves in and out of multiple worlds, crossing thresholds without indoctrination by specific worldviews), border crossings, and liminality (Anzaldúa, 1987, 2015a, 2015b). These notions teach me that engaging in inquiry means engaging in a recursive relationship with what I inquire. When I frame the data, I am simultaneously framed by it. Translating and transforming data analytically to represent my understanding of it inevitably translates and transforms me, similar to Ruth Behar's (1993) work. In the next section, I discuss how my approach to understanding data influences my approach to developing analytic insights.

Un/learning "Data Collection"

I recognize how distracting it is to add slashes or hyphens to perfectly good English words. However, given their value in expressing certain hybridized sensibilities, I ask the readers' indulgence—and promise to keep them to a minimum, heeding Saldaña's (2014) reminder to "bring it down a notch."[1] *Un/learning* indicates my need to learn and unlearn simultaneously when engaging with critical and de/colonial approaches to qualitative inquiry.

Critical perspectives have illuminated how power functions in relation to social structures, infrastructures, institutions, narratives, cultural histories, and discourses in people's lives (Freire, 1973; Giroux, 2009). Such perspectives make it clear that research is an undeniably exploitative process. Researchers have treated their fellow human beings as data (information) repositories, and training in research methodologies situates researchers as extractors of information from participants. Many qualitative researchers even contend that once a participant verifies the accuracy of an interview transcript the participant no longer owns the data—the researcher does. That someone would lose ownership of their own words is the type of exploitative thinking that maintains hierarchical relationships between researchers and participants.

I approach research as a journey of relationship-building that requires relinquishing the predetermined will to know (Bhattacharya, 2009). This sounds counterintuitive, given the expectation that a research purpose and set of questions must guide inquiry. To that I say, yes, one could have those while engaging in

---

[1]Saldaña (2014) states, "If you put prefixes in parentheses, like (re)search or (de)construction, or separate 'em with slashes like un/conditional or mis/appropriation, you need to bring it down a notch" (p. 979).

inquiry. But one also needs the intellectual humility to recognize that building relationships with research participants may illuminate paths of inquiry different from those initially projected.

Relationship-building requires a reverence for the sacredness of others' experience. This means we have no "right" to information, consent forms notwithstanding (Bhattacharya, 2007). Consent forms are a western concept that disregards how people build relationships and the fluidity of those relationships. For example, participants in my dissertation study refused to engage in member-checks, despite agreeing to do so on their consent forms. They refused because, as Indian graduate students who were younger than me, they saw me as their elder sister. From a culturally situated perspective, they were unwilling to "police" my work. They trusted me to do no wrong (a perspective that made me feel perpetually anxious and unworthy) and it was not their place to correct me. I could have reminded them of the consent form, but that would have compromised the relationships we developed during the research that allowed me to genuinely engage with them.

Therefore, I propose that we not "collect data" and claim ownership, like the British collected precious treasures from India and claimed ownership, showcasing them in British museums. I propose instead that we approach participants as people with whom we work collaboratively to advance an agenda of mutual interest. If we are justice-minded, these participants should benefit from this engagement in some form. If we have reverence for this relationship, we humbly accept what the participants choose to offer, even if it differs from our predetermined path of inquiry. We approach relationship-building with a sense of curiosity, discovery, wonder, and unconditional positive regard, without taking these relationships for granted or crossing certain boundaries for the sake of inquiry, even if this was authorized by a signed consent form. Enacted words from signed paperwork have caused tremendous harm to various communities across the world.

Un/learning for me involves how I cultivate relationships with participants and accept that I might not discover what I initially intended to know. If inquiry involves relationship-building with participants, then I am not "collecting data" but documenting my understanding of our relationship and what was shared through relationship-building. Above all, I am acknowledging that the participant is a fellow human being with full ownership and control over what is shared with me and, eventually, with a broader audience.

While this shift may seem intuitively obvious and ethically justified, it is challenging to disrupt years of qualitative research practice and understanding to say, "I enter the research space to humbly learn what my fellow human beings offer." There is a massive distinction between trained inquirers who "collect data" using tools and techniques versus humble learners. For the former, rapport-building is typically performed to extract information and obtain academic mileage. For the latter, entering the research space without a determined will to know and with a desire to learn and accept what is offered through sincere relationship-building implies that "data analysis" analyzes the outcome of relationship-building and that which is shared in the process. Inevitably, this process becomes a recursive analysis of how narratives of self and other intersect and diverge in varied ways, and how perspective-taking requires shuttling between one's own worldview and those of the participants, creating some kind of intelligibility between them.

The next section details a specific interview project, my data analysis process, and some points for consideration.

Creative, Critical, and Contemplative Approach to "Data Analysis"

In summer 2015, I undertook an interview project with doctoral students from my spring 2015 Introduction to Qualitative Research class. As a faculty of color, certain white students in my classes struggle with accepting my position and expertise. To subvert the power difference, some students have challenged my authority, accused me of "reverse racism," submitted caustic course evaluations devoid of constructive suggestions, spread rumors, or even lied about their interactions with me. I have written about one such incident (Bhattacharya, 2018) that finally made me incorporate overtly justice-oriented readings into my class. Previously, I was unsure how much hostility I might provoke by conveying an overtly justice-oriented approach to qualitative research. However, after being sensitive to the resistance I encountered in the past, I decided to be more direct, open, vulnerable, and transparent about my orientation to qualitative research, with the understanding that students were free to disagree with me and find their own paths.

In spring 2015, I introduced various decolonial, critical, creative, contemplative, philosophical, and culturally situated methodological readings (Bhattacharya, 2020). Most of these decentered whiteness and the western superiority of knowledge building, disrupting heteropatriarchal, ableist approaches that have been centered for decades. I engaged students in creative, critical, and contemplative activities during class: holding press conferences to discuss readings; performing plays, songs, and poems; and creating photo essays, short documentaries, and musical compositions to demonstrate their understanding of the readings.

As an educator I have always known that no matter how good my pedagogy is, not everyone will respond the same and there will always be dissenters. Yet on this inaugural attempt, I was surprised at the students' receptivity to my pedagogy and content. This unique combination of students intrigued me and I engaged them in an interview project that summer after our grading relationship ended. Thirteen of the 15 students participated; the other two had schedule conflicts and their availability did not match mine.

The interviews were conversational and easy, characterized by a sense of mutual trust and acceptance. The students knew of my eagerness to learn how they experienced the class, which was radically different from previous semesters and also from their experiences in other classes. They spoke about their experiences with the readings, assignments, activities, and final duoethnography[2] project. Yet the conversation inevitably turned to how the students' personal beliefs, values, assumptions, and worldviews were challenged, reinforced, or expanded through a sense of interconnectivity.

In class I had introduced the students to a mixed medium, contemplative, arts-based data analysis approach. I have written about this approach and outcome elsewhere (Bhattacharya, 2018, 2020; Bhattacharya & Cochrane, 2017). Here, I offer a narrative of that approach followed by some points for consideration when engaging in this form of recursive art- and sense-making.

After Transcription

Each time I began working with participants' narratives, I lit a candle and drew an imaginary circle in my living room that included my partner and my dog. I prayed and invited creative muses, wisdom keepers, and ancestral guides to work through me and protect me, keeping away detrimental energies, so I could remain open to receiving inspiration. My partner played music that harmonized with my creative energy for 5–6 hours, the time it took to work through one interview conversation.

My process was intuitive and iterative. I had taken some mixed medium art-making classes and combined what I learned in those classes with my knowledge of qualitative research, remaining open to a process that would provide analytic insights. I had created an artistic mirror window earlier using this process and highlighted the steps in a prior publication (Bhattacharya & Payne, 2016).

To begin art- and sense-making, I read the interview transcript, then drew representative icons and symbols based on my understanding of it (see Figure 21.1).

I tried to create connections between these symbols visually. Then I played with paint, ink, and parts of interview transcripts pasted on the canvas. I would turn the canvas around, letting paint drip, and while it dried I engaged in free writing, delving deeper into what arose for me in those moments (see Figure 21.2).

In these in-between times, as I wrote I began to see connections between the transcripts, the participants' stories, the ways I know and understand the world, and the ways I had yet to see and understand people's ways of being and how they unravel and arrive at new and different insights.

In a recent article (Bhattacharya, 2020), I wrote:

---

[2]Richard Sawyer and Joe Norris (2012) coined the term duoethnography, a recursive process of two or more researchers engaged in relational, stratified, and nested autoethnographic work in which they play the role of participant and researcher alternatively.

FIGURE 21.1 ● Icons and Images on Canvas

During this art-making process, I played with ink without any predetermined goal. This intuitive process of releasing control connected me to tacit ways of being and knowing for which there are no linguistic markers, allowing me to be present in the current moment. Based on how the ink dripped as I kept turning the canvas around and spraying the drips with water, I was able to see the art from multiple perspectives, through different worldviews, and in liminality simultaneously. I considered this process deeply contemplative, as in that moment of presence I was connected to parts within me, the world, and perhaps beyond spaces of consciousness that exceeded this realm. It was as if I was seeing narratives in their parts, whole, buried, revealed, focused, blurred, and morphing into new forms through color, movement, dripped paint, and my embodied connection. (p. 79)

In some ways this was a process-driven inquiry and analysis. In other ways, this art-making constituted inquiry in and of itself. By bringing forward multiple elements of the interview that had a strong pull for me, I investigated the reasons for this pull while making art (see Figure 21.3).

FIGURE 21.2 ● Pasting Interview Transcripts, Painting, Writing, and Connecting

My goal throughout this process was to inquire into what was going on while remaining open and expansive. I also asked, "What *else* is going on?" I would rotate my canvas and view it from multiple directions to see varied perspectives. In my free writing I inquired into and interrogated my hunches, insights, assumptions. Then I looked at the canvas with dripped paint, collaged interview transcripts, and icons symbolizing parts of the narrative and tried to intuit a composition.

How a composition came forward for me is difficult to put into words. It was a process of trusting my intuition, knowing that the knowledge and insights spilling out of me, onto my free writing or the canvas, appeared for a reason. I would pause, meditate, and sit in silence with the narrative's contradictions and tensions. I tried to feel these tensions in my body to engage in perspective-taking. I asked myself,

FIGURE 21.3 ● Layering, Painting, Dripping, Writing, and Diving Deeply Within

"What arises for you now?" and lived that question until I had an awareness of some answers.

By the end of such inquiry I would trace what inspired me most and, as I began to work with the art, I would intuitively create a composition. The image might be human or inanimate—whatever became salient in my mind's eye. As I outlined and drew the composition, it would encompass the prior collaging in some form within and outside the image. Then I would choose the image's foreground and background, deciding whether the background should be opaque, transparent, or translucent. I chose the background based on how I made sense of the relationship that elicited the narratives and the narratives themselves (see Figure 21.4).

Elsewhere I explained the narrative that inspired the image in Figure 21.4:

For this picture, I recalled that Amelia shared her adoption story, describing how deeply hurt she was upon learning that her birth mother gave only her up for adoption, keeping her older and younger biological siblings, leaving

FIGURE 21.4 ● The Trauma of Abandonment and Adoption

her with some letters. Amelia's mother was addicted to drugs at the time she was pregnant with Amelia. The adoption agency discounted the price of Amelia's adoption due to her mother's drug usage and her biracial heritage. As I began to think about the composition, Amelia's pain, the mother's womb, and the letters all culminated in this one canvas. (Bhattacharya, 2020, p. 80)

When I began creating this composition, the way the water and paint dripped, my color choices, and my artistic skills compelled me to draw river-like wavy lines framing the woman's face. Once I did that, the face and red paint began to reveal pain, largely in the center of the woman's being. In the corner of the picture was what stood out to me that captured Amelia's pain of being *discounted*. This juxta-position of not mattering and then mattering, with cellular-level trauma and pain from both the mother's and child's perspective, became the heaviness Amelia had carried all her life, even as she was about to become a mother herself.

At the onset, when I read the narratives, reflecting on our relationship and conversations, I never knew I would arrive at this point and in this way. Leaving myself open to possibilities and surprises offered a pathway for insight building. In the next section I discuss how a conversation that unfolded with one participant reflects how analyzing "data" can take its own recursive form.

Working with Michelle

Michelle, a white woman in her mid-30s, grew up in the rural Midwest. She told me her family uses the racist n-word frequently and she is uncomfortable with it. She began to unpack some of her white privilege when she realized her Black peers had different life trajectories, including the death of some of her childhood friends. While identifying as poor, Michelle noticed that she was able to take advantage of opportunities to overcome poverty that were not available to her Black friends. During our conversation, Michelle was honest, sometimes tearful, sometimes just sitting still with the heaviness of understanding the complicity of her whiteness, even though she herself had never harmed anyone knowingly.

As I worked with Michelle's narrative and began to create a composition, for some reason, a picture of a leaf came into my consciousness. I traced that awareness and created my composition (see Figure 21.5).

I showed the composition to Michelle and, to my surprise, she started weeping. Then she asked, "How did you know?"

"Know what?" I responded.

"My family is racist and I don't like that. I'd taken an interest in gardening so I wouldn't have to stay in the house with them when I am with family."

"Okay," I said.

"And I've always considered myself as branching out and turning over a new leaf with new possibilities of what I will teach my children, my students. This leaf is exactly how I think of myself." Michelle looked at me. "But how did you know? I didn't share this with you."

I do not know how I knew. I stayed open and reflected on our relationship and on what I heard and did not hear from Michelle. I was not trying to be right or perform some parlor trick of psychic revelation. I simply engaged with what I knew sincerely, intuitively, and iteratively.

Our conversation then went deeper into the ways Michelle was challenging her own complicity and taking risks. Michelle talked about difficult conversations with her family and her children. She expressed her embarrassment about her family and how compelled she felt to disrupt whiteness. In an earlier interview, she summarized her familial narrative rather quickly. Yet when she saw my composition, we paused and talked about our roots and routes in depth.

Michelle's reaction taught me the value of buried, tacit narratives, shared with muted emotions, that can exist in such intensity that they become the centerpiece in navigating one's life. What was unsaid and left in-between words, paragraphs, and sentences became a fertile site of analysis. In the next section, I offer some

FIGURE 21.5 ● Turning Over a New Leaf

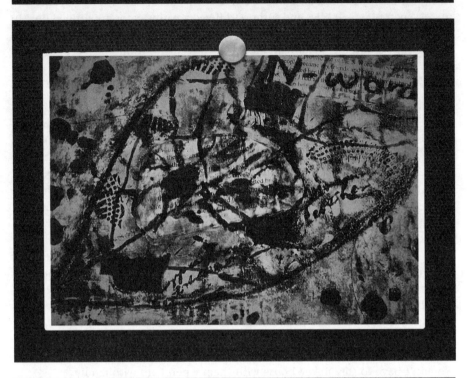

points for consideration when engaging with creative, contemplative, and critical approaches to narrative analysis.

Points for Consideration

The process of art- and sense-making described in this chapter is immensely personal. I offer some points to consider for those wishing to explore this approach in their own inquiry.

Replication Does Not Yield the Same Results

Detailing one's process of inquiry in qualitative research makes one vulnerable to accusations of being prescriptive and reductive instead of exploratory. While all pathways need not be dismissed as prescriptive, there is value in making certain processes transparent and illuminating the researcher's engagement with the outlined processes. Importantly, however, following the processes described here will not yield the same results. How can they when these processes are personal, driven by researcher–participant relationships and trust developed over months of conversation, learning, and growing? This process is *intuitive* and one must trust their own instincts and impulses to see what unfolds.

I encourage those interested in this process to become mindful of what calls them to engage with it. Even if one cannot language the "call," it is important to have some critical awareness. Perhaps it is an inclination toward a process that merges criticality, creativity, and contemplation; a sense of readiness to engage in mindfulness practices; or a reawakening of the creativity one has lost in the drudgery of higher education. Whatever the reason, engaging in this process requires raw honesty with oneself before engaging in sense-making of participants' narratives.

Understanding the Recursive Nature of Self–Other Relationships

Individuals interested in this approach to sense-making must interrogate who they are in the world, how the world frames them, and how they frame the world in response. Excavating one's place in the world requires understanding with humility the multiplicity and intersection of privilege and oppression and one's relationship with them. Performing such excavation requires an openness to certain contemplative practices of stillness, presence, and introspection.

As odd or mystical as this might sound, engaging in perspective-taking with others' narratives requires examining one's own narratives with utter honesty, understanding how those narratives have contributed to an authoring of self. Only when one excavates deeply within can another's storytelling offer in-depth insight. In other words, researchers must engage in practices that cultivate in-depth insight before they can attain insight into others' experiences or the documents, media, or other sources they analyze.

It is impossible to fully remove the self when analyzing one's relationship with others, just as it is unreasonable to expect human inquiry to decenter the human. Therefore, any positivist discomfort with relationship-building in qualitative inquiry should be disposed of quickly. Relationship-building should not be inherently transactional. Instead, researchers should value relationship-building for its own sake. By valuing our relationship with a fellow human being, we learn how to treat the relationship's unfolding with dignity and humility, even if it does not yield the exact "data" that advances our work. Only when we abandon posturing with a will to know can we cultivate sincere relationships that generate reflective opportunities to understand the relationship between self and other.

Contemplative Creativity as a Portal of Possibilities

Importantly, those seeking to engage in contemplative creative forms of sense-making must give themselves permission to do creative works badly, at first. One's artwork, poem, or photo essay does not need to be museum- or award-worthy. Instead, it is critical to see these engagements as portals to journeys that take one elsewhere, opening expansive possibilities, and to remain receptive to those possibilities and their relevance for one's work. The focus is not on creating a masterpiece, but on learning through engaging in the process.

Often people are intimidated by creative work because they think it requires some mastery of a set of skills. I believe we are all capable of being creative thinkers and doers, even if our creations may not meet certain aesthetic standards. A bad aesthetic is still an aesthetic, but more importantly, the process of creating *becomes* the process of inquiry and analysis, generating new insights.

If you are interested in experimenting with creative forms of sense-making, I urge you to embrace the call and go for it. If you end up enjoying this creative play, I encourage you to learn the craft more diligently. In other words, do not put forward your first poem as a creative masterpiece. Study the art of writing poems, discover your creative and aesthetic sensibilities, and elevate your work. Your inquiry will gain depth and your work will create numerous entry points for its multidimensionality.

Below, I offer some guidelines for experimentation. These guidelines are not meant to be prescriptive; this process is immensely personal and, before pursuing it, please consult the points for consideration offered earlier. Embrace the generative and expansive possibilities, instead of replication of similar results. This is an offering of transparency, as much as possible, while engaging in iterative and intuitive forms of sense making.

Crawford (2017, p. 77) documents several instructional guidelines from my pedagogy (Bhattacharya, 2015) applicable to contemplative creativity. Among them are the following:

1. Read the transcript closely. Connect to the transcript, not for identifying codes, categories, or themes, but to become deeply empathic about what the participant states in the conversation. Feel the words in your mouth; read them slowly as you become aware of how your body and mind are reacting to these words.

2. Select passages from the transcript that stand out after a close reading.

3. Draw visual icons, in any form that you like, on the passages that stand out to you. These icons do not have to be high in aesthetic quality but they have to connect your thoughts, emotions, and insights to the selected passage.

4. Cut out your selected portions of transcripts and glue them on a canvas in any orientation you like.

5. Turn your canvas around in another orientation so you can have a different perspective.

6. Use any form of art and mark-making instruments to connect the excerpts of transcripts you have on the canvas.

7. Turn your canvas around in another orientation so you can have a different perspective.

8. On a separate piece of paper, write about the experiences, emotions, and thoughts that arise for you in response to seeing your symbols and your connections. Freewrite in response to the following prompt: "The narratives that arise for me in this artwork in this moment are...."

9. Reflect on the following questions:

    a. What did you discover/understand/sharpen/deepen better through this activity?

    b. How did covering, uncovering, writing, and drawing allow you to gain insight into how you work with qualitative data?

    c. How might this activity change or inform the way you think about conducting your qualitative research?

    d. What insights about yourself did you discover as you worked with the narratives the participant shared with you?

I recommend keeping a notebook with you at all times to record your thoughts in whatever form you prefer. It might even be helpful to document dreams, inspirations, hunches—anything that arises that has some emotional charge for you. This way you can trace your own journey and articulate how you have attended to creativity, intuition, and instinct as ways of informing your analysis.

Conclusion

Writing about data analysis in qualitative research is challenging because it is a personal process and replication does not yield similar results. At the ICQI meeting, I was shot down for asserting that data analysis is part self-analysis. In this chapter, I have gone deep into the claim that self-analysis is a key element of data analysis because relationship-building is a central aspect of qualitative research—even more so if informed by critical and/or de/colonial frameworks.

From these perspectives, relationship-building exceeds the traditional transactional expectation of research as scholars enter into relationship-building for its own sake. I propose that any inquiry emerging from such relationship-building requires humility and abandoning the will to know. As researchers, we should not see our fellow human beings as data repositories from whom *it is our right to* extract information. Instead, we can learn from participants that which they choose to offer us, engaging in a journey of learning, curiosity, and discovery that may at times reveal alternate paths and insights.

The exemplars detailing various processes of mixed medium arts-based data analysis revealed in-depth insights, some of which were tacit and not articulated in interviews. In Michelle's case, a throwaway remark conveyed a central part of how she authored her life, illuminating the value of being mindful of intuitive and instinctive insights during data analysis.

I have argued that data analysis, at least in part, is an analysis of the relationship between participant and researcher—an analysis of self and other. To execute such analysis requires some contemplative engagement with criticality and the narratives that inform one's own worldviews, beliefs, assumptions, and identities. Only when engaging in recursive relationships with our participants can we become aware of intersected and specifically located privileges in our entangled narratives.

Nothing presented in this chapter should be taken prescriptively. These are simply guidelines, offerings one can engage with and even alter. For example, if the instructions call for drawing spirals but you want to draw triangles, trapezoids, or teacups, please give yourself permission to do so. This is a personal journey of inquiry and cultivation of in-depth insights.

Qualitative research cannot be divorced from its inherent whiteness and privileged western locations, given that the celebrated scholars of qualitative research are located in the Global North or predominantly white countries. Thus, to conduct data analysis from critical and/or de/colonial perspectives, it is vital to disrupt status quo understandings of qualitative research and exceed traditional boundaries of inquiry and analysis. In this chapter such boundary crossings have been presented as invitational moves, encouraging readers to take intellectual and creative risks and engage in their own insight-driven discoveries.

Supplemental Readings

Bhattacharya, K. (2018). Contemplation, imagination, and post-oppositional approaches in qualitative inquiry. *International Review of Qualitative Research, 11*(3), 271–285. https://doi.org/10.1525/irqr.2018.11.3.271

Bhattacharya, K. (2019). Theorizing from the streets: De/colonizing, contemplative, and creative approaches and consideration of quality in arts-based qualitative research. In N. Denzin & M. Giardina (Eds.), *Qualitative inquiry at a crossroads: Political, performative, and methodological reflections* (pp. 109–125). Routledge.

Bhattacharya, K. (2020). Understanding entangled relationships between un/interrogated privileges: Tracing research pathways with contemplative art-making, duoethnography, and pecha kucha. *Cultural Studies ↔ Critical Methodologies, 20*, 75–85. https://doi.org/10.1177/1532708619884963

Reflection and Activities

As I invite readers to engage in their own creative, contemplative, and critical approaches to data analysis, I suggest the following questions for consideration and discussion. These have no good, bad, right, or wrong answers; they are simply designed for thoughtful contemplation.

1. In what ways (other than those noted in this chapter) could you approach inquiry as a form of humility? Perhaps think in terms of research purpose, questions, design, data collection, analysis, representation, and ethics.

2. If data analysis is relationship analysis, what introspective analyses are necessary for your relationship-building approaches? In other words, what do you carry within you that facilitates and/or obstructs humility-oriented relationship building free of transactional expectations?

3. Regardless of which form of data analysis you engage in, how might you attend to the intuitive nature of data analysis and sense-making? What does that look like for you? What might you do to embrace and activate your own instincts and intuition for data analysis?

4. All forms of inquiry are framed by an organizing lens. As you engage in critical, creative, and contemplative approaches to data analysis, what theoretical and methodological approaches frame your analysis? These framings can come from established scholarship or from knowledge constructed outside traditional spaces in academia.

References

Anzaldúa, G. E. (1987). La conciencia de la Mestiza: Towards a new consciousness. In W. Kolmar & F. Bartkowski (Eds.), *Feminist theory: A reader* (pp. 398–402). Mayfield Publishing.

Anzaldúa, G. E. (2015a). Flights of the imagination: Rereading/rewriitng realities. In A. Keating (Ed.), *Light in the dark/Luz en lo oscuro: Rewriting identity, spirituality, reality* (pp. 23–46). Duke University Press.

Anzaldúa, G. E. (2015b). Geographies of selves—reimagining identity: Nos/otras (us/other), las nepantleras, and the new tribalism. In A. Keating (Ed.), *Light in the dark/Luz en lo oscuro: Rewriting identity, spirituality, reality* (pp. 65–94). Duke University Press.

Behar, R. (1993). *Translated woman: Crossing the border with Esperanza's story.* Beacon Press.

Bhattacharya, K. (2006). De/colonizing methodologies and performance ethnography: Extending and legitimizing qualitative approaches to "scientific" inquiry. *Paper presented at the American Educational Research Association, San Francisco, CA.*

Bhattacharya, K. (2007). Consenting to the consent form—What are the fixed and fluid understandings between the researcher and the researched? *Qualitative Inquiry, 13*(8), 1095–1115. https://doi.org/10.1177/1077800407304421

Bhattacharya, K. (2009). Othering research, researching the other: De/colonizing approaches to qualitative inquiry. In J. Smart (Ed.), *Higher education: Handbook of theory and research* (Vol. XXIV, pp. 105–150). Springer.

Bhattacharya, K. (2015). The vulnerable academic: Personal narratives and strategic de/colonizing of academic structures. *Qualitative Inquiry, 22*(5), 309–321. https://doi.org/10.1177/1077800415615619

Bhattacharya, K. (2018). Contemplation, imagination, and post-oppositional approaches: Carving the path of qualitative inquiry. *International Review of Qualitative Research, 11*(3), 271–285. https://doi.org/10.1525/irqr.2018.11.3.271

Bhattacharya, K. (2019). Theorizing from the streets: De/colonizing, contemplative, and creative approaches and consideration of quality in arts-based qualitative research. In N. K. Denzin & M. D. Giardina (Eds.), *Qualitative inquiry at a crossroads: Political, performative, and methodological reflections* (pp. 109–125). Routledge.

Bhattacharya, K. (2020). Understanding entangled relationships between un/interrogated privileges: Tracing research pathways with contemplative art-making, duoethnography, and pecha kucha. *Cultural Studies ↔ Critical Methodologies, 20*(1), 75–85. https://doi.org/10.1177/1532708619884963

Bhattacharya, K., & Cochrane, M. (2017). Assessing the authentic knower through contemplative arts-based pedagogies in qualitative inquiry. *Journal of Contemplative Inquiry, 4*(1). https://journal.contemplativeinquiry.org/index.php/joci/article/view/76

Bhattacharya, K., & Payne, R. (2016). Mixing mediums, mixing selves: Arts-based contemplative approaches to border crossings. *International Journal of Qualitative Studies in Education, 29*(2), 1100–1117. https://doi.org/10.1080/09518398.2016.1201163

Crawford, B. L. (2017). *Lights up when plugged in, the superpower of disability: An arts-based narrative* (Publication No. 10619664) (Doctoral dissertation). Kansas State University: Proquest Dissertations Publishing.

Freire, P. (1973). *Education for critical consciousness*. Seabury Press.

Giroux, H. (2009). Critical theory and educational practice. In A. Darder, M. P. Baltodano, & R. D. Torres (Eds.), *The critical pedagogy reader* (2nd ed., pp. 27–51). Routledge.

Saldaña, J. (2014). Blue-collar qualitative research: A rant. *Qualitative Inquiry, 20*(8), 976–980. https://doi.org/10.1177/1077800413513739

Sawyer, R. D., & Norris, J. (2012). *Duoethnography: Understanding qualitative research*. Oxford University Press.

Smith, L. T. (1999/2002). *Decolonizing methodologies: Research and indigenous peoples*. Zed Books Ltd.

Smith, L. T. (2005). On tricky ground: Researching the native in the age of uncertainty. In N. K. Denzin & Y. S. Lincoln (Eds.), *The SAGE handbook of qualitative research* (3rd ed., pp. 85–107). SAGE.

Follow the Headlights: On Comics-Based Data Analysis

Sally Campbell Galman

FOLLOW THE HEADLIGHTS:
on comics-based data analysis

◉ Sally Campbell Galman

SO... let's review: What is this data analysis?

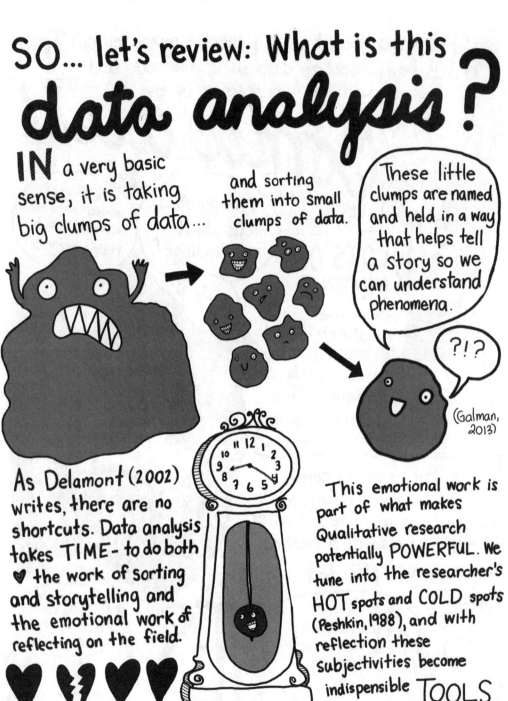

IN a very basic sense, it is taking big clumps of data...

and sorting them into small clumps of data.

These little clumps are named and held in a way that helps tell a story so we can understand phenomena.

?!?

(Galman, 2013)

As Delamont (2002) writes, there are no shortcuts. Data analysis takes TIME- to do both ♡ the work of sorting and storytelling and the emotional work of reflecting on the field.

This emotional work is part of what makes Qualitative research potentially POWERFUL. We tune into the researcher's HOT spots and COLD spots (Peshkin, 1988), and with reflection these subjectivities become indispensible TOOLS (Galman, 2018b)

BUT HOW DO COMICS FIT IN?

Comics and other visual arts can be forms of ARTS BASED RESEARCH! (ABR)

That is where researchers "make systematic use of the artistic process, the actual making of artistic expressions in all the different forms of the arts, as a primary way of understanding and examining experience by both researchers and the people that they involve in their studies" (McNiff, 2008, p29)

And one of these visual ABR methods is

COMIC BASED RESEARCH

WHOA!!

THIS AIN'T YO MAMA'S COMIC STRIP!!

CBR is "a broad set of practices that use the comic form to collect, analyze, and/or disseminate scholarly research" (Kuttner, Sousanis & Weaver-Hightower, 2018 p397)

NB: do not confuse CBR with CPR. Though the comic arts sure as hell save lives.

Data analysis is about holding and making sense of PARTS and the WHOLE at the same time *dynamically*.

It can be a COMPLICATED MENTAL GYMNASTICS

10

You stuck the dismount!

Writing and drawing can help! Comics offer "a multimodal way of scaffolding the analyst's cognition" (weaver-hightower 2013)

Comics tell a story. And as the analytic story emerges, comic writing allows the author to EXPLORE feelings, data, themes and ideas in linear and non linear ways. Comics "give access to EMPATHY AND INSIGHT INTO EXPERIENCE that resides centrally in the aims of qualitative research" (weaver-hightower 2017 p229)

Okay but HOW DO I DO IT?

A LITTLE BACK STORY

I had been conducting a qualitative study of transgender children since 2015. I was collecting data in the midwestern U.S. in the aftermath of the 2016 presidential election.

The whole post-election experience was PAINFUL for me as a researcher. When I got home and needed to analyze data, I found that I wanted to explore emerging ideas using tools from my training as a cartoonist.

I ended up writing a short comic vignette as an analytic task—to put what I had seen and felt into a coherent story. As Kuttner et al (2018) write, "word-picture interaction can be a useful tool for exploring other sorts of relationships... it can be an opportunity to investigate uncertainty and ambiguity"... (p. 411)

"This kid at school says that the new president all the ender people.

(Galman, 2019)

Remember the whole thing about hot spots and cold spots and subjectivity? WELL.

When I was thinking about and reading and reflecting on that data I KNEW there was something going on, something important there, and making a comic about it

EVEN IF IN DOING SO I COULD ONLY SEE AS FAR AHEAD AS THE METAPHORICAL HEADLIGHTS

... could do the analytic work of OPENING UP THE DATA!

As a comic artist I must attend to how the PARTS & the WHOLE of the data HANG TOGETHER. This means careful piecing & stitching

Weaver-Hightower (2017) calls this process "RE-STORYING." This is when the comic artist holds all the pieces and ideas and words and images in her hands and mind and arranges and rearranges them until they are in a logical (or extralogical ☺) order...

As I read through my fieldnotes, memos, and interview transcripts from that time in the field, I spent time exploring the words and images that came to mind as I read. The first thing I felt was a powerful sense of DOOM. As per Delamont (2002), I read widely in the field and this time it was Bob Dylan's (1991) Last Thoughts on Woody Guthrie and THIS was the image that appeared in the headlights. And I drew it again and again and FOLLOWED IT AS I READ ONWARD.

I COULD FEEL THE TEETH

... UNDER MY FEET

Drawing had become a kinesthetic questioning: WHAT IS THE STORY HERE? Is it precarity? Fear? Doom? The image came to me as I read and its meaning wouldn't be far behind.

In this process I found an organizing theme:

And as I wrote and drew and worked on figuring out where the headlights were taking me, I realized— as I drew those teeth and the gaping maw again and again— this is NOT the story of doom or of danger— this is the story of **BRAVERY** (Galman, 2018a)

THE COMIC DRAWING PROCESS CAN WORK FOR YOU TOO IN THESE

THREE STEPS

step one: READ HARD

Like, REALLY hard.

TRUST THE PROCESS

DATA ♥

I know all the hard copy is not the most efficient thing BUT THE WORK OF DISCOVERY IS NOT EFFICIENT

I print out hard copy of all my data and organize it in BIG 3 ring BINDERS. Then I READ & DRAW

And while I read I sketch the images and ideas that come to mind, including short narrative sequences, in my trusty sketchbook.

← a million eraser shavings

← favorite pens and highlighters.

← so many post its

Memo

3. People tend to get a bit twitchy about standards of rigor. And there are plenty of these in CBR (see Kuttner, Sousanis & Weaver-Hightower, 2018) but the standard of greatest resonance to me in analytic work is how we act in "fidelity to researcher experience and subjectivity — which is sometimes addressed by inserting the researcher into the piece as a character..." (p. 413)

Another good and simple rule: to make good **ART** you must make good **SCIENCE**

AND VICE VERSA

OBVIOUSLY NOT REAL

You can also use little animals or creatures to represent other voices!

YES! JUST START DRAWING!

And while you are mustering the courage, consider these exercises to whet your CBR appetite:

1. Think about your own work and try to *draw* a short story from either your data or your experience in the field.

Beginning 1	Middle 2	End 3

Keep it simple at first!

Did you discover any new things?

2. Head over to the bookstore or library and check out one of my comic books about research methods. What feels different about engaging with COMICS? What's different about how the material is organized and presented?

3. Describe something from your data OR your life using only pictures. Then share it with someone and see what *new* ideas *emerge*...

SHANE THE LONE ETHNOGRAPHER

THE GOOD, THE BAD, AND THE DATA
SHANE THE LONE ETHNOGRAPHER'S BASICS GUIDE TO QUALITATIVE DATA ANALYSIS
SALLY CAMPBELL GALMAN

have fun!

References

Delamont, S. (2002). *Fieldwork in educational settings: Methods, pitfalls and perspectives.* (2nd ed.). Routledge.

Dylan, B. (1991). Last thoughts on Woody Guthrie. [Song]. On: *The Bootleg series: Rare and unreleased 1961–1991.* Columbia Records.

Galman, S.C. (2018a). This is Vienna. In C. Kray, H. Mandell, & T. Carroll (Eds.), *Nasty Women and Bad Hombres: Historical Reflections on the 2016 Presidential Election.* (pp. 276–290). University of Rochester Press.

Galman, S.C. (2018b). *Naptime at the O.K. Corral: A beginner's guide to the ethnography of childhood.* Routledge.

Galman, S.C. (2018c). *Shane the Lone Ethnographer: A beginner's guide to ethnographic research.* (2nd ed.). Rowman & Littlefield.

Galman, S.C. (2017). Research in Pain. *Anthropology News,* 14–17. http://www.anthropology-news.org/index.php/2017/05/08/research-in-pain.

Galman, S.C. (2013). *The Good, the Bad, and the Data: A beginner's guide to Qualitative Data Analysis.* Routledge.

Galman, S.C. (2009). The truthful messenger: Visual methods and representation. *Qualitative Research.* 9(2), 197–217. https://doi.org/10.1177/1468794108099321

Kuttner, P., Sousanis, N. & Weaver-Hightower, M.B. (2018). How to draw comics the scholarly way: Creating comics-based research in the academy. In P. Leavy (Ed.) *Handbook of arts-based research.* (pp. 396–423). Guilford.

McNiff, S. (2008). Arts based research. In J.G. Knowles & A.L. Cole. (Eds.) *Handbook of the arts in Qualitative Research: Perspectives, methodologies, examples and issues.* (pp. 29–40). SAGE.

Peshkin, A. (1988). In search of subjectivity—one's own. *Educational Researcher* 17(1), 17–21. https://doi.org/10.3102/0013189X017007017

Weaver-Hightower, M.B. (2017). Losing Thomas & Ella: A father's story. *Journal of Medical Humanities,* 38(3), 215–230. https://doi.org/10.1007/s10912-015-9359-2

Weaver-Hightower, M.B. (2013). Comics and the narrative/ethnographic moment. Paper given at the annual meeting of the American Educational Research Association, San Francisco, CA.

want more cbr? sallycampbellgalman.com

Writing-Up Practices

Paul Mihas

Introduction

Qualitative researchers do more than "write up" their findings, they write *through* and *toward* discovery. As a practice, not simply a phase at the eleventh hour, the work of writing and rewriting continually activates knowledge and channels growing comprehension. Writing is a representation of experience (Bruner, 1986)—it communicates the understandings of both the researcher and the participants. Notes, memos, transcriptions, proposals, concept papers, and other forms of research writing build on each other. There are many writing strata reflected in the final "product," which is often a weigh station along a larger program of inquiry.

During the interview, we inhabit the participant's aural telling, already removed from a larger experience. In transcription, we then transform this oral event into a textual one (see Chapters 4–6 regarding practices in transcription). In analysis, we discern what narratives signify, working toward meaning—writing memos on quotations, transcripts, and codes—and by doing so develop our writing voice and locate the distinctive language of the study (see Chapters 13–15). In writing the final product—a dissertation, article, blog, or book—we attend to a particular audience of practitioners, academicians, or the general public (or to all these). Each of these written representations of experience moves us toward investigative breakthroughs and to writing as a *method of knowing* (Richardson, 2000).

Readers also participate in this knowledge production, as they have their own experiences of writers' narrative framing, curated evidence, and claims to meaning. Readers translate our words—our constructions and "findings"—to meanings based on their own discipline and positionality. When we consider all the layers of experience we bring to bear in writing-up practices, finding a way to communicate participants' intimations and pivotal moments as they see them can be daunting. Remembering to speak *with* participants, not *for* them, keeps us closer to the research context and site of exploration. Writing invites us to make claims and to articulate these claims with illustrative data and logical sensemaking, in some fields called a "chain of evidence" (Yin, 2014).

As a tool for conveying experience, writing has its limitations. Written text cannot allow the reader to hear participants' voices or see their faces as they puzzle through their responses. Nonetheless, in our written accounts, we have an opportunity to share the implications of an embodied social world and to engage an audience in our telling. Poet Paul Connolly states that "it is not arguing well, but speaking differently that changes the culture" (Retallack & Spahr, 2006). Even if our objective is not to change "culture" per se, but engage in discovery and to change what we once thought we (or our discipline) understood, speaking "differently" is a practice worth nurturing. We develop these skills in effective writing as we question assumptions, resist academic clichés, and employ incisive language as a new way of knowing. Because qualitative research gives us pathways to build knowledge from participants' own words and spoken awareness, the opportunities for "speaking differently" abound. We can also use different narrative formats—prosaic, poetic, dramatic, and technical (Saldaña, 2018)—selecting the one that perhaps best showcases phenomena in new ways, presenting the participant's social world, as much as is possible, through their eyes.

Definitions of publishing include to "make generally known" and to "disseminate to the public" (Merriam-Webster, 2020). Publishing traditionally concerns itself with the production and dissemination of knowledge, but qualitative researchers are not only concerned with study "results." We are also concerned with *understanding* the participants' complex reality, lived experiences, and meaning making.

Whether our work has overtones of ethnography, phenomenology, or narrative analysis, we are called upon to construct a compelling narrative, not simply an informative one. We must communicate how our study refines, contradicts, and expands upon what has come before. By drawing attention to the connective tissue that holds seemingly conflicting accounts together, we gain the readers' attention and, we hope, their trust. Our task is to use the written word to convey understanding by being storytellers that spark interest in a phenomenon whose dimensions are yet unknown or continuously evolving. A compressed journal abstract might adequately convey the findings of a quantitative article, but the same is not true for qualitative research. Readers need to experience the unfolding research journey and hear, as best they can, the participants' voices to gain not just condensed knowledge but an experiential grasp of a phenomenon, occasion, or passage. As poet Muriel Rukeyser (1968) reminds us, "the universe is made of stories, not of atoms," and it is these stories that invite the reader to lean in closer and participate in this nuanced knowledge production.

At the beginning of a qualitative article or arts-based creation, the researcher makes an implicit contract with the reader. The reader learns quickly whether and how the author will partner with them on this journey, and whether and how the author will help them find their way through evidence, claims, and stories from the data. In many ways, authors signal to readers how to read their work. They do this by the power of example, by sensitizing readers to context, and by raising doubts readers might themselves raise. In assessing a piece of qualitative writing, Richardson (2000) reminds us to ask ourselves whether it accomplishes the following:

- *substantive contribution* (a discovery worth sharing)

- *aesthetic merit* (a compelling researcher voice)

- *reflexivity* (adequate self-awareness)

- *impact* (does this affect the reader?)

- *expression of a reality* (an embodied sense of experience) (Richardson, 2000).

At its best, reading generates an intellectual and social partnership between author and reader to accomplish these objectives.

This section presents approaches and insights to writing practices and to addressing a range of audiences. In Chapter 23, Aishath Nasheeda, Haslinda Binti Abdullah, Steven Eric Krauss, and Nobaya Binti Ahmed discuss using practices from narrative analysis to transform interview transcripts into stories, using strategies to sequence and organize the written work around major turning points while communicating the voice of the storyteller. In Chapter 24, Jessica Smartt Gullion walks us through what it means to communicate to the public via concept papers, blogs, and OpEds for a range of audiences. She shares strategies and practices on how to ensure our work has a longer shelf life and greater impact than it might have in scholarly journals alone. Readers, she tells us, are always asking why a topic is important and, when we have done our job, wondering what will happen next. In Chapter 25, Mitchell Allen highlights the critical and complex relationship between author and editor as he celebrates publishing as a *social act*, one which often begins with a conversation.

Reflection and Activities

1. After reading Nasheeda et al. (Chapter 23) and Gullion (Chapter 24), rewrite a passage from one of your research studies or an excerpt from an interview transcript first as a narrative vignette and then as a concept paper or OpEd. What discoveries did you make from engaging in these writing practices and what meanings do they communicate to readers?

2. After reading Allen (Chapter 25), compose an email to a publishing company's acquisitions editor about a book idea based on your research.

References

Allen, M. (2022). Sophie's choices: The social act of publishing a qualitative study. In C. Vanover, P. Mihas, & J. Saldaña (Eds.), *Analyzing and interpreting qualitative research: After the interview*. SAGE.

Bruner, J. (1986). *Actual minds, possible worlds*. Harvard University Press.

Gullion, J. S. (2022). Writing for a broad audience: Concept papers, blogs, and OpEds. In C. Vanover, P. Mihas, & J. Saldaña (Eds.). *Analyzing and interpreting qualitative research: After the interview*. SAGE.

Merriam-Webster. (2020). Merriam-Webster.com dictionary. https://www.merriam-webster.com/

Nasheeda, A., Abdullah, H. B., Krauss, S. E., & Ahmed, N. B. (2022). Turning transcripts into stories. In C. Vanover, P. Mihas, & J. Saldaña (Eds.), *Analyzing and interpreting qualitative research: After the interview*. SAGE.

Retallack, J., & Spahr, J. (2006). *Poetry and pedagogy: The challenges of the contemporary*. Macmillan.

Richardson, L. (2000). Writing: A method of inquiry. In N. K. Denzin, & Y. S. Lincoln (Eds.), *The SAGE handbook of qualitative research* (2nd ed., pp. 923–948). SAGE.

Rukeyser, M. (1968). *The speed of darkness: Poems*. Random House.

Saldaña, J. (2018). *Writing qualitatively: The selected works of Johnny Saldaña*. Routledge.

Yin, R. K. (2014). *Case study research*. SAGE.

Turning Transcripts Into Stories

Aishath Nasheeda, Haslinda Binti Abdullah, Steven Eric Krauss, and Nobaya Binti Ahmed

Abstract

Narratives are written accounts or spoken or remembered words that are representations of events. Interviews contain narratives that may be analyzed through multiple approaches. However, few authors describe the process of transforming interviews into stories. Using transcripts from the first author's PhD study of young adults' experiences with life skills education programs in Maldives as an exemplar, the chapter describes the process of reconstructing narratives of one of the participant's experiences from their interviews. We provide a step-by-step illustration of how a set of transcripts were structured and organized to produce stories for analysis. This content is presented in a four-phased progression that describes how the participant's story was developed from interview transcripts through drafting a chronological plot to co-creating and revising the text and making meaning from the transcripts. The revised transcript became the focus of the qualitative analysis.

Keywords: Narratives; experiences; stories; multimethod progression in qualitative data analysis; transcripts

What Is a Narrative?

Most definitions of narrative include a spoken or written account of events, chronicles, or stories. Labov and Waletzky (1997) define narrative as temporal moments that match with the events that are narrated. Polkinghorne (1985) defines narrative as a process that gives meaning to a series of events by connecting these episodes to a theme or plot. Hence, narratives are representations that describe human experiences as they unfold over time (Clandinin & Rosiek, 2007).

Representations of Narratives

In qualitative research, narratives are collected and analyzed with a wide range of procedures and practices. Researchers may collect narratives through interviews, observations, textual analyses, and by taking samples of their own writing and self-talk.

The collected narratives may be analyzed through contemporary approaches such as thematic, structural, and performance analysis (Riessman, 2005). In thematic analysis, the emphasis is on the gist of a text, i.e., what is communicated rather than how a story is written or spoken. Making meaning in thematic analysis focuses on the content of speech. Language is treated as a universal art whereby readers assume that the themes grouped together in the analysis represent the narrators' experience (Riessman, 2005). In contrast, structural analysis emphasizes the way a story is told and tries to draw out the essential meanings relevant to the spoken or written language in order to understand how the narrative is composed (Hyvärinen, 2008). Therefore, the representations of storytelling in structural analysis tend to be limited to efforts to analyze how things are said, rather than investigating the institutional and interactional forces that shape the lives of the participants (Ahmed & Rogers, 2017). Dialogic/performance analysis moves beyond storytelling into performance and is focused on the societal/cultural setting rather than the individual story (Riessman, 2001, 2005).

Most narrative inquiries and other research that use stories collected from interviews are developed from commitments to specific genres such as biography, autoethnography, life history, and oral history. Each of these genres has different practices for guiding data collection (Creswell & Poth, 2018), and these practices influence how narratives are co-constructed by the interviewer and participant(s) (Breheny & Stephens, 2015) to become recorded and/or transcribed data.

Though many studies feature narrative inquiry as a design (see Clandinin & Connelly, 2000; Clandinin & Rosiek, 2007) and many provide guides on narrative interviewing (Anderson & Kirkpatrick, 2015; Jovchelovitch & Bauer, 2000), few authors have written about the process of transforming interviews to construct stories (Jeppesen, 2016). There are many different ways to represent and analyze stories (e.g., Connelly & Clandinin, 1990; Cortazzi, 1994; Ollerenshaw & Creswell, 2002; Riessman, 1993); however, the process of turning an oral interview into a story that is ready for analysis is often taken for granted (McCormack, 2000).

The methodological process of transcript analysis and story development described in this chapter has been constructed from multiple strategies for transforming narratives (Clandinin & Rosiek, 2007; Czarniawska, 2004; Riessman, 2005). The goal of the restorying framework (see Nasheeda, Abdullah, Krauss, & Ahmed, 2019) is to sequence transcripts chronologically to represent the participants' story while continuing to stay connected with the participant's understanding of their experiences. Check-ins and follow-up interviews might be used to develop and understand participants' stories as the analysis progresses. The framework consists of a four-phase progression that moves from the live interview to transcripts, to drafting a chronological plot from the initial interview transcript, to co-creating and revising the text, and to making meaning from the revised transcript. The following sections will provide readers with step-by-step illustrations of this progression; we will show how a set of transcripts were structured and reorganized to produce stories for analysis.

Study Description

Life skills education programs for young people have been critical for bringing about constructive adjustments to individual well-being from the early years of childhood and adolescence through their transition to adulthood (Nasheeda, 2008). The aim of the study was to describe how life skills education program experiences shaped a single participant's life. The participant shared her experience in a 60-minute interview and then, as we discuss, provided feedback to the team's questions and comments in a series of follow-up interviews and social media interactions. The interview transcripts from the participant's interviews were used to craft a story that reconstructed the meaning of the participant's experiences while keeping the original voice.

Transforming Interviews Into Stories

This chapter presents a four-phased progression that describes how the participant's story was developed from interview transcripts. The initial drafts of the participant's interview transcripts were read several times to understand the chronological sequence she shared in her interview and to develop a coherent story. Collaboration with the participant during this process added meaning to the narratives shared in the original interview. Practices and strategies from multiple forms of narrative analysis such as holistic-content reading (Lieblich, Tuval-Mashiach, & Zilber, 1998), elements of the story (Clandinin & Connelly, 2000; Clandinin & Rosiek, 2007; Czarniawska, 2004; Imabuchi & Ogata, 2012), narrative inquiry (DiCicco-Bloom & Crabtree, 2006), and structural analysis (Riessman, 1993, 2001, 2005) were adapted to develop the restorying framework. Figure 23.1 illustrates the multimethod approach.

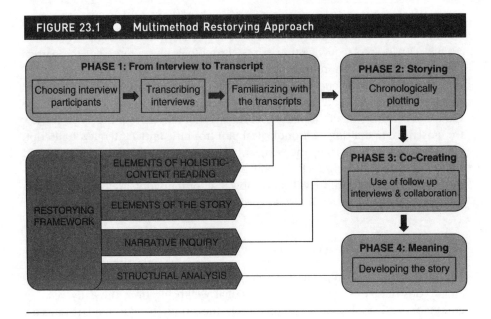

FIGURE 23.1 ● Multimethod Restorying Approach

Phase 1: From Interview to Transcript

Choosing Whom to Interview, Collecting Data, and Conducting the Sessions

The initial step in the progression deals with choosing the right participant to interview. In qualitative research, samples are selected with an intention/purpose to understand the central phenomenon. Because this study is about adolescents' experiences with a life skills education program, it was crucial to select a participant who had been involved in such a program.

The primary sources of data are a semi-structured face-to-face interview, follow-up interviews, and informal conversations through social media platforms such as Facebook instant messaging, Viber, and e-mails (Table 23.1 illustrates the number of engagements with the participant). All interviews were audio recorded and transcribed upon completion. The original interview guide can be found in Nasheeda (2020).

Transcribing Interviews

Each of the interviews was transcribed by the first author. The transcribed interviews were carefully checked by the first author against the audio recordings to ensure accurate accounts of the interviews. The transcriptions included the verbatim speech spoken during the interviews as well as verbal cues (smiles, nods),

TABLE 23.1 ● Type of Conversations and Time Spent With Shau Cocreating the Story		
Participant	**Types of Conversations**	**Time/Days Spent**
Shau (21-year-old female, living in Malé city, Maldives)	Semi-structured face-to-face interview	60 minutes, one interview
	Face-to-face follow-up interviews	45 minutes, two interviews
	Viber messages between January and April 2018	11 messages, around 15–20 minutes each conversation, 11 days
	E-mails	3 e-mails
	Facebook instant messaging	30 minutes, one day

extraneous words (e.g., "like"), and utterances ("hmms"). The transcripts were also sent to the participant to check for accuracy. This careful work is crucial to the success of a narrative analysis. Comprehensive transcriptions provide detailed features of interactions that are useful in negotiating story boundaries and relevance (Riessman, 2001).

Familiarizing With the Transcripts

The next step was to become familiar with the first transcript by reading and rereading it. Holistic content reading allows researchers to recognize and identify how the participants integrate events in the context of what has happened during the interview (Czarniawska, 2004). This process facilitates the researcher's ability to recognize and organize the repertoire of chronological events communicated in the participants' speech. Below is the first interview transcript from Shau (pseudonym), a 21-year-old describing her life skills education program experiences during adolescence.

[I: So you have recently completed your A' levels?]

Shau: Yes, I completed my [London, GCE] A/levels and then I worked for a bit and then I went to do my per-university level. So I am currently waiting for my admission process to get into med school.

[I: How long were you enrolled in life skills education program?]

Shau: I was exposed to Life Skills when I was in primary, secondary and in higher secondary and when I was doing my pre-university as well. So in primary it was, when I was in grade six, seven, then in secondary once I think when I was in grade 10 and then in higher secondary it was before beginning my grade 11.

[I: When you were in grade six, you'd be 11 years is it?]

Shau: I was 13 or 14, NO! 12, 13

[I: How would you describe your adolescence?]

Shau: I was (hesitated a bit) told I'm pretty big in size (gave an uncomfortable smile). So I actually faced a bit of bullying while I was in primary. That's actually when my parents started telling me, everything wouldn't go as I wish. I would have to face criticism, people wouldn't always say things that would please me. So when I was bullied, I was bullied for a bit but from the initial stage itself my parents were pretty supportive of everything I did, they said even if I am big and if I am different from the rest of the people, I can do anything I put my mind into. So, my adolescence from the very beginning from when I faced bulling, to when I got over it, when I (hesitated to search for the right word) figured out to tackle everything that I didn't like, I would describe as a whole as a very good period in my life. I was able to confide in my mother before I did something wrong, she would guide me to the right thing. I was actually able to learn things without doing big mistakes. Even when I made mistakes, I did do things wrong, I had my fair share of mistakes, but the thing is my mum and my dad, both, were always there for me. I know if I'm doing something wrong or even if I did anything or before attempting to do something I would ask for their opinion. So, it was a pretty good time. Even now, nothing has changed but, I would meet different people at different times but they keep on giving me advice on how to do things, how to deal with certain things, so overall I would say it's was very good. I mean, I don't have any regrets as such.

[I: How would you describe the life skills education program?]

Shau: Yeah, the life skills program, the set up was different for primary, secondary and higher secondary. So when I was in primary they would teach me how to be compassionate towards others, how to deal with certain things. I remember, when I was in grade 5, I kind of felt, so full of myself, I sometimes, neglected other peoples' perspectives.

So one day, my mum she came to pick me up and there is this specific girl I really didn't like in my class for some reason. She was like asking about something. I got really frustrated and annoyed with the fact and I was like "It's not your business why are you asking me this," (her voice raised a bit) mum was like, "That's not how you deal with something." *(pause)* From what mum had taught me and from what I learnt in the life skills program I was able to apply it there. After that I made a promise to myself. Not to say anything rude to anyone, even somebody said something rude to me I would always try to be the person who is kind, who is listening to the other person before passing on a judgement or a comment. So at that stage when I went to secondary, even if anybody said anything to me I would just brush it off, because, I know I'm better than that. That's their perspective. They are just putting something that they feel like they are going through on me. So that was something I learn when I went from primary to secondary. And when I was in secondary it was the same thing basically, everything thing (*the life skills program and the way it was conducted—mass session, same topics*) was pretty much the same. There was nothing new. But when I went to higher secondary they started telling us, "This is the age where you will get intimate with someone, where you would create bond of intimacy with someone, so you will find a companion or a life partner in someone, so when you are on that phase, the path to find someone you will meet different kind of people who will ask you different kind of questions." One thing, which is still fresh in my head is my LS program teacher. She was telling me that "In your age this is very common, sexting is very common," so even if I am on, lot of social platforms, err I was restricted to only family members and very close friends. My mum will know all my friends.

The transcript excerpt presents a chain of events consisting of three different time periods: primary, secondary, and higher secondary schooling. It is also evident the participant did not narrate incidents in a specific chronological order and most of the events described were related to life skills experiences in school. The flow of the interview consists of a recollection of thoughts and experiences in response to the interviewer's questions.

Phase 2: Drafting a Chronological Plot From the First Interview Transcript

Stories are comprised of chronological and non-chronological dimensions (Jovchelovitch & Bauer, 2000). The chronological dimension is about sequencing the story and the non-chronological dimension is about the elements of the story such as form, function, and phenomenon.

Sequencing Narratives

Sequencing narratives from transcripts is essential to storytelling. This process reveals significant events, major turning points, and the voice of the storyteller (Feldman, Sköldberg, Brown, & Horner, 2004). To aid the chronological plot development, the following questions were used to organize and sequence the material in the transcript:

1. Who are the main characters in this story?

2. What are the main events?

3. When and where did these events take place?

4. How has the participant positioned herself in the story?

The data were then chunked into events and reorganized by omitting the interview questions to understand the participant's narratological process to emplot their story. Emplotting a narrative text is a means to establish a sense-making mechanism on how events are connected and related; in other words, emplotting develops a narrative structure that makes sense of what happened then (Czarniawska, 2004). The following excerpts demonstrate how the transcripts were organized to understand the plot of the participant's stories. Many other excerpts were placed into these three major chronological categories.

> **Early years–primary (10, 11, 12, 13 years).** I remember, when I was in grade 5, I kind of felt, so full of myself, I sometimes, neglected other peoples' perspectives. So when I was in primary they would teach me how to be compassionate toward others, how to deal with certain things.

> **Adolescence (secondary years—14, 15, 16).** Even if anybody said anything to me I would just brush it off, because, I know I'm better than that. That is their perspective. When I was in secondary it was the same thing basically, everything thing was pretty same. There was nothing new.

> **Higher secondary years (17, 18, 19 years).** When I went to higher secondary they started telling us "This is the age where you will get intimate with someone, where you would create bond of intimacy with someone, so you will find a companion or a life partner in someone, so when you are on that phase, the path to find someone you will meet different kind of people who will ask you different kind of questions." One thing, which is still fresh in my head is my LS program teacher. She was telling me that "In your age this is very common, sexting is very common."

Once the participant's narrative had been chronologized, her transcript was read to see if the chronology made sense of what was represented. However, the many excerpts chunked together at this stage were still not a story. A story is an instantiation of a sequence of actions and experiences of an individual (Feldman, Sköldberg, Brown, & Horner, 2004) with significant elements such as conflicts, struggles, a protagonist, and a sequenced plot. Since the participant narrated her experiences in retrospect, our task was to retell her story out of the materials she had shared with us in a way that met the goals for our inquiry.

Story Dimensions

The narrative texts (from the first interview) were analyzed to identify story dimensions such as form, function, and phenomenon (see, Kurtz, 2014). Below is a critical story excerpt that was used as the form of the story. Form in a story consists of the communicative structure. The ideas and content the participant said she learned in her life skills education program became part of how she understood her life:

> I was bullied for my size, and for being different. I was told I was big in size. I was aware that people noticed me within a crowd as I was much taller than my peers. However, my parents were very supportive of me, they said that even though I am big and I am different from the rest of the people, I can do anything I put mind into. They also told me that everything wouldn't go as I wish. I would have to face criticism; people wouldn't always say things that would please me. I took this to heart.

With this illustrative excerpt in mind, we revised the chronological series of events and identified how the life skills education program was said to influence the experiences Shau had while she was in primary, secondary, and high school.

In the following excerpt, the core competencies of life skills education (WHO, 1997) provide values, thoughts, and emotions that enable the participant to cope with life challenges. The participant makes direct connections between her life skills education and her experience; these connections become part of her story. Hence, the excerpt helps in understanding the function of the story. The function of a story deals with connections between story characters and their plans, goals, and actions.

> I would have my setbacks and I would just wait till somebody comes and open up to me. Even if anybody said anything to me I would just brush it off, because, I know I'm better than that. That is their perspective. They are just putting something that they feel like they are going through on me. That was something I learnt when I went from primary to secondary, and when I was in secondary it was the same thing basically, everything thing was pretty much the same. There was nothing new.

Stories Within Stories

An important aspect of narrative is stories within stories. People live more than one story. Multiple stories happen within the same narrative as the person moves through time and society (Czarniawska, 2004; Kurtz, 2014; Singer & Blagov, 2004). Individuals tell stories within their narratives to give more emphasis to their experiences. The following excerpt uses a story within a story, as Shau described how a particular incident had an impact on her:

> One day, my mum came to pick me up from school, she noticed I was talking to a girl from my class from many encounters, she knew I didn't like her for some reason. She was asking, about something, I got really frustrated and annoyed with the fact that she was asking too many questions, and I

snapped at her, "It's not your business why are you asking me this." My mum was horrified, she told me, "That's not how you deal with something." I was 11 years old then.

Character Shifts

Narratives begin to make sense when character shifts are identified. An individual's character can change based on the situation and circumstances. The individual can take on two or more roles. They may understand themselves as a villain who creates disruptions in the narrative equilibrium while feeling victimized by their own actions and blaming themselves. The same individual can make amendments to these thoughts by seeking help or by modifying their behavior. These character shifts are the participant's internal conflicts. Here is an excerpt from a transcript that elaborates on the roles of the character and how these roles changed:

> I was really mad at myself, when I left. I was like … because my A level results didn't turn out as I would like it to be. I was pretty frustrated. I was like ok, now I have to do something with my life. I have to work hard. I was like so desperate, to like be employed at that point and earn money and be something on my own. So I was doing one permanent job and then a part time job. So I would be always occupied. I wouldn't have time to think about…useless things. I was like working. I would save all the money I earned. I would never go out to coffee so I would be like so determined.

The participant blamed herself for the events in her life. She also realized she had to take responsibility for her actions. This character shift helped in understanding how the participant was trying to resolve internal conflicts. Conflict resolutions are an important component of life skills education, and thus important issues for our analysis.

Although the function of the stories was identified, up to this point the narrative as a whole still made little sense. The next phase gives us strategies for addressing these gaps.

Phase 3: Follow-ups and Co-creating

The meanings produced by narratives are provisional. There are always gaps and ellipses in the account that might be explored. One way to deepen understanding and create links between events is to conduct follow-up interviews to confirm, clarify, and elaborate on the information obtained from the earlier interviews (Bolderston, 2012). In our study, follow-up interviewing was used for the purpose of collaboratively cocreating the chronological plot into a story. Once the transcript was chronologically plotted, it was sent to the participant to check the story plot to confirm whether the story sequence made sense. Several questions were asked, for instance: (a) Is this you? (b) Do you see yourself? These questions helped to clarify if the voice of the participant was still present in the chronological plot.

Many parts of the transcript presented us with puzzles that we tried to understand. In these cases our questions were more elaborate. We might send or ask follow-up questions for clarification on gaps in the story, such as examples of silences and contradictions. We probed for the meanings of words and phrases within the narratives. We also attempted to explore the surface meanings that were implied but not stated directly. For example, we asked questions such as, "What is the meaning of 'yes, yeah'?" or "Does the word 'like' mean anything different to you?" (the word "like" was used often in the conversation).

Several back-and-forth interactions took place during the co-construction process. Instant message via Viber and Facebook were useful in clarification as the story was unfolding. Some of the words the participant used were collaboratively examined to determine if they had embedded meaning within the narrative. Collaborating and co-creating the story with the participant facilitated giving meaning to the chronological plot.

At the conclusion of this phase, we had coconstructed a rich transcript by integrating the initial interview and the follow-ups for analysis along with a set of excerpts in the chronological plot. At this point, the transcripts were trimmed to the narratives that evolved around the participant's life skills education program experience. There were still many gaps and puzzles, but we had narrowed the range of possible meanings from the original interview (Feldman, Sköldberg, Brown, & Horner, 2004) and had confirmed or disconfirmed some of our initial hunches.

Phase 4: Making Meaning

In this final phase of crafting the story, it was crucial to analyze all the transcripts, including the follow-up interviews, Viber messages, emails, and instant messages to know how the chunks of narratives fit into the broader context. The transcribed narration was examined from various perspectives to understand how the participant spoke about herself. We would regularly listen to the original interviews to make sense of the written words in the transcript and compare the chronological plot to get a sense of how the story was unfolding.

Careful listening and reading are critical to developing the story. During storytelling, individuals may change their use of pronouns and begin talking in first, second, or third person. These changes frequently signal critical turns of events within the story (Kurtz, 2014).

To understand the structure of the narrative compositions, the transcripts were analyzed for person shifts used in the transcript. Table 23.2 illustrates examples of narrative compositions from the transcript:

TABLE 23.2 ● Examples of Narrative Composition	
Transcript	**Narrative Composition and What It Represents**
they are just putting something, that **they feel like they are going through on me**. so … that was something I learn when I went from primary to secondary	**Evaluation:** *personal touch to the lived experiences.*
She was telling me that **"in your age this is very common, sexting is very common"** so even if I am on, lot of social platforms, err I was restricted to only family members and very close friends. My mum will know all my friends. Even my dad.	**Direct speech:** *offers more realness to the narratives.*
when I went to higher secondary **they** started like .. telling us this is the age **where you** will get intimate with someone, where you would create bond of intimacy with someone…	**Shifting pronoun:** *indication of important narrative events that the participant wants to retell.*
She is like in the school post and **she would be a bit too full** of herself."	**Talking about the self but in third person:** *representing the view of someone else*
I always believe that my ideas cannot be forced from somebody else so, I would always tell "ok, why is he doing this amount of work, why am in doing a huge amount of work here." **I didn't believe in stereotypes—a girl should be this, a boy should do that.**	**Opinions/values/biases/judgments:** *represents the participant's awareness of the self and identity.*

The different narrative compositions in the above table facilitated in understanding the participant and how she constructed her life skills education program experiences.

Many forms of analysis might be performed at this stage. Researchers might use digital storytelling (Cunsolo Willox, Harper, & Edge, 2013; Lang, Laing, Moules, & Estefan, 2019), researcher's metaphors (Bell, 2003), and poetry (Furman, 2007; Shenfield & Prendergast, Chapter 20). All these analyses might then be opportunities for further co-construction and story development. In the case of Shau, we developed a chronology, a person shift analysis and, most importantly, a co-constructed transcript along with a rich sense of Shau's experience. The story we developed from this work exists in these texts and in the minds of the research team. Eventually, the story becomes part of our writings about life skills education (Nasheeda, Abdullah, Krauss, & Ahmed, 2019). As Feldman, Sköldberg, Brown, & Horner (2004) wrote, no story can represent the totality of a person's experience. Our work allowed us to deepen our understanding of how life skills education shaped Shau's life. Figure 23.2 illustrates an excerpt of the story that was cocreated from Shau's narratives.

FIGURE 23.2 ● An Excerpt of the Story

THE TRANSIT

Shau was in grade 6 when her school conducted life skills education program. Since then she has been in the life skills education program from secondary to higher secondary school. Shau was able to recall some components of life skills education program and her experiences of growing up. Shau has a very confident personality.

Growing up

I was 10 years old, when my parents moved to our own apartment. ... Having lived in an extended family for ten years, I knew my life just began.

Primary School – My Whole Life

My primary years was in Giyasuddin School. ... I liked school. I was very popular in school, ...so even though I was being bullied for being big in size, it didn't matter, at least I thought it didn't matter. Whenever something bothered me I always confide in my mum. She was my biggest supporter. My parents always told me that everything wouldn't go as I wish. I have to face criticism. People wouldn't always say things that would please me. So I refused to become a victim to these acts. I put all my energy into my studies. In a way I guess, I was so full of myself. I sometimes neglect other people's perspectives. I remember, one day my mum came to pick me up from school. I was talking to a girl in my class, whom I didn't really like. She was asking me too many questions and I got frustrated and annoyed and I snapped at her, "It's none of your business..." My mum was horrified. She was like, " That's not how you deal with something." On that day, I made a promise to myself never to be rude to anyone, even if someone is rude to me.

Conclusion

In the example presented we wove a narrative from the transcripts by following a phased progression. Individual transcripts were created and then excerpts from the data were reorganized into a chronological sequence to identify the time and place of critical events. This sequence led to the development of a more coherent story that was shared with the participant and used to coconstruct revisions to the transcript and the chronology. This revised transcript became the focus of the analysis. The story that we created was evident in the transcript, the analytic products, and in the minds of the participant and the research team.

Our work implies that while crafting a story may be time-consuming and daunting, it is a rewarding process to deeply engage with the participant. The process of crafting stories from interviews expanded our understanding of the structure and function of stories. A future direction for our research team is in-depth explorations of how story structures and functions are connected with participants' descriptions of their feelings, thoughts, and behaviors.

Supplemental Readings

Boyd, R. L., Blackburn, K. G., & Pennebaker, J. W. (2020). The narrative arc: Revealing core narrative structures through text analysis. *Science Advances, 6*(32). https://doi.org/10.1126/sciadv.aba2196

Ford, E. (2020). Tell me your story: Narrative inquiry in LIS research. *College & Research Libraries, 81*(2), 235. https://doi.org/10.5860/crl.81.2.235

Jeppesen, J. (2016). From interview to transcript to story: Elucidating the construction of journalistic narrative as qualitative research. *The Qualitative Report, 21*(9), 1636–1650. https://nsuworks.nova.edu/tqr/vol21/iss9/5

Reflection and Activities

1. Try listening to an audio of an interview and read along the transcript and identify how participants integrate events in the narratives.

2. Identify the narrative process such as language, stories within stories, and narrative compositions for a meaningful interpretation from an interview transcript.

3. Look over a piece of narrative data and create a set of follow-up questions that will help you understand and create the story. To whom might you ask these questions and on what platforms might you use to communicate? How would you integrate these data into your analysis?

References

Ahmed, A., & Rogers, M. (2017). Polly's story: Using structural narrative analysis to understand a trans migration journey. *Qualitative Social Work, 16*(2), 224–239. https://doi.org/10.1177/1473325016664573

Anderson, C., & Kirkpatrick, S. (2015). Narrative interviewing. *International Journal of Clinical Pharamacy,* February 2016. https://doi.org/10.1007/s11096-015-0222-0

Bell, A. (2003). A narrative approach to research. *Canadian Journal of Environmental Education, 8*(Spring), 95–110. https://cjee.lakeheadu.ca/article/view/240

Bolderston, A. (2012). Conducting a research interview. *Journal of Medical Imaging and Radiation Sciences, 43*(1), 66–76. https://doi.org/10.1016/j.jmir.2011.12.002

Breheny, M., & Stephens, C. (2015). Approaches to narrative analysis: Using personal, dialogical and social stories to promote peace. In D. Bretherton & S. Law (Eds.), *Peace psychology book series. Methodologies in peace psychology: Peace research by peaceful means* (Vol. 26, Issue September, pp. 275–291). Springer International Publishing. https://doi.org/10.1007/978-3-319-18395-4_14

Clandinin, D. J., & Connelly, F. M. (2000). *Narrative inquiry: Experience and story in qualitative research.* Jossey-Bass.

Clandinin, D. J., & Rosiek, J. (2007). Mapping a landscape of narrative inquiry: Borderland spaces and tensions. In D. J. Clandinin (Ed.), *Handbook of narrative inquiry: Mapping a methodology* (Issue 2001, pp. 37–75). SAGE. https://doi.org/10.4135/9781452226552.n2

Connelly, F. M., & Clandinin, D. J. (1990). Stories of experience and narrative inquiry. *Educational Researcher, 19*(5), 2–14. https://doi.org/10.2307/1176100

Cortazzi, M. (1994). State of the art article: Narrative analysis. *Language Teaching, 27*(3), 157. https://doi.org/10.1017/S0261444800007801

Creswell, J. W., & Poth, C. N. (2018). *Qualitative inquiry and research design: Choosing among five approaches.* SAGE.

Cunsolo Willox, A., Harper, S. L., & Edge, V. L. (2013). Storytelling in a digital age: Digital storytelling as an emerging narrative method for preserving and promoting indigenous oral wisdom. *Qualitative Research, 13*(2), 127–147. https://doi.org/10.1177/1468794112446105

Czarniawska, B. (2004). *Narratives in social science research: Introducing qualitative methods.* SAGE.

DiCicco-Bloom, B., & Crabtree, B. F. (2006). The qualitative research interview. *Medical Education, 40*(4), 314–321. https://doi.org/10.1111/j.1365-2929.2006.02418.x

Feldman, M. S., Sköldberg, K., Brown, R. N., & Horner, D. (2004). Making sense of stories: A rhetorical approach to narrative analysis. *Journal of Public Administration Research and Theory, 14*(2), 147–170. https://doi.org/10.1093/jopart/muh010

Furman, R. (2007). Poetry and narrative as qualitative data: Explorations into existential theory. *Indo-Pacific Journal of Phenomenology, 7*(1), 1–9. https://doi.org/10.1080/20797222.2007.11433939

Hyvärinen, M. (2008). Analyzing narratives and story-telling. In P. Alasuutari, L. Bickman, & J. Brannen (Eds.), *The Sage handbook of social research methods* (Vol. First, pp. 447–460). SAGE. https://dx.doi.org/10.4135/9781446212165.n26

Imabuchi, S., & Ogata, T. (2012). A story generation system based on propp theory: As a mechanism in an integrated narrative generation system. In H. Isahara & K. Kanzaki (Eds.), *Advances in natural language processing: 8th international conference on NLP, JapTAL 2012* (pp. 312–313). Springer.

Jeppesen, J. (2016). From interview to transcript to story: Elucidating the construction of journalistic narrative as qualitative research. *The Qualitative Report, 21*(9), 1636–1650. https://nsuworks.nova.edu/tqr/vol21/iss9/5

Jovchelovitch, S., & Bauer, M. W. (2000). Narrative interviewing. In M. Bauer & G. Gaskell (Eds.), *Qualitative researching with text, image and sound: A practical handbook.* SAGE. https://doi.org/10.1300/J021v28n01

Kurtz, C. F. (2014). *Working with stories in your community or organization: Participatory narrative inquiry* (3rd ed.). Kurtz-Fernhout Publishing. http://www.workingwithstories.org/

Labov, W., & Waletzky, J. (1997). Narrative analysis: Oral versions of personal experience. *Journal of Narrative and Life History, 7*(1–4), 3–38. https://doi.org/10.1075/jnlh.7.1-4.02nar

Lang, M., Laing, C., Moules, N., & Estefan, A. (2019). Words, camera, music, action: A methodology of digital storytelling in a health care setting. *International Journal of Qualitative Methods, 18*, 1–10. https://doi.org/10.1177/1609406919863241

Lieblich, A., Tuval-Mashiach, R., & Zilber, T. (1998). *Narrative research: Reading, analysis, and interpretation.* SAGE.

McCormack, C. (2000). From interview transcript to interpretive story: Part 1- viewing the transcript through multiple lenses. *Field Methods, 12*(4), 282–297. https://doi.org/10.1177/1525822X0001200402

Nasheeda, A. (2008). Life skills education for young people: Coping with challenges. *Counselling, Psychotherapy and Health, 4*(1), 19–25.

Nasheeda, A. (2020). *Exploring social construction experiences through life skills education program during adolescence in Maldives.* University Putra Malaysia.

Nasheeda, A., Abdullah, H. B., Krauss, S. E., & Ahmed, N. B. (2019). Transforming transcripts into stories: A multimethod approach to narrative analysis. *International Journal of Qualitative Methods, 18*, 1–9. https://doi.org/10.1177/1609406919856797

Ollerenshaw, J. A., & Creswell, J. W. (2002). Narrative research: A comparison of two restorying data analysis approaches. *Qualitative Inquiry, 8*(3), 329–347. https://doi.org/10.1177/10778004008003008

Polkinghorne, D. E. (1985). Narrative knowing and the practicing psychologist. *Paper presented at the annual convention of the American Psychological Association, August 23*, Los Angeles, CA. https://doi.org/10.1017/CBO9781107415324.004

Riessman, C. K. (1993). *Narrative analysis.* SAGE.

Riessman, C. K. (2001). Analysis of personal narratives. In J. F. Gubrium & J. A. Holstein (Eds.), *Handbook of interview research: Context and method* (pp. 695–710). Sage Publications. https://dx.doi.org/10.4135/9781412973588

Riessman, C. K. (2005). *Narrative analysis: Narrative, memory and everyday life.* University of Huddersfield.

Shenfield, R., & Prendergast, M. (2022). What makes an effective teacher? Revealing good teaching practice through interview poetic transcription. In C. Vanover, P. Mihas, & J. Saldaña (Eds.), *Analyzing and interpreting qualitative research: After the interview.* SAGE.

Singer, J. A., & Blagov, P. (2004). The integrative function of narrative processing: Autobiographical memory, self-defining memories, and the life story of identity. In D. Beike, J. Lampinen, & D. Behrend (Eds.), *The self and memory* (pp. 117–138). The Psychology Press. https://doi.org/10.4324/9780203337974

WHO. (1997). *Life skills education for children and adolescents in schools.* WHO/MNH/PSF/93.7A.Rev.2.

Writing for a Broad Audience: Concept Papers, Blogs, and OpEds

Jessica Smartt Gullion

Abstract

While academics want to publish peer-reviewed journal articles, we know those are not necessarily the best way to get information back to communities who might benefit from our research. Writing for the general public is a different skill than writing for our fellow academics. In this chapter, I provide tips and techniques for how to get your writing to a broader audience.

Keywords: Writing; concept papers; blogs; editorials

Though academics need to write for scholarly outlets, the general public has little access to those outlets (and, let's be honest, has little interest in reading scholarly articles). This is unfortunate because qualitative researchers often have insights and recommendations that would be directly beneficial to the public. How sad if you think about it—we pour our souls into creating knowledge that an elite handful of people can access, and that very few do access.

I looked at some of the statistics about the readership of my own work to give you an example of what I mean. According to ResearchGate, one of my favorite articles, "The Cheerleader: A feminist mom, her pre-teen daughter, and the spaces for girls in American football" (2016), which was published in a prestigious peer-reviewed journal, has been downloaded 10 times from ResearchGate, and cited by someone else once. Over on the journal's webpage, I can see it was accessed there

207 times, so that's a little more encouraging. Meanwhile, one of my books, *Writing Ethnography*, has been downloaded from libraries more than 12,000 times. An opinion piece that I wrote about guns on college campuses in *Newsweek* got hundreds of thousands of reads.

I will talk more about these projects, along with some others, as we move through the content below. Together, we will explore how to write the findings of your qualitative research for venues the general public actually reads, such as concept papers, blogs, opinion pieces, and editorials.

Literature Review: Going Public

We will begin where most scholarly publication begins, with the literature review. When we write for an academic audience, it's important for us to connect our work with the larger academic conversation on whatever issue we are writing about. There are scholarly lineages that a learned person should be aware of and that should be reflected in their writing.

Here's the thing with writing for the general public: *no one cares*. Sorry, but it's true. General audiences want you to get to the point. Of course, you will want to reference current events or link to data as appropriate, but the vast majority of people won't care how your research interconnects with Deleuze's; and your Marxist perspective could be construed as socialist, which as we know from Fox News, is a big no-no. They are looking for information that they can use themselves, or articles they find entertaining or interesting. They aren't interested in spending time reading a lot of gobbledygook (and let's be honest, how many of us don't read boring articles in detail?).

Writing for General Audiences

As we think about different places to publish our qualitative work outside of peer-reviewed journals, the most important consideration is the audience we hope to reach. Your writing should change for different audiences.

Let's look first at how to write for a general audience. Writing for a general audience is a skill we can develop, just like we developed the skill of writing for other academics.

In the United States, the average American reads at about a sixth-grade level. If you want a general audience to read your work, you've got to write it at this level. Many word processing programs can tell you the grade level of your writing (do this through the tools), or you can find free readability analyzers online. I ran this chapter through one and found that it's written between a ninth and tenth grade level.

Let's do this math: If the average American adult reads at a sixth grade level, then there are lots of adults who would find this chapter too difficult to comprehend.

One of the big things that will throw off your readability is jargon. In academic writing, we use keywords that signal our writing is in conversation with important ideas in our fields. For example, in a qualitative research book such as this one, I can use words like *epistemology*, *triangulation*, and even *qualitative*, and assume that the reader understands what I mean by those words. As fellow qualitative scholars, you and I probably share similar understandings of what is involved when we encounter these terms. I don't need to explain them to you. But I don't expect my mom or my next-door neighbor to understand these terms in the same way that you and I do. Nothing against my mom or my neighbors, they are intelligent people, but they don't have the same background as we do. So, when I'm writing for them, it's important that I get rid of all that jargon. If I absolutely have to use it, then I need to be sure I explain what I mean.

Creative Nonfiction

Of course, there is more to writing for the general public than simply writing at the correct grade level. I've long been an advocate of creative nonfiction (Gullion, 2016). This involves using storytelling techniques when writing the results of our qualitative research.

Let's face it, a lot of academic writing is boring. And while fellow academics will slog through boring writing, the general public won't. If you want to cultivate a broad audience, you need to make your writing engaging. You need to be a good storyteller.

Hart (2011) writes that a good story has relatable characters who want something and overcome obstacles to get it. A good story evokes sensory details (images, sounds, sensations) and draws on our emotions. A good story also follows a story arc or plotline. It unfolds as we read, and we want to keep reading to find out what happens.

Lucky for us, qualitative research gives us all these elements. This is a passage from an ethnography I conducted on natural gas development (i.e., fracking) in North Texas (Gullion, 2015). As you read, you can see how I made use of the elements of creative nonfiction:

> I sit in a large lecture hall struggling out of my coat when the Texas Railroad Commissioner approaches me. He is working the crowd. He sticks out his hand to shake mine, which is tangled in my sleeve. I try to shake hands, but the movement is awkward, and part of my bra flashes from the neck of my shirt. He ignores my distress (if he even noticed it) and continues along the audience row. The entire exchange exemplified what activists tell me about their interactions with his agency. Oblivious to my personal struggle, this man is here to get a job done. (p. 135)

The information (or data) for this passage came out of my field notes. I use sensory and emotional details (I'm in a large lecture hall, I am struggling, I am in distress). The plight is relatable (hello, I'm totally having a clothing malfunction). There's a main character (me) and an antagonist (the Railroad Commissioner), and a power differential between us. The last sentence of the paragraph begs the question of what will happen next; that should keep the reader reading to find out the answer.

As you write for a broad audience, think about how to best communicate with them. What is their motivation for reading your work? Are they reading you work for entertainment? Are they looking for guidance on policy decisions? Do they want practical tips about something? Consider why they would be interested in what you have to say, and what will entice them to read to the end. Just as we were trained in graduate school to write for academic audiences, we need to train ourselves to write for the general public.

Concept Papers

Now let's discuss writing Concept papers. These are informative briefs given to policy makers to guide them in decision-making.

For the last few years, I've been collecting ethnographic data on cheerleading in the United States. Cheerleading has a nebulous distinction—it's not officially considered a sport by most schools, yet cheerleading is very physical and is known for increasingly complex gymnastics stunts. Because it is considered an "activity" instead of a sport, school-based cheerleading does not require the specialized safety equipment and regulation that other sports are subjected to.

There are two types of cheerleading in the United States—competitive and football. Competitive cheer organizations (such as the National Cheerleaders Association and the American Cheerleaders Association) have safety standards and regulations that teams must comply with. Athletes perform on a spring floor similar to those used by gymnasts. In contrast, football cheerleaders perform on the sidelines during football games, and perform stunts and tumbling on the school's track (which is often made of blacktop, although they can range from a rubberized surface to gravel, depending on the school district). There are much fewer safety regulations for football cheerleaders relative to competitive cheerleaders.

Cheerleading is the number one cause of sports-related catastrophic injury to girls (Mueller, Kucera, & Cox, 2013). During my fieldwork, I witnessed cheerleaders receive concussions, fractures, sprains, strains, bruising, and other minor injuries. One of the findings of this work is that the nebulous question of sport versus activity may be leading to increased injury as football cheerleading incorporates more of the stunts used in competitive cheer.

While peer-reviewed journal articles exist on this subject, let's get real: The local school board official is probably not going to conduct a literature review on cheerleading before making policy decisions related to this issue. One service that academics can provide to the community is to do that work for them and translate that literature into language and sound bites that are easy to read and understand. This then allows them to make a better-informed decision. We can do this by writing a concept paper.

Generally speaking, this audience wants a brief summary of information and, more importantly, to know *why this issue is important to them*. By brief, I mean give them a bulleted list of points when possible. Then include support materials as appendices (or as links to a website). This way readers can access the background information if they want or need to, but the key points are readily available to them.

If I were writing a concept paper about cheerleading, say to give to a school board, there are some facts I would want to highlight. Even though we are qualitative researchers, some numbers would be helpful for school board officials to know. In addition to telling them that cheer is the leading cause of catastrophic (i.e., life-threatening) injury to female athletes, I could include data about injuries at schools within their district. This makes the broader data more concrete. I would want them to understand that when discussing injuries, we are talking about children in their district, and to make the connection that their policy changes could prevent those injuries. I could also provide information from national organizations about what we should be doing at a local level, and the cost ramifications (because they will want to know how much this will cost).

I am a PhD researcher who has been studying cheerleading for several years. It's important that I make sure this information is on the page—it lets them know that I am a credible expert on this subject.

I would also include photos of local cheerleaders doing stunts on hard surfaces, so they can clearly see what I am writing about. Finally, I would use my qualitative skills to have two or three quotes from cheerleaders that highlighted this issue. A quote from a parent might be good as well. In total, the concept paper would only be a page or two long, although I can use links to connect the information I provide to as many support documents as I want. The paper should be visually interesting, eye-catching, with enough information to get and hold their attention, yet not tedious to read.

This type of writing is meant to be persuasive; you are advocating for a particular social change. Keep in mind that many policy makers are elected officials. They are responsible to their constituents, and to be reelected they need to show positive outcomes of their work. I would leverage this into the cheerleading argument by noting how many students are involved in cheerleading annually at each school. I would also include something about the role of cheerleaders in creating school spirit and their visibility at football games. I might also throw in something that compares the benefits the football players get with the costs to the cheerleaders. That juxtaposition shows a pretty clear gender disparity (since most football players are boys and most cheerleaders are girls), and I will ask them to address that.

In doing so, I am not only asking them to do something for the parents of cheerleaders (who might or might not vote for them in the next election), but to show their support for gender equality across the school district (now we're talking about a whole lot more voters).

Opinions/Editorials

While concept papers are a means of reaching out to elected officials, it is also important for researchers to participate in publication platforms developed by and for nonscholars. Opinion pieces and editorials (which I'm going to shorten to OpEd) have a basic structure. The first sentence of an OpEd is called the lede. The lede should catch people's attention and make them want to read further. This is followed by main points with supporting evidence. Instead of including citations, insert hyperlinks into your piece. For print media, briefly explain the source (i.e., according to...). For online writing, hyperlinks have the dual role of bringing readers back to your piece from other websites that you have linked, so including a lot of links can raise your number of readers.

After your evidence, include a "to be sure." This is something I learned from the OpEd Project (www.theopedproject.org) and I now incorporate in all my writing. The "to be sure" is a way to cut off your detractors. It's how you signal that you already know what their counterargument to your argument will be, and it allows you to address it. For this chapter, a "to be sure" might look like this:

> To be sure, academics have to write for journals. Publish or perish is real, and we have to publish in peer-reviewed venues for tenure and promotion. However, writing for a broader audience gets our work into the hands of people who can use it to improve their daily lives.

Including the "to be sure" makes it more difficult for detractors to tear your piece apart. You acknowledge that you've already considered (and dismissed) their objections.

Conclude your OpEd by telling the reader what you want them to do after reading your post. This can be anything from a call to arms or, more subtly, giving them a takeaway to consider.

Example of an OpEd

Below is an OpEd I wrote that went viral. It first appeared in *The Conversation*, and was then picked up by *Newsweek* and *The Houston Chronicle*. Each block in the table is a new paragraph. To the right, I have commentary about the structure of the piece so that you can see how it is organized (Table 24.1).

There are all sorts of places for you to publish OpEds. Of course, newspapers publish them, but so do lots of different websites. Like writing for a journal, you

TABLE 24.1 ● OpEd Analysis[a]	
Original Text	**Analysis**
Will guns on campus lead to grade inflation?[a]	The editor wrote this title
Jessica Smartt Gullion Assistant Professor of Sociology, Texas Woman's University	My academic title justifies my credentials, and why I am the right person to write this piece.
Texas college professors may soon face a dilemma between upholding professional ethics and protecting their lives.	This is the lede.
On Thursday, December 10, a task force at the University of Texas at Austin *recommended* restricting guns in residence halls, at sporting events and in certain laboratories, but allowed them in classrooms.	This sentence ties the piece to what was happening in the news, the "hook."
The 19-member task force was set up following a *"Campus Carry" law* passed by the state in Spring 2015. The law, which will come into effect on August 1, 2016, will allow people with handgun licenses to carry concealed firearms on college campuses.	Instead of citations, use hyperlinks to show the reader where you got information.
With the recommendation to allow firearms in classrooms, a question coming up for many academics is whether they would be forced to give As to undeserving students, just so they can avoid being shot.	This is the crux of the argument.
This is not as far fetched as it sounds. In my five years as a college professor, I have had experience with a number of emotionally distressed students who resort to intimidation when they receive a lesser grade than what they feel they deserve.	Here the argument begins to be backed up with data.
Threats on campus	The editor added the sub-headers.
Here is an example of one such threatening experience: one evening in a graduate course, after I handed back students' papers, a young woman stood up and pointed at me. "This is unacceptable!" she screamed as her body shook in rage.	This is the first point in support of the main argument: students get upset and really do threaten or harm faculty.
She moved toward the front of the class waving her paper in my face and screamed again, "unacceptable!" After a heated exchange, she left the room, and stood outside the door sobbing.	
All this was over receiving a B on a completely low-stakes assignment.	

Table 24.1 *(Continued)*

Original Text	Analysis
What followed was even more startling. The following week, the student brought along a muscle-bound man to class. He watched me through the doorway window for the entire three hours of the class, with his arms folded across his chest.	
And if this wasn't enough, the young woman's classmates avoided me on campus because, they said, they were afraid of getting caught in the crossfire should she decide to shoot me.	
After that, every time she turned in a paper I cringed and prayed that it was good so that I wouldn't have to give her anything less than an A.	
Learning from this experience, now I give papers back only at the end of the class or just "forget" to bring them with me.	
I was lucky that the student didn't have a gun in my classroom. Other professors have not been so lucky.	
In 2014 a student at Purdue *shot his instructor* in front of a classroom of students. In another *incident* in 2009, a student at Northern Virginia Community College tried to *shoot* his math professor on campus. And, in 2000, a graduate student at the University of Arkansas *shot his English professor*.	Beyond my personal example, here are some examples of students shooting their professors.
In each of these states, carrying handguns on campus was illegal at the time of the shooting, although a *bill was introduced in Arkansas* earlier this year to allow students to carry guns.	
Grade inflation	
Despite these and other shootings, a new *trend* has emerged across the US that supports guns on college campuses.	This is a second set of evidence about this issue.
Nine states allow firearms onto college campuses and *11 states* are now considering similar legislation.	I use some quantitative data to give context
We know that some students will carry guns whether it is legal or not. *One study found* that close to 5% of undergraduates had a gun on campus and that almost 2% had been threatened with a firearm while at school.	

Table 24.1 *(Continued)*

Original Text	Analysis
Allowing students to carry weapons to class strips off a layer of safety. Students are often emotional and can be volatile when it comes to their GPAs.	
Who would want to give a student a low grade and then get shot for it?	
Many majors are highly competitive and require certain GPAs for admission. Students on scholarships and other forms of financial aid must maintain high grades to keep their funding. It's no surprise that some might students resort to any means necessary to keep up their GPAs.	And here we have a third set of evidence.
An international student once cried in my office and begged me to change his F to an A, as without it, his country would no longer pay for him to be in the US. I didn't. He harassed me by posting threatening messages on Facebook.	
So, the question is, will we soon see a new sort of grade inflation, with students earning a 4.0 GPA with their firepower rather than brain power? And if so, what sort of future citizenry will we be building on our campuses?	While this is not a specific call to action, it is a call to consider the ethical ramifications of the policy.

ªThe original article may be found at https://www.newsweek.com/will-guns-campus-lead-grade-inflation-327047.

will send a query to the editor about your OpEd. Keep in mind that news moves fast; much faster than journals.

Don't query an editor until you are ready to go. They will probably want your piece that day. Once you submitted your query, be on standby. You may be asked to do some immediate editing if it is accepted. Like journal publishing, do not query more than one editor at a time. That being said, if you haven't heard anything in a day or two, move on to another editor.

Keep your pitch brief—three or four sentences are enough. Tell the editor why this article is important, why it is important right now, and why you are the right person to write this article. Paste your completed article below your signature line.

Editors look for some sort of hook to your piece. This shows why your work is relevant to their readers. Try to connect your work to something else that is happening in the news or in pop culture. In the case of my OpEd on campus carry, university officials in Texas were in the middle of trying to address new legislation—that had just been in the news. Even though my idea (guns and grades make uncomfortable bedfellows) could have been offered at any time, the connection with a recent news event made it more relevant to readers. If I were writing an OpEd about the cheerleading issue I mentioned above, I would link it to the opening of football season. I would probably write something like, "As legions of young men begin a new season of tossing around a football, young women are on the sidelines tossing each other into their air..." and continue into my safety argument. The same piece would be less relevant to readers in the spring, when football is not in season.

Blogs

Writing a blog is a good way to highlight your academic work for your peers who may not have come across it yet. In other words, it's good advertising for you and your ideas.

When writing a blog, we tend to write more informally to our colleagues and others who are interested in the subject we're writing about. Just as the other types of writing I've highlighted in this chapter, you need to think about your intended audience and write to them.

One of the great things about writing a blog is that you do not have to go through an editor or through peer review to get your words out into the world. There are many different platforms for writing a blog, and many of them are free. Of course, this also means that you need to edit your work yourself—you can publish sloppy writing yourself just as easily as you can publish polished writing.

A blog is also a useful tool if you think you might like to write a book with a trade press. Trade publishers often want to know that you have an audience before they decide to publish your book. There is a lot of interest in blog-to-book publishing because they know that many of your blog followers will purchase your book—publishers know they can make money off this project. Obviously, the more followers your blog has, the more enticing your work is to publishers.

If you plan on writing a blog, it's important that you update it regularly. People will stop coming to your site if they aren't getting new content. Many bloggers put up new posts once a week, if not more often. This is also important for search engines and social media—the more often you post, the higher up you will be in searches and news feeds. Keep this in mind if you are thinking about writing a blog (the same goes with a podcast or videocast). Make sure you can keep up with providing new content.

As with writing a concept paper, you should make use of images in your blogs. Images catch people's attention. Use them. Think about the design and layout of your blog. You want it to be eye-catching without being overcrowded. Make use of white space as a design element. It can be helpful to look at how the blogs you enjoy are designed, or to work with a web designer to help you make your blog as professional as you would like it.

You can also use many, if not all, of the techniques I discussed for writing an opinion piece. One of the nice things about blogs is that we can use them to communicate with small academic communities. If you own the blog, you can invite people to write an entry for you, or conduct an interview with them (and don't forget you can embed your own videos or audio files in your blogs).

With this thought we should also talk about professional and project webpages. Many academics maintain a webpage with their CV, links to where to buy their books, and information about speaking engagements. If you are working as a member of a lab or team, you can have a website dedicated to that organization. Have members of your research team contribute. You can also invite other writers and people working within the field of study to write guest posts—which brings us back to networking.

This gives you a fantastic platform for increased visibility. You can link up your blog with the various social media and repositories that you use. Journals and presses typically won't market our work; it's up to us to get our ideas into the hands of people who can use them.

The Dark Side of Publishing for a General Audience; or, How I Pissed off the NRA

I would be remiss if I didn't extend a caveat to publishing for the general public. When we write for academic outlets, we expect a certain level of decorum. Though someone may disagree with what we write, those disagreements rarely turn into death threats (although mistakes have probably been made). Publishing for the public, however, opens you up to trolls.

The scourge of public venues, trolls have the potential to cause you a lot of havoc. I speak from personal experience.

Let's go back to my example about campus carry. As I said that piece went viral. The National Rifle Association saw it and posted a rebuttal on their website, along with a link to my university website. Many NRA chapters reposted the NRA rebuttal along with their own commentary on their websites.

The first rule of publishing online is: Don't read the comments on your writing. While you might think the comments would be a good way to interact with people, I suggest you avoid them. If you are the type of faculty member to be upset about a student evaluation of your teaching, then you really don't want to go anywhere near the comments about your public writing. The comments can be vicious. Once you publish a piece, back away from it.

Some people will use the comment section to harass writers. It's like a game to them to get arguments going, and those arguments have the potential to get pretty nasty. My OpEd got a lot of comments. While many were positive, there were a lot of haters as well.

Harassment doesn't stop at the comments, however. Following the flurry of excitement over my OpEd, I received death threats on all my social media accounts, via email, snail mail, and voicemail. I also received lots of "I will rape you at gunpoint" threats (which only solidified my feelings about guns on campus). In addition, trolls contacted my chair, dean, provost, chancellor, and elected officials demanding my termination.

I wish I had been more prepared for this onslaught, which is why I am telling you about it now. I'd be lying if I said it didn't bother me. I temporarily turned off my social media accounts. I have changed the settings now so that I approve comments whenever possible before they are made public. I also had a neutral person review my emails and phone messages and delete threats. I reported all this to both the administration and the campus police, who worked to ensure my safety.

If you are going to publish something that might be controversial, have a plan in place for how you will handle the fallout. And note that the fallout may be good—along with the trouble I had, I also heard from a lot of faculty who were as concerned as I was about the matter, and I got to be on National Public Radio (Fox News also wanted to interview me, but I declined their offer). Going viral can definitely boost your visibility, and you can move from the handful of readers of journal articles to hundreds of thousands (if not more) of readers. You can get your message out into the public; just be aware that not everyone will be receptive to your message.

Conclusion

We know that most journal articles have a limited readership. While scholars debate just how limited this is (see Jago, 2018), given that much academic writing is kept behind the firewalls of journal and library websites, and that so much of the writing is dense (often impenetrable) and written for specific audiences, this should not surprise anyone.

As qualitative researchers, we gather plenty of information to help us write for the general public. Once we fine-tune that skill, we can see our readership grow. For those of us who do qualitative inquiry with a social justice mindset, cultivating a broad audience can go a long way toward advocating for social change.

Supplemental Readings

Gullion, J. S. (2016). *Writing ethnography*. Sense Publishers.

Klinkenborg, V. (2012). *Several short sentences about writing*. Vintage.

Lamott, A. (1995). *Bird by bird: Some instructions on writing and life*. Anchor.

Reflection and Activities

1. In what ways is academic knowledge hidden from the public? How does that relate to mistrust of experts?

2. How accepting is your academic discipline to alternative publishing venues?

3. Take one major paper that you have written and rewrite it as an opinion piece, a concept paper, and a blog entry. Check the reading level of a paper that you have written. Reframe the information so that it can be read at a sixth grade level or lower but still get the major points across.

References

Gullion, J. S. (2015). *Fracking the neighborhood: Reluctant activists and natural gas drilling*. The MIT Press.

Gullion, J. S. (2016). *Writing ethnography*. Sense Publishers.

Hart, J. (2011). *Storycraft: The complete guide to writing narrative nonfiction*. University of Chicago Press.

Jago, A. G. (2018, June 1). Can it really be true that half of academic papers are never read? *The Chronicle of Higher Education*. https://www.chronicle.com/article/Can-It-Really-Be-True-That/243564

Mueller, F. O., Kucera, K. L., & Cox, L. M. (2013). *Catastrophic sports injury research thirty-first annual report*. National Center for Catastrophic Sport Injury Research. https://nccsir.unc.edu/files/2015/02/NCCSIR-31st-Annual-All-Sport-Report-1982_2013.pdf

Sophie's Choices: The Social Act of Publishing a Qualitative Study

Mitchell Allen

Abstract

This chapter works to demystify the black box of scholarly publishing of qualitative research for data-intensive publications. The key contention is that publishing, like every other part of the research process, is a social act, an interaction between a gatekeeper—book publisher or journal editor—and an author. In these interactions, the author has agency and influence. The process of having a book published is traced through a specific case, that of Sophie Tamas's *Life Without Leaving*, published by Left Coast Press, an experimental text populated with data from Tamas's dissertation. Correspondence and interaction between the author, publisher, and series editor during the process of developing this book provide a narrative line supplemented by the publisher's suggestion to authors on how they can best influence getting a book accepted, write the manuscript, work with the publisher's production department, and help market the work.

Keywords: Publishing; social interaction; scholarly writing; book marketing

May[1]

It starts the way most things do, with a conversation and a story.

In this case, it was on the lawn outside the Krannert Center at the University of Illinois Urbana-Champaign. I had taught a publishing workshop that day and Sophie got my attention with some perceptive questions. Worth sharing a spot of trampled grass with her to hear more while eating the traditional Congress feast of fried chicken, potato salad, and string beans. A glass of nondescript wine accompanied dinner.

> Publishing is a social act. Book editors and journal editors are always looking for good things to publish. If you can present your work to them effectively, your chances of getting published are increased. What better way to convince them your work is good than through a conversation—by phone, email, or in person? The informal setting of the International Congress of Qualitative Inquiry is ideal for this conversation to begin. You want the gatekeeper as your friend, not as your judge.

My question was an open-ended one, the kind favored by qualitative researchers: What are you working on? Most scholars take that bait to expound on their current research project. Not a specialist in their areas, I often reach saturation—theoretical or otherwise—within 5 minutes. But not with Sophie's tale. An autoethnographer, a theorist, and a compelling storyteller, she wove a very personal tale of domestic abuse, personal uncertainty, cultural marginalization, motherhood, tossing in delicious side tales of the Bahai faith, the Yukon, and West Africa. All of these stories were somehow designed to find their way into her dissertation. The story needed no additional spice, and I was easily convinced that her dissertation had the makings of a book I would want to publish.

---

[1]In traditional ethnographic fashion, the pedagogical information provided is embedded in the story. If you are mostly interested in descriptive advice on getting published, read the sections to the right. The book described here was published by Left Coast Press, the publishing house I founded and ran from 2005 to 2016. Left Coast Press is now part of Routledge, and Tamas's book can be obtained from them.

I selected this case as an example of how data-driven work, like Sophie's dissertation, can also be turned into an arts-based theoretical project when it comes to publication. While this chapter focuses largely on her book, most of the advice provided here works equally well for those trying to get a journal article published. The pedagogical material included in this chapter was first presented in publishing workshops at the International Congress of Qualitative Inquiry, The Qualitative Research Summer Intensive workshops, Thinking Qualitatively workshops, and other conference and training venues. Some of it appears in the book on publishing qualitative research that I wrote (Allen, 2016).

My thanks to Sophie Tamas, now an Assistant Professor at Carleton University, and to Carolyn Ellis for allowing me to publish private email correspondence between us. While the quotes are direct and the issues reflect those in developing Sophie's book, I have taken some liberties in the timeline of the events and other details in order to simplify the narrative. Some of the material presented here was developed in cooperation with my colleague, C. Deborah Laughton of Guilford Press, though any errors or idiocies remaining are solely mine.

"Just have a conversation." It was much easier for me, an older white male in a position of power than it was for Sophie, she reminds me. For Sophie, the story of getting her first book published had more nuances, interweaving relational, embodied, embedded personal histories, and shaped cultural scripts that continue to act on and within each of us. Was my attention to her and her book idea merely flirtation? If she responded in a similar fashion, would it call into question her sense of the worth of her work? "Both of us were handed social scripts in these scenes, and did our best to improvise around them in order to achieve our relational and professional goals," she wrote me recently. "Care and power are inevitably entangled." She also pointed out contributions by Carolyn Ellis and Laurel Richardson, two founding figures of her field and longstanding friends of mine, who provided us both with guidance and support.

I asked to see the dissertation when it was done.

More typically, you will be asked to submit a book proposal rather than a full manuscript. Every book publisher has guidelines for a book proposal on their website. When submitting a journal article, if you start with a conversation, you'll often want to submit a title and abstract to the journal editor to help direct the conversation. Full manuscripts, book or article, usually come later.

In the succeeding couple of years, Sophie became Dr. Sophie, and *Life After Leaving* (Tamas, 2011) appeared on the Left Coast Press book list. But it started with this conversation between an editor and an author.

June

"Are you sure you want to do this, Sophie?"

That was my first question as our email exchanges heated up, knowing that the additional work involved in transforming her dissertation into a viable book would take her many months, months in which she could be sending out articles to journals to build up her CV and improve her chances of finding an academic job.

Young scholars love the idea of having their dissertation published as a book—a payoff for all those years of work. But dissertations are written for an audience of three to five committee members. Books and even journal articles need to address larger audiences. A good committee chair continually pushes the doctoral student to constrict their study into something smaller and more manageable than the Big Question they started with, so that the student will finish writing before she becomes eligible for retirement benefits. A publisher and a journal editor want the reverse, to have the work unwind into addressing the Big Question again. There is usually a lot of work involved in that unwinding process. Sophie's choice was to do that work, which took her almost two years to complete.

She wrote:

I am wondering: if I start pulling apart my dissertation and working on articles based on bits of it, and publishing them in various journals, do I reduce the chances of the whole thing ever getting published (because it's old gum by then, or already out there, or copyright issues get messy, or whatever?)

The answer was neither simple nor short but, overall, I encouraged her to proceed with both the articles and the book.

> If your decision, like Sophie's, is to pursue book publication, producing first an article or two to publish is usually a good idea. It will rarely deter a publisher from publishing the entire manuscript. Just the reverse, it confirms to the publisher that you are doing good work if several articles are accepted from the dissertation, and it helps build an audience for your work by creating anticipation of publication of the full study.

July

Tamas's study raised the important question of whether women ever really recover from domestic violence. In addition to her personal journey through spousal violence, betrayal, its aftermath, and her struggle to write an autoethnographic dissertation about this journey, Sophie interviewed 18 survivors and service providers who lived and worked nearby. Weaving these data into a complex personal narrative became one of Sophie's challenges. Her choice was to select quotes from the various participants and place them thematically in a single chapter, positioned as a magical realist scene at her dissertation defense, where she gave voice to these women while addressing her committee members. How to format these voices in an informative yet nonlinear fashion became the issue. Voices spoke in sequence, in harmony, in cacophony against each other. Concepts and themes rose and fell with the words. Crescendos. Quiet moments. Silences. Visual representations. The story became a musical score of overlapping texts with Sophie the conductor. She and I struggled over how to place these multiple voices together on a traditional 6″ × 9″ page. We created and discarded solutions, finally settling on one that fit our standard book formats.

I thought of Bach and of Stoppard:

The sonata will be dense, no doubt about it. Kinda like Bach, I think you're not supposed to concentrate on every note. Do you ever watch Tom Stoppard plays? His dialogue is so full of puns, ideas, wordplays, double entendres that no one can absorb them all as the play is going on. It's intentional. A reason to read the script, or go to the theatre a second time and pick up on things you missed the first time. I doubt most readers will pore over every last line in this chapter, at least not without a good dose of aspirin. But that's ok. It's the nature of baroque word sonatas.

> Editors can be helpful to the author in shaping their work in a way the audience will be most receptive. By building a relationship, making the journal editor or book publisher your partner in the journey, their expertise in the pragmatics of publishing what you envision may help you to reach your goal.

December

A key actor in Sophie's work was Cricket. Wrestling with the theoretical ideas undergirding her research, Sophie and Cricket carried out long late-night discussions on how to talk about abuse. Cricket was able to cite Judith Butler, Linda Tuhiwai Smith, and Donna Haraway from memory. Impressive for someone so young and for being "a scruffy, cream-colored dog" (Tamas, 2011, p. 61). Sophie's choice to debate theory with Cricket is one of the more attractive features of her book. But Cricket's contributions to Sophie's book did not come without struggle. The author's portrayal of Cricket as a postmodern theorist worked much better than her description of Cricket as a dog. I sent Sophie back to give her more dogness, make her more grounded, more interested in scratching and licking her butt than in citing Foucault. It paid off. Shortly after publication a year later, I received an email from Sophie quoting her young daughter: "I'm reading your book to Cricket," Dora explained. "The part she's in. You got her voice just right, Mum. That is *exactly* how Cricket talks."

> Structuring a data-driven publication, whether an article or a book, has a predefined format, one that even has its own acronym: IMRaD (Introduction, Method, Results, and Discussion), leaving out a few critical elements like theory and conclusions (e.g., George Mason University Writing Center, n.d.). In publishing a data-driven study, this format is the default structure for your paper or book. But qualitative research prides itself on its storytelling, its demonstration of the complexities of research, and its literary merit. Authors can vary from the standard IMRaD formula, depending on the publication outlet. You'll have more luck with experimenting with format in a journal like *Qualitative Inquiry* than in *American Educational Research Journal*. Does your desired publication outlet allow for more creativity? Doing research on the journals to which you are considering submitting your article and asking questions of the editor will answer that. But a note of caution: To be a literary social scientist is twice as hard as being either a literary writer or a social scientist alone. Professional writers spend much time perfecting their craft, participating in writing groups, and attending writing workshops. Qualitative researchers with aspirations in this direction need to invest the same amount of effort working on their writing skills as on their research skills.

January

Carolyn Ellis, who coedited the *Writing Lives: Ethnographic Narrative Series* for Left Coast Press, entered the conversation. Her eye for evocative, thoughtful, and informed writing and her knowledge of autoethnography are unmatched. Carolyn's sympathetic, perceptive comments to Sophie gave the author confidence that her work was good. It also confirmed for me that my uninformed assessment of Sophie's project was not misplaced. Carolyn's note to Sophie began:

> Dear Sophie, I loved your manuscript and read it in one sitting, lying today in bed with my two dogs at my side! It was heaven. I think it is creative, smart, and deals with some very thorny issues in intelligent, humane, complex ways. I love the way you confront the issues head on, never (rarely anyway) taking the easy way out and refusing to say something without interrogating the deeper meaning/implications. Bravo. This certainly is a book I would use in my classes to show how autoethnography can be blended with poetry, art, interviewing and presented both in creative/poetic and more traditional/ grounded forms, all of it fitting together beautifully. So I'm willing to take it as is, but here are my comments if you want to think about doing some revisions. None of them would take a lot of effort—but feel free to pick and choose as you see fit.

Scholars who serve as series editors for publishers or as editorial board members and advisors of journal editors can often become your conduit toward publication. If you can enlist one of these people, often your friend or mentor, in helping you approach your desired publication outlet, it will serve you well. If publishing is a social act, then these intermediaries, trusted advisors of the gatekeepers, will give the decision maker confidence that your work should be considered seriously. These people can also provide you with trustworthy advice on how to rework your writing that will make it more appealing for publication.

I sent Sophie a contract for her book.

This is an important step. The publisher is not committed to your work until you receive a contract and all parties sign it. For journals it is often a paperwork formality once the journal editor has accepted the article. It is very important when it comes to books in demonstrating the publisher's commitment to the project. But heed this: Every publishing contract contains an escape clause for the publisher. The work needs to be "satisfactory" to the publisher to get to print. On rare occasion, the publisher can back out. If you've built a relationship with the decision maker, this is extremely unlikely. Do look over the contract. It will indicate what rights you have for reusing your own material, for example. If that is unclear or not to your liking, ask the editor.

May Comes Again

More fried chicken. Another glass of wine at a local bar. A walk around the quad with Sophie. Catching up on kids and postdocs and publishing issues. And how to handle revisions. Drop the academic chapter at the end, written to appease her dissertation committee, I told her. Make Cricket more doglike. Embed the metaphors of music and haunting more deeply in the manuscript. We agreed, and she went home the next day, ready to do the work required.

> Revisions are always daunting for the younger scholar; older ones too. If you remember that publishing is a social process and that you have agency in the relationships, you can better accomplish your publication goals while still appeasing the decision maker. That itself is crucial: Reviewers don't decide if you get your article or book published, the book or journal editor does. When you receive reviews, look at the comments openly and honestly. Which ones improve your argument? Which will make your work better? And which are unproductive or require you to write something that doesn't meet your goals? From there, make a list of reviewer suggestions and your choices as to which to revise and which you'll ignore. Present this list to the editor and get him to agree to these changes, or at least negotiate them with you. If you come to agreement, then do what you promised you would do and send the agreed-upon list back to the editor with the revised manuscript. The editor should accept your revision if you did what you promised the editor you would do, rather than trying to accommodate every comment from every reviewer.

A Second July

Sophie wrote:

> As to the larger question of what I do now. The review makes me want to quit my job immediately, clear the table, lay out the text, and start performing a long and careful surgery. Because my post doc is so intertwined with my dissertation, it doesn't feel like a tangent or waste to take time sorting out what I really think, learning to speak more directly, sharpening the points, developing more elegant presentation ... I also feel like there's stuff my diss states or demonstrates that could be helpful—things I wish I'd found when I was scouring the literature in the field.

Sophie's revision took a long time as she struggled with finding an academic home, performed her job and fulfilled teaching commitments, lived her life ... and searched for free time to work on the manuscript:

> I guess the question that I can't answer is, could the work ever be brilliant, original, insightful, helpful, interesting, engaging (etc.) enough to be

worthwhile? Is there a worthy book in there? I think there could be, but I don't see enough manuscripts to be able to compare. I am, of course, wondering if you are humoring me because you don't want to hurt my feelings.

> The editor can, and often does, serve simultaneously as your psychologist, cheerleader, and taskmaster. What writer hasn't had those moments of doubt about their work? Ram headlong into a mental roadblock? Lose focus as other, quicker, more immediate tasks appear on the to-do list? An experienced, skilled journal editor or publisher can become your academic partner, knowing when to give you comforting strokes, when to threaten you with deadlines, when to spend the hour listening to how you had to put down your ailing cat. But, given the number of projects these editors handle at any time, they can't always be there when you need them. A support group for the novice writer is more common and more reliable. Create a writing group. Find a friend willing to do the pulling, pushing, coaxing, stroking, when you need it, and read the first drafts you're afraid to show anyone else. For all the rhetoric about the lone-wolf writer, writing—even more than publishing—is a social act and requires a social support system.

September

I wrote Sophie, asking for help on someone else's manuscript I was considering for publication. Her thoughtful response was helpful.

> Building a relationship for the sole purpose of getting an article or book published is selfish and easily ignored. If the journal is one you wish to publish in regularly, or the publisher one you hope will publish the next book too, be a responsive partner. Volunteer to review for them, send good projects their way, offer compliments when they publish something that you find particularly inventive or useful. Editors will remember those kindnesses when it comes time to work with you on your own project.

Fall

Sophie wrote:

> When/if you publish, do you print from PDF files? And—therefore—does it matter if the pages are all typed text, or a mix of text and images, assuming it's all black and white? I might want to play with mixing text and hand writing or images—not sure it will work or if I'll want to go with it, but the first step is to see if it's a logistical possibility.

She must be far along in her revisions if she's now worried about formatting. I replied:

Delete any and all formatting from the Word files. Make it as simple as you can. Our designer is pouring it into another program and has to strip out all the format codes before she can do so.

Every book publisher and every journal have their own style and reference guide. Most of these guides are posted online to make it easier for the author to produce a document that goes through production quickly and easily. This is not the place to fight battles about Oxford commas, odd formatting, or English vs. American spellings. Those discussions should take place before the final manuscript is submitted, just as Sophie has done here. If there are design elements that require special handling, like Sophie's data "sonata," make sure the editor agrees to it early and provides clear instructions to the production department as to how to handle it when the manuscript is submitted.

January

She's done! I wrote:

Please send me a hard copy of the final manuscript and a disk with the images and text on it. Carolyn only wants an email version with a note from you telling her where you've made significant changes. She probably won't read the whole thing again.

The manuscript is complete. But what to call this work?

That question generated more conversation between myself, Sophie, and Carolyn than any other element of the book. Dozens of choices flew back and forth: *Playing the Survivor. Love Me Not. Wreckovery. Songs of Everyday Sorrows. Writing Survival. Unpicked. Ghost Songs. Ghostly Survivors. Get Well, Shut Up, Go Away. Intimate Passages. Recovering from Recovery. Journeys in Abuse and Wreckovery. Abuse, Recovery, and Zombies* (everything was about zombies that year). *Songs of Survivors. Singing Our Survival. A Symphony of Abuse. Survivor's Sonata* (the metaphor of music ran through the manuscript). *Afterword* (dropped, Virginia Woolf wrote a book with this title). *Sweet Nothings. Life After Leaving.*

And a subtitle. *Do Women Recover from Spousal Abuse? Songs of a Survivor of Spousal Abuse. The Haunted Life of Abuse Survivors. The Paradox of Recovering from Spousal Abuse. Abused Women Reconstructing Lives. The Remains of Spousal Abuse.*

Carolyn had her own method for titling a work:

I always find it helpful to read through my manuscript one time for the purpose of looking for the title. Now that you are almost done, you might want to do that. Look for words, phrases, turn of phrases, and write them down. Some of Mitch's suggestions are better, though none has grabbed me yet.... I like "the paradox of recovering" ... but is it a paradox really?

> The title is crucial to the success of any publication. It should signal to the reader what the piece is about and who should read it. For most data-rich academic articles, it is best just to stick with the subject of the work, being sure to include your most important keywords, so you can be found by someone searching on your topic. In cases of a literary work like Sophie's, a more metaphoric title can be used, but even in this case a subtitle with the right keywords is critical. And the metaphoric title should still connote the topic of the work. *Life After Leaving* does that; not all of the rest we tossed around did so.

And Another April Arrives

Yes, the publisher will almost always make you do the index. Sophie asks:

> I'm a little hazy on the line between (1) an author whose work I discuss, (2) an author I name in the text while citing them, (3) an author who appears as a speaker in the script (as in the pool scene), and (4) an author whose name only appears in the endnotes. Do I index them all, Herr Boss?

I answered:

> No one I have ever met liked doing their index. It's a despicable practice ... until you need to find something in someone else's book. Anyone whose work you discuss in the book should be in the index. After all, they'll start there to see if you have cited them before they deign to read any of it.

> Many publishers have created their own brief indexing guides. The *Chicago Manual of Style Online* (University of Chicago Press, 2017) has a lengthy chapter that is most helpful. And there is at least one good book on the process of indexing (Mulvany, 2005).

May Comes Yet Again

Another Qualitative Congress, more fried chicken. But a big difference this year: *Life After Leaving* is sitting at the Left Coast Press book exhibit. Sophie's job is done. Now it's up to the publisher's marketing department. Or is it?

Sophie's dissertation won an award from the International Institute for Qualitative Methodology in Canada. I urged her to accept the offer to give a keynote speech at their conference as a way of building an audience for the book. Could she hold up a copy of the book when she made her presentation at the Congress that week and ask people to come to our table to look at it? Did she have a list of contacts with whom she had corresponded about the book so we could send them information on it? Were there people who might give us an endorsement for the advertising? Did she plan any local talks with women's groups where she could pass around flyers about the book?

Sophie's book was published before social media became ubiquitous. Those channels—your Facebook, Twitter, Instagram accounts—are key to announcing your publication. If you have a blog, or can contribute as a guest to someone else's, it could have an important impact. Every university has a public information office that may be interested in advertising your work broadly if you can convince them of its importance. If you write a book, research some potential awards for which you might submit it. If an article, make sure you send digital copies to select "influencers" in your field who might find it of interest and help you get more exposure. Don't leave the announcements of your work just to the publisher. The best results are when marketing is done in tandem with them.

> Most scholars think that marketing of a book, or announcing the publication of an article, is the job of the publisher. It is. But publishers might be marketing dozens or hundreds of books and thousands of articles at the same time that yours comes out. The publisher will do lots of invisible marketing of your work for you—getting it into key reference and indexing services, providing metadata to the wholesalers who reach librarians who might buy the book, placing your work in aggregations of books and articles that might be sold to libraries around the world. These institutional channels are invisible to most scholars. The more specific audiences are harder for the publisher to reach but easier for you: the newsletter of the specialized interest group of the professional organization you belong to; your network of professional colleagues and friends who have been asking about the book; the community groups you consult with. In tandem with the publisher, you should develop a strategy to reach each of the audiences who might be interested in your work. Some of the work will be theirs, some of it should end up on your shoulders. This is even more important with any article you publish as the publisher is mostly concerned with advertising the journal, not your particular contribution to it.

Summer

"What are you working on?"

Sophie responded,

> I have an idea that I have been stewing on.... I think it would end up as a book, probably called "Scrap." If, as my research has suggested, we may not actually recover from some traumas and losses, the question becomes, how do we process or make use of our pasts? I want to explore this question, using photos and interviews, in two very different sites: rural scrapyards and

suburban scrapbooking stores.... I love the contrast between the masculinity and dirt and unruliness of those spaces, and the hyper-orderly femininity of scrapbooking. Both seem, to me, like systems for putting the past in its place and finding something useful in it, but they take such different approaches.

One of the key points about establishing a relationship with a publisher or journal editor is that the second time becomes easier. If they like your work, they will be more receptive to the second piece you offer them, and the entire publication process will be easier for both of you. You've learned the culture, process, and systems of that press, and they've learned that you're a talented, reliable author with an audience for your work. Sophie's second (and third) book ideas were sent to me as soon as she was willing to share them. I was happy to publish the second one but the third was designed for a different audience. Instead, I gave her suggestions as to who to approach to get Book 3 published. Left Coast Press closed down before she could send me Book 2 for publication, so I only had one opportunity of working with this talented scholar.

And it begins all over again, a conversation between author and editor.

Supplemental Readings

Allen, M. (2016). *Essentials of publishing qualitative research.* Left Coast Press.

Luey, B. (Ed.). (2007). *Revising your dissertation: Advice from leading editors.* University of California Press.

Rabiner, S., & Fortunato A. (2003). *Thinking like your editor: How to write great serious nonfiction and get it published.* Norton.

Reflection and Activities

1. You run across the editor from your favorite book publisher at a conference reception and want her to consider your dissertation for publication. Prepare a thirty-second "elevator speech" to get her attention to your work. Thirty seconds, no cheating.

2. Take an article that you are currently working on or considering writing. Using web research, create a list of three journals that might best meet your goals for that article.

3. Create a short list of questions you would ask one of those journals' editor via phone or email to determine if the journal meets your publication goals.

References

Allen, M. (2016). *Essentials of publishing qualitative research.* Left Coast Press.

George Mason University Writing Center. (n.d.). *Writing a scientific research report (IMRaD).* https://writingcenter.gmu.edu/guides/writing-an-imrad-report

Mulvany, N. (2005). *Indexing books* (2nd ed.). University of Chicago Press.

Tamas, S. (2011). *Life after leaving: The remains of spousal abuse.* Left Coast Press.

University of Chicago Press. (2017). *The Chicago manual of style online* (17th ed.). University of Chicago Press. https://www.chicagomanualofstyle.org/home.html

Conclusion

Paul Mihas, Johnny Saldaña, and Charles Vanover

Qualitative Research in the Age of Data Science[1]

This volume and its editors have celebrated the qualitative research life cycle and its unique form of knowledge acquisition. We began our journey with a set of chapters that describe how to prepare interview data for analysis, and then we moved through the process of transcription, coding, interpretive strategies, and writing practices. Quality in qualitative inquiry is a product of strategic decisions made at every stage of the qualitative life cycle (Maietta, Hamilton, Swartout, & Petruzzelli, 2019). Quality is also a product of efforts necessary to get the message out to our audiences, including the public. Sally Campbell Galman's inventive comics, in Chapter 22, ask us to consider an important question: in a field where discussions of method are frequently obtuse, what if we worked to communicate the passion of qualitative inquiry to everyone? Jessica Smartt Gullion, in Chapter 24, asks us to imagine the benefits and the vulnerability that come from using forms of writing that allow research findings to be read by hundreds of thousands of people. Mitchell Allen, in Chapter 25, reminds us that developing publishable qualitative studies requires complex social and technical choices. Finding the right audience is complicated but necessary work.

We conclude *Analyzing and Interpreting Qualitative Research* by asking what qualitative research might have to offer people within and outside of the university given developments in other innovative fields of research in social and behavioral inquiry. Research using data science and big data analytics has grown in popularity in both industry and academia, with schools of (and majors in) data science popping up across universities in the U.S. and internationally. We might ask ourselves where this emerging trend and focus on "big" leaves qualitative researchers with our, by comparison, much smaller studies that might not seem as ground-breaking as machine learning and artificial intelligence.

It is true that big data can accommodate heretofore unimaginable amounts of text. For example, researchers from the University of Vermont used values assigned to words contained in 4.6 billion tweets from September 2008 to September 2011 to track levels of happiness (Parry, 2011). They determined that the last months of each year, Saturdays, and the early mornings are happy times, while January, the

[1]This chapter was inspired by a short course, Doing Qualitative Research in the Big Data Era, taught by Dr. Mario Small, at the Qualitative Research Summer Intensive, 2017.

first days of the week, and late-nights are less so. Their data and analytic methods afford them incredible precision. Daily happiness generally "peaked at 5 a.m.–6 a.m. local time, then declined, at first rapidly, then more gradually, to the average low of 10 p.m.–11 p.m., returning to its peak overnight" (n.p.). These findings might be helpful to clinical psychologists (and marketers) researching the daily cycle from high to diminishing happiness, but in being far removed from the lived experience of people in the study, this approach calls attention only to broad trends rather than unveiling social mysteries or understanding the contextualized lives of people experiencing these cycles of happiness, both daily and annually. Context-dependent knowledge, necessarily absent in this big data study, allows researchers and practitioners to develop from rule-based thinking to more refined, qualified expertise (Flyvbjerg, 2006).

Qualitative research by definition moves closer to the research problem and population being studied. This is the nature of a purposive, typically small sample, but one that provides a deep well of layered phenomena and contexts. In being in the same room (or video call) with participants, the distance between researcher and participant is bridged by the act of listening, not simply collecting. Listening is a "dangerous act," one that generates vulnerability for both participant and situated researcher-knower (Karner & Warren, 1995, p. 81). As Craig M. McGill, Drew Puroway, and Mark Duslak, in Chapter 13, discuss, "without a sense of vulnerability, there are walls around the data," often the case with studies focusing too heavily on quantitative variables. Big data researchers scrape data "out there" on the Web or on e-mail servers, but qualitative researchers tend to *generate* data "in there," in the voices and actions of individuals. Captured data have already happened; interview data unfold before our very eyes.

In using tailored probes to open up telling moments in interviews, qualitative researchers more deeply investigate the well of meaning. Jaime Fiddler, in Chapter 16, reminds us that to "explore a phenomenon that is continuous requires prolonged engagement rather than a 'snapshot' approach." In engaging several teachers in research conversations over a one-year period, she discovered how qualitative practices allowed her and her co-researchers to "delve deeper: we could look back, look forward, or speak of present experiences as we talked over time." No part of life was "disregarded." Instead, these life accounts—with unexpected detours—were *condensed* into a shared interpretation (Fiddler). Though a 140-character tweet can reveal someone's state of mind—and billions of tweets can perhaps do so for the globe—qualitative research slows down to *look at* what others might look *through* (Vagle, 2018).

McGill et al. (Chapter 13) state that putting their autoethnographic work "out there in the world is an exciting and extremely vulnerable act," and Kakali Bhattacharya, in Chapter 21, claims that qualitative data analysis is "part self-analysis." Calling attention to the assumed guise of neutrality, these authors point to researcher reflexivity, an invaluable mode that researchers adopt during the qualitative research life cycle. Though big data researchers must also question their methods, their own lens—their researcher stance and actions—is not always addressed in the research product, perhaps with little indication why they might be "privileging one order of the 'facts' over others" (Richardson, 2000, p. 927). As Janet Richards, in Chapter 9, reminds us, "at every step of the process, researchers need to examine and consciously acknowledge the assumptions and biases they bring to their inquiries that impact their decisions and interpretations."

Big data are, for better or worse, distant data, sometimes revealing the map more than the territory. Qualitative data—interviews, observations, focus groups, diaries—position the researcher closer to the "noise" and experience as it is lived. Data science allows us to document when people tweet happier thoughts, but we still largely do not know *why*. Furthermore, happiness is contextual; what makes each one of us happy is complex and deeply personal. Social scientists and applied practitioners alike are invested in *why* questions so that they can theorize human behavior or offer practical interventions to vexing behavioral problems and social injustice. By going analytically deeper with fewer people, qualitative researchers undertake a deep diving mission to uncover multiple layers of the *what, how, in what ways*, and *why* of social inscrutabilities.

Rather than viewing big data and qualitative data as competitors, however, we can instead view them as different bases of knowledge. Our research questions, as knowledge questions, can seek out both big data and complex qualitative data to help us build theory and know the lifeworld through the eyes of our participants as well as through trends discerned through big data. Fiddler (Chapter 16) states that experience is storied, continuous, and constructed through social influences on a person's inner life and their unique personal history. Qualitative inquiry can delve into complex matters of this inner life and the "between space" of person and lifeworld (Vagle, 2018, p. 8).

In *Someone To Talk To,* sociologist Mario Small (2017) combines social network analysis, up-close interviews with adults undergoing major life changes, and general surveys of Americans to study how we select confidants—people we confide in regarding intimate and complex matters. His works show us that confidants are not always best friends or spouses, but sometimes the stranger sitting next to us on an airplane. Interviews with participants revealing these unfolding confidential moments expose the mysteries of the human heart—how a stranger with kind eyes might allow us to open up more than our best buddy from high school. Survey data and big data, in contrast, might document the larger facts of disclosure, with scales of likelihood and measures of trust. Qualitative data, the lived experience of telling, allow us a more precise glimpse into the motivations of disclosing certain secrets—our shoplifting days as teenagers or how lonely we might feel in a marriage. Big data can leave our findings in factoid-land, where we remain *outside* a phenomenon, whereas the attentive listening and deep well of qualitative research brings us *into* the lives and impulses of disclosure.

Charmaz (2002), in studying people living with chronic illness, goes even further than analyzing what people reveal and to whom. She studies silences, examines disparities between lived experience and accounts of it, and "brings the body into analytic purview" (p. 302). Her work showcases what qualitative research is best poised to do, to study immensely challenging terrain such as silences and identity, and *give meaning to* abstract topics such as the potential loss of self. We need more than the large-surface lens of big data to address these perplexing questions. We need to develop a partnership with participants and study narrative layers, multiple voices within the same individual—a difficult task for a computer algorithm, but a challenge that an experienced qualitative researcher with rich and storied data can uncover.

In his classes, Ray Maietta (Maietta et al., 2019), sociologist and president of ResearchTalk, often recalls an interview of a woman whose broken leg was in a cast, elevated on a chair with her toes exposed. Whenever Maietta, as the interviewer, entered challenging emotional territory, her toes would clench. This is the human body as vessel. Words are not simply text; they are embodied. What we learn from participant observation and embodied data collection cannot be gleaned from 4.6 billion disembodied tweets. As Mariaelena Bartsaghi, in Chapter 5, reminds us, there are many ways that qualitative researchers attempt to remain close to the interview episode as a lived encounter. Though a transcription may appear to be a text that is removed from its context, transcripts are also "very much embodied. They are entangled in how we listen and capture what we hear, which is itself inextricable from our cultural understandings of how to re-present speech and how micro-discourse is done" (Bartesaghi, Chapter 5). In moving closer to a phenomenon and the intricacies of the spoken word, and in laboring to create an embodied transcript, we are moving closer to what Mario Small (2018) calls "cognitive empathy," the ability to "understand another person's predicament as they understand it" (n.p.). In Chapter 10, James Bernauer's approach to cognitive empathy is to listen to the audio recordings of interviews repeatedly and make mental notes, reflexively considering his own awareness. This attentiveness to the aural nature of data is another example of edging closer to participants' beliefs, logic, and values, a difficult task, to be sure, in the world of big data.

Though qualitative analysis has its software tools to automate text searches and expedite coding, as Jessica N. Lester and Trena M. Paulus, in Chapter 2, state, QDAS packages are simply tools, whereas big data analysis could not be done without automation; data acceleration is often the point. Data science applications give us massive amounts of textual data at our disposal and automated procedures for clustering documents and comparing frequencies across time or groups.

For example, consider a research question focusing on whether the Supreme Court's rulings reflect the language and understanding of the lower courts. Using data science, researchers can explore thousands of Supreme Court rulings to determine whether the language of the higher court reflects the language of lower courts. This would involve using programming tools such as R, rather than reading thousands of pages of court rulings to code data, writing memos, and using interpretive analysis. We cannot deny the efficiency of spending simply a day or two answering this research question without even reading data! However, the shift toward understanding and meaning making must still involve an interpretive understanding discerned by a human being, not simply through automation.

For many, numbers are seductive and big data especially so. Social scientists have long been concerned with sample sizes, statistical power, and representative samples. As computing power becomes more available to the average researcher, where does that leave the qualitative researcher who wants to *understand*, not just back up a correlational claim with a huge *n*? There are many kinds of *n*'s—not just the number of people in a study, but the number of contexts (or layers of voices) that a researcher is able to draw from and analyze during the research life cycle. Big data automation may allow us to analyze millions or even billions of e-mails but, as Small reminds us, the context is still just one—the single context of e-mails (Small, 2017). Because qualitative data can use multiple data-collection media—interviews, observations, diaries, and so on—and activate stories revealing multiple social contexts, the contextual *n* is potentially rich. In analyzing, through automation, thousands of e-mails in an organization, we miss interaction that does not happen in e-mails (Small, 2017). In interviews, we learn about these undocumented encounters—hallway chats and information shared at the bathroom sink. Narrative data—stories activated by interviews—teach us about process—what activates a process, what keeps a process in place, what destabilizes it—in ways that augment or challenge findings from massive datasets. The wide-angle lens and computing power of big data studies accelerate information, but if we are seeking to unlock the enigmas of process, to become listeners and not simply consumers of data, then we are invited to take on qualitative research practices to make room for competing and unanticipated contexts.

In McGill et al.'s words, the researcher engages in an "intake of that person's world and inner contemplation of that data." Qualitative researchers attempt to create analytic bridges—practices, strategies, and lenses—to bring us closer to meaning in the data. Keane (Chapter 15) discusses using different logics, such as abductive reasoning, to explore surfacing complexities. Memo writing "enables us to see gaps in our analyses" and to perhaps return to the field to fill "conceptual gaps in—or between—categories." Memos are a place to make conjectures, and we use data to test these conjectures. It is not possible for a big data researcher to read millions of tweets; dwelling in the data and adding another layer of "data," memos, is unthinkable. These practices—coding, memo writing, drawing—are not imbued with acceleration. They are invested in attentiveness, moments of unearthing that, when shared with participants in member checking or other means, can lead to further connection and collaboration.

In arts-based research, researchers create an artistic product—poetry, ethno-theatre, and cartoon panels—from qualitative data (e.g., see Campbell Galman, Chapter 22). Visual, dramatic, and literary approaches are ways of representing the complex social world for a scholarly audience or the public (see Saldaña, Chapter 19). Shenfield and Prendergast (Chapter 20) showcase the illustrative power of poems—found poems and erasure poems—and remind us that not all social scientific research leads to tables, charts, and PowerPoint slides. Art allows us to see through facts and findings; in drawing a picture or "finding" a poem, we know our data differently, and so do our audiences. Indeed, as this book's introduction reminds us, qualitative research is a big tent with many performers (Tracy, 2010).

Even if not taking advantage of arts-based practices, researchers engaging in analytic processes, such as theme building, can be creative as well. In Fiddler's chapter, she and her research collaborators construct the theme "heavy hours," crystalizing the experiences teachers have in their induction years. Of these creative moments of synthesis, she says that "sometimes there was just a certain energy to our discussion, a generative feeling in the room, heightened interest from everyone, questioning, circling, laughing." This is the language of discovery, of a "certain energy" that is both analytic and inspired, a feeling that experienced qualitative researchers know well.

Tim Huffman, in Chapter 19, reminds us that different types of studies require different types of invention, sometimes leading to "eureka" moments. Qualitative researchers make claims and deepen them with intentional methods. But let's not forget the shadow of big data. Over the last two years alone, 90% of the data in the world was generated (Marr, 2020). More data have likely been collected in the time it took to read this sentence than was collected in the entire nineteenth century. With this astounding volume of data and accelerated methods to analyze it, we will have exponential knowledge at our disposal. But let us also remember that the "larger the island of knowledge, the longer the coastline of wonder" (Sockman, n.d.). Qualitative researchers are uniquely positioned to address this coastline, to acknowledge what we know, question what we think we know, and dwell more intentionally in the lived experience of the ordinary and extraordinary alike. Strategies for analysis and interpretation—approaches that bring us closer to the experiential world—allow us to make sense and make meaning of the social mysteries still unfolding around us.

References

Allen, M. (2022). Sophie's choices: The social act of publishing a qualitative study. In C. Vanover, P. Mihas, & J. Saldaña (Eds.), *Analyzing and interpreting qualitative research: After the interview*. SAGE.

Bartesaghi, M. (2022). Theories and practices of transcription from discourse analysis. In C. Vanover, P. Mihas, & J. Saldaña (Eds.), *Analyzing and interpreting qualitative research: After the interview*. SAGE.

Bernauer, J. A. (2022). Oral coding: An alternative way to make sense of interview data. In C. Vanover, P. Mihas, & J. Saldaña (Eds.), *Analyzing and interpreting qualitative research: After the interview*. SAGE.

Bhattacharya, K. (2022). Embedding critical, creative, and contemplative data analysis in interview studies. In C. Vanover, P. Mihas, & J. Saldaña (Eds.), *Analyzing and interpreting qualitative research: After the interview*. SAGE.

Charmaz, K. (2002). Stories and silences: Disclosures and self in chronic illness. *Qualitative Inquiry, 8*(3), 302–328. https://doi.org/10.1177/107780040200800307

Fiddler, J. L. (2022). Listening deeply: Indexing research conversations in a narrative inquiry. In C. Vanover, P. Mihas, & J. Saldaña (Eds.), *Analyzing and interpreting qualitative research: After the interview*. SAGE.

Flyvbjerg, B. (2006). Five misunderstandings about case-study research. *Qualitative Inquiry, 12*(2), 219–245. https://doi.org/10.1177/1077800405284363

Galman, S. C. (2022). Follow the headlights: On comics-based data analysis. In C. Vanover, P. Mihas, & J. Saldaña (Eds.), *Analyzing and interpreting qualitative research: After the interview*. SAGE.

Gullion, J. S. (2022). Writing for a broad audience: Concept papers, blogs, and op-eds. In C. Vanover, P. Mihas, & J. Saldaña (Eds.), *Analyzing and interpreting qualitative research: After the interview*. SAGE.

Huffman, T. (2022). Making claims using qualitative data. In C. Vanover, P. Mihas, & J. Saldaña (Eds.), *Analyzing and interpreting qualitative research: After the interview*. SAGE.

Karner, T., & Warren, C. A. B. (1995). The dangerous listener: Unforseen perils in intensive interviewing. *Clinical Sociology Review, 13*(1), 80–105. http://digitalcommons.wayne.edu/csr/vol13/iss1/9

Keane, E. (2022). Critical analytic memoing. In C. Vanover, P. Mihas, & J. Saldaña (Eds.), *Analyzing and interpreting qualitative research: After the interview*. SAGE.

Lester, J. N., & Paulus, T. M. (2022). Using qualitative data analysis software to manage the research process. In C. Vanover, P. Mihas, & J. Saldaña (Eds.), *Analyzing and interpreting qualitative research: After the interview*. SAGE.

Maietta, R., Hamilton, A., Swartout, K., & Petruzzelli, J., ResearchTalk. (2019). *Qualitative data analysis camp*. ResearchTalk Inc.

Marr, B. (2020). *How much data do we create every day? The mind-blowing stats everyone should read*. Forbes. https://www.forbes.com/sites/bernardmarr/2018/05/21/how-much-data-do-we-create-every-day-the-mind-blowing-stats-everyone-should-read/#99fa3960ba99

McGill, C. M., Puroway, D., & Duslak, M. (2022). On being a researcher-participant: Challenges with the iterative process of data production, analysis and (re)production. In C. Vanover, P. Mihas, & J. Saldaña (Eds.), *Analyzing and interpreting qualitative research: After the interview*. SAGE.

Parry, W. (2011). *Twitter reveals when we're happiest*. Livescience. https://www.livescience.com/17552-happiness-measured-twitter.html

Richards, J. (2021). Coding, categorizing, and theming the data: A reflexive search for meaning. In C. Vanover, P. Mihas, & J. Saldaña (Eds.), *Analyzing and interpreting qualitative research: After the interview*. SAGE.

Richardson, L. (2000). Writing: A method of inquiry. In N. K. Denzin & Y. S. Lincoln (Eds.), *Handbook of qualitative research* (2nd ed., pp. 923–948). SAGE.

Saldaña, J. (2021). Dramatizing interviews. In C. Vanover, P. Mihas, & J. Saldaña (Eds.), *Analyzing and interpreting qualitative research: After the interview.* SAGE.

Shenfield, R., & Prendergast, M. (2021). What makes an effective teacher? Revealing good teaching practice through poetic transcription. In C. Vanover, P. Mihas, & J. Saldaña (Eds.), *Analyzing and interpreting qualitative research: After the interview.* SAGE.

Small, M. L. (2017). *Someone to talk to.* Oxford University Press.

Small, M. L. (2018). Rhetoric and evidence in a polarized society. Harvard University Public lecture, Coming to Terms with a Polarized Society Lecture Series, ISERP, Columbia University, March 1.

Sockman, R. (n.d.). Wikipedia. https://en.wikipedia.org/wiki/Ralph_Washington_Sockman

Tracy, S. J. (2010). Qualitative quality: Eight "big-tent" criteria for excellent qualitative research. *Qualitative Inquiry, 16*(10), 837–851. https://doi.org/10.1177/1077800410383121

Vagle, M. (2018). *Crafting phenomenological research* (2nd ed.). Routledge.

• About the Contributors •

Haslinda Binti Abdullah is Associate Professor and Deputy Dean for Research and Innovation in the Faculty of Human Ecology, University Putra Malaysia. Her teaching and research concentrate on Applied and Developmental Psychology.

Nobaya Binti Ahmed is Associate Professor and currently Head of Department of the Social and Developmental Sciences in the Faculty of Human Ecology, University Putra Malaysia. Her research focuses on social issues in urban areas including housing, well-being of urban residents, and marginalized groups in urban areas.

Mitchell Allen runs Scholarly Roadside Service, a publishing consulting service for scholars and publishers. During his 45-year publishing career, he founded two independent scholarly presses specializing in qualitative research, AltaMira Press (1995–2005) and Left Coast Press (2005–2016), and worked at Sage Publications, where he created their qualitative research publishing program. Mitch's own academic work is in archaeology, and he is affiliated with UC Berkeley and the Smithsonian. He is author of *Essentials of Publishing Qualitative Research* and regularly teaches publishing workshops to scholars and students. Allen is recipient of career achievement awards from the International Congress on Qualitative Inquiry and the Society for the Study of Symbolic Interaction.

Mariaelena Bartesaghi is Associate Professor of Communication at The University of South Florida. She studies institutionalization, or how social discourses of authority can be traced in spoken and written discourse. Her research on therapy, psychiatry, crisis settings, academia, and qualitative research as practice has been published in journals such as *Discourse Studies, Management Communication Quarterly, Communication Studies, The Review of Communication, Communication & Medicine and Language under Discussion*. She is the Editor in Chief of *Qualitative Research in Medicine and Healthcare*.

James A. Bernauer is Professor of Education at Robert Morris University in Pittsburgh, PA. He teaches preparatory courses for teachers at the undergraduate and masters levels and qualitative and quantitative methodology at the doctoral level. His major interests include integrating methodologies as well as exploring a broad range of topics and issues impacting teaching and learning. He especially likes to coauthor with his doctoral graduates as well as with colleagues at his own university and across the world and he will continue to do so as long as the creative juices keep flowing!

Kakali Bhattacharya is a multiple award-winning professor at University of Florida housed in Research, Evaluation, and Measurement Program. She is the 2018 winner of AERA's Mid-Career Scholar of Color Award and the 2018 winner of AERA's Mentoring Award from Division G: Social Context of Education. Her coauthored text with Kent Gillen, *Power, Race, and Higher Education: A Cross-Cultural Parallel Narrative* has won a 2017 Outstanding Publication Award from AERA (SIG 168) and a 2018 Outstanding Book Award from the International Congress of Qualitative Research. She is recognized by *Diverse Magazine* as one of the top 25 women in higher education.

Andrea J. Bingham is Assistant Professor of Leadership, Research, and Foundations in the College of Education at the University of Colorado, Colorado Springs. Dr. Bingham's research focuses on applications of qualitative methodologies, policy implementation and instructional reform, and organizational change. In recent studies, she has used qualitative research methods to understand how teachers and leaders implement innovative K–12 school models aimed at improving educational equity. Much of her research focuses on personalized learning models, including teacher practices, implementation challenges, and sustainability.

Gerardo L. Blanco is Associate Professor of Educational Leadership and Higher Education, and

Academic Director of the Center for International Higher Education at the Lynch School of Education and Human Development, Boston College. His research focuses on international higher education and on the application of qualitative methods on international contexts. His teaching, research and consulting have taken place in 15 countries and 5 continents. An interdisciplinary scholar, his research has been published in leading journals, such as *Cultural Studies-Critical Methodologies,* the *International Journal of Qualitative Studies in Education,* the *Comparative Education Review,* and the *Review of Higher Education.*

Sheryl L. Chatfield is Assistant Professor in the College of Public Health at Kent State University and serves as co-coordinator of Kent State University's Graduate Certificate in qualitative research. She is also the Editor of Ohio Journal of Public Health. Sheryl conducts primary and secondary qualitative and mixed methods research on a variety of public health topics.

Mark Duslak is Associate Dean of Students at Lake-Sumter State College. He is currently finishing his doctoral studies in the Educational Leadership and Policy Studies program at Florida State University. Mark's research interests include qualitative and quantitative methodologies—with a focus on topics relating to administrator-service provider dynamics in education, academic advisor role articulation, and academic advisor identity formation. Mark can be reached at Duslakm@lssc.edu.

Cori Egan is a research associate at the George Washington University's Graduate School of Education and Human Development. Over the last seven years, she has conducted research into the Tennessee Achievement School District and, more recently, a three-year mixed methods study of Shelby County Schools' turnaround district, the iZone, in Memphis. Prior to joining George Washington University, she worked as a researcher for the Tennessee Department of Education and as a Teach For America Corps Member in North Carolina.

Jaime Leigh Fiddler is the Academic Program Coordinator for the MEd research program at the University of Calgary, a program in which she also instructs. She has been interested in arts-based and narrative methodologies since her own MA journey and has published work on and within research-based theatre and arts-based, design-based, and narrative methodologies. She is also the Managing Editor of *Art/Research International: A Transdisciplinary Journal.* Jaime's research interests include emergency teaching, teacher mentorship, beginning teacher induction and attrition, and teacher professional learning and growth.

Joshua L. Glazer is Associate Professor of Education Policy at George Washington University. Dr. Glazer's research examines multiple approaches to improving underperforming schools in high-poverty environments. He recently directed two multiyear studies into school turnaround in Memphis, including the state-run Achievement School District, and the locally operated iZone in which the district devised and

Sally Campbell Galman is Professor of Child and Family Studies @ the University of Massachusetts @ Amherst. She wrote and illustrated this piece while at home as a single parent of three children during the COVID-19 Pandemic, which continues to disproportionately affect female academics. Her work has been generously supported by the Spencer Foundation. You can learn more about her arts-based scholarship at sallycampbellgalman.com.

directed its own improvement effort. In addition, Dr. Glazer was also principal investigator for a multiyear study of research-practice partnerships in two mid-Atlantic cities. He is coeditor of the recently released *Choosing Charters: Better Schools or More Segregation?*

Elsa M. Gonzalez is Assistant Professor of Higher Education in the Department of Educational Leadership and Policy Studies in the University of Houston, where she also serves as Program Director of the Higher Education PhD program. She served as Energy Fellow for the UH Energy initiative of the University of Houston. She received her MBA from the National University of Mexico (UNAM), and a PhD from Texas A&M University (College Station). She is the author of 73 publications; her research interests include higher education leadership, methodological issues in cross-language qualitative data analysis, women in higher education, and access, resilience, and retention of underrepresented students.

Silvana di Gregorio, PhD, is Research Director at QSR International, the developers of NVivo. She is a sociologist and a former academic. She has been training, consulting, and publishing about qualitative data analysis software since 1995. For 16 years she had her own training/consultancy business—SdG Associates. She is author of Using Web 2.0 Tools for Qualitative Analysis and coauthor with Judith Davidson of *Qualitative Research Design for Software Users* and *Qualitative Research and Technology: In the Midst of a Revolution*, and coauthor with Linda Gilbert and Kristi Jackson of *Tools for Qualitative Analysis*. She is part of the product development team at QSR.

Jessica Smartt Gullion is Associate Dean of Research for the College of Arts and Sciences and Associate Professor of Sociology at Texas Woman's University. She has published more than thirty-five peer-reviewed journal articles and book chapters, and seven books. Her most recent books include *Researching With: A Decolonizing Approach to Community-Based Action Research*, the award-winning *Diffractive Ethnography: Social Sciences in the Ontological Turn,* and *Writing Ethnography.*

Tim Huffman received his PhD from Arizona State University and is Associate Professor in Communication Studies at Saint Louis University. Tim uses participatory action, qualitative approaches to understand and promote justice in society. He is particularly committed to homelessness and radical urban poverty and tries to leverage the structures and processes of knowing in society for the benefit of the most marginalized and oppressed. Tim has engaged in community-based qualitative research projects in various organizations across the homeless/housing human services sector. His scholarship on inquiry offers paradigmatic, methodological, and analytic tools with which communication researchers can pursue, imagine, and build more just societies.

George Kamberelis earned his PhD at the University of Michigan and is Professor, Department Chair, and Graduate Program Director in the Department of Education at Western Colorado University. Most of Dr. Kamberelis' research focuses on literacy education (especially genre studies) and qualitative inquiry (especially the use of focus groups in research). He is published widely in journals and handbooks including *Qualitative Inquiry, International Journal of Qualitative Studies in Education, Annals of the American Academy of Political and Social Sciences, Handbook on Promoting Social Justice in Education, SAGE Handbook of Qualitative Research,* and *Oxford Handbook of Qualitative Research Methods.*

Elaine Keane is Senior Lecturer (Sociology of Education and Research Methods) and Director of Doctoral Studies in the School of Education at the National University of Ireland, Galway. Her research and publications center on widening participation in higher education, including in teacher education, with a particular focus on social class, ethnicity, and intercultural education. She is lead editor of a book about diversifying the teaching profession (Routledge, 2022). Elaine serves on the Editorial Board of *Teaching in Higher Education.* Her research interests also include research methodology, especially constructivist grounded theory, on which she has collaborated and published with Professor Kathy Charmaz and taught workshops internationally.

Steven Eric Krauss is Professor in the Faculty of Educational Studies, University Putra Malaysia. His teaching and research focus on positive youth development in diverse cultural settings with a particular interest in intergenerational partnership as a support for youth thriving and well-being.

Adrian Larbi-Cherif is Associate Scholar at the Learning Research and Development Center at the University of Pittsburgh. Dr. Larbi-Cherif's research uses different methodologies to understand what it takes to improve instructional quality and equitable student learning opportunities in large, urban school districts. His prior research investigated what school leaders need to know and do to support math teachers in developing ambitious instructional practices in mathematics. He is currently examining how school systems can use improvement science and continuous improvement methods to improve instruction and equitable learning opportunities both with and without an external intermediary organization.

Jessica N. Lester is Associate Professor of Inquiry Methodology (Qualitative Track) at Indiana University, Bloomington, Indiana. Her scholarship centers on qualitative methodologies and methods, with a particular focus on language-based methodologies. Most recently, she coauthored *Doing Qualitative Research in a Digital World* (2021) and *Applied Conversation Analysis: Social Interaction in Institutional Settings* (2019).

Yvonna S. Lincoln is Ruth Harrington Chair of Educational Leadership Emerita and University Distinguished Professor of Higher Education Emerita at Texas A&M University, where she also served as Program Chair for the higher education program area, Associate Department Head, and Department Head. She is the author or coauthor of more than 100 chapters and journal articles on aspects of higher education or qualitative research methods and methodologies. Her research interests include development of qualitative methods and methodologies, the status and future of research libraries, and the impact of the assemblage of neoliberalism, globalization, and corporatization on western higher education.

Craig M. McGill is Assistant Professor for the Department of Special Education, Counseling, and Student Affairs at Kansas State University. He holds a doctorate from Florida International University in adult education and human resource development. Dr. McGill is a qualitative researcher with an emphasis on identity (personal, professional, and organizational). His research agenda is focused on social justice and the professionalization of academic advising and he has also published articles in musical theatre and queer studies. He can be reached at cmcgill@ksu.edu.

Aishath Nasheeda is Senior Lecturer in Psychology at Villa College, Maldives. She completed her PhD in Social Psychology at the University Putra Malaysia in 2020. Her research focuses on adolescents' life skills education and psychosocial issues.

Trena M. Paulus is Professor and Director of Undergraduate Research and Creative Activity at East Tennessee State University. She holds a PhD from

Indiana University in Instructional Systems Technology, an MA from Ohio University in Applied Linguistics, and a BA from Franklin College in English and Philosophy. Her scholarship centers on methodological innovation, especially as it intersects with new technologies. She is coauthor *of Doing Qualitative Research in a Digital World* (2021), *Looking for Insight Transformation and Learning in Online Talk* (2019) and *Digital Tools for Qualitative Research* (2014).

Monica Prendergast is Professor of Drama/Theatre Education, Department of Curriculum & Instruction, University of Victoria. Her research interests include drama-based curriculum and pedagogy, drama/theatre in community contexts, and arts-based qualitative research methods. Dr. Prendergast's books include: *Applied Theatre and Applied Drama; Teaching Spectatorship; Poetic Inquiry; Staging the Not-yet; Drama, Theatre and Performance Education in Canada; Poetic Inquiry II; Teachers and Teaching on Stage and on Screen.* Her CV includes 50+ peer-reviewed journal contributions, 25+ chapters, book reviews and professional contributions. Monica also reviews theatre for *CBC Radio Canada* and writes a column on theatre *for Focus Magazine.*

Drew Puroway is Associate Director of Academic Counseling at the University of Saint Thomas in Minnesota. He holds a doctorate from the University of Saint Thomas in Educational Leadership with a concentration in Critical Pedagogy. He is a qualitative researcher whose interests include ethics in academic advising, campus ecology, and social justice. Dr. Puroway can be reached at dwpuroway@stthomas.edu.

Janet Richards is Professor of Literacy and Qualitative Research at the University of South Florida where she created three qualitative courses, Art-Based Research, Qualitative Research Pedagogy, and Writing as Inquiry. She is Senior Editor of *Literacy Practice and Research-Online* and received the Organization of Teacher Educators of Literacy's Outstanding Achievement Award for converting the OTEL journal from print to open access. She received two research awards from OTEL and served as an International Literacy Association Scholar working in emerging nations, such as Pakistan, Azerbaijan, Romania, Estonia, Hungary, and in the jungles between Myanmar and Thailand.

Gretchen B. Rossman is Professor Emerita at the University of Massachusetts Amherst. She has expertise in qualitative research design and methods. Rossman has coauthored 15 books, two are major qualitative research texts (*An Introduction to Qualitative*

Research: Learning in the Field, 4th ed. with Sharon F. Rallis *and Designing Qualitative Research,* 7th ed. in preparation, with Catherine Marshall and Gerardo Blanco). She has also authored or coauthored more than 50 articles, book chapters, and technical reports.

Robyn Shenfield is a PhD candidate in the Department of Curriculum and Instruction in the Faculty of Education at the University of Victoria. She has taught in public and independent schools in Australia and Canada, and at the undergraduate level to preservice elementary school teachers. She has published work in a number of journals including *Research in Drama Education: The Journal of Applied Theatre and Performance, Art/Research International,* and *NJ: Drama Australia Journal.* Her research interests are varied and include drama education, applied theatre, moral education, and arts-based qualitative research.

Daniel Turner started as a qualitative researcher in health, healthcare delivery, and long-term conditions, and he engaged in collaborations with national bodies and universities across the UK. He left academia in 2014 to start up Quirkos, when he found an unmet need for simple and reliable qualitative analysis software. He is founder and director of Quirkos and writes a popular blog on qualitative methods.

Alyson Welker received her PhD in Educational Sciences from Colorado State University and her MA in Rhetoric and the Teaching of Writing from the University of Colorado at Denver. Dr. Welker has taught composition courses at the university level for the last nine years, and she is currently a Senior Instructor of English at Colorado State University. Just beginning her publishing career, Dr. Welker has published articles and chapters in *SAGE Handbook of Qualitative Research, Journal of Curriculum Theorizing, Dialogic Pedagogy: An International Online Journal,* and *Journal of Technical Communication Online.*

Patricia Witkowsky is Assistant Professor of Leadership, Research, and Foundations at the University of Colorado, Colorado Springs. Dr. Witkowsky conducts qualitative research focusing on college student transitions and student affairs professionals in higher education. She is active with various student affairs professional associations, including NASPA: Student Affairs Administrators in Higher Education and ACPA: College Student Educators-International.

• Index •